MANUAL OF ARTICULATORY PHONETICS

Revised Edition

by

WILLIAM A. SMALLEY

Cartoons by George Ivan Smith

William Carey Library

SOUTH PASADENA, CALIF.

Library of Congress Cataloging in Publication Data

Smalley, William Allen.
Manual of articulatory phonetics.

Bibliography: p.
1. Phonetics. I. Title.
P221.S55 1973 421'.5 73-14763
ISBN 0-87808-139-9

Eleventh Printing, 1977

William Carey Library
533 Hermosa Street
South Pasadena, California 91030
Telephone (213) 798-0819

PRINTED IN THE UNITED STATES OF AMERICA

TAPE RECORDINGS

Each of the thirty-three regular lessons of the *Manual of Articulatory Phonetics* has been recorded and tape copies are available for purchase. Recordings run from forty to sixty minutes per lesson and are available on a seven inch reel at 7.5 inches per second. Scotch 1/4" X 1200' reel to reel is used as well as Scotch low noise cassettes.

	Cassettes	Reels
Complete set of 33 tapes delivered in the U.S.	$148.50	$198.50
Outside the U.S.A. add $13.50 for surface delivery of reel tapes, $8.90 for surface delivery of cassettes.		
Individual tapes in orders of six tapes or more, delivered in the U.S.A, any combination of lessons. Each tape.	4.80	5.75
Individual tapes in orders of <u>under</u> six tapes delivered in the U.S.A. Each tape.	5.00	6.50
Outside the U.S.A. add for each tape or cassette	.40	.60

Religious organizations purchasing tapes should state the intended use of the tapes on their letterhead in order to receive a discount from Sound Recording Service.

The cassettes should be played back on a good machine having a large speaker. The cassettes are recorded on high speed machines and the response is almost equal to the reel to reel recordings. The small (two inch) speakers in the portable cassette recorders do not render the full response. Prices subject to change without notice.

Send orders only to: SOUND RECORDING SERVICE
977 Creekdale Drive
Clarkston, Georgia 30021
U.S.A.

CONTENTS

Appendix

OH, HIS TONGUE IS PLENTY FLEXIBLE!
HE JUST HAS TROUBLE WITH THE STOPS!

PREFACE

The *Manual of Articulatory Phonetics* has been designed for courses in practical phonetics for beginning students.[1] The point of view behind this book is that general phonetics is a primary skill of great importance to language students who want to acquire a fluent and accurate spoken mastery of a language in adulthood, as well as to linguists who need it as a basic tool of their profession. To that end one of the goals of this course is to sharpen the student's hearing of sounds which may be exotic and strange to him, and to make him conscious of sounds which he may use constantly in his own speech, but of which he is unaware. A second goal is the development of a flexibility of the speech apparatus such that the student can control the various parts of the mouth and throat which are used in pronunciation. He can learn to manipulate them and produce combinations of movement which he does not use in his own speech but which are necessary for other languages. Another goal is the development of the skill of mimicry. This is the skill of being able to reproduce quickly and accurately a sound, a word, a sentence, in a language which the student is in the process of learning.

A lesser goal for the language learner (but not any less for the linguist) and one which is involved in the reaching of the previous goals, is the development of a sound-symbol association. This means the ability to correlate a given segment of sound in a stream of speech with some symbol which is consistently used to represent it on paper. English spelling habits are such that many speakers of English are not conditioned to a sound-symbol association of high consistency.

---

[1]This *Manual* has been in preparation since 1955, primarily as a textbook for intensive courses offered at the Toronto Institute of Linguistics and at the language section of the Missionary Training Conference held in Meadville, Pennsylvania. Both of these courses are designed to introduce prospective missionaries to some of the techniques and skills of learning a language on the field. As such they place a heavy emphasis upon practical general phonetics. This *Manual* provides a skeleton of material on which the phonetics drill sessions are built. Although this *Manual* is prepared with a specific teaching situation in mind, it should be useful in other phonetics courses as well. There is nothing in it but what is adaptable to any course in general phonetics, whether for embryo linguists, language teachers, or any other group.

The symbols which are used in this *Manual* have no particular value in themselves. They are arbitrary, just as are phonetic symbols in any other system. The system is basically that used by many American linguists working on American Indian languages. It is derived directly from publications of Kenneth L. Pike and Eugene A. Nida with certain modifications. These modifications are in the direction of easier teaching (that is, of eliminating inconsistencies in sound-symbol association), or they may be easier to produce on a typewriter or easier to use in some other way.

Phonetic Theory

The phonetic theory which lies behind this *Manual* is derived directly and almost completely from Kenneth L. Pike.[1] It takes up the formation of sounds by the human speech mechanism. It uses what Pike calls the imitation-label technique to a large degree; it strives to help students produce a variety of sounds and gives them information about the mechanics of articulation so that they learn to make an association between what they hear and what they do. It introduces the sound types in a pedagogical progression which is based on their articulations rather than on their occurrence in any language. The phonetics offered, therefore, is *general* rather than related to any particular language. However, in the *Manual* and in the recordings which accompany it, there are exercises drawn from actual languages, and most of these exercises are recorded by native speakers of those languages. In each such case the purpose is not to teach anything about that particular language but simply to illustrate realistically the sounds under study.

We keep phonetic terminology to a minimum. We use that terminology (usually following Pike) which we find necessary for talking with students about articulations which they are being taught to make. The terminology which is introduced in the beginning is extensively drilled in the first lesson, because it comes in a proportionately larger amount at that time than at later points in the course. After the first lesson terminology is introduced more gradually and is not drilled as extensively, although at certain points, such as at the introduction of vowels, there is some drill on the new terminology needed.

---

[1]For his principal work on phonetics see Kenneth L. Pike, *Phonetics*. For full information on works cited in this *Manual* see the Bibliography.

At a few points the terminology does differ from that used by Pike, largely for pedagogical reasons. An example is the labeling of the various tongue heights of vowels as in Lesson 14. The system used here[1] has been found much easier to teach than the more usual system of rating vowels as "close" or "open." In Appendix C we include a condensed summary description of speech articulation presented so as to bring together in one place an outline of the information about speech production which is scattered through the book among the several hundred drills.

Content and Use of This Manual

The *Manual of Articulatory Phonetics* is designed to provide one lesson for each 50 to 55 minute class drill session. That is, the drill sessions follow the progression of the *Manual*, introducing the new material covered in the new lesson. In these lessons there are sometimes more drills and exercises than can possibly be done in an hour. However, the drill session introduces the new sound type, drills it with a representation of exercises, and then any students who have not fully caught the point or had sufficient practice to get the new sound may continue with other exercises in the lesson, using tape recordings or extra drill sessions as an aid in their practice.

The *Manual* is designed for a schedule of two such drill sessions per day, which accounts for the fact that lessons are alternated, first between consonants and pitch, and then between consonants and vowels. Consonant lessons are always odd-numbered lessons, pitch and vowel lessons even-numbered lessons. The *Manual* may well be used on a different schedule from this, of course.

For the teacher, the *Manual* provides a large assortment of graded drills for each new sound-type introduced, and thus makes it possible to lead a class through much more oral drill than is usually possible in phonetics classes. For the student it is intended to be used in drill sessions where some drills are of a reading nature, or where the diagrams may be helpful, but for the most part it serves as a supplement to the class period.

The *Manual* is intended also to be useful on the field to any students who have previously had some phonetic training. It may serve as a reference work to help with the practice of sound types in which the students are not skilled.

---

[1]After H. A. Gleason, *Introduction to Descriptive Linguistics*, p. 203.

The Tape Recordings

Tape recordings have been made of the exercises contained in the *Manual*. They are intended to be used with the *Manual* at any point where the student feels that his mastery of the sound type or combinations of sounds is not adequate. There are definite problems in connection with the use of tapes for phonetics materials, however. For one thing certain types of sounds do not record in an adequate fashion. This is particularly true of fricatives. The tape recording also obliterates or nearly obliterates contrasts between other sounds in some instances. At such points the usefulness of recordings is relatively small except that they may give some guidance to the student as to the pace, tempo, and rhythm of the pronunciation and utterance. The other difficulty is that when it comes to mimicry and other forms of production a tape machine cannot correct the student, and if the student continues to mimic the tape machine inaccurately he is simply drilling bad habits. Copies of the tape recordings are available, as announced on p. i.

Workbook Supplement

A workbook is available to accompany this *Manual* (see p. ii for further details). It is 8 1/2" x 11", with perforated pages so that individual sheets may be taken out and handed in to the instructor when required. Included in the *Workbook Supplement* are Blank Sammies (see p. 79 below for more information), blanks for transcription exercises of various kinds (both phonetics and phonemics lessons), a tally form for transcription errors, and some exercises designed to strengthen the recall of phonetic symbols. It totals 106 pages. The *Manual* may be used without the *Workbook Supplement* but the latter strengthens the pedagogical efficiency of the former.

Teacher's Guide

We have found that effective classroom presentation makes an enormous difference to student progress in phonetics. Several good linguists who have worked in our programs have shown little sense of the timing, closely graded progression, and variety which is needed in a phonetics drill section until they had been trained and had developed some experience in these techniques. The procedures, and the detailed lesson plans, that have been used in teaching from this *Manual* have been compiled in a *Teacher's Guide*, as announced on p. ii. It contains suggestions for conducting the various kinds of drills in class, and tested lesson plans for presenting each lesson in a class period.

The Place of Phonemics

In this *Manual* it is assumed that the concept of phonemics is being introduced to the student in conjunction with his phonetics work. Phonemic notation is occasionally used where it is pertinent, but is kept to a minimum. The appendix contains two lessons on the phonemic transcription of English, the one on English consonants and the other on English vowels. The first is intended as a supplementary lesson to be prepared before Lesson 3. Its purpose is to help the student develop a repertoire of consonant symbols as rapidly as possible, and to develop the concept and practice of a consistent sound-symbol association (the student at this stage generally being unaware of sub-phonemic phonetic differences). Unlike other chapters in this book, the "lesson" on English vowel phonemes is really a series of lessons. Suggestions for dividing it up and teaching it are contained in the *Teacher's Guide*. These lessons are intended to come after Lesson 20. They are designed to show the functional validity of the phonemic concept as a way of making order out of the enormous phonetic variety in English vowel nuclei, as well as to sharpen the student's (phonetic) skill in hearing and identifying these nuclei.

Changes in the Present Edition

In this revised edition of the *Manual of Articulatory Phonetics* the most common changes have been in the correction of errors. In addition, what was previously published in two parts is now combined into a single volume. The preface and Lesson B have been partly rewritten and expanded. Lesson C and the Index are new.

Plans for Future Development

Except for the standardized tests which are being prepared and tested, whether or not I will be able to give any more time to this book and related materials in the future is uncertain. I would like very much, however, sometime to include about twelve new lessons at the end, each built around the phonetic problems in a specific language. The approach to drilling would be the same as in the present work, but all of the material in one of these lessons would be drawn from the same language, graded according to difficulty, and drilled in progressive order. A chapter summarizing some of the insights of acoustic phonetics would also be helpful.

Acknowledgments

My debts in the preparation of this book are enormous. Eugene A. Nida has provided constant stimulus and encouragement,

as well as many ideas which have been woven into the teaching of phonetics formalized in this Manual. The American Bible Society gave me much of the time needed in its preparation. Lyndora Smith contributed to the writing of Lessons 10, 12, 14, 16, 18, and 22, and offered suggestions for the remainder. Jane Smalley wrote some of the drills, and typed the pages for photographing the lithoprinted editions, as well as stencils of previous mimeographed editions. Richard O. Crane served as recording technician for all thirty-three tapes. Anna-Lisa Madeira prepared the index. Judy Wood drew the "Sammies." Garner Hoyt prepared models for some exercises. The thirty or more different people who served as drill instructors with me, teaching these lessons and earlier versions of them over the past eight years, have contributed by their criticisms and suggestions. Of these, several deserve particular mention: G. Linwood Barney, Esther Cummings, Robert E. Maston, Fred C. C. Peng, and Earl W. Stevick. But more than anyone else, Donald N. Larson brought his skill in teaching phonetics, his keen sense of pedagogical progression, and his faculty for creative criticism to bear on these lessons and greatly influenced their development.

William A. Smalley
January, 1963

The cartoons introduced in the 1964 reprinting are the work of George Ivan Smith, who recorded his reactions to his first contact with phonetics by drawing the cartoons and posting them for the edification of students and staff. He very kindly agreed to share them with other students and other staff by redrawing them for the Manual.

William A. Smalley
June, 1964

After ten years of publication, the *Manual* has now been taken over by a new publisher, and I have used the occasion to make a few minor corrections. It is gratifying to know that the book is still in steady demand, having gone through a series of reprintings, and that it is still useful to many students of introductory phonetics even though there have been important developments in research and theory in the mean time.

William A. Smalley
August, 1973

LESSON ONE

Description of Sounds

The main purpose of this lesson is to get started off fast in the study of phonetics. To do that we begin the study of how sounds are formed, and learn some of the vocabulary needed in talking about sounds. Although the technical vocabulary of phonetics has no particular value for some of you in your work, during this course we need some way of discussing our subject matter, and that requires some useful words, although we will keep them to a minimum.

Facial Diagrams

This will introduce Sam Mansfield. Sammy is a gentleman who always looks westward (if you think of the paper on which his picture appears as being a map), but his "leftist" look is not the most significant thing about Sammy nor the most convenient. The importance of Sammy lies in the fact that you can see inside his head. Sammy is the result of what would happen if you carefully sliced right down through a man's head from front to back and then drew a rough schematized diagram of what you saw, particularly emphasizing those parts of Sam's exposed anatomy which are especially significant for the production of speech sounds.[1]

Sammy has holes in his head. The three principal "holes", which we call cavities, are the oral cavity, the nasal cavity, and the pharyngeal cavity. These cavities change in shape by the movements of the vocal organs and thus influence the air stream which passes through them to create differences of sound. More about this later. Even though Sammy has been cut in two, he has not lost his capacity for moving his vocal organs. In Sammy 1.2 you can see him pronouncing a [p] as in English pill. In Sammy 1.3, however, he is pronouncing a [k] as in English call.

Although Sammy is useful in helping us to learn the parts of the vocal apparatus and to visualize the movements involved in making speech sounds, it is important to remember that Sammy is very unrealistic in many ways. Speech consists of a

---

[1]In case you are wondering about the significance of Sammy's name, there is none. However, Sammy's initials also stand for Speech Mechanism.

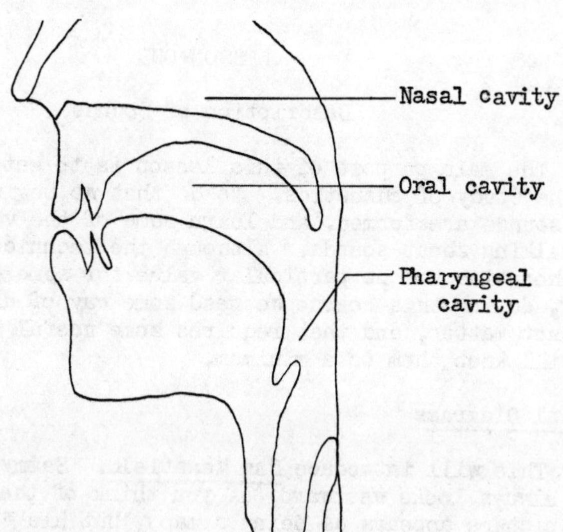

Sammy 1.1: Introducing Sammy

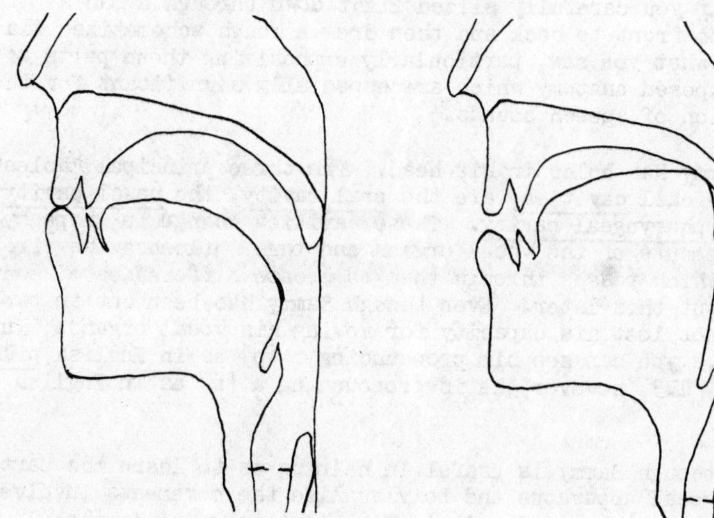

Sammy 1.2: Pronouncing [p] as in <u>pill</u>

Sammy 1.3: Pronouncing [k] as in <u>call</u>

continuous movement of many muscles simultaneously. This we cannot picture on Sammy because Sammy is static. Sammy is really a tremendous oversimplification, but with that reserva-

tion in mind we will use him profitably throughout this book.

Major Points of Articulation

If you move your face and mouth into various contortions, you will soon realize that there are certain parts of the mouth which can be moved and others which cannot. In talking, for example, your lower jaw moves but your upper jaw does not; therefore, your lower teeth attached to your lower jaw move but your upper teeth do not. Your tongue moves but the surface of the mouth just above the tongue (the hard palate) does not move. It is a safe generalization to say that of the interior surfaces of the mouth the upper ones move less than the lower ones.

If you will continue this process of contortion in your mouth and face, you will notice that the moving lower surfaces in the mouth can approach and touch the immovable or less moving upper surfaces or they can withdraw to some distance from them. On Sammy 1.2 and 1.3 the highly movable lower lip and tongue have touched the less movable upper lip and roof of the mouth respectively. You ought to be able to feel this sort of thing very clearly if you say asa several times over to yourself. You should be able to feel the tongue come up to the top of the mouth, almost touch it, and then recede again up and down, up and down. We call these less movable points along the upper part of the mouth to which the more movable parts approach points of articulation.

Actually there is an unbroken continuum of points of articulation from Sammy's upper lip back to the back wall of his throat. However, for practical purposes we divide this continuum into some useful segments to which we give names. You will find the points of articulation which you will need to know labeled on the following diagram.

The naming of certain ones of these points of articulation should give no difficulty whatsoever. You will not have any trouble remembering upper lip, upper teeth, nor probably palate. It will be well to point out that in our terminology palate here refers to the region which you can feel from the point where the hump of gum behind your upper teeth stops to the point where the soft palate begins. The other terms may give you a little more difficulty. The alveolar ridge is the gum just behind the upper teeth. The alveopalatal region[1] is the back side of that gum as it rises toward the top of the mouth. You

---

[1]At a few points such as this, standard linguistic usage differs from medical usage.

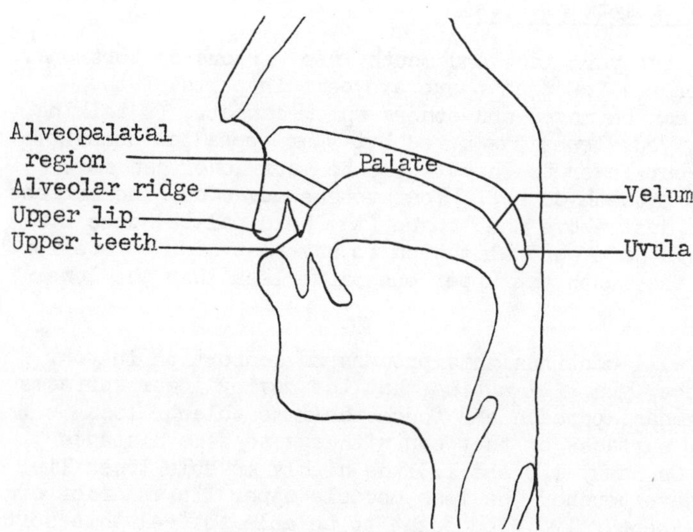

Sammy 1.4: Points of Articulation

can feel these configurations with your tongue. Just remember that the surface immediately behind the teeth is the alveolar ridge and that the surface which rises behind that is the alveopalatal region. This continues until you get to the top of the mouth which is the palate. The velum is what we often know as the soft palate and it continues on down in back to that little peninsula which you can see in the mirror (if you open your mouth wide), a little cone of flesh called the uvula. The uvula is attached at the lower extremity of the velum. The uvula hangs free in the back of the mouth.

Recorded Exercises 1.1-1.9. Points of Articulation[1]

In order to help you learn the points of articulation, and to make sure that the labels are mastered to the point that they can be used in talking about sounds without any hesitation, a set of nine recorded exercises follows. The text of the exercises may be found below, but you should

---

[1]Numbering of Sammy diagrams, recorded exercises, tables, etc., is in sequence for each type, and is preceded by the number of the lesson. Thus Sammy 1.5 is the fifth Sammy diagram in Lesson 1, while RE 1.1 is the first recorded exercise in Lesson 1.

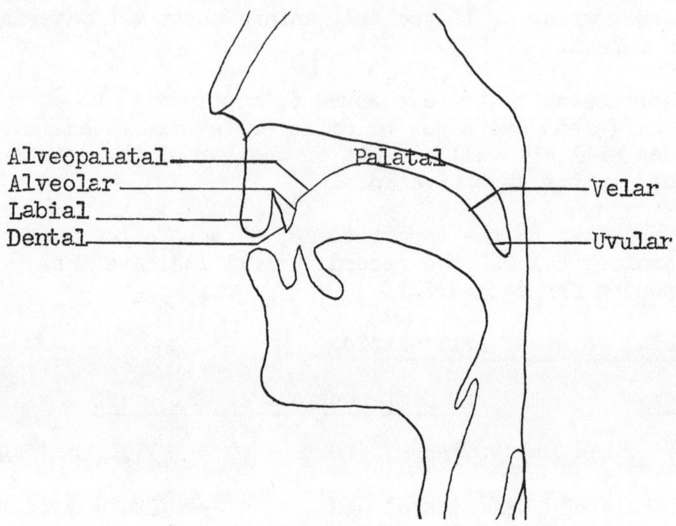

Sammy 1.5: Points of Articulation
(Adjective forms)

preferably do the exercises without referring to the written text except in problem cases. Read the directions before you turn on the tape.

The first five of these exercises will have two parts. The first part will be a mimicry drill, in which you will mimic the utterances you hear on the tape. These will contain only English sounds, but will be nonsense (meaningless) utterances. In mimicking them pay close attention to the point of articulation. Each mimicry drill will contain only those English sounds which are natural in this kind of sequence. You will repeat each item twice in the silent space provided for you on the tape.

The mimicry sections, which are designed to help you get a feel for the point of articulation, are followed by the drill proper, in which you hear an utterance on the tape and respond by naming the point of articulation. You will hear an utterance which consists of a syllable or two. That utterance will be repeated twice and then there will be a pause. In that pause you respond orally or on paper. Following the pause for your response, the tape will give the correct response. In this way you will know immediately whether or not you were right in your response. Do not stop the machine but continue through the whole exercise in this manner. If you get all of the items right in the exercise, go on to the next exercise.

If you get them wrong or if you felt unsure about the material, go back and repeat.

The response which you are asked to supply will be different for different exercises or different groups of exercises. The responses will all call for one or another of the points of articulation, in the adjective form.

After you turn on the tape recorder do not follow the written exercises below. The recording will indicate the proper responses for each drill.

RE 1.1. Labial Point of Articulation

a. Mimicry	b. Differential: LABIAL or NO			
1. [ɑp^{h}ɑ]	9. [ɑp^{h}ɑ]	LA	17. [ɑbɑ]	LA
2. [ɑbɑ]	10. [ɑk^{h}ɑ]	NO	18. [ɑžɑ]	NO
3. [ɑmɑ]	11. [ɑsɑ]	NO	19. [p^{h}ɑ]	LA
4. [p^{h}ɑ]	12. [ɑmɑ]	LA	20. [mɑ]	LA
5. [bɑ]	13. [ɑbɑ]	LA	21. [ɑd]	NO
6. [mɑ]	14. [ɑp^{h}ɑ]	LA	22. [ɑθ]	NO
7. [ɑp^{h}]	15. [ɑfɑ]	NO	23. [ɑb]	LA
8. [ɑb]	16. [ɑlɑ]	NO	24. [ɑš]	NO

RE 1.2. Dental Point of Articulation

a. Mimicry	b. Differential: DENTAL or NO			
1. [ɑfɑ]	8. [ɑθɑ]	DE	15. [ɑfɑ]	DE
2. [ɑθɑ]	9. [ɑvɑ]	DE	16. [θɑ]	DE
3. [ɑvɑ]	10. [ɑp^{h}ɑ]	NO	17. [d̪ɑ]	DE
4. [ɑd̪ɑ]	11. [ɑd̪ɑ]	DE	18. [vɑ]	DE
5. [fɑ]	12. [ɑmɑ]	NO	19. [ɑθ]	DE
6. [θɑ]	13. [ɑk^{h}ɑ]	NO	20. [ɑŋ]	NO
7. [vɑ]	14. [ɑšɑ]	NO	21. [ɑl]	NO

RE 1.3. Velar Point of Articulation

a. Mimicry	b. Differential: VELAR or NO			
1. [ɑk^{h}ɑ]	8. [ɑŋɑ]	VE	15. [t^{h}ɑ]	NO
2. [ɑgɑ]	9. [ɑp^{h}ɑ]	NO	16. [đɑ]	NO
3. [ɑŋɑ]	10. [ɑgɑ]	VE	17. [gɑ]	VE
4. [ɑk^{h}ɑ]	11. [ɑsɑ]	NO	18. [k^{h}ɑ]	VE
5. [ɑgɑ]	12. [ɑlɑ]	NO	19. [zɑ]	NO
6. [ɑŋɑ]	13. [ɑk^{h}ɑ]	VE	20. [ɑk^{h}]	VE
7. [ɑk^{h}ɑ ɑgɑ ɑŋɑ]	14. [žɑ]	NO	21. [ɑŋ]	VE

RE 1.4. Alveolar Point of Articulation

a. Mimicry	b. Differential: ALVEOLAR or NO			
1. [ɑsɑ]	8. [ɑdɑ]	AL	15. [mɑ]	NO
2. [ɑzɑ]	9. [ɑnɑ]	AL	16. [p^{h}ɑ]	NO
3. [ɑt^{h}ɑ]	10. [ɑsɑ]	AL	17. [ɑb]	NO
4. [ɑdɑ]	11. [ɑk^{h}ɑ]	NO	18. [ɑn]	AL
5. [ɑnɑ]	12. [fɑ]	NO	19. [ɑl]	AL
6. [ɑlɑ]	13. [lɑ]	AL	20. [ɑz]	AL
7. [ɑsɑ ɑzɑ]	14. [žɑ]	NO	21. [ɑt^{h}]	AL

RE 1.5. Alveopalatal Point of Articulation

a. Mimicry	b. Differential: ALVEOPALATAL or NO			
1. [ɑšɑ]	6. [ɑlɑ]	NO	11. [ɑŋɑ]	NO
2. [ɑžɑ]	7. [ɑnɑ]	NO	12. [bɑ]	NO
3. [ɑšɑ]	8. [ɑθɑ]	NO	13. [šɑ]	AP
4. [ɑžɑ]	9. [ɑšɑ]	AP	14. [vɑ]	NO
5. [ɑšɑ ɑžɑ]	10. [ɑžɑ]	AP	15. [đɑ]	NO

16. [žɑ] AP
17. [ɑš] AP
18. [ɑp^h] NO

For the next drills you will not have any NO responses. Instead you will differentiate between two or more different points of articulation, as will be indicated for each drill. In RE 1.6, for example, you will respond LABIAL or DENTAL according to the consonant you hear. As before, do not follow in your book.

RE 1.6. Differential: LABIAL or DENTAL

1. [ɑfɑ] DE
2. [ɑðɑ] DE
3. [ɑmɑ] LA
4. [ɑvɑ] DE
5. [ɑθɑ] DE
6. [ɑp^{h}ɑ] LA
7. [ɑvɑ] DE
8. [ɑbɑ] LA
9. [mɑ] LA

RE 1.7. Differential: ALVEOLAR or VELAR

1. [ɑnɑ] AL
2. [ɑgɑ] VE
3. [ɑŋɑ] VE
4. [lɑ] AL
5. [zɑ] AL
6. [ɑt^h] AL
7. [ɑk^h] VE
8. [ŋɑ] VE
9. [ɑs] AL
10. [ɑdɑ] AL
11. [gɑ] VE
12. [ɑd] AL
13. [zɑ] AL
14. [ɑŋɑ] VE
15. [ɑgɑ] VE

RE 1.8. Differential: ALVEOLAR or ALVEOPALATAL

1. [ɑnɑ] AL
2. [sɑ] AL
3. [šɑ] AP
4. [ɑl] AL
5. [ɑd] AL
6. [ɑt^{h}ɑ] AL
7. [zɑ] AL
8. [žɑ] AP
9. [ɑšɑ] AP
10. [ɑs] AL
11. [ɑl] AL
12. [ɑnɑ] AL
13. [zɑ] AL
14. [žɑ] AP
15. [ɑš] AP
16. [ɑz] AL
17. [ɑs] AL
18. [šɑ] AP

RE 1.9. Differential: LABIAL, DENTAL, ALVEOLAR, ALVEOPALATAL, or VELAR

1. [ɑšɑ] AP
2. [ɑlɑ] AL
3. [ɑnɑ] AL
4. [ɑp^{h}ɑ] LA
5. [ɑðɑ] DE
6. [ɑgɑ] VE

7. [aŋa]	VE	13. [va]	DE	19. [al]	AL
8. [asa]	AL	14. [da]	AL	20. [aŋ]	VE
9. [aža]	AP	15. [fa]	DE	21. [až]	AP
10. [aza]	AL	16. [k^ha]	VE	22. [ad]	AL
11. [ba]	LA	17. [θa]	DE	23. [ak^h]	VE
12. [t^ha]	AL	18. [ma]	LA	24. [am]	LA[1]

Major Articulators

The more movable lower portions of the mouth which were mentioned above we call articulators. This time again we have to be a bit arbitrary as we divide the tongue up into sections for purposes of discussion. Sammy 1.6 gives you the terms for these articulators.

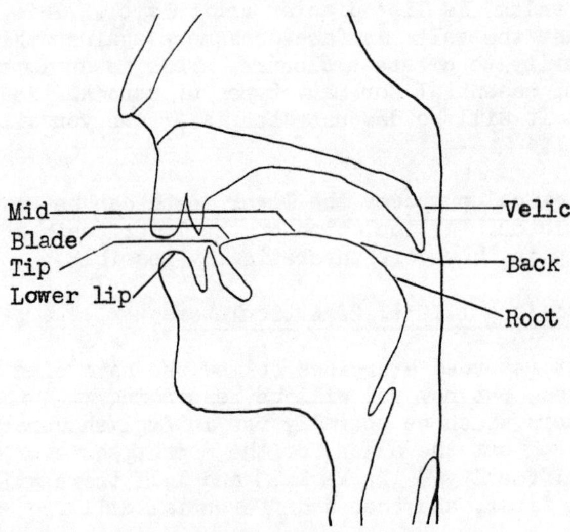

Sammy 1.6: Articulators
(Noun forms)

---

[1]Note that we have not included the palatal or uvular points of articulation. We omitted them because we want to use English sounds only in these drills, and these points of articulation do not lend themselves to our purposes for now.

By the tip of the tongue we mean its very point. This is the part most of us would use in feeling for some unevenness along the ridge of our teeth. It is the articulator most of us use in English for the t in take. (If you do not think that your articulation of take fulfills this description, be sure to check with your teacher so that you can know for sure whether or not it is a safe guide for you.)

The blade of the tongue is that part immediately behind the tip. If you clench your teeth and put the tip down behind the lower teeth touching the back of the lower teeth with the tip, then the blade is the part which touches up against the alveolar ridge. In that position also, the middle of the tongue is the part below the palate, and the back of the tongue is the part below the velum. The root is down in the upper part of the throat.

One item on the list of articulators does not fully conform to the description we have so far given. You will notice that the velic (the back part of the velum, or the northeast side of the velum) is listed as an articulator. This is done simply because the velic surface does move against the back of the nasal cavity to create a closure. This is an important articulation, essential for many types of sounds. You may not feel it, but it will be demonstrated later and you will learn to control it.

For practical purposes the lower teeth can be disregarded as an articulator. Articulation of the lower teeth against the upper lip is, however, theoretically possible.

Recorded Exercises 1.10-1.12. Articulators

The next recorded exercises follow the same plan as the preceding ones, but now you will be responding with the names of articulators which we normally use in English consonants. (We are leaving out the blade for the moment, however, as it presents a difficulty.) In RE 1.10 and 1.11 there will be a mimicry part first, and then a differential drill.

RE 1.10. Tip and Back Articulators

a. Mimicry: Tip		b. Mimicry: Back
1. [ɑtʰɑ]	4. [ɑlɑ]	5. [ɑkʰɑ]
2. [ɑdɑ]		6. [ɑgɑ]
3. [ɑnɑ]		7. [ɑŋɑ]

c. Differential: TIP or BACK

8.	[ɑgɑ] BACK	13.	[ɑt^{h}ɑ] TIP	18.	[dɑ] TIP
9.	[ɑnɑ] TIP	14.	[ɑk^{h}ɑ] BACK	19.	[lɑ] TIP
10.	[ɑlɑ] TIP	15.	[ɑŋɑ] BACK	20.	[nɑ] TIP
11.	[ɑdɑ] TIP	16.	[ɑt^{h}ɑ] TIP	21.	[k^{h}ɑ] BACK
12.	[ɑŋɑ] BACK	17.	[gɑ] BACK	22.	[ɑŋ] BACK

RE 1.11. Lip and Back Articulators

a. Mimicry: Lip

1. [ɑp^{h}ɑ]
2. [ɑbɑ]
3. [ɑmɑ]
4. [ɑfɑ]
5. [ɑvɑ]

b. Differential: LIP or BACK

6. [ɑfɑ]	LIP	13. [mɑ]	LIP
7. [ɑgɑ]	BACK	14. [k^{h}ɑ]	BACK
8. [ɑmɑ]	LIP	15. [p^{h}ɑ]	LIP
9. [ɑp^{h}ɑ]	LIP	16. [ɑf]	LIP
10. [ɑbɑ]	LIP	17. [ɑŋ]	BACK
11. [ɑŋɑ]	BACK	18. [ɑg]	BACK
12. [vɑ]	LIP	19. [ɑb]	LIP

RE 1.12. Differential: LIP, TIP, or BACK

1. [ɑk^{h}ɑ]	BACK	7. [ɑfɑ]	LIP	13. [ɑθ]	TIP
2. [ɑdɑ]	TIP	8. [ɑp^{h}ɑ]	LIP	14. [ɑb]	LIP
3. [ɑmɑ]	LIP	9. [ɑk^{h}ɑ]	BACK	15. [ɑg]	BACK
4. [ɑlɑ]	TIP	10. [gɑ]	BACK	16. [ɑd]	TIP
5. [ɑt^{h}ɑ]	TIP	11. [nɑ]	TIP	17. [fɑ]	LIP
6. [ɑŋɑ]	BACK	12. [vɑ]	LIP	18. [ŋɑ]	BACK

Some Manners of Articulation

In order to get started in the discussion of the speech sounds, we have to have terminology not only for the articulators and the points to which those articulators move, but we also need to be able to say something about the ways in which

they articulate. These ways of articulation we call manners of articulation. Some of these manners of articulation have to do with the actual relationship between the articulator and the point of articulation. Others have to do with simultaneous features in other parts of the vocal system.

Stops

For example, one manner of articulation which has to do with the relationship between the articulator and the point of articulation is that which we call a stop. A stop is a manner of articulation in which the articulator so completely touches the point of articulation that no air can escape. (We should also mention that all of the other avenues of escape for the air stream are also closed off. This means in the case of most stops that the velic must close off the escape avenue into the nasal cavity. See Sammy 1.2 and 1.3, both of which are stops.) If you contrast the initial sound in English take with the initial sound in English say, you will realize that the t in take is a stop and that the s in say is not. If you exaggerate your pronunciation and prolong the initial sound, you will realize that the air is stopped off by the articulation of the t but it is not stopped off by the articulation of the s. Perhaps you can see this even more clearly if you pronounce ata and asa. You can prolong the s as long as you like, getting asssssssa, but the longer you prolong the t the more silence you get because the t is a stop and the air stream is shut off. It is not until the t is released, when the air stream will have to move again, that sound begins once more.

The stop, then, is a very important manner of articulation. The stops in English are /p, t, k, b, d, and g/[1], as in the words pill, till, kill, bill, dill, and gill. Do not let the English spelling fool you. The initial sound in cat is a /k/ just like the initial sound in kill. Our spelling inconsistency sometimes tends to give us misconceptions about the way we speak.

---

[1]We will use three different sets of symbols for speech in this course. Symbols within brackets [ ] will represent speech as it is articulated or heard. We call this phonetic symbolization. Symbols within slant lines / / represent the significant sound distinctions of the language. We call this phonemic symbolization. Symbols underlined represent the conventional spelling used normally in that language. The meaning of these distinctions will come to you more clearly later, and is not crucial to your understanding at the present point. For symbolization of English consonant phonemes see The Appendix, Lesson A.

Some of you may feel that the initial sound in <u>chill</u> and in <u>Jill</u> are also stops. They are, but they are a complicated kind of stop which we will not discuss until Lesson 9.

RE 1.13. Differential: STOP or NO

Most students have no trouble understanding and identifying the difference between a stop and other manners of articulation. However, in order to help those individuals who may need it, we provide the following drill as a recorded exercise. If you find the drill very simple, sample it and go on. If the utterance which you hear on the tape contains a stop, you respond with STOP. If it does not contain a stop, you respond with NO.

1.	[ɑp^{h}ɑ]	S	10.	[bɑ]	S	19.	[ɑp^{h}]	S
2.	[ɑk^{h}ɑ]	S	11.	[t^{h}ɑ]	S	20.	[ɑŋ]	NO
3.	[ɑmɑ]	NO	12.	[nɑ]	NO	21.	[ɑb]	S
4.	[ɑbɑ]	S	13.	[k^{h}ɑ]	S	22.	[θɑ]	NO
5.	[ɑwɑ]	NO	14.	[p^{h}ɑ]	S	23.	[ɑt^{h}]	S
6.	[ɑgɑ]	S	15.	[ɑg]	S	24.	[ɑθɑ]	NO
7.	[ɑhɑ]	NO	16.	[ɑf]	NO	25.	[ɑt^{h}ɑ]	S
8.	[t^{h}ɑ]	S	17.	[ɑθ]	NO	26.	[gɑ]	S
9.	[dɑ]	S	18.	[ɑk^{h}]	S	27.	[ɑðɑ]	NO

Fricatives

A second manner of articulation which we can now take up is that which we call <u>fricative</u>. In contrasting the difference of pronunciation between <u>asa</u> and <u>ata</u>, we said that the second one contained a stop. The first one is a <u>fricative</u>. The difference lies in the fact that the fricative does not make a complete stoppage of the air stream. The articulator instead reaches a point very close to the point of articulation, so close that the air forcing through sets up a turbulence and makes a hissing or buzzing sound. Try the English fricatives in Sammies 1.7-1.10.

Remember that the distinguishing characteristic of a fricative is that the space between the articulator and the point of articulation is so narrow that the air forcing through is impeded and is caused to set up extra vibrations.

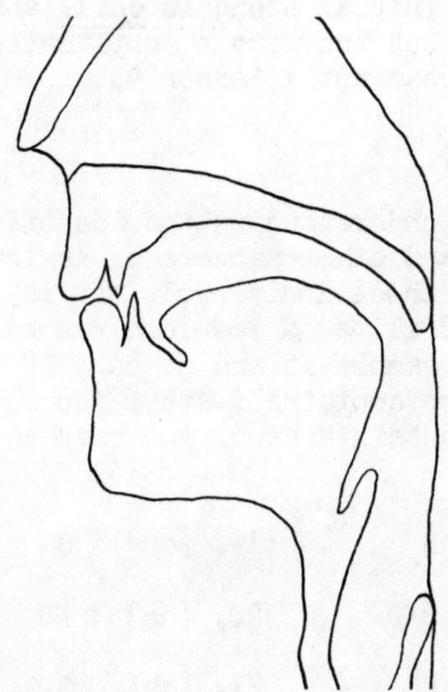

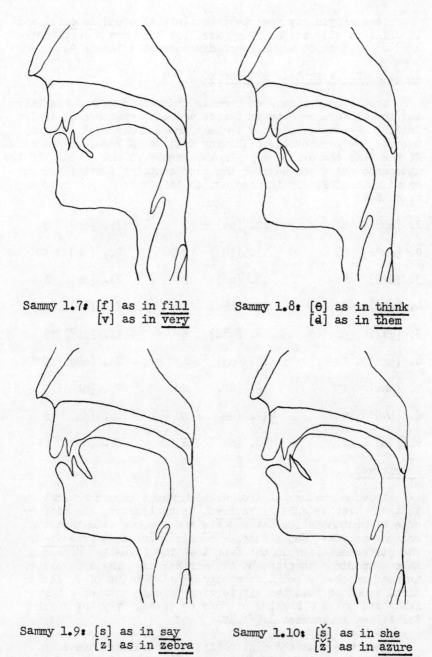

Sammy 1.7: [f] as in fill
[v] as in very

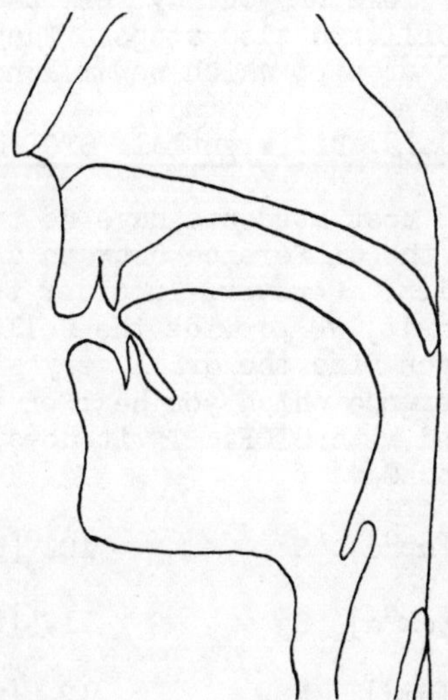

Sammy 1.8: [θ] as in think
[ð] as in them

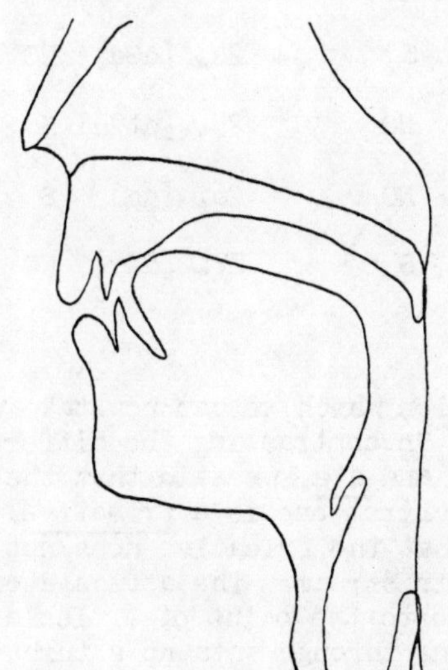

Sammy 1.9: [s] as in say
[z] as in zebra

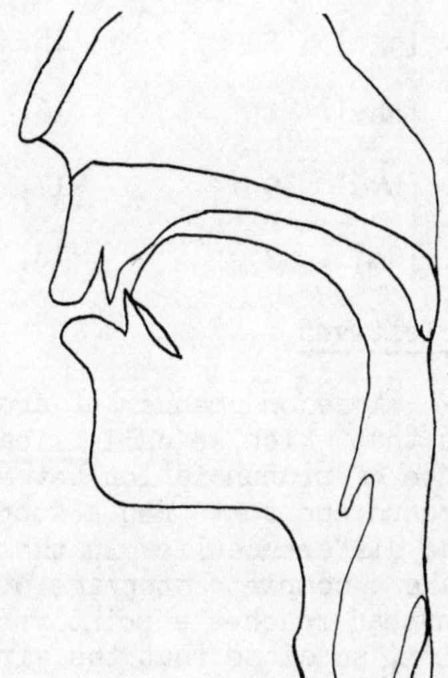

Sammy 1.10: [š] as in she
[ž] as in azure

This is like air coming through a crack around a door. A strong wind will cause the air to whistle through that crack, whereas if the door is wide open the air comes in without any such noise.

RE 1.14. Differential: FRICATIVE or NO

1. [ɑp^{h}ɑ]	NO	8. [sɑ]	F	15. [ɑθ]	F
2. [ɑfɑ]	F	9. [žɑ]	F	16. [ɑfɑ]	F
3. [ɑθɑ]	F	10. [dɑ]	NO	17. [k^{h}ɑ]	NO
4. [ɑzɑ]	F	11. [ɑš]	F	18. [ɑw]	NO
5. [ɑmɑ]	NO	12. [ɑž]	F	19. [nɑ]	NO
6. [θɑ]	F	13. [ɑl]	NO	20. [bɑ]	NO
7. [đɑ]	F	14. [ɑf]	F	21. [ɑz]	F

RE 1.15. Differential: STOP or FRICATIVE

Here your response will be either STOP or FRICATIVE for every utterance. There will be no utterances which do not contain either a stop or fricative. There will, however, be included some sounds which do not occur in English.

1. [ɑvɑ]	F	8. [xɑ]	F	15. [ɑθɑ]	F
2. [ɑdɑ]	S	9. [ɑb]	S	16. [ɑž]	F
3. [ɑp^{h}ɑ]	S	10. [ɑt^{h}]	S	17. [ɑg]	S
4. [ɑžɑ]	F	11. [ɑv]	F	18. [đɑ]	F
5. [k^{h}ɑ]	S	12. [ɑg]	S	19. [ɑzɑ]	F
6. [šɑ]	F	13. [ɑdɑ]	S	20. [ɑθ]	F
7. [gɑ]	F	14. [sɑ]	F	21. [ɑš]	F

RE 1.16. Differential: STOP, FRICATIVE, or NEITHER

1. [ɑk^{h}ɑ]	S	4. [lɑ]	N	7. [ɑb]	S
2. [ɑz]	F	5. [p^{h}ɑ]	S	8. [ɑgɑ]	S
3. [mɑ]	N	6. [ɑx]	F	9. [wɑ]	N

Nasals

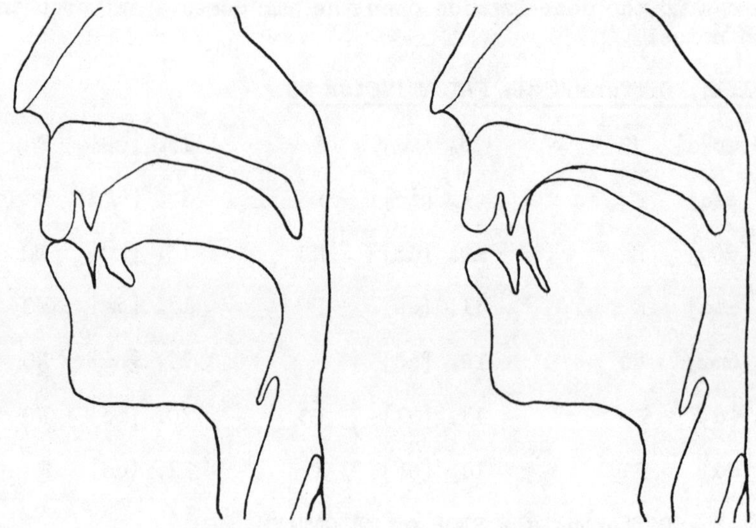

Sammy 1.11: [m]   Sammy 1.12: [n]

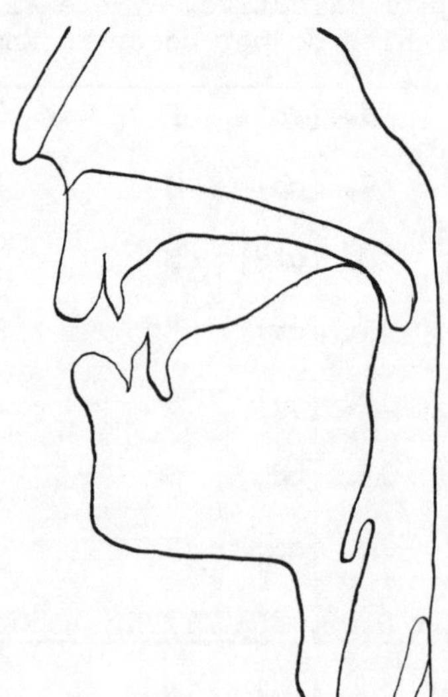

Sammy 1.13: [ŋ]

A third manner of articulation is <u>nasal</u>. English nasals are /m n ŋ/. (/ŋ/ is often spelled <u>ng</u> in English standard spelling.) If you experiment for a minute you will see that these three sounds are made with the same points of articulation in the mouth as /p t k/. The difference lies in the fact that for /m n ŋ/ the velic is open, letting the air stream go out the nose.

Notice that for a nasal the oral cavity has to be stopped off at some point, and the velic must be open. Although the oral cavity is stopped off, nasals are not stops. By definition, a stop must have both a velic closure and an oral closure. Nasals do not have the velic closure. Neither are nasals fricatives. By definition, a fricative must leave a narrow slot through which the air stream whistles or buzzes. The opening into the nose through the velic is not such a narrow opening as that in a normal fricative sound. The nasals then form a third manner of articulation in addition to the stops and fricatives.

RE 1.17. Differential: STOP, FRICATIVE, or NASAL

1. [ɑmɑ] N
2. [ɑŋɑ] N
3. [ɑk^{h}ɑ] S
4. [ɑnɑ] N
5. [ɑsɑ] F
6. [ɑgɑ] S
7. [ɑt^{h}ɑ] S
8. [ɑŋɑ] N
9. [ɑnɑ] N
10. [ɑfɑ] F
11. [ɑp^{h}ɑ] S
12. [ɑšɑ] F
13. [ɑnɑ] N
14. [ɑžɑ] F
15. [ɑdɑ] S
16. [ɑmɑ] N
17. [ɑbɑ] S
18. [ɑgɑ] S

Laterals

The fourth (and last) manner of articulation which will be taken up in this lesson is lateral. It has to do with a formation of the tongue such that the air comes over the sides (one or both) rather than over the center of the tongue. Compare the following pairs of English words: let vs. set, law vs. gnaw, loot vs. toot. If you say these pairs slowly to yourself you will feel the difference (in the initial sounds) between lateral articulation and others. In the case of let vs. set, for example, you can prolong the initial sounds. In let the tongue tip remains up, touching the point of articulation. The velic is also closed. But the airstream continues to move anyhow, because the sides of the tongue are down enough to let it out. In set there is a groove down the center of the tongue and the sides are up against the teeth. English /l/ is a lateral. (On Sammy [l] cannot be distinguished from [d] because the sides of the tongue do not show.)

RE 1.18. Differential: STOP, FRICATIVE, NASAL, or LATERAL

1. [ɑlɑ]	L	8. [ɑpʰ]	S	15. [sɑ]	F
2. [gɑ]	S	9. [ɑtʰ]	S	16. [lɑ]	L
3. [ŋɑ]	N	10. [ɑθ]	F	17. [ɑd]	S
4. [vɑ]	F	11. [ɑš]	F	18. [ɑg]	S
5. [bɑ]	S	12. [đɑ]	F	19. [ɑfɑ]	F
6. [ɑlɑ]	L	13. [ɑnɑ]	N	20. [žɑ]	F
7. [ɑmɑ]	N	14. [ɑkʰ]	S	21. [ɑl]	L

Recorded Exercises 1.19-1.26. Description of Sounds

We will now begin to describe sounds in the terminology which you have been learning. We will begin this process on a gradual cumulative basis to make the description of sounds habitual for you as quickly as possible.

RE 1.19. Point and Manner

Respond with the manner of articulation as you did just previously, but also with the point of articulation. That is, for the utterance asa you will respond with ALVEOLAR FRICATIVE. Please note the order in which these different elements are included in the description and use the same order in your response.

Here is the total inventory of your possible responses. (Take one from each column.) Keep these before you temporarily if you need them, but as quickly as possible work toward responding without looking at these lists.

LABIAL	STOP
DENTAL	FRICATIVE
ALVEOLAR	NASAL
ALVEOPALATAL	LATERAL
VELAR	

1. [ɑfɑ]	DENTAL F	3. [ɑđɑ]	DENTAL F
2. [ɑvɑ]	DENTAL F	4. [ɑtʰɑ]	ALVEOLAR S

5. [ɑbɑ] LABIAL S
6. [ɑžɑ] ALVEOPALATAL F
7. [ɑŋɑ] VELAR N
8. [ɑšɑ] ALVEOPALATAL F
9. [ɑmɑ] LABIAL N
10. [ɑlɑ] ALVEOLAR L
11. [ɑs] ALVEOLAR F
12. [ɑn] ALVEOLAR N
13. [ɑpʰ] LABIAL S
14. [ɑd] ALVEOLAR S
15. [ɑz] ALVEOLAR F
16. [ɑž] ALVEOPALATAL F
17. [ɑθ] DENTAL F
18. [ɑkʰ] VELAR S
19. [ɑŋ] VELAR N
20. [ɑð] DENTAL F
21. [ɑlɑ] ALVEOLAR L
22. [ɑnɑ] ALVEOLAR N
23. [ɑsɑ] ALVEOLAR F
24. [ɑtʰɑ] ALVEOLAR S
25. [ɑŋ] VELAR N
26. [ðɑ] DENTAL F
27. [vɑ] DENTAL F
28. [fɑ] DENTAL F
29. [tʰɑ] ALVEOLAR S
30. [kʰɑ] VELAR S
31. [gɑ] VELAR S
32. [nɑ] ALVEOLAR N
33. [šɑ] ALVEOPALATAL F
34. [ðɑ] DENTAL F
35. [gɑ] VELAR S
36. [ɑlɑ] ALVEOLAR L
37. [ɑm] LABIAL N
38. [ɑθɑ] DENTAL F
39. [ɑŋɑ] VELAR N
40. [ɑn] ALVEOLAR N
41. [ɑž] ALVEOPALATAL F
42. [šɑ] ALVEOPALATAL F
43. [ɑbɑ] LABIAL S
44. [ɑs] ALVEOLAR F

RE 1.20. Differential: BILABIAL or LABIO-DENTAL

RE 1.20 begins to add information about the articulator to what you have just been doing. When the articulator is the lower lip, and the point of articulation is the upper lip, we speak of bilabial articulation. When the lower lip articulates against the upper teeth we speak of labio-dental articulation. Thus, if you hear afa, respond with LABIO-DENTAL. If you hear ama, respond with BILABIAL.

1.	[ɑfɑ]	L-D	4.	[ɑvɑ]	L-D	7.	[ɑpʰɑ]	BIL
2.	[ɑpʰɑ]	BIL	5.	[ɑbɑ]	BIL	8.	[ɑvɑ]	L-D
3.	[ɑmɑ]	BIL	6.	[ɑfɑ]	L-D	9.	[ɑbɑ]	BIL

RE 1.21. Differential: BILABIAL, LABIO-DENTAL, TIP-DENTAL

RE 1.21 adds a new relationship between articulator and point of articulation, such as we have in English *thin* and *then*. The tongue tip (or even the blade in more exaggerated pronunciation) articulates against the edge of the upper teeth. We will call this articulation *tip-dental*.[1]

1.	[ɑθɑ]	T-D	4.	[ɑðɑ]	T-D	7.	[ɑθɑ]	T-D
2.	[ɑfɑ]	L-D	5.	[ɑvɑ]	L-D	8.	[ɑpʰɑ]	BIL
3.	[ɑbɑ]	BIL	6.	[ɑmɑ]	BIL	9.	[ɑðɑ]	T-D

RE 1.22. Differential: BILABIAL, LABIO-DENTAL, TIP-DENTAL, BACK VELAR

RE 1.22 adds the *back-velar* articulation. Here the back of the tongue articulates in respect to the velar region. The exercise works just like the preceding ones.

1.	[ɑŋɑ]	B-V	6.	[ɑθɑ]	T-D	11.	[ɑkʰɑ]	B-V
2.	[ɑðɑ]	T-D	7.	[ɑkʰɑ]	B-V	12.	[ɑgɑ]	B-V
3.	[ɑpʰɑ]	BIL	8.	[ɑbɑ]	BIL	13.	[ɑŋɑ]	B-V
4.	[ɑgɑ]	B-V	9.	[ɑðɑ]	T-D	14.	[ɑθɑ]	T-D
5.	[ɑvɑ]	L-D	10.	[ɑfɑ]	L-D	15.	[ɑmɑ]	BIL

RE 1.23. Differential: TIP-(or BLADE-) ALVEOLAR or ALVEOPALATAL

RE 1.23 introduces a new type of complication peculiar to the articulation of certain English sounds. Some sounds, namely the consonants in *asa* and *aza* are *tip-alveolar* by some speakers of English, and *blade-alveolar* by others. The difference lies in the position of the tongue tip. In the tip-

---

[1]A very common term for this articulation is *interdental*, but we are using *tip-dental* simply because it is more analogous to our other terminology, and thus presents less of a learning problem.

alveolar articulation the tongue tip is up very near the alveolar ridge, leaving only the narrow slit for the fricative. In the blade-alveolar articulation the tongue tip is behind the lower teeth, and the blade is up near the alveolar ridge. The narrow slit is between the blade and the alveolar ridge. The two articulations can be pronounced so as to be indistinguishable to the ear. They make no functional difference for English. However, you should figure out what you do (with the help of your instructor, if necessary) so as to better get the feel and understanding of the articulatory process. Prolong the initial sounds in <u>see</u> and <u>zee</u> to feel the way in which you articulate: <u>sssssee</u>, <u>zzzzzee</u>.

Furthermore, there is a similar problem with the English fricative sounds in <u>fission</u> and <u>vision</u>. Some English speakers pronounce these with <u>tip-alveopalatal</u> articulation, and others with <u>blade-alveopalatal</u> articulation. Figure out what you do by pronouncing <u>fisssssssion</u> and <u>visssssssion</u>.

Here are the possibilities from which you are to select your responses in this drill: TIP-ALVEOLAR, BLADE-ALVEOLAR, TIP-ALVEOPALATAL, or BLADE-ALVEOPALATAL.

At any point where you respond TIP someone else may correctly respond BLADE in this exercise. It all depends on what you or the other person actually does in pronunciation. Remember that in this drill you are responding by <u>your</u> articulation of the English sound, regardless of which of the alternatives (tip or blade) may have actually been used on the tape. You could not possibly hear the difference.

The answer given on the tape will give both possible correct responses. But remember, only one of them is correct for you, unless you actually fluctuate in your pronunciation between the one and the other.

1. [ɑsɑ]	TIP-(or BLADE-) AL	6. [ɑžɑ]	TIP-(or BLADE-) AP
2. [ɑzɑ]	TIP-(or BLADE-) AL	7. [ɑsɑ]	TIP-(or BLADE-) AL
3. [ɑšɑ]	TIP-(or BLADE-) AP	8. [ɑšɑ]	TIP-(or BLADE-) AP
4. [ɑžɑ]	TIP-(or BLADE-) AP	9. [ɑzɑ]	TIP-(or BLADE-) AL
5. [ɑzɑ]	TIP-(or BLADE-) AL	10. [ɑšɑ]	TIP-(or BLADE-) AP

RE 1.24. Differential: TIP-(or BLADE-) ALVEOLAR or ALVEOPALATAL

RE 1.24 adds now some tip-alveolar articulations in English for which there are not normally speakers who use a blade articulation. For example, in <u>ata</u>, most speakers of English will have tip-alveolar articulation, as contrasted with <u>asa</u> where a large percentage have blade-alveolar. Remember that for some of these sounds the tape will have to give two responses, but only one of them is correct for you. The responses are the same as for the preceding exercise.

1. [αtʰα] TIP-AL
2. [αšα] TIP-(or BLADE-) AP
3. [αlα] TIP-AL
4. [αnα] TIP-AL
5. [αsα] TIP-(or BLADE-) AL
6. [αdα] TIP-AL
7. [αžα] TIP-(or BLADE-) AP
8. [αzα] TIP-(or BLADE-) AL
9. [αtʰα] TIP-AL
10. [αlα] TIP-AL

<u>RE 1.25. Description of Sounds</u>

Now you finally get the opportunity to put all of this together, to drive home the terminology we have introduced so far, and to test your use of it. Here is the total inventory of your possible responses. (Take one from each column.)

BILABIAL	STOP
LABIO-DENTAL	FRICATIVE
TIP-DENTAL	NASAL
TIP-ALVEOLAR	LATERAL
BLADE-ALVEOLAR	
TIP-ALVEOPALATAL	
BLADE-ALVEOPALATAL	
BACK-VELAR	

It takes a little practice to get used to the terminology for the description of new sounds, but that is what the drills here presented are for. This is not all we could say about sounds. However, we do not yet know enough about them to say anything more, and what we do have gives us a very useful means of talking about them and of building other information.

1. [αšα] TIP-(or BLADE-) ALVEOPALATAL F
2. [αgα] BACK-VELAR S
3. [αŋα] BACK-VELAR N

4. [ɑθɑ] TIP-DENTAL F

5. [ɑžɑ] TIP-(or BLADE-) ALVEOPALATAL F

6. [ɑnɑ] TIP-ALVEOLAR N

7. [ɑdɑ] TIP-ALVEOLAR S

8. [ɑp^{h}ɑ] BILABIAL S

9. [ɑfɑ] LABIO-DENTAL F

10. [ɑlɑ] TIP-ALVEOLAR L

11. [zɑ] TIP- (or BLADE-) ALVEOLAR F

12. [p^{h}ɑ] BILABIAL S

13. [šɑ] TIP-(or BLADE-) ALVEOPALATAL F

14. [gɑ] BACK-VELAR S

15. [žɑ] TIP-(or BLADE-) ALVEOPALATAL F

16. [mɑ] BILABIAL N

17. [lɑ] TIP-ALVEOLAR L

18. [ðɑ] TIP-DENTAL F

19. [vɑ] LABIO-DENTAL F

20. [fɑ] LABIO-DENTAL F

21. [ɑŋ] BACK-VELAR N

22. [ɑð] TIP-DENTAL F

23. [ɑš] TIP-(or BLADE-) ALVEOPALATAL F

24. [ɑs] TIP-(or BLADE-) ALVEOLAR F

25. [ɑp^h] BILABIAL S

26. [ɑk^h] BACK-VELAR S

27. [ɑt^h] TIP-ALVEOLAR S

28. [ɑf] LABIO-DENTAL F

29. [ɑv] LABIO-DENTAL F

30. [ɑð] TIP-DENTAL F

31. [ɑš] TIP- (or BLADE-) ALVEOPALATAL F

32. [ɑm] BILABIAL N

33. [mɑ] BILABIAL N

34. [ɑθ] TIP-DENTAL F

35. [ɑn] TIP-ALVEOLAR N

36. [k^{h}ɑ] BACK-VELAR S

37. [nɑ] TIP-ALVEOLAR N

38. [ɑŋ] BACK-VELAR N

39. [ɑl] TIP-ALVEOLAR L

40. [ɑm] BILABIAL N

RE 1.26. Description of Sounds

RE 1.26 reverses the above procedure. This time the tape will give you the description and you pronounce the sound in the space provided. Then the tape will follow with the sound between two vowels. If more than one sound is possible for the description, both will be given. This is just another way of practicing the same material.

1. BILABIAL S [ɑbɑ] or [ɑp^{h}ɑ]

2. TIP-ALVEOLAR N [ɑnɑ]

3. BACK-VELAR S [ɑgɑ] or [ɑk^{h}ɑ]

4. TIP-DENTAL F [ɑðɑ] or [ɑθɑ]

5. LABIO-DENTAL F [ɑvɑ] or [ɑfɑ]

6. TIP-(or BLADE-) ALVEOLAR F [ɑzɑ] or [ɑsɑ]

7. TIP-(or BLADE-) ALVEOPALATAL F [ɑžɑ] or [ɑšɑ]

8. TIP-(or BLADE-) ALVEOLAR F [ɑzɑ] or [ɑsɑ]

9. BACK-VELAR S [ɑgɑ] or [ɑk^{h}ɑ]

10. LABIO-DENTAL F [ɑvɑ] or [ɑfɑ]

11. TIP-DENTAL F [ɑðɑ] or [ɑθɑ]

12. TIP-(or BLADE-) ALVEOPALATAL F [ɑžɑ] or [ɑšɑ]

13. BILABIAL N [ɑmɑ]

14. TIP-ALVEOLAR L [ɑlɑ]

15. LABIO-DENTAL F [ɑvɑ] or [ɑfɑ]

Suggested Reading

Further discussion on the subjects of this lesson will be found in the following references. There are usually some differences of terminology which, however, are usually translatable from one author to another. This list is intended to suggest representative readings which are not overly difficult, and which parallel the treatment of our Lesson 1 closely enough to be useful. Full bibliographic information on these and other books mentioned in the _Manual_ will be found in the bibliography.

Charles F. Hockett, <u>A Course in Modern Linguistics</u>, pp. 62-74.

W. Nelson Francis, <u>The Structure of American English</u>, pp. 51-70.

Bernard Bloch and George L. Trager, <u>Outline of Linguistic Analysis</u>, pp. 10-16, 25-28.

A LOWER-LOW CENTRAL UNROUNDED ORAL VOWEL FOLLOWED BY A VOICELESS GROOVED ASPIRATED ALVEOPALATAL AFFRICATE WITH EGRESSIVE LUNG AIR FOLLOWED BY AN EXTENDED HIGH BACK ROUNDED ORAL VOWEL ......OR IN THE VERNACULAR, A SNEEZE!

LESSON TWO

Hearing Pitch Distinctions

One of the most common mistakes of English-speaking people learning another language is the neglect of the way speakers of the second language modulate their voices as they speak. We are, of course, aware of the fact that in English we raise and lower our voices as we talk. Most of us realize, for example, that we can signal a difference between a question and an answer of certain types by change in the pitch of our voice. We know that the sequence "John is coming" can be said either as a statement or as a question. If it is said as a question, there is a rise at the end of the sentence.

We do not usually have it called to our attention, however, that we are capable of making distinctions of the following kind.

Speaker 1: "I saw it there."

Speaker 2: "What?" (with a rising voice)

Speaker 1: "I saw it there."

In this case, if Speaker 2 says "what" with a rising intonation, the first speaker repeats his initial statement. However, look at the following exchange.

Speaker 1: "I saw it there."

Speaker 2: "What?" (with a falling intonation)

Speaker 1: "A chair."

It is very clear that by two different pitch contours the whole implication of the word "what" is changed. We do not have time here to demonstrate the fact that the English intonation system contains a large number of important distinctions.[1]

For some reason or other, when we learn another language, even though we may learn the consonants and vowels well, we tend to take our intonation distinctions over from English into

---

[1]Kenneth L. Pike, Intonation of American English; George L. Trager and Henry Lee Smith, Jr., An Outline of English Structure, pp. 41-52.

the other language. Perhaps because these are not written in English or the other language they seem less real, and we are less conscious of them. But whatever the reason, we tend to speak French or German or Hindi or Zulu words and sentences with English intonation. This is bad for any number of reasons. In the first place, some languages are so constructed in their pitch systems that a change in pitch makes a much greater meaning difference even than in English, and a difference of another kind. The difference between 'I' and 'he' may be a difference of pitch. Pitch does not make this kind of meaning difference in English, but if we carry our English intonation patterns over into a language like that, they may result in our saying things which are either utter nonsense or completely different from what we intended to say.

Then, on the other hand, even for languages which do not use pitch distinctions to distinguish words, it is safe to say that by carrying English intonation patterns over we speak with a foreign accent, or we may even occasionally be misunderstood. People may also misunderstand our mood and attitude by such a fault on our own part.

If, however, we make a diligent attempt to reproduce the pitch patterns of the language we are learning from the beginning of our study, in most cases they will not be nearly as difficult as we thought. Native speakers of the language are impressed with our learning ability and the "naturalness" of our speech.

Care in the mimicry of pitch is not something which can be put off in language study. It has to begin from the very first day. It has to be a basic part of our mimicry of the speech of the language being learned. It has to occupy a focal point in our attention. We should never be content to say a sentence or a word in the second language without having the intonation or the tone just as correct as we have the consonants and vowels. We can never be said to speak a language well if we do not control its pitch patterns to an important degree.

One of the important things about learning to use correct pitch is the fact that the language cannot be practiced orally without some pitch or other. Either English pitch will be used or some other pitch. This is because we cannot talk without pitch. If we use English pitch in practicing the new language, we are simply reinforcing bad habits which become nearly impossible to break. If to the best of our ability we mimic the pitch of the new language, we are on the way toward building new habits which will mean clear and pleasant speech.

The purpose, then, of this lesson is to begin to train the student's ears to hear pitch distinctions. At first the work will consist simply of listening for pitch sameness or difference. Listening for difference of kind (whether the pitch is rising, falling, or level) will follow. Both nonsense syllables with English sound characteristics and actual foreign language materials will be used in these exercises.

Follow the directions carefully and keep going over this material repeatedly until you are confident of it. If you find the drills fairly easy try writing the pitch as you respond. Write from left to right, drawing a line upward for a rising pitch [/], downward for a falling pitch [\ ], and level for a level pitch [—].

Recorded Exercises 2.1-2.2. Discrimination Drill: Which is Different?

On the tape you will now work with exercises which are different from those you have found up to the present. In RE 2.1 each utterance will consist of three syllables in the sequence [mo pi su]. This sequence will be repeated twice. You will be asked to decide which of the three syllables in the sequence is different in pitch from the other syllables of the sequence. You are to listen to the utterances and in the space following them you are to respond by pronouncing the syllable which is different. That is, if the first syllable is different from the other two, you will respond with [mo]. If the second syllable is different, you will respond with [pi], etc. If they are all the same, you will respond with NONE, because none of the syllables is different.

Now turn on the tape recorder and try the exercise without watching the transcription below. A demonstration is given to you first before the exercises actually begin. If this gives you difficulty, try humming them in imitation of the tape. If you still do not get them, watch the transcription of the exercise and watch the drawings of the pitch levels as you listen and hum.

RE 2.1. Discrimination: Name the Syllable Which is Different

1. [mopisu]	[pi]	4. [mopisu]	NONE	7. [mopisu]	NONE
2. [mopisu]	[mo]	5. [mopisu]	[su]	8. [mopisu]	[pi]
3. [mopisu]	[su]	6. [mopisu]	[su]	9. [mopisu]	[mo]

10. [mopisu] [pi]
11. [mopisu] [pi]
12. [mopisu] [mo]
13. [mopisu] [su]
14. [mopisu] NONE
15. [mopisu] [su]
16. [mopisu] [su]
17. [mopisu] NONE
18. [mopisu] [pi]
19. [mopisu] [mo]
20. [mopisu] [pi]
21. [mopisu] NONE

In RE 2.2 each utterance will consist of five syllables. Your response, however, is to be called out in exactly the same way. Remember that all you have to listen for is which syllable is different and to respond with that syllable.

RE 2.2. Discrimination: Name the Syllable Which is Different

1. [somebikuna] [na]
2. [somebikuna] [na]
3. [somebikuna] [me]
4. [somebikuna] [ku]
5. [somebikuna] NONE
6. [somebikuna] [so]
7. [somebikuna] [bi]
8. [somebikuna] [ku]
9. [somebikuna] [na]
10. [somebikuna] [so]
11. [somebikuna] [so]
12. [somebikuna] [me]
13. [somebikuna] NONE
14. [somebikuna] [ku]
15. [somebikuna] [bi]
16. [somebikuna] [bi]
17. [somebikuna] [ku]
18. [somebikuna] [me]
19. [somebikuna] [na]
20. [somebikuna] [so]

Recorded Exercises 2.3-2.10. Discrimination: Same or Different

In the following exercises you are to listen to each pair of utterances. This is a change in procedure from what you have been doing before. Instead of hearing the same utterance twice, you will now hear two different utterances in sequence, and you are to decide whether or not the pitch of the two is the same. You are to respond with SAME or DIFFERENT.[1] The tape leaves you space for reply, and then indicates the correct response.

Those who find these exercises easy should simply sample them. Those who find them more difficult should go over them again and again until they become easier. There will, of course, be opportunity for practice in later lessons.

These exercises are written in a phonemic or nearly phonemic transcription. The tone is indicated by extra marks, called diacritics, above or below the word. You are not responsible for these diacritics or for the transcription used for the words. Listen selectively to the pitch.

Do not watch the transcription as you try the exercises.

RE 2.3: Amoy[2]. Discrimination: SAME or DIFFERENT

1.	kho·	'class. for dollars'	khó·	'bitterness'	D
2.	ám	'rice water'	ám	'rice water'	S
3.	bak	'to defile'	bák	'wood'	D
4.	thāu	'to poison'	thâu	'the head'	D
5.	su	'inferior,	sū	'a matter'	D
6.	soa^{n}	'a mountain'	soá^{n}	'to disperse'	D
7.	bān	'slowly'	bān	'slowly'	S
8.	bī	'taste'	bī	'taste'	S
9.	eng	'an eagle'	éng	'a wave'	D

[1] These exercises are modeled after ones prepared by Dr. William E. Welmers.

[2] Amoy is spoken on Taiwan. Data and tape recording for this and succeeding exercises by Fred C.C. Peng, U. of Buffalo.

10.	hiòng	'towards'	hiòng	'towards'	S
11.	gōa	'outside'	gōa	'outside'	S
12.	gô	'a goose'	gô	'a goose'	S
13.	gán	'the eye'	gàn	'to cool, as in water'	D
14.	bé	'to buy'	bē	'to sell'	D
15.	sng	'ache, sore'	sńg	'to play about'	D
16.	siū^{n}	'to think'	siū^{n}	'to think'	S
17.	lāng	'to sport with'	lâng	'a person'	D
18.	ńg	'shade'	n̂g	'yellow'	D
19.	mî	'night'	mî	'cotton'	S
20.	khiat	'to strike, as match'	khiat	'to strike, as match'	S

RE 2.4: Amoy. Discrimination: SAME or DIFFERENT

Remember that you are discriminating between the words on the basis of tone only. In this exercise consonants and vowels will differ, but disregard such differences.

1.	chháu	'grass'	cháu	'to run'	S
2.	hiong	'vehement'	khióng	'to be afraid of'	D
3.	chhân	'a field'	thàn	'to obey'	D
4.	tui	'a heap'	thui	'a ladder'	S
5.	n̂g	'yellow'	hn̂g	'a field'	S
6.	hong	'wind'	khong	'empty'	S
7.	tsôa	'a snake'	tsoa^{n}	'to boil'	D
8.	phâng	'to carry with two hands'	tháng	'a pail'	D
9.	phi	'to spread out'	khi	'to lean over'	S
10.	thâng	'a worm'	hang	'to bake'	D

11.	kiù	'to save'	iù	'tender'	S
12.	siū^{n}	'to think'	kiu^{n}	'ginger'	D
13.	siōng	'a picture'	hiong	'vehement'	D
14.	tòa	'to stay'	koa	'a song'	D
15.	mn̄g	'to ask'	nn̄g	'an egg'	S
16.	kng	'high'	mn̂g	'hair'	D
17.	khò·	'trousers'	thò·	'to vomit'	S
18.	oan	'a curve'	khoan	'to forgive'	S
19.	tōng	'a cave'	ông	'a king'	D
20.	chhàt	'a thief'	chat	'to wrap up'	D
21.	hoàt	'to punish'	thoat	'to escape'	D
22.	kam	'sweet'	am	'to cover'	S

RE 2.5: Amoy. Discrimination: SAME or DIFFERENT

1.	su	'defeated'	tóng	'a company'	D
2.	siu^{n}	'a box'	sng	'sour'	S
3.	that	'to kick'	suh	'to suck'	S
4.	the	'to lean'	sóa	'to remove'	D
5.	soa^{n}	'a mountain'	sǹg	'to reckon'	D
6.	bâng	'bewildered'	gô·	'a goose'	S
7.	hiông	'violence'	gōa	'outside'	D
8.	chháu	'grass'	êng	'leisure'	D
9.	èng	'to fulfill'	góa	'I'	D
10.	â^{n}	'to guard'	â^{n}	'Eh?, What?'	S
11.	chheh	'a book'	bak	'to defile'	S
12.	khò·	'trousers'	chháu	'grass'	D

13. chhàu	'to rot'	hiòng	'towards'	S
14. bān	'slowly'	khó•	'bitter'	D
15. lâi	'to come'	bê	'to get lost'	S
16. bī	'taste'	ám	'rice water'	D
17. bàk	'wood'	chhèh	'to sink down'	S
18. gōng	'stupid'	tsôa	'a snake'	D
19. ti	'a pig'	lai	'sharp'	D
20. kim	'gold'	chhau	'to copy a writing'	S

RE 2.6: Hausa[1]. Discrimination: SAME or DIFFERENT

1. gídá	'compound'	kífí	'fish'	S
2. kúká	'cry'	náma	'meat'	D
3. ɗáki	'hut'	kazá	'chicken'	D
4. ubá	'father	karé	'dog'	S
5. náma	'meat'	ído	'eye'	S
6. tsóhó	'old'	jakí	'donkey'	D
7. ragó	'ram'	bakó	'guest'	S
8. ído	'eye'	kífí	'fish'	D
9. záki	'lion'	karé	'dog'	D
10. úwá	'mother'	ráná	'day'	S
11. kífí	'fish'	aíki	'work'	D
12. záki	'lion'	sárkí	'chief'	D
13. úwá	'mother'	ubá	'father'	D

[1]Hausa is an important language of West Africa, centering in Nigeria. Data are from Rev. Charles Kraft, Kennedy School of Missions. Informant for RE 2.6 and 2.7 is Hamalai Mubi.

14.	tsóhó	'old'	záfí	'hot'	S
15.	addá	'machete'	yáro	'boy'	D
16.	fará	'grasshopper'	addá	'machete'	S
17.	ído	'eye'	aíki	'work'	S
18.	tsóhó	'old'	náma	'meat'	D
19.	záki	'lion'	ɗáki	'hut'	S
20.	giwá	'elephant'	fará	'grasshopper'	D

RE 2.7: Hausa. Discrimination: SAME or DIFFERENT

1.	cókúla	'spoons'	ɗákúna	'huts'	S
2.	túfáfi	'clothes'	labári	'news'	D
3.	binciké	'investigate'	littinîn	'Monday'	D
4.	gonakí	'farms'	labarú	'news (pl.)'	S
5.	fúskókí	'faces'	láfíya	'well'	D
6.	líttáfi	'book'	júmá'a	'Friday'	S
7.	ɗákúna	'huts'	asára	'misfortune'	D
8.	tawáda	'ink'	ƙankáne	'small'	S
9.	cókúla	'spoons'	bíndíga	'gun'	S
10.	littinîn	'Monday'	labarú	'news (pl.)'	D
11.	taláta	'Tuesday'	sabúlu	'soap'	S
12.	gonakí	'farms'	tawáda	'ink'	D
13.	labarú	'news (pl.)'	ídanú	'eyes'	D
14.	kújerá	'chair'	ƙáfafú	'feet'	S
15.	fúskókí	'faces'	ítacé	'wood'	D
16.	cókúla	'spoons'	ídanú	'eyes'	D
17.	júmá'a	'Friday'	máfárkí	'dream'	D

18. dúwatsú	'stones'	túgwayé	'twins'	S
19. sabúlu	'soap'	amfaní	'usefulness'	D
20. asára	'misfortune'	labarú	'news (pl.)'	D

RE 2.8: Hausa.[1] Discrimination: SAME or DIFFERENT

1. áyóyí	'verses'	ƙófófí	'doors'	S
2. hányóyí	'paths'	ígíya	'rope'	D
3. áyyúka	'works'	yárínya	'girl'	S
4. gaísúwá	'greetings'	ásálí	'lineage'	S
5. líttáfi	'book'	ɗánúwá	'brother'	D
6. túfáfi	'clothes'	ámínci	'peacefulness'	S
7. iyáli	'family'	garajé	'haste'	D
8. shari'ú	'judgments'	alhéri	'goodness'	D
9. dangána	'depends'	akwataí	'boxes'	D
10. wahála	'trouble'	magána	'word'	S
11. alkálí	'judge'	aljíhú	'pocket'	S
12. garajé	'haste'	shinkáfá	'rice'	D
13. abínci	'food'	shari'ú	'judgments'	D
14. taimákó	'help'	takalmí	'shoe'	D
15. ƙokárí	'trying'	kasúwá	'market'	S
16. tabarmí	'mats'	shekarú	'years'	S
17. daríyá	'laugh'	asubâ	'dawn time'	D
18. ciníkí	'barter'	kadarkaí	'bridges'	D
19. áyyúka	'works'	dángúna	'clans'	S

[1]The informant for this and succeeding Hausa exercises is Ishmaila Mubi.

20.	kujéra	'stool'	iyáli	'family'	S

RE 2.9: Hausa. Discrimination: SAME or DIFFERENT

1.	dalíli	'reason'	tálaúci	'poverty'	D
2.	aláma	'sign'	ígíya	'rope'	D
3.	aléwa	'onion'	bukáta	'need'	S
4.	ámínci	'peacefulness'	alhéri	'goodness'	D
5.	makáho	'blind man'	allúra	'needle'	S
6.	fártánya	'hoe'	áddú'a	'prayer'	S
7.	ajíya	'savings'	jarába	'test'	S
8.	gáfára	'forgiveness'	magána	'word'	D
9.	láfíya	'well'	túfáfi	'clothes'	S
10.	kádárko	'bridge'	yárínya	'girl'	S
11.	halítta	'creation'	sabúlu	'soap'	S
12.	tákálma	'shoes'	shekára	'year'	D
13.	hádíri	'storm'	wahála	'trouble'	D
14.	ígíya	'rope'	faraúta	'hunting'	D
15.	dangána	'depends'	líttáfi	'book'	D
16.	abíncí	'food'	iyáli	'family'	D
17.	shekára	'year'	takalmí	'shoe'	D
18.	túkúnyá	'cook pot'	túnkiyá	'sheep'	D
19.	láfíya	'well'	ajíya	'savings'	D
20.	daríyá	'laugh'	tabármá	'mat'	S

RE 2.10: Hausa. Discrimination: SAME or DIFFERENT

1.	jagabá	'leader'	adíko	'towel'	D
2.	hánkalí	'character'	fáraúta	'hunting'	D

3. zúciyá	'heart'	kasúwá	'market'	D
4. gánúwá	'rampart'	ázáncí	'meaning'	S
5. ílimí	'knowledge'	taimákó	'help'	D
6. ídanú	'eyes'	aláma	'sign'	D
7. fártánya	'hoe'	amfaní	'usefulness	D
8. wahála	'trouble'	táláka	'poor man'	D
9. ítacé	'wood'	dangána	'depends'	D
10. tásóshí	'dishes'	állúna	'needles'	D
11. ásálí	'lineage'	agwagwá	'duck'	D
12. alhéri	'goodness'	sabúlu	'soap'	S
13. mútané	'people'	íyaká	'end'	S
14. bukáta	'need'	ajiyé	'put'	D
15. saúrayí	'young man'	dalíli	'reason'	D
16. gaisúwá	'greetings'	gáfára	'forgiveness'	D
17. dúwatsú	'stones'	líttáfi	'book'	D
18. tálaúci	'poverty'	asubâ	'dawn time'	D
19. ínúwa	'shade'	makáho	'blind man'	D
20. allúra	'needle'	fártánya	'hoe'	D

Recorded Exercises 2.11-2.21. Level or Glided Pitch

In this set of exercises you are asked to distinguish between level pitch and glided pitch. A glided pitch is a pitch which moves either up or down. A level pitch is one which is level throughout its duration. You will be allowed space to make your oral response and the tape will correct you. In RE 2.11-2.16 each drill will have a constant frame. This means that whereas the pitch differs from one item of the exercise to the next, other features of the utterance are constant throughout. In this case the frame which is constant consists of the consonants and the vowels.

RE 2.11. Differential: LEVEL or RISING

1. well L	7. well R	13. well R
2. well R	8. well R	14. well R
3. well R	9. well R	15. well R
4. well L	10. well L	16. well L
5. well L	11. well R	17. well L
6. well L	12. well L	18. well R

RE 2.12. Differential: LEVEL or FALLING

1. mine L	7. mine L	13. mine L
2. mine L	8. mine F	14. mine F
3. mine F	9. mine F	15. mine L
4. mine F	10. mine F	16. mine L
5. mine L	11. mine F	17. mine F
6. mine F	12. mine L	18. mine L

RE 2.13. Differential: RISING or FALLING

1. up R	3. up F	5. up R
2. up R	4. up F	6. up F

7. up	R	11. up	R	15. up	F
8. up	R	12. up	R	16. up	F
9. up	R	13. up	F	17. up	R
10. up	F	14. up	F	18. up	R

RE 2.14. Differential: LEVEL, RISING, or FALLING

1. some	F	7. some	R	13. some	R
2. some	L	8. some	R	14. some	R
3. some	R	9. some	L	15. some	F
4. some	L	10. some	F	16. some	L
5. some	L	11. some	L	17. some	F
6. some	R	12. some	L	18. some	F

RE 2.15-2.16 contain longer sequences. In these exercises we now give you longer stretches of utterance, but we control them so that you listen only to the last syllable of each utterance. You are to respond to the last syllable of each utterance with the same responses that you had in the immediately preceding exercises, that is, LEVEL, RISING, or FALLING. Do not be confused by the syllables preceding the last one. They will be kept constant, as the frame. Listen only to the pitch on the last syllable.

RE 2.15. Differential: LEVEL, RISING, or FALLING

1. Will you come here R   2. Will you come here L

3. Will you come here F
4. Will you come here F
5. Will you come here R
6. Will you come here L
7. Will you come here R
8. Will you come here F
9. Will you come here R
10. Will you come here R
11. Will you come here R
12. Will you come here L
13. Will you come here L
14. Will you come here F
15. Will you come here F
16. Will you come here F
17. Will you come here L
18. Will you come here R
19. Will you come here F
20. Will you come here L

RE 2.16. Differential: LEVEL, RISING, or FALLING

1. I didn't see John F
2. I didn't see John L
3. I didn't see John R
4. I didn't see John F
5. I didn't see John R
6. I didn't see John F
7. I didn't see John R
8. I didn't see John L
9. I didn't see John R
10. I didn't see John R
11. I didn't see John L
12. I didn't see John F
13. I didn't see John F
14. I didn't see John R

15. I didn't see John F
16. I didn't see John L
17. I didn't see John L
18. I didn't see John F
19. I didn't see John R
20. I didn't see John L

RE 2.17: Mano.[1] Differential: LEVEL, RISING, or FALLING

1. /gɛ̀ɛ̀/ 'spirit' F
2. /gɛɛ/ 'cotton tree' L
3. /gɛ́ɛ́/ 'green snake' L
4. /gɛ́ɛ̀/ 'Gio (a neighboring tribe)' F
5. /gɛ̀ɛ/ 'country devil' R
6. /gɛɛ̀/ 'rattle' F

RE 2.18: Mano. Differential: LEVEL, RISING, or FALLING

1. /kɔ̀/ 'arm, hand' F
2. /sɔ̄/ 'cloth' L
3. /gɔ̄́/ 'leopard' L
4. /lɔ̄́ɔ̄́/ 'week' L
5. /yɔ̄́ɔ̄/ 'brother-in-law' F
6. /bɔ̄́ɔ̄̀/ 'two-cent piece' F
7. /wɔ̄ɔ̄/ 'to lie down' L
8. /dōṓ/ 'one'
9. /pɔ̄ɔ̄̀/ 'load' F
10. /tɔ̄̀ɔ̄̀/ 'chicken' F
11. /kɔ̄̀ɔ̄́/ 'first daughter' R
12. /lɔ̄̀ɔ̄/ 'hunger' R
13. /ñ̄ɔ̂ɔ̄/ 'better' FR
14. /wɛ̀ɛ̄/ 'how much' RF
15. /lṑô/ 'one's own mother' RF
16. /gɔ̄̌ɔ̄̀/ 'water snail' RF

---

[1] Mano is spoken in Liberia and Guinea. The informant recorded in this lesson is See Diagbɛ from Gbuuyi, Liberia. The material was recorded with the cooperation of Dr. Charles White and Miss Mildred Black of the Methodist Mission, Ganta, Liberia.

RE 2.19: Vietnamese.[1] Differential: LEVEL, RISING, or FALLING

1.	/cĩ/	'to be only'	R	8.	/cín/	'nine'	R
2.	/ñĩ/	'isn't that so?'	R	9.	/sin/	'please'	L
3.	/t^{h}î/	'then'	F	10.	/ñîw/	'much, many'	F
4.	/mî/	'wheat'	F	11.	/t^{h}íw/	'lack'	R
5.	/xi/	'when'	L	12.	/tiw/	'be digested'	L
6.	/ɗi/	'go'	L	13.	/hĩw/	'understand'	R
7.	/cị/	'older sister'	R				

RE 2.20: Vietnamese. Differential: LEVEL, RISING, or FALLING

1.	/gé/	'chair'	R	4.	/t^{h}ẽ/	'ability'	R
2.	/t^{h}é/	'manner'	R	5.	/vè/	'to return home'	F
3.	/ɗẽ/	'place'	R				

RE 2.21: Vietnamese. Differential: LEVEL, RISING, or FALLING

1.	/ɓǽ/	'small'	R	4.	/xwæ̃/	'be well'	R
2.	/sæ/	'conveyance'	L	5.	/mæ̣/	'mother'	R
3.	/ṣæ̃/	'fut. indicator'	R				

Suggested Readings

Eugene A. Nida, Learning a Foreign Language, pp. 110-118.

---

[1] Vietnamese data and recordings in this lesson are from William A. Smalley and Nguyễn-văn-Vạn, Vietnamese for Missionaries.

LESSON THREE[1]

Voiced and Voiceless Fricatives

We said in Lesson 1 that one kind of manner of articulation had to do with the relationship between the articulator and the point of articulation. Stops, fricatives, nasals, and laterals are examples of this kind of manner. Another kind of manner we said had to do with other activity in the vocal tract simultaneously with the articulation. An example of this is the distinction which we will now discuss between voicing and voicelessness.

If you make a long English [s] or a long [f], prolonging these sounds for several seconds, and cup the palms of your hands over your ears, you will not feel any buzzing or vibration in your ears. If, however, you pronounce a long [z] or a long [v] in the same manner, prolonging them for several seconds, and hold your hands over your ears in this way, you will feel such a vibration and hear a buzzing in them. This will be very clear if you pronounce first the [f] and then the [v], the [s] and then the [z]. Be sure to prolong them long enough to be able to feel and hear the difference. The sounds which do not have this vibration or buzzing are called voiceless sounds. Those which do are called voiced sounds. All speech sounds are either voiced or voiceless, no matter what the articulation.

RE 3.1. Demonstration: English Fricatives

Here are some examples of voiceless and voiced fricatives in English. Pronounce the examples to yourself with your hands over your ears, and then listen to them in RE 3.1, as they are pronounced on the tape. When the voiced or voiceless fricative is said with a vowel immediately preceding or following, it is harder to hear the voicing than if it is said alone. This is caused by the fact that the vowel is voiced and the duration of the consonant when spoken naturally is very short. If you cannot feel or hear the voicing in normal speech, exaggerate the words by prolonging the fricatives. Follow the transcription.

---

[1] This lesson and succeeding ones presuppose the study of Lesson A (Appendix) on the phonemic transcription of English consonants so that students have learned the values of the symbols used for English consonants and their names.

Voiceless fricatives:	Voiced fricatives:
/fɑ/ as in fie	/vɑ/ as in vie
/θɑ/ as in thigh	/đɑ/ as in thy
/sɑ/ as in see	/zɑ/ as in Z
/šɑ/ as in Asshur	/žɑ/ as in azure[1]

In the following you may find that you have little or no voicing in the fricative. With your hands over your ears, try to determine what happens in your voicing of the words in the second column.[2]

/ɑf/ as in life	/ɑv/ as in alive
/ɑθ/ as in lath	/ɑđ/ as in lathe
/ɑs/ as in cross	/ɑz/ as in cause
/ɑš/ as in lush	/ɑž/ as in garage

Be careful about garage. It is pronounced with /ž/ on the tape, and is so pronounced by some speakers of English. Others, however, use another sound. Listen carefully to the tape.

The Nature of Voicing

In order to understand more about voicing and voicelessness, we have to add to our Sam Mansfield. In Sammy 3.1 we see drawn and labeled the larynx areas of the speech tract, including the vocal cords. The vocal cords are twin membranes in the throat, such that they can be pulled tight against each other or allowed to relax loosely in the throat. Control of them is completely automatic, of course, in our speech in English, and usually we are not conscious of it. When a voiceless sound is pronounced the membranes are opened and relaxed, allowing the air to come through unimpeded. On a voiced sound

---

[1]/ž/ does not occur initially in English.

[2]This does not mean that the final sounds in the first column are necessarily the same as the final sounds in the second, even though they are voiceless, made at the same point of articulation, etc. There are other characteristics of these phonemes in English which also differentiate them in most people's speech.

the membranes are drawn taut but are not completely closed off. They are drawn so taut and so close together that the air going through is impeded in a manner similar to that which a fricative creates in the mouth. The resulting effect is the buzzing that you hear in [v], [z], etc.

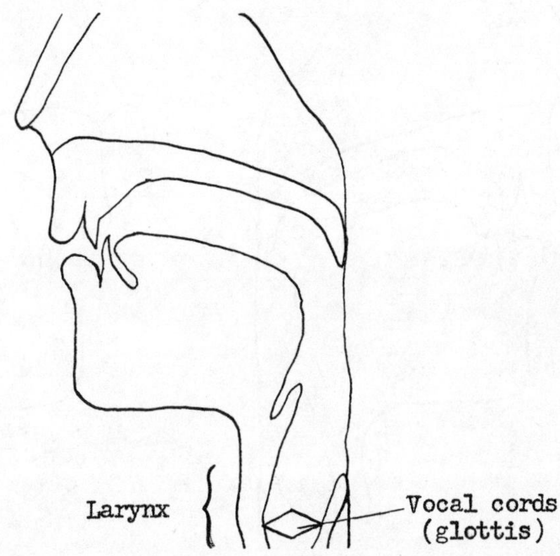

Sammy 3.1: Larynx and Vocal Cords

The vocal cords serve several functions in speech. Some of them will be taken up later.

Here is a picture of what the vocal cords look like, roughly, from above. Remember that these are not the only positions the vocal cords can take, but they are the positions which they assume in voicelessness and voicing.

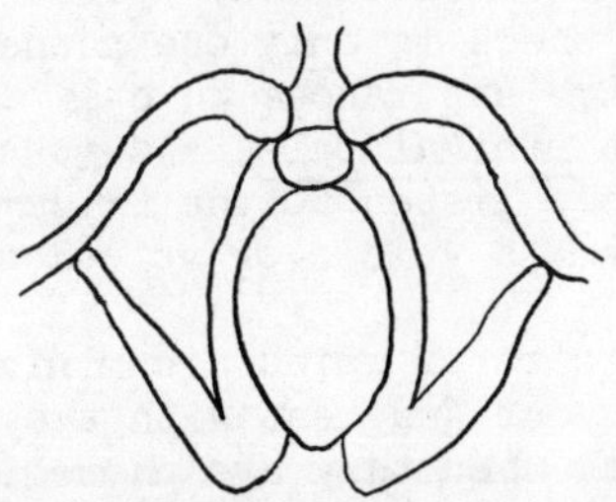

Sammy 3.2: Larynx Open for Voicelessness

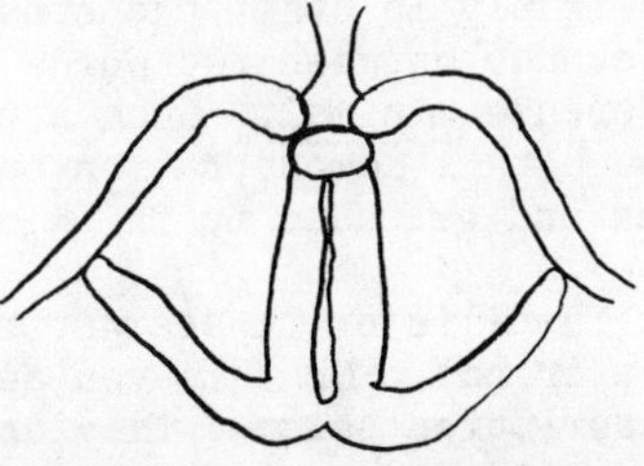

Sammy 3.3: Larynx Nearly Closed for Voicing

In drawing Sammies to represent speech sounds we indicate voicing or voicelessness by arbitrary symbols at the larynx. Voicing is indicated by a wavy line, and voicelessness by a broken line.

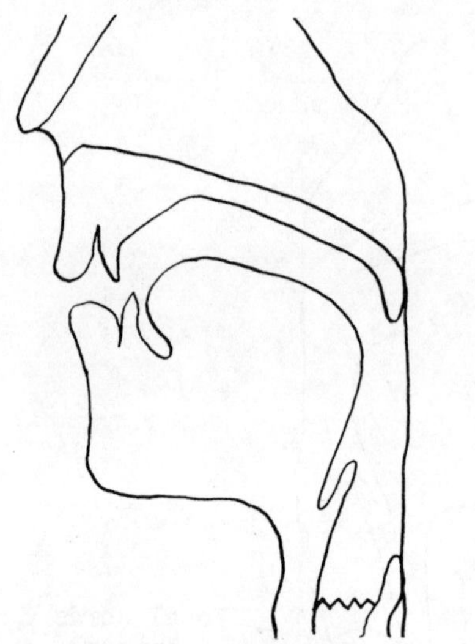

Sammy 3.4: Wavy Line to Indicate Voicing

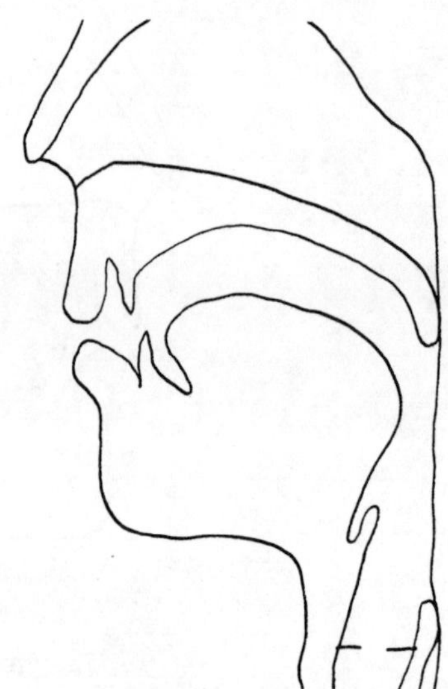

Sammy 3.5: Broken Line to Indicate Voicelessness

RE 3.2. Demonstration: English /š ž/

Because the voiced fricative /ž/ is not too common in English, it sometimes gives students a little more trouble in identification than the others. For that reason we are demonstrating it here in contrast with /š/. In my speech the pairs of words are very close in pronunciation. In some cases they differ only by the /š/ and /ž/. In other cases they differ also slightly in other phonemes. When there is only one phoneme difference between two words or any two utterances we call the difference minimal. Such a pair is a minimal pair. As you go through this demonstration on the tape, listen to the fricatives and get used to thinking of them as voiced or voiceless.

Then listen to see whether the pairs of words are minimal pairs or not. On this you can check your judgment with the transcription below. They are minimal when they are phonemically identical except for the /š/ and /ž/. There are only two minimal pairs in this exercise. Which are they?

Finally, pronounce these words to yourself, with your

hands over your ears to feel and hear the buzzing or lack of it on the fricatives. Follow the transcription.

1a. dilution	/ˌdɨ'lɨwšɨn/	vs.	1b. delusion	/dɨ'lɨwžɨn/
2a. glacier	/'glɛyšɨr/	vs.	2b. glazier	/'glɛyžɨr/
3a. Aleutian	/ʌ'lɨwšɨn/	vs.	3b. allusion	/ˌʌ'lɨwžɨn/
4a. fishin'	/'fɨšɨn/	vs.	4b. vision	/'vɩžɨn/
5a. Asshur	/'æšɨr/	vs.	5b. azure	/'æžɨr/

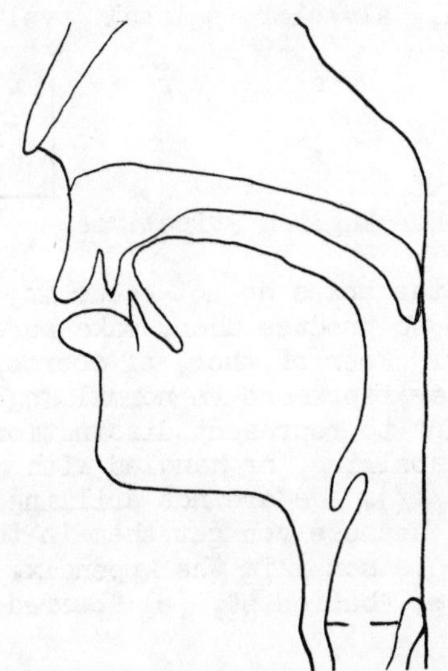

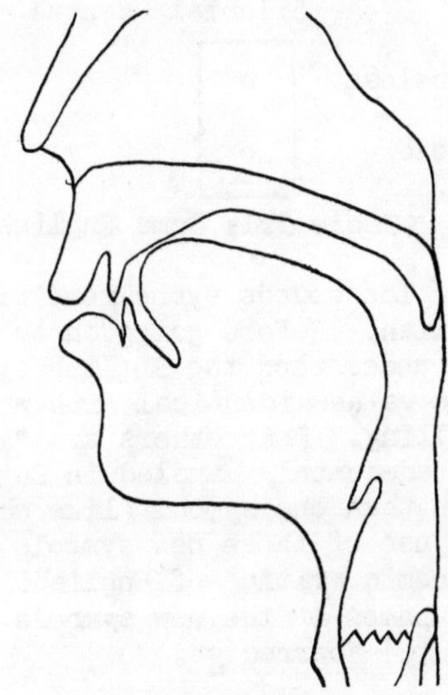

Sammy 3.6: [š]

Sammy 3.7: [ž]

RE 3.3. Differential: VOICED or VOICELESS

This exercise is constructed in the same way as the exercises in Lesson 1. This time your response is to be VOICED or VOICELESS. As in previous exercises, you disregard the [ɑ] vowel. Don't peek!

1. [ɑfɑ]	VL	4. [ɑžɑ]	VD	7. [ɑsɑ]	VL
2. [ɑđɑ]	VD	5. [ɑfɑ]	VL	8. [ɑθɑ]	VL
3. [ɑzɑ]	VD	6. [ɑđɑ]	VD	9. [ɑšɑ]	VL

10. [αfα]	VL	15. [đα]	VD	20. [αθ]	VL
11. [αžα]	VD	16. [fα]	VL	21. [αš]	VL
12. [vα]	VD	17. [žα]	VD	22. [αđ]	VD
13. [zα]	VD	18. [αv]	VD	23. [αf]	VL
14. [šα]	VL	19. [αž]	VD	24. [αz]	VD

<u>Production and Recognition of [ᵽ ƀ x ǥ]</u>

	Bilabial	Labio-dental	Tip-dental	Tip-(or blade-) alveolar	Tip-(or blade-) alveo-palatal	Back-velar
Voiceless	ᵽ	f	θ	s	š	x
Voiced	ƀ	v	đ	z	ž	ǥ

Table 3.1: Some English and Non-English Fricatives

The sounds symbolized within the boxes do not occur in English. Before going on to learn to produce them, make sure you understand the English symbols. Four of them, of course, have values identical with what they represent in normal English spelling. Four others are "made up" to represent distinctions not adequately handled in English spelling, or handled with more than one symbol (like <u>sh</u> for /š/). We are not drilling the use of these new symbols here, because you get them in the phonemic writing of English. (See Lesson A in the Appendix.) The names of the new symbols are [ᵽ] "barred <u>p</u>", [ƀ] "barred <u>b</u>", and [ǥ] "barred <u>g</u>".

The four new sounds are completely parallel to the English sounds in that they are fricatives, and in that they come in pairs, voiced and voiceless. However, they have different points of articulation from any English fricatives. To emphasize the relationship of this chart to Sam Mansfield, study it in relation to Sammy 3.8 on the next page. (The articulators are left off.)

<u>Learning the Bilabial Fricatives: [ᵽ ƀ]</u>

For many students the best way of learning a new sound is first by mimicry. If you find that you can make these sounds, after practice, by mimicry of an instructor, you may avoid a great deal of trial and error. The following suggestions have been found helpful for students who do not have such ready

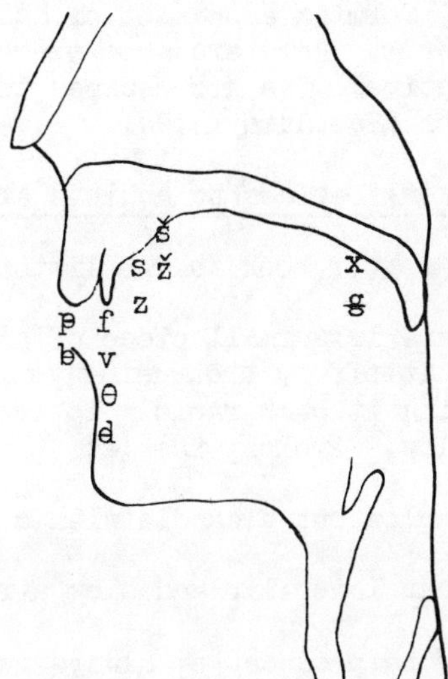

Sammy 3.8: Some Fricatives and Their Points of Articulation

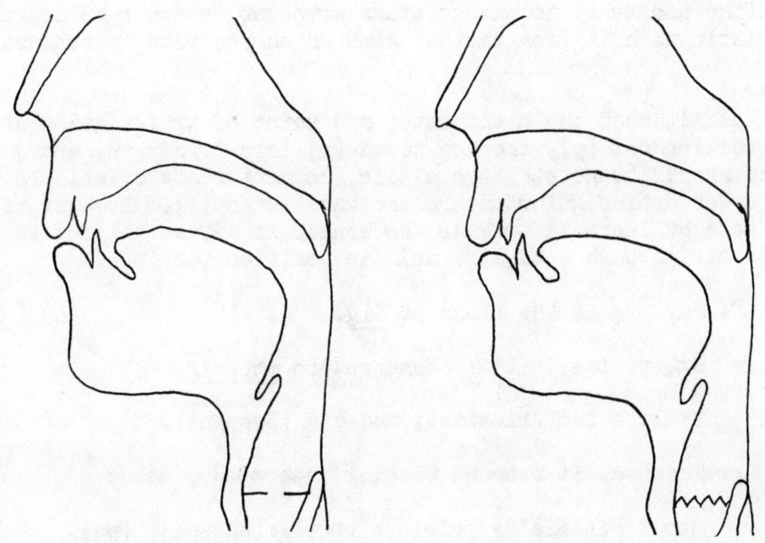

Sammy 3.9: [p]

Sammy 3.10: [b]

success with mimicry, however, and they provide drills for strengthening the new articulatory habits of those who do.

When you learn a new speech sound remember that you are

developing a skill, forming a new set of habits, new muscle coordination and control. Here are some exercises for [ᵽ]. It is a bilabial fricative. The air escapes through a slot made between the two lips (See Sammy 3.9).

RE 3.4. Demonstration: Devices to Achieve Articulation of [ᵽ]

Follow along in your book as you listen to the tape.

a. Pretend there is a small piece of grass on the tip of your tongue. Spit it off by protruding your tongue between your lips and pulling it back rapidly to leave a narrow slit through which to blow. Prolong the [ᵽ].

b. Pretend to blow out a candle with a smile on your face.

c. Protrude your lower lip and blow air up your nose.

d. In learning to produce [ᵽ] always remember that it is to be kept distinct from [f]. If you have a temptation to make an [f], practice protruding your lower lip beyond your upper lip as you make the sound at first. The normal position for the lower lip, however, is roughly in the position for [p]. It is often necessary to exaggerate a movement in order to learn to distinguish it from another with which you tend to confuse it.

e. Although the articulator and point of articulation are in position for [p], the new sound [ᵽ] is a fricative, and there should be no stoppage of air, no matter how brief. In manner of articulation the resemblance is to [f]. However, for the sake of learning to make the sound, it may be helpful to force air through your lips held in position for [p].

f. Say *ᵽig* in the place of *fig*.

Extend the initial consonant to *ᵽᵽᵽᵽᵽig*.

Isolate the fricative, and say [ᵽᵽᵽᵽᵽᵽᵽ].

Then say it between vowels: [aᵽᵽᵽᵽᵽa], [aᵽa].

Say it initially before a vowel: [ᵽᵽᵽᵽᵽa], [ᵽa].

Say it finally after a vowel: [aᵽᵽᵽᵽᵽ], [aᵽ].

These are demonstrated for you on the tape. Unfortunately, fricatives do not record too well on less than high-fidelity equipment, so the distinctions do not come through as clearly a as they do in a face-to-face situation.

RE 3.5. Demonstration: Devices to Achieve Articulation of [ƀ]

Once you can do [ᵽ], you simply add voicing to produce [ƀ]. Follow the transcription.

a. Hum while you say [ᵽ]. This will give you [ƀ].

b. Get the feel of the contrast between [f v], and produce the same contrast with the lips articulating [ᵽ]. Practice long sequences [fvfvfvfvfvfvfv] and then [ᵽƀᵽƀᵽƀᵽƀᵽƀᵽƀᵽƀ] with no vowels intervening. Articulator and point of articulation do not move!

c. Try for the same effect by practicing ha-ha-ha-ha-ha, and then doing the same thing with lips set for [ᵽ]. If done right, this will give you [ᵽƀᵽƀᵽƀᵽƀᵽƀ].

d. Try the following sequence:

hhhhhhhhhhaaaaaaaaa

[sssssssssszzzzzzzzz]

[ffffffffffvvvvvvvvv]

[ᵽᵽᵽᵽᵽᵽᵽᵽᵽᵽƀƀƀƀƀƀƀƀƀ]

e. Mimic the tape on this sequence:

[fvfvfvfvfvfvfvfvfvfv]

[szszszszszszszszszsz]

hahahahahahahahahaha

[ᵽƀᵽƀᵽƀᵽƀᵽƀᵽƀᵽƀᵽƀᵽƀᵽƀ]

f. Pronounce very deliberately, several times: boy.

Prolong the [b]: bbboy (as though you were not sure you wanted to finish it, or as though you were waiting for the word "Go!" to finish it. Be sure it is the initial consonant you prolong, not the vowel. You cannot prolong it for long, as your mouth will fill up with air.)

Say a vowel simultaneously with the [b] held loosely: ƀƀƀƀoy.

Say it before other vowels: [ƀƀƀƀƀa], [ƀa].

Say it between vowels: [aƀƀƀƀa], [aƀa].

Say it finally, after a vowel: [aƀƀƀ], [aƀ].

Say it in isolation: [ƀƀƀƀƀ].

Recorded Exercises 3.5a-3.6. Differential: [f ᵽ] [v ƀ]

This group of exercises is to help you to distinguish between [f] and [ᵽ] and between [v] and [ƀ]. Although it is relatively easy to produce the difference, pronouncing the sounds with different points of articulation, it is much harder to hear the difference. You are not very likely to find contrasts between these pairs in any one language, but the exercises will focus your attention on the differences to prepare you for whichever sound you meet. In all these exercises your response is to be the articulation involved: BILABIAL or LABIO-DENTAL. You will hear each utterance twice. Don't peek!

RE 3.5a. Differential: BILABIAL or LABIO-DENTAL

1.	[ɑfɑ]	L-D	7.	[ɑᵽɑ]	BIL	13.	[ᵽɑ]	BIL
2.	[ɑfɑ]	L-D	8.	[ɑfɑ]	L-D	14.	[ᵽɑ]	BIL
3.	[ɑᵽɑ]	BIL	9.	[ɑfɑ]	L-D	15.	[ɑᵽ]	BIL
4.	[ɑᵽɑ]	BIL	10.	[ɑᵽɑ]	BIL	16.	[ɑf]	L-D
5.	[ɑᵽɑ]	BIL	11.	[ᵽɑ]	BIL	17.	[ɑᵽ]	BIL
6.	[ɑfɑ]	L-D	12.	[fɑ]	L-D	18.	[ɑf]	L-D

RE 3.6. Differential: BILABIAL or LABIO-DENTAL

1.	[ɑvɑ]	L-D	7.	[ɑvɑ]	L-D	13.	[ƀɑ]	BIL
2.	[ɑƀɑ]	BIL	8.	[ɑƀɑ]	BIL	14.	[vɑ]	L-D
3.	[ɑvɑ]	L-D	9.	[ƀɑ]	BIL	15.	[ƀɑ]	BIL
4.	[ɑƀɑ]	BIL	10.	[vɑ]	L-D	16.	[ƀɑ]	BIL
5.	[ɑƀɑ]	BIL	11.	[ƀɑ]	BIL	17.	[vɑ]	L-D
6.	[ɑƀɑ]	BIL	12.	[ƀɑ]	BIL	18.	[ƀɑ]	BIL

Learning the Velar Fricatives [x ǥ]

The voiceless velar fricative [x] occurs in German in

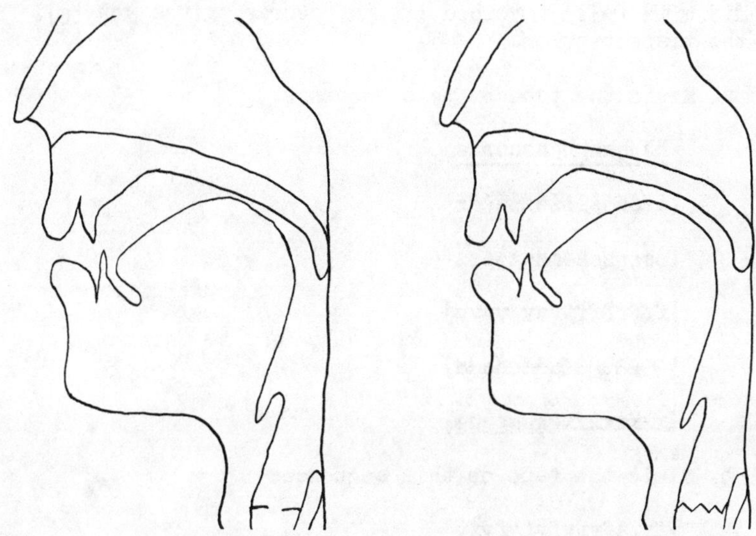

Sammy 3.11: [x] Sammy 3.12: [g]

such words as <u>ach</u>. If you have not studied German, or did not learn to pronounce this sound then, or if you do not succeed in learning the velar fricatives by mimicry of an instructor, try the following exercises.

RE 3.7. Demonstration: Devices to Achieve Production of [x]

Follow in the text as you listen to the tape.

a. Say what the cat says when it spits at a dog: [xxxxx].

b. Do what small boys do when they shoot a "six-shooter": [kxxx]. Then practice eliminating the [k] from this to get [xxx].

c. Think [k], but relax the tongue to blow air through the slot.

d. Start with [ɑ], raising the back of the tongue almost to [k], and lowering it again. If done correctly, this gives [ɑxɑ]. When you get this down, work on [ɑx] and [xɑ].

e. "Whistle" a tune with the back of the tongue.

RE 3.8. Demonstration: Devices to Achieve Production of [g]

Now practice adding the voicing to [x], in just the way

you did with [ɸ]. A voiced [x], of course, gives you [g]. Follow the transcription.

a. Mimic the tape on this sequence:

hhhhhhhhaaaaaaa

[šššššššžžžžžžžž]

[sssssssszzzzzzz]

[ffffffffvvvvvvvv]

[θθθθθθθθdddddddd]

[xxxxxxxxgggggggg]

b. Mimic the tape on this sequence:

[fvfvfvfvfvfvfvfv]

hahahahahahahaha

[xgxgxgxgxgxgxgxg]

c. Think [g], but relax the tongue and blow air through the slot.

d. Start with [ɑ], raising the back of the tongue almost to [g], and lowering it again. If done correctly, this gives [ɑgɑ]. When you get this, work on [ɑg] and [gɑ].

e. Pronounce very deliberately several times: good.

Prolong the [g]: ggggood.

Say a vowel simultaneously with the initial sound: ggggood.

Say it before other vowels: [ggga], [ga].

Say it between vowels: [aggga], [aga].

Say it finally, after a vowel: [aggg], [ag].

Recorded Exercises 3.9-3.10. Differential: Velar Fricatives

Unlike [ɸ β], the velar fricatives are not usually confused with any English sounds. You do, however, need practice hearing them and recognizing them immediately. Don't peek!

RE 3.9. Differential: VOICED or VOICELESS

1. [αxα]	VL	7. [αǥα]	VD	13. [ǥα]	VD
2. [αǥα]	VD	8. [ǥα]	VD	14. [ǥα]	VD
3. [αǥα]	VD	9. [xα]	VL	15. [αǥ]	VD
4. [αǥα]	VD	10. [xα]	VL	16. [αǥ]	VD
5. [αxα]	VL	11. [ǥα]	VD	17. [αx]	VL
6. [αxα]	VL	12. [xα]	VL	18. [αǥ]	VD

RE 3.10. Differential: VELAR or NO

1. [αsα]	NO	7. [αxα]	VE	13. [žα]	NO
2. [αxα]	VE	8. [ƀα]	NO	14. [θα]	NO
3. [αǥα]	VE	9. [zα]	NO	15. [αđ]	NO
4. [αfα]	NO	10. [xα]	VE	16. [αǥ]	VE
5. [αžα]	NO	11. [šα]	NO	17. [αx]	VE
6. [αǥα]	VE	12. [ǥα]	VE	18. [αf]	NO

Recorded Exercises 3.11-3.12. Differential: Right or Wrong?

A very common mistake in learning velar fricatives is to pronounce [x] as [kx], and [ǥ] as [gǥ], that is, to pronounce a velar stop followed by a velar fricative. These exercises are designed to help you hear the difference, so that you can make sure you are not making this mistake yourself. Your response is to be FRICATIVE if the sound pronounced is a pure fricative, and WRONG if it is not. Don't peek!

RE 3.11. Differential: FRICATIVE or WRONG

1. [αxα]	F	6. [αxα]	F	11. [kxα]	WRONG
2. [αkxα]	WRONG	7. [αkxα]	WRONG	12. [xα]	F
3. [αkxα]	WRONG	8. [kxα]	WRONG	13. [kxα]	WRONG
4. [αxα]	F	9. [xα]	F	14. [xα]	F
5. [αxα]	F	10. [xα]	F	15. [αx]	F

16. [ɑkx] WRONG
17. [ɑx] FR
18. [ɑkx] WRONG

RE 3.12. Differential: FRICATIVE or WRONG

1. [ɑggɑ] WRONG
2. [ɑgɑ] FR
3. [ɑgɑ] FR
4. [ɑggɑ] WRONG
5. [ɑggɑ] WRONG
6. [ɑgɑ] FR
7. [ɑggɑ] WRONG
8. [gɑ] FR
9. [gɑ] FR
10. [ggɑ] WRONG
11. [gɑ] FR
12. [ggɑ] WRONG
13. [ggɑ] WRONG
14. [ɑg] FR
15. [ɑgg] WRONG
16. [ɑgg] WRONG
17. [ɑg] FR
18. [ɑgg] WRONG

RE 3.13. Differential: FRICATIVE or WRONG

In this exercise you will again distinguish between fricatives and non-fricatives, but now you will have the additional complication of [h] which often sounds like [x]. Don't peek

1. [ɑxɑ] FR
2. [ɑhɑ] WRONG
3. [ɑxɑ] FR
4. [ɑkxɑ] WRONG
5. [ɑhɑ] WRONG
6. [ɑxɑ] FR
7. [ɑkxɑ] WRONG
8. [ɑxɑ] FR
9. [ɑxɑ] FR
10. [ɑhɑ] WRONG
11. [ɑkhɑ] WRONG
12. [ɑhɑ] WRONG

RE 3.14. Demonstration: Tongue Twisters

In order to get facility in the use of the new fricatives, practice the following, or make up others like them. Listen to the demonstration on the tape, and follow the transcription below.

a. ᵽeter ᵽiᵽer ᵽicked a ᵽeck of ᵽickled ᵽeᵽᵽers.

b. A ƀig ƀad ƀoy ƀuilt ƀulging ƀoats.

c. xween xatherine xissed her xrotchety xousin.

d. get gus's grandmother some great green gooey gumdrops.

Recorded Exercises 3.15-3.16. Differential: Recognition and Labeling

Give the technical label for the consonant you hear, just as you did for Lesson 1.

RE 3.15. Description of Sounds

Here you will have only the new fricatives you have learned in this chapter. That means that you have the following choice of responses (one item from each list):

VOICED	BILABIAL	FRICATIVE
VOICELESS	BACK-VELAR	

Don't peek!

1. [ɑƀɑ] VD BILABIAL F
2. [ɑǥɑ] VD BACK-VELAR F
3. [ɑxɑ] VL BACK-VELAR F
4. [ɑᵽɑ] VL BILABIAL F
5. [ɑxɑ] VL BACK-VELAR F
6. [ɑƀɑ] VD BILABIAL F
7. [ɑᵽɑ] VL BILABIAL F
8. [ǥɑ] VD BACK-VELAR F
9. [xɑ] VL BACK-VELAR F
10. [ᵽɑ] VL BILABIAL F
11. [ƀɑ] VD BILABIAL F
12. [xɑ] VL BACK-VELAR F
13. [ǥɑ] VD BACK-VELAR F
14. [ƀɑ] VD BILABIAL F
15. [ɑx] VL BACK-VELAR F
16. [ɑǥ] VD BACK-VELAR F
17. [ɑᵽ] VL BILABIAL F
18. [ɑx] VL BACK-VELAR F
19. [ɑƀ] VD BILABIAL F
20. [ɑᵽ] VL BILABIAL F

RE 3.16. Description of Sounds

In this drill you may have any English fricative as well. If you need a list of possible responses to refer to as you do this drill, take one from each of the following lists:

VOICED	BILABIAL	FRICATIVE
VOICELESS	LABIO-DENTAL	
	TIP-DENTAL	
	TIP-(or BLADE-) ALVEOLAR	
	TIP-(or BLADE-) ALVEOPALATAL	
	BACK-VELAR	

1. [αšα] VL TIP-(or BLADE-) ALVEOPALATAL F
2. [αxα] VL BACK-VELAR F
3. [αzα] VD TIP-(or BLADE-) ALVEOLAR F
4. [αđα] VD TIP-DENTAL F
5. [αƀα] VD BILABIAL F
6. [αvα] VD LABIO-DENTAL F
7. [αǥα] VD BACK-VELAR F
8. [đα] VD TIP-DENTAL F
9. [fα] VL LABIO-DENTAL F
10. [sα] VL TIP-(or BLADE-) ALVEOLAR F
11. [ᵽα] VL BILABIAL F
12. [xα] VL BACK-VELAR F
13. [zα] VD TIP-(or BLADE-) ALVEOLAR F
14. [žα] VD TIP-(or BLADE-) ALVEOPALATAL F
15. [αǥ] VD BACK-VELAR F
16. [αθ] VL TIP-DENTAL F
17. [αᵽ] VL BILABIAL F
18. [αf] VL LABIO-DENTAL F
19. [αƀ] VD BILABIAL F
20. [αf] VL LABIO-DENTAL F

Recorded Exercises 3.17-3.19. Mimicry Drills: Nonsense Syllables

Follow along as you listen to the tape and mimic it. You will hear each utterance twice, but you will mimic the tape in the silent space provided, rather than respond to it. The exercises increase in complexity. As you listen and watch the page before you, try to associate the sound with the symbol, as well as to mimic the syllable.

RE 3.17. Mimicry

1. [αᵽα]
2. [αƀα]
3. [αxα]
4. [αǥα]
5. [αxα]
6. [αƀα]
7. [αᵽα]
8. [αǥα]
9. [αxα]
10. [αǥα]
11. [ǥα]
12. [ƀα]
13. [ᵽα]
14. [xα]
15. [ƀα]
16. [xα]
17. [αᵽ]
18. [αƀ]
19. [αǥ]
20. [αx]
21. [αᵽ]

RE 3.18. Mimicry

1. [ᵽαᵽ]
2. [ƀαƀ]
3. [ǥαǥ]
4. [xαx]
5. [ǥαǥ]
6. [ƀαƀ]
7. [xαx]
8. [ᵽαᵽ]
9. [ǥαǥ]
10. [xαx]
11. [ᵽαǥ]
12. [xαƀ]
13. [ƀαᵽ]
14. [ƀαx]
15. [ǥαƀ]
16. [ǥαᵽ]
17. [ƀαƀ]
18. [xαǥ]
19. [ᵽαƀ]
20. [ƀαƀ]
21. [ƀαx]
22. [ᵽαǥ]
23. [đαš]
24. [đαž]
25. [žαs]
26. [ǥαz]
27. [αθ]
28. [đα]
29. [fαᵽ]
30. [vαƀ]

RE 3.19. Mimicry

1. [αƀđα]
2. [αxšα]
3. [šαᵽαθ]
4. [vαƀα]
5. [fαǥαx]
6. [ᵽαǥαž]
7. [ᵽαƀαƀ]
8. [žαzđαƀ]
9. [xαšθαs]

RE 3.20. Mimicry: Vietnamese

This exercise gives you actual language materials, spoken by a native informant. Drill it so that you can mimic it with accuracy. If it helps you to do so, watch the transcription of the exercise and follow along as you mimic. Remember that this will be more difficult for you than the previous exercise because it contains other unfamiliar sounds, in addition to the ones you are working on. Concentrate on the fricatives as you work.

1. /xwaay/ 'sweet potato'
2. /xinàaw/ 'when?'
3. /xɔ́/ 'to be difficult'
4. /xá^{k}p/ 'to cry'
5. /xwæ̃/ 'to be strong'
6. /xʌ^{ŋ}m/ 'no, not'
7. /ǥaa/ 'railway station'
8. /ǥé/ 'chair'
9. /ǥɔ̣y/ 'to call'
10. /ǥɔ̣k/ 'to peel, sharpen'

Transcription Exercises

With your book closed, transcribe RE 3.18 and RE 3.19. Correct your transcription by comparing it with the printed transcription in the Manual. When you transcribe, be sure to write all the consonants and vowels which you hear.

Reading Exercises

Check your skill in reading the new sounds by the use of RE 3.17-3.19. Read off the syllable before the tape says it, and compare your reading with the tape. The dialogue will sound like this:

You: [ɑp̶ɑ]

Tape: Number one, [ɑp̶ɑ], [ɑp̶ɑ].

You: [ɑb̶ɑ]

Tape: Number two, [ɑb̶ɑ], [ɑb̶ɑ].

Suggested Reading

Page numbers in parentheses may not apply specifically to the points of this lesson, but have been listed in previous lessons, and you may want to read them while you have the book.

H.A. Gleason, Jr., An Introduction to Descriptive Linguistics, pp. 187-193 (14-26).

Kenneth L. Pike, Phonemics, pp. 24-28.

LESSON FOUR

Finer Distinctions in Hearing Pitch

Recorded Exercises 4.1-4.2. Discrimination: Same or Different

Here are more tone drills, such as you had in Lesson 2 (RE 2.3ff). Respond with SAME or DIFFERENT according to what you hear on the tape. The items in these exercises will be a little more complicated than what you heard in Lesson 2. Don't peek!

RE 4.1: Amoy[1]. Discrimination: SAME or DIFFERENT

1.	Ko Hiông Chhī 'Kaoshiung City'	Pîn Tong Koān 'Pingtung County'	S
2.	Góa khì hia 'I go there'	Lí lâi chia 'You come here'	D
3.	eng âm sî 'at night'	tsa khí sî 'in the morning'	D
4.	lāi-bīn tsē 'come in and sit (lit.)'	m̄ hō· lí 'don't give you'	S
5.	siu óa^n-pôa^n 'to collect the dishes (e.g. after meal)'	tsin hó thi^n 'very good weather'	D
6.	la̍k lia̍p lê 'six shells'	chhit tsiah kâu 'seven monkeys'	D
7.	pō-lê poe 'a drinking glass'	kā-pi au 'coffee cup'	S
8.	o· pe̍h kóng 'to say any old thing'	o· pe̍h lâi 'to get anything disordered'	D
9.	tse sī to 'This is a knife'	i tī tsia 'He is here'	S
10.	i tsin gâu 'He (is) very clever'	i bô lâi 'He didn't come'	S

---

[1] For sources see fn. p. 30.

RE 4.2: Amoy. Discrimination: SAME or DIFFERENT

1.	tsit pun chheh 'this book'	tsi̍t pun chheh 'one book'	D
2.	âng m̂ng thô· 'cement'	hóe sio thn̂g 'burnt sugar'	D
3.	hit tsiah tsôa 'that snake'	hit tsiah thâng 'that worm'	S
4.	n̄ng tè pía^{n} 'two cakes'	gō· ê kía^{n} 'five sons'	D
5.	Bí-kok-á 'the Americans'	tseng-thâu-á 'finger(s)'	D
6.	tsit óa^{n} pn̄g 'this bowl of rice'	peh óa^{n} pn̄g 'eight bowls of rice'	S
7.	lák keng chhù 'six houses'	pa̍t keng chhù 'another house'	S
8.	iáu bē kàu 'has not arrived yet'	bô lōa àm 'not so dark'	D
9.	tsū-otōng-chhia 'automobile'	bô tī tsia '(he) is not here'	D
10.	iáu bē lâi 'has not come yet'	i bē lâi 'he doesn't come'	S

RE 4.3. Levels and Glides

The English word Johnny can be said in the four following ways, among others. Listen to the tape, and watch the transcription.

1. 3 / 2 Johnny / 1

3. 3 / 2 Johnny / 1

2. 3 / 2 Johnny / 1

4. 3 / 2 Johnny / 1

Notice that we have indicated three pitch levels for this example, although English has an additional fourth (highest) pitch which is more rarely used. We have indicated a change between level pitches by the vertical dotted line which shows the abrupt change. The down-turn at the end of 1 and 2 indicates the normal fade-off of voice and pitch at the end of some phrases. We will ignore it for the present.

Now listen to the word John as pronounced in four corresponding ways on the tape, and watch the transcription.

```
   3                         3
5. 2  John                7. 2  John
   1                         1

   3                         3
6. 2  John                8. 2  John
   1                         1
```

Notice that this time there was a glide between pitch levels, and that some of the glides were longer than others, depending on the distance between the levels.

The distinction between long and short glides applies whether the glides start at the same point or not. If one starts higher than the other, and they both rise to the same pitch, the one which started lower is the longer. Or if one starts lower than the other and both fall to the same pitch, the one which started higher is the longer. We can illustrate that by the next items of the exercise. Notice that we include a comparison of the same rise or fall as a step in Column b. Compare this group with the preceding group.

```
     Glide                      Step

     3                          3
9a.  2  John              9b.   2  Johnny
     1                          1

     3                          3
10a. 2  John              10b.  2  Johnny
     1                          1

     3                          3
11a. 2  John              11b.  2  Johnny
     1                          1

     3                          3
12a. 2  John              12b.  2  Johnny
     1                          1
```

By length of glide we do not mean to imply anything about the length (duration) of the vowel on which the glide occurs. You may have a long glide on a very short vowel, and an equally long one on a long vowel. These points are illustrated by analogy with music in Figures 4.1-4.2. Do not get the impression from these illustrations that speech pitch is sung. This notation simply points out the lack of relation between length of glide and length of vowel (its duration).

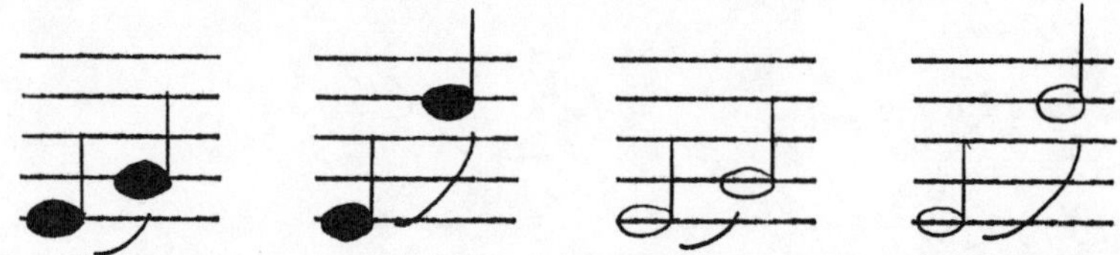

Fig. 4.1: Short and Long Rising Glides with Different Durations

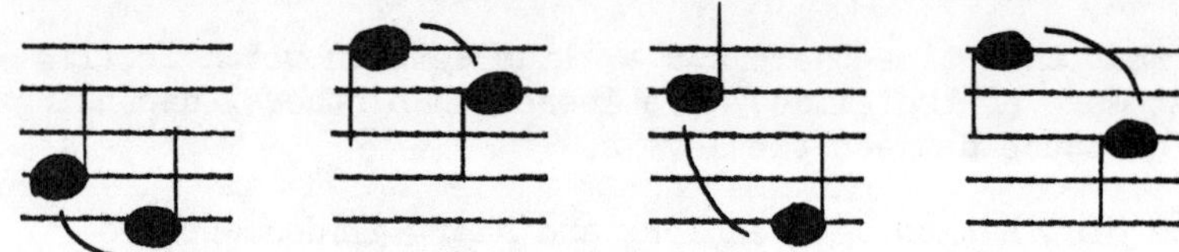

Fig. 4.2: Two Short Falls and Two Long Falls

RE 4.4. Differential: LONG or SHORT

In this exercise you will be asked principally to distinguish between long glides and short glides on the frame one. You are to respond with LONG for long rises, and SHORT for short rises. A demonstration will be given you before the exercise begins. The first five examples will be exaggerated. The second five will not be exaggerated, but will be slow. The last ones will be faster, and each utterance will be given only once. Do not watch the text of the exercise.

1. one LONG
2. one LONG
3. one SHORT
4. one LONG
5. one SHORT
6. one SHORT
7. one LONG
8. one SHORT
9. one SHORT
10. one LONG
11. one SHORT
12. one SHORT
13. one LONG
14. one LONG
15. one LONG
16. one SHORT
17. one SHORT
18. one LONG

RE 4.5. Differential: LONG or SHORT

1. three SHORT	7. three SHORT	13. three SHORT
2. three SHORT	8. three LONG	14. three SHORT
3. three LONG	9. three LONG	15. three SHORT
4. three SHORT	10. three SHORT	16. three LONG
5. three LONG	11. three LONG	17. three LONG
6. three LONG	12. three LONG	18. three SHORT

RE 4.6. Differential: LONG RISE, SHORT RISE, LONG FALL, SHORT FALL

1. go LONG R	7. go SHORT R	13. go LONG F
2. go LONG F	8. go SHORT F	14. go LONG R
3. go SHORT F	9. go LONG F	15. go SHORT F
4. go LONG F	10. go SHORT R	16. go SHORT R
5. go SHORT R	11. go SHORT F	17. go SHORT F
6. go LONG R	12. go SHORT F	18. go LONG F

RE 4.7. Differential: LONG RISE, SHORT RISE, LONG FALL, SHORT FALL, LEVEL

1. high SHORT R	2. high LONG R	3. high LEVEL

4. high SHORT F
5. high SHORT R
6. high SHORT F
7. high LEVEL
8. high LONG F
9. high LEVEL
10. high SHORT R
11. high LONG F
12. high LEVEL
13. high SHORT R
14. high LONG R
15. high SHORT R
16. high LONG F
17. high SHORT F
18. high LONG F

RE 4.8. Differential: LONG RISE, SHORT RISE, LONG FALL, SHORT FALL, LEVEL

Re 4.8 has longer sequences. You are to listen to the final syllable for the long or short glide, or level pitch. The rest of the sentence will be held approximately constant.

1. That'll be fine LEVEL
2. That'll be fine LONG R
3. That'll be fine SHORT R
4. That'll be fine LEVEL
5. That'll be fine LONG F
6. That'll be fine LONG R
7. That'll be fine LONG F
8. That'll be fine LEVEL
9. That'll be fine SHORT F
10. That'll be fine LEVEL
11. That'll be fine LONG R
12. That'll be fine SHORT F
13. That'll be fine LEVEL
14. That'll be fine LONG R
15. That'll be fine SHORT R
16. That'll be fine LONG R
17. That'll be fine SHORT F
18. That'll be fine LONG F

19. That'll be fine SHORT F   20. That'll be fine SHORT R

Recorded Exercises 4.9-4.12. Differential: One Direction or Two

The pitch glides on which you have been working up to now have been unidirectional. That is, they have either simply risen, fallen, or remained level. In the present exercise you are to distinguish between unidirectional glides and bidirectional glides. In RE 4.9, for example, all examples will either rise, or rise and then fall. You are to respond with RISE or RISE-FALL according to whether the glide has one direction or two. Do not watch the text of the exercise.

RE 4.9. Differential: RISE or RISE-FALL

1. John RISE
2. John RISE-FALL
3. John RISE-FALL
4. John RISE
5. John RISE-FALL
6. John RISE
7. John RISE-FALL
8. John RISE-FALL
9. John RISE
10. John RISE
11. John RISE
12. John RISE-FALL
13. John RISE
14. John RISE
15. John RISE-FALL
16. John RISE-FALL
17. John RISE-FALL
18. John RISE

RE 4.10. Differential: FALL or FALL-RISE

1. why FALL-RISE
2. why FALL
3. why FALL
4. why FALL-RISE
5. why FALL
6. why FALL-RISE
7. why FALL
8. why FALL
9. why FALL-RISE
10. why FALL-RISE
11. why FALL-RISE
12. why FALL

13. why FALL-RISE 15. why FALL 17. why FALL

14. why FALL-RISE 16. why FALL 18. why FALL-RISE

RE 4.11. Differential: RISE, FALL, RISE-FALL, or FALL-RISE

1. so FALL 7. so RISE-FALL 13. so RISE-FALL

2. so FALL-RISE 8. so FALL-RISE 14. so RISE

3. so FALL 9. so FALL 15. so RISE

4. so RISE-FALL 10. so FALL 16. so FALL-RISE

5. so RISE-FALL 11. so RISE 17. so FALL

6. so RISE 12. so RISE 18. so FALL-RISE

RE 4.12: Differential: LEVEL, RISE, FALL, RISE-FALL, or FALL-RISE

1. large RISE 7. large FALL-RISE

2. large RISE-FALL 8. large RISE-FALL

3. large LEVEL 9. large RISE-FALL

4. large LEVEL 10. large RISE

5. large FALL-RISE 11. large LEVEL

6. large FALL 12. large FALL-RISE

13. large RISE-FALL

14. large LEVEL

15. large FALL

16. large RISE

17. large RISE-FALL

18. large LEVEL

Recorded Exercises 4.13-4.16. Mimicry by Humming

For the exercises which follow on the tape, you will hear approximately the same material as you have in RE 4.9-4.12, according to the following table. However, try to do the exercises without turning back to the transcription.

4.13 is the same as 4.9.

4.14 is the same as 4.10.

4.15 is the same as 4.11.

4.16 is the same as 4.12.

This time you mimic the stimulus by humming. A humming response will also be heard on the tape to help you. Compare your humming with what you hear on the tape, and, if possible, have someone else listen to you hum, and compare it with the tape response.

Recorded Exercises 4.17-4.21. Mimicry Drills

In these exercises you will mimic the tape. Each utterance consists of four syllables, with a constant frame [mu so pa fu]. This means that the consonants and vowels, and the tone of the initial syllable are held the same throughout. The tone of the initial syllable gives you something to peg the tones of the other syllables to. Do these exercises without watching the book.

RE 4.17. Mimicry

The tones used will be low level, high level, and falling. You are to mimic the tape, the first time through by humming, and then through by articulating the consonants and vowels also.

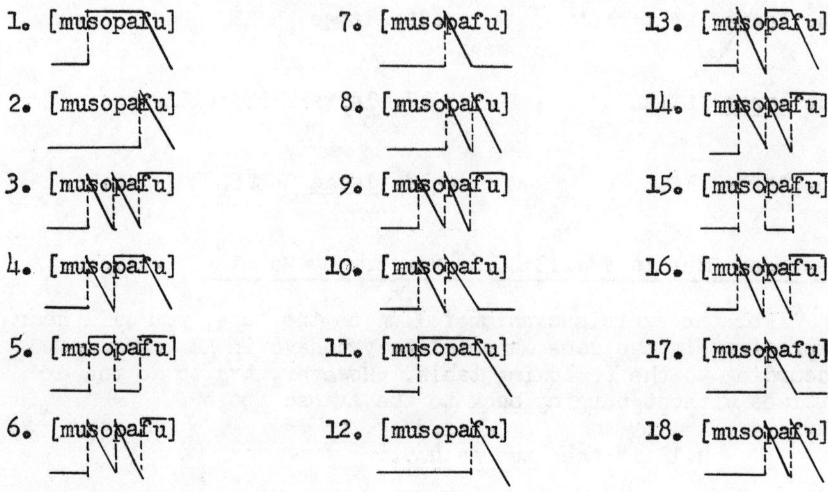

RE 4.18. Mimicry

Your directions are the same, except that this time the glide tone will be rising instead of falling.

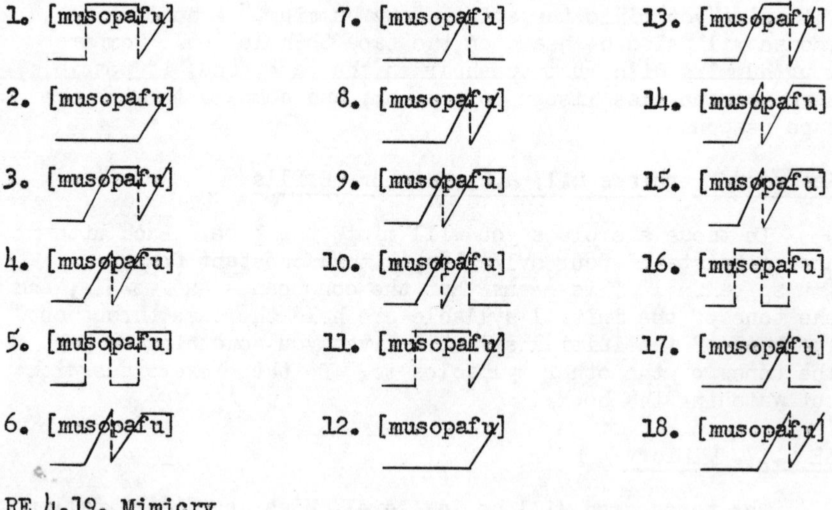

RE 4.19. Mimicry

The glide may be either rising or falling.

1. [musopafu] 2. [musopafu] 3. [musopafu]

4. [musopafu] 9. [musopafu] 14. [musopafu]

5. [musopafu] 10. [musopafu] 15. [musopafu]

6. [musopafu] 11. [musopafu] 16. [musopafu]

7. [musopafu] 12. [musopafu] 17. [musopafu]

8. [musopafu] 13. [musopafu] 18. [musopafu]

RE 4.20: Vietnamese[1]. Mimicry: Humming only

1.	['loŋ hoŋ]	'louder'	11.	[kɔ'du]	'enough'
2.	[noy'maaw]	'speak fast'	12.	[kɔ'tʰe]	'may, can'
3.	[tiʌŋ'ʌⁿm]	'your language'	13.	[kʌy'yɨʌ]	'dish'
4.	[cuⁿm'toy]	'we(exclusive)'	14.	[noy'laay]	'repeat'
5.	[tʰɨ'haay]	'Monday'	15.	[cuʌ'ñɨk]	'Sunday'
6.	[tʰɨ'ɓaa]	'Tuesday'	16.	[kʌy'ñaa]	'house'
7.	[tʰɨ'tɨ]	'Wednesday'	17.	[kʌy'ɓaaŋ]	'table'
8.	[tʰɨ'naam]	'Thursday'	18.	[kʌy'kwɨŋ]	'trousers'
9.	[kʌy'kiʌ]	'that'	19.	[kʌy'nʌy]	'this'
10.	[kɔ'hiw]	'understood'	20.	['nɨʌk'nʌy]	'this water'

[1]For source, see fn. p. 42.

21. [ˈtʰe naaw] 'how?'

22. [ˈaawˈkwɨŋ] 'clothes'

23. [ˈboŋ dʌⁿm] 'four piastres'

24. [ˈsaaw dʌⁿm] 'six piastres'

25. [ˈtaam dʌⁿm] 'eight piastres'

26. [ˈcin dʌⁿm] 'nine piastres'

RE 4.21: Kpelle (Liberia)[1]. Mimicry: Humming only

1. [pɛrɛ ka ti] 'That's a house'

2. [kwala ka ti] 'That's a monkey'

3. [kali ka ti] 'That's a hoe'

4. [kona ka ti] 'That's a mortar'

5. [pɛrɛ lɔɔlu] 'Five houses'

6. [kwala lɔɔlu] 'Five monkeys'

7. [kali lɔɔlu] 'Five hoes'

8. [kona lɔɔlu] 'Five mortars'

Transcription Exercises

Listen to RE 4.13-4.19 again, this time drawing the contour as you hum. Use the following symbolization:

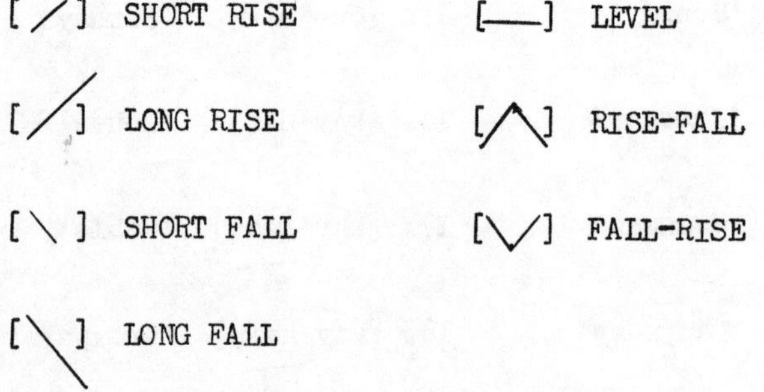

The correct transcription is given in the text.

[1]Data from William E. Welmers' lessons in Kpelle [multilith], p. 6. The recording was read by Moses Peter of Parakwelle, Liberia.

Reading Exercises

Check your skill in reading the pitch contours by the use of RE 4.13-4.19. Read off the contour (by humming, or by articulating) before the tape says it, and compare your reading with the tape, just as you did in Lesson 3.

"BOOM BIDDY BOOM DIDDY BOOM BOOM BOOM..."

LESSON FIVE

Facial Diagrams; Voiced Stops

In this lesson you are going to learn to make your own facial diagrams of various sounds. One purpose in doing this is for convenience of communication in this course. We want to make sure that you are able to read those we draw for you in explanation, and are able to express your understanding of speech articulations through drawing diagrams. Thus the drawing of diagrams serves both as a means of communication and as a testing device. However, the other reason is basically much more important. In the drawing of diagrams, you are forced to pay attention to the various inter-playing movements of the speech tract. It is one thing to understand in a vague way what is going on, but it is another to be able to represent it specifically in a schematized diagram.

In Sammy 5.1 you see the three basic articulations which must be drawn in on all Sammy diagrams. They are the lips, the tongue, and the velic.

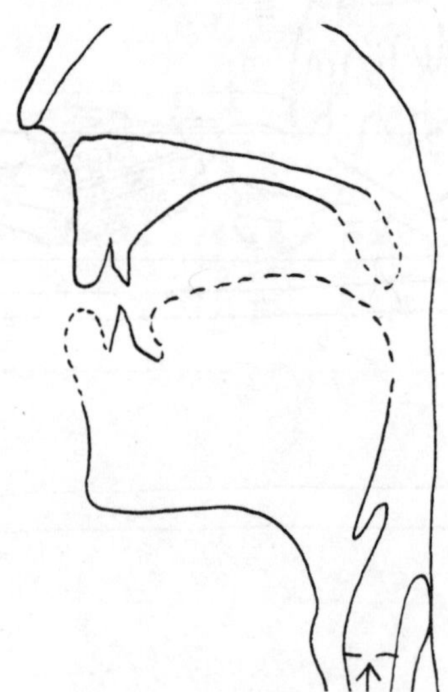

Sammy 5.1: Basic Articulations to be Drawn

In making Sam Mansfields of stops there are two things particularly to remember. The velic must be closed to show that the air is not going out through the nose, and the articulator must be shown closed against the point of articulation. To show this complete closure we draw the line of the velic and of the articulator tightly against the point of articulation, letting no white space show. Sammy 5.2 will show you a correct drawing of the articulation of a [t].

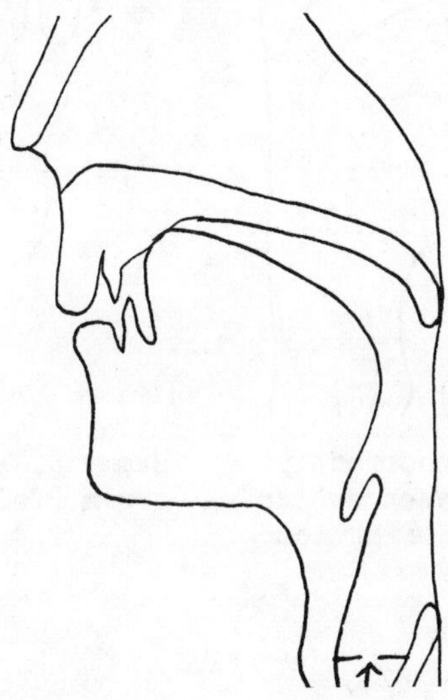

Sammy 5.2: [t] correctly drawn

Sammy 5.3 is incorrect because the articulation is not shown as being closed in stop position. Sammy 5.4 is incorrect because the velic is not closed. Study these diagrams. Be sure that you understand the principle that a stop [t] implies full closure at both these points. A diagram of a [p] or a [k] would be the same except that the point of articulation would differ in relation to the articulator. Sammies 5.3 and 5.4 are on the next page.

Fricatives are diagrammed as in Sammy 5.5. A narrow slit is left between the articulator and the point of articulation to show the fricative nature of the sound being diagrammed. Sammy 5.6 is incorrect because too little space is left, making a stop. Sammy 5.7 shows too much space. For the time being we will draw fricatives with the velic closed as we do stops. It is, however, perfectly possible to pronounce fricatives with the velic open.

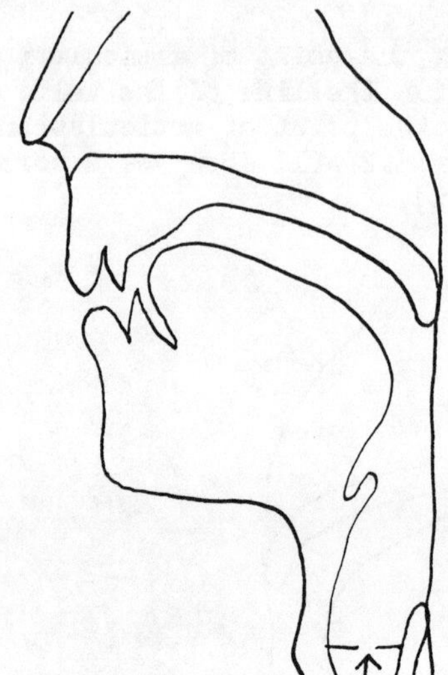

Sammy 5.3: [t] incorrectly drawn (space between articulator and point of articulation)

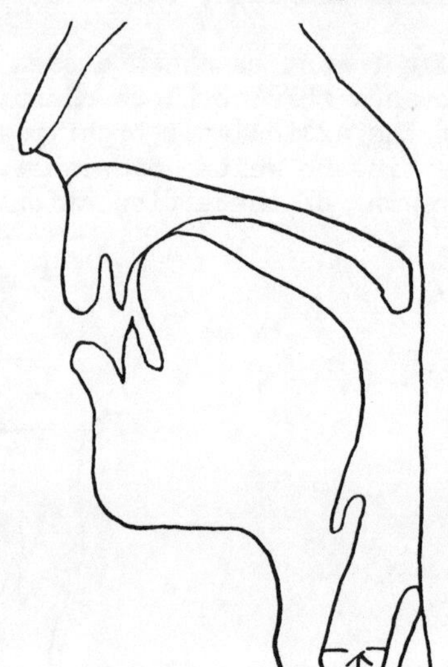

Sammy 5.4: [t] incorrectly drawn (velic open)

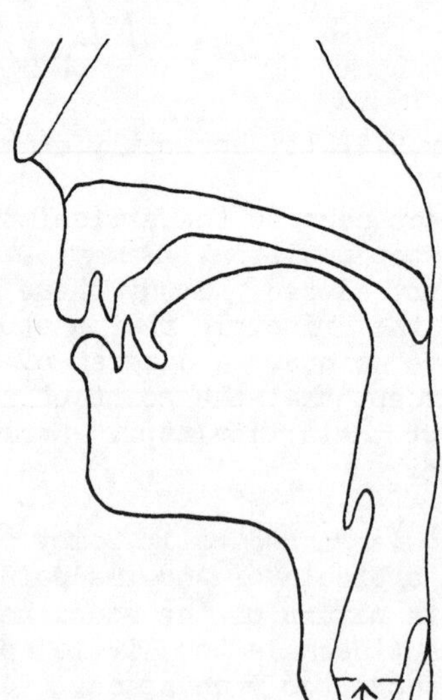

Sammy 5.5: [x] correctly drawn

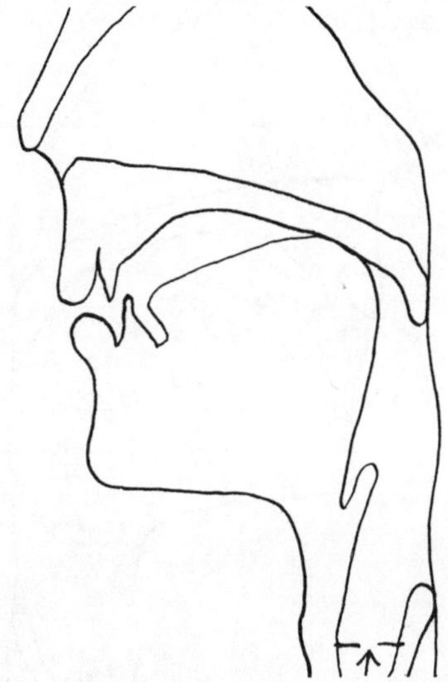

Sammy 5.6: [x] incorrectly drawn (no space between articulator and point of articulation)

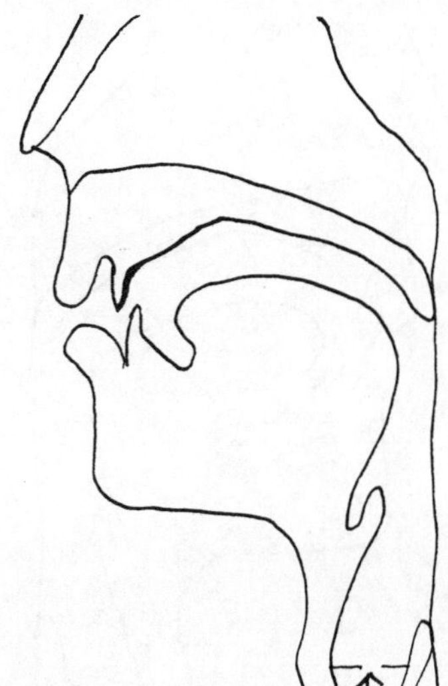

Sammy 5.7: [x] incorrectly drawn (too much space between articulator and point of articulation)

Of course voicing and voicelessness must be drawn simultaneously with the other articulations. They are therefore indicated on all of the diagrams of the articulations which we have illustrated earlier in this lesson. The indication of the voicing or lack of it is in the larynx at the vocal cords. A wavy line shows voicing. A broken line shows voicelessness. (See Sammies 5.8 and 5.9 on the next page.)

The direction and source of the air stream must also be represented. Up to the present we have not studied any other air stream than one coming out of the lungs. Therefore, for the present we will simply draw the air stream as an arrow pointing upward from the lungs to the larynx. Notice that it should not extend through the larynx. You will later have other kinds of air stream to represent. (See Sammies 5.10 and 5.11 on the next page.)

The final Sammy diagram in this lesson is a "blank Sammy." This is the kind of Sammy on which, from time to time, you will be asked to diagram specific sounds.

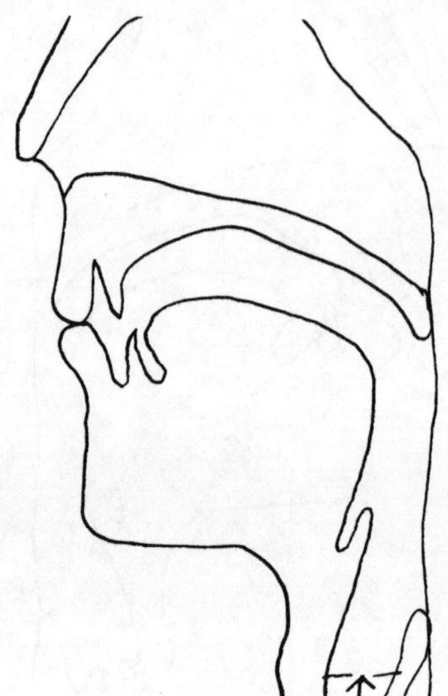

Sammy 5.8: [p]
note voicelessness

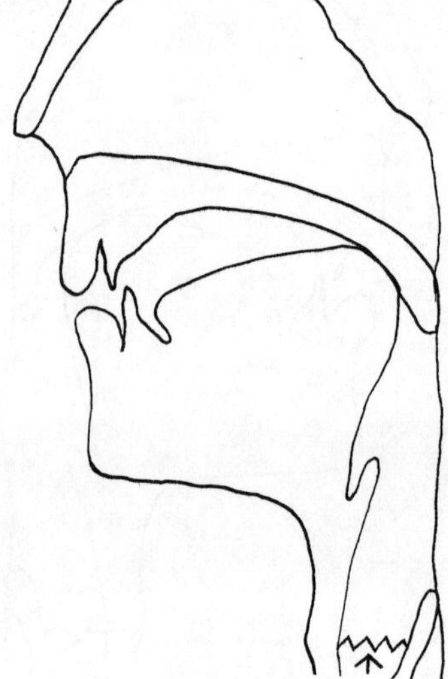

Sammy 5.9: [g]
note voicing

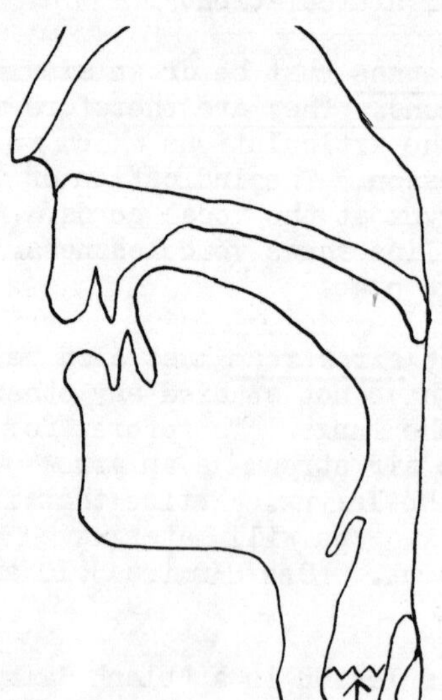

Sammy 5.10: [z]
note voicing and placement of arrow indicating air stream

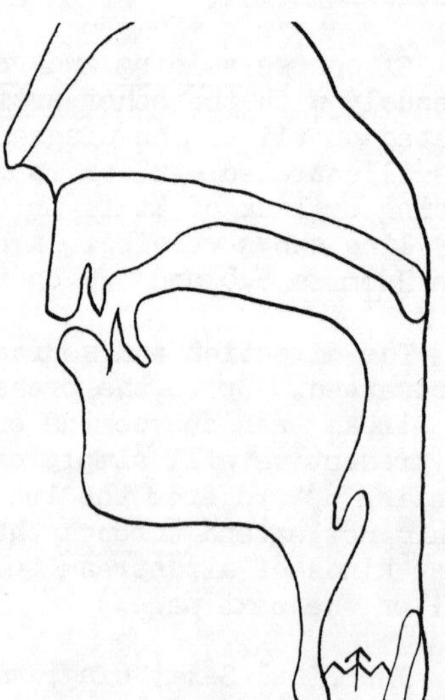

Sammy 5.11: Air stream incorrectly drawn through larynx

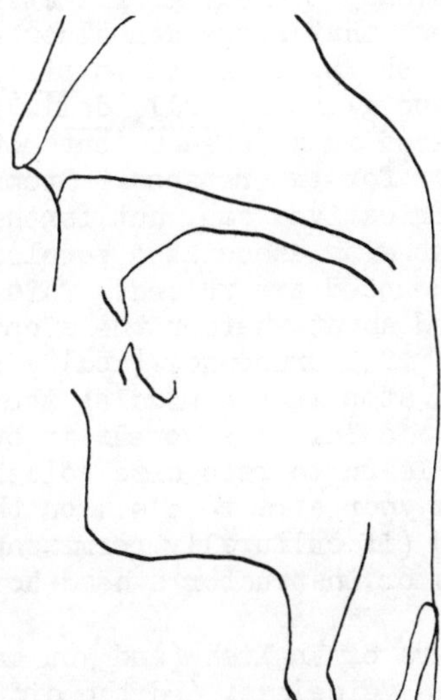

Sammy 5.12: Blank Sammy

In Sammy 5.12 you are introduced to Blank Sammy. In the Workbook (p. 7ff.) copies are available in large size (Big Blank Sammy, one to a page) or small size (Little Blank Sammy, four to a page) to save you time. The general configurations of Sammy are drawn except for certain parts such as the articulators, the velum, and the larynx. You have to fill in the missing parts. If you do not have some Blank Sammies to use, you can trace Sammy 5.12 or draw it freehand. When you are given an exercise in which you draw the articulation for more than one sound, using different colored pencils or different kinds of lines to do so, it is more convenient to use a Big Blank Sammy. When you are asked to draw individual specific sounds, you will find a Little Blank Sammy more convenient.

Sammy Exercises 5.1-5.3

On a Big Blank Sammy, draw [b] and [m], using two different colored pencils, pencil and ink, or different kinds of lines (like regular line and dotted line). On another Big Blank Sammy do the same for [d] and [n] and on a third do the same for [g] and [ŋ]. What constitutes the difference between these pairs of sounds in each diagram?

Voiced Stops

In Lesson 3 you learned to distinguish between voicing and voicelessness. We used fricatives as examples because voicing or voicelessness is easy to hear in fricatives. However, it should be pointed out that stops can also be either voiced or voiceless. In English /p, t, k/ as in pill, till, and kill are voiceless; /b, d, and g/ as in ball, doll, and gall are often at least partly voiced in my speech (but not in everybody's). This is hard to hear for two reasons. Stops cannot be prolonged as much as fricatives can, but furthermore they cannot be pronounced except with associated vowels. The vowels with which they are pronounced are voiced. This may lead you at first to be confused about whether the stop is voiced or voiceless. For example, if I pronounce [ɑpɑ] versus [ɑbɑ], the first one has a voiceless stop in the middle; the second one has a voiced stop in the middle. The vowels in both cases are voiced. You simply have to learn to recognize voiceless and voiced stops by practice. Cover your ears to check on the voicing in your own production, and (if culturally permissable) put your hand on your informant's or instructor's head to feel his voicing.

In many speakers of English (and you may be one of them), both /p/ and /b/ are voiceless, and the difference is due only to other factors. You should check with an instructor if you want to know what your pronunciation of /b, d, and g/ is.

We can line up English stop phonemes according to whether they are voiceless or sometimes voiced (in my speech) as in the following diagram:

Voiceless stops	/p	t	k
(Sometimes) voiced stops	b	d	g/

In phonetics work, however, when we are discussing sounds without relation to the phonemic system of any language, [b, d, g] will always represent voiced stops, giving us this diagram:

Voiceless stops	[p	t	k
Voiced stops	b	d	g]

RE 5.1. Demonstration: English Stops and Fricatives

Listen to RE 5.1 to hear the voicing and voicelessness on stops. On the tape /b d g/ are pronounced with voicing whether they so occur in your speech or not. Notice the symbols as you go along, but do not try to memorize them now. You are concentrating on the difference between voicing and voicelessness at this point. Each sound is given medially first in a nonsense syllable, (with /ɑ/ because stops cannot be pronounced without a vowel), and then initially, medially, and finally in English words. Follow the transcription.

Voiceless Stops	Voiced Stops
/ɑpɑ/ as in pea, appear, ape	/ɑbɑ/ as in buy, about, ebb
/ɑtɑ/ as in tea, attack, ate	/ɑdɑ/ as in die, adorn, Ed
/ɑkɑ/ as in key, acclaim, ache	/ɑgɑ/ as in guy, again, egg

Students who do not voice English /b d g/ should be careful not to become confused at this point. In all of our phonetics work, where we are dealing with sounds as sounds, regardless of the language in which they occur, we will use the symbols [b d g] for voiced stops only. For your English phonemic transcription you will continue to use these symbols for the initial sounds in buy, die, and guy, regardless of whether in your actual pronunciation you voice them or not. In other words for English phonemic transcription continue to use the symbols as you have learned to do. But for phonetics work you will have to learn to make fully voiced stops for use in other languages, and you will transcribe such voiced stops with these symbols.

Recorded Exercises 5.2-5.5. Demonstration: Voicing [b d g]

Listen to the following demonstration exercises on tape, and practice them yourself, following the directions, to help you get a good, full voicing on [b d g] such as you may need in some other languages than English. Remember that the voicing is a rumble which is very audible in your ears when you cover them with the palms of your hands. You can also sense it by feeling the top of another person's head as he speaks.

RE 5.2. Negative Practice: Exaggerating the Voicing on English Stops

This exercise is built around English words which have /b d g/ in the middle of the words, with a following unstressed syllable. These are more likely to be voiced than in most positions in English. Listen to the tape as it says the words first naturally, then in elongated fashion, preserving the voicing. (The raised dots indicate the lengthening.) Follow the transcription.

1a. baby	1b. b•a•b•y	1c. b•y
2a. able	2b. a•b•l•e	2c. b•l
3a. adder	3b. a•dd•er	3c. d•r

4a. puddle 4b. pu•dd•le 4c. d•l

5a. ugly 5b. ug•ly 5c. g•ly

6a. August 6b. Aug•ust 6c. g•ust

In Column c prolong the stop as long as you can. Your mouth will fill up with air so you cannot pronounce it very long. Be sure you are not making a nasal instead of a stop.

RE 5.3. Demonstration: Avoiding Substitution of Nasal for Stop

Here we will try to help you distinguish between a long voiced stop and a long nasal. This is important because some people tend to substitute a nasal when they are trying to learn to voice a stop. For this exercise pinch your nose shut with your fingers and feel the degrees of vibration in your nose as you say the utterances suggested. You should get heavy vibration on the [m] but little on the [b]. If it continues when you think you have switched to the [b] you are fooling yourself. The same applies to [n] vs. [d] and [ŋ] vs. [g]. Follow the transcription.

1. [ɑm•ɑ ɑm•ɑ ɑb•ɑ ɑb•ɑ]
2. [ɑn•ɑ ɑn•ɑ ɑd•ɑ ɑd•ɑ]
3. [ɑŋ•ɑ ɑŋ•ɑ ɑg•ɑ ɑg•ɑ]
4. [ɑm•ɑ ɑb•ɑ ɑm•ɑ ɑb•ɑ]
5. [ɑn•ɑ ɑd•ɑ ɑn•ɑ ɑd•ɑ]
6. [ɑŋ•ɑ ɑg•ɑ ɑŋ•ɑ ɑg•ɑ]
7. [ɑm• ɑb• ɑm• ɑb• ɑm• ɑb•]
8. [ɑn• ɑd• ɑn• ɑd• ɑn• ɑd•]
9. [ɑŋ• ɑg• ɑŋ• ɑg• ɑŋ• ɑg•]
10. [m•ɑ b•ɑ m•ɑ b•ɑ m•ɑ b•ɑ]
11. [n•ɑ d•ɑ n•ɑ d•ɑ n•ɑ d•ɑ]

RE 5.4. Demonstration: Voicing of Stops by Analogy with Fricatives

Here is another approach to the problem of full voicing of stops. Start with long voiced fricatives at the same point of articulation and cut them off into stops in the manner indicated below. Listen to the tape and follow the transcription. Then try it for yourself.

1. [ɑƀ• ɑƀ•b• ɑƀ•b• ɑb•]
2. [ɑz• ɑz•d• ɑz•d• ɑd•]
3. [ɑg̶• ɑg̶•g• ɑg̶•g• ɑg•]
4. [ɑƀ•ɑ ɑƀ•b•ɑ ɑb•ɑ]
5. [ɑz•ɑ ɑz•d•ɑ ɑd•ɑ]
6. [ɑg̶•ɑ ɑg̶•g•ɑ ɑg•ɑ]

7. [ƀ•α ƀ•b•α b•α]

8. [z•α z•d•α d•α]

RE 5.5. Negative Practice: Exaggerated English Voicing of Stops

Work on English phrases such as the ones below, striving for exaggerated voicing on all of the stops.

1. b•ig• b•ad• b•oy

2. g•ooey g•reen g•rapes

3. d•oes D•otty d•ream

RE 5.6. Differential: VOICED OR VOICELESS

In this exercise you are asked to recognize voicing or voicelessness, as you did in Lesson 3, but now, of course, stops are included in the drill. Be sure to listen for voicing or voicelessness in the utterance on the tape. Do not rely on your own pronunciation of the corresponding English phoneme. Your pronunciation may not be what is on the tape. Listen to voicing on the tape. Try to do the exercise without watching the transcription.

1. [αsα] VL
2. [αŋα] VD
3. [αvα] VD
4. [αtʰα] VL
5. [αdα] VD
6. [αθα] VL
7. [αmα] VD
8. [αlα] VD
9. [αgα] VD
10. [αgα] VD
11. [zα] VD
12. [žα] VD
13. [bα] VD
14. [pʰα] VL
15. [kʰα] VL
16. [αpʰ] VL
17. [αb] VD
18. [αθ] VL
19. [αm] VD
20. [αtʰ] VL
21. [αǥ] VD
22. [ƶα] VD
23. [αđα] VD
24. [αpʰα] VL
25. [dα] VD
26. [αkʰ] VL
27. [αŋ] VD
28. [αsα] VL
29. [gα] VD
30. [αlα] VD

Recorded Exercises 5.7-5.10. Differential: Description of Sounds

In this series we take you through a progression toward the labeling of sounds, as we did in Lesson 1. This will be review of much of the material, but the distinction between voicing and voicelessness will be added.

RE 5.7

Use one term from each column below. Listen to the tape and give the label. Do not consult the transcription which follows unless you have to do so.

VOICED	STOP
VOICELESS	FRICATIVE
	NASAL
	LATERAL

1.	[αsα] VL F	13.	[đα] VD F	25.	[αŋ] VD N
2.	[αŋα] VD N	14.	[tʰα] VL S	26.	[αx] VL F
3.	[αpʰα] VL S	15.	[bα] VD S	27.	[αs] VL F
4.	[αdα] VD S	16.	[žα] VD F	28.	[αš] VL F
5.	[αzα] VD F	17.	[gα] VD S	29.	[αđ] VD F
6.	[αlα] VD L	18.	[šα] VL F	30.	[αg] VD S
7.	[αθα] VL F	19.	[pʰα] VL S	31.	[θα] VL F
8.	[αkʰα] VL S	20.	[lα] VD L	32.	[αm] VD N
9.	[αǥα] VD F	21.	[αđ] VD F	33.	[αbα] VD S
10.	[αmα] VD N	22.	[αv] VD F	34.	[ǥα] VD F
11.	[nα] VD N	23.	[αf] VL F	35.	[αž] VD F
12.	[vα] VD F	24.	[αtʰ] VL S	36.	[αd] VD S

RE 5.8

Take one term from each column. Don't peek!

VOICELESS	LABIAL	STOP
VOICED	DENTAL	FRICATIVE
	ALVEOLAR	NASAL
	ALVEOPALATAL	LATERAL
	VELAR	

1. [ɑfɑ] VL DENTAL F
2. [ɑvɑ] VD DENTAL F
3. [ɑðɑ] VD DENTAL F
4. [ɑtʰɑ] VL ALVEOLAR S
5. [ɑbɑ] VD LABIAL S
6. [gɑ] VD VELAR S
7. [nɑ] VD ALVEOLAR N
8. [šɑ] VL ALVEOPALATAL F
9. [ðɑ] VD DENTAL F
10. [gɑ] VD VELAR S
11. [ɑlɑ] VD ALVEOLAR L
12. [ɑm] VD LABIAL N
13. [ɑθɑ] VL DENTAL F
14. [ɑŋɑ] VD VELAR N
15. [ɑn] VD ALVEOLAR N
16. [ɑž] VD ALVEOPALATAL F
17. [šɑ] VL ALVEOPALATAL F
18. [ɑbɑ] VD LABIAL S
19. [ɑs] VL ALVEOLAR F
20. [ɑθ] VL DENTAL F
21. [ɑŋ] VD VELAR N
22. [ɑg] VD VELAR S
23. [kʰɑ] VL VELAR S
24. [lɑ] VD ALVEOLAR L

RE 5.9

Take one term from each column. Don't peek!

VOICELESS	BILABIAL	STOP
VOICED	LABIO-DENTAL	FRICATIVE
	TIP-DENTAL	NASAL
	TIP-ALVEOLAR	LATERAL
	BLADE-ALVEOLAR	
	TIP-ALVEOPALATAL	
	BLADE-ALVEOPALATAL	
	BACK-VELAR	

1. [ɑfɑ] VL LABIO-DENTAL F
2. [ɑvɑ] VD LABIO-DENTAL F
3. [ɑðɑ] VD TIP-DENTAL F
4. [ɑtʰɑ] VL TIP-ALVEOLAR S
5. [ɑbɑ] VD BILABIAL S
6. [gɑ] VD BACK-VELAR S

7. [nɑ] VD TIP-ALVEOLAR N
8. [šɑ] VL TIP-(or BLADE-) ALVEOPALATAL F
9. [đɑ] VD TIP-DENTAL F
10. [gɑ] VD BACK-VELAR S
11. [ɑlɑ] VD TIP-ALVEOLAR L
12. [ɑm] VD BILABIAL N
13. [ɑθɑ] VL TIP-DENTAL F
14. [ɑŋɑ] VD BACK-VELAR N
15. [ɑn] VD TIP-ALVEOLAR N
16. [ɑž] VD TIP-(or BLADE-) ALVEOPALATAL F
17. [šɑ] VL TIP-(or BLADE-) ALVEOPALATAL F
18. [ɑbɑ] VD BILABIAL S
19. [ɑs] VL TIP-(or BLADE-) ALVEOLAR F
20. [ɑθ] VL TIP-DENTAL F
21. [ɑŋ] VD BACK-VELAR N
22. [ɑg] VD BACK-VELAR S
23. [k^{h}ɑ] VL BACK-VELAR S
24. [lɑ] VD TIP-ALVEOLAR L

RE 5.10.

This exercise reverses the previous procedure, giving you the technical name and asking you to pronounce the sound between vowels. The tape follows with the correct response. Don't peek!

1. VD BILABIAL N [ɑmɑ]
2. VD TIP-ALVEOLAR N [ɑnɑ]
3. VD BACK-VELAR N [ɑŋɑ]
4. VD BILABIAL S [ɑbɑ]
5. VL BACK-VELAR F [ɑxɑ]
6. VL TIP-(or BLADE-) ALVEOPALATAL F [ɑšɑ]
7. VD LABIO-DENTAL F [ɑvɑ]
8. VD BACK-VELAR N [ɑŋɑ]
9. VL TIP-DENTAL F [ɑθɑ]
10. VL BILABIAL F [ɑɸɑ]
11. VD BACK-VELAR S [ɑgɑ]
12. VD TIP-DENTAL F [ɑđɑ]
13. VL BACK-VELAR S [ɑk^{h}ɑ]
14. VD BILABIAL N [ɑmɑ]
15. VL LABIO-DENTAL F [ɑfɑ]
16. VD TIP-ALVEOLAR N [ɑnɑ]
17. VD TIP-(or BLADE-) ALVEOLAR F [ɑzɑ]
18. VD TIP-(or BLADE-) ALVEOPALATAL F [ɑžɑ]
19. VD BACK-VELAR N [ɑŋɑ]
20. VD TIP-ALVEOLAR S [ɑdɑ]

RE 5.11. Differential: [f v ᵽ ƀ] (Review)

In this drill you will be asked to respond with any one of the following: VOICELESS BILABIAL, VOICED BILABIAL, VOICELESS LABIO-DENTAL, VOICED LABIO-DENTAL. This drill is difficult because the tape does not fully record the slight difference of sound between the two voiceless fricatives and the two voiced fricatives. You can also use this exercise as a mimicry exercise, with your Manual open to the transcription of the exercise, to practice the production of these fricatives. Remember that when you pronounce the bilabial fricatives you cannot let your lower lip touch your upper teeth. If you have any difficulty, review Lesson 3. Don't peek!

1.	[ɑfɑ]	VL LABIO-DENTAL	11.	[ɑᵽ]	VL BILABIAL
2.	[ɑᵽɑ]	VL BILABIAL	12.	[ɑv]	VD LABIO-DENTAL
3.	[ɑᵽɑ]	VL BILABIAL	13.	[ɑv]	VD LABIO-DENTAL
4.	[ɑfɑ]	VL LABIO-DENTAL	14.	[ɑƀ]	VD BILABIAL
5.	[ɑvɑ]	VD LABIO-DENTAL	15.	[ƀɑ]	VD BILABIAL
6.	[ɑvɑ]	VD LABIO-DENTAL	16.	[vɑ]	VD LABIO-DENTAL
7.	[ɑƀɑ]	VD BILABIAL	17.	[fɑ]	VL LABIO-DENTAL
8.	[ɑƀɑ]	VD BILABIAL	18.	[fɑ]	VL LABIO-DENTAL
9.	[ɑᵽ]	VL BILABIAL	19.	[ᵽɑ]	VL BILABIAL
10.	[ɑf]	VL LABIO-DENTAL	20.	[fɑ]	VL LABIO-DENTAL

RE 5.12. Mimicry: Fricatives

This exercise is designed to help you get facility in the use of non-English fricatives studied so far. Practice in mimicry of the tape. You may follow along by reading the utterances as you mimic if you care to do so. Each item will be given twice, with space for your mimicry after each repetition.

1. [ɑv vɑ ɑvvɑ]	5. [ɑs vɑ ɑsvɑ]	9. [ɑx vɑ ɑxvɑ]
2. [ɑf vɑ ɑfvɑ]	6. [ɑš vɑ ɑšvɑ]	10. [ɑg vɑ ɑgvɑ]
3. [ɑđ vɑ ɑđvɑ]	7. [ɑᵽ vɑ ɑᵽvɑ]	11. [ɑv xɑ ɑvxɑ]
4. [ɑθ vɑ ɑθvɑ]	8. [ɑƀ vɑ ɑƀvɑ]	12. [ɑf xɑ ɑfxɑ]

13. [ɑđ xɑ ɑđxɑ]

14. [ɑθ xɑ ɑθxɑ]

15. [ɑs xɑ ɑsxɑ]

16. [ɑš xɑ ɑšxɑ]

17. [ɑᵽ xɑ ɑᵽxɑ]

18. [ɑƀ xɑ ɑƀxɑ]

19. [ɑx xɑ ɑxxɑ]

20. [ɑǥ xɑ ɑǥxɑ]

21. [ɑv ǥɑ ɑvǥɑ]

22. [ɑf ǥɑ ɑfǥɑ]

23. [ɑđ ǥɑ ɑđǥɑ]

24. [ɑθ ǥɑ ɑθǥɑ]

25. [ɑs ǥɑ ɑsǥɑ]

26. [ɑš ǥɑ ɑšǥɑ]

27. [ɑᵽ ǥɑ ɑᵽǥɑ]

28. [ɑƀ ǥɑ ɑƀǥɑ]

29. [ɑx ǥɑ ɑxǥɑ]

30. [ɑǥ ǥɑ ɑǥǥɑ]

RE 5.13. Transcription

In the following exercise you are to write what you hear on the tape, using the phonetic symbols you have been learning. The vowels in these utterances will be kept constant as a frame, and will be [ɑ]. You, however, should write the vowel every time you hear it, along with the correct consonants. Check your work with the key below after you finish your transcription to your satisfaction.

1. [mɑđɑ]

2. [šɑzɑ]

3. [bɑnɑ]

4. [xɑŋɑ]

5. [žɑǥɑ]

6. [θɑvɑ]

7. [ǥɑǥɑ]

8. [šɑmɑ]

9. [xɑdɑ]

10. [sɑŋɑ]

11. [mɑnɑŋ]

12. [fɑđɑŋ]

13. [wɑzɑm]

14. [ᵽɑŋɑǥ]

15. [nɑƀɑž]

16. [xɑmdɑz]

17. [lɑbsɑǥ]

18. [θɑnfɑŋ]

19. [ƀɑǥšɑm]

20. [đɑnxɑǥ]

Reading Exercise

Use RE 5.13 as a reading exercise by reading off the transcription of each utterance before the tape recording sounds the pronunciation.

LESSON SIX

Controlled Intonation

In this lesson we narrow our requirements in the hearing, mimicry, and control of pitch. We do this largely by setting artificial limits on English pitch in the exercises we use.

As we pointed out in Lesson 2, English has an extremely complicated pitch system which is used in every utterance by every speaker of the language. We mentioned that learners of another language must learn to use a different pitch system as a part of their learning process.

The English pitch system is of a kind which we call <u>intonation</u>. We distinguish this from <u>tone</u>, which is the kind of pitch system which makes Chinese, Vietnamese, Thai, and many languages of Africa so difficult for English-speaking learners. Both intonation systems and tone systems employ pitch, but the use to which they put them is different.

In general, in a tone system the pitches are related to a single syllable or to a word. In an intonation system the pitches are related to the whole phrase or sentence. Tone serves a function like that of consonants and vowels, helping to keep words from sounding the same, and so being confused. Intonation superimposes an additional meaning on the whole phrase or sentence.

RE 6.1: Vietnamese. Demonstration: Five Tone Contrasts

For example, here are five Vietnamese words with five different tones (but no difference of consonants and vowels). If in doubt, listen to them on the tape and follow the transcription.

Meaning	Vietnamese Spelling	Phonetic Transcription
cheek	má	[ma·]
ghost	ma	[ma·]
tomb	mả	[ma·]
rice plant	mạ	[ma·]
but	mà	[ma·]

RE 6.2: English. Demonstration: Range of a Contour

English does not distinguish between words on the basis of pitch in this way, but it spreads an intonation contour out over a phrase, whether that phrase consists of one word or many. Notice how the same contours, with the same meanings, can occur on many words, or few. The tape will help you hear the contours if the transcription is not enough. When the rise or fall occurs on a syllable, the result is a glide [/] or [\ ]. When it is between syllables it is a step [_|¯] or [¯|_]. The part of the contour preceding the stress mark ['] is relatively non-significant.

1a. Did you go 'yesterday?	1b. Did you go 'yesterday?
2a. Did you 'go?	2b. Did you 'go?
3a. Did 'you?	3b. Did 'you?
4a. 'You?	4b. 'You.
5a. 'Yesterday?	5b. 'Yesterday.
6a. You 'did?	6b. You 'did.
7a. 'Hm?	7b. 'Hm!

Notice that the intonation used in Column a means question all the way through, no matter whether it is on one word or on several, or on none (as in 7a). The intonation used in Column b is more general, however. If there is a question word in the utterance the result is a question, but if there is not, the result is an affirmative statement.

RE 6.3: English. Demonstration: Contrasting Intonations

Now listen to the following English examples in which a variety of intonations are used down the list. Here it is not the lexical meaning which changes, as in Vietnamese, but the added meaning which shows the attitude of the speaker, or indicates something about the grammar (like question vs. statement).

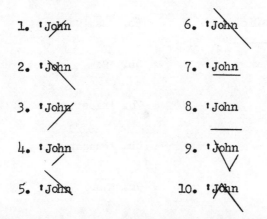

1. 'John
2. 'John
3. 'John
4. 'John
5. 'John
6. 'John
7. 'John
8. 'John
9. 'John
10. 'John

RE 6.4. Mimicry: Contours in "The Hat with the Bird"

On p. 93 you will find part of "The Hat with the Bird," a brief story about Sally Mansfield (Sam's wife). It has been transcribed with lines to indicate the intonation (pitch) contours. In this transcription, however, only a very limited number of pitch contours is used. Although normal English has an enormous repertoire of pitch contours, in this exercise only a small number of them is allowed. The contours used are demonstrated first in RE 6.4. Following that (in RE 6.5) the full page is read off at various speeds to help you learn to control your own intonation in exactly the way indicated by the transcription.

In practicing these exercises you should not only seek to control your intonation pitch contours in the ways indicated, but also to keep your voice from trailing off or rising at the end of phrases in the English fashion. Your purpose is to help gain mastery and control of your own pitch on English material.

1a. 'Mansfield
1b. 'Mansfield
2a. 'husband
2b. 'husband
3a. 'very
3b. 'very
4a. 'women's
4b. 'women's

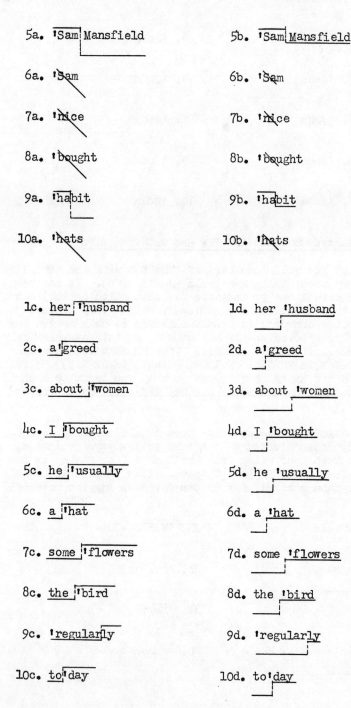

5a. 'Sam Mansfield	5b. 'Sam Mansfield
6a. 'Sam	6b. 'Sam
7a. 'nice	7b. 'nice
8a. 'bought	8b. 'bought
9a. 'habit	9b. 'habit
10a. 'hats	10b. 'hats
1c. her 'husband	1d. her 'husband
2c. a'greed	2d. a'greed
3c. about 'women	3d. about 'women
4c. I 'bought	4d. I 'bought
5c. he 'usually	5d. he 'usually
6c. a 'hat	6d. a 'hat
7c. some 'flowers	7d. some 'flowers
8c. the 'bird	8d. the 'bird
9c. 'regularly	9d. 'regularly
10c. to'day	10d. to'day

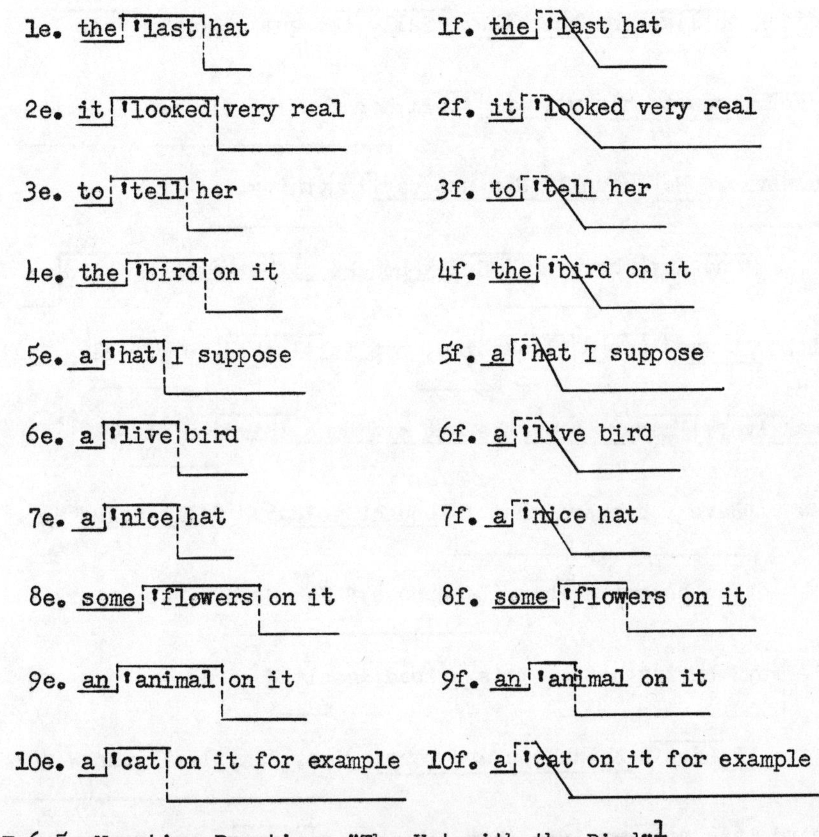

RE 6.5. Negative Practice: "The Hat with the Bird"[1]

Listen to the tape demonstration of the reading of Sally Mansfield with the restricted contours indicated. Then practice reading it yourself until you can follow the transcription of the contours perfectly.

'Sally 'Mansfield and her 'husband, 'Sam Mansfield,

disa'greed 'very much about 'women's 'hats. 'Sam Mansfield

[1]By Frank Fletcher. Story and intonation contours adapted from Kenneth L. Pike, The Intonation of American English, Ann Arbor: U. of Mich. Press, 1947. pp. 129-131. Used by permission of the publisher.

did not 'like the hats that 'Sally 'bought. He was 'too 'courteous to his wife to 'tell her that he did not like them, however. He 'usually did not say 'anything.

'One day, however, 'Sally bought a 'hat with a 'bird on it. It was 'not a 'live bird, but it 'looked very real. Sally was 'very 'happy about the hat with the 'bird on it.

"Have you heard what I 'bought to'day?" Sally asked Sam.

"You bought a 'hat, I suppose," Sam said. "Women are 'always buying hats. It's a 'bad 'habit."

"I 'don't think you are very 'nice, Sam," Sally answered. "And it's a 'very 'nice hat. It has a 'bird on it."

"Do you have to 'feed the bird 'regularly?" Sam asked, but 'Sally didn't 'answer him. "The 'last hat you bought," Sam continued, "had some 'flowers on it. 'This hat has a 'bird on it. The 'third 'hat is going to have an 'animal on it, I suppose. 'Why don't you buy a 'hat that has a 'cat on it, for example?" (Continued in Lesson 8)

RE 6.6. Review of Pitch Glides (Self Test)

Number your paper from 1 - 5.

Listen to the tape, and mark your paper with a symbol to represent the pitch contour of each item, as follows:

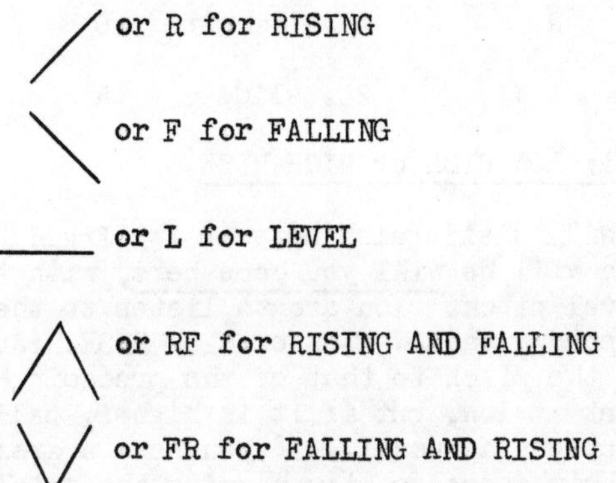
or R for RISING
or F for FALLING
or L for LEVEL
or RF for RISING AND FALLING
or FR for FALLING AND RISING

You will hear five warmup utterances, each given three times. Write the pitch you hear for each utterance by using one of the codes above. You will then hear the answers for these warmup examples on the tape, followed by a repeat demonstration of the warmup so you can check your mistakes.

Then number from 1 - 20 and take the test in the same manner. The answers will then be given at the end of the test. Don't peek!

Warmup

1. 'never	F	4. gow'pɪy	RF
2. Hi!	R	5. 'sɪmʌn	FR
3. Ouch!	L		

Test

1. well	F	5. good	RF
2. no	R	6. mine	R
3. John	R	7. some	F
4. yes	L	8. gɑs	L

9.	sɛmp	FR	15. 'wɛwgɑ	F
10.	zwɩŋ	R	16. sɩym'pɩy	RF
11.	I 'don't	F	17. 'gowtɛy	L
12.	He'll 'run	FR	18. cʌ'nɔk	R
13.	Who's 'there	R	19. 'wɑhɑnt	L
14.	I'll 'see you	L	20. slide	R

RE 6.7. Differential: LOW RISE or HIGH RISE

In RE 6.7 you will distinguish between two English pitch contours. The frame will be will you come here, with the first three words on a level pitch. You are to listen to the last word and are to respond with LOW RISE or HIGH RISE. Judge the height by comparing the pitch to that of the preceding words. If it is lower, count it low, but if it is higher, call it high. The tape will correct you as usual. If you have a great deal of difficulty with this exercise, try humming the pitch. Have a friend listen to you hum to see whether or not you are really mimicking the tape. Then go back and try the oral responses again. If this does not work, try speaking in mimicry of the tape. Say what the tape says, and with the same intonation. A demonstration will be given you before you begin.

If you prefer, you may draw the contours instead of responding orally. If you do so, number from one to twenty, and draw in the frame. Then as you hear the tape, draw in the pitch of the final syllable. Your possible responses will be as follows:

[ ] LOW RISE [ ] HIGH RISE

You can tell whether or not you were correct by listening to the correct answer given on the tape, and comparing it with your drawing, or you can correct your answers by referring to the transcription of the drill. Don't peek!

1. will you come here L R
2. will you come here L R
3. will you come here H R
4. will you come here H R
5. will you come here H R
6. will you come here L R

7. will you come here H R
8. will you come here L R
9. will you come here L R
10. will you come here L R
11. will you come here H R
12. will you come here L R

RE 6.8. Differential: LOW FALL or HIGH FALL

Follow the same procedure as for the preceding exercise. The pitch on the last word will now be falling. Don't peek!

1. will you come here H F
2. will you come here L F
3. will you come here H F
4. will you come here L F
5. will you come here L F
6. will you come here H F
7. will you come here L F
8. will you come here L F
9. will you come here H F
10. will you come here H F
11. will you come here L F
12. will you come here L F

RE 6.9. Differential: Various Contours

In RE 6.9 we add an additional complication of a long rise and long fall on the frame my book. The possibilities of responses are:

LONG	HIGH	FALL
SHORT	LOW	RISE

Choose one from each column. Or you may draw the contour if you prefer. In each case of a long fall, it will start high, and in each case of a long rise, it will start low. Don't peek!

1. my 'book LONG L R
2. my 'book SHORT L R
3. my 'book SHORT H R
4. my 'book SHORT H F
5. my 'book SHORT L F
6. my 'book LONG H F
7. my 'book SHORT H F
8. my 'book SHORT H R
9. my 'book SHORT L R
10. my 'book SHORT L R
11. my 'book LONG L R
12. my 'book SHORT L F
13. my 'book SHORT H F
14. my 'book SHORT H F
15. my 'book LONG H F
16. my 'book SHORT H R
17. my 'book SHORT L F
18. my 'book SHORT L R
19. my 'book SHORT L F
20. my 'book LONG L R

RE 6.10. Differential: Various Contours

RE 6.10 is the same as the preceding, except that this time the words of the frame change. The pitch of the frame does not change. Don't peek!

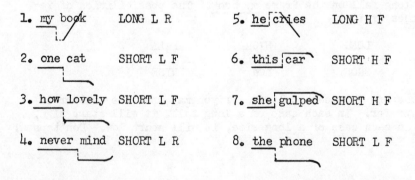

1. my book LONG L R
2. one cat SHORT L F
3. how lovely SHORT L F
4. never mind SHORT L R
5. he cries LONG H F
6. this car SHORT H F
7. she gulped SHORT H F
8. the phone SHORT L F

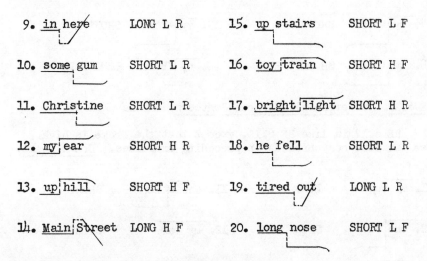

9. in here	LONG L R	15. up stairs	SHORT L F
10. some gum	SHORT L R	16. toy train	SHORT H F
11. Christine	SHORT L R	17. bright light	SHORT H R
12. my ear	SHORT H R	18. he fell	SHORT L R
13. up hill	SHORT H F	19. tired out	LONG L R
14. Main Street	LONG H F	20. long nose	SHORT L F

RE 6.11. Differential: Various Contours

RE 6.11 is like RE 6.9, except that the frame is higher. This gives you a different point of reference for deciding on the height of the final pitch. Use the same responses as in preceding exercises. Don't peek!

1. my 'book	LONG L R	9. my 'book	SHORT L R
2. my 'book	SHORT L R	10. my 'book	SHORT L R
3. my 'book	SHORT H R	11. my 'book	LONG L R
4. my 'book	SHORT H F	12. my 'book	SHORT L F
5. my 'book	SHORT L F	13. my 'book	SHORT H F
6. my 'book	LONG H F	14. my 'book	SHORT H F
7. my 'book	SHORT H F	15. my 'book	LONG H F
8. my 'book	SHORT H R	16. my 'book	SHORT H R

17. my 'book SHORT L F

18. my 'book SHORT L R

19. my 'book SHORT L F

20. my 'book LONG L R

RE 6.12. Differential: Various Contours

RE 6.12 is like RE 6.10, except that the frame is high. Use the same responses as in preceding exercises. Don't peek!

1. my book LONG L R
2. one cat SHORT L F
3. how lovely SHORT L F
4. never mind SHORT L R
5. he cries LONG H F
6. this car SHORT H F
7. she gulped SHORT H F
8. the phone SHORT L F
9. in here LONG L R
10. some gum SHORT L R
11. Christine SHORT L R
12. my ear SHORT H R
13. up hill SHORT H F
14. Main Street LONG H F
15. up stairs SHORT L F
16. toy train SHORT H F
17. bright light SHORT H R
18. he fell SHORT L R
19. tired out LONG L R
20. long nose SHORT L F

RE 6.13. Transcription: Pitch Contours

RE 6.13 is a transcription exercise. It is made on the same pattern as the preceding exercises, but no response is recorded on the tape. Draw the contours as your response. Draw the frame as well as the final syllable. Check your answers against the text of the exercise.

1. Mary
2. had a
3. little
4. lamb its
5. fleece was
6. white as
7. snow and
8. every
9. where that
10. Mary
11. went the
12. lamb was
13. sure to
14. go she
15. followed
16. her to
17. school one
18. day which
19. was a
20. gainst the
21. rules it
22. made the
23. children
24. laugh and
25. the end

LESSON SEVEN

Voiceless Aspirated and Unaspirated Stops

If you pronounce the interjection Oh-oh! deliberately and carefully, you should be aware of a "break" or "catch" in the middle. This break or catch is called a glottal stop. Or, if you cough deliberately, the "catch" at the beginning is a glottal stop. Most speakers of English use the glottal stop constantly in some interjections and frequently also as an "attack" or "opening" for words beginning with a vowel phoneme. In addition, many dialects of American English have glottal stops as a substitute or replacement[1] for a [t] in certain combinations with other sounds. An example of this is the "Brooklynese" bottle [ˈbɑʔl̩], or kitten [kʰɩʔn̩]. Americans from all parts of the United States say some variety of [ˈsɛnʔn̩ts] or [ˈsɛʔɛnts] for sentence. The glottal stop is symbolized by [ʔ], the top part of a question mark without the dot.

Recorded Exercises 7.1-7.3: English. Demonstration: Uses of Glottal Stop

Listen to the tape demonstration of some English uses of the glottal stop. Mimic the tape.

RE 7.1

1.	[ˈʔoʔo]	Oh-oh!	8.	[ˈkʰɩʔn̩]	kitten
2.	[ˈm̩ʔm̩]	negative grunt	9.	[ˈsɩʔn̩]	sittin'
3.	[ˈMm̩ʔm̩]	negative grunt	10.	[ˈbɩʔn̩]	bitten
4.	[ˈʔʌ̨ʔʌ̨]	negative grunt	11.	[ˈbɑʔl̩]	bottle
5.	[ˈsɛnʔnts]	sentence	12.	[ˈkʰæʔl̩]	cattle
6.	[ˈsæʔr̩dɛy]	Saturday	13.	[ˈmɛʔl̩]	metal
7.	[ˈmɩʔn̩]	mitten	14.	[ˈlɩʔl̩]	little

[1]In technical terms (for those who understand them by now), [ʔ] is an allophone of /t/ in some English dialects. Do not let these English examples affect your phonemic transcription of English. Glottal stop is not a separate phoneme in most dialects of English, although it is in many languages. It should be indicated in phonetic transcription but not in phonemic transcription of English.

RE 7.2. Demonstration: Glottal Stop at Medial Word Boundary

The first column indicates pronunciation <u>with</u> the glottal stop, and the second without it. Both are common pronunciations. The tape recordings read from left to right so that you can hear the same phrase with and without glottal stop.

1a. [ˌt^{h}ʊw ˈʔæpl̩z]	1b. [ˌt^{h}ʊw ˈæpl̩z]	<u>two apples</u>
2a. [ˌmɑy ˈʔιyr̩z]	2b. [ˌmɑy ˈιyr̩z]	<u>my ears</u>
3a. [ˈsowfɨ ˌʔɑHrmz]	3b. [ˈsowfɨ ˌɑHrmz]	<u>sofa arms</u>
4a. [ˈp^{h}ɑHpʌ ˌʔιz]	4b. [ˈp^{h}ɑHpʌ ˌιz]	<u>papa is</u>
5a. [ˌsʌm ˈʔʌys]	5b. [ˌsʌm ˈʌys]	<u>some ice</u>
6a. [ˈʔænʌ ˈʔæsks]	6b. [ˈʔænʌ ˈæsks]	<u>Anna asks</u>
7a. [ˌθrιy ˈʔɛgz]	7b. [ˌθrιy ˈɛgz]	<u>three eggs</u>
8a. [ˌdr̩ďιy ˈʔæŋk^{h}l̩z]	8b. [ˌdr̩ďιy ˈæŋk^{h}l̩z]	<u>dirty ankles</u>
9a. [ˌblʊw ˈʔɑyz]	9b. [ˌblʊw ˈɑyz]	<u>blue eyes</u>
10a. [ˌyɛlow ˈʔɔtow]	10b. [ˌyɛlow ˈɔtow]	<u>yellow auto</u>

RE 7.3. Demonstration: Initial Glottal Stop

1. [ˈʔæpl̩z]	<u>apples</u>	6. [ˈʔæHsks]	<u>asks</u>
2. [ˈʔιyr̩z]	<u>ears</u>	7. [ˈʔɛgz]	<u>eggs</u>
3. [ˈʔɑHrmz]	<u>arms</u>	8. [ˈʔɑyz]	<u>eyes</u>
4. [ˈʔιz]	<u>is</u>	9. [ˈʔæŋk^{h}l̩z]	<u>ankles</u>
5. [ˈʔʌys]	<u>ice</u>	10. [ˈʔɔtow]	<u>auto</u>

For English-speaking people glottal stop is hardest to hear in initial position. Listen again carefully to RE 7.3. You will get more drill on initial glottal stop later.

Producing Glottal Stops

In producing the glottal stop the vocal cords are briefly closed, and air pressure from the lungs builds up behind them. The sudden opening of the glottis releases the air. Note that in a glottal stop the air stream is cut off at the larynx, below all of the articulators. This means that for the duration

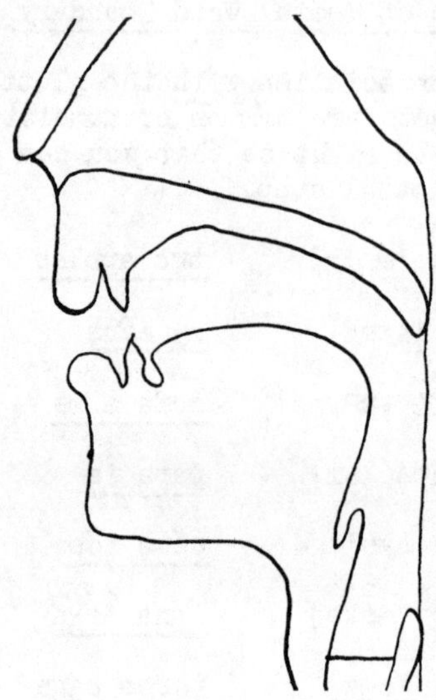

Sammy 7.1: Glottal Stop in the sequence [ɑʔɑ]

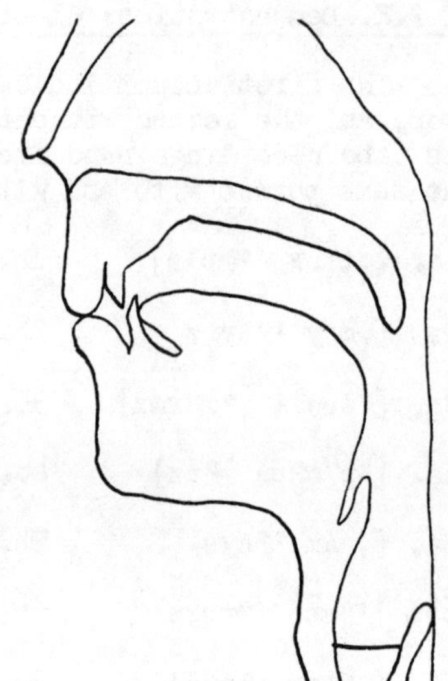

Sammy 7.2: Glottal Stop in the sequence [m̩ʔm̩]

of this stop the position of the articulators is irrelevant to the sound. The position is governed by preceding and/or following sounds. Compare Sammies 7.1 and 7.2. Most students have very little difficulty producing glottal stops, but for those who do, we provide the following exercises.

RE 7.4. Mimicry: Producing Medial [ʔ]

Mimic the tape, pronouncing the words, and exaggerating or lengthening the [ʔ] in Column b.

1a. [so'ʔo] 1b. [so'ʔ·o]

2a. [sɑ'ʔɑ] 2b. [sɑ'ʔ·ɑ]

3a. [si'ʔi] 3b. [si'ʔ·i]

4a. [su'ʔu] 4b. [su'ʔ·u]

5a. [se'ʔe] 5b. [se'ʔ·e]

RE 7.5. Mimicry: Producing Final [ʔ]

In order to learn to produce a glottal stop in final position, start with the sequence of RE 7.4 and add a third column without a final vowel.

1a. [so'ʔo]	1b. [so'ʔ•o]	1c. ['soʔ]
2a. [sɑ'ʔɑ]	2b. [sɑ'ʔ•ɑ]	2c. ['sɑʔ]
3a. [si'ʔi]	3b. [si'ʔ•i]	3c. ['siʔ]
4a. [su'ʔu]	4b. [su'ʔ•u]	4c. ['suʔ]
5a. [se'ʔe]	5b. [se'ʔ•e]	5c. ['seʔ]

RE 7.6. Mimicry: Producing Initial [ʔ]

Learn to pronounce an initial glottal stop in the same way, except that this time you leave off the first syllable of Column b to form Column c.

1a. [so'ʔo]	1b. [so'ʔ•o]	1c. ['ʔ•o]
2a. [sɑ'ʔɑ]	2b. [sɑ'ʔ•ɑ]	2c. ['ʔ•ɑ]
3a. [si'ʔi]	3b. [si'ʔ•i]	3c. ['ʔ•i]
4a. [su'ʔu]	4b. [su'ʔ•u]	4c. ['ʔ•u]
5a. [se'ʔe]	5b. [se'ʔ•e]	5c. ['ʔ•e]

Eliminating Initial [ʔ]

As you will see in the Toʔa'baʔita (Solomon Islands) data in RE 7.12, languages occasionally require a phonemic distinction between initial [ʔ] and lack of it before vowels. Such contrasts in medial and final position are much more common, and are easier for English-speaking people to learn. In the next exercises we will concentrate on producing clear initial vowels without a glottal stop.

RE 7.7. Mimicry: Initial Presence and Absence of [ʔ]

Listen to the tape and mimic. The exercise reads across. Follow in your text. As you mimic items in Column a be sure you feel the [ʔ] in your throat. As you mimic items in Column b be sure there is no [ʔ] in your throat.

1a. [ʔo•]	1b. [o•]
2a. [ʔɑ•]	2b. [ɑ•]
3a. [ʔi•]	3b. [i•]

4a. [ʔu·]	4b. [u·]
5a. [ʔe·]	5b. [e·]

RE 7.8. Mimicry: Producing Initial Vowel

Another way to learn to make an initial vowel without a glottal stop is by making a slight [h] just as you begin the vowel. This opens the glottis. Listen to, and practice the contrast between Column a (with [ʔ]), Column b (with [h]), and Column c (with initial vowel). Say Column c like Column b, except that there is no audible [h]. Let the [h] open your glottis for you, but do not sound it.

1a. [ˈʔo]	1b. [ˈho]	1c. [ˈo]
2a. [ˈʔɑ]	2b. [ˈhɑ]	2c. [ˈɑ]
3a. [ˈʔi]	3b. [ˈhi]	3c. [ˈi]
4a. [ˈʔu]	4b. [ˈhu]	4c. [ˈu]
5a. [ˈʔe]	5b. [ˈhe]	5c. [ˈe]

Another variety of the same exercise is to breathe in slightly for Column b in place of the [h]. Breathe in to open the glottis and then say the vowel.

Recognizing Glottal Stops

In the following exercises you should listen for any glottal stop which may be pronounced. Each of the exercises will focus on a different position in the word. In RE 7.9, when there is a [ʔ] it will be medial; in RE 7.10 it will be final; and in RE 7.11 it will be initial. Do not watch the text of the exercises in your books.

RE 7.9. Differential: GLOTTAL or NO

1. [ˈmɑʔɑ]	GLOTTAL	7. [ˈkɑ·kɑ]	NO
2. [ˈmɑ·]	NO	8. [ˈkɑkɑkɑ]	NO
3. [ˈmɑ·m]	NO	9. [ˈkɑʔɑkɑ]	GLOTTAL
4. [ˈmɑʔɑm]	GLOTTAL	10. [ˈkɑkɑʔɑ]	GLOTTAL
5. [ˈmɑʔɑ]	GLOTTAL	11. [ˈfɑlɑʔɑtʰɑ]	GLOTTAL
6. [ˈkɑʔɑkɑ]	GLOTTAL	12. [ˈfɑlɑ·tʰɑ]	NO

13. [ˈfalakatʰa]	NO	15. [ˈfalatʰaʔa]	GLOTTAL
14. [ˈfalaʔatʰa]	GLOTTAL	16. [ˈpatakaʔala]	GLOTTAL

RE 7.10. Differential: GLOTTAL or NO

Listen for final position only. Don't peek!

1. [ˈmaʔ]	GLOTTAL	8. [ˈmakaʔ]	GLOTTAL
2. [ˈma·]	NO	9. [ˈmaʔak]	NO
3. [ˈma·ʔ]	GLOTTAL	10. [ˈmaʔaʔ]	GLOTTAL
4. [ˈmakaʔ]	GLOTTAL	11. [ˈpataka·laʔ]	GLOTTAL
5. [ˈmaka]	NO	12. [ˈpatala·lak]	NO
6. [ˈmaka·]	NO	13. [ˈpataka·la]	NO
7. [ˈmaka]	NO	14. [ˈpataʔalak]	NO

RE 7.11. Differential: GLOTTAL or NO

Listen for initial position only. Don't peek!

1. [ˈʔa]	GLOTTAL	8. [ˈʔaʔ]	GLOTTAL
2. [ˈa]	NO	9. [ˈaʔaʔak]	NO
3. [ˈʔafa]	GLOTTAL	10. [ˈʔakaʔak]	GLOTTAL
4. [ˈʔa·fa]	GLOTTAL	11. [ˈa·ʔaʔak]	NO
5. [ˈafa]	NO	12. [ˈʔakalakaʔ]	GLOTTAL
6. [ˈafaʔ]	NO	13. [ˈakalakaʔ]	NO
7. [ˈkafaʔ]	NO	14. [ˈkaʔalakaʔ]	NO

RE 7.12: Toʔaˈbaʔita (Solomons).[1] Mimicry

Pay particular attention to the pairs of words which differ only by [ʔ]. Mimic the tape.

1. ˈilia ˈdoˈ 2. ˈʔilia ˈdigˈ

---

[1]Data from lesson plans in use at the Summer Institute of Linguistics, Norman, Oklahoma, 1956.

3. ai 'woman' 7. oe 'you (sg.)'

4. ʔai 'tree' 8. 'abu 'flood'

5. e'aʔi 'it is not' 9. 'ʔabu 'holy'

6. 'oʔe 'act of adultery'

Voiceless Aspirated and Unaspirated Stops

When native speakers of English pronounce the words spill, still, and skill, they normally do so with a simple voiceless stop as the second sound. When they pronounce the words pill till, and kill, they do so with a voiceless stop, but one which has an additional phonetic feature not present in spill, still, and skill. This feature is a slight puff of air immediately after the stop. This puff of air is called aspiration. A stop which has this puff of air is called an aspirated stop. One which does not have it is called an unaspirated stop. The puff of air is symbolized by a raised [h] immediately after the stop symbol.

You can sense the difference in the aspiration of the /p/[1]

---

[1]For those who have learned enough about phonemics to understand it, the following statement may be helpful. In English the distinction between aspirated and unaspirated stops is not phonemic. That is why as speakers of English we do not need to be conscious of the /p/ in spill ['spɩl] being different from the /p/ in pill ['pʰɩl]. English speakers make the difference automatically, according to the sound environment in which the stop phonemes /p t k/ occur. The presence of a preceding /s/, for example, is one environment which automatically causes the stop to be pronounced without aspiration in English.

Other languages do not have the same patterning of aspirated and unaspirated stops. In many languages they are phonemically distinctive, making all the difference between some words. See, for example, the Thai words in RE 9.15: /pìt/ 'to close,' /pʰìt/ 'wrong,' etc.

In your phonemic writing of English be sure not to transcribe the aspiration. [p] and [pʰ] belong to the same phoneme /p/ in English (but not necessarily in other languages). Similarly [t] and [tʰ] belong to the same English phoneme /t/, and [k] and [kʰ] to the same English phoneme /k/. In your phonetics work, however, where you want to be aware of various differences of pronunciation within a phoneme, or of sound differences which constitute phonemic differences in other languages, you need to write the aspiration where it occurs.

in spill and pill if you hold the back of your hand close to your mouth as you pronounce the two words in turn. Or, you can hold a light slip of paper in front of your lips. You can feel the puff of air (or see it if you use a slip of paper). You need to learn to produce it at will and to hear it wherever it occurs.

Perhaps you can hear the difference between aspiration and lack of it in pairs like the following:

(a) loose pill [lʊws pʰɪl] vs. (let) Lou spill (it) [lʊw spɪl]

Diagrammatically, the difference between an aspirated stop and an unaspirated one may be shown as follows. The "word" being diagrammed is shown in the first line. The dashes show the occurrence of the feature (articulation or manner of articulation) shown in the left column.

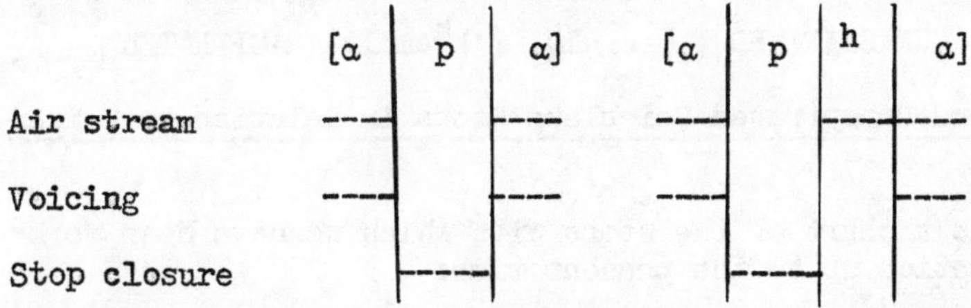

In the unaspirated stop the voiceless stop release coincides very closely with the onset of voicing in the vowel. In the aspirated stop the release of the stop is followed by a brief period of continued voicelessness before the voicing of the vowel begins. It is this voiceless current of air which is called aspiration.

RE 7.13. Differential: ASPIRATED or UNASPIRATED

Distinguishing between aspirated and unaspirated voiceless stops is not difficult when you hear the two in a controlled sequence as in the following drill. Listen for the stops alone. Do not let other consonants confuse you. Don't peek!

1. [ˈapʰa]	ASPIRATED	6. [ˈakʰa]	ASPIRATED
2. [ˈapa]	UNASPIRATED	7. [ˈapa]	UNASPIRATED
3. [ˈata]	UNASPIRATED	8. [ˈakʰama]	ASPIRATED
4. [ˈatʰa]	ASPIRATED	9. [ˈatʰasa]	ASPIRATED
5. [ˈaka]	UNASPIRATED	10. [ˈapʰala]	ASPIRATED

11. ['amata]	UNASPIRATED	13. ['at^{h}ana]	ASPIRATED
12. ['avaka]	UNASPIRATED	14. ['ak^{h}asa]	ASPIRATED

RE 7.14. Differential: ASPIRATED or UNASPIRATED

1. ['p^{h}a]	ASPIRATED	8. ['tama]	UNASPIRATED
2. ['pa]	UNASPIRATED	9. ['k^{h}ala]	ASPIRATED
3. ['ka]	UNASPIRATED	10. ['p^{h}asa]	ASPIRATED
4. ['k^{h}a]	ASPIRATED	11. ['kama]	UNASPIRATED
5. ['p^{h}a]	ASPIRATED	12. ['pala]	UNASPIRATED
6. ['t^{h}a]	ASPIRATED	13. ['tasama]	UNASPIRATED
7. ['ta]	UNASPIRATED	14. ['k^{h}amala]	ASPIRATED

Aspirated and Unaspirated Voiceless Stops in Relation to Voiced Stops

Here is a chart of the stops with which we have been working in phonetics up to the present time:

	Bilabial	Alveolar	Velar	Glottal[1]
Voiced	b	d	g	
Voiceless unaspirated	p	t	k	ʔ
Voiceless aspirated	p^h	t^h	k^h	

It is quite likely that as you were working on the previous exercises you noticed that the unaspirated stops sounded to you very much like voiced stops. There are at least two reasons for this. One lies in the phonetic facts, which we could diagram as follows:

---

[1]The glottal stop belongs here with the others because it patterns as a regular stop consonant in many languages. It can occur aspirated (as in a cough), but that is more rare in languages, so we do not include that possibility here.

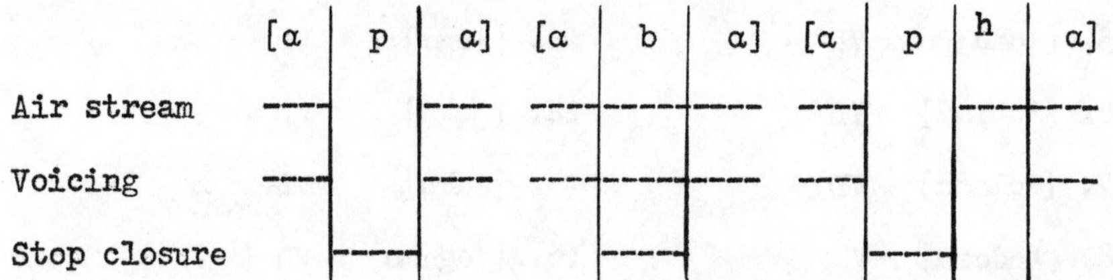

The vertical lines mark the different segments, or pieces into which the utterance is divided by the articulations. The aspirated stop has an extra segment, whereas the voiced stop and the voiceless unaspirated stop have the same number of segments and seem more alike.

Another reason lies in a fact we referred to in Lesson 5, when voiced stops were being discussed. It is that English-speaking people do not voice their /b d g/ very fully, and some of them do not voice them at all. In fact, such people who do not voice them actually have phonetic voiceless unaspirated stops for /b d g/. This stop differs from their unaspirated variety of /p t k/ in the strength with which it is articulated, but this difference is very slight.

Because of the tendency on the part of English-speaking people to confuse voiced stops (which in some languages are strongly voiced) and voiceless unaspirated stops (which in some languages contrast phonemically with them), this distinction needs particularly careful practice. It is the source of many pronunciation mistakes in learning a second language.

RE 7.15. Differential: VOICED or VOICELESS

Listen for the voicing (or lack of it) in the stops of the following exercise. Remember that you are listening for a "rumble" in the stop. Do not watch the text of the exercise.

1.	['ɑbɑ]	VD	8.	['ɑsɑbɑ]	VD
2.	['ɑpɑ]	VL	9.	['ɑpɑnɑ]	VL
3.	['ɑpɑ]	VL	10.	['ɑlɑpɑ]	VL
4.	['ɑbɑ]	VD	11.	['ɑtɑ]	VL
5.	['ɑpɑ]	VL	12.	['ɑdɑ]	VD
6.	['ɑbɑlɑ]	VD	13.	['ɑtɑ]	VL
7.	['ɑbɑmɑ]	VD	14.	['ɑtɑ]	VL

15.	['ada]	VD	23.	['aga]	VD
16.	['atana]	VL	24.	['aka]	VL
17.	['alada]	VD	25.	['aka]	VL
18.	['adasa]	VD	26.	['agama]	VD
19.	['adama]	VD	27.	['akala]	VL
20.	['anata]	VL	28.	['asaga]	VD
21.	['aka]	VL	29.	['anaga]	VD
22.	['aga]	VD	30.	['agama]	VD

RE 7.16. Differential: VOICED or VOICELESS

1.	['ap]	VL	16.	['amanab]	VD
2.	['ad]	VD	17.	['alasat]	VL
3.	['ak]	VL	18.	['analag]	VD
4.	['ag]	VD	19.	['asamad]	VD
5.	['ab]	VD	20.	['avasab]	VD
6.	['ta]	VL	21.	['basa]	VD
7.	['ka]	VL	22.	['dava]	VD
8.	['da]	VD	23.	['gala]	VD
9.	['ba]	VD	24.	['tama]	VL
10.	['pa]	VL	25.	['bafa]	VD
11.	['amat]	VL	26.	['kamala]	VL
12.	['alap]	VL	27.	['tasafa]	VL
13.	['asag]	VD	28.	['gamana]	VD
14.	['cnad]	VD	29.	['pavama]	VL
15.	['alak]	VL	30.	['kalasa]	VL

Producing Voiceless Aspirated and Unaspirated Stops

You use voiceless aspirated stops in your English speech all of the time. All you need to do is to learn to produce them at will in environments where they do not normally occur in English (like after /s/) and to control the amount of aspiration, making it more or less pronounced, according to the language you are learning.

You also use voiceless unaspirated stops in your English speech. You need now to take sounds which are conditioned by their environment in English, and produce them at will in any sound environment.

RE 7.17. Mimicry: Developing Strong Aspiration

Mimic the tape, maintaining its rhythm and speed. Exaggerate the amount of aspiration more than you would for normal English.

1. [hɑhɑhɑhɑ]

   [p^{h}ɑp^{h}ɑp^{h}ɑp^{h}ɑ]

   [sp^{h}ɑsp^{h}ɑsp^{h}ɑsp^{h}ɑ]

2. [hɑhɑhɑhɑ]

   [t^{h}ɑt^{h}ɑt^{h}ɑt^{h}ɑ]

   [st^{h}ɑst^{h}ɑst^{h}ɑst^{h}ɑ]

3. [hɑhɑhɑhɑ]

   [k^{h}ɑk^{h}ɑk^{h}ɑk^{h}ɑ]

   [sk^{h}ɑsk^{h}ɑsk^{h}ɑsk^{h}ɑ]

4. [hɑp^{h}ɑt^{h}ɑk^{h}ɑ]

5. [hɑsp^{h}ɑst^{h}ɑsk^{h}ɑ]

RE 7.18. Negative Practice: Exaggerated Aspiration

Practice the following English words, exaggerating all of the normal aspiration, and adding aspiration to any voiceless stop which does not normally have it.

1. ['p^{h}ɛy] pay
2. ['t^{h}ʊw] two
3. ['nɑt^{h}] not
4. ['ɔt^{h}ow] auto
5. ['p^{h}owgow] pogo
6. ['sæt^{h}] sat
7. ['st^{h}ɛp^{h}] step
8. ['t^{h}ɑt^{h}] tot
9. [p^{h}ʌ'rɛyd] parade
10. ['bowt^{h}] boat
11. ['ɔp^{h}ɨrɛyt^{h}] operate
12. ['st^{h}rɪyt^{h}] street

13. [ɛkʰsˈtʰɛnd] extend 15. [ɪnˈkʰlɨwdɨd] included

14. [ˈstʰʊwdɨntʰ] student 16. [ɪnˌtʰɨrpʰrɨˈtʰɛyšɨn] interpretation

Practice other English words in the same way.

RE 7.19. Demonstration: Producing Voiceless Unaspirated Stops

In this and the following exercises keep the back of your hand in front of your lips so that you can feel the aspiration if there is any.

1. Start by making a long voiceless stop, holding the closure a second or so:

[ɑp·ɑ ɑp·ɑ ɑt·ɑ ɑt·ɑ ɑk·ɑ ɑk·ɑ]

2. Now be sure you put the greatest stress on the second vowel. Try to keep off every trace of aspiration:

[ɑp·ˈpɑ ɑt·ˈtɑ ɑk·ˈkɑ]

3. "Think" the first syllable of the utterances above but do not say it. Just pronounce the second syllable, and keep all aspiration off:

[pɑpɑpɑpɑ] [tɑtɑtɑtɑ] [kɑkɑkɑkɑ]

Now again, fast!

Go thru RE 7.19 again, this time starting with the "words" [ɑb·ɑ], [ɑd·ɑ], and [ɑg·ɑ] and whispering each part of the exercise before you say it aloud. As you whisper, your whole utterance will automatically be voiceless. Get the feel of the voiceless stops. As you change back to regular speech, continue to "whisper" the stops even though you voice the vowels.

RE 7.20. Demonstration: Producing Voiceless Unaspirated Stops

This exercise is based on the English words spill, still, and skill. The stops in these words are normally unaspirated in English because they follow /s/. This exercise is designed to help you take the /s/ off the words without losing the unaspirated quality. Mimic the speed and timing of the tape. Be careful that the words do not come to sound like the English words pill, till, and kill.

1. Make a long [s]: sssssssssssˈpill

sssssssssss'till

sssssssssss'kill

2. Make a break between the [s] and the rest of the word:

sssssssssss 'pill

sssssssssss 'till

sssssssssss 'kill

3. Just do the last part alone. Watch out for aspiration! Think the [s] but do not pronounce it:

'pill

'till

'kill

4. Run through the sequence rapidly:

sssssssssss'pill

sssssssssss 'pill

'pill

'pill 'pill 'pill

Do the same for [t k].

5. ['pɩHl pɑ pi po pu]

['tɩHl tɑ ti to tu]

['kɩHl kɑ ki ko ku]

In the following exercises listen carefully to the tape, repeating after it exactly what you hear, maintaining the rhythm, stress, and speed, but paying particular attention to the articulation of the consonants. You may use your printed text with these drills.

RE 7.21. Mimicry: Buildups to Longer Sequences with Stops

In this exercise each item on the tape will be given only once. Mimic in the space provided. The items grouped together with the same number build on each other and become cumulatively longer. The first number is written out in full to show the sequence. Those which follow are built on exactly the same pattern. Follow the transcription.

1. [ˈʔɑʔɑ]

   [ˈʔɑʔɑʔɑ]

   [ˈʔɑʔɑʔɑʔɑ]

2. [ˈp^{h}ɑp^{h}ɑp^{h}ɑp^{h}ɑ]

3. [ˈpɑpɑpɑpɑ]

4. [ˈbɑbɑbɑbɑ]

5. [ˈt^{h}ɑt^{h}ɑt^{h}ɑt^{h}ɑ]

6. [ˈtɑtɑtɑtɑ]

7. [ˈdɑdɑdɑdɑ]

8. [ˈk^{h}ɑk^{h}ɑk^{h}ɑk^{h}ɑ]

9. [ˈkɑkɑkɑkɑ]

10. [ˈgɑgɑgɑgɑ]

RE 7.22. Mimicry: Buildups to Longer Sequences with Stops and Fricatives

This time the tape will repeat each item more than once when it comes to the longer sequences. Mimic after each repetition. As in the previous exercise, the first number is written out in full so that you can see the progression. From there on, however, only the sequence to which you are building is written out. You will build toward it in the same fashion as in number one. Follow the transcription.

1. [ˈʔɑp^{h}ɑ]

   [ˈʔɑp^{h}ɑt^{h}ɑ]

   [ˈʔɑp^{h}ɑt^{h}ɑk^{h}ɑ]

2. [ˈʔɑpɑtɑkɑ]

3. [ˈʔɑbɑdɑgɑ]

4. [ˈʔɑt^{h}ɑtɑdɑzɑsɑ]

5. [ˈʔɑp^{h}ɑpɑbɑbɑpɑ]

6. [ˈmɑlɑfɑbɑp^{h}ɑ]

7. [ˈpɑkɑxɑbɑt^{h}ɑ]

8. [ˈʔɑbɑgɑsɑdɑ]

9. [ˈpɑkɑp^{h}ɑbɑlɑ]

10. [ˈgɑp^{h}ɑdɑlɑxɑ]

RE 7.23. Transcription

Listen to the tape, and write down the utterances you hear. The vowels will all be [ɑ], but be sure to write them in in their proper places. Watch for the new sounds or sound distinctions which you have been drilling. Check your transcription afterwards against the correct transcription below, but do not peek until you are satisfied with your transcription.

1. [ˈpɑx]

2. [ˈdɑf]

3. [ˈgɑp]

4. [k^{h}ɑs]

5. [ˈmɑt^h]

6. [ˈzɑp^{h}ɑ]

7. [ˈtɑvɑ]

8. [ˈnɑkɑ]

9. [ˈbɑxɑ]

10. ['pɑʔɑ] 12. ['fɑʔɑp] 14. ['pɑnɑs]

11. ['lɑsɑg] 13. ['gɑxɑb] 15. ['tʰɑvɑl]

Read off the items in RE 7.23 before you hear them pronounced on the tape. Then listen to the tape to compare with what you have just said. Stop the machine between items if necessary to give yourself the time to read them off.

"Buddy System" for Phonetic Study

You can work to considerable advantage, and perhaps help avoid at least the grosser mistakes in practicing phonetics, by working in a team with another student. As you practice together you can point out to each other where you do not correspond to the tape. You can also get practice in reading and transcribing by dictating to each other.

Sammy Exercise 7.1

Draw articulations of [v ƀ x š] on Little Blank Sammies.

Suggested Reading

Page numbers in parentheses may not apply specifically to the points of this lesson, but have been listed in previous lessons, and you may want to read them while you have the book.

W. Nelson Francis, The Structure of American English, pp. 72-78 (51-70).

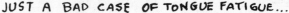

JUST A BAD CASE OF TONGUE FATIGUE...

LESSON EIGHT

Longer Sequences of Pitch

RE 8.1. Reading: "The Hat with the Bird" (continued)[1]

The following material continues with the Sally Mansfield story, read with artificially controlled English intonation. Remember that your purpose here is to be able to say something without the intonation which you would usually attach to it, but with an intonation which is prescribed for you, and which will seem unnatural at times.

Before you turn on the tape recorder for this exercise, read over the remainder of "The Hat with the Bird" which is given here, practicing the intonation contours indicated. When you think you have the reading down fairly well, turn on the recorder and check yourself against it. You read each numbered sentence aloud in the space provided on the tape, and the tape will give it correctly after you. Listen to the tape and compare it with what you said. Have a classmate listen to you and the tape to help you realize where you are off. Turn on the tape recorder before you begin to read. You should read the first sentence after the tape says "Number One."

(1) 'Sally was 'angry. (2) She was 'sensitive when Sam talked about 'hats. (3) He 'always 'tried to be 'funny.

(4) "'That i'dea is ab'surd," she said. (5) "I have never 'heard of it before."

(6) "'I haven't 'either," said Sam, (7) "but it's an o'riginal idea, 'anyway. (8) I am going to write a 'poem about women's 'hats. (9) It is going to go like 'this:

[1]Continued from Lesson 6, p. 94

(10) A 'bird can sit upon a 'hat,

(11) But a 'hat can't have a 'cat upon it;

(12) To have a 'cat would be ab'surd

(13) But a 'hat can have a 'bird upon it.

(14) I 'wonder if it's 'possible that

A 'bird can have a 'cat upon it?

(15) 'Sally went 'out of the 'room because her 'feelings were hurt. (16) She re'turned 'quickly and she was 'crying.

(17) "'Sam, 'Sam," she said, "Our 'cat is trying to eat, the 'bird on my 'hat. (19) The 'cat thought the 'bird was, a'live and she 'jumped upon it. (20) 'What shall I 'do, Sam?"

(21) 'Sam tried 'not to 'laugh but he could 'hardly, pre'vent himself.

(22) "'Where is the cat 'now?" he asked.

(23) "It is 'sitting on my 'hat in the 'chair in the, 'living room, 'eating the 'bird on the 'hat." (24) 'Sally

began to 'cry more than be'fore. (25) "I 'think you are 'terrible, Sam. (26) I think the cat 'really 'heard what you 'said about 'hats."

(27) 'Sam did not 'say anything, (28) but he tried to appear un'happy about the 'hat, the 'cat, and the 'bird. (29) He knew he would 'laugh if he opened his mouth to 'say anything.

Mimicry of Pitch Combinations.

For the remainder of this lesson you will concentrate primarily on the mimicry of tone drills of various kinds. The emphasis will be on three level tones, two glide tones, and combinations of these.

RE 8.2. Mimicry: Three Levels

In this drill you will be helped by the fact that a part of your frame will be the words low, mid, and high, each corresponding with the pitch level of that particular syllable. For example, if the pitch sequence is low-high-low, the syllables of your drill will be the words low, high, low as well. In this exercise the first syllable will always be low to give you an additional peg point. Mimic the tape. Try to avoid a "singing" quality. Each item will be given twice.

1. low mid high
2. low high high
3. low high mid
4. low mid mid
5. low low mid
6. low mid low
7. low low high
8. low low low
9. low high low

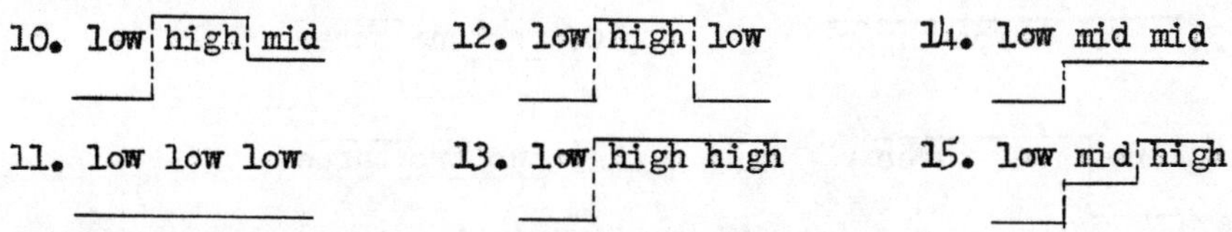

RE 8.3. Mimicry: Three Levels

Here the words of your frame are one, two, and three. As in the last exercise, these words will correllate with the pitches you will hear. One will be low pitch, two mid, and three high. The initial syllable will always be low.

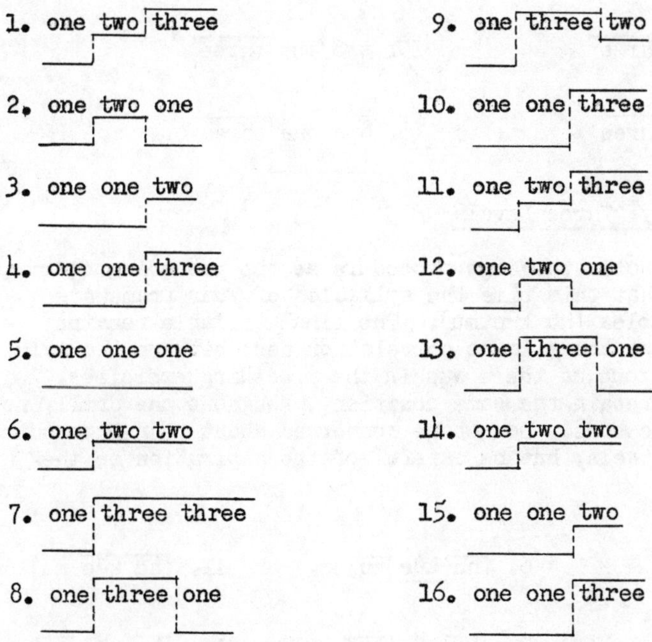

RE 8.4. Mimicry: Three Levels

This exercise will be the same as the preceding one, except that the tone of the last syllable (rather than the first) will be the frame tone, and it will be high.

1. three one three

2. two two three

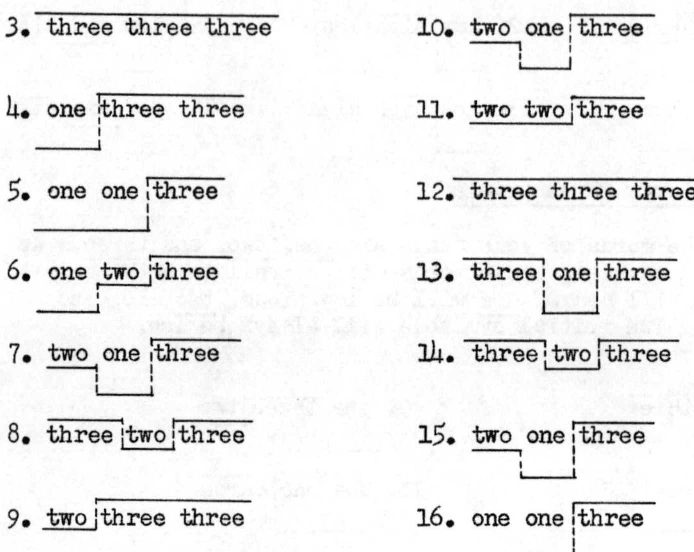

3. three three three
4. one three three
5. one one three
6. one two three
7. two one three
8. three two three
9. two three three
10. two one three
11. two two three
12. three three three
13. three one three
14. three two three
15. two one three
16. one one three

RE 8.5. Mimicry: Three Levels

Follow exactly the same procedure as the preceding exercise, except that this time the syllables of your frame are nonsense syllables [ha k^he mu]. The final syllable remains high. Note that there is no correlation here between the syllable and the tone as there was in the preceding exercises. The syllables retain the same position throughout the drill, no matter what the tone. Do not be concerned about your pronunciation of the vowels, but be careful of the aspiration on the [k^h].

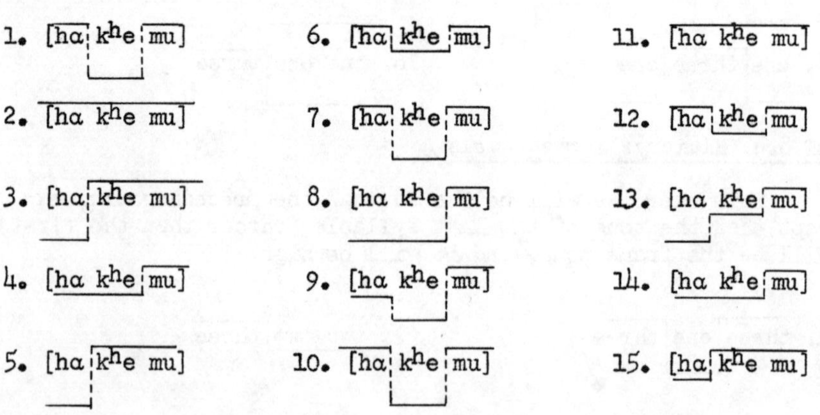

1. [ha k^he mu]
2. [ha k^he mu]
3. [ha k^he mu]
4. [ha k^he mu]
5. [ha k^he mu]
6. [ha k^he mu]
7. [ha k^he mu]
8. [ha k^he mu]
9. [ha k^he mu]
10. [ha k^he mu]
11. [ha k^he mu]
12. [ha k^he mu]
13. [ha k^he mu]
14. [ha k^he mu]
15. [ha k^he mu]

RE 8.6. Buildup: Three Levels

There now follows a series of exercises in which you will be working with the same kinds of pitches as the preceding ones, but this time your sequences will be longer, and you will build up to those sequences by adding a syllable at a time. The tape gives three repetitions for each item.

The text of the first item in this exercise is written out in full, showing each step of the buildup. The remaining items have only the final utterance transcribed for you here. In this exercise the buildups will begin with the final syllable of the long utterance and add preceding syllables one by one. The tape has the full buildup recorded for each item. This drill corresponds to RE 8.2 in that there is a correlation between the syllables high, mid, low and the pitches they contain. Mimic the tape; watch the transcription.

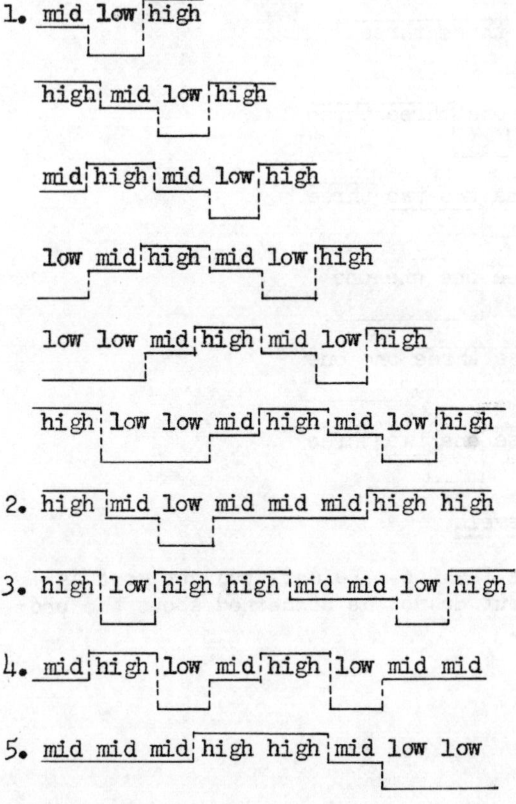
1. mid low high
high mid low high
mid high mid low high
low mid high mid low high
low low mid high mid low high
high low low mid high mid low high
2. high mid low mid mid mid high high
3. high low high high mid mid low high
4. mid high low mid high low mid mid
5. mid mid mid high high mid low low

RE 8.7. Buildup: Three Levels

Follow the same buildup procedure with this exercise, which is patterned after RE 8.3.

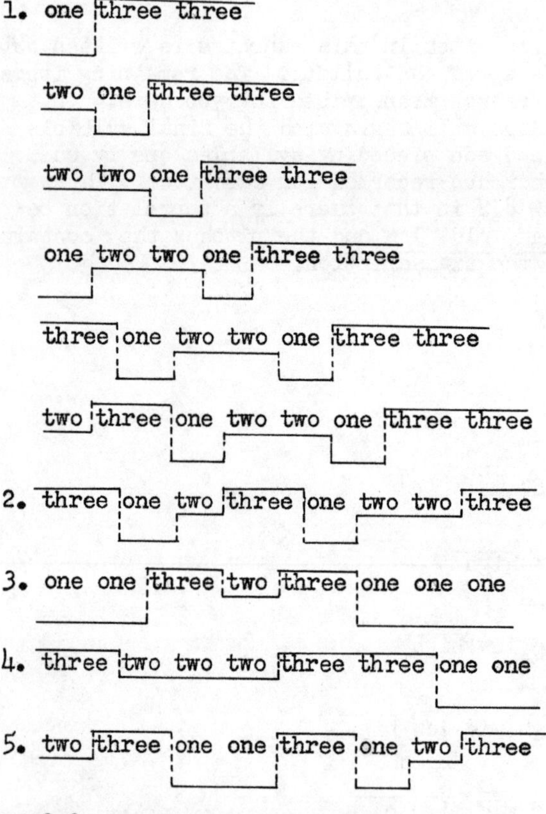

1. one three three
two one three three
two two one three three
one two two one three three
three one two two one three three
two three one two two one three three
2. three one two three one two two three
3. one one three two three one one one
4. three two two two three three one one
5. two three one one three one two three

RE 8.8. Buildup: Three Levels

Continue in the same fashion. Be sure you get good aspiration on your stops, but do not be concerned about the pronunciation of the vowels.

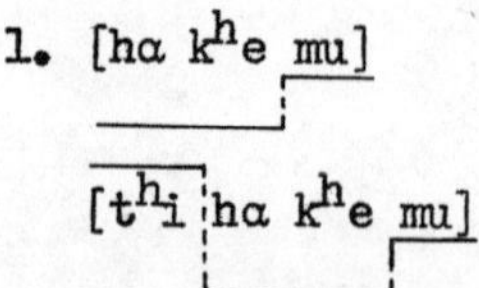

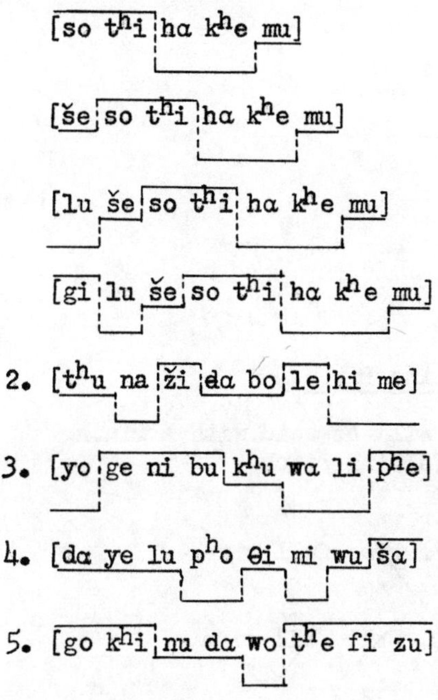
[so tʰi ha kʰe mu]
[še so tʰi ha kʰe mu]
[lu še so tʰi ha kʰe mu]
[gi lu še so tʰi ha kʰe mu]
2. [tʰu na ži da bo le hi me]
3. [yo ge ni bu kʰu wa li pʰe]
4. [da ye lu pʰo θi mi wu ša]
5. [go kʰi nu da wo tʰe fi zu]

RE 8.9. Buildup: Three Levels

This exercise is of the same principle as the preceding one except that the pattern of buildup is reversed, building from the beginning of the final utterance rather than from the end. The consonants used this time are not restricted to English ones. In this exercise, therefore, you will have to pay close attention not only to the tone, but also to the non-English consonants.

1. [xe ša po]

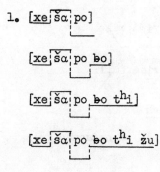

[xe ša po ɓo]

[xe ša po ɓo tʰi]

[xe ša po ɓo tʰi žu]

[xe ša po ɓo tʰi žu θe]

[xe ša po ɓo tʰi žu θe ʔu]

2. [pα θe ʔi te du gu žα kʰi]

3. [ke gi kʰu xu gα ʔi kʰα ge]

4. [ši θα tʰi du tʰo tα so du]

5. [pʰo be pi be vi po fa pʰo]

RE 8.10. Mimicry: Rising and Falling Pitch

In this drill the word rise will be said with a rising pitch, and the word fall with a falling pitch.

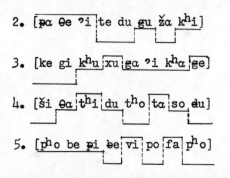

1. rise fall rise
2. rise rise rise
3. fall rise fall
4. fall fall fall
5. fall rise rise
6. fall fall rise
7. rise fall fall
8. rise rise fall
9. rise fall rise
10. fall fall rise
11. fall rise fall
12. rise fall fall
13. rise fall rise
14. fall fall fall
15. fall rise rise
16. rise rise fall

RE 8.11. Mimicry: Rising and Falling Pitch

You will now do the same kind of drill on nonsense syllables.

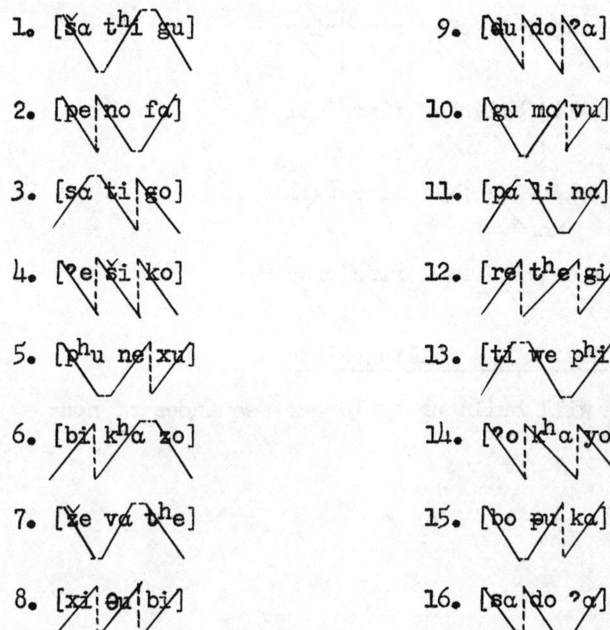

RE 8.12. Buildup: Rising and Falling Pitch

In this exercise you will use the words rise and fall again, but will build up to longer sequences.

1. rise rise fall

   rise rise fall rise

   rise rise fall rise fall

   rise rise fall rise fall fall

   rise rise fall rise fall fall rise

   rise rise fall rise fall fall rise rise

2. fall rise rise rise fall rise rise rise

3. rise fall fall fall fall rise rise fall

4. rise fall rise fall rise fall rise fall

5. fall fall rise rise rise fall rise rise

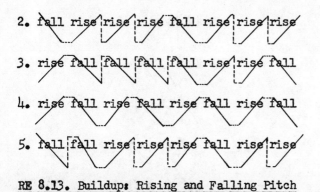

RE 8.13. Buildup: Rising and Falling Pitch

This time you will build up to longer sequences of nonsense syllables.

1. [la re pi]

[la re pi tʰo]

[la re pi tʰo gu]

[la re pi tʰo gu mu]

[la re pi tʰo gu mu to]

[la re pi tʰo gu mu to ši]

2. [ze ne bi bu yi po me da]

3. [pʰo di lo na te so xa go]

4. [la tʰi ža ru ke ki šu mu]

5. [ʔu me kʰo ge wi ʔa bu fi]

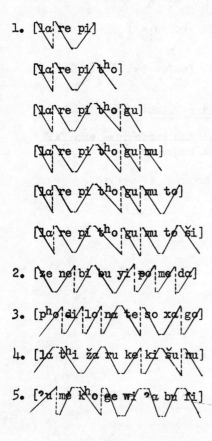

RE 8.14. Mimicry: Levels and Glides

In this drill you will hear three levels plus rising and falling pitches. The syllables will consist of the words which describe the pitch: high, mid, low, rise, fall. Each item will consist of three syllables. The last syllable will be the constant frame.

1. high high mid
2. rise low mid
3. low fall mid
4. mid rise mid
5. fall mid mid
6. fall high mid
7. mid mid mid
8. low low mid
9. high fall mid
10. rise rise mid
11. fall high mid
12. mid low mid
13. high mid mid
14. low fall mid
15. high rise mid
16. fall high mid

RE 8.15. Mimicry: Levels and Glides

Now you will do the same thing with nonsense syllables. Initial low tone will be the constant frame.

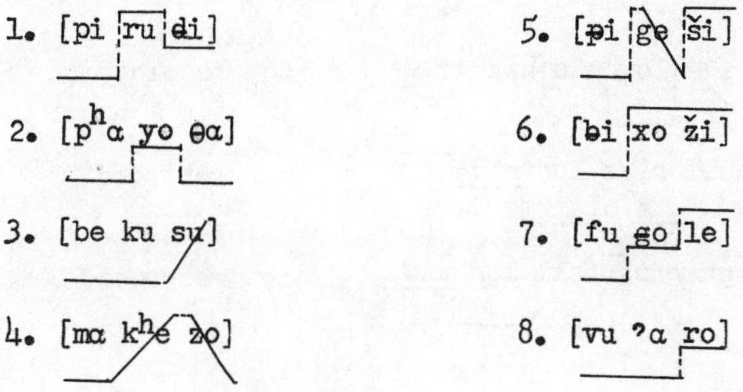

9. [wɑ pɑ ne]

10. [tu p^{h}i ye]

11. [t^{h}o bi wu]

12. [do ƀu kɑ]

13. [đo ᵽu k^{h}ɑ]

14. [θe me gɑ]

15. [si fe xi]

16. [zi vo ǥi]

RE 8.16. Buildup: Levels and Glides

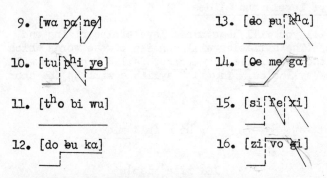

This drill is like RE 8.14 except that it builds up to longer sequences.

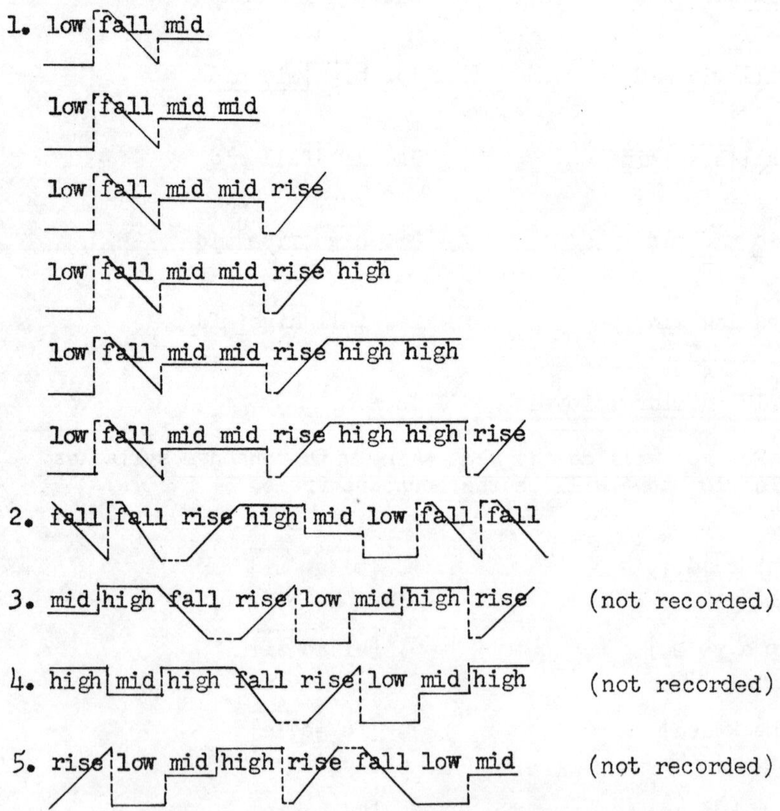
1. low fall mid
low fall mid mid
low fall mid mid rise
low fall mid mid rise high
low fall mid mid rise high high
low fall mid mid rise high high rise
2. fall fall rise high mid low fall fall
3. mid high fall rise low mid high rise (not recorded)
4. high mid high fall rise low mid high (not recorded)
5. rise low mid high rise fall low mid (not recorded)

RE 8.17. Buildup: Levels and Glides

This time the drill will be like RE 8.15, except that you will build up to longer sequences.

1. [bɑ le fɑ]

   [bɑ le fɑ xi]

   [bɑ le fɑ xi šu]

   [bɑ le fɑ xi šu mo]

   [bɑ le fɑ xi šu mo ɓo]

   [bɑ le fɑ xi šu mo ɓo ʔu]

2. [te ro θu ti vɑ po ki žɑ]

3. [yi mu go ze pʰe wi ge tʰe] (not recorded)

4. [bo dɑ ni ʔɑ ši ʔe xɑ si] (not recorded)

5. [ɓu ʔɑ fe kʰu po lu wu ɗo] (not recorded)

RE 8.18. Gola (Liberia).[1] Mimicry: Tone

The following drills constructed from phrases in the Gola language of Liberia consist primarily of level pitches, but with a downward glide in some phrase-final positions. Gola has three phonemic tone levels, marked as follows in the phonemic transcription: /´/ high, /-/ (or unmarked) mid, and /`/ low. You will see these in the phonemic transcription. As you drill this group of exercises, however, you should concentrate on the

---

[1]The informant who supplied the data for this exercise, and whose voice is heard on the tape, is Miss Amelia Mitchell, Suehn Mission, Liberia. The phonemic analysis represented is tentative.

phonetic transcription (in brackets). Listen selectively for the tone. Some of the consonants and vowels may be difficult for you, but try not to let them bother you. Mimic the tone. If the consonants and vowels get in your way, hum the tone, or whistle it. The recording is at an unnaturally slow speed of utterance, which makes it easier for you, though less realistic.[1]

Part 1: /́ ́/ tone sequence

1. [fali syɛ̨ syɛ̨] /fálí syɛ́ syɛ̀/ 'very good pail'

2. [kana syɛ̨ syɛ̨] /káná syɛ́ syɛ̀/ 'very good chief'

3. [siyɩ syɛ̨ syɛ̨] /síyé syɛ́ syɛ̀/ 'very good Palm nut'

4. [bʋla syɛ̨ syɛ̨] /búlá syɛ́ syɛ̀/ 'very good side'

5. [fɛla syɛ̨ syɛ̨] /fɛ́lá syɛ́ syɛ̀/ 'very good man'

6. [ñawa syɛ̨ syɛ̨] /nyáwá syɛ́ syɛ̀/ 'very good bush rope'

Part 2: /-́/ tone sequence

1. [ᵍbaŋᵍba syɛ̨ syɛ̨] /gbaŋgbá syɛ́ syɛ̀/ 'very good stock fish'

2. [dɔmɔ syɛ̨ syɛ̨] /dɔmɔ́ syɛ́ syɛ̀/ 'very good beads'

3. [gɔlɔ syɛ̨ syɛ̨] /gɔlɔ́ syɛ́ syɛ̀/ 'very good palm cabbage'

4. [dono syɛ̨ syɛ̨] /donó syɛ́ syɛ̀/ 'very good net'

Part 3: /̀ ́/ tone sequence

1. [ᵍbetu syɛ̨ syɛ̨] /gbètú syɛ́ syɛ̀/ 'very good play devil'

[1]The recording is incomplete in this lesson for lack of space on the tape. The full recording will be found as RE 32.13 (p. 449).

2. [gbɨli syɛ̨ syɛ̨] /gbìlí syɛ̃́ syɛ̃̀/ 'very good cat'

3. [gelɩ syɛ̨ syɛ̨] /gèlé syɛ̃́ syɛ̃̀/ 'very good hawk'

4. [golo syɛ̨ syɛ̨] /sòló syɛ̃́ syɛ̃̀/ 'very good hole'

5. [gbemee syɛ̨ syɛ̨] /gbèméé syɛ̃́ syɛ̃̀/ 'very good door'

6. [mɔtu syɛ̨ syɛ̨] /mɔ̀tú syɛ̃́ syɛ̃̀/ 'very good friend'

Part 4: /--/ tone sequence

1. [tuwa syɛ̨ syɛ̨] /tuwa syɛ̃́ syɛ̃̀/ 'very good leaf'

2. [komą syɛ̨ syɛ̨] /komã syɛ̃́ syɛ̃̀/ 'very good seed'

3. [fali syɛ̨ syɛ̨] /fali syɛ̃́ syɛ̃̀/ 'very good comb'

4. [tawa syɛ̨ syɛ̨] /tawa syɛ̃́ syɛ̃̀/ 'very good tobacco'

5. [tombo syɛ̨ syɛ̨] /tombo syɛ̃́ syɛ̃̀/ 'very good work'

6. [mąmą syɛ̨ syɛ̨] /mãmã syɛ̃́ syɛ̃̀/ 'very good grandmother'

Part 5: /\`-/ tone sequence

1. [gəlɩ syɛ̨ syɛ̨] /gèle syɛ̃́ syɛ̃̀/ 'very good peanut'

2. [dada syɛ̨ syɛ̨] /dàda syɛ̃́ syɛ̃̀/ 'very good father'

3. [gbʋmą syɛ̨ syɛ̨] /gbùmã syɛ̃́ syɛ̃̀/ 'very good bed'

4. [golo syɛ syɛ] /gòlo syɛ̂ syɛ̀/ 'very good cola nut'

Part 6: /´`/ tone sequence

1. [gbɔli syɛ syɛ] /gbɔ́lì syɛ́ syɛ̀/ 'very good bowl'

2. [sali syɛ syɛ] /sálì syɛ́ syɛ̀/ 'very good fly'

3. [sɛmɛ syɛ syɛ] /sɛ́mɛ̀ syɛ́ syɛ̀/ 'very good fan'

4. [jina syɛ syɛ] /jínà syɛ́ syɛ̀/ 'very good spirit'

Part 7: /-`/ tone sequence

1. [kuma syɛ syɛ] /kumà syɛ́ syɛ̀/ 'very good shirt'

2. [gbɔdi syɛ syɛ] /gbɔdì syɛ́ syɛ̀/ 'very good hat'

3. [kɨlɛ syɛ syɛ] /kilɛ̀ syɛ́ syɛ̀/ 'very good pepper'

4. [bana syɛ syɛ] /banà syɛ́ syɛ̀/ 'very good banana'

5. [ñawa syɛ syɛ] /nyawà syɛ́ syɛ̀/ 'very good onion'

Part 8: /``/ tone sequence

1. [gaŋɩ syɛ syɛ] /gàŋè syɛ́ syɛ̀/ 'very good monkey'

2. [gbař̌a syɛ syɛ] /gbàlà syɛ́ syɛ̀/ 'very good cassava'

3. [gbama syɛ syɛ] /gbàmà syɛ́ syɛ̀/ 'very good gun'

4. [vaña syɛ syɛ] /vànyà syɛ́ syɛ̀/ 'very good apron'

5. [zuwɛñ syɛ syɛ] /zùwɛ̀ny syɛ́ syɛ̀/ 'very good bull frog'

Part 9: tone changes (odd numbers are the same as Part 1)

1. [fali syɛ syɛ] 2. [fali gʊdn] /gún/ 'one pail'

3. [kana syɛ syɛ] 4. [kana gʊdn] /gún/ 'one chief'

5. [siyɩ syɛ syɛ] 6. [siyɩ gʊdn] /gún/ 'one Palm nut'

7. [bʊla syɛ syɛ] 8. [bula gʊdn] /gún/ 'one side'

9. [fɛla syɛ syɛ] 10. [fɛla gʊdn] /gún/ 'one man'

11. [ñawa syɛ syɛ] 12. [ñawa gʊdn] /gún/ 'one bush rope'

RE 8.19. Reading Exercise

In this exercise you are to read the material of RE 8.15 before the tape gives it to you. Compare the tape utterance with your own.

Transcription Exercises

Use any of the following exercises as transcription exercises: RE 8.5, 8.8, 8.9, 8.11, 8.13, 8.15, 8.17, 8.18. Instead of mimicking the tape, transcribe what you hear. Then check your transcription by comparing it with the text in your book.

LESSON NINE

Affricates

Whenever any two consonant sounds occur in immediate sequence we call the sequence a consonant cluster (abbreviated CC). In this as in all phonetics work, we are, of course, concerned with spoken consonants, not written ones. Notice the consonant clusters in the following English words: [bɛgz] begs, [θæŋk] thank, ['mɛnšɨn] mention. In many languages, including English, one important kind of consonant cluster is a sequence of a stop plus a fricative. Such clusters sometimes work together very tightly, and sometimes even work phonemically like a single unit, even though they are phonetically a sequence of two segments. This particular sequence of stop plus fricative, when it is in the same syllable, and pronounced tightly together, we call an affricate[1] /'æfrɨkɨt/.

Read over to yourself the following English words, paying attention to the transcription of the consonants as you do so. Note the final CC which is an affricate in each case. Sense the stop sound followed by a fricative sound in each of these.

1.	kicks	[kʰɪks]	6.	tax	[tʰæks]
2.	ships	[šɪps]	7.	adze	[ædz]
3.	bags	[bægz]	8.	Zipf	[zɪpf]
4.	boards	[boHrdz]	9.	Ritz	[rɪts]
5.	lymph	[lɪmpf]	10.	drugs	[drʌgz]

Now try the same procedure on the following words, paying particular attention to the final CC of Column a and the initial CC of Column b. The alternative forms given in the phonetic transcription are not alternative pronunciations, but alternative symbolization.[2]

---

[1]Please note that although this word is obviously related to the word fricative, and with good reason, it is not simply fricative with an af- on the front, as some students seem tempted to pronounce it.

[2]These sequences are affricates, just as much as are the sequences in 1 - 10. Some of you may notice, however, that the affricates in 11 - 15 (a and b) seem more nearly like a

11a. beach [bιytš] (or [bιyč]) 11b. cheap [tšιyp] (or [čιyp])

12a. bridge [brιdž] (or [brιǰ]) 12b. jeep [džιyp] (or [ǰιyp])

13a. etch [ɛtš] (or [ɛč]) 13b. chip [tšιp] (or [čιp])

14a. edge [ɛdž] (or [ɛǰ]) 14b. gyp [džιp](or [ǰιp])

15a. church [tšr̩tš] (or [čr̩č]) 15b. judge [džʌdž] (or [ǰʌǰ])

Here are segmental diagrams showing the interplay of different features involved in these affricates.

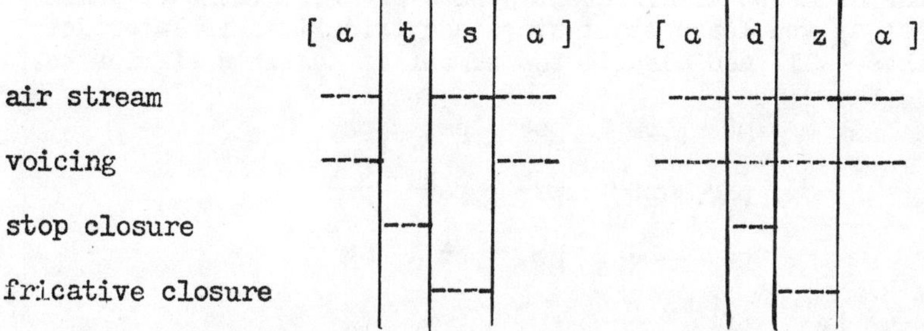

You may have noticed that the stop and fricative in some of the affricates had the same point of articulation, and in others had different points of articulation. For example, [ps] has a stop with a labial point and a fricative with alveolar, whereas [ts] has both stop and fricative at the same point. Table 9.1 gives you the possibilities so far of affricates with both segments at the same point of articulation. Note that the tongue tip actually changes point of articulation to coincide with the point of [θ], [s], and [š] on the stop part of the affricate in which it is involved.

---

single unit to you than do the ones in 1 - 10. This, and other more sophisticated reasons we cannot mention here, make many linguists analyze these particular affricates in English as single units phonemically (although they are complex phonetically). See Archibald A. Hill, Introduction to English Structures, pp. 36-37. This is why we asked you to transcribe these sequences as /č ǰ/ in your phonemic writing of English. In the examples above we included the [tš dž] transcription to emphasize the phonetic complexity of the affricates. From here on, however, we will transcribe these affricates as [č ǰ] wherever we find them in this course, on the analogy of English, simply to avoid the confusion of double symbolization.

	Labial	Dental	Alveolar	Alveopalatal	Velar
Voiceless					
Unaspirated	pᵽ	tθ	ts	č (or tš)	kx
Aspirated	pᵽ^h	tθ^h	ts^h	č^h (or tš^h)	kx^h
Voiced	bƀ	dđ	dz	ǰ (or dž)	gǥ

Table 9.1: Affricates with Both Segments at Same Point

Table 9.2 gives some of the possibilities of affricates with the segments at different points of articulation. Remember that as you learn other stops and fricatives in later lessons these will add also to the number of possible affricates.

	pf	pθ	ps	pš	px
	pf^h	pθ^h	ps^h	pš^h	px^h
	bv	bđ	bz	bž	bǥ
tᵽ	tf				tx
tᵽ^h	tf^h				tx^h
dƀ	dv				dǥ
kᵽ	kf	kθ	ks	kš	
kᵽ^h	kf^h	kθ^h	ks^h	kš^h	
gƀ	gv	gđ	gz	gž	

Table 9.2: Affricates with Segments at Different Points

Affricates in Initial Position

/č ǰ/ are the only affricates which we commonly use in initial position in English. A few borrowed words like tsetse are exceptions. The other affricates need to be practiced in that position for other languages. Do not forget to practice these drills on the "buddy system" (see p. 117) as well as with the recording.

RE 9.1. Demonstration: Affricates in Initial Position

Listen, read, and mimic as you go through this exercise. Then use it as a model to practice all of the affricates in the charts above. We will be working on the unaspirated-aspirated differences below.

1. tsetse	6. [ksaksa]	11. [gvagva]
2. [tsatsa]	7. [gzagza]	12. [pšapša]
3. [dzadza]	8. [pfapfa]	13. [bžabža]
4. [psapsa]	9. [bvabva]	14. [kšakša]
5. [bzabza]	10. [kfakfa]	15. [gžagža]

RE 9.2. Differential: AFFRICATE or FRICATIVE

Respond to the tape, but do not watch your Manual on this exercise.

1. [tsα] A	7. [xα] F	13. [pɸʰα] A
2. [sα] F	8. [dɣα] A	14. [bvα] A
3. [šα] F	9. [čα] A	15. [žα] F
4. [txα] A	10. [kɸα] A	16. [ǰα] A
5. [kxα] A	11. [ƀα] F	17. [ksʰα] A
6. [kθα] A	12. [ɸα] F	18. [kfʰα] A

Aspirated, Unaspirated, and Voiced Affricates

A little experimentation will show you that some of the same problems which apply to the regular stops in English apply to affricates as well. English /č/ in church, for example, is aspirated. Phonetically, therefore, we write [čʰr̥čʰ]. English /ǰ/ in judge is often very lightly voiced, or not voiced at all. For application to some other languages, therefore, we need to practice the same kinds of drills on these affricates as we do on English stops, learning to make unaspirated voiceless ones, fully aspirated ones, and fully voiced ones.

You can get the feeling of aspirated, unaspirated and voiced affricates by saying the following English sequences to yourself.

Aspirated	Unaspirated	Voiced
1a. change [čʰ]	1b. exchange [č]	1c. Jane [ǰ]
2a. cat's here [tsʰ]	2b. cat's ear [ts]	2c. Ed's own [dz]

3a. Mac's house [ks^h] 3b. Maxwell [ks] 3c. exact [gz]

RE 9.3. Differential: ASPIRATED or UNASPIRATED

Do not watch the text.

1. [ts^{h}α] A	6. [pᵽα] U	11. [tᵽα] U
2. [tsα] U	7. [pᵽ^{h}α] A	12. [kᵽα] U
3. [č^{h}α] A	8. [kš^{h}α] A	13. [txα] U
4. [čα] U	9. [ṱθ^{h}α] A	14. [ps^{h}α] A
5. [pxα] U	10. [pθα] U	15. [pf^{h}α] A

RE 9.4. Differential: VOICED or VOICELESS

Don't peek!

1. [dzα] VD	6. [kxα] VL	11. [txα] VL
2. [čα] VL	7. [pfα] VL	12. [gvα] VD
3. [tsα] VL	8. [bžα] VD	13. [kθα] VL
4. [bvα] VD	9. [ḓđα] VD	14. [pxα] VL
5. [gžα] VD	10. [pšα] VL	15. [ṱθα] VL

Recorded Exercises 9.5-9.6. Demonstration: Producing Strongly Aspirated Affricates

These drills will parallel closely those used to demonstrate the approach to the production of aspirated stops. Mimic the tape and watch the text. Keep the back of your hand in front of your mouth to feel the aspiration. When you have learned the sequence, try it with other voiceless affricates in Tables 9.1 and 9.2.

RE 9.5. Mimicry

1. [hαhαhαhα]	2. [hαhαhαhα]	3. [hαhαhαhα]
[p^{h}αp^{h}αp^{h}αp^{h}α]	[t^{h}αt^{h}αt^{h}αt^{h}α]	[k^{h}αk^{h}αk^{h}αk^{h}α]
[pᵽ^{h}αpᵽ^{h}αpᵽ^{h}αpᵽ^{h}α]	[č^{h}αč^{h}αč^{h}αč^{h}α]	[kf^{h}αkf^{h}αkf^{h}αkf^{h}α]

RE 9.6. Negative Practice

Practice the following English words, exaggerating the aspiration on the voiceless alveopalatal affricate.

1.	[ˈčʰr̩čʰ]	church	6.	[ˈčʰɔpʰ]	chop
2.	[ˈčʰɛyn]	chain	7.	[ˈsr̩čʰ]	search
3.	[ˈčʰɩldrɨn]	children	8.	[ˈlr̩čʰ]	lurch
4.	[ˈpʰr̩čʰ]	perch	9.	[ˈčʰɩmnɩy]	chimney
5.	[ˈɛyčʰ]	H	10.	[ˈčʰɑym]	chime

Practice other English words in the same way.

Recorded Exercises 9.7-9.8. Producing Unaspirated Affricates

Mimic the tape and watch the text. Be careful to keep all aspiration off the stops and affricates.

RE 9.7. Mimicry

1. [pɑpɑpɑpɑ]	4. [kɑkɑkɑkɑ]	7. [tsɑtsɑtsɑtsɑ]
2. [tɑtɑtɑtɑ]	5. [pɑtɑčɑkɑ]	8. [pfɑpfɑpfɑpfɑ]
3. [čɑčɑčɑčɑ]	6. [kɑčɑtɑpɑ]	9. [kθɑkθɑkθɑkθɑ]

RE 9.8. Negative Practice

Practice the following English words, removing the aspiration on the voiceless alveopalatal affricates.

1.	[ˈčr̩č]	church	6.	[ˈčɔpʰ]	chop
2.	[ˈčɛyn]	chain	7.	[ˈsr̩č]	search
3.	[ˈčɩldrɨn]	children	8.	[ˈlr̩č]	lurch
4.	[ˈpʰr̩č]	perch	9.	[ˈčɩmnɩy]	chimney
5.	[ˈɛyč]	H	10.	[ˈčɑym]	chime

Recorded Exercises 9.9-9.10. Demonstration: Producing Voiced Affricates

RE 9.9. Negative Practice

Exaggerate the voicing in the /ǰ/ of the following English words. Prolong it, and get a good rumble of voicing. Follow the transcription.

1. [ˈǰʌǰ] *judge*
2. [ˈslɛǰ] *sledge*
3. [ˈæǰɩl] *agile*
4. [ˈǰæm] *jam*
5. [ˈmæǰ] *Madge*
6. [ˈp^{h}ɩǰn̩] *pidgeon*
7. [ˈǰɑyɨnt^{h}] *giant*
8. [ˈɛyǰ] *age*
9. [ˈmɩǰɨt^{h}] *midget*
10. [ˈǰɛlow] *jello*

RE 9.10. Mimicry

Cup your hands over your ears to hear the voicing as you work this exercise. Keep the voicing for the full duration of each "word".

1. [ɑdɑ ɑdɑ ɑdɑ ɑdɑ]
2. [ɑžɑ ɑžɑ ɑžɑ ɑžɑ]
3. [ɑǰɑ ɑǰɑ ɑǰɑ ɑǰɑ]
4. [ɑdɑ ɑžɑ ɑǰɑ]

Practice the other affricates in the same manner if you have difficulty in developing adequate aspiration, or voicing, or in keeping the sequence unaspirated.

RE 9.11. Buildup: Stops and Affricates

These exercises parallel RE 7.21-7.22, with the addition of the three affricates studied above. Mimic the tape. You may watch the transcription below or not, just as you find most helpful.

1. [ʔɑʔɑ]

   [ʔɑʔɑʔɑ]

   [ʔɑʔɑʔɑʔɑ]
2. [p^{h}ɑp^{h}ɑp^{h}ɑp^{h}ɑ]
3. [tɑtɑtɑtɑ]
4. [dɑdɑdɑdɑ]
5. [č^{h}ɑč^{h}ɑč^{h}ɑč^{h}ɑ]
6. [čɑčɑčɑčɑ]
7. [ǰɑǰɑǰɑǰɑ]
8. [ts^{h}ɑts^{h}ɑts^{h}ɑts^{h}ɑ]
9. [pfɑpfɑpfɑpfɑ]
10. [bzɑbzɑbzɑbzɑ]

Velar Fricatives and Affricates

Velar affricates, like velar fricatives, require special attention for speakers of English, although they seem somewhat less difficult than fricatives. Continue careful practice of both fricatives and affricates through the use of the following exercises.

RE 9.12. Buildup: Sequence with Velar Fricatives and Affricates

Listen to the tape, and watch your text. Mimic carefully, working for a clear articulation.

1. [xɑxɑ]
   [xɑxɑxɑ]
   [xɑxɑxɑxɑ]
2. [kxɑkxɑkxɑkxɑ]
3. [kxʰɑkxʰɑkxʰɑkxʰɑ]
4. [ɡɑɡɑɡɑɡɑ]
5. [gɡɑgɡɑgɡɑgɡɑ]
6. [pxɑpxɑpxɑpxɑ]
7. [txɑtxɑtxɑtxɑ]
8. [bɡɑbɡɑbɡɑbɡɑ]
9. [pxʰɑpxʰɑpxʰɑpxʰɑ]
10. [txʰɑtxʰɑtxʰɑtxʰɑ]

RE 9.13: Huli (Papua).[1] Mimicry

1. [ˈpɸini] 'root'
2. [ˈpɛdia] 'eleven'
3. [ˈkxadia] 'seven'
4. [ˈkɛmbobβɛ] 'front of throat'
5. [ˈtʰandagaba] 'painful'
6. [ˈnogo] 'pig'
7. [yaˈkxɒndi] 'star'
8. [pɸuˈdaβu] 'wind'
9. [piˈaŋgo] 'dog'

RE 9.14. Buildup: Random Sequences

1. [ˈmakačabapʰɑ]
2. [ˈpakaxabaǰɑ]
3. [ˈtsɑʔaβagasɑ]
4. [ˈɸakapʰakfalɑ]
5. [ˈgadzapʰadaxɑ]
6. [ˈkxatʰaβavagɑ]
7. [ˈfalabapɸʰaǰɑ]
8. [ˈdasakʰabaxɑ]

---

[1] Data from lesson plans in use at The Summer Institute of Linguistics, Norman, Oklahoma, 1956.

9. ['pxɑṭ͓θɑp^{h}ɑdɑtɑ] 10. ['k^{h}ɑbvɑkfɑbzɑp̣ɑ]

Recorded Exercises 9.15-9.24. Review: Thai Drills on Stops

The following are actual language drills from Thai.[1] They are simple in syllable structure and length. Some of the vowel qualities will be new to you. Do not let them bother you, as you are working selectively on the stops. However, mimic the vowel quality as best you can as you go along. Note the tone as well, and mimic it closely. The written transcription of these exercises is a phonemic transcription rather than a phonetic one. You may notice some difference in quality of some of the phonemes. This will not affect your work with the stops. The diacritic marks over the vowels are tone marks.

RE 9.15: Thai. Listening

This is a listening exercise. Listen, and follow along the text of the exercise below. Pay close attention to the contrasts between voiced, voiceless unaspirated, and voiceless aspirated stops. Note the phonemic contrasts involved. Make sure you can hear the distinctions.

1. /bît/ 'twist'	11. /pît/ 'to close'	21. /p^{h}ît/ 'wrong'
2. /bàat/ 'to wound'	12. /pàak/ 'mouth'	22. /p^{h}àak/ 'forehead'
3. /baw/ 'light' (not heavy)	13. /pàw/ 'to blow with mouth'	23. /p^{h}ǎw/ 'to burn' (trans.)
4. /bâa/ 'crazy'	14. /pâa/ 'older sister of father or mother'	24. /p^{h}âa/ 'cloth'
5. /bèt/ 'fishhook'	15. /pèt/ 'duck'	25. /p^{h}èt/ 'peppery'
6. /bay/ 'leaves'	16. /pay/ 'to go'	26. /p^{h}ày/ 'bamboo'

[1] These exercises were prepared and recorded by Rev. and Mrs. Richard Johnston. The Thai speaker in RE 9.15-9.16 is Nay Daeng, a judge of Srisaket Province, originally from Bangkok. The speaker in the remainder is Nay Prasan of Surin Province.

7. /bòk/ 'dry land'

8. /bòn/ 'complain'

9. /bɔ̀ɔt/ 'blind'

10. /bàt/ 'papers, cards'

17. /pòk/ 'cover' (as of book)

18. /pon/ 'to mix, adulterate'

19. /pɔ̀ɔt/ 'lungs'

20. /pàt/ 'to dust'

27. /p^hòk/ 'to turn face'

28. /p^hón/ 'to be free from'

29. /p^hɔ̀ɔt/ 'to inhale'

30. /p^hàt/ 'to fry in small pieces'

RE 9.16: Thai. Listening

Follow the same procedure for the following exercise.

1. /dam/ 'black'

2. /duaŋ/ 'particle for stamps, stars'

3. /dɔɔŋ/ 'to pickle'

4. /daŋ/ 'loud'

5. /dâam/ 'handle'

6. /dòk/ 'fertile'

7. /dom/ 'to smell'

8. /dàk/ 'to ensnare'

9. /duu/ 'to look at'

11. /tam/ 'to pound (in mortar)'

12. /tuaŋ/ 'measure (bulk)'

13. /tɔ̂ɔŋ/ 'must'

14. /tâŋ/ 'to set, place'

15. /taam/ 'to follow'

16. /tòk/ 'fall'

17. /tôm/ 'to boil'

18. /tàk/ 'to draw water'

19. /tûu/ 'cupboard, closet'

21. /t^ham/ 'to do, make'

22. /t^hûan/ 'complete, entire'

23. /t^hɔɔŋ/ 'gold'

24. /t^hǎŋ/ 'bucket'

25. /t^hǎam/ 'ask'

26. /t^hòk/ 'flay, skin'

27. /t^hǒm/ 'fill in a hole with earth'

28. /t^hàk/ 'plait, braid'

29. /t^hǔu/ 'to rub'

10. /dâay/ 'can, to be able'

20. /tây/ 'torch'

30. /t^hǎy/ 'to plough'

RE 9.17: Thai. Mimicry

This is a mimicry exercise in which you will mimic a series of words each of which has the same Thai stop. The series will be the first column of RE 9.15 (Nos. 1-10). Turn to that exercise and follow down the column, mimicking the tape. Pay particular attention to the stops.

RE 9.18-9.19: Thai. Mimicry

Follow the same procedure with the second and third columns of RE 9.15.

RE 9.20

This time you will be drilling across the columns in RE 9.15. Follow the same procedure of mimicking after the utterances on the tape.

RE 9.21-9.24

Follow the same procedures as for RE 9.17-9.20, but this time use RE 9.16 as the text.

RE 9.25. Transcription

Transcribe the utterances on the tape. When you are sure of your transcriptions compare them with the answers below. Don't peek until you are ready to check your answers!

1. ['šɑk^h]
2. ['pɑθ]
3. ['ǰɑg]
4. ['rɑp]
5. ['mɑdz]
6. ['p^hɑxɑ]
7. ['lɑ$č^h$ɑ]
8. ['fɑtsɑ]
9. ['ɓɑsɑ]
10. ['dɑžɑ]
11. ['nɑkɑs]
12. ['bɑt^hɑv]
13. ['bvɑʔɑm]
14. ['psɑdɑp^h]
15. ['šɑlɑx]

RE 9.26. Reading

1. ['gɑm]
2. ['pɑ$č^h$]
3. ['t^hɑf]
4. ['bzɑθ]
5. ['sɑk]
6. ['ʔɑɗɑ]

Affricates

7. ['čɑgɑ]   10. ['b̵ɑǰɑ]   13. ['dɑtkʰɑp̵]

8. ['dɑp̵ɑ]   11. ['tɑʔnɑ]   14. ['bɑpʰsɑg̵]

9. ['lɑšɑ]   12. ['kɑgrɑkx]   15. ['žɑɑkfɑd]

note elongation

Suggested Reading

Archibald A. Hill, Introduction to Linguistic Structures, pp. 36-37.

W. Nelson Francis, The Structure of American English, pp. 79-81 (51-70, 72-74).

NO, MISS TAKE! IT'S AN ASPIRATED AFFRICATE, NOT AN EXASPERATED AFRICAN!

LESSON NINE R

Review

Review lessons in the Manual merely give condensed summaries of the material covered to the present. They are intended to be supplemented by extensive review of exercises in the previous lessons.

	Bilabial	Labio-dental	Tip-dental	Alveolar	Alveo-palatal	Back-velar	Glottal
STOPS							
Voiceless							
Unaspirated	p			t		k	ʔ
Aspirated	p^h			t^h		k^h	
Voiced	b			d		g	
AFFRICATES							
Voiceless							
Unaspirated	pᵽ	pf		ts	č	kx	
Aspirated	pᵽ^h	pf^h		ts^h	čh	kxh	
Voiced	bƀ	bv		dz	ǰ	gǥ	
FRICATIVES							
Voiceless	ᵽ	f	θ	s	š	x	
Voiced	ƀ	v	đ	z	ž	ǥ	
NASALS	m			n			
LATERAL				l			

Check List of Review Items

1. Technical labels of consonants

2. Drawing of Sammies

3. Recognition, production, and mimicry of pitch

4. Recognition, production, and mimicry of all consonants so far studied, including both English consonants and the

others so far taught. See the chart on p. 148.

5. Other affricates: Table 9.2 (p. 138)

6. Reading and mimicry control of the various exercises in the Manual.

TE 9R.1. Matching Symbols

After you have reviewed the above chart try TE 9R.1 in the Workbook Supplement (pp. 31-32). It will help you learn the relationship between the symbols.

NOW TRY FOR A LITTLE LESS ASPIRATION....

LESSON TEN

Syllables and Some of Their Characteristics

Now we come to a new characteristic of speech which has been implicit in the work done on pitch and on the articulation of the consonants studied so far. It is the division of the speech stream into syllables, which are groupings of sounds such that each grouping carries its own beat.

The division between syllables is indicated in this lesson (and in following lessons when necessary) by [.], which is spoken of as "period" or "syllable division." The sequences of sounds separated by [.], therefore, are syllables, and each carries its own separate beat.

RE 10.1. Demonstration: Syllable Beat

Listen to the tape and follow along in the book. Count the beats in each utterance as you go along, and see if your count agrees with the count indicated. Tap out the count with your finger if that helps. In the second repetition of the last utterance you will hear the beat tapped out on the tape.

	No. of Beats (Syllables)
1. [ʔɑ]	1
2. [ʔɑ.pʰɑ]	2
3. [ʔɑ.pʰɑ.tʰɑ]	3
4. [ʔɑ.pʰɑ.tʰɑ.xɑ]	4
5. [ʔɑ.pʰɑ.tʰɑ.xɑ.mɑ]	5

In the above example, each of the syllables was characterized by one of the consonants you have been practicing followed by an [ɑ]. Any other vowel would do just as well as [ɑ]. Any other consonant would do just as well as the consonants used.[1] We can call this kind of syllable a CV syllable (with C representing consonant and V representing vowel). Other kinds of syllables also occur, some of which are illustrated in the following exercise.

---

[1]The phonetic distinction between vowel and consonant will be discussed in Lesson 12.

RE 10.2. Demonstration: Some Other Syllable Patterns

In this exercise each utterance will have three syllables, and each of the syllables within a particular utterance will be similar in consonant-vowel sequence. Listen to the tape and beat out the syllables as you study the syllable structure of each syllable transcribed below. You will hear two repetitions of each utterance on the tape.

	Syllable Structure
1. [pɑm.t^{h}ɑk.sɑf]	CVC
2. [glɑ.ksɑ.šnɑ]	CCV
3. [fθɑs.mrɑk^{h}.smɑʔ][1]	CCVC
4. [ɑ.e.i]	V
5. [ɑp.et.ik]	VC

RE 10.3. Demonstration: Consonants as Syllables

Syllables may consist of single vowels or of certain single consonants. Listen to the tape, count the beats, and study the syllable structure of each utterance, and mimic.

	Syllable Structure
1. [bɑ.bɑ.bɑ.bɑ.bɑ.bɑ.bɑ.bɑ]	CV
2. [ɑ.ɑ.ɑ.ɑ.ɑ.ɑ.ɑ.ɑ]	V
3. [u.u.u.u.u.u.u.u]	V
4. [m̩.m̩.m̩.m̩.m̩.m̩.m̩.m̩]	C
5. [l̩.l̩.l̩.l̩.l̩.l̩.l̩.l̩]	C
6. [s̩.s̩.s̩.s̩.s̩.s̩.s̩.s̩]	C

Notice how the syllables have no break in sound between them, but there is still an audible pulse, even when the same vowel or consonant quality carries through.

---

[1]For many languages, and from some points of view in phonetic theory, aspirated consonants could be considered CC. For convenience, however, we handle them as single consonants.

Syllables and Syllabicity

In the preceding exercise you saw transcribed a short vertical line [̩] under the consonants which were independent syllables. This mark is a "syllabic indicator," or "indicator of syllabicity." Every syllable has a syllabic, that is, one sound which carries the beat, or which is the most prominent sound of the syllable. If there is only one sound in a syllable, then that sound is, of course, the syllabic.

Most commonly, vowels are syllabics. For this reason we do not mark the syllabicity of vowels with an extra sign. Any unmarked vowel is assumed to be syllabic. Some kinds of consonants, on the other hand, may be syllabic or non-syllabic. In phonetic transcription we assume they are non-syllabic unless they are marked with [̩].

Syllabic sounds are most commonly sounds where the articulation allows a fairly wide opening for the air stream to move out relatively unimpeded. This is true of vowels. It is also true of nasals (where the air stream comes unimpeded through the nose), laterals (where it comes unimpeded over the sides of the tongue), or even fricatives (where it is partially impeded, but where it may be less impeded than stop consonants around it.[1]

The following exercises are to help you distinguish between syllabic consonants (which carry the beat and are the most prominent sound of a syllable) and non-syllabic consonants.

RE 10.4. Demonstration: English Syllabic Consonants

Listen to the tape and mimic. Each utterance is given twice. Follow the phonetic transcription below as well to help you focus on those consonants which are syllabic as opposed to those which are not.

1.	[ˈsmɪ.ʔn̩]	smitten	6.	[ˈbɑ.tl̩]	bottle
2.	[ˈæm.pʰl̩]	ample	7.	[ˈkʰɑ.ʔn̩]	cotton
3.	[ˈkʰɑr.ʔn̩]	carton	8.	[n̩ˈlɛs]	unless
4.	[ˈkʰr̩.ʔn̩]	curtain	9.	[m̩ˈpʰowz]	impose
5.	[ˈtʰr̩.tl̩]	turtle	10.	[m̩ˈpʰɑ.sɨ.bl̩]	impossible

[1] See Kenneth L. Pike, *Phonetics*, pp. 118ff.

11. [m̩'pʰr̩tn̩ɨnt] impertinent
12. ['m̩Mm̩] mhm
13. [ps̩t] pst
14. [ˌɑy kn̩ 'sιy] I can see
15. ['dεytʰr̩] date her
16. [ˌhιyn̩'ɑy] he 'n' I

RE 10.5. Differential: SYLLABIC or NON-SYLLABIC

In this drill listen to the nasal consonant in each utterance and respond with SYLLABIC or NON-SYLLABIC, according to what you hear. Do not watch the text.

1. [pɑm] N-S
2. [pʰm̩] S
3. [kʰm̩] S
4. [kʰn̩] S
5. [m̩] S
6. [mɑm] N-S
7. [sɑŋ] N-S
8. [sŋ̩] S
9. [ɑŋkʰ] N-S
10. [ŋ̩kʰ] S
11. [n̩'tɑtʰ] S
12. [ɑ'tn̩tʰ] S
13. [ɑ'tɑntʰ] N-S
14. [ɑn̩'tɑtʰ] S
15. [ɑn'tɑtʰ] N-S

RE 10.6. Buildup: Syllables with Syllabic Consonants

Mimic the tape as you follow the transcription below. Each utterance will be given twice. This is a buildup exercise, so you will begin with the last three syllables of each item for the first utterance, and then add a syllable for each succeeding one.

1. [kl̩ km̩ kn̩ kf̩ ks̩ kš̩ kx̩ kr̩]
2. [ps̩tʰ pf̩tʰ pš̩tʰ pv̩tʰ pl̩tʰ pr̩tʰ pƀ̩tʰ pn̩tʰ]
3. [ʔɑ lɑ tʰr̩ vɑ tʰl̩ rɑ pʰn̩ ɑ]
4. [tʰs̩ vɑ ɑ l̩ ʔɑ pʰr̩ tʰn̩ šɑ]
5. [xɑ lɑ v̩ tš̩ ɑ pz̩ kɑ tʰm̩]
6. [dɑ šn̩ mn̩ sr̩ ʔɑk zɑz strɑ gɑ]
7. [šn̩ zɑz mn̩ dɑ sr̩ ʔɑk xɑ stl̩]
8. [dɑ mn̩ stz̩ šn̩ ʔɑt sr̩ gɑ zɑz]

Boundaries Between Syllables

As you learn to recognize the beats of the syllables and the syllabics, you can identify the center or crest of the syllable without any difficulty. The syllabic is the crest. In some cases it is equally easy to identify the syllable boundaries, and in some of the exercises above these boundaries were marked by [.] or by space. It is not always possible, however, to determine an exact syllable boundary. A consonant between two syllables may belong phonetically to both. We can diagram it this way, using the English word money.

It is clear what the syllabics and non-syllabics are. However, the [n] in the middle is a boundary between two syllables, and does not belong more completely with one than with the other, unless you pronounce the word in an over-precise way. When you do you can pronounce it either way: ['mʌn.ɩy] or ['mʌ.nɩy]. At other times, however,(and in some languages this is always true) syllable division is clearly audible.

In this book we mark syllable division when it is necessary or helpful. Many times syllable division will be obvious, and we will not mark it. At other times it will make no difference to the exercise, and we will often leave it unmarked in that case as well. Then again, it may simply be impossible to mark a precise boundary, for the reasons just indicated.

Stress

In languages different syllables have different degrees of loudness or prominence. Just as one sound within a syllable constitutes the syllabic, and carries the greatest degree of prominence within the syllable, so some syllables in a sequence carry greater prominence than the surrounding ones. This we speak of as different degrees of stress.

Stress, then, is a matter of relative prominence of one or more syllables in a sequence of syllables.[1] Actually, no

---

[1]Not all speech sounds themselves are, of course, equally loud; some speech sounds have what is called high phonetic power and others have low phonetic power. That is to say, the loudness actually measurable in terms of microwatts varies greatly from sound to sound in any one speaker. Sounds such as the vowels, for example, may have up to as much as 680 times the power of the weakest consonant in English (θ). This innate power of the sounds of any one syllable may be modified by the general level of loudness of the speech of a given speaker; it may also be modified by the degree of stress occurring on that

syllable can be produced in any language without some degree of stress. Stress phenomena, therefore, are conveniently referred to in terms of degrees such as primary stress, secondary stress, tertiary stress, weak stress, etc.

In this course we will usually work with only two levels of stress: 1) <u>primary stress</u> (the loudest) which will be symbolized by [ˈ] before the beginning of the syllable which carries the stress, and 2) degrees less than primary, which will be left unmarked for stress. This, however, is not very realistic for many languages (including English) which have more different degrees of stress than that, and so in this lesson we illustrate <u>secondary stress</u> as well, although we do not continue to insist on its recognition in subsequent lessons.[1] Secondary stress is marked by [ˌ] before the beginning of the syllable which carries the stress.

<u>RE 10.7. Demonstration: Some English Stress Contrasts</u>

Here are some simple cases of stress difference in English. Listen to the tape and watch the transcription below. Listen to the difference in stress between the syllables of any one word, and also the difference in the placement of the loudest stress in the two columns. Remember the symbolization: [ˈ] primary stress, [ˌ] secondary stress, and [unmarked] less than secondary stress.

1a.	/ˈɔgmɨnt/	<u>AUGment</u>	1b.	/ˌɔgˈmɛnt/	<u>augMENT</u>
2a.	/ˈrιyfr̩/	<u>REEfer</u>	2b.	/ˌrιyˈfr̩/	<u>reFER</u>
3a.	/ˈtɔrmɨnt/	<u>TORment</u>	3b.	/ˌtɔrˈmɛnt/	<u>torMENT</u>
4a.	/ˈpr̩mιt/	<u>PERmit</u>	4b.	/ˌpr̩ˈmιt/	<u>perMIT</u>
5a.	/ˈtrænsfr̩/	<u>TRANSfer</u>	5b.	/ˌtrænsˈfr̩/	<u>transFER</u>
6a.	/ˈιmpoHrt/	<u>IMport</u>	6b.	/ˌιmˈpoHrt/	<u>imPORT</u>

---

syllable. These facts reveal something of the relative nature of the feature of loudness. See H. L. Barney and H. K. Dunn, "Speech Analysis" in L. Kaiser, <u>Manual of Phonetics</u>, p. 188ff.

[1]Concern about more than two levels of stress (primary stress and "other") distracts from the heavy volume of new phonetic material being introduced in each lesson.

RE 10.8. Discrimination: Two Degrees of Stress

Answer SAME or DIFFERENT as the utterances are contrasted in each item. Listen for difference of stress and stress placement. Sustained level pitch will be maintained throughout the following exercises. Do not watch the book!

1.	['lalɑ]	[lalɑ]	D
2.	[lɑ'lɑ]	[lɑ'lɑ]	S
3.	[lɑ'lɑ]	['lalɑ]	D
4.	['lalɑ]	['lalɑ]	S
5.	[lɑ'lɑ]	[lɑ'lɑ]	S
6.	[lɑ'lalɑ]	['lalalɑ]	D
7.	[lalɑ'lɑ]	['lalalɑ]	D
8.	['lalɑ'lɑ]	['lalalɑ]	D
9.	[lɑ'lɑ'lɑ]	[lɑ'lɑ'lɑ]	S
10.	[lɑ'lalɑ]	[lɑ'lɑ'lɑ]	D

RE 10.9. Negative Practice: Three Degrees of Stress

Mimic the tape and follow the transcription below. In each column you have a different sequence of English words. Both can be said with different placement of our three degrees of stress, with differences of meaning. Mimic them through once noting the stress differences and reproducing them. Then follow the tape as it goes on through the items again with controlled pitch, keeping the pitch level, but preserving the stress pattern.

1. ˌelevator 'operator
2. 'elevator ˌoperator
3. 'eleˌvator ˌopeˌrator
4. ˌeleˌvator 'opeˌrator
5. ˌdemon'stration ˌexercises
6. ˌdemonstration 'exercises
7. 'demonstration ˌexer'cises
8. 'demonˌstration 'exerˌcises

RE 10.10. Differential: PRIMARY, SECONDARY or WEAK

Do not watch your text. Listen to the tape, and respond in the time provided. For each item you will hear an utterance of four syllables which will have varying degrees of stress. Listen selectively to the third syllable of the utterance and respond according to the degree you hear. The difference will be demonstrated first.

1.	[ˈsazaˌsaza]	S	11.	[ˈtagataˌga]	W
2.	[ˌsazaˈsaza]	P	12.	[ˌtagaˈtaga]	P
3.	[saˌzaˈsaza]	P	13.	[tagaˌtaˈga]	S
4.	[sazaˈsaza]	P	14.	[ˈtagaˌtaga]	S
5.	[sazaˌsaˈza]	S	15.	[ˈtagataga]	W
6.	[ˌsazaˈsaza]	P	16.	[ˈtagaˈtaga]	P
7.	[saˈzaˌsaza]	S	17.	[ˈtaˌgaˌtaga]	S
8.	[sazaˌsaˈza]	S	18.	[ˈtaˌgataˌga]	W
9.	[saˌzaˈsaza]	P	19.	[ˈtagaˌtaˈga]	S
10.	[ˈsazaˈsaza]	P	20.	[ˌtagaˈtaga]	P

RE 10.11. Mimicry: Stress

Mimic the tape, following along in your book. The text of this exercise is the same as the preceding one. Pay particular attention to distinguishing the degrees of stress. Keep your pitch constant.

RE 10.12. Demonstration: Onset of Stress

We mentioned earlier in this lesson that it was sometimes impossible to tell exactly where a boundary between syllables came, that sometimes a single sound belonged to both syllables. Sometimes, however, the place where stress begins marks off the beginning of a syllable. This is called the onset of the stress. Listen to the following English examples, and notice the placement of the stress marker at the onset of stress. Note the contrasts in meaning that are possible in English by shifting the onset.[1]

1a. [ʌˈnɛym] a name   1b. [ʌnˈɛym] an aim

---

[1]The position of the onset of stress is not necessarily the only distinction you can hear between these pairs.

2a. [ˈtʰɩy,mɩytɩŋ] tea meeting 2b. [ˈtʰɩym,ɩytɩŋ] team eating

3a. [ˈɑy,skrɩym] I scream 3b. [ˈɑys,kʰrɩym] ice cream

4a. [ˈnʌy,tʰrɛyt] nitrate 4b. [ˈnʌyt,rɛyt] night rate

5a. [ˈpʰlɛy,tʰræk] play track 5b. [ˈpʰlɛyt,ræk] plate rack

Juncture

Sometimes the division between syllables can be heard as an audible break. This break we call juncture. When we need it for our purposes in this Manual we will symbolize it by a space between the symbols. Juncture, of course, like stress, is a relative matter. There are varying degrees of break between syllables, ranging from those where we cannot distinguish the exact syllable boundary, to a relatively long and audible break. We shall speak of juncture wherever we hear an audible break, whether long or short.

RE 10.13. Demonstration: Some Examples of Juncture

Listen to the following sentences, and watch the transcription. In this transcription space will always represent the juncture for which you are listening, whether it comes between words or within a word. The sentences are taken from different languages, and the particular language is indicated in parentheses after the meaning is given. After each sentence is read twice there will be a third utterance substituting [ʔɑ] for each syllable, but maintaining the juncture, stress, intonation and timing of the sentence. Mimic this utterance.

1. /ˈtenah pɨʔ tsaʔ ˈpiɓia nakI katɨ ˈpuʔetu ˈmiʔaarɨ/ 'The man with the big ears is walking in the road.' (Comanche)[1]

2. /ˈname wah sɨkʷI tɨɨ ˈpiɓia kahni nɨɨ/ 'eight big houses' (Comanche)

3. /ˈʔorii ˈnɨmɨ kuh tsuʔ nii ˈpuuni/ 'Look at those buffalo!' (Comanche)

4. /ʌwŋˈnôy kʌwnʌ̂ytrɨ̂ak/ 'You (sir) say it first' (Vietnamese)[2]

---

[1]Comanche data from William A. Smalley, "Phonemic Rhythm in Comanche." The language is spoken by Indians of the American Southwest.

[2]Vietnamese data from William A. Smalley and Nguyễn-văn-Vạn, Vietnamese for Missionaries, Book 1, Part 1, pp. 13, 50.

5. /'toy šə̃nɔ́y'laay 'šaaw'bàa/ 'I shall repeat after you (madam)' (Vietnamese)

6. /mọk'cɯwk 'yáabaawm̃iw/ 'How much for ten?' (Vietnamese)

7. /sɨ'lii gɔʔhn,duum/ 'The corn ripened.' (Khmuʔ)[1]

8. /bɨŋgə'taay ,law ci,yɔh 'phaan/ 'The oldest said he would go and kill it.' (Khmuʔ)

9. /,yɔh 'gaa da,tuup 'hreʔ gə,niʔ/ 'He went and climbed into this same ricefield house.' (Khmuʔ)

10. /'mæɾɪy 'ǰɛyn 'pɪytɨrsɨn ,kæntɑy'trʌstyɨwa'mɪnɨt/ Mary Jane Peterson, can't I trust you a minute? (English)

Juncture, as illustrated in these examples, is closely tied in with stress, intonation, and other features, some of them difficult to sort out. An ear quick to detect these features, and a ready mimicry of them can go a long way toward naturalness of speech.

Rhythm

Stress, the point of onset of stress, syllable structure, and the kind of juncture between syllables, together with intonation pattern and other features combine to give sentences a rhythm, and to give different languages different characteristic rhythms. Good pronunciation involves a close approximation of this rhythm, running syllables together, separating them by juncture, "slurring" them, keeping them discreet and distinct, and in every way maintaining the timing which native speakers do.

RE 10.14: English. Demonstration: Stress-Timing

English has a characteristic rhythm pattern which often produces bad pronunciation when carried over into another language. It is based on a rhythm of primary stresses, between which are squeezed varying numbers of lesser stresses. This contrasts with many languages which give each syllable a more nearly even timing. Listen to the English example, and follow the transcription. On the tape you hear a beat which follows the rhythm of the primary stresses.

---

[1]Khmuʔ data from William A. Smalley, Outline of Khmuʔ Structure, pp. 96,97.

1. The 'program was 'boring

2. The 'program was not 'boring

3. The 'program was very 'boring

4. The 'program we saw was 'boring

5. The 'program we saw was very 'boring

6. The 'program we saw was not very 'boring

Notice how the syllables are rushed or spaced out to fill in the space between the beats. Now listen to RE 10.13 again and note the characteristic rhythm of the different sentences from the different languages. Mimic the sentences once more, paying attention to the rhythm.

RE 10.15. Negative Practice: Syllable Timing

This exercise takes the sentences of RE 10.14 and pronounces them now in non-English fashion to mimic the rhythm of Spanish and some other languages. In these languages each syllable gets much the same timing. Mimic the tape.

Practice reciting English with syllable timing. Beat out the timing with your finger as you do so. Work on the buddy system, and get your buddy to help you know when your syllable timing breaks down.

RE 10.16. Transcription: Juncture and Primary Stress

In this transcription exercise the sequence of syllables each time will be [mopɑseni]. Transcribe the sequence, leaving space for juncture, and marking primary stress by ['] at the point of onset. Take transcription from the tape without looking at the text below. When you are satisfied with your transcription, check it with the transcription below.

1. [mopɑ 'seni]	6. [mopɑ'se 'ni]
2. ['mo pɑse'ni]	7. ['mopɑ 'seni]
3. ['mo 'pɑ 'se 'ni]	8. [mo'pɑseni]
4. [mo pɑ 'seni]	9. ['mo pɑseni]
5. [mo'pɑse 'ni]	10. ['mo 'pɑ se'ni]

RE 10.17. Transcription: Syllabic Consonants, Syllable Division, and Primary Stress

Transcribe the following items. The vowel [ɑ] will be used along with a variety of consonants which you have had, both syllabic and non-syllabic. Mark any syllabic consonants with a [ˌ] under the consonant. Mark syllable division with [.]. Mark the onset of primary stress with [']. When you have transcribed the tape utterances to your satisfaction, check them with the text below.

1. ['bɑ.dl̩]	6. ['k^{h}m̩.p^{h}m̩]
2. ['k^{h}ɑ.ʔn̩]	7. [fɑ.'nm̩]
3. ['p^{h}ɑ.tr̩]	8. ['ʔm̩p^h.tɑ]
4. [k^{h}r̩.'gɑ]	9. [bɑ.k^{h}n̩.'dl̩]
5. [p^{h}r̩.'nɑ]	10. [prɑ.'tɑ.gl̩]

Syllable Characteristics and This Manual

In this lesson you have been introduced briefly to some of the more important characteristics of syllables and syllable sequences, all of which contribute to effective pronunciation when properly used in any language. All of these features should be carefully observed and mimicked both in the materials of this course and in actual language work. In this introductory course, however, we will not be able to pay full attention to all of these features in an overt way by transcribing them in every case.

Primary stress ['] will always be indicated at the point of onset, and should be so indicated in any student transcription. Other stresses will be indicated only when necessary or convenient, and students will not be required to transcribe them unless specifically instructed to do so.

Syllable boundary and juncture, likewise, will not always be directly indicated in the transcription in the Manual, and will not be required in student transcription except where the instructions so indicate.

RE 10.18: Hausa. Mimicry: Tone Review[1]

In the following exercises mimic as best you can, paying

[1]Data from Rev. Charles Kraft. The informant is Hamalai Mubi.

particular attention to the tone, but not neglecting also the rhythm, stress, timing, etc. If the consonants and vowels are too much for you, mimic on [lɑ] or hum, maintaining the tone and rhythm. The words are written in the normal spelling used for Hausa, which does not distinguish between long and short vowels which you will hear on the tape. Tone marks have been added. /´/ represents high tone, and low tone is unmarked.

High-High		High-Low		Low-High	
1a. sárkí	'chief'	1b. dóki		1c. jakí	'donkey'
2a. gídá	'compound'	2b. yáro	'boy'	2c. ubá	'father'
3a. kífí	'fish'	3b. báwa	'slave'	3c. karé	'dog'
4a. kúká	'cry'	4b. záki	'lion'	4c. ragó	'ram'
5a. rúwá	'wafer'	5b. ɗáki	'hut'	5c. baƙó	'guest'
6a. tsóhó	'old'	6b. náma	'meat'	6c. rafí	'brook'
7a. záfí	'hot'	7b. jéji	'bush country'	7c. gorá	'bamboo'
8a. úwá	'mother'	8b. ído	'eye'	8c. kazá	'chicken'
9a. ráná	'day'	9b. áiki	'work'	9c. addá	'machete'
10a. gíwá	'elephant'			10c. fará	'grass-hopper'

The following lists continue with the same words, but in different groupings.

H-H and H-L	L-H and H-L	H-H and L-H	H-H, H-L, and L-H
1d. kúká	1e. ubá	1f. kífí	1g. gíwá
2d. náma	2e. karé	2f. úwá	2g. ragó
3d. jéji	3e. ɗáki	3f. ubá	3g. baƙó
4d. ráná	4e. kazá	4f. tsóhó	4g. tsóhó
5d. kífí	5e. náma	5f. jakí	5g. náma
6d. áiki	6e. ído	6f. gíwá	6g. ído
7d. gídá	7e. addá	7f. fará	7g. kífí

H-H and H-L	L-H and H-L	H-H and L-H	H-H, H-L, and L-H
8d. záki	8e. yáro	8f. addá	8g. záki
9d. sárkí	9e. fará	9f. ráná	9g. karé
10d. báwa	10e. bakó	10f. kazá	10g. jakí

Suggested Reading

Page numbers in parentheses may not apply specifically to the points of this lesson, but have been listed in previous lessons, and you may want to read them while you have the book.

Eugene A. Nida, Learning a Foreign Language, pp. 108-110 (110-118).

Kenneth L. Pike, Phonetics, pp. 107-120.

Charles F. Hockett, A Course in Modern Linguistics, pp. 33-61 (15-32, 62-74).

Archibald A. Hill, Introduction to Linguistic Structures, pp. 13-30 (36-37).

LESSON ELEVEN

Dental, Retroflexed, Grooved, and Flat Articulations

	Labial	Dental	Alveolar	Alveopalatal	Alveopalatal[1] (retroflex)	Velar
Stops						
Voiceless unasp.	p	ṱ	t		ṭ	k
Voiceless asp.	p^h	ṱ^{h}	t^h		ṭ^h	k^h
Voiced	b	ḓ	d		ḍ	g
Fricatives						
Grooved						
Voiceless		s̭	s	š	ṣ̌	
Voiced		z̭	z	ž	ẓ̌	
Flat						
Voiceless	ᵽ	θ				x[2]
Voiced	ƀ	đ				ǥ
Affricates						
Grooved						
Voiceless unasp.		ṱs̭	ts	č	ṭṣ̌	
Voiceless asp.		ṱs̭^{h}	ts^h	č^h	ṭṣ̌^{h}	
Voiced		ḓz̭	dz	ǰ	ḍẓ̌	
Flat						
Voiceless unasp.	pᵽ	ṱθ				kx[2]
Voiceless asp.	pᵽ^h	ṱθ^h				kx^h
Voiced	bƀ	ḓđ				gǥ

---

[1] Tip-palatal articulation is also used for retroflex sounds.

[2] Velar fricatives and affricates may be made with grooved or flat articulation. There is an audible difference, but we will not deal with it in this _Manual_.

Study the above consonant chart carefully. Notice the new consonant symbols (enclosed in boxes), and study their relation to the surrounding symbols. Notice that the fricatives have been divided now into two groups, *grooved fricatives* and *flat fricatives*. Notice the symbols for new sounds at dental point of articulation, and the new retroflex column at alveopalatal (or palatal) point of articulation. These new distinctions will be taken up in this lesson. Although nineteen new sounds are represented by the symbols within the boxes, these few new distinctions account for them all, and only two new symbols [̭] "circumflex under the letter" and [̣] "dot under the letter" need to be learned, so long as their meaning is clearly understood.

Dental Stops, Fricatives, and Affricates

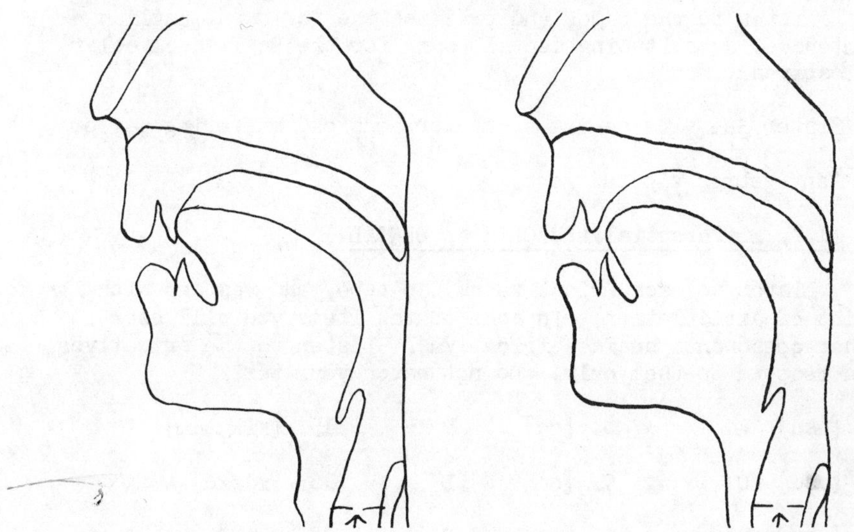

Sammy 11.1: Dental Stop [ṱ] Sammy 11.2: Dental Fricative [s̭]

Place the tip of your tongue firmly against the back of your upper teeth, and pronounce [ḓɑ], [ṱʰɑ], [ṱɑ]. These are dental stops. Your articulation is now forward from the alveolar position most characteristic of English /t d/ into the dental position characteristic of Spanish /t/ and that of many other languages. The difference can be made very easily, and can often be seen as you watch a native speaker talk, but the distinction between dental stops and alveolar stops is so slight accoustically that we will not require students to hear the difference. You must learn to make it, however. Practice by making dental stops on the following English sentences and others like them:

Ṱake Ṱommy ṱo the ṱrain. Ḓear Ḓaḓdy, ḓon't ḓo thaṱ.

Read whole paragraphs of English material substituting dental stops for English alveolar ones. Practice with your buddy by talking to him in this fashion.

But, whereas the difference between dental and alveolar stops is so slight that we expect students to make the difference but not to hear it, the difference between dental and alveolar [s̭ z̭] vs. [s z] is easy to hear, and students should learn both to hear and to produce it.

RE 11.1. Negative Practice

Listen to the tape, and practice the following English sentences, substituting dental [s̭ z̭] for the English alveolar fricatives.

1. S̭is̭ter S̭ue s̭its̭ s̭ewing s̭ocks for s̭eas̭ick, s̭uffering s̭ailors̭.

2. Z̭any z̭ebras̭ z̭ip and z̭oom.

RE 11.2. Differential: ALVEOLAR or DENTAL

Listen to each fricative on the tape, and respond with its point of articulation. In some of the items you will hear other consonants besides fricatives. Listen to the fricatives, and respond to them only. Do not watch your text.

1.	[ɑsɑ]	A	8.	[z̭ɑ]	D	15.	[sikɑtɑm]	A
2.	[ɑs̭ɑ]	D	9.	[s̭ɑ]	D	16.	[maskɑ]	A
3.	[ɑz̭ɑ]	D	10.	[ɑs̭]	D	17.	[mɑs̭kɑ]	D
4.	[ɑsɑ]	A	11.	[sɑtɑ]	A	18.	[dɑz̭kɑ]	D
5.	[s̭ɑ]	D	12.	[z̭ɑtɑ]	D	19.	[gɑkɑsp]	A
6.	[z̭ɑ]	D	13.	[s̭ɑkɑʔ]	D	20.	[dɑlɑzb]	A
7.	[zɑ]	A	14.	[s̭tɑmɑ]	D	21.	[ɑspɑkɑ]	A

The dental affricates present no special problem as they are again simply a combination of stop and fricative, at this point of articulation.

To summarize: For every alveolar sound there is a corresponding dental sound. To make it you simply move the tongue forward from alveolar position to dental position. The symbol for this forward tongue position is [̭].

Flat and Grooved Fricatives and Affricates

We now have two different kinds of voiceless dental fricatives [s̭ θ] and two different kinds of voiced ones [z̭ đ]. If you pronounce them you may notice a slight difference in the point of articulation on the upper teeth. [θ đ] may be lower down on the teeth, at the edge. The tongue may even protrude between the teeth.

In addition to the difference in point of articulation on the teeth, however, there is an important difference in the shape of the tongue. If we could look in at the top of the tongue from the front we would see a groove the length of the tongue on [s̭ z̭ s z š ž] which is not there for [θ đ]. Look at Fig. 11.1.

Tongue as a flat articulator [θ đ] | Tongue as a grooved articulator [s z]

Fig. 11.1

It is the articulating surface of the tongue which is either flat or grooved. The placing of [ᵽ ƀ] in the flat category in the consonant chart at the beginning of the lesson was somewhat arbitrary. Velar fricatives may be either flat or grooved, but we will not insist on this distinction.

RE 11.3. Differential: FLAT or GROOVED

Listen to the fricative in each of the items on the tape, and respond with FLAT or GROOVED according to the shape of the tongue in their articulation. Do not watch the text.

1.	[αθα] F	6.	[αžα] G	11.	[zαmα] G
2.	[αđα] F	7.	[αz̭α] G	12.	[z̭αmα] G
3.	[αθα] F	8.	[αs̭α] G	13.	[žαmα] G
4.	[αsα] G	9.	[αđα] F	14.	[θαmα] F
5.	[αs̭α] G	10.	[đαmα] F	15.	[mαškα] G

16. [maθkɑ] F 18. [mɑđgɑ] F 20. [hɑlɑs̭] G

17. [mɑθ̵kɑ] F 19. [hɑlɑđ] F 21. [hɑlɑš] G

Retroflexed Stops, Fricatives, and Affricates

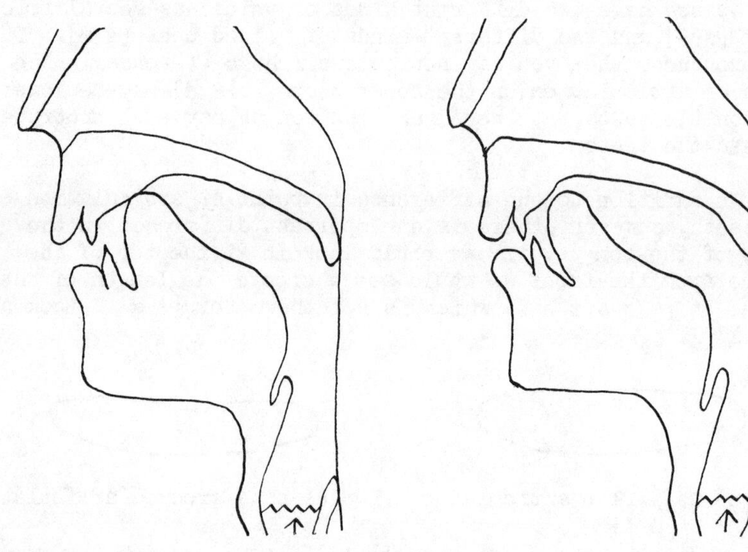

Sammy 11.3: Retroflexed Stop [ḍ]

Sammy 11.4: Retroflexed Fricative [ẓ̌]

To achieve a retroflexed articulation simply curl your tongue tip back from alveolar or alveopalatal [š] position, until it points upward and touches against the alveopalatal region near the palate, or on the palate itself. Study Sammies 11.3 and 11.4 to see the formation. Be sure to curl your tongue tip back and up to get the articulation. The result is a cup in the surface of the tongue. It it this cupped, curled position of the tongue which is called retroflexed.

RE 11.3a. Demonstration: Making and Practicing Retroflexed Sounds

Here are some ways of getting the feel of retroflexed stops, fricatives, and affricates. Read the directions for each one, and mimic the tape. In many cases you can use the same kind of exercises on other English words and phrases.

a. Say car slowly, exaggerating the /r/. Many (but not all) speakers of English curl the tongue tip and sides upward as they pronounce the /r/, making a cup in their tongues. Try real, again exaggerating the /r/. Many speakers of English start the word with the tongue in this cupped position. Now say car top, making the /t/ in the same position as the curled-up /r/, but closing the gap to the point of articulation, of course, to make a stop. The result should be [ṭʰ]. Try the same with car seat to get [ṣ̌]. Listen to the tape, and mimic these words with retroflexed tongue whether you normally pronounce English /r/ in this fashion or not.

b. Mimic the tape in the pronunciation of the following English words:

tree [ṭṣ̌ʰ·ɩy], extricate ['ɛksṭṣ̌·ɨˌkɛyt], dream [ḍẓ̌·ɩym]

This gives you the affricates [ṭṣ̌ʰ ṭṣ̌ ḍẓ̌]. This pronunciation (though not so exaggerated in length) is normal for /tr dr/ with many speakers of English.

c. Deliberately retroflex your alveolar and alveopalatal stops, fricatives and affricates as you read a paragraph from a book, practice with your buddy, or drill on the following sentences which are demonstrated on the tape.

1. Ṭake Ṭommy ṭo ṭhe ṭrain. [ṭṣ̌ʰɛyn]

2. Ḍear Ḍaḍḍy, ḍon't ḍo thaṭ.

3. Ṣ̌iṣ̌ter Ṣ̌ue ṣ̌iṭṣ̌ ṣ̌ewing ṣ̌ockṣ̌ for ṣ̌eaṣ̌ick ṣ̌uffering ṣ̌ailorṣ̌.

4. Ẓ̌any ẓ̌ebraẓ̌ ẓ̌ip and ẓ̌oom.

RE 11.4. Differential: RETROFLEXED or NO

Listen to the consonant in the taped utterance, and decide whether it is retroflexed or not. You may have noticed that many retroflexed sounds seem to have a little r-like quality to them which also modifies the surrounding vowels. This is one of the principal ways in which you can detect retroflexed articulation. Do not watch the text.

1. [ɑṣ̌ɑ]	R	6. [ɑz̭ɑ]	NO	11. [tsɑ]	NO
2. [ɑšɑ]	NO	7. [ɑṱɑ]	NO	12. [čɑ]	NO
3. [ɑṭʰɑ]	R	8. [ḍẓ̌ɑ]	R	13. [ṭɑ]	R
4. [ɑṭṣ̌ʰɑ]	R	9. [ḓɑ]	NO	14. [ḍɑ]	R
5. [ɑẓ̌ɑ]	R	10. [ṭṣ̌ɑ]	R	15. [ɑd]	NO

16. [ɑṭ]	R	18. [ɑẓ̆]	NO	20. [ɑṭṣ̌]	R
17. [ɑṣ̌]	R	19. [ɑṭʰ]	R	21. [ɑž]	NO

RE 11.5. Differential: ALVEOLAR or RETROFLEXED

1. [ɑsɑ]	A	6. [zɑ]	A	11. [ɑṭʰ]	R
2. [ɑṣ̌ɑ]	R	7. [dzɑ]	A	12. [ɑs]	A
3. [ɑṭṣ̌ɑ]	R	8. [sɑ]	A	13. [ɑts]	A
4. [ɑẓ̌ɑ]	R	9. [ṣ̌ɑ]	R	14. [ɑṭʰ]	R
5. [ɑtsɑ]	A	10. [ḍẓ̌ɑ]	R	15. [ɑẓ̌]	R

RE 11.6. Differential: ALVEOPALATAL or RETROFLEXED

1. [ɑšɑ]	A	5. [čɑ]	A	9. [ɑš]	A
2. [ɑṣ̌ɑ]	R	6. [ǰɑ]	A	10. [ɑẓ̌]	R
3. [ɑẓ̌ɑ]	R	7. [ẓ̌ɑ]	R	11. [ɑṭṣ̌ʰ]	R
4. [ɑṭṣ̌ɑ]	R	8. [šɑ]	A	12. [ɑǰ]	A

RE 11.7. Differential: VELAR or RETROFLEXED

1. [ɑkʰɑ]	V	5. [xɑ]	V	9. [ɑg]	V
2. [ɑgɑ]	V	6. [ṣ̌ɑ]	R	10. [ɑẓ̌]	R
3. [ɑṭʰɑ]	R	7. [ẓ̌ɑ]	R	11. [ɑx]	V
4. [ɑḍɑ]	R	8. [ḍẓ̌ɑ]	R	12. [ɑkx]	V

RE 11.8: Vietnamese. Mimicry: [ṣ̌ ẓ̌ ṭ][1]

Listen through the exercise, and then mimic the tape as the words are read down each column. Concentrate particularly on the retroflexed initial consonants, but do your best to get the tone and the remainder of the syllable as well.

1a. /ṣ̌áaw/ 'six'	1b. /ẓ̌aa/ 'go out'	1c. /ṭáŋ/ 'white'
2a. /ṣ̌áaŋ/ 'morning'	2b. /ẓ̌aaw/ 'vegetable'	2c. /ṭáay/ 'fruit'

[1]Data for this and succeeding exercises from William A. Smalley and Nguyễn-văn-Vạn, Vietnamese for Missionaries.

3a. /ṣ̌aay/ 'incorrect'		3b. /ẓ̌õ/	'clear'	3c. /ṭɨ́ŋ/	'egg'
4a. /ṣ̌aaw/	'follow'	4b. /ẓ̌ồy/	'already'	4c. /ṭɨʌk/	'precede'
5a. /ṣ̌oy/	'boil'	5b. /ẓ̌ɨ̃ʌ/	'to wash'	5c. /ṭam/	'100'
6a. /ṣ̌o/	'notebook'			6c. /ṭa^{ŋ}m/	'in'
7a. /ṣ̌ɨ̌ʌ/	'correct'			7c. /ṭen/	'on'
8a. /ṣ̌æ̃/	'future'			8c. /ṭàa/	'tea'
				9c. /ṭõ̤/[1]	'return'

RE 11.9: Vietnamese. Mimicry: [s ṣ̌]

Continue, as in the preceding exercise.

1. /ṣ̌æ̃/	'future'	5. /sa^{ŋ}m/	'finish'
2. /sæ/	'conveyance'	6. /ṣ̌aaw/	'to be after'
3. /súʌŋ/	'go down'	7. /ṣ̌ák/	'high tone'
4. /ṣ̌ɨ̃ʌ/	'correct'	8. /súp/	'soup'

RE 11.10: Vietnamese. Mimicry: [t ṭ t^{h}]

1. /tɨ̂/	'leave'	8. /t^{h}ɨ́/	'order, rank'
2. /ṭɨ̂/	'exclude'	9. /ṭɨ́ʌk/	'precede'
3. /ṭõ̤/[1]	'return'	10. /t^{h}ɨ́'tɨ'ṭɨ́ʌk/	'last Wednesday'
4. /t^{h}ù^{ŋ}m/	'large container'	11. /tiw/	'digested'
5. /ṭu^{ŋ}m/	'center'	12. /t^{h}íw/	'lack, be short'
6. /tɨ/	'fourth'	13. /yó̤y't^{h}ịw/[2]	'introduce
7. /tɨ̂/	'leave, go'	14. /ṭáay/	'fruit'

---

[1]Two dots under the [o] mark a difference of vowel quality which you will study later.

[2]A single dot under a vowel in Vietnamese examples is a tone mark, following the Vietnamese system of representing tone.

RE 11.11. Review: Fricatives

Practice mimicry of the following sequences, as you read along in your text. Work especially on [x ǥ].

1. [ɑpxɑ] 10. [ɑxθɑ] 19. [ɑvƀɑ]

2. [ɑfxɑ] 11. [ɑxƀɑ] 20. [ɑđƀɑ]

3. [ɑθxɑ] 12. [ɑxvɑ] 21. [ɑǥƀɑ]

4. [ɑƀxɑ] 13. [ɑxđɑ] 22. [ɑƀpɑ]

5. [ɑvxɑ] 14. [ɑxǥɑ] 23. [ɑƀfɑ]

6. [ɑđxɑ] 15. [ɑpƀɑ] 24. [ɑƀθɑ]

7. [ɑǥxɑ] 16. [ɑfƀɑ] 25. [ɑƀxɑ]

8. [ɑxpɑ] 17. [ɑθƀɑ] 26. [ɑƀvɑ]

9. [ɑxfɑ] 18. [ɑxƀɑ] 27. [ɑƀđɑ]

RE 11.12. Substitution

The following drill uses a long frame, substituting a different sequence in it each time. The steady repetition of the frame through the whole exercise helps to give intensive practice to the articulations. On the first utterance there is a buildup to help you learn the sequence. On succeeding ones a buildup should not be necessary because only a small part of the sequence is new.

1. ['t^{h}ɑ.ṣ̌ɑ.psɑ.'mɑ.xɑ.s̭ɑn.'zɑ]
2. 'kxɑ.lɑ
3. 'ppɑ.nɑ
4. 'čɑ.ǰɑ
5. 'tsɑ.dzɑ
6. ['t^{h}ɑ.šɑ.psɑ.'z̭ɑ.ṱɑ.šɑn.'zɑ]
7. 't̤šɑ.žɑ
8. 'ggɑ.ḍɑ
9. 'pṣ̌ɑ.yɑ
10. 'd̤žɑ.tsɑ

RE 11.13. Buildups

Mimic the tape and follow in your book. The buildups will begin with the first syllables in each case.

1. ['t^{h}ɑ.bƀɑ.vɑx.gɑ.pɑ] 2. ['ẓ̌ɑ.lɑ.bɑ.ḍɑ.ṭɑ]

3. [ˈdɑ.tsɑ.k^{h}ɑ.bɑ.kxɑ]   7. [ˈpɑṭ^h.bɑg.mɑṣ̌.dɑx]

4. [ˈk^{h}ɑ.vɑ.pɑ.bzɑ.ᵽɑ]   8. [ˈfɑs̭.ḓɑl.ᵽɑṭ.kɑʔ]

5. [ˈpsɑx.k^{h}ɑs.bɑ.čɑ]   9. [ˈḍɑp.s̭ɑb.vɑk^h.ṱs̭ɑḓ]

6. [ˈʔɑ.gɑl.gɑm.d̤ž̤ɑ]   10. [ˈk^{h}ɑ.gɑx.kɑps̭.ǰɑpf]

RE 11.14. Transcription

Listen to the tape, and transcribe the full utterances without looking at the text below. When you are satisfied with your transcriptions, check them with the text of the exercise.

1. [kxɑǥ]   6. [mɑˈt̥š̥ɑf]   11. [ˈḍɑƀṭ^{h}ɑl]

2. [pṣ̌ɑm]   7. [ṱθɑˈs̭ɑǥ]   12. [ˈkɑnxɑp^h]

3. [ṭɑd̤ž̤]   8. [bgɑˈkṣ̌ɑn]   13. [ˈṣ̌ɑᵽmɑts]

4. [s̭ɑbv]   9. [čɑˈʔɑpx]   14. [ˈlɑfk^{h}ɑb]

5. [z̭ɑgz]   10. [z̭ɑˈtsɑš]   15. [ˈggɑʔpɑm]

RE 11.15. Reading

Read off the following items before you hear them pronounced on the tape. Then listen to the tape to compare with what you have just said.

1. [ˈḍɑmɑ]   7. [ˈpɑ.kxɑm]   13. [ˈgɑʔ.p^{h}ɑ]

2. [ˈxɑbɑ]   8. [ˈlɑṣ̌ɑǥ]   14. [ˈpɑn.vɑ]

3. [ˈp^{h}ɑṱɑ]   9. [ˈp^{h}ɑʔɑd]   15. [ˈtsɑƀ.lɑ]

4. [ˈnɑkɑ]   10. [ˈggɑbɑᵽ]   16. [ˈp^{h}ɑx.pɑn]

5. [ˈxɑpᵽɑ]   11. [ˈmɑf.xɑ]   17. [ˈčɑs.ǥɑk^h]

6. [ˈt^{h}ɑƀɑn]   12. [ˈṭɑs̭.ḓɑ]   18. [ˈdɑʔ.lɑks]

LESSON TWELVE

Vowels and Vowel Glides

We come at last to the beginning of the study of vowels. For them we need a new framework of reference, for the points of articulation useful in describing consonants do not fit vowels. The characteristic which distinguishes vowels from consonants phonetically is the fact that there is no stoppage or friction in the oral cavity or throat of the kinds previously defined. The articulation of vowels is, therefore, more open than that of consonants.

Different vowel qualities are produced primarily by changing the shape of the oral and pharyngeal cavities by altering the position and configuration of the tongue, lips, and velic. Sammies 12.1-12.3 show different positions for the tongue on three different vowels, and Sammy 12.3 shows also the different lip position for one of these vowels. Sammy 12.4 shows these three tongue positions superimposed on each other. You can see that for the different vowels the highest part of the tongue is in different positions. For [ɛ] the highest part of the tongue is in the _front_ part of the mouth. For [ɑ] it is in the _central_ part of the mouth, and for [o] it is in the _back_ part of the mouth. Wherever its position, front to back, the tongue may take different heights, to give _high_ tongue position, _mid_ tongue position and _low_ tongue position. We also have the distinction between _rounded_ and _unrounded_ lips. This can be charted, as in Table 12.1. We have entered on the chart the three vowels pictured in the Sammies, and in future lessons you will be taught to distinguish vowels for other parts of the chart. Note the relation between the position of the vowel in the chart, and the position of the highest part of the tongue in the Sammy. For the time being the velic is closed and the vowels are voiced.

	Front Unrounded	Central Unrounded	Back Rounded
High			
Mid	ɛ		o
Low		ɑ	

Table 12.1: Chart of Basic Vowel Articulations

The names of the vowel symbols are [ɛ] "epsilon" (from Greek) /ˈɛpsɨˌlɑHn/, [ɑ] "script _a_" or "written _a_", and [o] _o_.

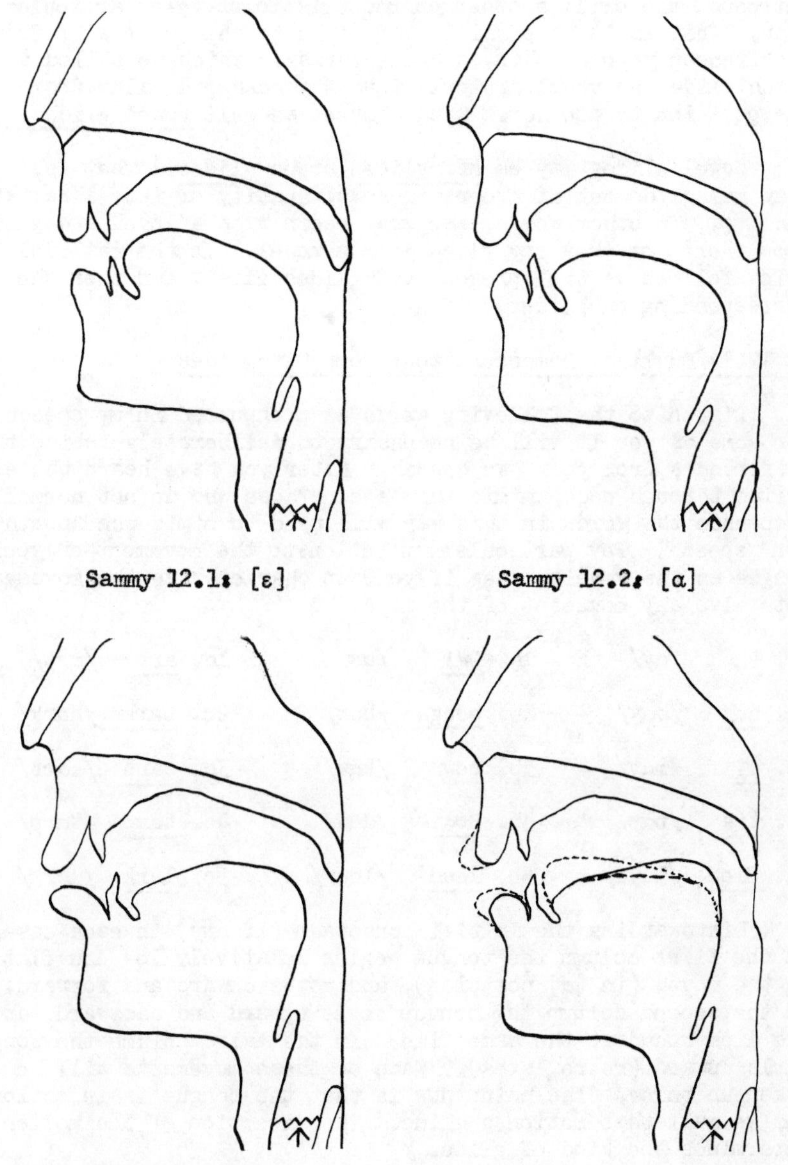

Sammy 12.1: [ɛ]

Sammy 12.2: [ɑ]

Sammy 12.3: [o]

Sammy 12.4: [ɛ ɑ o] superimposed

Vowel Glides

Later on in this lesson we will practice the pronunciation of the three vowels charted above. First, however, we need to introduce and drill another characteristic of vowel articulation. Just as it is possible for pitch to change or slur from one frequency to another, a characteristic which we called a pitch glide, so vowel articulations may change or slur from one position to another. Such changes we call vowel glides.

Vowel glides may be off-glides or on-glides. That is, they may glide out of a certain vowel quality or into a certain quality. In other words, they may begin with a vowel and glide from there, or they may glide into a vowel. In the material which follows we will present off-glides first, and then the corresponding on-glides.

RE 12.1: English. Demonstration: Some Off-glides

Listen to the following words as pronounced in my speech. For some of you it will be necessary to deliberately notice the differences from your own speech. After you have heard the exercise through once, mimic the tape. Those who do not normally pronounce the words in this way will need to mimic the "northern" speech. Pay particular attention to the movement of your tongue on the vowels. See if you can characterize the movement. Note also any movement of the lips.

1a.	I	/ɑy/	1b.	Ow!	/ɑw/	1c.	art	/ɑrt/
2a.	buy	/bɑy/	2b.	bough	/bɑw/	2c.	bark	/bɑrk/
3a.	my	/mɑy/	3b.	cow	/kɑw/	3c.	cart	/kɑrt/
4a.	tie	/tɑy/	4b.	Dow	/dɑw/	4c.	tarp	/tɑrp/
5a.	lied	/lɑyd/	5b.	loud	/lɑwd/	5c.	lark	/lɑrk/

Disregarding the initial consonant (if any) in each case, in the first column the tongue begins relatively low and flat in the mouth (in [ɑ] position), and moves upward and forward. In the second column the tongue moves upward and backward, and the lips round at the same time. In the third column the tongue curls upward (retroflexes). Each of these movements will be taken up below. The point now is that the tongue is in motion, and we call that motion a glide. The direction of the motion determines the kind of glide.

[y] Off-glide, Tongue Upward and Forward

The [y] off-glide begins with any vowel position and moves upward and forward, as illustrated in Sammies 12.5 and 12.6. We are not concerned with any exact point to which it moves, but the glide consists in the audible upward and forward movement, as in Table 12.2.

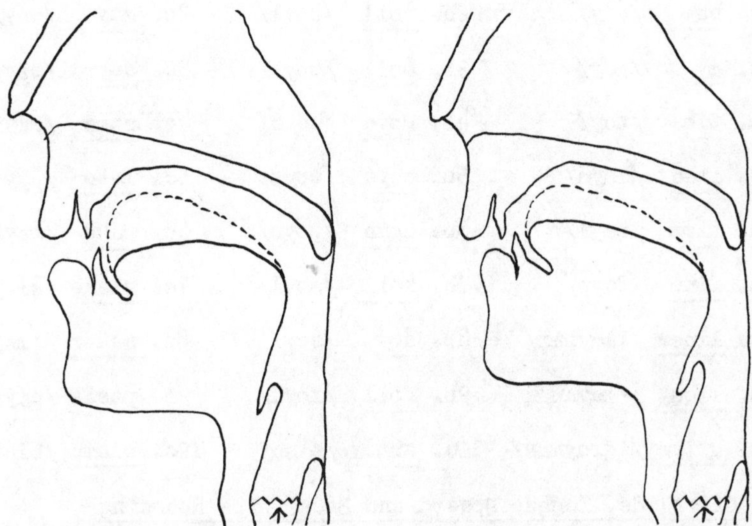

Sammy 12.5: Articulation of [ɑy] Showing Tongue at Beginning and at End of Glide

Sammy 12.6: Articulation of [ɛy] Showing Tongue at Beginning and at End of Glide

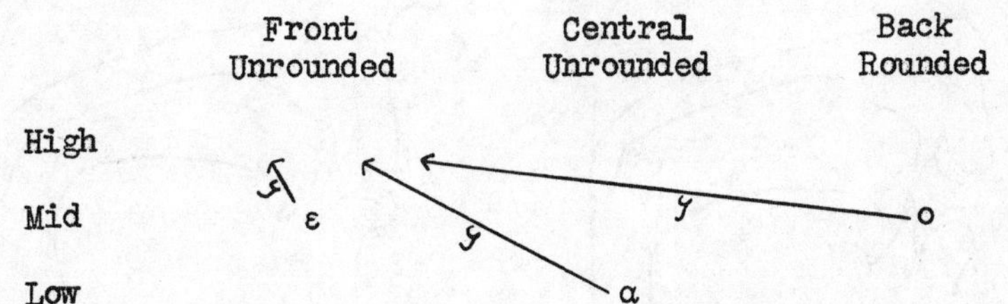

Table 12.2: Movement Which Constitutes the [y] Off-glide

RE 12.2: English. Demonstration: [y] Off-glides

The following English words contain [y] off-glides as they are pronounced on the tape. They may not necessarily in your speech. If these do not, see if you can find some words in your own speech which demonstrate [y] off-glide. There certainly are many. Mimic the tape, and feel the glide. It is easiest to feel in Column a and Column b because it has farther to travel (see Table 12.2), but make sure you learn to feel it in Column c as well. Watch yourself in a mirror, and see your tongue move.

1a. I	/ɑy/	1b. boy	/boy/	1c. hey!	/hɛy/
2a. buy	/bɑy/	2b. coil	/koyl/	2c. may	/mɛy/
3a. my	/mɑy/	3b. boil	/boyl/	3c. say	/sɛy/
4a. tie	/tɑy/	4b. Boyd	/boyd/	4c. same	/sɛym/
5a. lied	/lɑyd/	5b. boys	/boyz/	5c. late	/lɛyt/
6a. time	/tɑym/	6b. coin	/koyn/	6c. rake	/rɛyk/
7a. fine	/fɑyn/	7b. soil	/soyl/	7c. slake	/slɛyk/
8a. liner	/ˈlɑynɨr/	8b. soy	/soy/	8c. maker	/ˈmɛykɨr/
9a. lion	/ˈlɑyʌn/	9b. foil	/foyl/	9c. paste	/pɛyst/
10a. grimey	/ˈgrɑymɨy/	10b. annoy	/ʌˈnoy/	10c. blame	/blɛym/

[w] Off-glide, Tongue Upward and Back, Lips Rounding

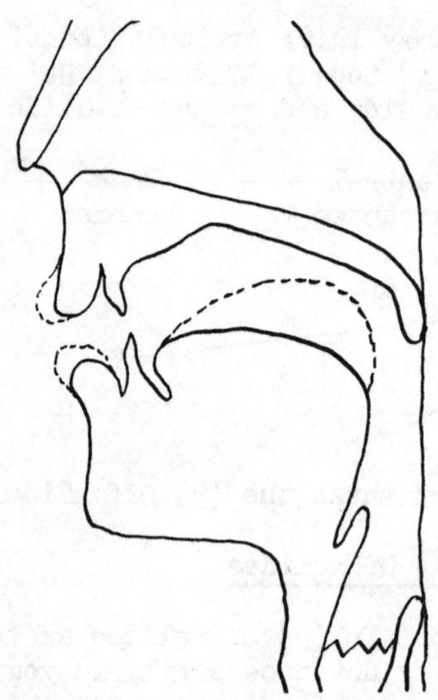

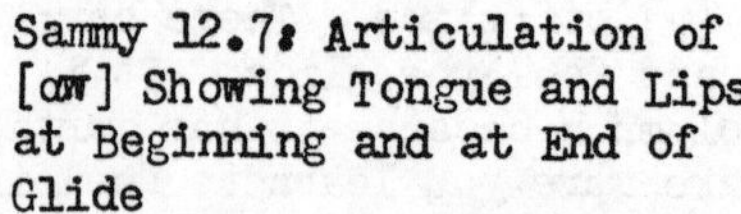

Sammy 12.7: Articulation of [ɑw] Showing Tongue and Lips at Beginning and at End of Glide

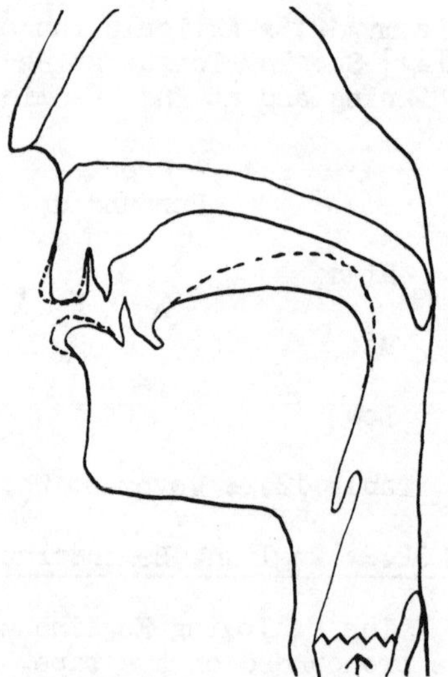

Sammy 12.8: Articulation of [ow] Showing Tongue and Lips at Beginning and at End of Glide

The [w] off-glide begins with any vowel position and moves upward and back, together with a lip rounding, as illustrated in Sammies 12.7 and 12.8. As in the case of the [y] off-glide, we are not concerned with the exact point to which it moves, but with the audible upward and back movement, together with the lip movement. See Table 12.3.

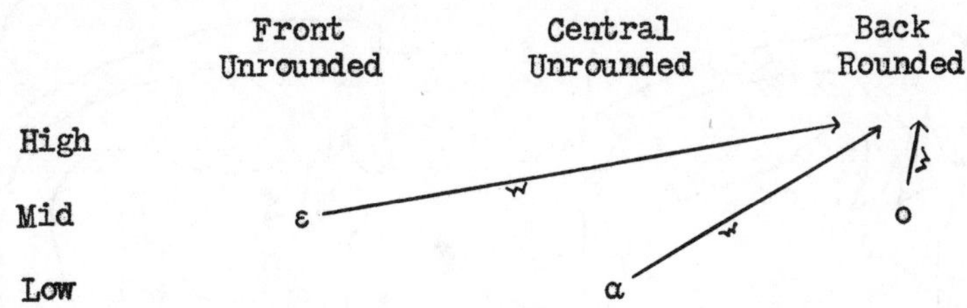

Table 12.3: Movement Which Constitutes the [w] Off-glide

RE 12.3: English. Demonstration: [w] Off-glides

The following English words contain [w] off-glides as they are pronounced on the tape. These words may not necessarily contain them in your speech. If they do not, see if you can find some words in your own speech which demonstrate the [w] off glide. There certainly are many. These pronunciations do not all represent the same dialect of English. Mimic the tape, and feel the glide. Whereas the [y] off-glide was harder to feel with [ε] than with the other vowels, the [w] off-glide may be harder to feel with [o], again because the tongue does not have as far to travel. You can watch your lips in a mirror, however, and have no trouble detecting the glide. Get your buddy to watch you, also.

1a. Ow! /ɑw/	1b. house /hεws/	1c. Oh! /ow/
2a. bough /bɑw/	2b. note /nεwt/	2c. note /nowt/
3a. cow /kɑw/	3b. coat /kεwt/	3c. coat /kowt/
4a. Dow /dɑw/	4b. own /εwn/	4c. own /own/
5a. loud /lɑwd/	5b. notice/'nεwtɨs/	5c. notice/'nowtɨs/
6a. crown /krɑwn/	6b. so /sεw/	6c. so /sow/
7a. allow /ʌ'lɑw/	7b. go /gεw/	7c. go /gow/
8a. grouse/grɑws/	8b. throne/θrεwn/	8c. throne/θrown/

[r] Off-glide, Tongue to Retroflexed Position

The [r] off-glide begins with any vowel position and moves

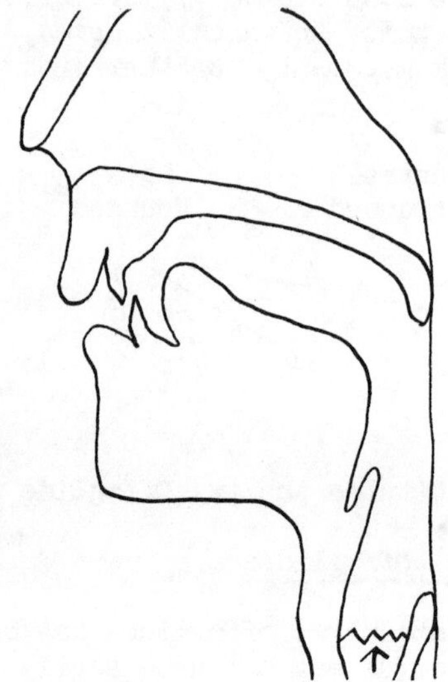

Sammy 12.9: One Typical English Retroflexed Position for [r]

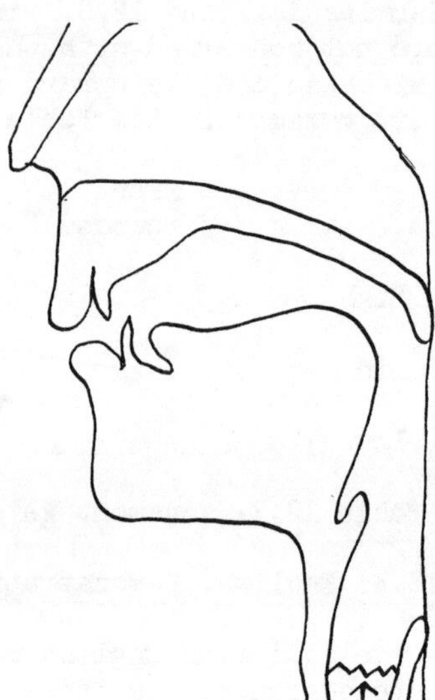

Sammy 12.10: A Second Typical English Retroflexed Position for [r]

into a retroflexed position. In Lesson Eleven you learned to make retroflexed consonants, and you learned that the distinguishing characteristic of a retroflexed sound was the cup-like surface of the tongue, created by the fact that the tongue tip turned upward to articulate. Retroflexed glide position again has a cup in the surface of the tongue, but because it is a vowel type of articulation rather than a consonant type of articulation, there is more space between the tongue and the top of the mouth.

In English the [r] glide is made by different speakers with two characteristic different tongue formations, both of which have a cup in them to produce the retroflex quality. See Sammies 12.9 and 12.10. In the one case the back of the tongue is low, with the tip and sides curling up. In the other case the back of the tongue is high, with the tip curling up slightly, as illustrated in the Sammies. There is no audible difference between the two, and either is satisfactory for the [r] glide. Again, as with all previous glides, it is a movement, this time into retroflexed position, which constitutes the glide.

RE 12.4: English. Demonstration: [r] Off-glides

The following English words contain [r] off-glides as they

are pronounced on the tape. They may not necessarily in your speech. If they do not, see if you can find some words in your own speech which demonstrate the [r] off-glide. It is possible that you do not have any, for some dialects of English do not. Learn to produce this off-glide if you do not have it in your speech. Get the feel of the tongue movement into retroflexed position.

1a. art	/ɑrt/	1b. ferry	/ˈfɛrɩy/	1c. story	/ˈstorɩy/
2a. cart	/kɑrt/	2b. merry	/ˈmɛrɩy/	2c. sort	/sort/
3a. mark	/mɑrk/	3b. Sperry	/ˈspɛrɩy/	3c. pork	/pork/
4a. startle	/ˈstɑrtɨl/	4b. Gerry	/ˈǰɛrɩy/	4c. fort	/fort/
5a. partner	/ˈpɑrtnɨr/	5b. berry	/ˈbɛrɩy/	5c. orchard	/ˈorčɨrd/

[H] Off-glide, Tongue to Central Position

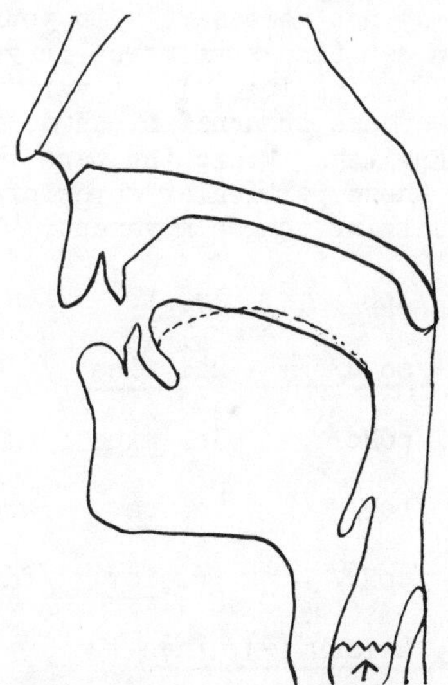

Sammy 12.11: Articulation of [ɛH] Showing Tongue at Beginning and at End of Glide

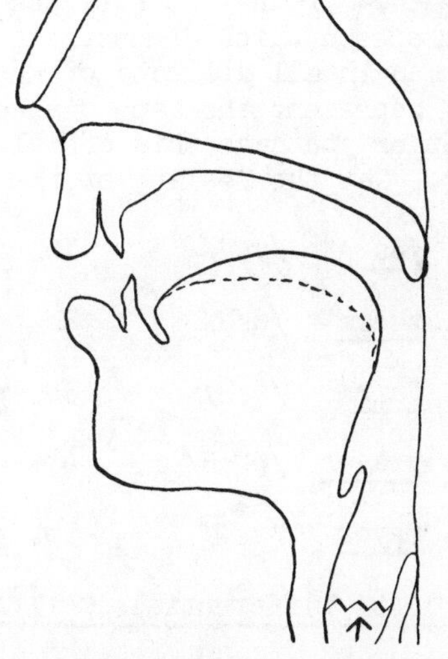

Sammy 12.12: Articulation of [oH] Showing Tongue at Beginning and at End of Glide

The fourth and last off-glide which we will take up begins with any vowel position and moves into mid-central position, as illustrated in Sammies 12.11 and 12.12. Again we are not concerned with the exact point to which it moves, but with the audible movement into the mid-central area. See Table 12.4. Do not let the choice of the capital H as a symbol for this glide confuse you. It has no relation to [h] in our work. Neither does it have any relation to the sign of aspiration [ʰ]. It is simply a symbol not otherwise used in our work, and available to represent the centralizing glide.[1]

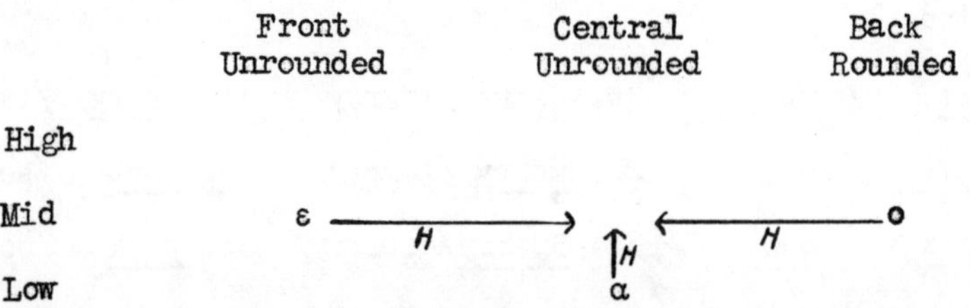

Table 12.4: Movement Which Constitutes the [H] Off-glide

RE 12.5: English. Demonstration: [H] Off-glides

The following English words contain [H] off-glides as they are pronounced on the tape. They may not necessarily in your speech. If they do not, see if you can find some words in your own speech which demonstrate the [H] off-glide. It is very common in all dialects of English. These pronunciations do not all represent the same dialect of English. Mimic the tape whether you have this off-glide on these particular words or not. Get the feeling of the centralizing tongue movement.

1a.	yea	/yɛH/	1b.	four	/foH/	1c.	I	/ɑH/
2a.	there	/ðɛH/	2b.	sword	/soHd/	2c.	fine	/fɑHn/
3a.	fair	/fɛH/	3b.	porch	/poHč/	3c.	mine	/mɑHn/
4a.	prayer	/prɛH/	4b.	boa	/boH/	4c.	car	/kɑH/
5a.	mayor	/mɛH/	5b.	pork	/poHk/	5c.	far	/fɑH/

RE 12.6. Differential: CAPITAL [H], RAISED [ʰ], [h]

The following drill is to help you fix the three symbols [H ʰ h] so you will not confuse them. You have not yet had [h] in final position, but it sounds just like [h] in initial

---

[1]Some linguists maintain that [H] and [h] are actualizations of the same phoneme in English. Whether one holds to that interpretation of English or not, these sounds are phonetically different, and have no relation to each other in our phonetics work.

position, and it is demonstrated for you on the tape before the exercise begins. In this exercise you respond with the name of the symbol, because it is the different use of the symbols which you want to learn to keep straight. Do not watch the text.

1. [mɑp^h] R
2. [mɑh] h
3. [mɑH] C
4. [t^{h}ɛm] R
5. [sok^h] R
6. [hoz] h
7. [loh] h
8. [loH] C
9. [fɛH] C
10. [p^{h}rɛl] R
11. [rɑh] h
12. [zɛh] h
13. [lop^h] R
14. [tɑk^h] R
15. [tɑH] C
16. [tɑh] h
17. [ḍɛH] C
18. [xoh] h

RE 12.7. Differential: [y w r H]

In this drill you are to distinguish the kind of off-glide which you hear. Call out the name of the symbol used to represent it.

1. [mɛy] y
2. [mɛw] w
3. [mɛH] H
4. [mɛr] r
5. [lɑyk^h] y
6. [sowk^h] w
7. [fɛHm] H
8. [psoyd] y
9. [tsɛrk^h] r
10. [bzork^h] r
11. [t̤šoHk^h] H
12. [stɑHv] H
13. [hɑwk^h] w
14. [hɑyp^h] y
15. [žɛyn] y
16. [čɑwd] w
17. [fɛrn] r
18. [zɑwl] w

Up to the present we have dealt only with off-glides, glides which begin with a syllabic vowel, and move to one or another of the four defined positions in a non-syllabic movement. On-glides are just the reverse. They move to the position of the syllabic vowel. The position from which they come defines the glide. In other words, any Sammy above which represents an off-glide can be made to represent an on-glide by having the dotted line represent the non-syllabic beginning point, and the solid line the syllabic vowel to which the glide moves. See also Table 12.5.

RE 12.8: English. Demonstration: On-glides

Listen to the tape, and mimic. Notice how the on-glide (the glide coming before the vowel) in Column a is just the

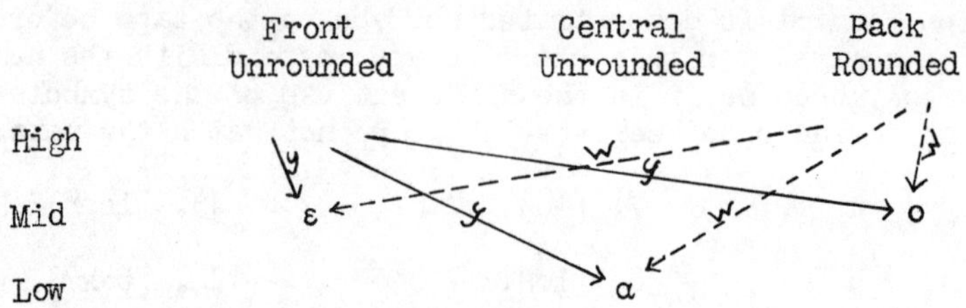

Table 12.5: Movements Which Constitute the [y] and [w] On-glides

reverse in tongue movement of the off-glide in Column b. The tape will read across. Follow the transcription as you mimic. These pronunciations do not all reflect the same dialect of English.

1a.	yes	/yεs/	1b.	say	/sεy/
2a.	yacht	/yɑt/	2b.	tie	/tɑy/
3a.	Wes	/wεs/	3b.	so	/sεw/
4a.	wan	/wɑn/	4b.	now	/nɑw/
5a.	woe	/wow/	5b.	woe	/wow/
6a.	wreck	/rεk/	6b.	care	/kεr/
7a.	rock	/rɑk/	7b.	car	/kar/

We do not drill [H] as an on-glide.

RE 12.9. Demonstration: Lack of Syllabicity on Glides

One of the characteristics of the glides as they have been discussed above has been the fact that they are non-syllabic vowel movement. In order to help you feel the non-syllabic character of the glides we provide the following drill. Mimic the tape and watch the transcription. In order to help you visualize what is happening, study the following diagram in relation to the first utterance.

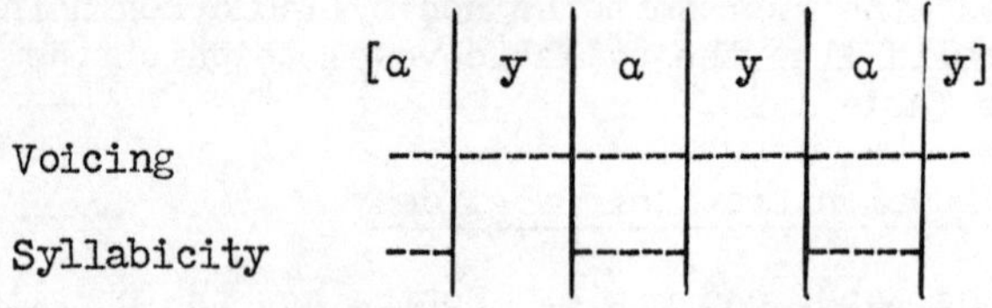

1. [yɑyɑyɑyɑyɑyɑyɑy] 2. [yoyoyoyoyoyoyoyoy]

3. [yɛyɛyɛyɛyɛyɛyɛy]

4 [wowowowowowowowow]

5. [wɑwɑwɑwɑwɑwɑwɑw]

6. [wɛwɛwɛwɛwɛwɛwɛw]

7. [rɛrɛrɛrɛrɛrɛrɛr]

8. [rororororororor]

9. [rɑrɑrɑrɑrɑrɑrɑr]

10. [ɑHɑHɑHɑHɑHɑHɑH]

11. [ɛHɛHɛHɛHɛHɛHɛH]

12. [oHoHoHoHoHoHoH]

As you drilled the above did you notice that sometimes you could not tell whether the glide was off-glide or on-glide? Actually it slurred imperceptibly from one to the other. This illustrates the point made about syllables in Lesson 10, that the syllabic is easy to identify, but the point of syllable boundary may not be audible. Note also that the tongue stops just as long at the end of the glide position as it does at the vowel position. The fact that the vowel is syllabic, however, helps to distinguish the glide.[1]

RE 12.10: English. Demonstration: Glide Onsets with Preceding Consonant

Mimic the following English words, paying particular attention to the on-glides, and to the consonant which precedes each one. Notice that the articulation of the glide begins before the release of the consonant, and that the glide articulation continues after the release of the consonant in the following manner.

---

[1]You have probably noticed that all of the glides except [H] have previously been identified as consonants in your English transcription (Appendix A). Phonetically they are vowel glides in English, as in any other language. Phonemically they pattern as consonants in English and in some (though not all) other languages. Some linguists prefer to use the term *consonant* and *vowel* for phonemic classes, and *vocoid* and *non-vocoid* for what we are calling phonetic vowel (and vowel glide) and consonant. As valuable as this terminological distinction is, we have not burdened you with it in this *Manual*. See Kenneth L. Pike, *Phonetics*, pp. 66-79. You will remember from Lesson 10 that just as some vowels operate in some languages as consonants (the glides we have been studying), so some consonants can be syllabic, and can therefore operate in some languages as vowels. If we were dealing seriously with the classification of sounds on the phonemic level it would be worthwhile to maintain Pike's distinction in terminology.

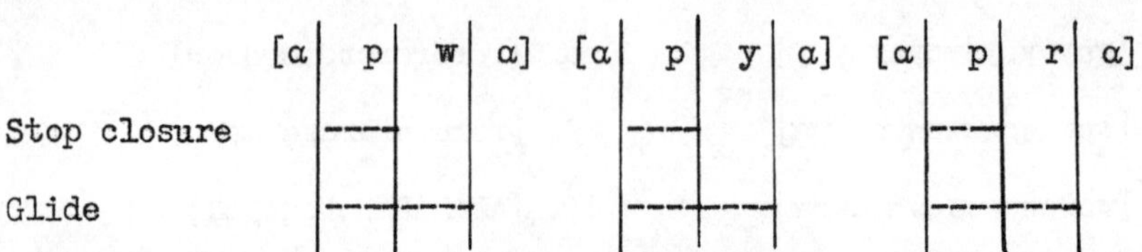

This is especially easy to notice in English with the [w] on-glide because the lips round for the preceding consonant. Notice how your lips round for the /k/ in quick. Column b contains words without the on-glide so that you can feel and hear the difference. The tape recording reads across. Follow the text as you mimic.

1a.	dwell	/dwεHl/	1b.	dell	/dεHl/
2a.	swell	/swεHl/	2b.	sell	/sεHl/
3a.	twenty	/'twεntιy/	3b.	tent	/tεnt/
4a.	quotient	/'kwowšɨnt/	4b.	cogent	/'kowǰɨnt/
5a.	pure	/pyʊHr/	5b.	poor	/pʊHr/
6a.	cute	/kyɨwt/	6b.	coot	/kɨwt/
7a.	beauty	/'byɨwtιy/	7b.	booty	/'bɨwtιy/
8a.	few	/fyɨw/	8b.	foo	/fʊw/
9a.	break	/brεyk/	9b.	bake	/bεyk/
10a.	pray	/prεy/	10b.	pay	/pεy/
11a.	shred	/šrεd/	11b.	shed	/šεd/
12a.	fray	/frεy/	12b.	Fay	/fεy/

RE 12.11. Negative Practice: On-glides Following Consonants

Practice each of the following sentences with an inserted [y] on-glide after the alliterative consonant. Then practice them with [w] and then with [r]. These are written out in the first example to make the exercise clear. The tape demonstrates them for you. You can read whole paragraphs of English in this way as well.

1. Pyeter Pyipyer pyicked a pyeck of pyickled pyeppyers.

Pweter Pwipwer pwicked a pweck of pwickled pweppwers.

Preter Priprer pricked a preck of prickled prepprers.

2. Tiny Tim took ten tin tubs to Toronto.

3. Keen cool cats kick kittens constantly.

4. Many mothers made much money Monday morning.

Pure vowels [ɑ o ɛ]

The glides which you have been studying in this chapter may glide into or out of any of the many vowel qualities which you will be studying in the remainder of this course. With very few exceptions, however, we have restricted our examples and drills in this lesson to three vowels as the end point or starting point of glides. These three vowels are [ɑ o ɛ]. See Table 12.1. We now go on to practice these three vowels as unglided vowels, or "pure" vowels. We want to be able to say them without the slightest audible trace of any of our four glides.

The importance of gaining such control over all vowels that you can keep them pure, or glide them at will, cannot be over-emphasized. You will soon discover that you have an automatic tendency to glide certain vowels in certain ways in English. This carries over into your learning of another language in ways that sound atrocious. It is not that other languages do not glide their vowels. Every language has its own patterns of glided and unglided vowels, and you must learn to control your speech so that English patterns are not applied to the other language.

It is very important that you learn the vowel qualities of this and succeeding lessons by mimicking your teacher and the tape. Do not depend on English words as models or guides for certain vowel qualities until you have checked your pronunciation of them with a competent person. The pronunciation of different speakers of English varies so much that you have to be careful here. Furthermore, what may pattern as a phoneme in English and be symbolized in a certain way, such as /ɛ/, may have several different pronunciations in any one person's speech. In our phonetics work we are striving for phonetic norms, and as much as possible we will seek for a uniform pronunciation. The choice of this uniform pronunciation is a bit arbitrary, and it is not possible in any absolute way, but we can come close to it for practical purposes.

RE 12.12. Demonstration: [ɑ o ɛ]

Look back at Table 12.1, and read the first two paragraphs

of this lesson again. Get a clear picture of the table in your mind, and then do the following exercise. Listen to the tape, and mimic it, following along in your text. Try to sense the position of your tongue and lips, in accordance with the chart. Be very careful not to get any glides. [•] indicates a prolonging of the vowel. For the [h] just blow out without changing the articulation. Each item will be given three times.

1. [ʔɑ• ʔɑ ʔɑ ʔɑ ʔɑ] 4. [ʔɑ•h]

2. [ʔo• ʔo ʔo ʔo ʔo] 5. [ʔo•h]

3. [ʔɛ• ʔɛ ʔɛ ʔɛ ʔɛ] 6. [ʔɛ•h]

For each of these pure vowels there are characteristic traps which speakers of English are likely to be caught in when they mean to produce pure vowels. For [ɑ] the temptation is to change the quality between the long and short pronunciations. There is also the problem of tending to substitute your own English pronunciation, which in many dialects of English is considerably different from what you hear on the tape.

The trap in the [o] is the temptation to add the English [w] off-glide. Watch your lips in the mirror as you pronounce it. If there is any movement toward greater rounding you are adding the glide.

The trap in the [ɛ] is the temptation to add the English [H] off-glide. Be especially careful of this. You cannot see it in a mirror. You must learn to hear it and feel it.

Now go through this exercise again, remembering the traps, and trying to avoid them. Work with your buddy so that you can listen to each other and help each other find the points at which you differ from the tape.

RE 12.13. Negative Practice: [ow o]

In the following exercise we are going to pronounce the same English words with [ow] in Column a, and with [o] in Column b. Neither of these pronunciations may be your natural pronunciation of the word in some cases. The purpose is to mimic the tape and learn to produce a glided or unglided [o] at will.

1a. [sow]	1b. [so]	so
2a. [ʔow]	2b. [ʔo]	oh
3a. [low]	3b. [lo]	low

4a. [bow]	4b. [bo]	bow
5a. ['mowtr̩]	5b. ['motr̩]	motor
6a. [lowf]	6b. [lof]	loaf
7a. ['gowɩŋ]	7b. ['goɩŋ]	going
8a. [ʌ'lown]	8b. [ʌ'lon]	alone

RE 12.14. Negative Practice: [εH ε]

This exercise follows the same procedure and purpose as the preceding one, except that the vowel and glide are different.

1a. [yεH]	1b. [yε]	yea
2a. [wεHl]	2b. [wεl]	well
3a. [lεHt]	3b. [lεt]	let
4a. [mεHnt]	4b. [mεnt]	meant
5a. [frεHnd]	5b. [frεnd]	friend
6a. [bεHst]	6b. [bεst]	best
7a. [εHnd]	7b. [εnd]	end
8a. [frεHt]	8b. [frεt]	fret

RE 12.15. Differential: GLIDED or NO

If you hear [w y H r] respond with GLIDED. Otherwise respond with NO. You get the same vowel with or without the same glide in both syllables of each utterance in Nos. 1-14. This gives you more opportunity to hear and identify the glide. Do not watch the text.

1. [kεHsεH]	G	7. [kεysεy]	G	13. [koHsoH]	G
2. [kεsε]	NO	8. [kεsε]	NO	14. [koso]	NO
3. [kowsow]	G	9. [kεwsεw]	G	15. [kɑH]	G
4. [kɑysɑy]	G	10. [kowsow]	G	16. [kɑy]	G
5. [kɑHsɑH]	G	11. [koysoy]	G	17. [kɑ]	NO
6. [kasɑ]	NO	12. [kɑHsɑH]	G	18. [kε]	NO

19. [kɛH] G   20. [kɑw] G   21. [ko] NO

RE 12.16. Mimicry: [ɑ ɛ o]

Follow the tape in mimicking the following items, first down the columns, and then across. Be sure to get pure vowels.

1a. ['lɑlɑ]	1b. ['lɛlɛ]	1c. ['lolo]
2a. ['bɑbɑ]	2b. ['bɛbɛ]	2c. ['bobo]
3a. ['nɑnɑ]	3b. ['nɛnɛ]	3c. ['nono]
4a. ['ḍɑḍɑ]	4b. ['ḍɛḍɛ]	4c. ['ḍoḍo]
5a. ['žɑžɑ]	5b. ['žɛžɛ]	5c. ['žožo]
6a. ['tsɑtsɑ]	6b. ['tsɛtsɛ]	6c. ['tsotso]
7a. ['s̭ɑs̭ɑ]	7b. ['s̭ɛs̭ɛ]	7c. ['s̭os̭o]
8a. ['gɑgɑ]	8b. ['gɛgɛ]	8c. ['gogo]
1d. [lɑ]	1e. [lɛ]	1f. [lo]
2d. [bɑ]	2e. [bɛ]	2f. [bo]
3d. [nɑ]	3e. [nɛ]	3f. [no]
4d. [ḍɑ]	4e. [ḍɛ]	4f. [ḍo]
5d. [žɑ]	5e. [žɛ]	5f. [žo]
6d. [tsɑ]	6e. [tsɛ]	6f. [tso]
7d. [s̭ɑ]	7e. [s̭ɛ]	7f. [s̰o]
8d. [gɑ]	8e. [gɛ]	8f. [go]

RE 12.17. Mimicry: Glides Again

Mimic the tape, and practice saying the following English words with the glided vowels shown for each item. Notice that No. 6 contains some British pronunciation, Nos. 7, 8, 9 some Deep South pronunciation, etc.

1. [ɛy]: bay, say, may   3. [ɑy]: buy, pie, lie

2. [oy]: boil, coin, choice   4. [ɑw]: how, cow, now

5. [ɑw]: so, bow, low

6. [ɛw]: go, no, oh

7. [ɛH]: layer, mayor, bed

8. [oH]: boa, Noah, four

9. [ɑH]: choir, lies, lion

10. [ɛr]: their, fair, pear

11. [or]: chore, door, core

12. [ɑr]: choir, part, barn

RE 12.18. Buildups: Pure Vowels and Glides

Mimic the tape. These longer utterances will be built up from the end. Be very careful of your pure vowels and glides.

1. ['dɑ.nɑw.frɑm.'kʰɛy.mo.bɛn.'pʰɛr.gɑy.sɛH.'soy]

2. ['šo.sɛn.tʰɑf.'mɑpʰ.mɛH.fɛH.'žɛHkʰ.bol.wɑ.'broH]

3. ['čʰɑyv.ǰɑw.gɛd.'vɑHl.mɛyn.ṭṣ̌ɛw.'goy.do.dow.'hɑH]

RE 12.19. Buildups: Review of Stress and Timing

Follow along in your text, and mimic the tape on these buildups. The consonants and vowels are kept simple so that you can concentrate on the stress, juncture, syllabicity, timing, etc.

1. ['nɑnɑ nɑ'nɑnɑ nɑ nɑ 'nɑ nɑ nɑ'nɑ]

2. [bn̩bn̩'bn̩bn̩ bn̩bn̩ 'bn̩ bn̩ 'bn̩'bn̩ 'bn̩bn̩bn̩]

3. ['sr̩tsr̩tsr̩t'sr̩t 'sr̩tsr̩t sr̩t sr̩t 'sr̩t 'sr̩tsr̩tsr̩t]

4. [m̩bɑ'bɑ 'm̩bɑm̩bɑm̩ 'm̩ 'm̩ bɑ'm̩ m̩ m̩ 'm̩m̩m̩bɑ 'bɑ]

RE 12.20. Reading

To help you associate the symbols and the glide sounds you have learned to produce, listen to the correct form on tape after you have read it. Practice aloud and with another student if possible. Be prepared for class dictation.

1. [sow'so]
2. [soH'so]
3. [soy'so]
4. [sɑy'sɑ]
5. [sɑ'sɑy]
6. [sɑy'sɑH]
7. [sɑH'sɑy]
8. [sɑy'sɑw]
9. [sɑw'sɑ]
10. [sɑw'sɑy]
11. [so'soH]
12. [so'soy]
13. [sow'sow]
14. [sɛy'sɛy]
15. [sɛ'sɛ]
16. [sɛw'sɛ]
17. [sɛ'sɛw]
18. [sɛH'sɛy]
19. [sɛH'sɑH]
20. [sɑw'sɛH]

LESSON THIRTEEN

Nasals

	Bilabial	Dental	Alveolar	Alveopalatal	Retroflexed	Velar
Nasals						
Voiced	m	n̪	n	ñ	ṇ	ŋ
Voiceless	M	(N̪)[1]	N	Ñ	(Ṇ)	Ŋ

The nasal manner of articulation was explained in Lesson 1 (p. 16). It consists of a closure in the oral cavity, and an open velic to allow the air stream to come out through the nose. We need now to learn to produce some nasals in positions where they do not occur in English, and to learn some new nasals which do not normally occur in English.

Names of new symbols in this lesson are [~] "tilde" /ˈtɩldʌ/, [ñ] "enya" /ˈɛnyɑ/, [ŋ] "eng" /ɛŋ/ or "velar n", [n̪ ṇ] "dental n", "retroflexed n", [M] "capital m", etc.

[ŋ] in Initial Position

You are already familiar with [ŋ] in final position and some medial positions in such English words as sing [sɩŋ], singer [ˈsɩŋ.r̩], and finger [ˈfɩŋ.gr̩] (see Appendix). We now introduce it in initial position, where it also occurs in many languages.

RE 13.1. Negative Practice: Learning to Make Initial [ŋ]

Mimic the stress, timing, and length as demonstrated on the tape, to help you get the rhythm, and you will find yourself making initial [ŋ] with no difficulty. Follow the transcription.

1. Start by saying singing•ing•ing•ing [ˈsɩŋɩŋ•ˈɩŋ•ˈɩŋ•ˈɩŋ]

2. Change the stress placement: [sɩŋɩˈŋ•ɩˈŋ•ɩˈŋ•ɩ]

3. Then change to: [ˈŋɩˈŋɩˈŋɩˈŋɩ]

---

[1]The voiceless dental nasal and voiceless retroflexed nasal articulations in parentheses are perfectly possible, but we will not drill them in this course.

4. [ˈŋɛˈŋɛˈŋɛˈŋɛ]

5. [ˈŋoˈŋoˈŋoˈŋo]

6. [ˈŋɑˈŋɑˈŋɑˈŋɑ]

RE 13.2. Mimicry: Initial [ŋ]

Follow the transcription as you mimic the tape.

1a. [ˈŋɑ]	1b. [ˈŋɑŋɑ]	1c. [ˈŋɑŋɑŋ]	1d. [ˈŋɑŋ ˈŋɑŋɑŋ]
2a. [ˈŋɛ]	2b. [ˈŋɛŋɛ]	2c. [ˈŋɛŋɛŋ]	2d. [ˈŋɛŋ ˈŋɛŋɛŋ]
3a. [ˈŋo]	3b. [ˈŋoŋo]	3c. [ˈŋoŋoŋ]	3d. [ˈŋoŋ ˈŋoŋoŋ]

RE 13.3. Differential: STOP, NASAL, or BOTH

Say the following words to yourself, and analyze the medial consonants: bigger [ˈbɩgr̩], singer [ˈsɩŋr̩], finger [ˈfɩŋ.gr̩]. Note that they have [g] STOP, [ŋ] NASAL, and [ŋg] BOTH, respectively. In the following exercise respond to the tape with one of these labels according to what you hear. Don't peek.

1. [ɑgɑ]	S	6. [oŋo]	N	11. [ɑgɑ]	S
2. [ɑŋɑ]	N	7. [ɛŋɛ]	N	12. [ɛgɛ]	S
3. [ɑŋgɑ]	B	8. [ɑŋɑ]	N	13. [oŋgo]	B
4. [ɑŋgɑ]	B	9. [ɛgɛ]	S	14. [ɛŋgɛ]	B
5. [ɑgɑ]	S	10. [ɛŋgɛ]	B	15. [oŋo]	N

Now go back and practice in mimicry of the tape.

Production of [ñ]

Be sure your tongue tip is down behind your lower teeth. Hold it there with the tip of your finger. Articulate with your blade where it naturally touches the alveopalatal region.

In many, if not most, languages where [ñ] occurs it has a [y] automatically associated with it, making an on-glide into a following vowel or an off-glide from a preceding one. In such languages the [y] helps to distinguish [ñ] from [n]. Other languages have no such off-glide. In this course, however, (except for the following exercise) [ñ] will always be accompanied with a slight [y] glide which will not be transcribed, but will be considered a feature of the [ñ]. The glide movement

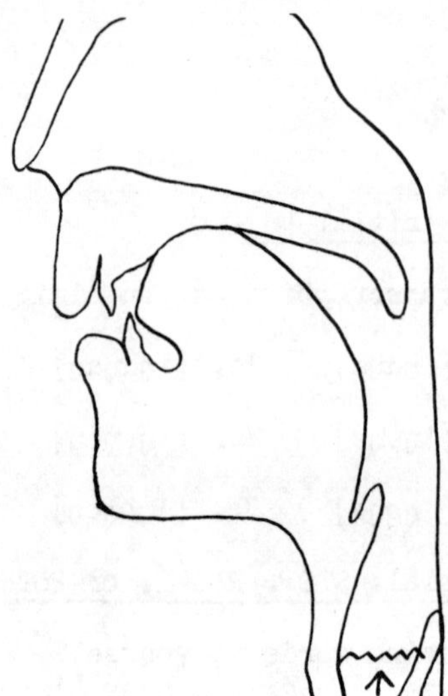

Sammy 13.1: [ñ]

of [y] comes very close to [ñ] articulation.

RE 13.4. Demonstration: [ñ] With and Without [y] Glides

Listen and mimic to hear and feel the presence and absence of the [y] glide. Follow the transcription.

Without Glide	Following Glide	Preceding Glide
1a. [ɑñɑ]	1b. [ɑñyɑ]	1c. [ɑyñɑ]
2a. [ɛñɛ]	2b. [ɛñyɛ]	2c. [ɛyñɛ]
3a. [oño]	3b. [oñyo]	3c. [oyño]

RE 13.5. Mimicry: [ñ]

Be very careful to see that your tongue tip stays behind your lower teeth. If necessary, place the tip of your finger lightly at the edge of your lower teeth to hold your tongue down. Follow the transcription.

1a. [ˈñɑ]	1b. [ˈñɑñɑ]	1c. [ˈñɑñɑñ]	1d. [ˈñɑñ ˈñɑñɑñ]
2a. [ˈñɛ]	2b. [ˈñɛñɛ]	2c. [ˈñɛñɛñ]	2d. [ˈñɛñ ˈñɛñɛñ]
3a. [ˈño]	3b. [ˈñoño]	3c. [ˈñoñoñ]	3d. [ˈñoñ ˈñoñoñ]

Production of [ṋ ṇ]

[ṋ ṇ] do not present any new articulation problem, but simply the control of dental and retroflexed articulations learned in Lesson 11, and their correlation with nasal manner of articulation. Some speakers of English will feel the articulation of [ṋ] in *ten things* [ˌt^{h}ɛṋˈθɪŋz]. Some, but not as many, will feel the articulation of [ṇ] in *door knob* [ˈdoHrṇɑ·b].

You will need to learn to make both these articulations, and to hear [ṇ]. As with [ṱ ḓ], however, you may learn to recognize [ṋ] more by seeing the tongue at the teeth than by its acoustic difference from [n].

RE 13.6. Mimicry: [ṋ ṇ]

Keep the proper articulation on the following items whether you hear the dental articulation or not. Follow the transcription.

1a. [ˈṋɑ] 1b. [ˈṋɑṋɑ] 1c. [ˈṋɑṋɑṋ] 1d. [ˈṋɑṋ ˈṋɑṋɑṋ]

2a. [ˈṇɑ] 2b. [ˈṇɑṇɑ] 2c. [ˈṇɑṇɑṇ] 2d. [ˈṇɑṇ ˈṇɑṇɑṇ]

3a. [ˈṋɛ] 3b. [ˈṋɛṋɛ] 3c. [ˈṋɛṋɛṋ] 3d. [ˈṋɛṋ ˈṋɛṋɛṋ]

4a. [ˈṇɛ] 4b. [ˈṇɛṇɛ] 4c. [ˈṇɛṇɛṇ] 4d. [ˈṇɛṇ ˈṇɛṇɛṇ]

5a. [ˈṋo] 5b. [ˈṋoṋo] 5c. [ˈṋoṋoṋ] 5d. [ˈṋoṋ ˈṋoṋoṋ]

6a. [ˈṇo] 6b. [ˈṇoṇo] 6c. [ˈṇoṇoṇ] 6d. [ˈṇoṇ ˈṇoṇoṇ]

RE 13.7. Negative Practice: [ṋ ñ ny ṇ ŋ]

In the following sentences the English /n/'s will be replaced with various kinds of nasals just drilled. [ny] will also be practiced. Remember that [ñ] when it has a following [y] glide, sounds very much like [ny]. The articulator and point of articulation are different. Make the proper articulation for each of the substituted sounds. Practice all of these variations until you can say them fluently. *Follow the transcription.*

1. Nyæ, nyæ, nyæ said the little fox.

   1a. ṋæ ṋæ ṋæ said the little fox

   1b. ñæ ñæ ñæ said the little fox

1c. nyæ nyæ nyæ said the little fox

1d. ṇæ ṇæ ṇæ said the little fox

1e. ŋæ ŋæ ŋæ said the little fox

2. Ned never knew Nancy's new number.

2a. ṋed ṋever ṋew ṋancy's ṋew ṋumber

2b. ñed ñever ñew ñancy's ñew ñumber

2c. nyed nyever nyew nyancy's nyew nyumber

2d. ṇed ṇever ṇew ṇancy's ṇew ṇumber

2e. ŋed ŋever ŋew ŋancy's ŋew ŋumber

3. Ten thin men man one gun.

3a. teṋ thiṋ meṋ maṋ oṋe guṋ

3b. teñ thiñ meñ mañ oñe guñ

3c. teṇ thin̥ meṇ maṇ oṇe guṇ

3d. teŋ thiŋ meŋ maŋ oŋe guŋ

RE 13.8. Differential: ALVEOPALATAL, RETROFLEXED, VELAR

Don't peek!

1.	[oño]	A	6.	[ɛŋɛ]	V	11.	[oŋo]	V
2.	[oṇo]	R	7.	[ɛñɛ]	A	12.	[ɛṇɛ]	R
3.	[oŋo]	V	8.	[ɛñɛ]	A	13.	[αñα]	A
4.	[oṇo]	R	9.	[αŋα]	V	14.	[ɛṇɛ]	R
5.	[ɛṇɛ]	R	10.	[αṇα]	R	15.	[αŋα]	V

Voiceless Nasals

You can produce any voiceless nasal by articulating for a voiced one, and simply blowing. Voiceless nasals often occur adjacent to voiced nasals of the same articulation, and in our drills we will follow this practice as it makes the voiceless nasals easier to identify. You should be prepared, however, to find such voiceless nasals without contiguous voiced nasals in languages you may study.

RE 13.9. Demonstration: English Exclamations with [M]

Listen, and mimic the tape on the following exclamations which have [M]. Get the feeling of the articulation of the voiceless nasal.

1. hm! [Mm̩] 2. hm-m [Mm̩ʔm̩] 3. mhm [ʔm̩Mm̩]

RE 13.10. Negative Practice: [N N͂ Ŋ M]

Mimic the tape, and follow the transcription.

1. Ned never knew Nancy's new number.

1a. Nned Nnever Nnew Nnancy's Nnew Nnumber

1b. N͂ñed N͂ñever N͂ñew N͂ñancy's N͂ñew N͂ñumber

1c. Ŋŋed Ŋŋever Ŋŋew Ŋŋancy's Ŋŋew Ŋŋumber

2. Ten thin men man one gun

2a. tenN thinN menN manN onNe gunN

2b. teñN͂ thiñN͂ meñN͂ mañN͂ oñN͂e guñN͂

2c. teŋŊ thiŋŊ meŋŊ maŋŊ oŋŊe guŋŊ

3. Mother, make me much more mush.

3a. Mmother Mmake Mme Mmuch Mmore Mmush

RE 13.11. Mimicry: Voiceless Nasals

Mimic the tape, and follow the transcription.

1a. ['Mmo] 1b. [ʔo'Mmo] 1c. [ʔom'Mmo] 1d. [ʔomM]

2a. ['Nno] 2b. [ʔo'Nno] 2c. [ʔon'Nno] 2d. [ʔonN]

3a. ['N͂ño] 3b. [ʔo'N͂ño] 3c. [ʔoñ'N͂ño] 3d. [ʔoñN͂]

4a. ['Ŋŋo] 4b. [ʔo'Ŋŋo] 4c. [ʔoŋ'Ŋŋo] 4d. [ʔoŋŊ]

RE 13.12. Buildup and Substitution

Mimic the tape. The frame remains constant, with one

syllable changing for each utterance. There is a buildup on the first one because the sequence is long and the combinations require practice. Work on them until you get them fluently. Follow the transcription.

1.	[gomMˈñɛw sɑtʰɑˈṇoñÑ]	6.	[gomMˈẓ̌ɛw sɑtʰɑˈṇonN]
2.	ˈtʰɑŋ	7.	ˈŊŋo
3.	ˈŋoz	8.	ˈḍɑṇɑ
4.	ˈnɛnN	9.	ˈṋɛs̭o
5.	ˈtsɑñ	10.	ˈxɛŋŊ

RE 13.13: Khmuʔ[1]. Mimicry: Voiced Nasals

Mimic the tape and follow the transcription.

1a. /naa/ 'she'	1b. /ñaak/ 'poor'	1c. /ŋaa/ 'tusk'
2a. /naay/ 'that'	2b. /ñaam/ 'time when'	2c. /ŋaam/ 'part of a plow'
3a. /naaŋ/ 'Miss'	3b. /ñaaŋ/ 'crawl'	3c. /ŋaak/ 'nursing'
4a. /nɛɛw/ 'kind'		4c. /ŋɛɛp/ 'roof overhang'

RE 13.14: Khmuʔ. Mimicry: Voiceless Nasals

Mimic the tape and follow the transcription.

	1b. [Nna·y] 'there'	1d. [Ŋŋa·p] 'yawn'
2a. [Mman] 'hold'	2b. [Nnam] 'be large'	2d. [Ŋŋat] 'recede'
3a. [Mmɔ·ŋ] 'sad'	3b. [Nnɔ·ŋ] 'be remaining'	

---

[1]Khmuʔ is a mountain minority language spoken in northern Laos. Data from William A. Smalley, Outline of Khmuʔ Structure.

4a. [Mmu•c] 'ant'   4c. [N̄nip] 'grab, grasp'   4d. [Nŋε•k] 'hornbill'

RE 13.15: Khmu?. Final [ñ]

Mimic the tape and follow the transcription.

1. [ma•ñ] 'ask'   3. [ta•ñ] 'weave'   5. [piñ] 'shoot'

2. [ba•ñ] 'be drunk'   4. [gu•ñ] 'see'   6. [kiñ] 'full'

RE 13.16: Black Bobo[1]. Mimicry: Nasals with Tone

Mimic the tape and follow the transcription. Note the syllabic nasals, and the tones on them.

1. [gŋ] 'oven'   6. [n] 'grease'

2. [gŋ] 'yesterday'   7. [n] 'head'

3. [gŋ] 'black'   8. [n] 'sleep'

4. [kŋ] 'skin'   9. [Nn] 'sun'

5. [ñ] 'odor'   10. [Nn] 'man'

RE 13.17. Review Buildups: General

1. [θα.ddyε'po.mαŋ.'α.ɲo]   4. [dα.čε'thon.tšεŋ'džow.Nnα]

2. [gwαx.?α'fα.ñεg.'ppoŋN]   5. [psho.kε'ǰαŋ.ñom 'n.Nnε?]

3. [tsε.pom'pwα m'bo.N̄ñε.doz]   6. [phαd.syεx'bočh.žεŋ.sεm.ton.'Mmε]

---

[1]Black Bobo is spoken in Mali, West Africa. Data obtained with the help of Rev. Grant Crooks. Recording simulated from notes.

RE 13.18. Review: [x ǥ ŋ]

By now you should be getting the velar fricatives. Practice the following utterances repeatedly. Mimic the tape and follow the transcription.

1. [ǥɛŋ'xoŋɑ]
2. ['ŋɑǥoǥɛx]
3. [xɛ'ŋæŋɛŋo]
4. [ǥɛǥo'ǥæxæŋ]
5. [ŋɛŋ'xɑǥ.ŋoŋ.xɑ]
6. [xɛx'xæxoŋ.ǥoxo]

RE 13.19. Transcription

Transcribe the utterances on the tape. When you are satisfied with your transcription, check it with the transcription below. Until then, don't peek!

1. [Nnɛm]
2. [ŋæmM]
3. [ṭṣ̌o'ṇḁn]
4. [ñɛ'Mmæŋ]
5. [ṣ̌ɛ'ñɛñ]
6. [θɑs̭ɑ'Ŋŋoǥ]
7. [čɛʔoǥ'k^{h}oʔ]
8. [moŋ.Ŋŋɛƀ.'t^{h}ɑʔ]
9. [ᵽæx.'ẓ̌ɛmM.ṇæḍ]
10. [ǰok^h.ƀa͠n.'gɛñ]

RE 13.20. Reading

Read off each of the following items, and listen to the correct reading on the tape. Go through the exercise several times if necessary.

1. ['mæŋɛ]
2. ['Nnɛño]
3. ['xɛṇɑ]
4. [s̭o'Mmɛ]
5. [pᵽɛs̭'t^{h}æŋ]
6. [ḍẓ̌o'ṭṣ̌ɛṇ]
7. ['Ŋŋɛf.tsɑ]
8. [mok^h'N͠ñɛᵽ]
9. [Mmæŋ'k^{h}oŋŊ]
10. [ñɑǥ'tsɛŋŊ]

LESSON FOURTEEN

Some Back and Central Vowels

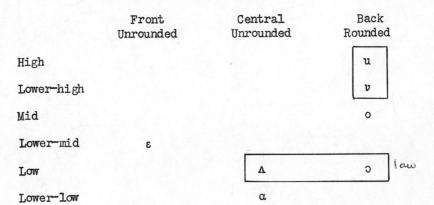

	Front Unrounded	Central Unrounded	Back Rounded
High			u
Lower-high			ʊ
Mid			o
Lower-mid	ɛ		
Low		ʌ	ɔ
Lower-low		ɑ	

Table 14.1: Vowels to Date

The names of the new vowel symbols on this chart (those enclosed in boxes) are [ʌ] "caret" or "upside-down v", [ʊ] "upsilon" (from Greek), and [ɔ] "open o" or "backwards c".

In Lesson 12 we discussed vowel qualities in terms of three levels (high, mid, and low) as well as three regions from front to back. Three levels were enough for our purposes at that time, but now that we need to introduce more vowel qualities we have further subdivided the levels as you can see in the chart.[1]

Do not let this chart, and the careful drilling which you will be doing give you a false sense of absolute precision on these vowel qualities and positions we chart for them. You will be working toward enormously increased control over vowel articulation, but even so you should think of the areas of the vowel chart and the positions of the various symbols as "target areas." In actual languages there is a considerable variation in the pronunciation of a single vowel phoneme, the various pronunciations clustering in an area of the chart, giving a scatter-shot effect. In this course we will be working toward

---

[1] This system of labels is modified from H. A. Gleason, An Introduction to Descriptive Linguistics, p. 203. Many phoneticians use the terms high close, high open, mid close, mid open, low close, low open.

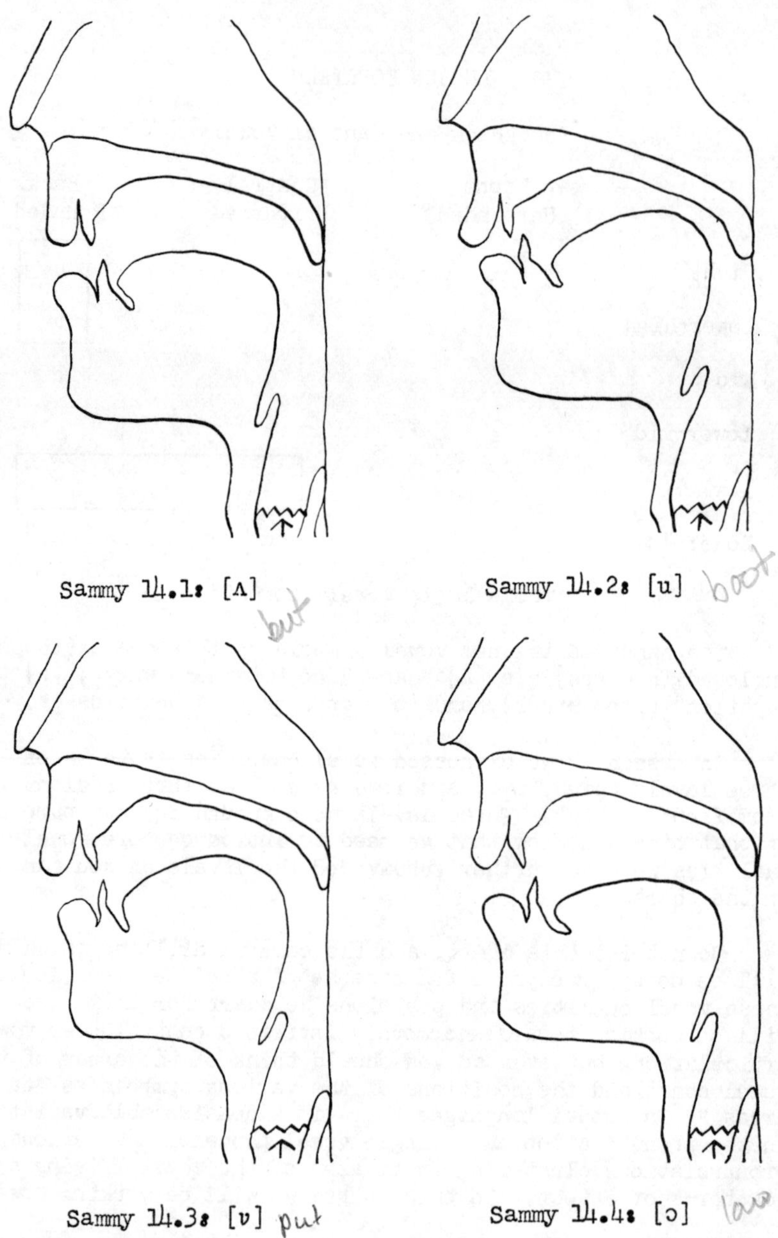

Sammy 14.1: [ʌ]

Sammy 14.2: [u]

Sammy 14.3: [ʊ]

Sammy 14.4: [ɔ]

greater control, so that you can discriminate and produce sounds in more of the areas of the chart than you have been able to do at will before. In order to do this we set up a kind of phonetic norm for each vowel we teach. Equally important is to learn to vary away from this "norm" at will in any direction to mimic any variation you hear.

Remember that these "target area" qualities are also selected from an infinite number of possibilities. Listen to the different qualities created by the "slur" in RE 14.1, Nos. 4-5.

If you still have any problems about the principles of vowel formation, study Sammies 14.1-14.4 in relation to the above chart.

RE 14.1. Demonstration: Vowel Qualities in Table 14.1

Listen to the exercise through several times, and mimic. Follow along in your text, and by watching Table 14.1. Be careful to try to eliminate all glides. You will have more work on that in a later exercise. The "slurs" in Nos. 4 and 5 demonstrate that the vowels you are now drilling are only selected points out of a continuum.

1. [ɛ ʌ ɑ ɔ o ʊ u]
2. [ʔu ʔʊ ʔo ʔɔ ʔɑ ʔʌ ʔɛ]
3. [sɔ so sʊ su sɑ sʌ sɛ]
4. slur from [u] to [ɔ]
5. slur from [ɑ] to [u]
6. [mɑ mʌ mɔ mɔ mɑ mʌ]
7. [du dʊ do do dʊ du]
8. [xɛ xʌ xɑ xɔ xo xʊ xu]

Learning [u] and [ʊ]

Now you will have special practice in hearing and producing the high and lower-high back rounded vowels. Do not be deceived by any similarity to vowels in your English speech. Mimic what you hear on the tape, and learn to control both the quality and the tendency to glide.

RE 14.2. Discrimination: SAME or DIFFERENT

Listen to the paired words, and answer SAME or DIFFERENT. After you have completed the exercise, listen again and mimic. Column a will pair the vowels [u o], Column b [u ʊ], and Column c [ʊ o]. Don't peek!

1a. [gom gum] D
2a. [gom gom] S
3a. [gum gum] S
4a. [gum gom] D
5a. [gom gum] D
6a. ['mugi 'mogi] D
7a. ['mugi 'mugi] S
8a. ['mogi 'mugi] D
9a. ['mogi 'mogi] S
10a. ['mugi 'mogi] D

1b.	[wʊf wuf] D		1c.	[los lʊs] D
2b.	[wʊf wuf] D		2c.	[lʊs los] D
3b.	[wʊf wʊf] S		3c.	[lʊs lʊs] S
4b.	[wuf wʊf] D		4c.	[lʊs los] D
5b.	[wʊf wuf] D		5c.	[los los] S
6b.	[wuf wuf] S		6c.	['sola 'sʊla] D
7b.	[wuf wuf] S		7c.	['sola 'sola] S
8b.	[wʊf wʊf] S		8c.	['sʊla 'sola] D
9b.	[wuf wʊf] D		9c.	['sʊla 'sʊla] S
10b.	[wʊf wʊf] S		10c.	['sola 'sola] S

In producing [u] you must be very careful not to make a glided sound. [u] is deceptively similar to the way many of us pronounce boot (actually often pronounced more like [bɨwt]). [u] must be unglided, with the tongue high in back and the lips closely rounded.

To produce [ʊ] lower the back of the tongue slightly from [u] and lessen the rounding slightly. Or, raise the back of the tongue slightly from [o] and increase the rounding slightly.

RE 14.3. Mimicry: [u ʊ o]

In the following exercise mimic the tape and watch in a mirror to see that you do not get a [w] glide. On all of these sounds experiment with the position of the back of your tongue to get the same quality you hear on the tape. Work with your buddy so that he can tell you when you don't sound like the tape. Watch the transcription.

1a. [butʰ]	1b. [bʊtʰ]	1c. [botʰ]
2a. [kupʰ]	2b. [kʊtʰ]	2c. [kotʰ]
3a. [sum]	3b. [sʊm]	3c. [som]
4a. [šuz]	4b. [šʊz]	4c. [šoz]
5a. [xuf]	5b. [xʊf]	5c. [xof]
6a. ['gudfɛn]	6b. ['gʊdfɛn]	6c. ['godfɛn]

7a. ['gudfɑn]	7b. ['gʋdfɑn]	7c. ['godfɑn]
8a. ['gudfon]	8b. ['gʋdfon]	8c. ['godfon]
9a. ['gudfʋn]	9b. ['gʋdfʋn]	9c. ['godfʋn]
10a. ['gudfun]	10b. ['gʋdfun]	10c. ['godfun]

RE 14.4. Negative Practice: "This Is the House that Jack Built"

Recite the following verse, substituting first [u], then [ʋ], then [o] in the underlined words. A transcription is given you at the side for the words to be changed. Do the whole verse through with one vowel before going on to another. The tape will demonstrate how each set starts, but will not provide mimicry material for the full drill. Be especially careful to avoid slipping into English sounds. Keep the distinct qualities on which we are working for each of the substituted sounds.

	a	b	c
This is the House that Jack built.	[hus]	[hʋs]	[hos]
This is the Malt	[mult]	[mʋlt]	[molt]
That lay in the House that Jack built.	[hus]	[hʋs]	[hos]
This is the Rat	[rut]	[rʋt]	[rot]
That ate the Malt	[mult]	[mʋlt]	[molt]
That lay in the House that Jack built.	[hus]	[hʋs]	[hos]
This is the Cat	[k^hut]	[k^hʋt]	[k^hot]
That killed the Rat	[rut]	[rʋt]	[rot]
That ate the Malt	[mult]	[mʋlt]	[molt]
That lay in the House that Jack built.	[hus]	[hʋs]	[hos]
This is the Dog	[dug]	[dʋg]	[dog]
That worried the Cat	[k^hut]	[k^hʋt]	[k^hot]
That killed the Rat	[rut]	[rʋt]	[rot]

	a	b	c
That ate the Malt	[mult]	[mɒlt]	[molt]
That lay in the House that Jack built.	[hus]	[hɒs]	[hos]
This is the Cow with the crumpled horn	[k^huw]	[k^hɒw]	[k^how]
That tossed the Dog	[dug]	[dɒg]	[dog]
That worried the Cat	[k^hut]	[k^hɒt]	[k^hot]
That killed the Rat	[rut]	[rɒt]	[rot]
That ate the Malt	[mult]	[mɒlt]	[molt]
That lay in the House that Jack built.	[hus]	[hɒs]	[hos]
This is the Maiden all forlorn	['mudn̩]	['mɒdn̩]	['modn̩]
That milked the Cow with the crumpled horn	[k^huw]	[k^hɒw]	[k^how]
That tossed the Dog	[dug]	[dɒg]	[dog]
That worried the Cat	[k^hut]	[k^hɒt]	[k^hot]
That killed the Rat	[rut]	[rɒt]	[rot]
That ate the Malt	[mult]	[mɒlt]	[molt]
That lay in the House that Jack built.	[hus]	[hɒs]	[hos]
This is the Man all tattered and torn	[mun]	[mɒn]	[mon]
That kissed the Maiden all forlorn	['mudn̩]	['mɒdn̩]	['modn̩]
That milked the Cow with the crumpled horn	[k^huw]	[k^hɒw]	[k^how]
That tossed the Dog	[dug]	[dɒg]	[dog]
That worried the Cat	[k^hut]	[k^hɒt]	[k^hot]

	a	b	c
That killed the Rat	[rut]	[rɒt]	[rot]
That ate the Malt	[mult]	[mɒlt]	[molt]
That lay in the House that Jack built.	[hus]	[hɒs]	[hos]
This is the Priest, all shaven and shorn	[p^{h}rust]	[p^{h}rɒst]	[p^{h}rost]
That married the Man all tattered and torn	[mun]	[mɒn]	[mon]
That kissed the Maiden all forlorn	[ˈmudn̩]	[ˈmɒdn̩]	[ˈmodn̩]
That milked the Cow with the crumpled horn,	[k^{h}uw]	[k^{h}ɒw]	[k^{h}ow]
That tossed the Dog	[dug]	[dɒg]	[dog]
That worried the Cat	[k^{h}ut]	[k^{h}ɒt]	[k^{h}ot]
That killed the Rat	[rut]	[rɒt]	[rot]
That ate the Malt	[mult]	[mɒlt]	[molt]
That lay in the House that Jack built.	[hus]	[hɒs]	[hos]
This is the Cock that crowed in the morn	[k^{h}uk]	[k^{h}ɒk]	[k^{h}ok]
That waked the Priest all shaven and shorn	[p^{h}rust]	[p^{h}rɒst]	[p^{h}rost]
That married the Man all tattered and torn	[mun]	[mɒn]	[mon]
That kissed the Maiden all forlorn	[ˈmudn̩]	[ˈmɒdn̩]	[ˈmodn̩]
That milked the Cow with the crumpled horn	[k^{h}uw]	[k^{h}ɒw]	[k^{h}ow]
That tossed the Dog	[dug]	[dɒg]	[dog]
That worried the Cat	[k^{h}ut]	[k^{h}ɒt]	[k^{h}ot]

	a	b	c
That killed the Rat	[rut]	[rʋt]	[rot]
That ate the Malt	[mult]	[mʋlt]	[molt]
That lay in the House that Jack built.	[hus]	[hʋs]	[hos]
This is the Farmer who sowed the corn	[ˈfumr̩]	[ˈfʋmr̩]	[ˈfomr̩]
That fed the Cock that crowed in the morn	[k^huk]	[k^hʋk]	[k^hok]
That waked the Priest all shaven and shorn	[p^hrust]	[p^hrʋst]	[p^hrost]
That married the Man all tattered and torn	[mun]	[mʋn]	[mon]
That kissed the Maiden all forlorn	[ˈmudn̩]	[ˈmʋdn̩]	[ˈmodn̩]
That milked the Cow with the crumpled horn	[k^huw]	[k^hʋw]	[k^how]
That tossed the Dog	[dug]	[dʋg]	[dog]
That worried the Cat	[k^hut]	[k^hʋt]	[k^hot]
That killed the Rat	[rut]	[rʋt]	[rot]
That ate the Malt	[mult]	[mʋlt]	[molt]
That lay in the House that Jack built.	[hus]	[hʋs]	[hos]

Learning [ɔ] and [ʌ]

To produce [ɔ] the back of the tongue is lowered from [o], and the rounding is lessened. Be careful not to get an [H] glide. Some speakers of English will tend to confuse [ɔ] and [ɑ]. They should work especially hard on these drills.

To produce [ʌ] the center of the tongue is raised from [ɑ] very slightly.

RE 14.5. Discrimination: SAME or DIFFERENT

1a.	[ˈsofɑ ˈsofʌ]	D	1b.	[fɔt^h fɑt^h]	D
2a.	[ˈsofʌ ˈsofʌ]	S	2b.	[fɑt^h fɑt^h]	S
3a.	[ˈsofʌ ˈsofɑ]	D	3b.	[fɑt^h fɔt^h]	D
4a.	[ˈsofɑ ˈsofʌ]	D	4b.	[fɔt^h fɑt^h]	D
5a.	[ˈsofɑ ˈsofɑ]	S	5b.	[fɔt^h fɔt^h]	S
6a.	[ˈsofʌ ˈsofɑ]	D	6b.	[fɑt^h fɑt^h]	S
7a.	[ˈsofɑnɛ ˈsofʌnɛ]	D	7b.	[nuˈfɑt^h nuˈfɔt^h]	D
8a.	[ˈsofɑnɛ ˈsofɑnɛ]	S	8b.	[nuˈfɑt^h nuˈfɑt^h]	S
9a.	[ˈsofʌnɛ ˈsofɑnɛ]	D	9b.	[nuˈfɔt^h nuˈfɔt^h]	S
10a.	[ˈsofʌnɛ ˈsofʌnɛ]	S	10b.	[nuˈfɔt^h nuˈfɑt^h]	D

1c.	[hos hɔs]	D	6c.	[hos hos]	S
2c.	[hos hos]	S	7c.	[ˈhosmon ˈhɔsmon]	D
3c.	[hɔs hos]	D	8c.	[ˈhosmon ˈhɔsmon]	D
4c.	[hɔs hɔs]	S	9c.	[ˈhosmon ˈhosmon]	S
5c.	[hɔs hos]	D	10c.	[ˈhɔsmon ˈhɔsmon]	S

RE 14.6. Mimicry: [ɔ o ɑ ʌ]

Mimic carefully, striving for the same pronunciation as that which you hear on the tape. Get your buddy to listen to you and help you compare.

1a. [bɔt^h]	1b. [bot^h]	1c. [bʌt^h]	1d. [bɑt^h]
2a. [kɔt^h]	2b. [kot^h]	2c. [kʌt^h]	2d. [kɑt^h]
3a. [sɔm]	3b. [som]	3c. [sʌm]	3d. [sɑm]
4a. [šɔz]	4b. [šoz]	4c. [šʌz]	4d. [šɑz]
5a. [xɔf]	5b. [xof]	5c. [xʌf]	5d. [xɑf]
6a. [ˈzɔglɛn]	6b. [ˈzoglɛn]	6c. [ˈzʌglɛn]	6d. [ˈzɑglɛn]

7a. [ˈzɔglɑn]	7b. [ˈzoglɑn]	7c. [ˈzʌglɑn]	7d. [ˈzɑglɑn]
8a. [ˈzɔglon]	8b. [ˈzoglon]	8c. [ˈzʌglon]	8d. [ˈzɑglon]
9a. [ˈzɔglɒn]	9b. [ˈzoglɒn]	9c. [ˈzʌglɒn]	9d. [ˈzɑglɒn]
10a. [ˈzɔglun]	10b. [ˈzoglun]	10c. [ˈzʌglun]	10d. [ˈzɑglun]

RE 14.7. Negative Practice: "This Is the House that Jack Built"

Refer to the text of RE 14.4, if you need to. The sounds to be substituted are indicated in the columns below. The tape will start you off for each one.

	a	b	c
House	[hɔs]	[hɑs]	[hʌs]
Malt	[mɔlt^{h}]	[mɑlt^{h}]	[mʌlt^{h}]
Rat	[rɔt^{h}]	[rɑt^{h}]	[rʌt^{h}]
Cat	[k^{h}ɔt]	[k^{h}ɑt]	[k^{h}ʌt]
Dog	[dɔg]	[dɑg]	[dʌg]
Cow	[k^{h}ɔw]	[k^{h}ɑw]	[k^{h}ʌw]
Maiden	[ˈmɔdn̩]	[ˈmɑdn̩]	[ˈmʌdn̩]
Man	[mɔn]	[mɑn]	[mʌn]
Priest	[p^{h}rɔst^{h}]	[p^{h}rɑst^{h}]	[p^{h}rʌst^{h}]
Cock	[k^{h}ɔk^{h}]	[k^{h}ɑk^{h}]	[k^{h}ʌk^{h}]
Farmer	[ˈfɔmr̩]	[ˈfɑmr̩]	[ˈfʌmr̩]

RE 14.8. Differential: ROUNDED vs. UNROUNDED

Turn to Table 14.1, p. 201, and watch it as you go through this drill or part of it. When you no longer need it, cover it up and continue the drill, or do the drill again. Listen to the vowel sound on the tape, and respond with ROUNDED or UNROUNDED. Do not watch the text of the exercise. A demonstration of the qualities on the chart down the columns from left to right will precede the drill. This is to "tune you up" to the distinctions again.

Demonstration: [ʔɛ ʔʌ ʔɑ ʔu ʔʋ ʔo ʔɔ]

[k^{h}ɛm k^{h}ʌm k^{h}ɑm k^{h}um k^{h}ʋm k^{h}om k^{h}ɔm]

1. [ʔu] R
2. [ʔɑ] U
3. [ʔo] R
4. [ʔʋ] R
5. [ʔɔ] R
6. [ʔɛ] U
7. [k^{h}ʌm] U
8. [k^{h}ɑm] U
9. [k^{h}ʋm] R
10. [k^{h}om] R
11. [k^{h}um] R
12. [k^{h}ɔm] R
13. [žʌg] U
14. [žug] R
15. [žɑg] U
16. [žɛg] U
17. [žog] R
18. [žʋg] R

RE 14.9. Differential: FRONT UNROUNDED, CENTRAL UNROUNDED, or BACK ROUNDED

Follow the same instructions as for the preceding exercise, except for the enlarged response.

1. [ʔɛ] F U
2. [ʔɔ] B R
3. [ʔu] B R
4. [ʔo] B R
5. [ʔʋ] B R
6. [ʔʌ] C U
7. [tsɑf] C U
8. [tsʋf] B R
9. [tsʌf] C U
10. [tsɛf] F U
11. [tsɔf] B R
12. [tsuf] B R
13. [ḍẓ̌uṇ] B R
14. [ḍẓ̌oṇ] B R
15. [ḍẓ̌ɑṇ] C U
16. [ḍẓ̌ʌṇ] C U
17. [ḍẓ̌ɔṇ] B R
18. [ḍẓ̌ʋṇ] B R

RE 14.10. Differential: Tongue Height

Respond with one of the following: HIGH, LOWER-HIGH, MID, LOWER-MID, LOW, LOWER-LOW.

1. [ʔu] H
2. [ʔʌ] L
3. [ʔɔ] L
4. [ʔɛ] L-M
5. [ʔɑ] L-L
6. [ʔʋ] L-H
7. [ṣ̌uŋ] H
8. [ṣ̌oŋ] M
9. [ṣ̌ɔŋ] L
10. [ṣ̌ʌŋ] L
11. [ṣ̌ɑŋ] L-L
12. [ṣ̌ʋŋ] L-H
13. [pɔgz] L
14. [pogz] M
15. [pugz] H
16. [pʋgz] L-H
17. [pɛgz] L-M
18. [pugz] H

RE 14.11. Differential: Full Labels

Select one term from each column to make up your response.

HIGH	FRONT	ROUNDED
LOWER-HIGH	CENTRAL	UNROUNDED
MID	BACK	
LOWER-MID		
LOW		
LOWER-LOW		

1. [ʔɑ] L-L C U
2. [ʔu] H B R
3. [ʔʌ] L C U
4. [ʔo] M B R
5. [ʔɔ] L B R
6. [ʔɛ] L-M F U
7. [ʔʊ] L-H B R
8. [ʔu] H B R
9. [rɛg] L-M F U
10. [rɔg] L B R
11. [rog] M B R
12. [rʌg] L C U
13. [rug] H B R
14. [rog] M B R
15. [rʊg] L-H B R
16. [rɔg] L B R
17. [Mmɔč^h] L B R
18. [Mmuč^h] H B R
19. [Mmɑč^h] L-L C U
20. [Mmʊč^h] L-H B R
21. [Mmɛč^h] M F U
22. [Mmɔč^h] L B R
23. [Mmʌč^h] L C U
24. [Mmʊč^h] L-H B R

Off-glides on the New Vowels

Any of the new vowels in this lesson (and all other vowels) may have any of the four off-glides [w y H r]. We will not drill [w] glide on [u], as the distinction is very close if you have a proper [u].

RE 14.12. Differential: GLIDED or NO

The new vowel sounds occur with off-glides in some words in this exercise. Listen to the tape and respond accordingly. Then listen again and mimic. Don't peek!

1. [sut] NO
2. [sʊt] NO
3. [sʌyt] G
4. [sɔt] NO
5. [surt] G
6. [sʌt] NO
7. [sut] NO
8. [soyt] G
9. [sʊwt] G

10. [suHt] G	17. [sɔt] NO	24. [sʌwt] G
11. [sʌt] NO	18. [surt] G	25. [surt] G
12. [sʌrt] G	19. [sʌt] NO	26. [sʌt] NO
13. [sʊwt] G	20. [sut] NO	27. [sɔt] NO
14. [sʊt] NO	21. [suyt] G	28. [sɔwt] G
15. [sʊHt] G	22. [sɔHt] G	29. [sɔyt] G
16. [sʊyt] G	23. [sʊt] NO	30. [sɔrt] G

RE 14.13. Mimicry: Vowels With and Without Glides

Mimic the tape, and watch the transcription.

1a. [t^{h}u]	1b. [t^{h}uy]		1d. [t^{h}uH]	1e. [t^{h}ur]
2a. [t^{h}ʊ]	2b. [t^{h}ʊy]	2c. [t^{h}ʊw]	2d. [t^{h}ʊH]	2e. [t^{h}ʊr]
3a. [t^{h}o]	3b. [t^{h}oy]	3c. [t^{h}ow]	3d. [t^{h}oH]	3e. [t^{h}or]
4a. [t^{h}ɔ]	4b. [t^{h}ɔy]	4c. [t^{h}ɔw]	4d. [t^{h}ɔH]	4e. [t^{h}ɔr]
5a. [t^{h}ʌ]	5b. [t^{h}ʌy]	5c. [t^{h}ʌw]	5d. [t^{h}ʌH]	5e. [t^{h}ʌr]
6a. [t^{h}ɑ]	6b. [t^{h}ɑy]	6c. [t^{h}ɑw]	6d. [t^{h}ɑH]	6e. [t^{h}ɑr]
7a. [t^{h}ɛ]	7b. [t^{h}ɛy]	7c. [t^{h}ɛw]	7d. [t^{h}ɛH]	7e. [t^{h}ɛr]

RE 14.14. Negative Practice: "This Is the House that Jack Built"

This time substitute various vowels with off-glides like those indicated below. These are not all of the possibilities. You can take others from the preceding exercise. The tape will demonstrate these briefly.

	a	b	c	d
House	[hʊys]	[hows]	[hɔHs]	[hurs]
Malt	[mʊylt^h]	[mowlt^h]	[mɔHlt^h]	[murlt^h]
Rat	[rʊyt^h]	[rowt^h]	[rɔHt^h]	[rurt^h]
Cat	[k^{h}ʊyt^h]	[k^{h}owt^h]	[k^{h}ɔHt^h]	[k^{h}urt^h]
Dog	[dʊyg]	[dowg]	[dɔHg]	[durg]

Cow	[k^{h}ʊy]	[k^{h}ow]	[k^{h}ɔH]	[k^{h}ur]
Maiden	['mʊydn̩]	['mowdn̩]	['mɔHdn̩]	['murdn̩]
Man	[mʊyn]	[mown]	[mɔHn]	[murn]
Priest	[p^{h}rʊyst^h]	[p^{h}rowst^h]	[p^{h}rɔHst^h]	[p^{h}rurst^h]
Cock	[k^{h}ʊyk^h]	[k^{h}owk^h]	[k^{h}ɔHk^h]	[k^{h}urk^h]
Farmer	['fʊymr̩]	['fowmr̩]	['fɔHmr̩]	['furmr̩]

RE 14.15. Differential: MID or LOW

This is a differential drill on [oy] and [ɔy]. Disregard any other vowels or vowel glides in the words. Don't peek!

1. [boy] M
2. [bɔy] L
3. [bɔy] L
4. [boy] M
5. ['k^{h}ɔyn] L
6. ['k^{h}oyn] M
7. ['k^{h}ɔyn] L
8. ['k^{h}ɔyn] L
9. ['foystlɛy] M
10. ['foystlɛy] M
11. ['foystlɛy] M
12. ['fɔystlɛy] L

RE 14.16. Differential: LOW or LOWER-LOW

This is a differential drill on [ʌH] and [ɑH]. Follow the same procedure as in the preceding exercise.

1. [k^{h}ʌHm] L
2. [k^{h}ɑHm] L-L
3. [k^{h}ʌHm] L
4. [k^{h}ɑHm] L-L
5. [sʌH't^{h}u] L
6. [sʌH't^{h}u] L
7. [sɑH't^{h}u] L-L
8. [sʌH't^{h}u] L
9. ['xʌHfɛgz] L
10. ['xɑHfɛgz] L-L
11. ['xɑHfɛgz] L-L
12. ['xɑHfɛgz] L-L

RE 14.17. Differential: LOWER-HIGH and MID

This is a differential drill on [ʊw] and [ow]. Follow the same procedure as in the preceding exercise.

1. [nʊw] L-H
2. [nʊw] L-H
3. [now] M
4. [now] M
5. ['bzʊwk] L-H
6. ['bzowk] M
7. ['bzowk] M
8. ['bzowk] M
9. ['brʊwsNnɑ] L-H
10. ['brʊwsNnɑ] L-H
11. ['browsNnɑ] M
12. ['brʊwsNna] L-H

RE 14.18. Review: Glided Pitch and Glided Vowels

The purpose of this exercise is to reinforce the independence of pitch glides and vowel glides. The exercise consists of longer sequences to which you build up. You will mimic the pitch as well as the consonants and vowels. Note that pure vowels may have rising or falling pitch, and that glided vowels may have level pitch. Watch the transcription as you mimic.

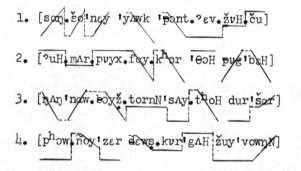

1. [sɑŋ.šø'nɛy 'yʌwk 'pɔnt.ʔɛv.žʊH.ču]

2. [ʔuH.mʌr.pʊyx.fɑy.kʰɔr 'θɔH pʊg'bɛH]

3. [ŋʌŋ'nɑw.bɔyž.tornN'sʌy.tʰoH dur'šɑr]

4. [pʰɔw.nɔy'zɛr dɛws.kʊr'gʌH žuy'vowŋN]

RE 14.19. Review: Pitch and Stress

In most languages, pitch and stress are to some degree related. Stressed syllables often tend to have higher pitch, etc. They are not so closely related, however, but what they do have independent occurrence. In this exercise you will practice changing pitch and stress patterns relative to each other.

1. ['θɑ θɛ θo θu θɔ θʊ]
2. [θɑ θɛ θo 'θu θɔ θʊ]
3. [θɑ 'θɛ θo θu θɔ θʊ]
4. [θɑ θɛ θo θu θɔ 'θʊ]
5. [θɑ θɛ 'θo θu θɔ θʊ]
6. [nɑ nɛ 'no nu nɔ nʊ]
7. [nɑ 'nɛ no nu nɔ nʊ]
8. [nɑ nɛ no nu 'nɔ nʊ]
9. [nɑ nɛ no nu nɔ 'nʊ]
10. ['nɑ nɛ no nu nɔ nʊ]

RE 14.20. Substitution

Mimic the tape in the following utterances. The first one

will be built up, and the remainder will consist of substitutions made in the first one. Practice for fluency. Work on pitch, stress, timing, etc., as well as on consonants and vowels.

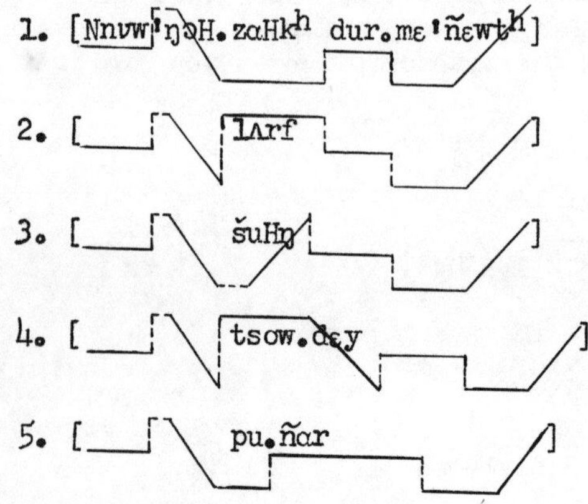

RE 14.21. Transcription

Transcribe the utterances you hear on the tape. When you are satisfied with your transcriptions, check them against the text below. Until then, don't peek!

1. [Mmvŋk]
2. [tšoyf]
3. [gɑwtθ]
4. [pso'dvy]
5. ['žʌwt^hɔnN]
6. ['pɔytsʌpf]
7. [tvH'yɔHŋ]
8. [pšɛ'ksur]
9. ['ñɑyNŋɑwkx]

RE 14.22. Reading

Read off the item and check your reading with the tape in the usual manner.

1. [mʌyn]
2. [duyf]
3. [šoHŋN]
4. [pɔrž]
5. [bɛw'tɛθ]
6. ['m̃uH.guš]
7. ['voy.k^hoz]
8. [t^hɔw'ppɔ]
9. [sɑl'Nnɑrd]
10. ['dɛg.p^hɛHš]
11. [ǰʌx'bʌrč^h]
12. [vož'koHts]

LESSON FIFTEEN

Laterals

	Dental	Alveolar	Alveo-palatal	Retroflexed	Velar
Laterals					
Oral					
Voiced					
High tongue	ḽ˄	l˄	l̃		(l̡)[1]
Low tongue	ḽ˅	l˅		(ḷ)	
Voiceless	(Ḽ)	L	(L̃)	(Ḷ)	(L̡)
Fricative					
Voiced	(ł̭)	ł	(ł̃)	(ł̣)	(ł̡)
Voiceless	(Ł̭)	Ł	(Ł̃)	(Ł̣)	(Ł̡)
Affricate					
Voiced	(ḓł̭)	dł		(ḍł̣)	(gł̡)
Voiceless					
Unaspirated	(ṱŁ̭)	tŁ		(ṭŁ̣)	
	(kŁ̭)	(kŁ)	(kŁ̃)	(kŁ̣)	(kŁ̡)
Aspirated	(ṱŁ̭^{h})	tŁ^h		(ṭŁ̣^{h})	
	(kŁ̭^{h})	(kŁ^h)	(kŁ̃^{h})	(kŁ̣^{h})	(kŁ̡^{h})

Table 15.1: Some Lateral Articulations

The lateral manner of articulation was explained in Lesson 1 (p. 17). It differs from other articulations in that one or both of the sides of the tongue are open to allow the airstream to pass, but some part of the tongue (usually the tip) is touching a point of articulation so that the airstream cannot come over the center of the tongue. Whereas in English there is one lateral phoneme /l/, this has several different

---

[1]Symbols in parentheses represent sounds which are perfectly possible and are included for the sake of the record, but which will not be drilled in this course. Brief descriptions are included in the lesson.

pronunciations in the speech of any one individual, depending on the position in the word. Some languages have more than one kind of lateral in phonemic contrast. Others which have only one lateral phoneme have a different selection of allophones from English. The pronunciation of laterals is one of the principal characteristics of the foreign accent of Americans speaking many languages.

Although the array of symbols in the above chart may look imposing, there is nothing much new by way of symbolization, if analogy with the symbols for nasals (p. 192) is kept in mind. All of the symbols in the chart are built around two basic ones: [l] (for voiced lateral) and [L] "capital l" (for voiceless lateral). The use of the capital is analogous to the symbolization of the voiceless nasals. Around these two symbols are arranged a variety of diacritics exactly analogous to those used for the nasals, to indicate points of articulation: [̪] "dental," [˜] "alveopalatal," [.] "retroflexed," and the tail on the symbol (like the tail on the [ŋ]) for "velar." The line through the symbols to indicate the fricatives is analogous to [đ ǥ].

Actually there are only two really new symbols in this chart. They are the diacritics on [l^ lˇ] "high tongue l" and "low tongue l." The articulatory significance of these will be discussed and drilled below, but for the moment notice the symbolization. The diacritic for the "high tongue l" points high, and that for the "low tongue l" points low. [l^] is sometimes called "clear l," or "light l," and [lˇ] "dark l" or "velarized l" in other linguistic materials.

RE 15.1. Demonstration: High and Low Tongue Laterals

Pronounce these English words, and notice the difference in tongue position for the /l/: William [ˈwɩl^yʌm] and callous [ˈkʰælˇʌs]. Prolong the lateral in each case: [l^· lˇ·], and alternate them. Note that the point of articulation does not necessarily change (although it may change slightly in some speakers), but for many speakers of American English the surface of the tongue behind the point of articulation is noticeably higher (nearer the palate) for the /l/ in William than for the one in callous. It is because of this difference in tongue height that the one is called "high tongue l" [l^], and the other "low tongue l" [lˇ]. Now pronounce the English word little, and see if you have a difference between the two /l/'s: [ˈl^ɩtl̩ˇ], as many American speakers do.

In these dialects of American English the choice between high and low tongue laterals is made for the speaker by the

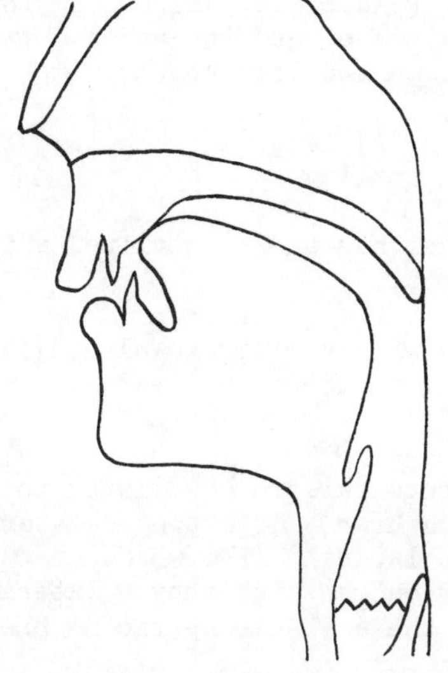

Sammy 15.1: [l^]. Note the relatively high position of the tongue surface behind the point of articulation.

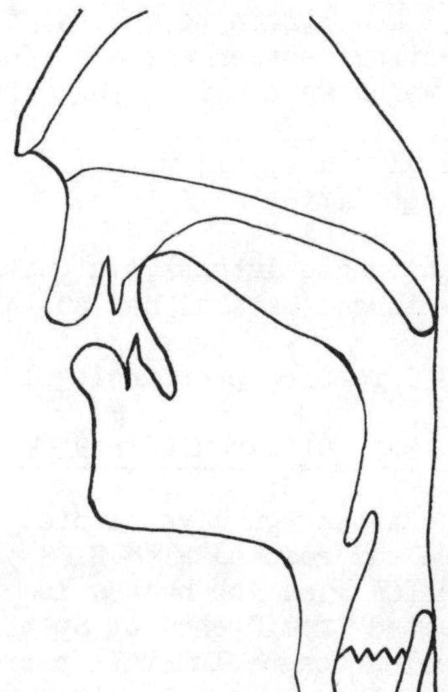

Sammy 15.2: [lˇ]. Note the relatively low position of the tongue surface behind the point of articulation.

language system. [l^] occurs before high front vowels (p. 232) and the [lˇ] in other positions, making them allophones of one phoneme. Many languages, such as French and Spanish, do not have this use of [lˇ], and the carryover of this unconscious English habit is one of the causes of an undesirable pronunciation.

Actually, a lateral at a given point of articulation may be said with a variety of different tongue contours, giving it different sounds. Listen to the tape as you follow along in the Manual, and watch for the different qualities associated with the laterals pronounced. This is done by changing the configuration of the tongue behind the point of articulation and of the lips. Nos. 7-10 are vowel qualities which you have not yet had.

1. [l] with [u] quality
2. [l] with [ʊ] quality
3. [l] with [o] quality
4. [l] with [ɔ] quality
5. [l] with [ʌ] quality
6. [l] with [ɑ] quality
7. [l] with [ɛ] quality
8. [l] with [i] quality
9. [l] with [e] quality
10. [l] with [æ] quality

Now listen to the two following laterals, which show the relation between these different kinds of quality and the two on which we are focusing (high tongue and low tongue).

11. [l^] ie., [l] with [i] quality
12. [lˇ] ie., [l] with [ʌ] quality

High tongue lateral, in other words, has an [i] quality, while low tongue lateral has an [ʌ] quality.

Practice pronouncing laterals with various vowel qualities.

RE 15.2. Differential: HIGH or LOW

After you have studied the above paragraphs, listen to the tape and respond with HIGH when you hear a high tongue lateral and LOW when you hear a low tongue lateral. The words are adapted from French or Spanish, which use high tongue laterals. The low tongue laterals represent the way some Americans speak these languages. Don't peek!

1. [ɛl^]	H	6. [l^ɑ]	H	11. ['l^opɛz]	H
2. [ɑlˇ]	L	7. [lˇɑ]	L	12. ['lˇopɛz]	L
3. [ɑl^]	H	8. [lˇo]	L	13. [l^e'te]	H
4. [mɑl^]	H	9. [lˇu]	L	14. [ku'l^e]	H
5. [mɑlˇ]	L	10. [l^u]	H	15. [ku'lˇe]	L

When you have practiced this exercise enough so that you can respond orally to the tape, run through it again, this time transcribing the items on a transcription form. Check your transcription against the exercise above, and tally your errors on the Transcription Tally Form in your Workbook Supplement, p. 27 ff. Repeat the exercise at intervals if you need to do so.

RE 15.3. Negative Practice: [l^ lˇ]

Practice saying each of the following sentences first with high tongue laterals, and then with low tongue laterals. Be careful to keep the laterals the same in any one repetition of a sentence, and not mix them in English fashion. As with any negative practice drill, you can practice this at odd moments when you are not otherwise engaged in phonetics study.

1. Let me call little Lil later. 2. Will Nell feel ill all day?
3. Little Lulu loaned Lynn the lumber.

RE 15.4: French.[1] Mimicry: [l^]

Mimic the tape, striving for a clear [l^] in each case. Follow the transcription if you care to do so.

1. [mɔḽ^ə̬]	molle	'soft (fem.)'
2. [fɔḽ^ə̬]	folle	'insane (fem.)'
3. [kuḽ^ə̬]	coule	'flows'
4. [fuḽ^ə̬]	foule	'crowd'
5. [ḽ^o]	l'eau	'the water'
6. [ḽ^u]	loup	'wolf'
7. [ḽ^ɛnə̬]	laine	'wool'
8. [ḽ^ɔmə̬]	l'homme	'the man'

RE 15.5. Demonstration: [L]

Listen to the tape, and try the English words for yourself. Notice how the /l/ is voiceless because it coincides with the aspiration from the stop, or at times there is a voiceless lateral followed by a brief voiced lateral [Ll]. This is the third allophone of English /l/ demonstrated in this lesson. Listen to the examples, and practice the words until you can sense the voiceless [L] in the examples below. Follow the transcription, reading across.

1a. please [pLi›yz] or [pLl^i›yz]	1b. [Li›yz]	1c. [Li›y]
2a. play [pLe˅y] or [pLl˅e˅y]	2b. [Le˅y]	2c. [Le]
3a. plunder ['pLʌndr̩] or ['pLl˅ʌndr̩]	3b. ['Lʌndr̩]	3c. [Lʌ]
4a. clock [kLɑk^{h}] or [kLl˅ɑk^{h}]	4b. [Lɑk^{h}]	4c. [Lɑ]
5a. claw [kLɔH] or [kLl˅ɔH]	5b. [LɔH]	5c. [Lɔ]

Fricative Laterals

The laterals demonstrated to the present have all been characteristic allophones of the /l/ phoneme of many speakers of American English. As such they are not "new" sounds, but nevertheless present a learning problem for a second language because the English phonemic habits must not be carried over. We turn now, however, to another pair of laterals which are not so characteristic of American English, but which may be heard in the speech of some individuals. Of these fricative laterals, the voiceless one in particular is very common in languages around the world.

---

[1]Recording by Rénate Wiesmann. Mimic the final sound of the first words as best you can.

RE 15.6. Demonstration: [Ⱡ ɬ]

Listen to the tape and follow along in the Manual. Mimic and imitate until you can make clear fricative laterals like those on the tape.

a. Say the English word leaf, and isolate the [l^•]. Then say it with greater force of air from the lungs. This may produce [ɬ•].

b. Say [l^•], but instead of a greater thrust of air, raise the sides of the tongue slightly to get [ɬ•].

c. Whisper William, and then isolate a whispered [L^•]. Say it with greater force of air. This may produce [Ⱡ•].

d. Raise the sides of the tongue from a whispered [L^•] to produce [Ⱡ•].

e. If you find it easy to produce [ɬ], but not [Ⱡ], say [ɬ] and then "whisper" it, or stop the voicing.

f. If you find it easy to produce [Ⱡ], but not [ɬ], say [Ⱡ] and voice it, or "buzz around it."

g. One kind of lisp in English consists of producing [Ⱡ] for /s/ and [ɬ] for /z/. Usually people who lisp in this way make their laterals on one side only, rather than on both sides simultaneously, as you probably did above, and as you should practice for most languages. Mimic the following English words "lisped" with lateral fricatives.

1. see	[Ⱡi› y]	4. zebra	['ɬi›ybrʌ]
2. set	[Ⱡɛt]	5. zeplin	['ɬɛplɩn]
3. sunny	['Ⱡʌni›y]	6. zone	[ɬown]

RE 15.7. Differential: VOICED or VOICELESS

In this drill we will include both oral and fricative laterals, high tongue, low tongue, etc., but your response is to be only VOICED or VOICELESS, according to what you hear. When you can do well on the oral response to this drill, try transcribing what you hear. Transcribe the laterals only, or transcribe each whole utterance, with its vowels as well as consonants. To do the latter you will have to stop the machine after each longer utterance to have time to write. Check your transcription against the exercise below. Don't peek.

1. [l^] VD
2. [ł] VD
3. [L] VL
4. [Ł] VL
5. [L] VL
6. [Ł] VL
7. [αlᵛα] VD
8. [εLε] VL
9. [oło] VD
10. [ɔl^ɔ] VD
11. [uŁu] VL
12. [ʌl^ʌ] VD
13. [ˀʋ'mʌŁ] VL
14. [ˀε'dʋł] VD
15. [ˀu'koL] VL
16. [ˀo'ŋαŁ] VL
17. [ˀʌ'gεl^] VD
18. [ˀɔ'xʌl^] VD

RE 15.8. Differential: FRICATIVE or NO

In this drill there will be the same variety of stimuli as in the last, but your response is different. Again you can try your hand at transcription after you do the oral practice. Pay particular attention to the laterals. Don't peek.

1. [l^] NO
2. [ł] F
3. [L] NO
4. [Ł] F
5. [L] NO
6. [Ł] F
7. [αlᵛα] NO
8. [εLε] NO
9. [oło] F
10. [ɔl^ɔ] NO
11. [uŁu] F
12. [ʌl^ʌ] NO
13. [łε'son] F
14. [Łα'duH] F
15. [lᵛɔ'mʌñ] NO
16. [Lʋ'fαr] NO
17. [l^o'pʰɔy] NO
18. [Łʌ'rεH] F

RE 15.9. Differential: ONE segment or TWO

Voiceless laterals, whether fricative or oral, often occur adjacent to voiced laterals, although they do not necessarily do so in all cases. Here is a segmental diagram of what happens.

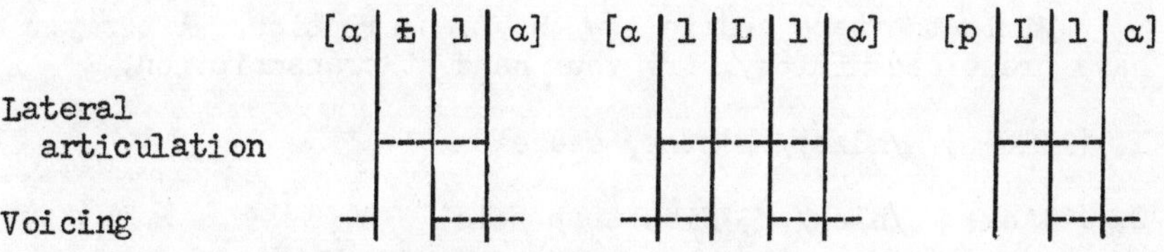

In other words, the lateral articulation holds throughout two or more segments, with and without voicing.

Listen to the following exercise and respond with ONE or TWO, depending on whether or not you hear two lateral segments.

After you have worked the exercise orally, try transcription of it. Don't peek.

1.	[Łl^ɑ]	TWO	5.	['ʌ.Łu]	ONE	9.	[pɑm'Llˇor]	TWO
2.	[Ło]	ONE	6.	['u.Łl^ɛ]	TWO	10.	[zuŋ'Łʌw]	ONE
3.	[Lɛ]	ONE	7.	['ʋ.Ll^ɛ]	TWO	11.	[fɛz'Łl^ʋt^{h}]	TWO
4.	[Llˇɔ]	TWO	8.	['ɔ.Lʌ]	ONE	12.	[dog'Lɑv]	ONE

RE 15.10. Mimicry: [L Ł ł]

Mimic the tape on the following exercise, following along in your Manual as you do so. Pay just as much attention to getting clear, unglided vowels as you do to the articulation of the consonants. Read across.

1a. ['ɑŁɑ]	1b. ['ɑ.Łl^ɑ]	1c. ['ɑl^.Łɑ]	1d. ['ɑl^.Łl^ɑ]
2a. ['ɑłɑ]	2b. ['ɑ.łl^ɑ]	2c. ['ɑl^.łɑ]	2d. ['ɑl^.łl^ɑ]
3a. ['ɑLɑ]	3b. ['ɑ.Ll^ɑ]	3c. ['ɑl^.Lɑ]	3d. ['ɑl^.Ll^ɑ]
4a. ['uŁu]	4b. ['u.Łl^u]	4c. ['ul^.Łu]	4d. ['ul^.Łl^u]
5a. ['ułu]	5b. ['u.łl^u]	5c. ['ul^.łu]	5d. ['ul^.łl^u]
6a. ['uLu]	6b. ['u.Ll^u]	6c. ['ul^.Lu]	6d. ['ul^.Ll^u]
7a. ['ɔŁɔ]	7b. ['ɔ.Łl^ɔ]	7c. ['ɔl^.Łɔ]	7d. ['ɔl^.Łl^ɔ]
8a. ['ʋłʋ]	8b. ['ʋ.łl^ʋ]	8c. ['ʋl^.łʋ]	8d. ['ʋl^.łl^ʋ]
9a. ['ʌLʌ]	9b. ['ʌ.Ll^ʌ]	9c. ['ʌl^.Lʌ]	9d. ['ʌl^.Ll^ʌ]

RE 15.11: Khmuʔ. Mimicry: [Łl]

Mimic the tape and follow the transcription. After you have practiced mimicry, try your hand at transcription.

1. [Łl^ɑ•p] /hlaap/ 'stop, cease'
2. [Łl^ɑk] /hlak/ 'fish trap pole'
3. [Łl^ʌŋ] /hlaŋ/ 'building
4. [Łl^aʔ] /hlaʔ/ 'leaf'
5. [Łl^ɛ•ŋ] /hlɛɛŋ/ 'tether'

6. [Ɫl^ɒk] /hlok/ 'chicken's nesting basket'

7. [Ɫl^ɒbm] /hlom/ 'capsize'

8. [Ɫl^ɒŋ] /hloŋ/ 'to forget'

9. [Lɫ^da•t] /hldaat/ 'scatter'

Alveopalatal Lateral

Some speakers of American English produce [l̃] for /l/ in William, or will ya? The articulator and point of articulation are the same as for /ñ/ (see Sammy 13.1, on p. 194), though the velic is closed and the sides of the tongue are open. Remember that in any blade-alveopalatal articulation the tongue tip is down behind the lower teeth. There is often a slight [y] onglide to the following vowel or off-glide from the preceding vowel with the alveopalatal laterals, as there is with alveopalatal nasals.

[l̃], then, occurs as another allophone of English /l/ for some speakers. However, in some dialects of Spanish, Portuguese, and Italian, for example, it occurs in contrast with the alveolar (or dental) lateral, and constitutes a separate phoneme.

RE 15.12. Demonstration: [l̃]

Listen to the tape and practice the suggestions below for the production of [l̃].

a. If you can produce a clear [ñ] start with that, and switch to lateral articulation without changing the point of articulation:

[ɑñɑ ɑñɑ ɑñɑ ɑl̃ɑ ɑl̃ɑ ɑl̃ɑ] [ɑñɑ ɑl̃ɑ ɑñɑ ɑl̃ɑ ɑñɑ ɑl̃ɑ]

b. Say the following words, being careful to keep your tongue tip down behind the lower teeth: William, will ya?, billion. Prolong the [l̃] and isolate it.

RE 15.13. Differential: ALVEOLAR or ALVEOPALATAL

After you listen to the tape and respond orally, transcribe the utterances.

1. [ɑl̃ɑ] AP 3. [ɑl^ɑ] AL 5. [ɑl̃ɑ] AP

2. [ɑl^ɑ] AL 4. [ɑl^ɑ] AL 6. [l^ɑ] AL

7. [l̃ɑ]	AP	10. [ɑl̃]	AP	13. [su'l̃ɛŋ]	AP
8. [l^ɑ]	AL	11. [ɑl^]	AL	14. [ti'l̃ɔz]	AP
9. [ɑl̃]	AP	12. [fo'nɑl^]	AL	15. [wi'l^ux]	AL

RE 15.14. Mimicry: [l^ lˇ l̃]

Mimic the tape and follow the transcription.

1a. [l^ɑ]	1b. [lˇɑ]	1c. [l̃ɑ]	1d. [ɑl̃]
2a. [l^ɛ]	2b. [lˇɛ]	2c. [l̃ɛ]	2d. [ɛl̃]
3a. [l^o]	3b. [lˇo]	3c. [l̃o]	3d. [ol̃]
4a. [l^ʌ]	4b. [lˇʌ]	4c. [l̃ʌ]	4d. [ʌl̃]
5a. [l^ɔ]	5b. [lˇɔ]	5c. [l̃ɔ]	5d. [ɔl̃]
6a. [l^u]	6b. [lˇu]	6c. [l̃u]	6d. [ul̃]
7a. [l^ɒ]	7b. [lˇɒ]	7c. [l̃ɒ]	7d. [ɒl̃]
8a. [ɑl^o]	8b. [ɑlˇo]	8c. [ɑl̃o]	8d. [ɑl̃ol̃]
9a. [ɛl^ɔ]	9b. [ɛlˇɔ]	9c. [ɛl̃ɔ]	9d. [ɛl̃ɔl̃]
10a. [ul^ʌ]	10b. [ulˇʌ]	10c. [ul̃ʌ]	10d. [ul̃ʌl̃]

Dental Laterals

All varieties of laterals which may be articulated in alveolar position may have counterparts with dental articulation, such as has previously been presented for stops, fricatives, and nasals. The symbol used to represent dental articulation [‸] is the same as well. As with the stops, the difference between alveolar and dental articulation is impossible to hear, but it may be seen. Its importance lies in the fact that by mimicking it closely in languages where it occurs, the tongue has a much better chance of developing a total set of articulations which will result in good pronunciation.

RE 15.15. Mimicry: [ḽ^ ḽˇ l̃]

Run the tape back and repeat RE 15.14, this time substituting a dental lateral for each of the alveolar ones in that exercise. The acoustic result will not be any different, perhaps, but you should consciously place the tip of your tongue solidly behind the upper teeth.

RE 15.16: Italian.[1] Mimicry: [l̃ ḽ^]

Mimic the tape and follow the transcription, reading across. Be very conscious of your articulation.

1a.	[l̃i]	gli	'him, it'	1b.	[ḽ^i]	li	'there'
2a.	['pal̃a]	paglia	'straw'	2b.	['paḽ^a]	pala	'shovel'
3a.	['fɔl̃a]	foglia	'leaf'	3b.	['foḽ^a]	fola	'fairy tale'
4a.	['l̃ene]	gliene	'some of it to him'	4b.	['ḽ^yɛve]	lieve	'light'
5a.	['l̃el^o]	glielo	'it to him'	5b.	['ḽ^yɛto]	lieto	'happy'
6a.	['el̃ino]	eglino	'they'	6b.	['eḽ^ika]	elica	'ship's screw'
7a.	['ǰil̃o]	giglio	'lily'	7b.	['ḽ^iḽ^o]	Lilo	(proper name)
8a.	['el̃i]	egli	'he, it'	8b.	[eḽ^imi'nare]	eliminare	'eliminate'
9a.	[ba'gal̃o]	bagaglio	'baggage'	9b.	['baḽ^ya]	balia	'wet nurse'
10a.	[pa'l̃ac·o]	pagliaccio	'clown'	10b.	[paḽ^a'taḽ^i]	palatali	'palatal'

Retroflexed and Velar Laterals

Retroflexed and velar laterals will not be drilled simply because of insufficient time in the course. Here, however, are some brief descriptive notes on them. (See Table 15.1.)

Retroflexed laterals are self-explanatory. As on all retroflexed sounds, the tongue curls up somewhat to articulate with the tip on or behind the alveolar ridge. A retroflexed lateral in alveolar position is virtually the same as an extremely low tongue lateral. When the point of articulation is

---

[1] Data from Claude Merton Wise, *Applied Phonetics*, and from Rénate N. Wiesmann, who made the recording.

palatal, however, there is a distinctly retroflexed quality.

A true velar lateral is articulated with the back of the tongue against the velum, leaving space for the airstream to come around the articulation. There is another articulation, however, which sounds much like it. It is really a vowel glide, however, and does not have lateral articulation. This consists of a backing and raising of the back of the tongue, together with a configuration of the tongue which sounds like a low tongue lateral. The articulation remains oral, however. This "pseudo-lateral" glide is used by some speakers of English for an /l/ in final position, in such a word as *ill*. It may be represented as [l˒], but will not be further treated in this course. It is a notable allophone in some dialects of Brazilian Portuguese, occurring with simultaneous lip rounding in words like *Brazil*.

Affricates with Lateral Release

Lateral fricatives follow stops to make affricates with lateral release. Note the varieties in the chart at the beginning of the lesson. Combinations with other stops are, of course, possible, as are aspirated affricates. Combinations of stops with other laterals also occur, but are not affricates as the laterals are not fricatives.

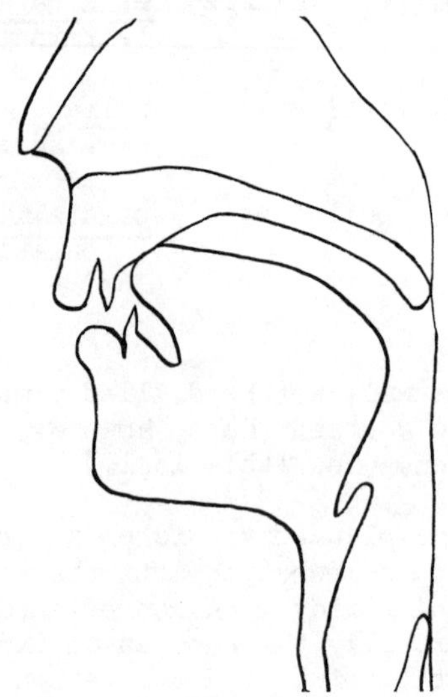

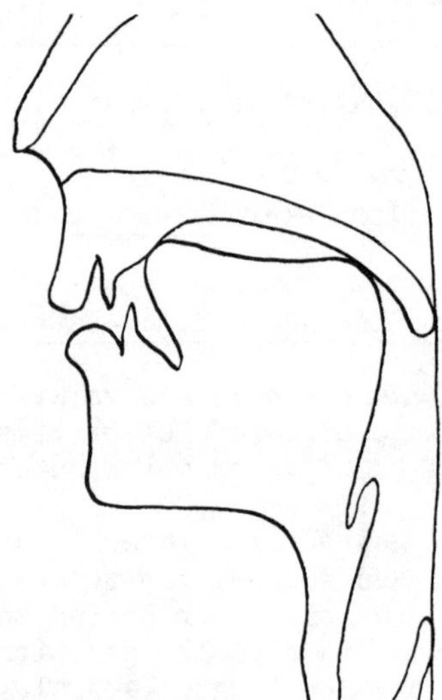

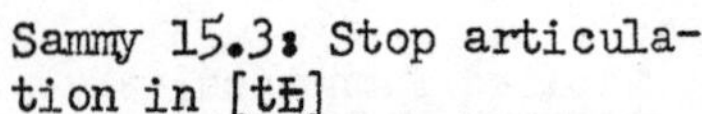

Sammy 15.3: Stop articulation in [tɬ]

Sammy 15.4: Stop articulation in [kɬ]

Sammies 15.3 and 15.4 illustrate the articulation of the affricates [tł] and [kł], which often sound very much alike, depending on just how the release of the stop is made. In [tł] the [t] is released simply by lowering the sides of the tongue slightly to give [ł], keeping the tongue-tip point of articulation. However, in [kł] the [k] is articulated with a simultaneous tip-alveolar lateral articulation. The [k] is released, leaving the lateral fricative. These laterals therefore end the same way, but begin differently.

RE 15.17. Differential: VOICED or VOICELESS

Listen for the lateral affricate in each utterance and respond with VOICED or VOICELESS. After you are able to respond orally to the tape, transcribe the utterances. Don't peek.

1. [oˈdło] VD	5. [ˈtłamɑs] VL	9. [ˈxʌzɛdł̩] VD
2. [ɛˈtłɛ] VL	6. [ˈtłogɛy] VL	10. [ˈts^{h}ʋvɔdł̩] VD
3. [uˈdłɔ] VD	7. [ˈdłuš.mʌt] VD	11. [ˈʔɔwĩɑdł̩] VD
4. [ʌˈtłʋ] VL	8. [ˈtłoH.ŋʋʔ] VL	12. [ˈMmʋ.ṭ̈šɛtł̩] VL

RE 15.18. Differential: ASPIRATED or UNASPIRATED

Listen for the lateral affricate in each utterance and respond with ASPIRATED or UNASPIRATED. After you are able to respond orally to the tape, transcribe the utterances.

1. [uˈtłu] UNA	5. [ˈtł^{h}ɑmɑs] A	9. [ˈxʌzɛ.tł^{h}o] A
2. [ɔˈtłɔ] UNA	6. [ˈtł^{h}ogɛy] A	10. [ˈts^{h}ʋvɔ.tłɛ] UNA
3. [uˈtł^{h}ʋ] A	7. [ˈtł^{h}uš.mʌt] A	11. [ˈʔɔwĩɑ.tł^{h}u] A
4. [ʌˈtłɛ] UNA	8. [ˈtłɔH.ŋʋʔ] UNA	12. [ˈMmʋ.ṭ̈šɛ.tło] UNA

RE 15.19. Mimicry: Affricates

Mimic the tape and follow in the Manual. Be careful to get full voicing, clear aspiration, or lack of it, as the case may be. Read across.

1a. [ɛˈdło]	1b. [ɛˈtło]	1c. [ɛˈtł^{h}o]
2a. [ɔˈdzɑ]	2b. [ɔˈtsɑ]	2c. [ɔˈts^{h}ɑ]
3a. [uˈd̂ðʌ]	3b. [uˈt̂θʌ]	3c. [uˈt̂θ^{h}ʌ]

4a. [o'ggɒ]	4b. [o'kxɒ]	4c. [o'kxʰɒ]
5a. [ʌ'bƀɛ]	5b. [ʌ'pp̶ɛ]	5c. [ʌ'pp̶ʰɛ]
6a. [ɑ'ǰɔ]	6b. [ɑ'čɔ]	6c. [ɑ'čʰɔ]
7a. [ɒ'd̤ž̤o]	7b. [ɒ't̤š̤o]	7c. [ɒ't̤š̤ʰo]
8a. [ɛ'bvu]	8b. [ɛ'pfu]	8c. [ɛ'pfʰu]
9a. [ɒ'bžʌ]	9b. [ɒ'pšʌ]	9c. [ɒ'pšʰʌ]
10a. [ɔ'dłɛ]	10b. [ɔ'tŁɛ]	10c. [ɔ'tŁʰɛ]

RE 15.20. Buildups

Mimic the tape, repeating those parts which give you difficulty as often as necessary. Follow along in your Manual. When you have gained oral fluency, transcribe the utterances, running the tape back as many times as necessary.

1. [ḽ^ ɛ'tŁɔ.šu ñow.ḽ^ u.ŋʌ'fʌḽ^ .MmʌŁ]

2. ['gutʰ.pLɑs ñɛž'l̃ɒx.kɑ.mɑ 'ḽ^ʌpf.l̃ɒkʰ]

3. [Łlʌŋ.go.ḽ^ɛ'l̃ɔƀ 'Mmʌŋ.kɒč.tŁol̃.yɑg]

4. [ŋo'l̃ɑ.ñɛ.šow.ŋɛtŁ kʰɒz.Łlˇɑ.'zɛŋŊ]

Transcription

Use RE 15.2, 15.4, 15.7, 15.9, 15.10, 15.11, 15.13, 15.14, 15.17, 15.18, 15.19, and 15.20 as transcription exercises. Transcribe them after you drill them orally, and then return to them another time for retranscription. Transcribe repeatedly those which give you trouble. Do your transcription on a transcription form in the Workbook Supplement and keep track of your errors on the Transcription Tally Form, p. 27ff. Watch to see whether or not you are improving in the transcription of sounds which give you difficulty, or of symbols which tend to confuse you. If you are having consistent trouble, go back to the lesson where the sound was taken up and transcribe some of the exercises in that lesson for practice.

Remember that in any transcription where there are small differences indicated by diacritics, (like [l^ lˇ]), write as much as you hear. That is, if you hear a voiced lateral, write [l], whether or not you can distinguish its high tongue or low tongue position. If you do hear that it is high tongue, add the [^], or if you hear that it is low tongue, add the [ˇ], etc.

Reading

Use RE 15.7 and 15.8 as reading exercises, reading off the utterances before the machine gives them, and checking yourself against the production on the tape.

... AND THIS IS THE SYMBOL FOR THE VOICELESS FRICATIVE ALVEOPALATAL LATERAL!

LESSON SIXTEEN

Some Front Vowels

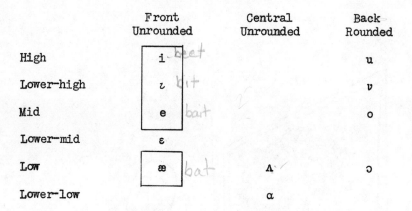

	Front Unrounded	Central Unrounded	Back Rounded
High	i		u
Lower-high	ι		υ
Mid	e		o
Lower-mid	ε		
Low	æ	ʌ	ɔ
Lower-low		α	

Table 16.1: Vowels to Date

The names of the new vowel symbols on this chart are [ι] "iota" /ˌιyˈowtʌ/ (symbol and name taken from Greek), and [æ] "digraph" (meaning two symbols written as one).

In transcribing these vowel symbols by hand there are a few cautions to observe, so that the symbols do not become confused with each other, or with ones to follow.

[ι] may be written as [ι]. It must not have a dot in order to keep it distinct from [i]. A tail on the bottom helps.

[υ] may be written as [ʊ]. It must not have a tail in order to keep it distinct from [u].

[α] may be written as [ɑ]. It should not be written as [a] to keep it distinct from another vowel we will have later.

[æ] can be written with a single stroke if you follow this pattern:

In this lesson we do not add any categories of vowel articulation, but fill in some of the sounds in front unrounded position to correspond with those already drilled in back rounded position.

RE 16.1 Demonstration: Table 16.1

Listen to the demonstration of the vowel chart repeatedly, studying Table 16.1 as you do so. When you are familiar with it, read off the chart simultaneously with the tape. It is especially valuable to work with your "buddy" on vowel articulations as it is difficult sometimes to hear where your mimicry is off. The practicing in slurring from one vowel position to another distant one on the chart is to help you realize that vowels make up an unbroken continuum with an enormous variety of possible modification in tongue configurations.

RE 16.2 Discrimination: SAME or DIFFERENT

Continue tuning up your ears to these new vowel qualities by responding SAME or DIFFERENT to the following pairs. Concentrate on the differences to help you become familiar with them. Don't peek.

1a.	[k^{h}rιk^h k^{h}rik^h]	D	1b.	[pιn pεn]	D
2a.	[k^{h}rιk^h k^{h}rik^h]	D	2b.	[pιn pιn]	S
3a.	[k^{h}rιk^h k^{h}rιk^h]	S	3b.	[pεn pεn]	S
4a.	[k^{h}rik^h k^{h}rιk^h]	D	4b.	[pεn pεn]	S
5a.	[k^{h}rik^h k^{h}rik^h]	S	5b.	[pεn pιn]	D
6a.	['k^{h}riklˇow 'k^{h}rιklˇow]	D	6b.	['pεnsιlˇ 'pιnsιlˇ]	D
7a.	['k^{h}rιklˇow 'k^{h}rιklˇow]	S	7b.	['pιnsιlˇ 'pεnsιlˇ]	D
8a.	['k^{h}riklˇow 'k^{h}riklˇow]	S	8b.	['pιnsιlˇ 'pεnsιlˇ]	D
9a.	['k^{h}rιklˇow 'k^{h}riklˇow]	D	9b.	['pεnsιlˇ 'pιnsιlˇ]	D
1c.	[žef žef]	S	1d.	[dε dʌ]	D
2c.	[žεf žef]	D	2d.	[dʌ dʌ]	S
3c.	[žef žεf]	D	3d.	[dε dε]	S
4c.	[žef žεf]	D	4d.	[dε dʌ]	D
5c.	[žef žef]	S	5d.	[dε dʌ]	D
6c.	['žεf.tsɔb 'žεf.tsɔb]	S	6d.	['sʌndε 'sʌndʌ]	D

7c.	['žef.tsɔb 'žef.tsɔb]	S	7d.	['sʌndʌ 'sʌndʌ]	S
8c.	['žɛf.tsɔb 'žef.tsɔb]	D	8d.	['sʌndʌ 'sʌndɛ]	D
9c.	['žef.tsɔb 'žɛf.tsɔb]	D	9d.	['sʌndɛ 'sʌndɛ]	S
1e.	[xɛmM xæmM]	D	1f.	[l^æl^ l^æl^]	S
2e.	[xɛmM xæmM]	D	2f.	[l^æl^ l^æl^]	S
3e.	[xæmM xæmM]	S	3f.	[l^ɑl^ l^æl^]	D
4e.	[xæmM xɛmM]	D	4f.	[l^ɑl^ l^ɑl^]	S
5e.	[xɛmM xɛmM]	S	5f.	[l^ɑl^ l^æl^]	D
6e.	[pl̩'xæmM pl̩'xɛmM]	D	6f.	[m̃u'l^æl^ m̃u'l^æl^]	S
7e.	[pl̩'xɛmM pl̩'xæmM]	D	7f.	[m̃u'l^ɑl^ m̃u'l^ɑl^]	S
8e.	[pl̩'xɛmM pl̩'xɛmM]	S	8f.	[m̃u'l^æl^ m̃u'l^æl^]	S
9e.	[pl̩'xɛmM pl̩'xæmM]	D	9f.	[m̃u'l^æl^ m̃u'l^ɑl^]	D

Production of [i ɩ e æ]

The new vowel sounds of this lesson may seem deceptively easy to the English speaker who identifies them with sounds in his own speech. There are pitfalls in them, however. One danger is that the English speaking person will put an [H] off-glide on [ɩ] and [æ], that he will put a very slight [y] off-glide on [i], and a strong [y] off-glide on [e]. A second difficulty is that many will not make the vowels truly front, but slightly centralized, and not make the [i] high enough. In relation to the normal habits of many speakers of English, in other words, the [i] quality which we will be striving for will be very high, very front, and unglided. The [ɩ] and [e] qualities will be front and unglided. The [æ] will be unglided and will be higher than some speakers of English want to make it.

If you look at Sammy 16.1 you will notice that it is not actually the tip of the tongue which is high for front vowels. The tip of the tongue is generally behind the lower teeth. "Front" refers to the blade and areas just behind it, as opposed to the central and back parts of the tongue.

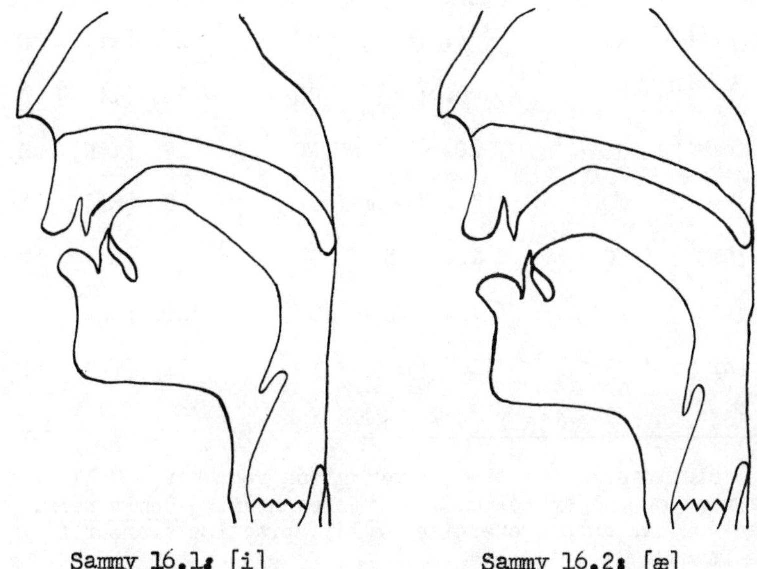

Sammy 16.1: [i] Sammy 16.2: [æ]

RE 16.3. Demonstration: Producing Unglided [i ɩ e æ]

Throughout the remainder of this course unglided vowels must be practiced until control is mastered. Many of the suggestions below apply to vowels introduced in Lesson 14, and should be practiced with them as well. A mirror is extremely valuable when practicing pure vowels or vowel glides. Your buddy should watch as well. It is often possible to see movements which produce glides you are not yet able to hear.

a. Practice each of the vowels in the sequence [ʔe· ʔe ʔe ʔe ʔe], [ʔi· ʔi ʔi ʔi ʔi], etc. Maintain this rhythm, controlling the tendency to glide.

b. Follow this same exercise with other frames such as [sɩ· sɩ sɩ sɩ sɩ], [tɩ·m tɩm tɩm tɩm tɩm], etc.

c. Practice eliminating the glide by devoicing the vowel at the end, thus in effect replacing the glide by [h]: [ʔæ·h [ʔe·h ʔɩ·h ʔi·h].

d. Then practice unglided vowels in alternation with those followed by [h]: [ʔe·h ʔe· ʔe·h ʔe·], etc.

RE 16.4 Differential: GLIDED or NO

Listen for the [H] off-glide on [ɩ æ], and the [y]

off-glide on [i e]. Respond with GLIDED or NO.[1]

1. [hιtʰ]	NO	8. [eym]	G	15. [ti]	NO
2. [hιHtʰ]	G	9. [em]	NO	16. [ti˃y]	G
3. [hæHtʰ]	G	10. [æm]	NO	17. [tæH]	G
4. [hætʰ]	NO	11. [i˃ym]	G	18. [tæ]	NO
5. [hetʰ]	NO	12. [ιHm]	G	19. [te]	NO
6. [hitʰ]	NO	13. [eHm]	G	20. [tey]	G
7. [hi˃ytʰ]	G	14. [im]	NO	21. [tι]	NO

RE 16.5. Differential: [y w r H]

Distinguish the kind of off-glide you hear. Call out the name of the symbol used to represent it. Don't peek. When you can do the exercise orally, practice transcribing the items.

1. [zιy]	y	7. [l^ewn]	w	13. [tsiwx]	w
2. [zιr]	r	8. [l^εwn]	w	14. [cιrm]	r
3. [zιH]	H	9. [niHf]	H	15. [xærmM]	r
4. [zιw]	w	10. [ŋæHp̶]	H	16. [t̤š̤εHv]	H
5. [kʰær]	r	11. [zeyd]	y	17. [d̤ž̤εyb̶]	y
6. [geH]	H	12. [zæyd]	y	18. [tɬiHθ]	H

RE 16.6. Negative Practice: Removing [y] Off-glides

All of the following words contain a [y] off-glide in some dialects of English. Column a transcribes the pronunciation.[2] In Column b they are transcribed without glides, but

---

[1]In the transcription of this exercise [˃] represents a pronunciation which is not articulated at the norm indicated by the symbol, but slightly back from it. Thus, [i˃] is slightly back from [i], etc. If the [i] is pronounced in truly high front position a [y] off-glide is virtually impossible. [i˃y] is a more characteristic English pronunciation.

[2]In the transcription of this exercise [ˇ] represents a

with the nearest pure vowel on our vowel chart. Read across as you mimic the tape.

1a. [ˈʔe˅ybl̩]	1b. [ˈʔebl̩]	able
2a. [ʔe˅yt^h]	2b. [ʔet^h]	eight
3a. [le˅yt^h]	3b. [let^h]	late
4a. [spe˅yd]	4b. [sped]	spade
5a. [we˅y]	5b. [we]	way
6a. [pLe˅y]	6b. [pLe]	play
7a. [be˅yt^h]	7b. [bet^h]	bait
8a. [me˅yd]	8b. [med]	made
9a. [wɑy]	9b. [wɑ]	why
10a. [dɑy]	10b. [dɑ]	die
11a. [t^{h}ɑyp^h]	11b. [t^{h}ɑp^h]	type
12a. [ʔʌys]	12b. [ʔʌs]	ice
13a. [rʌyt^h]	13b. [rʌt^h]	right
14a. [k^{h}wʌyt^h]	14b. [k^{h}wʌt^h]	quite
15a. [ˈʔɑydl̩]	15b. [ˈʔɑdl̩]	idle
16a. [ʔɑyz]	16b. [ʔɑz]	eyes

RE 16.7. Mimicry: [i ɩ e æ]

Follow the transcription as you mimic. Strive for the articulation described for the new vowels. Have your buddy listen to make sure your mimicry is accurate, and watch your

---

pronunciation which is not articulated at the norm indicated by the symbol, but slightly down from it. Thus [e˅] is slightly down from [e]. Remember that there are almost infinite numbers of vowel positions, and this provides a way of transcribing subtle differences without an infinite number of symbols. (See the previous footnote on p. 236, and note the analogy also to [l˅].)

mouth in a mirror. Practice down and across. Use this exercise for transcription also, when you have learned to mimic well.

1a. [dif]	1b. [dɩf]	1c. [def]	1d. [dæf]
2a. [nip^h]	2b. [nɩp^h]	2c. [nep^h]	2d. [næp^h]
3a. [l^iš]	3b. [l^ɩš]	3c. [l^eš]	3d. [l^æš]
4a. [tłis]	4b. [tłɩs]	4c. [tłes]	4d. [tłæs]
5a. [ŋil^]	5b. [ŋɩl^]	5c. [ŋel^]	5d. [ŋæl^]
6a. [Nnidz]	6b. [Nnɩdz]	6c. [Nnedz]	6d. [Nnædz]
7a. [pLiᵽ]	7b. [pLɩᵽ]	7c. [pLeᵽ]	7d. [pLæᵽ]
8a. [kiž]	8b. [kɩž]	8c. [kež]	8d. [kæž]
9a. [l̃iv]	9b. [l̃ɩv]	9c. [l̃ev]	9d. [l̃æv]
10a. [ǥi]	10b. [ǥɩ]	10c. [ǥe]	10d. [ǥæ]

RE 16.8. Negative Practice: "This is the House that Jack Built"

Refer to the text of RE 14.4, p. 205, if you need to. The sounds to be substituted are indicated in the columns below. The tape will start you off for each one.

	a	b	c	d
House	[his]	[hɩs]	[hes]	[hæs]
Malt	[mil^t]	[mɩl^t]	[mel^t]	[mæl^t]
Rat	[rit]	[rɩt]	[ret]	[ræt]
Cat	[k^{h}it]	[k^{h}ɩt]	[k^{h}et]	[k^{h}æt]
Dog	[dig]	[dɩg]	[deg]	[dæg]
Cow	[k^{h}iw]	[k^{h}ɩw]	[k^{h}ew]	[k^{h}æw]
Maiden	['midn̩]	['mɩdn̩]	['medn̩]	['mædn̩]
Man	[min]	[mɩn]	[men]	[mæn]
Priest	[p^{h}rist]	[p^{h}rɩst]	[p^{h}rest]	[p^{h}ræst]

	a	b	c	d
Cock	[kʰik]	[kʰɩk]	[kʰek]	[kʰæk]
Farmer	['firmr̩]	['fɩrmr̩]	['fermr̩]	['færmr̩]

RE 16.9. Mimicry: Vowels With and Without Off-glides

Mimic the tape and watch the transcription. When you have learned to mimic the material, use it for transcription practice as well.

1a. [zi]		1c. [ziw]	1d. [ziH]	1e. [zir]
2a. [ñib]		2c. [ñiwb]	2d. [ñiHb]	1e. [ñirb]
3a. [zɩ]	3b. [zɩy]	3c. [zɩw]	3d. [zɩH]	3e. [zɩr]
4a. [ñɩb]	4b. [ñɩyb]	4c. [ñɩwb]	4d. [ñɩHb]	4e. [ñɩrb]
5a. [ze]	5b. [zey]	5c. [zew]	5d. [zeH]	5e. [zer]
6a. [ñeb]	6b. [ñeyb]	6c. [ñewb]	6d. [ñeHb]	6e. [ñerb]
7a. [zæ]	7b. [zæy]	7c. [zæw]	7d. [zæH]	7e. [zær]
8a. [ñæb]	8b. [ñæyb]	8c. [ñæwb]	8d. [ñæHb]	8e. [ñærb]

Review of Vowels and Vowel Off-glides

Tune up on the vowel qualities of previous lessons, as well as of this lesson by listening to RE 16.1 again. Practice some of the vowels with off-glides as well.

RE 16.10. Negative Practice: "Old MacDonald Had a Farm"

The tape will demonstrate how this exercise goes, and then you can continue practicing with your buddy. It is a device for getting rather intensive practice of vowel qualities and associated glides.

The various vowels and combinations listed below are the "sounds" in Old MacDonald's farmyard. After the first start it will not be necessary to repeat the verse.

Old MacDonald had a farm.

/'ɩyɑy 'ɩyɑy 'ow/

And on that farm he had some sounds

/'ɩyɑy 'ɩyɑy 'ow/

a. With a [mi mi] here and a [mi mi] there
Here a [mi], there a [mi], everywhere a [mi mi]

b. [mɩ mɩ] here...

c. [me]

d. On around the whole vowel chart with pure vowels.

e. [miw]

f. [mɩw]

g. On around with [w] off-glides.

h. The same with [y] off-glides.

j. The same with [H] off-glides.

k. The same with [r] off-glides.

Review of On-glides

On-glides [y w r] occur with all vowels to date, except for the combinations [yi] and [wu] when the vowel qualities are truly high front and high back respectively.

RE 16.11. Mimicry: [y w r] On-glides

Follow the transcription as you mimic the tape. Make sure you have good on-glides, but no off-glides. When you have learned to mimic fluently, try transcribing the exercise.

1a. [če]	1b. [čye]	1c. [čwe]	1d. [čre]
2a. [ppæ]	2b. [ppyæ]	2c. [ppwæ]	2d. [ppræ]
3a. [ṭi]	3b. [ṭyi]	3c. [ṭwi]	3d. [ṭri]
4a. [ṣ̌ʌ]	4b. [ṣ̌yʌ]	4c. [ṣ̌wʌ]	4d. [ṣ̌rʌ]
5a. [ṭ̬θɩm]	5b. [ṭ̬θyɩm]	5c. [ṭ̭θwɩm]	5d. [ṭ̭θrɩm]
6a. [ŋɛǰ]	6b. [ŋyɛǰ]	6c. [ŋwɛǰ]	6d. [ŋrɛǰ]
7a. [Nnɔdz]	7b. [Nnyɔdz]	7c. [Nnwɔdz]	7d. [Nnrɔdz]
8a. [gɑmM]	8b. [gyɑmM]	8c. [gwɑmM]	8d. [grɑmM]

9a. [ñubƀ]	9b. [ñyubƀ]	9c. [ñwubƀ]	9d. [ñrubƀ]
10a. [l^ oñ]	10b. [l^ yoñ]	10c. [l^ woñ]	10d. [l^ roñ]
11a. [žʋtŁ]	11b. [žyʋtŁ]	11c. [žwʋtŁ]	11d. [žrʋtŁ]

RE 16.12. Negative Practice: "The Walrus and the Carpenter"

In the following exercise, read the stansa from "The Walrus and the Carpenter," changing the last syllable of each line to insert an on-glide if there is not one, or to replace it if there is. The three columns give the resulting pronunciation in one dialect. The tape will start you off. As with all negative practice, this is something you can do in spare moments without the recording, once you see how it goes.

"The time has come, the Walrus said	1a. [syɛd]	1b. [swɛd]	1c. [srɛd]
"To talk of many things	2a. [θyɩŋz]	2b. [θwɩŋz]	2c. [θrɩŋz]
Of shoes--and ships-- and sealing wax--	3a. [yæks]	3b. [wæks]	3c. [ræks]
Of cabbages-- and kings	4a. [k^hyɩŋz]	4b. [k^hwɩŋz]	4c. [k^hrɩŋz]
And why the sea is boiling hot--	5a. [hyɑt^h]	5b. [hwɑt^h]	5c. [hrɑt^h]
And whether pigs have wings.	6a. [yɩŋz]	6b. [wɩŋz]	6c. [rɩŋz]

\- - -

"A loaf of bread," the Walrus said	7a. [syɛd]	7b. [swɛd]	7c. [srɛd]
"Is what we chiefly need:	8a. [nyi›yd]	8b. [nwi›yd]	8c. [nri›yd]
Pepper and vinegar besides	9a. [syɑydz]	9b. [swɑydz]	9c. [srɑydz]
Are very good indeed--	10a. [dyi›yd]	10b. [dwi›yd]	10c. [dri›yd]
Now if you're ready, Oysters dear,	11a. [dyi›r]	11b. [dwi›r]	11c. [dri›r]

We can begin
to feed." 12a. [fyi˃yd] 12b. [fwi˃yd] 12c. [fri˃yd]

RE 16.13. Differential: Identification of Vowels

In this exercise respond to the tape by giving the name of the symbol with which the vowel sound is transcribed. That is, when you hear [i], say /ɑy/ or write i. When you hear [ɔ], say "backwards c" or write ɔ. The tape gives the correct oral response. Don't peek, but if you are responding by writing the symbol, check your responses after you finish the exercise.

1. [ˀo] o
2. [ˀɩ] IOTA
3. [ˀʌ] CARET
4. [ˀæ] DIGRAPH
5. [ˀi] i
6. [ˀɔ] BACKWARDS c
7. [l^ud] u
8. [l^ɑd] SCRIPT ɑ
9. [l^ɛd] EPSILON
10. [l^ɩd] IOTA
11. [l^ʋd] UPSILON
12. [l^ed] e
13. [xitȽ] i
14. [xʌtȽ] CARET
15. [xɑtȽ] SCRIPT ɑ
16. [xætȽ] DIGRAPH
17. [xʋtȽ] UPSILON
18. [xotȽ] o

RE 16.14. Differential: FRONT UNROUNDED, CENTRAL UNROUNDED, or BACK ROUNDED

Respond orally to the tape. Don't peek. Use this exercise for transcription after you are able to do it orally without hesitation.

1. [ñi] F U
2. [ñʌ] C U
3. [ñɛ] F U
4. [ñɑ] C U
5. [ñɔ] B R
6. [ñʋ] B R
7. [l̃upʰ] B R
8. [l̃ɩpʰ] F U
9. [l̃æpʰ] F U
10. [l̃ɑpʰ] C U
11. [l̃ipʰ] F U
12. [l̃ɛpʰ] F U
13. [tl̩æŋk] F U
14. [tl̩ɩŋk] F U
15. [tl̩ʌŋk] C U
16. [tl̩ʋŋk] B R
17. [tl̩ɔŋk] B R
18. [tl̩iŋk] F U

RE 16.15. Differential: Tongue Height

Respond with one of the following: HIGH, LOWER-HIGH, MID, LOWER-MID, LOW, LOWER-LOW.

1. [ẓ̌ʌ] L
2. [ž̥ɛ] L-M
3. [ẓ̌ɔ] L
4. [ẓ̌ʊ] L-H
5. [ẓ̌ɩ] L-H
6. [ẓ̌æ] L
7. [Ŋŋiv] H
8. [Ŋŋov] M
9. [Ŋŋuv] H
10. [Ŋŋɑv] L-L
11. [Ŋŋev] M
12. [Ŋŋɛv] L-M
13. [kxɩb] L-H
14. [kxub] H
15. [kxɔb] L
16. [kxʌb] L
17. [kxɑb] L-L
18. [kxeb] M

RE 16.16. Differential: Full Labels

Select one term from each column to make up your response. <u>Don't peek!</u>

HIGH	FRONT	ROUNDED
LOWER-HIGH	CENTRAL	UNROUNDED
MID	BACK	
LOWER-MID		
LOW		
LOWER-LOW		

1. [ʔe] M F U
2. [ʔu] H B R
3. [ʔɩ] L-H F U
4. [ʔɔ] L B R
5. [ʔʌ] L C U
6. [ʔo] M B R
7. [ʔi] H F U
8. [ʔæ] L F U
9. [swɑmp] L-L C U
10. [swomp] M B R
11. [swɩmp] L-H F U
12. [swæmp] L F U
13. [swump] H B R
14. [swʌmp] L C U
15. [swʊmp] L-H B R
16. [swimp] H F U
17. [krɛtš̤] L-M F U
18. [krʊtš̤] L-H B R
19. [krɩtš̤] L-H F U
20. [kræṭš̤] L F U
21. [kriṭš̤] H F U
22. [kretš̤] M F U
23. [krotš̤] M B R
24. [krʌtš̤] L C U

RE 16.17. Khmuʔ.[1] Mimicry: [i ɩ ε ʋ]

Mimic the tape as you follow the transcription. Pay particular attention to the vowels. You may hear fine differences in the pronunciation of the vowels transcribed with the same phonemic symbols. Mimic the fine differences. Remember that such differences may be due to free fluctuation, or to complementary distribution. The double vowels symbolize phonemic length.

a	b	c	d
1a. /liiw/ 'measure of width'	1b. /lɩɩw/ 'try'	1c. /lεεw/ 'already'	1d. /lʋʋl/ 'slide'
2a. /liit/ 'level off'	2b. /lɩɩt/ 'hide'	2c. /lεεp/ 'packet'	2d. /lʋʋp/ 'hold back part'
	3b. /lɩɩŋ/ 'wander'	3c. /lεεŋ/ 'dry season'	3d. /lʋʋŋ/ 'coffin'
4a. /hiip/ 'to ladle'	4b. /hɩɩt/ 'cause disaster'	4c. /hεεt/ 'call to'	
5a. /piik/ 'dark (liquid)'	5b. /pɩɩp/ 'push through'	5c. /pεεt/ 'seven'	5d. /pʋʋp/ 'call of deer'
	6b. /p^{h}ɩɩt/ 'dress up'	6c. /p^{h}εεk/ 'pine tree'	6d. /p^{h}ʋʋt/ 'too much'
7a. /siit/ 'rub'	7b. /sɩɩt/ 'left over'	7c. /sεεt/ 'apart'	
8a. /miit/ 'knife'	8b. /mɩɩp/ 'crawl under'	8c. /mεεt/ 'fish trap'	8d. /mʋʋt/ 'decayed'
9a. /tiiŋ/ 'fall over'		9c. /tεεŋ/ 'do'	9d. /tʋʋn/ 'jump down'
10a. /t^{h}iip/ 'born in succession'	10b. /t^{h}ɩɩt/ 'preach'	10c. /t^{h}εεn/ 'shelf'	10d. /t^{h}ʋʋt/ 'steal, lie'
11a. /ʔiik/ 'more, again'	11b. /ʔɩɩm/ 'kin term'	11c. /ʔεεk/ 'yoke'	11d. /ʔʋʋp/ 'gather in'

[1] Recording by Naay Muun and Naay Ngaa of Luang Prabang, Laos.

12a. /kiip/ 'board' 12c. /kεεp/ 'grasp with tongs' 12d. /kυυt/ '10 million'

RE 16.18. Transcription

For this exercise use the special transcription form for RE 16.18 (pp. 47-48 in the _Workbook Supplement_). Listen to the tape and fill in the blanks in the _Supplement_. If nothing goes in a particular blank, draw a vertical line through it like this sʌm/no. When you have completed the exercise, check your answers with the text below. You are given additional columns in the workbook to take the transcription four times, if necessary. If you find this easy, take a regular transcription form and transcribe the whole utterance for each item. If you find it difficult, use RE 16.2, 16.4, 16.5, 16.7, 16.9, 16.11, 16.13, 16.14, 16.15, and 16.16 instead.

Here are the answers. Don't peek!

1. [ŋʌ'ṭʰæ]	8. [či'goH]	15. ['tŧævwɑ]
2. ['tsoñu]	9. [guy'đwɩ]	16. [čʰʌᵽ'kež]
3. [vye'ge]	10. [ƀu'ʔυ]	17. [pʰυ'θɩx]
4. [Nnu'tɑŋ]	11. ['dyoǰur]	18. ['pæwLlᵛɑkʰ]
5. ['kuθɩw]	12. [ṭ̈šeH'ṭɔHlᵛ]	19. [šεg'bepʰ]
6. [bυ'swɔy]	13. ['Mmoŋzεʔ]	20. ['zɔlᵛtʰiHmM]
7. [ǰεr'Nŋʌtʰ]	14. ['fwʌysɩ]	21. [dɨim'šmæwkʰ]

Reading

Use RE 16.18 as a reading exercise. Practice each word to yourself first, and then listen to the tape recording of that word to check yourself. Work with your buddy.

Suggested Readings

Eugene A. Nida, _Learning a Foreign Language_, pp. 101-105 (108-118, 132-134).

H. A. Gleason, _An Introduction to Descriptive Linguistics_, pp. 201-204, (14-26, 37-39, 187-193).

Charles F. Hockett, _A Course in Modern Linguistics_, pp. 77-83 (15-74).

LESSON SEVENTEEN

Flaps and Trills

	Bilabial	Tip-dental	Tip-alveolar	Tip-alveopalatal (retroflexed)	Uvular
Flaps					
Nasal		(ṋ̌)	ň	(ṇ̌)	
Lateral		(ḽ̌)	ľ	(ḷ̌)	
Stop					
Flat tongue					
Voiced		(ḓ̌)	ď	(ḍ̌)	
Voiceless		(ṱ̌)	ť	(ṭ̌)	
Cupped tongue					
Voiced		(ř̭)	ř	(ṛ̌)	
Voiceless		(Ř̭)	Ř	(Ṛ̌)	
Trills					
Voiced	(b̃)	(r̭̃)	r̃		ṛ̃
Voiceless	(p̃)	(R̭̃)	R̃		Ṛ̃

Table 17.1: Some Flap and Trill Articulations

Study the above table to make sure that you understand the significance of the symbols. Note the use of capital R for voiceless articulation, by analogy with capitals for nasals and laterals. The diacritics here, however, are used with a different significance from the ways in which you have met them before. Be careful that it does not become a source of confusion. [ˇ] was used earlier as a sign of alveopalatal articulation on fricatives and affricates [š ž č], etc. It is used on other consonant symbols (and most frequently on ř] to represent flap articulation. [~] was used earlier as a sign of alveopalatal articulation on nasals and laterals [ñ l̃], etc. It is used with these new symbols to represent trill articulation. [̣] was used earlier to represent retroflexed articulation [ṭ ṣ̌ ẓ̌], etc. It is used with the trills to represent uvular articulation. (Note that there is an analogy here. This represents backing in both cases.) [r] was used earlier to represent a vowel glide. It is used now (with [ˇ] or [~])

to represent these new kinds of consonant articulation which have some acoustic similarity to the [r] glide.

There is not much point in presenting Sammies of these new sounds except for the uvular trills below, because the points of articulation and articulators are familiar. It is the manner of articulation which differs.

Flaps

Flap articulation differs only slightly from the corresponding nasal, lateral or stop articulation. Points and manner of articulation may be the same except for the additional flap characteristic.

RE 17.1 Demonstration: Flap Articulation

Mimic the tape and follow along in the Manual.

a. Listen to the tape on the pronunciation of the following words, and notice the pronunciation of the medial consonant. Practice making the same kind of articulation yourself, whether you consider this standard pronunciation for English or not, and whether you find it natural to your dialect or not.

1a.	[ˈmɪňi›y]	Minnie	1b.	[ˈfʌňi›y]	funny
2a.	[ˈmɪľi›y]	Millie	2b.	[ˈsʌľi›y]	sully
3a.	[ˈmɪďi›y]	middy	3b.	[ˈmʌďi›y]	muddy
4a.	[ˈkʰɪři›y]	kitty	4b.	[ˈpʰʌři›y]	putty

b. Now follow the tape, pronouncing each of these words in the same way, and abstracting the medial consonant, placing it between [ɑ...ɑ]. Maintain the flap articulation. This should be a short, rapid flick of the tongue against the point of articulation. The articulator, instead of deliberately going up and touching the point of articulation, flicks up against it or flicks it as it passes rapidly by. Figure 17.1 diagrams these kinds of movement.

Tongue tip flicking up against point of articulation and away	Tongue tip flicking point of articulation as it passes from front to back	Tongue tip flicking point of articulation as it passes from back to front

Fig. 17.1

c. In order to make [ř], give a little [r] quality to an English [ď]. Imitate the tape. You may find that you are working too hard at producing a flap. Relax. Be sure you are not wagging your chin. Hold your chin steady with your hand.

1a. [ˈmʌďi›y] 1b. [ˈmʌři›y] 1c. [ˈmʌřʌ] 1d. [ˈʌřʌ]

2a. [ˈmιďi›y] 2b. [ˈmιři›y] 2c. [ˈmιřι] 2d. [ˈιřι]

d. For another exercise in producing [ř], imitate the rapid repetition of these English words: city, pity, ditty. Also: got a lot [ˌgɑřɨˈlɑt]

e. Try water and butter [ˈwɑř̩] and [ˈbʌř̩].

RE 17.2. Differential: [ď ř]

Begin tuning up your ears to flaps by differentiating two kinds. Respond with d or r. The tape will demonstrate. When you find that you can answer orally, transcribe the exercise in order to be sure you learn the use of the flap diacritic.

1. [ɑďɑ] d 5. [ɔři] r 9. [ɑˈřeso] r

2. [oďo] d 6. [iďɔ] d 10. [uˈďiŋu] d

3. [ɛřɛ] r 7. [ʌřʊ] r 11. [eˈfɔďi] d

4. [uřu] r 8. [ιřæ] r 12. [ʊˈčoďʌ] d

RE 17.3. Differential: [ť ř]

Respond orally with t or r, and then transcribe. Be sure you transcribe the flap diacritic correctly.

1. [ɑřɑ] r 5. [ɔťi] t 9. [ɑˈřeso] r

2. [oťo] t 6. [iťɔ] t 10. [uˈřiŋu] r

3. [ɛřɛ] r 7. [ʌřu] r 11. [eˈfɔťi] t

4. [uťu] t 8. [ιťæ] t 12. [ʊˈčoťʌ] t

RE 17.4. Differential: [ď ť ř]

Respond orally with d, t, or r, and then transcribe.

1. [ιřι] r 3. [ʌďʌ] d 5. [ɑřɛ] r

2. [ɔťɔ] t 4. [æťæ] t 6. [uďo] d

7. [æřʋ] r 9. [ɔ'ďik^hɑ] d 11. [ʌ'řuxi] r

8. [ʌťɩ] t 10. [i'zɔřɛ] r 12. [ɩ'næťu] t

RE 17.5. Differential: [ň ľ ď ť ř]

Respond with n, l, d, t, or r until you can do the exercise well, and then transcribe.

1. [iňɑ] n 7. [ɛřʌ] r 13. [ɩ'ťɑƀ] t

2. [uťe] t 8. [ɔťi] t 14. [e'gæľɔ] l

3. [ɩřo] r 9. [eďɑ] d 15. [ɛ'zrɛďu] d

4. [ʋďæ] d 10. [oňæ] n 16. [ʋ'řewzʌ] r

5. [æřɩ] r 11. [iřɛ] r 17. [ɩ'xyořu] r

6. [ʌľɔ] l 12. [uľʌ] l 18. [ʋ'řɔviH] r

RE 17.6. Differential: FLAP or GLIDE

[r] and [ř] are very different in their articulation. Respond orally with FLAP or GLIDE, and then transcribe the exercise.

1. [ɛro] G 5. [iřɔ] F 9. [t^hæ'porɛy] G

2. [ɩřɑ] F 6. [ærʌ] G 10. [bi'sɛHro] G

3. [ʌře] F 7. [ɑře] F 11. [gʌw'yuřɩ] F

4. [æri] G 8. [ʋrɩ] G 12. [k^he'mɑrɔ] G

RE 17.7. Mimicry: [ř]

Mimic the tape, paying particular attention to clear flap articulation, especially in initial and final position. Follow along in the Manual.

1. [iři] 6. ['řɩřɑ] 11. [mu'řiř]

2. [ɛřɛ] 7. ['řʋřɔ] 12. [no'řɔř]

3. [ořo] 8. ['řʌřɛy] 13. [ŋe'řʋř]

4. [ʌřʌ] 9. ['řɑře] 14. [nʌ'řæř]

5. [æřæ] 10. ['řɛři] 15. [l^ɛ'řuř]

RE 17.8. Mimicry: [R̆]

To produce [R̆] simply turn off the voicing. Practice by mimicry of the following exercise. Follow along in the Manual.

1. [ɑR̆] 5. [ɾ̆ʊR̆] 9. [R̆ʌɾ̆i]

2. [oR̆] 6. [ɾ̆ɔR̆] 10. [R̆eɾ̆ʌ]

3. [iR̆] 7. [ɾ̆æR̆] 11. [R̆ɔɾ̆æ]

4. [uR̆] 8. [ɾ̆ɩR̆] 12. [R̆ɑɾ̆u]

RE 17.9. Differential: VOICED or VOICELESS

Listen to the flaps, and respond with VOICED or VOICELESS. When you can do the exercise orally, go back and transcribe the utterances until you are sure of them. Don't peek.

1. [sɑɾ̆] VD 5. [ˈR̆iño] VL 9. [ˈziɾ̆æ] VD

2. [tʰuR̆] VL 6. [R̆ɛˈŊŋɑ] VL 10. [ˈR̆ɛpyɩ] VL

3. [mɔɾ̆] VD 7. [R̆eˈtsɩ] VL 11. [ˈfyæR̆u] VL

4. [ĩɛɾ̆] VD 8. [ɾ̆ɔˈtƐʊ] VD 12. [ˈɾ̆etʰwʌ] VD

Trills

Most people have made tongue-tip trills all of their lives in play. Others can learn to do so. There is one important tip to remember, however. The trill is not created by voluntarily moving the tongue through use of your muscles. The tongue is moved by the air stream. One analogy is that of a tarpaulin on the back of a truck. As the truck moves along, the tarpaulin flaps repeatedly and rhythmically. This is not a movement made on its own part, but is made by the rushing of the air acting on the tarpaulin. Correspondingly, the muscles serve to hold the tongue in the right position and with the right degree of tension, so that when the air does rush out, the tongue flaps repeatedly, creating a rapid trill.

RE 17.10. Demonstration: [r̃ R̃]

Listen to the tape, mimic, and follow in your Manual.

a. Most people can make a voiced alveolar trill, having done so from childhood when they played cars or airplanes, or machine guns. Just make sure your trill is with the tongue tip in the alveolar region: [r̃·].

b. If you have no trouble with a voiced tip-alveolar trill, try doing the same thing without voicing: [R̃•].

c. If the voiced trill is difficult for you, try saying the following two phrases rapidly and repeatedly: put it on and butter up. For many speakers, when this is done naturally and in a relaxed manner it will give [pʰʋr̃'r̃ɑn] and [bʌr̃'r̃ʌp]. Work on these in odd moments, but frequently, over a period of several days, and you will probably find that very suddenly the tongue tip trill works.

d. Some people who have difficulty with [r̃] find it easier to make after [p], so you could try practicing [pr̃•].

e. All of these same devices can be used to get the voiceless trill as well if you whisper the items as you practice them.

RE 17.11. Mimicry: [r̃ R̃]

Mimic and follow the transcription.

1a. [ɑr̃ɑ]	1b. [r̃ɑr̃ɑr̃]	1c. [ɑR̃ɑ]	1d. [R̃ɑR̃ɑR̃]
2a. [ɛr̃ɛ]	2b. [r̃ɛr̃ɛr̃]	2c. [ɛR̃ɛ]	2d. [R̃ɛR̃ɛR̃]
3a. [ir̃i]	3b. [r̃ir̃ir̃]	3c. [iR̃i]	3d. [R̃iR̃iR̃]
4a. [ur̃u]	4b. [r̃ur̃ur̃]	4c. [uR̃u]	4d. [R̃uR̃uR̃]
5a. [ɔr̃ɔ]	5b. [r̃ɔr̃ɔr̃]	5c. [ɔR̃ɔ]	5d. [R̃ɔR̃ɔR̃]
6a. [ær̃æ]	6b. [r̃ær̃ær̃]	6c. [æR̃æ]	6d. [R̃æR̃æR̃]

RE 17.12. Demonstration: [ṛ̃ Ṛ̃]

Mimic and follow along in your Manual.

a. Many people have made uvular trills from childhood. Sometimes children who do not make tip-alveolar trills substitute uvular trills for them. If you can already do so, imitate the tape and produce a trill with your uvula vibrating against the back of your tongue: [ṛ̃•].

b. If you can make a voiced uvular trill, turn off the voicing and make a voiceless one: [Ṛ̃•]

c. If the uvular trill does not come easily, articulate your mouth for an [o], inhale deeply, and then exhale suddenly and sharply through this articulation. You may get an [ṛ̃]. Try

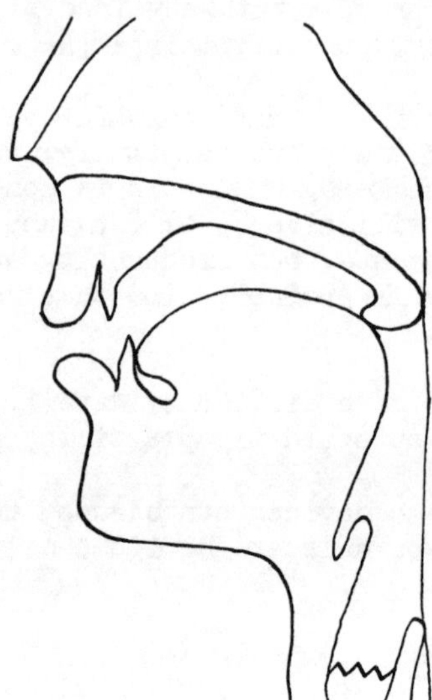

Sammy 17.1: Articulation of [r̥̃], Showing the Uvula Articulating on the Back of the Tongue

this repeatedly at various times. Keep relaxed as you do it, playing around with various combinations until you get one that works.

d. Some people who find a uvular trill difficult, make it most easily in the sequence [ɑ'r̥̃o], forcing the air out of the lungs forcefully on the [r̥̃o].

e. Try snoring, as you hold your nostrils shut with your fingers. Get the feel of your velic and uvula vibrating in the back of your mouth. Snore in, and then, without moving your tongue, breathe out through your mouth (nostrils held shut with your fingers). Sometimes this produces [r̥̃·].

f. Some people find the sequence [gr̥̃·] most useful for producing a uvular trill.

g. Some people have a tendency to make [x g] so far back that they produce [R̥̃ r̥̃]. Try approaching the uvular trill from the velar fricative.

h. Some people find it helpful to get the uvula into position in relation to the tongue by sitting in a chair and leaning their heads back to look up at the ceiling, and then forcing the air out of the lungs. Others lie on a bed with their head hanging off to create this same effect.

i. Whatever way works best with you, when you have begun to produce a voiced or voiceless uvular trill, then articulate it between vowels, before vowels, after them, etc.: [αṛ̃α ṛ̃α αṛ̃ oṛ̃o], etc.

RE 17.13. Mimicry: [ṛ̃ Ṛ̃]

When you can produce a uvular trill in isolation, work on mimicry of this exercise. Follow along in your Manual.

1a. [αṛ̃α]	1b. [ṛ̃αṛ̃αṛ̃]	1c. [αṚ̃α]	1d. [Ṛ̃αṚ̃αṚ̃]
2a. [εṛ̃ε]	2b. [ṛ̃εṛ̃εṛ̃]	2c. [εṚ̃ε]	2d. [Ṛ̃εṚ̃εṚ̃]
3a. [iṛ̃i]	3b. [ṛ̃iṛ̃iṛ̃]	3c. [iṚ̃i]	3d. [Ṛ̃iṚ̃iṚ̃]
4a. [uṛ̃u]	4b. [ṛ̃uṛ̃uṛ̃]	4c. [uṚ̃u]	4d. [R̥̃uṚ̃uṚ̃]
5a. [ɔṛ̃ɔ]	5b. [ṛ̃ɔṛ̃ɔṛ̃]	5c. [ɔṚ̃ɔ]	5d. [Ṛ̃ɔṚ̃ɔṚ̃]
6a. [ær̥̃æ]	6b. [ṛ̃æṛ̃æṛ̃]	6c. [æṚ̃æ]	6d. [Ṛ̃æṚ̃æṚ̃]

RE 17.14. Differential: FLAP or TRILL

Respond orally with FLAP or TRILL. When you have done the exercise orally, transcribe the utterances and check your transcription against the text below. Don't peek.

1. [ˈpiřæ]	F	6. [ˈR̃α.tsɔ]	T	11. [Mmeˈnʌřoz]	F
2. [ˈsɔr̃ʌ]	T	7. [ˈṚ̃ušɩ]	T	12. [k^hwɔˈŋεṛ̃uč]	T
3. [ˈger̃ʊ]	T	8. [ˈŘεtħα]	F	13. [ǰɩˈxæřup]	F
4. [ˈfuṛ̃o]	T	9. [ˈṚ̃ol^i]	T	14. [ñʌˈdzεṚ̃ʊt^h]	T
5. [ˈwεři]	F	10. [ˈR̃el̃æ]	T	15. [gαˈbɓoR̃ɔŋ]	T

RE 17.15. Differential: VOICED or VOICELESS

1. [ˈR̃α.tsɔ]	VL	5. [ˈpiřæ]	VD	9. [gαˈbɓoR̃ɔŋ]	VL
2. [ˈṛ̃ušɩ]	VD	6. [ˈger̃ʊ]	VD	10. [ñʌˈdzεṚ̃ʊt^h]	VL
3. [ˈṚ̃ol^i]	VL	7. [ˈsɔR̃ʌ]	VL	11. [ǰɩˈxæřup]	VD
4. [ˈřεtħα]	VD	8. [ˈfuṚ̃o]	VL	12. [k^hwɔˈŋεr̃uč]	VD

RE 17.16. Differential: ALVEOLAR or UVULAR

1. ['pir̆æ] A	5. ['Ṛ̃ušɩ] U	9. [k^{h}wɔ'ŋɛṛ̃uč] U
2. ['sɔr̆ʌ] A	6. ['Ř ɛtɫɑ] A	10. [ǰɩ'sær̆up] A
3. ['fuṛ̃o] U	7. ['R̃el̃æ] A	11. [gɑ'bƀoR̃ɔŋ] A
4. ['wɛr̆i] A	8. ['Ṛ̃ol˄i] U	12. [Mme'nʌr̆oz] A

RE 17.17. Negative Practice: Flaps and Trills

Practice saying these English words and phrases with the indicated substitutions of flaps and trills. Follow the transcription as you mimic the tape.

a. car	b. rat	c. near	d. park
1a. [k^{h}ɑr̃]	1b. [r̃æt^h]	1c. [ni˒yr̃]	1d. [p^{h}ɑr̃k^h]
2a. [k^{h}ɑR̃]	2b. [R̃æt^h]	2c. [ni˒yR̃]	2d. [p^{h}ɑR̃k^h]
3a. [k^{h}ɑr̆]	3b. [r̆æt^h]	3c. [ni˒yr̆]	3d. [p^{h}ɑr̆k^h]
4a. [k^{h}ɑŘ]	4b. [Řæt^h]	4c. [ni˒yŘ]	4d. [p^{h}ɑŘk^h]
5a. [k^{h}ɑṛ̃]	5b. [ṛ̃æt^h]	5c. [ni˒yṛ̃]	5d. [p^{h}ɑṛ̃k^h]
6a. [k^{h}ɑṚ̃]	6b. [Ṛ̃æt^h]	6c. [ni˒yṚ̃]	6d. [p^{h}ɑṚ̃k^h]

e. prowl	f. roaring	g. Rosa rarely ran
1e. [pr̃ɑwl]	1f. ['r̃oHr̃ɩŋ]	1g. ['r̃owzʌ 'r̃ɛHr̃l˅i˒y 'r̃æHn]
2e. [pR̃ɑwl]	2f. ['R̃oHR̃ɩŋ]	2g. ['R̃owzʌ 'R̃ɛHR̃l˅i˒y 'R̃æHn]
3e. [pr̆ɑwl]	3f. ['r̆oHr̆ɩŋ]	3g. ['r̆owzʌ 'r̆ɛHr̆l˅i˒y 'r̆æHn]
4e. [pŘɑwl]	4f. ['ŘoHŘɩŋ]	4g. ['Řowzʌ 'ŘɛHŘl˅i˒y 'ŘæHn]
5e. [pṛ̃ɑwl]	5f. ['ṛ̃oHṛ̃ɩŋ]	5g. ['ṛ̃owzʌ 'ṛ̃EHṛ̃l˅i˒y 'ṛ̃æHn]
6e. [pṚ̃ɑwl]	6f. ['Ṛ̃oHṚ̃ɩŋ]	6g. ['Ṛ̃owzʌ 'Ṛ̃ɛHṚ̃l˅i˒y 'Ṛ̃æHn]

RE 17.18: Khmuʔ.[1] Mimicry: [r̃]

Mimic the tape, and follow the transcription.

---

[1] The recording is not that of a native speaker.

1a. /r̃ɑɑ/ 'pour over'	1b. /bɑɑr̃/ 'two'	1c. /hr̃ɑɑŋ/ [R̃r̃ɑ•ŋ] 'tooth'
2a. /r̃ɑɑy/ 'fierce'	2b. /wɑɑr̃/ 'hot'	2c. /hr̃nɑɑ/ [R̃r̩̃'nɑ•] 'irrigated ricefield'
3a. /r̃ɑk/ 'love'	3b. /mɑr̃/ 'snake'	3c. /hr̃lɑp/ [R̃r̩̃'lʌp] 'fold up'
4a. /r̃ɑp/ 'grasp'	4b. /sɑr̃/ 'wild cat'	4c. /hr̃iin/ [R̃r̃i•n] 'to lead'
5a. /r̃iit/ 'custom'	5b. /wiir̃/ 'stare'	5c. /hr̃niip/ [R̃r̩̃•'ni•p] 'spoon'
6a. /r̃eeŋ/ 'abandoned ricefield'	6b. /wer̃/ 'turn over'	6c. /hr̃eʔ/ [R̃r̃ɩʔ] 'swidden'
7a. /r̃ɛɛŋ/ 'strong'	7b. /her̃/ 'intelligent'	7c. /hr̃oh/ [R̃r̃ʋh] 'to ripen'
8a. /r̃ɛɛw/ 'noose trap'	8b. /nɛɛr̃/ 'tiny'	8c. /hr̃ok/ [R̃r̃ʋk] 'six'
9a. /r̃ɔɔŋ/ 'line'	9b. /ŋɔɔr̃/ 'road'	9c. /hr̃lɔʔ/ [R̃r̩̃'lɔʔ] 'word'
10a. /r̃uup/ 'picture'	10b. /buɑr̃/ 'evening'	10c. /hr̃uuy/ [R̃r̃u•y] 'spirit'

RE 17.19. Review: Nasals, Laterals, Stops

In this exercise we will emphasize three kinds of articulation: bilabial, tip-alveolar, and blade-alveopalatal. Mimic the tape and follow along in your Manual. Make sure that your voicing, or voicelessness, or aspiration is clear, as well as your articulation.

1a. [mɑmem]	1b. [nɑnen]	1c. [ñɑñeñ]
2a. [Mmo.MmʌmM]	2b. [Nno.NnʌnN]	2c. [Ññо.ÑñʌñÑ]
	3b. [l^ɛl^ul^]	3c. [l̃ɛl̃ul̃]
	4b. [lˇɔlˇælˇ]	
	5b. [Llˇɑ.Llˇilˇ L]	
	6b. [dɬu.dɬɩdɬ]	

	7b. [tƀo.tƀɛtƀ]
	8b. [tƀʰæ.tƀʰɑtƀ]
9a. [bebʌb]	9b. [dedʌd]
10a. [pupɛp]	10b. [tutɛt]
11a. [pʰɑpʰʋpʰ]	11b. [tʰɑtʰʋtʰ]

RE 17.20. Substitution

Mimic the tape on the following exercise. The first one will be built up, and the remainder will consist of substitutions made in the first one. Practice for fluency. Work on pitch, timing, stress, juncture, etc., as well as consonants and vowels.

1. [Nnæw'ŋiH.pɔ.ñʌr̃ dɑ.ř̌ɛ'l^ ɩwtʰ]

2. [ĩɑ.xɛŋ]

3. [R̃of.šil̬]

4. [šʌr.př̌ʌtƀ]

Transcription

Use RE 17.2, 17.9, 17.13-17.17 as transcription exercises. Transcribe repeatedly those which give you trouble. Do your transcription on a transcription form, and keep track of your errors. Watch your progress on sounds which give you difficulty, and drill with those sounds and symbols which tend to confuse you, going back to the lesson where the sound was introduced, if necessary.

Reading

Use 17.14-17.16 as reading exercises, calling off the utterance before the machine gives it, and checking yourself against the production on the tape.

LESSON SEVENTEEN R

Review

Consonants

Here is the inventory of the symbols representing sounds drilled so far. You are responsible for production of all sounds to date except the flaps and trills, which may take a little more time for some people. You are not responsible for hearing the difference between dental and alveolar stops, nasals and laterals. You should hear this difference in fricatives and affricates.

	Labial	Dental	Alveolar	Alveo-palatal	Alveo-palatal[1] (retroflex)	Velar	Glottal
STOPS							
Vl. unasp.	p	ṱ	t		ṭ	k	ʔ
Vl. asp.	p^h	$ṱ^h$	t^h		$ṭ^h$	k^h	
Voiced	b	ḓ	d		ḍ	g	
Vl. flap			ť				
Vd. flap			ď				
FRICATIVES							
Lip articulation							
Voiceless	ᵽ	f					
Voiced	ƀ	v					
Tongue articulation							
Grooved							
Voiceless		s̭	s	š	ṣ̌		
Voiced		z̭	z	ž	ẓ̌		

[1]Tip-palatal articulation is also used for retroflexed sounds.

	Labial	Dental	Alveolar	Alveo-palatal	Alveo-palatal (retroflex)	Velar	Uvular
Flat							
Voiceless		θ				x	
Voiced		đ				ǥ	
Lateral							
Voiceless			Ł				
Voiced			ł				
AFFRICATES[1]							
Grooved							
Vl. unasp.		ṱs̭	ts	č	t̤š̤		
Vl. asp.		ṱs̭^{h}	ts^h	č^h	t̤š̤^{h}		
Voiced		ḓz̭	dz	ǰ	d̤ž̤		
Flat							
Vl. unasp.	pᵽ	ṱθ				kx	
Vl. asp.	pᵽ^h	ṱθ^h				kx^h	
Voiced	bƀ	ḓđ				gǥ	
Lateral							
Vl. unasp.			tŁ				
Vl. asp.			tŁ^h				
Voiced			dł				
NASALS							
Voiceless	M		N	Ñ		Ŋ	
Voiced	m	ṋ	n	ñ	ṇ	ŋ	
Vd. flap			ň				

[1] There are, of course, many affricates with different points of articulation for stop and fricative. Some are shown on p. 138.

	Labial	Dental	Alveolar	Alveo-palatal	Alveo-palatal (retroflex)	Velar	Uvular
LATERALS[1]							
Voiceless			L				
Vd. high tongue		ḽ^	l^	l̃			
Vd. low tongue		ḽˇ	lˇ				
Vd. flap			ľ				
TRILLS							
Voiceless			R̃				Ṛ̃
Voiced			r̃				ṛ̃
FLAPS (cupped tongue)[2]							
Voiceless			Ř				
Voiced			ř				

Table 17R.1. Consonants to Date

TE 17R.1. Matching Symbols

Since the number of consonant symbols is now becoming rather large, the problem of remembering symbols themselves, aside from the problem of hearing sound differences, needs some attention and practice. After you have reviewed the above chart, paying particular attention to the diacritic marks and the distinctions they represent, try TE 17R.1 in the Workbook Supplement (pp. 49-54).

Vowels

Table 16.1, p. 232, charts the vowel qualities to date. Review the vowel symbols and the qualities they represent from that lesson. Review also the on-glides [w y r] and the off-glides [w y r H] in Lesson 12, p. 175ff., and subsequent

---

[1]Lateral fricatives and affricates are shown above under fricatives and affricates, respectively.

[2]Nasal flaps are shown under nasals, lateral flaps under laterals, and flat tongue flaps under stops.

even-numbered lessons. Work on production, recognition, and transcription.

Syllables and Their Characteristics

Review Lesson 10 (p. 150ff.).

Pitch

If you have very much trouble with pitch, review Lesson 8, p. 118ff. If you do not, review exercises like RE 17.20, p. 256, and 14.20, p. 215f.

Transcription

a. For any sounds which you have difficulty recognizing, use the differential drills in the lessons where they were introduced as transcription drills, and check your answer with the Manual.

b. Transcribe drills containing longer sequences.

In all your transcription, study your mistakes in comparison with the correct form, and see the reasons for your errors if you can. Keep track of your errors on the Transcription Tally Form in your Workbook Supplement.

Reading

Practice reading items from exercises in the Manual, and checking your production against the tape. Work with your buddy so that a second person can hear your production.

LESSON EIGHTEEN

Lower-low Vowels; Length

	Front U.	Front R.	Central U.	Central R.	Back U.	Back R.
High	i					u
Lower-high	ɪ					ʊ
Mid	e					o
Lower-mid	ɛ					
Low	æ		ʌ			ɔ
Lower-low	a		ɑ		ɒ	

Table 18.1: Vowels to Date

The names for the new symbols on the chart are [a] "printed a" or "typewriter a" or "Boston a," and [ɒ] "upside-down a." In contrast, [ɑ] is called "written a" or "script a." The easiest way to write [ɒ] by hand is to start in the upper left-hand corner:

RE 18.1. Demonstration: Table 18.1

Listen to the demonstration of the vowel chart repeatedly, studying Table 18.1 as you do so. When you are familiar with it, read off the chart simultaneously with the tape. Work with your buddy.

RE 18.2. Discrimination: SAME or DIFFERENT

Continue tuning up your ears to these new vowel qualities by responding SAME or DIFFERENT to the following pairs. Concentrate on the differences to help you become familiar with them. Don't peek.

1a. [l^æl^ l^al^] D

2a. [l^æl^ l^æl^] S

3a. [l^al^ l^al^] S

4a. [l^al^ l^æl^] D

5a. [l^æl^ l^al^] D

6a. [tso'l^æl^ tso'l^æl^] S

7a.	[tso'l^æl^ tso'l^al^]	D	9a.	[tso'l^al^ tso'l^al^]	S
8a.	[tso'l^æl^ tso'l^al^]	D	10a.	[tso'l^al^ tso'l^æl^]	D

1b.	[vaθ vɑθ]	D	1c.	[gɒtŁ gɑtŁ]	D
2b.	[vɑθ vaθ]	D	2c.	[gɑtŁ gɒtŁ]	D
3b.	[vɑθ vaθ]	D	3c.	[gɒtŁ gɒtŁ]	S
4b.	[vaθ vɑθ]	D	4c.	[gɑtŁ gɑtŁ]	S
5b.	[vaθ vaθ]	S	5c.	[gɒtŁ gɒtŁ]	S
6b.	[pʰr̩'vɑθ pʰr̩'vɑθ]	S	6c.	[Ŋŋi'gɒtŁ Ŋŋi'gɒtŁ]	S
7b.	[pʰr̩'vɑθ pʰr̩'vaθ]	D	7c.	[Ŋŋi'gɑtŁ Ŋŋi'gɒtŁ]	D
8b.	[pʰr̩'vaθ pʰr̩'vaθ]	S	8c.	[Ŋŋi'gɒtŁ Ŋŋi'gɑtŁ]	D
9b.	[pʰr̩'vaθ pʰr̩'vɑθ]	D	9c.	[Ŋŋi'gɑtŁ Ŋŋi'gɑtŁ]	S
10b.	[pʰr̩'vaθ pʰr̩'vɑθ]	D	10c.	[Ŋŋi'gɑtŁ Ŋŋi'gɒtŁ]	D

1d.	[r̃ɔR̃ r̃ɔR̃]	S	1e.	[l̃al^ l̃ʌl^]	D
2d.	[r̃ɔR̃ r̃ɒR̃]	D	2e.	[l̃ʌl^ l̃ʌl^]	S
3d.	[r̃ɔR̃ r̃ɔR̃]	S	3e.	[l̃ʌl^ l̃al^]	D
4d.	[r̃ɒR̃ r̃ɒR̃]	S	4e.	[l̃ʌl^ l̃ʌl^]	S
5d.	[r̃ɒR̃ r̃ɔR̃]	D	5e.	[l̃al^ l̃al^]	S
6d.	[ñɛ'r̃ɒR̃ ñɛ'r̃ɒR̃]	S	6e.	[řɔ'l̃al^ řɔ'l̃al^]	S
7d.	[ñɛ'r̃ɔR̃ ñɛ'r̃ɒR̃]	D	7e.	[řɔ'l̃ʌl^ řɔ'l̃ʌl^]	S
8d.	[ñɛ'r̃ɒR̃ ñɛ'r̃ɔR̃]	D	8e.	[řɔ'l̃al^ řɔ'l̃ʌl^]	D
9d.	[ñɛ'r̃ɔR̃ ñɛ'r̃ɒR̃]	D	9e.	[řɔ'l̃al^ řɔ'l̃ʌl^]	D
10d.	[ñɛ'r̃ɔR̃ ñɛ'r̃ɔR̃]	S	10e.	[řɔ'l̃ʌl^ řɔ'l̃al^]	D

1f.	[ƀɒtʰ ƀʌtʰ]	D	3f.	[ƀʌtʰ ƀɒtʰ]	D
2f.	[ƀʌtʰ ƀɒtʰ]	D	4f.	[ƀɒtʰ ƀʌtʰ]	D

5f.	[ƀʌt^h ƀʌt^h]	S	8f.	['šuƀɒt^h 'šuƀɒt^h]	S
6f.	['šuƀɒt^h 'šuƀʌt^h]	D	9f.	['šuƀɒt^h 'šuƀɒt^h]	S
7f.	['šuƀʌt^h 'šuƀɒt^h]	D	10f.	['šuƀʌt^h 'šuƀʌt^h]	S

Production of [æ a ɑ ɒ ɔ]

All of these low and lower-low vowel qualities occur in one or another of the dialects of English, but they do not usually occur all in the same dialect, at least not with phonemic distinctiveness. Speakers of English, furthermore, differ in the degree of tongue height, fronting, and backing, with which they pronounce these vowels, as any others. For example, many speakers of English do not normally have [æ] or [a], but a vowel somewhere between: [æ˅] or [a˄]. Others have [æ] but not [a], others [a] but not [æ]. Some have both. In similar fashion, some English speakers have [ɑ] and [ɔ], others [ɒ] and [ɔ], and still others have only [ɑ˃], without either [ɒ] or [ɔ]. The learning problems in this area are therefore different for different English-speaking people.

[a] is famous in the United States as one of the ingredients of the "Harvard accent," speech of the Boston area, and of President Kennedy. It occurs, however, in other areas as well, notably the South. Some Americans in areas where it is not normal have it sporadically in certain words because of dialect influence. Some areas, like Western New England have a variety not quite so far front as the Boston variety. Some New York City dialects have a variety not quite so low as the Boston variety. We will strive in this course for a really lower-low front articulation. The sound occurs as the only lower-low vowel in many languages, including some dialects of French and Spanish, and along with [ɑ] in others, including some dialects of French.

[ɒ] occurs commonly in some British dialects of English, including some used in Canada. It occurs in the speech of many Americans as well.

RE 18.3. Demonstration: Producing [æ a ɑ ɒ ɔ]

a. One of the best ways to develop a feel for the lower-low front articulation represented in [a] or the lower-low back articulation represented in [ɒ], is to practice talking or reading English in a fronted articulation style, and in one which uses a lowered tongue-back position. Listen to the tape as it demonstrates both of these. It will read this paragraph first in fronted articulation style, and then in backed, lowered articulation style. Practice reading in this same way

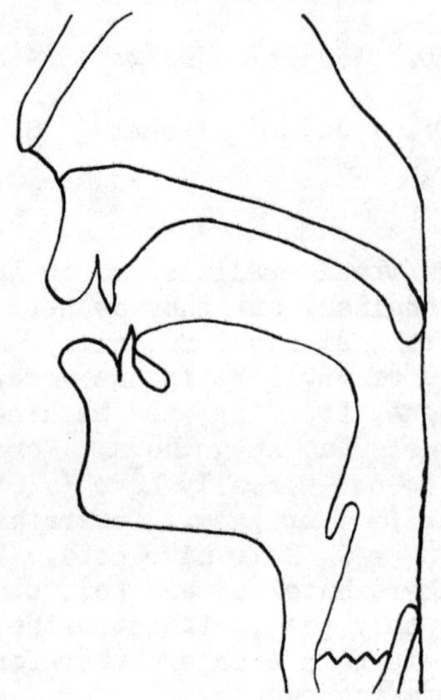

Sammy 18.1: [a]. Note that the whole tongue is low and flat, but that the highest point is in the front.

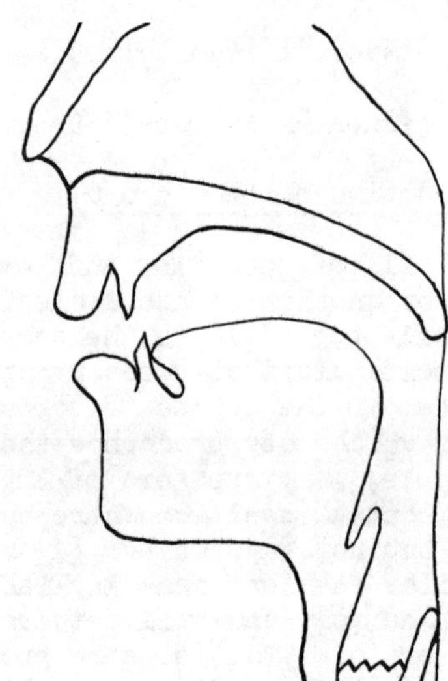

Sammy 18.2: [ɒ]. Note that the whole tongue is low and flat, but that the highest point is in the back.

yourself. Watch your tongue closely in the mirror on the fronted style. Make sure it does not slip back, but stays firmly bunched in the front of your mouth.

b. One way to achieve a clear distinction between [æ] and [a] is to go down the "front unrounded" column of the chart, opening the mouth slightly with each sound, and making sure the tongue does not slip back to [ɑ]. Mimic the tape, and watch in the mirror. If necessary at first, protrude your lower jaw on [a] to make sure it stays front.

c. The same approach can be taken for [ɔ] and [ɒ]. Go down the "back rounded" column with progressively more open mouth. Notice also that the amount of rounding decreases. When you go from [ɔ] to [ɒ] there is no more rounding. Be careful not to jump to [ɑ]. Mimic the tape.

c. Work on the sequence [æ a ɑ ɒ ɔ]. Watch your tongue in the mirror as you do so. There should be a clear movement of the hump of the tongue backwards on the sequence [a ɑ ɒ]. Listen to the tape and mimic.

d. Among some American ministers [ɒ] is sometimes used as a special pronunciation restricted to formal prayer or other occasions when they need to sound sanctimonious. [ˌɑwr ˈfɒdr̩] our Father, for example, is frequently heard in the prayers of some preachers who would say [ˌɑwr ˈfɑdr̩] under other circumstances. It is sometimes used facetiously by Americans who do not otherwise use it, as in [wɒˈhɒpn̩d] what happened? Some people say [ˈwɒfl̩] waffle or [ˈɒfl̩] awful. The tape demonstrates. Mimic the speech of someone in whom you detect this pronunciation.

e. For [a] mimic the speech of a Bostonian whom you know in such words as car, father. Or mimic the speech of a southerner who says [a·] or [aH] for I, [faHn] fine, [maHn] mine.

RE 18.4. Negative Practice: [æ a ɑ ɒ ɔ]

Mimic the tape, substituting the various vowel qualities in the English sentences. In the second sentence the substitutions will be made only in the underlined words. Follow in your Manual. When you have learned to do this in mimicry of the tape, use it as an exercise to practice in your spare minutes.

1. Park your car in Harvard Yard.

   1a. [ˈpʰæk yɨˈkʰæ ɪnˈhævɨd ˈyæd]

   1b. [ˈpʰak yɨˈkʰa ɪnˈhavɨd ˈyad]

   1c. [ˈpʰɑk yɨˈkʰɑ ɪnˈhɑvɨd ˈyɑd]

   1d. [ˈpʰɒk yɨˈkʰɒ ɪnˈhɒvɨd ˈyɒd]

   1e. [ˈpʰɔk yɨˈkʰɔ ɪnˈhɔvɨd ˈyɔd]

2. It made me laugh to see a calf go down the path to take a bath.

2a.	[læf]	[kʰæf]	[pʰæθ]	[bæθ]
2b.	[laf]	[kʰaf]	[pʰaθ]	[baθ]
2c.	[lɑf]	[kʰɑf]	[pʰɑθ]	[bɑθ]
2d.	[lɒf]	[kʰɒf]	[pʰɒθ]	[bɒθ]
2e.	[lɔf]	[kʰɔf]	[pʰɔθ]	[bɔθ]

RE 18.5. Mimicry: [æ a ɑ ɒ ɔ]

Follow the transcription as you mimic. Work with a buddy

so that you can check each other when you wander from close mimicry of the tape.

1a. [dæf] 1b. [daf] 1c. [dɑf] 1d. [dɒf] 1e. [dɔf]

2a. [næpʰ] 2b. [napʰ] 2c. [nɑpʰ] 2d. [nɒpʰ] 2e. [nɔpʰ]

3a. [l^æš] 3b. [l^aš] 3c. [l^ɑš] 3d. [l^ɒš] 3e. [l^ɔš]

4a. [tɬæs] 4b. [tɬas] 4c. [tɬɑs] 4d. [tɬɒs] 4e. [tɬɔs]

5a. [ŋæl^] 5b. [ŋal^] 5c. [ŋɑl^] 5d. [ŋɒl^] 5e. [ŋɔl^]

6a. [Nnæd] 6b. [Nnad] 6c. [Nnɑd] 6d. [Nnɒd] 6e. [Nnɔd]

7a. [pLæƥ] 7b. [pLaƥ] 7c. [pLɑƥ] 7d. [pLɒƥ] 7e. [pLɔƥ]

8a. [kæž] 8b. [kaž] 8c. [kɑž] 8d. [kɒž] 8e. [kɔž]

9a. [l̃ær] 9b. [l̃ar] 9c. [l̃ɑr] 9d. [l̃ɒr] 9e. [l̃ɔr]

10a. [R̥̃æm] 10b. [R̥̃am] 10c. [R̥̃ɑm] 10d. [R̥̃ɒm] 10e. [R̥̃ɔm]

RE 18.6. Mimicry: Vowels With and Without On-glides

Mimic the tape and watch the transcription.

1a. [ƀɔ] 1b. [ƀyɔ] 1c. [ƀwɔ] 1d. [ƀrɔ]

2a. [ƀɔŋkʰ] 2b. [ƀyɔŋkʰ] 2c. [ƀwɔŋkʰ] 2d. [ƀrɔŋkʰ]

3a. [ṛ̌ɒ] 3b. [ṛ̌yɒ] 3c. [ṛ̌wɒ] 3d. [ṛ̌rɒ]

4a. [ṛ̌ɒŋkʰ] 4b. [ṛ̌yɒŋkʰ] 4c. [ṛ̌wɒŋkʰ] 4d. [ṛ̌rɒŋkʰ]

5a. [d̤ž̤ɑ] 5b. [d̤ž̤yɑ] 5c. [d̤ž̤wɑ] 5d. [d̤ž̤rɑ]

6a. [d̤ž̤ɑŋkʰ] 6b. [d̤ž̤yɑŋkʰ] 6c. [d̤ž̤wɑŋkʰ] 6d. [d̤ž̤rɑŋkʰ]

7a. [ƚa] 7b. [ƚya] 7c. [ƚwa] 7d. [ƚra]

8a. [ƚaŋkʰ] 8b. [ƚyaŋkʰ] 8c. [ƚwaŋkʰ] 8d. [ƚraŋkʰ]

9a. [xæ] 9b. [xyæ] 9c. [xwæ] 9d. [xræ]

10a. [xæŋkʰ] 10b. [xyæŋkʰ] 10c. [xwæŋkʰ] 10d. [xræŋkʰ]

RE 18.7. Negative Practice: "Old MacDonald Had a Farm"

Practice in the manner of RE 16.10, p. 239. The tape

will demonstrate the beginning, and you can practice at odd moments.

a. With a [væ væ] here...

b. With a [vwæ vwæ] here...

c. Continue with other glides and other vowels.

RE 18.8. Differential: Vowel Symbols

Respond to the tape by giving the name of the symbol with which the vowel sound is transcribed, as you did in RE 16.13, p. 242. You may do this orally or in writing. Don't peek, but if you write your responses check them with the transcription below after you finish the exercise. When you can respond with the correct symbol in every case, transcribe the full utterance.

1. [ñɑ] SCRIPT ɑ
2. [ñæ] DIGRAPH
3. [ñɛ] EPSILON
4. [ñɔ] BACKWARDS c
5. [ño] o
6. [ñɒf] UPSIDE-DOWN ɑ
7. [ñaf] PRINTED a
8. [ñɩf] IOTA
9. [ñuf] u
10. [ñæf] DIGRAPH
11. [Ññʋfl̩ˇ] UPSILON
12. [Ññefl̩ˇ] e
13. [Ññæfl̩ˇ] DIGRAPH
14. [Ññifl̩ˇ] i
15. [Ññɑfl̩ˇ] SCRIPT ɑ
16. [šŋufl̩] u
17. [šŋɛfl̩] EPSILON
18. [šŋafl̩] PRINTED a
19. [šŋɔfl̩] BACKWARDS c
20. [šŋifl̩] i
21. [šŋoṚ̃] o
22. [šŋɩṚ̃] IOTA
23. [šŋɒṚ̃] UPSIDE-DOWN ɑ
24. [šŋʋṚ̃] UPSILON

RE 18.9. Differential: FRONT or CENTRAL UNROUNDED, BACK ROUNDED or UNROUNDED

Respond orally to the tape. Use the exercise for transcription when you can handle it as a differential drill.

1. [d̂dɑ] C U 2. [d̂dɛ] F U 3. [d̂dæ] F U

4. [ḓɑɒ]	B U	8. [přɔl^]	B R	12. [skyɑnt^{h}]	C U
5. [ḓɑa]	F U	9. [přɒl^]	B U	13. [skyænt^{h}]	F U
6. [přʊl^]	B R	10. [přʌl^]	C U	14. [skyɒnt^{h}]	B U
7. [přol^]	B R	11. [skyant^{h}]	F U	15. [skyɔnt^{h}]	B R

RE 18.10. Differential: Tongue Height

Respond with HIGH, LOWER-HIGH, MID, LOWER-MID, LOW, or LOWER-LOW. Then transcribe.

1. [t̤š^{h}a]	L-L	8. [sřʌñ]	L	15. [žl^ɔyk^{h}]	L
2. [t̤š^{h}ɒ]	L-L	9. [sřɒñ]	L-L	16. [žl^ɒyk^{h}]	L-L
3. [t̤š^{h}æ]	L	10. [sřɔñ]	L	17. [žl^æyk^{h}]	L
4. [t̤š^{h}ɛ]	L-M	11. [sřoñ]	M	18. [žl^ɑyk^{h}]	L-L
5. [t̤š^{h}ɑ]	L-L	12. [sřʊñ]	L-H	19. [žl^ayk^{h}]	L-L
6. [t̤š^{h}i]	H	13. [sřɪñ]	L-H	20. [žl^uyk^{h}]	H
7. [t̤š^{h}u]	H	14. [sřʊñ]	L-H	21. [žl^ɪyk^{h}]	L-H

RE 18.11. Differential: Full Labels

Select one term from each column to make up your response. Don't peek.

HIGH	FRONT	ROUNDED
LOWER-HIGH	CENTRAL	UNROUNDED
MID	BACK	
LOWER-MID		
LOW		
LOWER-LOW		

1. [ya]	L-L F U	4. [yɛ]	L-M F U	7. [ya]	L-L F U
2. [yo]	M B R	5. [yæ]	L F U	8. [yʌ]	L C U
3. [yɔ]	L B R	6. [yɪ]	L-H F U	9. [žyɒd]	L-L B U

10. [žyɑd] L-L C U

11. [žyʌd] L C U

12. [žyad] L-L F U

13. [žyʋd] L-H B R

14. [žyɔd] L B R

15. [žyæd] L F U

16. [žyɒd] L-L B U

17. [pẓ̌ard] L-L F U

18. [pẓ̌ʌrd] L C U

19. [pẓ̌ɛrd] L-M F U

20. [pẓ̌ʋrd] L-H B R

21. [pẓ̌ord] M B R

22. [pẓ̌ɔrd] L B R

23. [pẓ̌ɑrd] L-L C U

Length of Vowel and Consonant

Almost all speech sounds may vary perceptibly in length, duration of time in which the articulation is held. Some kinds of sounds like vowels, fricatives, nasals, and laterals may be held artificially until the speaker runs out of breath. In others, like voiced stops, the duration for which they can be held is short. When the stopped-off air chambers fill up with air, voicing is no longer possible, and the voiced stop can no longer be held as a voiced stop. A voiceless stop, on the other hand, may be held until the person gasps for breath. Such a stop, however, is completely noiseless. A voiceless stop cannot be heard during its closure.

Unlike most other sounds, flaps cannot be articulated with perceptibly different lengths. When you hold a flap it automatically becomes something else. [ř] becomes [t], [ň] becomes [n], etc.

It should be clear from this discussion that when we talk of long vowels or consonants, and short vowels or consonants, we are not referring to the same phenomenon as when some people say that beat contains a long vowel and bit a short vowel in English. From a phonetic point of view the difference between these two words is in vowel quality and glide, rather than in length. There may be a difference in length as well, but it is easy to confuse the glide in beat with length.

In the speech of many of us, however, there is a difference of length in bat and bad, bit and bid, lock and log. The shorter vowel comes before a voiceless consonant and the longer vowel before a voiced consonant. This demonstrates what is a non-phonemic difference in length for many of us.

All languages show perceptible differences of length on

some of their sounds. In some languages, differences in length create phonemic distinctions. In Khmuʔ, contrasts between long and short vowels of the same quality can be seen in pairs like [lo•ŋ] 'coffin' and [loŋ] 'branch,' [dɛ•k] 'flush at the end' and [dɛk] 'small, little.' (The [•] symbolizes the prolonged articulation, and is called a "raised dot.")

Differences in consonant length are also functional parts of some language systems. In English a long consonant is sometimes heard when a word ending with a certain consonant immediately precedes another beginning with the same consonant, with deliberate pronunciation but no break. Examples are [ˈwɑl•ɑytʰ] 'wall light,' or <u>team meeting</u> as against <u>team eating</u> or <u>tea meeting</u>.

Long consonants are also heard in English as a stylistic device in some speakers, particularly in public address. <u>He was there a l•ong time!</u> <u>N•ever have I seen such a sight!</u>

Some other languages use difference of length on consonants to distinguish words. In Finnish there is [mit•æ] 'measurement' and [mitæ] 'what.' Other examples of the use of long consonants in Finnish include [ɑk•ɑ] 'old lady,' [kʰis•ɑ] 'cat,' [mɑm•ɑ] 'mother,' [pʰuk•o] 'knife.'

RE 18.12. Mimicry: Sequences of Long and Short Vowels and Fricatives

Mimic the tape and follow the transcription. The tape will build up to the long sequences. Mimic the timing, rhythm, and length. Be very careful not to have different vowel quality on the short vowels from what you have on the long. Try to keep the stress even.

1. [sɑ•sɑsɑ ɑsɑ•sɑ sɑ•sɑ sɑ•sɑ sɑ•sɑsɑsɑ]

2. [sɑs•ɑs• s•ɑsɑs•ɑ ɑsɑs•ɑ ɑs•ɑs•ɑsɑ]

3. [sɑ•s•ɑsɑsɑs•ɑ ɑ•sɑs•ɑs•ɑ• s•ɑsɑsɑ•sɑ]

RE 18.13. Demonstration: Long Stops

a. To make a long voiceless stop, simply keep the articulation closed for the length of time you want to hold the stop. There is no sound during the stop. Mimic the tape: [ep•e] [et•e] [ek•e]

b. To make a long voiced stop, keep the articulation closed as with a voiceless stop, but keep the rumble of the voicing going. You will not be able to do this long as your air cavities will fill up with air. Mimic the tape: [eb•e] [ed•e] [eg•e].

c. Mimic the following sequences:

1. [ba•baba aba•ba ba•ba ba•ba ba•bababa]

2. [bab•aba b•abab•a abab•a ab•ab•aba]

3. [ba•b•abab•a a•bab•ab•a• b•ababa•ba]

RE 18.14. Negative Practice: "The Hat With the Bird"

Practice reading the following sentences with their artificially controlled length. When you have control over them turn on the tape recorder and read them before the tape does. Compare your reading with that on the tape.

1. [đʌ ˌhæt wɨđɨ ˈbr̩d ɑn ɪt]

2. [đʌ ˌhæ•t wɨđɨ ˈbr̩•d ɑn ɪt]

3. [đʌ• ˌhæt wɨđɨ ˈbr̩d ɑn ɪ•t]

4. [đʌ ˌhæt wɨ•đɨ ˈbr̩d ɑ•n ɪt]

5. [đʌ ˌh•æt wɨđɨ ˈbr̩d ɑn• ɪt]

6. [đ•ʌ ˌhæt wɨđɨ ˈb•r̩d ɑn ɪt]

7. [đ•ʌ• ˌhæt wɨđɨ ˈbr̩d• ɑ•n• ɪt]

8. [đʌ ˌhæt• wɨđɨ• ˈbr̩d ɑn ɪt]

RE 18.15. Differential: VOWEL or CONSONANT

Listen for whether the consonant or the vowel is long, and respond accordingly. Don't peek.

1. [nɑ•] V	5. [g•ɛ] C	9. [θ•a] C
2. [s•e] C	6. [d•ɔ] C	10. [ř̌ɪ•] V
3. [ži•] V	7. [f•æ] C	11. [ŋɒ•] V
4. [ƚ•ʌ] C	8. [r̃u•] V	12. [l^•ɒ] C

RE 18.16. Differential: VOWEL, CONSONANT, NEITHER, or BOTH

Listen for the second syllable of each item, and decide what is long, if anything.

1. [pɩˈs·ɩ] C
2. [tʰɛˈx·ɛ] C
3. [ḍʌˈƀʌ·] V
4. [fɑˈzɑ·] V
5. [ẓ̌uˈmu·] V
6. [bɔˈš·ɔ] C
7. [žʋˈl^ɔ·] V
8. [pʰæˈž·i] C
9. [diˈnu·] V
10. [ʂ̬oˈθ·e] C
11. [kɒˈlˇi·] V
12. [ᵽiˈR̃o·] V
13. [taˈŋ·ɩr̃ɛ] C
14. [ɓɩˈɫu·Nnɑ] V
15. [geˈg·ozu] C
16. [t̬ʌˈl̃·e.tƚɔ] C
17. [væˈñ·ʋři] C
18. [kʰɛˈɗɛ·.tš̤ʋ] V

RE 18.17. Differential: LONG or GLIDED

Listen for the first syllable of each item, and decide whether the vowel is long or glided. If it is both long and glided, answer long.

1. [sæ·ˈsæy] L
2. [sæHˈsæw] G
3. [sowˈso] G
4. [so·ˈsoy] L
5. [soHˈsoH] G
6. [sɔ·ˈsɔy] L
7. [sɔwˈsɔ] G
8. [sa·ˈsay] L
9. [sɛyˈsɩw] G
10. [sɛHˈsɩH] G
11. [sɛ·ˈsɩy] L
12. [siHˈsɩH] G
13. [siwˈsuH] G
14. [sʌ·ˈsʌw] L
15. [suyˈsuH] G

RE 18.18: Finnish.[1] Mimicry: Long Vowels and Consonants

Follow the transcription as you mimic the tape. Each item will be given once, and then the whole list repeated.

1a. [ku·l^a] 'bullet'

1b. [ɘul^a][2] 'melted'

---

[1]Finnish materials in this book are taken from recordings for the Special Phonetics of the Wycliffe Language Course (England), and used by permission. The speaker is Mr. Elias Pentti of the Finnish Mission in Angola.

[2]The initial consonant is not one you have had. Mimic it as best you can.

2a. [ku•l^•a]
'to hear'

2b. [ꞓul^α•]
'(it) melts'

3a. [kuol^a]
'drivel'

3b. [ꞓu•l^a]
'a kind of bird'

4a. [kuol^•a]
'to die'

4b. [ꞓu•l^α•]
'a kind of bird (partitive)'

5a. [muta]
'mud'

5b. [ꞓu•l^•a]
'with the mouth'

6a. [mut•a]
'but'

6b. [ꞓuil^•a]
'with the mouths'

7a. [muita]
'others'

7b. [ꞓuol^•a]
'on the swamp'

8a. [muit•a]
'without the others'

8b. [ꞓuol^a]
'salt'

9b. [ꞓuol^α•]
'(he, she) salts'

1c. [takα•]
'from behind'

2c. [takα•ʔ]
'(impera.) go surety'

3c. [tak•a]
'fireplace (nom. case)'

4c. [tak•α•]
'fireplace (partitive (case'

5c. [tα•k•a]
'burden (nom. case)'

6c. [tα•k•α•]
'burden (partitive)'

7c. [taika]
'witchcraft'

8c. [taikα•]
'witchcraft (partitive)'

9c. [taik•a]
'or'

RE 18.19: Finnish. Mimicry: Longer Sequences

This drill contains two pairs of Finnish sentences, different by long vowels and consonants. Within each pair the sentences are repeated several times, in mixed order. Follow the transcription as you mimic the tape. Concentrate on the combination of pitch and length.

1a. ['tæ^ea 'tul^e· 'l^ikɑ·] 'Here comes dirt.'

1b. ['tæ^ea 'tu·l^e· 'l^i·kɑ·] 'Here it blows too much.'

2a. [kül^amɛ'viɛl^a'toisɛmɛta'pɑ·m·ɛ][1]

'We shall meet each other later on.'

2b. [kül^amɛ'viɛl^a'toisɛmɛta'pam·ɛ][1]

'We shall kill each other later on.'

Transcription and Reading

Use RE 18.2, 18.5, 18.16, 18.8-18.11, 18.15-18.18.

---

[1]The first vowel is one you have not had, but mimic it as best you can.

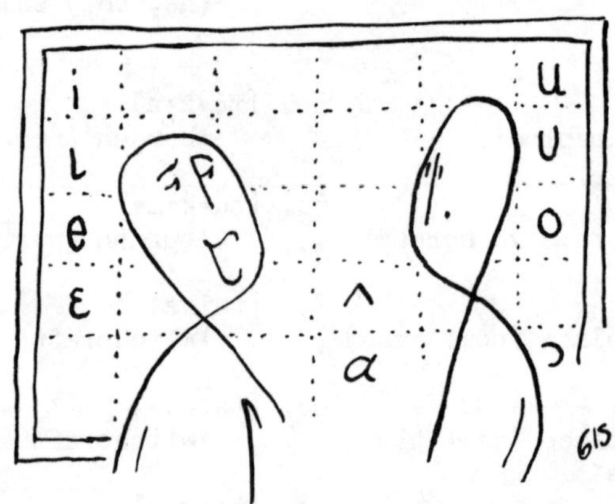

SURE I CAN HEAR THE "DIFFERENCE" BETWEEN "ɑ" AND "^" — AND WHAT'S MORE I CAN SEE THE EMPEROR'S NEW CLOTHES!

LESSON NINETEEN

Alveopalatal Stops

	Labial	Alveolar	Alveopalatal	Alveopalatal (retroflexed)	Velar
Stops					
Voiceless					
Unaspirated	p	t	c	ṭ	k
Aspirated	p^h	t^h	c^h	$ṭ^h$	k^h
Voiced	b	d	j	ḍ	g
Affricates					
Voiceless					
Unaspirated	pᵽ	ts	č (or tš)	t̤š̤	kx
Aspirated	$pᵽ^h$	ts^h	$č^h$ (or $tš^h$)	$t̤š̤^h$	kx^h
Voiced	bƀ	dz	ǰ (or dž)	d̤ž̤	gǥ
Vd. nasals	m	n	ñ	ṇ	ŋ
Vd. laterals		l	l̃		

Table 19.1: Alveopalatal Stops in Relation to Some Other Consonants

The three new consonants boxed in the chart above fill in a blank space in the consonant chart as it has been developing (see Table 17R.1, p. 257). This means that we do not have any new point or manner of articulation, but simply a new combination of these. Note the resemblance in the symbolization of these stops to that of the affricates [č $č^h$ ǰ] (which may also be represented [tš $tš^h$ dž]). This difference in symbolization represents the difference between stop and affricate, as indicated on the chart; it usually represents, however, a difference of articulator as well. Whereas the English affricates are usually pronounced with tongue tip articulation for the [t], dropping the tip for the [š], the alveopalatal stops of many languages are pronounced with blade articulator, the tongue tip being kept down at the lower teeth. (See Sammy 13.1, p. 194, for the articulation. The velic, of course, is closed for [c j], and voicing is absent for [c] and present for [j].)

RE 19.1. Demonstration: Alveopalatal Stops

Listen and mimic as you follow in your Manual.

a. If you make your normal [š] with blade-alveopalatal articulation (tongue tip down behind your lower teeth), try the following sequence: [ɑšɑ ɑšɑ ɑšɑ ɑcɑ ɑcɑ ɑcɑ ɑšɑ ɑcɑ ɑšɑ ɑcɑ ɑšɑ ɑcɑ]. The tongue movement up to the alveopalatal region should be the same in both cases, [š] resulting in a fricative and [c] in a stop, if the tongue tip is kept lightly touching the back of the lower teeth.

b. Try the same sequence using [ñ] and [j]: [ɑñɑ ɑñɑ ɑñɑ ɑjɑ ɑjɑ ɑjɑ ɑñɑ ɑjɑ ɑñɑ ɑjɑ ɑñɑ ɑjɑ].

c. Try articulating the English words cheap and jeep, church and judge with alveopalatal stops by keeping the tongue tip behind the lower teeth and then making your tongue movement otherwise as naturally as possible. Try eliminating most of the affrication as well: [cʰi›ypʰ ji›ypʰ] [cʰr̩cʰ jʌj].

d. The alveopalatal stops are usually articulated with a slight [y] on-glide to the following vowel, as are alveopalatal nasals and laterals. Work for this same degree of glide on these stops with this exercise: [ɑñɑ ɑcɑ ɑñɑ ɑjɑ], etc.

e. Work for a clear distinction between aspirated and unaspirated alveopalatal stops: [ɑcɑ ɑcʰɑ].

f. Work for a clearly voiced alveopalatal stop: [ɑjɑ ɑjɑ].

RE 19.2. Discrimination: SAME or DIFFERENT

Respond to each item with SAME or DIFFERENT. Don't peek. When you can do the exercise well, transcribe the items.

1a. ['eči 'eci] D

2a. ['eci 'eci] S

3a. ['eči 'eči] S

4a. ['eči 'eči] S

5a. ['eci 'eči] D

6a. ['ñæčo 'ñæco] D

7a. ['ñæco 'ñæco] S

8a. ['ñæco 'ñæčo] D

9a. ['ñæco 'ñæčo] D

10a. ['ñæco 'ñæco] S

1b. ['ujɔ 'ujɔ] S

2b. ['ujɔ 'uǰɔ] D

3b. ['uǰɔ 'uǰɔ] S

4b. ['uǰɔ 'ujɔ] D

5b. [ˈujɔ ˈuǰɔ] D

6b. [ˈšʌǰυ ˈšʌjυ] D

7b. [ˈšʌjυ ˈšʌjυ] S

8b. [ˈšʌǰυ ˈšʌǰυ] S

9b. [ˈšʌjυ ˈšʌjυ] S

10b. [ˈšʌjυ ˈšʌǰυ] D

1c. [ˈɛč^{h}o ˈɛc^{h}o] D

2c. [ˈɛc^{h}o ˈɛč^{h}o] D

3c. [ˈɛc^{h}o ˈɛc^{h}o] S

4c. [ˈɛc^{h}o ˈɛc^{h}o] S

5c. [ˈɛč^{h}o ˈɛc^{h}o] D

6c. [ˈflač^{h}ι ˈflač^{h}ι] S

7c. [ˈflac^{h}ι ˈflac^{h}ι] S

8c. [ˈflač^{h}ι ˈflac^{h}ι] D

9c. [ˈflac^{h}ι ˈflač^{h}ι] D

10c. [ˈflac^{h}ι ˈflač^{h}ι] D

RE 19.3. Differential: STOP or AFFRICATE

Distinguish between the alveopalatal stops and alveopalatal affricates by responding STOP or AFFRICATE in this exercise. Don't peek. When you can respond orally use this as a transcription exercise as well.

1. [ɛcɛ] S
2. [ɛčɛ] A
3. [ɛjɛ] S
4. [ɛc^{h}ɛ] S
5. [ɒjɒ] A
6. [jigʌ] S
7. [c^{h}igʌ] S
8. [č^{h}igʌ] A
9. [čigʌ] A
10. [ǰigʌ] A
11. [sɑč^{h}ol^] A
12. [sɑcol^] S
13. [sɑc^{h}ol^] S
14. [sɑjol^] S
15. [sɑčol^] A

RE 19.4. Differential: ASPIRATED or UNASPIRATED

1. [υˈcæ] U
2. [eˈc^{h}i] A
3. [ɔˈc^{h}ʌ] A
4. [oˈc^{h}ɛ] A
5. [ˈcʌŋgr̩] U
6. [ˈcaŋgr̩] U
7. [ˈc^{h}uŋgr̩] A
8. [ˈcɔŋgr̩] U
9. [Ĩɛñˈc^{h}iz] A
10. [Ĩuñˈcʌz] U
11. [Ĩιñˈcɔz] U
12. [Ĩɒñˈc^{h}ez] A

RE 19.5. Differential: VOICED or VOICELESS

1. [jeHlˇ] VD
2. [c^{h}uHlˇ] VL
3. [jʌHlˇ] VD
4. [cæHlˇ] VL
5. [ˈÑñʌjok^h] VD
6. [ˈÑñɛcιk^h] VL

7. ['Ñn̄ac^{h}ʋk^h] VL   9. [r̃ɔ'cɛtŁ] VL   11. [r̃ɒ'citŁ] VL

8. ['Ñn̄ɑjik^h] VD   10. [r̃ʋ'c^{h}ɩtŁ] VL   12. [r̃a'jætŁ] VD

RE 19.6. Differential: ALVEOLAR or ALVEOPALATAL

In this exercise we will contrast [c c^h j] with [ty t^{h}y dy]. Since the alveopalatal stops are characterized by a slight [y] on-glide to the following vowel, you should listen to the difference between that and a [y] on-glide from an alveolar stop. Respond with ALVEOLAR or ALVEOPALATAL. Don't peek. Use this exercise for transcription as well.

1. [i'ca] AP   7. [jɛ'řɑŘ] AP   13. [ḍɑ'dyuŋŊ] AL

2. [ɑ'dyæ] AL   8. [c^{h}ɒ'řɑŘ] AP   14. [ḍɑ'tyɒŋŊ] AL

3. [u'tyɩ] AL   9. [t^{h}yʋ'řɑŘ] AL   15. [ḍɑ'ceŋŊ] AP

4. [o'c^{h}ɔ] AP   10. [tyæ'řɑŘ] AL   16. [ḍɑ'tyæŋŊ] AL

5. [ɛ't^{h}yʋ] AL   11. [dye'řɑŘ] AL   17. [ḍɑ'jɒŋŊ] AP

6. [ʌ'jɑ] AP   12. [cʌ'řɑŘ] AP   18. [ḍɑ'cʋŋŊ] AP

RE 19.7. Differential: ALVEOPALATAL or VELAR

Depending somewhat on where it is articulated, the alveopalatal stops are sometimes confused with velar stops. Respond with ALVEOPALATAL or VELAR. Don't peek. This exercise may be used for transcription as well.

1. ['oci] AP   5. [gya'yɛbm̩] V   9. [r̥̃ul^'kyoĩ] V

2. ['ekyɔ] V   6. [jɔ'yɛbm̩] AP   10. [r̥̃ul^'caĩ] AP

3. ['ɩjɛ] AP   7. [kyæ'yɛbm̩] V   11. [r̥̃ul^'c^{h}uĩ] AP

4. ['ʋc^{h}ʋ] AP   8. [k^{h}yʌ'yɛbm̩] V   12. [r̥̃ul^'gyɩĩ] V

RE 19.8. Differential: Name the Symbol

This time your response is to be the name of the symbol used, which you may call out or write. Don't peek. The choice will be between [c c^h j č č^h ǰ ty t^{h}y dy ky k^{h}y gy]. When you can do this, transcribe the utterances.

1. [čɑw] č   3. [gyow] gy   5. [c^{h}ɩw] c^h

2. [ǰew] ǰ   4. [tyɔw] ty   6. [jæw] j

7. [tyɒw] ty
8. [cʌw] c
9. [šɩ'juñ] j
10. [šɩ'dyɔñ] dy
11. [šɩ'gyʌñ] gy
12. [šɩ'cañ] c
13. [šɩ'c^{h}ɛñ] c^h
14. [šɩ't^{h}yɒñ] t^{h}y
15. [šɩ'čeñ] č
16. [šɩ'k^{h}yɩñ] k^{h}y
17. [ḍat̬θ'č^{h}æž] č^h
18. [ḍaṱθ'k^{h}yuž] k^{h}y
19. [ḍaṱθ'c^{h}iž] c^h
20. [d̥aṱθ'jož] j
21. [ḍaṱθ'dyɔž] dy
22. [ḍat̬θ'kyaž] ky
23. [d̥aṱθ'cαž] c
24. [ḍaṱθ'ǰɩž] ǰ

RE 19.9. Negative Practice: Alveopalatal Stops

Practice the following sentences, making the indicated substitutions. Mimic the tape and watch the directions below.

1. Chuck chucked the champ a cheap chunk.

1a. Substitute [c^h] for the alveopalatal affricates. Do not get too much affrication. Be careful of your tongue position.

1b. Substitute [c] for the alveopalatal affricates. Get a slight [y] off-glide. Not too much affrication.

1c. Substitute [j]. Be sure to get good voicing, and a slight [y] off-glide.

2. Joe Jones gently jockeyed the jeepful of junk.

2a. Substitute [j].

2b. Substitute [c].

2c. Substitute [c^h].

RE 19.10. Mimicry: [c c^h j]

Follow the transcription as you mimic the tape. Note that the alveopalatal stops in final position are included, and listen for the slight [y] off-glide from the vowel which helps to signal them.

1a. [cα·]　　1b. [lˆ o'cα·]　　1c. [lˆ α·c]

2a. [cʰα·]　　2b. [lˆ o'cʰα·]　　2c. [lˆ α·cʰ]

3a. [jα·]　　3b. [lˆ o'jα·]　　3c. [lˆ α·j]

4a. [ce·m]　　4b. [ñu'ce·m]　　4c. [ñe·c]

5a. [cʰe·m]　　5b. [ñu'cʰe·m]　　5c. [ñe·cʰ]

6a. [je·m]　　6b. [ñu'je·m]　　6c. [ñe·j]

7a. [cu·Ṛ̃]　　7b. [za'cu·Ṛ̃]　　7c. [Ṛ̃u·c]

8a. [cʰu·Ṛ̃]　　8b. [za'cʰu·Ṛ̃]　　8c. [Ṛ̃u·cʰ]

9a. [ju·R̥̃]　　9b. [za'ju·Ṛ̃]　　9c. [Ṛ̃u·j]

RE 19.11: Kuy.[1] Mimicry: [c]

Mimic carefully. In addition to the [c] on which you are especially working, note the vowel qualities which are similar to, but usually not identical with those we have been practicing. Mimic as exactly as you can.

1. [ʔʌ'cɒ·] 'dog'　　7. [ciˇ·] 'go'

2. [ceˇ·m] 'bird'　　8. [ca·] 'to eat'

3. [ciˇʔ] 'don't'　　9. [ñ̩'ceˇ·] 'human lice'

4. [cam] 'to wait'　　10. [ñ̩'cɤt] 'ten'

5. [cat] 'to pierce'　　11. [ñ̩'ciˇ·n] 'ring'

6. [caw] 'come'

RE 19.12: Kuy. Mimicry: [ñ̩cʰ]

1. [ñ̩'cʰat] 'to put out fire'　　4. [ñ̩'cʰɒ·c] 'itching'

2. [ñ̩'cʰeˇ·ŋ] 'lard, oil, fat'　　5. [ñ̩'cʰɒ·ʔ] 'straw'

3. [ñ̩'cʰoˇʔ] 'rotten smell'

---

[1] Kuy is a minority language spoken in Eastern Thailand, with some speakers in Cambodia and Southern Laos as well. The informant recorded in these exercises is Leng of Samrongthab, Surin Province, Thailand. The recording was made by Rev. and Mrs. Richard Johnston of the Christian and Missionary Alliance.

RE 19.13: Maninka.[1] Mimicry: [j]

In this exercise practice the tone as well as [j], and the vowels.

1.	['jaña]	'to be long'	5.	[ja·]	(interjection)
2.	['jʌ˃ni]	'to burn'	6.	['jɛ·]	'fish'
3.	[ja'mɑ]	'a crowd'	7.	[jɛ˃'l˄ɪ˃]	'son'
4.	[ja'ra]	'lion'	8.	['jɛ˃l˄ɪ˃]	'how much?'

RE 19.14. Review: Flaps and Trills

Mimic the tape and follow the transcription.

1a. [r̃ɑ]	1b. [R̃ɑr̃]	1c. [r̃ɑ'R̃ɑr̃]
2a. [r̃u]	2b. [R̃ur̃]	2c. [r̃u'R̃ur̃]
3a. [R̃ɩ]	3b. [r̃ɩR̃]	3c. [r̃ɩ'R̃ɩR̃]
4a. [R̃o]	4b. [r̃oR̃]	4c. [R̃o'r̃oR̃]
5a. [řɛ]	5b. [Řɛř]	5c. [řɛ'ŘɛŘ]
6a. [řʌ]	6b. [Řʌř]	6c. [řʌ'Řʌř]
7a. [Ři]	7b. [řiŘ]	7c. [Ři'řiŘ]
8a. [Řʋ]	8b. [řʋŘ]	8c. [Řʋ'řʋŘ]
9a. [r̥̃æ]	9b. [R̥̃æ̥r̃]	9c. [r̥̃æ'R̥̃æ̥r̃]
10a. [r̥̃e]	10b. [R̥̃e̥r̃]	10c. [r̥̃e'R̥̃e̥r̃]

---

[1]Maninka is spoken in Guinea, West Africa. The informant recorded is Mamoudou Kaba, of Kankan. The material was collected and recorded with the help of Mrs. John Emary and other missionaries of the Christian and Missionary Alliance in Kankan, Guinea.

11a. [Ṛ̃a] 11b. [ṛ̃aṚ̃] 11c. [Ṛ̃a'ṛ̃aṚ̃]

12a. [Ṛ̃ɔ] 12b. [ṛ̃ɔṚ̃] 12c. [Ṛ̃ɔ'ṛ̃ɔṚ̃]

RE 19.15: Foe.[1] Review: [r̃ ř]

1. ['ar̃u]	'tongue'	6. ['tiřʌ]	'having spoken'
2. ['or̃o]	'bamboo'	7. ['for̃ɛ]	'big'
3. ['ir̃ʌ]	'tree'	8. ['fɛr̃ʌ]	'a hole'
4. ['hɛr̃ʌ]	'tomorrow'	9. ['ar̃ɛřʌ]	'palm-leaf bag'
5. ['sɛr̃ɛ]	'day'	10. [ir̃'lapo]	'sun'

RE 19.16: Erakor.[2] Review: [r̃ R̃]

1. [maR̃]	'to breathe'	6. [matʰʋR̃]	'to sleep'
2. ['n̩dr̃am]	'your blood'	7. [a'mur̃ɩn]	'I want it'
3. ['n̩dr̃oŋ]	'(to) hear'	8. ['fʌtʰfaR̃]	'coral (for lime'
4. ['n̩dR̃iR̃]	'to fly'	9. ['n̩dr̃ʋR̃n̩dr̃ʋR̃]	'to shake'
5. [naR̃ukʰ]	'my hand'	10. [n̩dr̃ɛR̃'n̩dr̃ɛR̃]	'to shine brilliantly'

RE 19.17. Substitution

Mimic the tape, and follow the transcription. The build-up of the first utterance will be from the end of the utterance. Practice these substitutions to gain real fluency.

1. [r̃ɔ·ŋ'xis.mMmɩn Ɨxαs'Ṛ̃o 'l̃ov·a]

---

[1]Foe is a Papuan language. The recording is simulated from data in lesson plans used at the Summer Institute of Linguistics, Norman, Oklahoma, 1956.

[2]Erakor is spoken in the New Hebrides Islands. The recording is simulated from data in lesson plans used at the Summer Institute of Linguistics, Norman, Oklahoma, 1956.

2. [f̃ɔ•ŋ'xis.mMmɩn 'ƚan.ř̌u 'l̃ov•a]

3. [ju'fæ]

4. [ksay'cʋH]

5. ['guƚi]

6. [zɛ'Mmą]

7. [jɩ'dƚo]

8. ['vɩ.tƚi]

RE 19.18. Transcription

To transcribe this exercise use the special transcription form for RE 19.18 (pp. 55-56 in the Workbook Supplement). Listen to the tape and fill in the blanks in the Supplement. Follow the same directions as for RE 16.18 (p.245). If you find this easy, take a transcription form and transcribe the whole utterance for each item. If you find it too difficult, use the following exercises as transcription exercises instead: RE 19.3-19.8.

1. ['so•.dzɑ]	8. [l^ɩw'r̃æ•f]	15. [yʌnN'ɖuH]
2. ['špin.či•]	9. [ŋ•ɔb'Mmɛt̂θ]	16. [dʋp'zwɒ•]
3. [kxo'cɛŋŊ]	10. ['waH.šyʋt^h]	17. ['kxwɔy.xi•Ř̌]
4. ['L̃ʌw.dza]	11. ['ñ̌ulæ•g]	18. ['c^heň̌ʌm]
5. [g•o'ts^hoy]	12. [rapf'kɔ•y]	19. [ƚ•ɩẓ̌'twær]
6. [r̃iŘ̃'dzɑ•k^h]	13. [syɑŋk^h'ged]	20. [brɒts'J̌ɛɖ̥ɖ]
7. [ṣ̂ṭθa'k^hʋƚ]	14. ['Ř̃ɛr.g•ɑŋŊ]	21. ['je•ɗ̌ʌw]

Reading

Use RE 19.18 as a reading exercise, checking your reading

with the tape after you have practiced it. If this is too difficult, try the same process with RE 19.2-19.8 first.

NO, IT WAS AN Ṛ̃ — I SAW HIS ADNOIDS TWITCH!

LESSON TWENTY

Some Central Vowels; Vowel Clusters

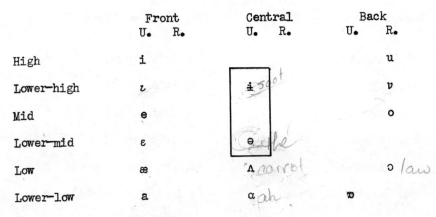

	Front U.	Front R.	Central U.	Central R.	Back U.	Back R.
High	i					u
Lower-high	ɩ		ɨ			ʊ
Mid	e					o
Lower-mid	ɛ		ə			
Low	æ		ʌ			ɔ
Lower-low	a		ɑ		ɒ	

Table 20.1: Vowels to Date

ɨ is called "barred i" and ə is called "shwa" /šwɑH/ or /šɨˈwɑH/. The easiest way to write ə by hand is to start in the upper left-hand corner: ə

RE 20.1. Demonstration: Table 20.1

Listen repeatedly, and study the vowel chart as you do so. When you are familiar with the material, read off the vowel chart with the tape. Work with your buddy.

RE 20.2. Discrimination: SAME or DIFFERENT

Respond to the pairs of utterances with SAME or DIFFERENT. Concentrate on the differences to help you become familiar with them. Don't peek!

1a.	[řɑlˇ řəlˇ]	D	1b.	[ǰʌd ǰəd]	D
2a.	[řəlˇ řəlˇ]	S	2b.	[ǰʌd ǰʌd]	S
3a.	[řɑlˇ řɑlˇ]	S	3b.	[ǰəd ǰəd]	S
4a.	[řɑlˇ řəlˇ]	D	4b.	[ǰəd ǰʌd]	D
5a.	[řəlˇ řɑlˇ]	D	5b.	[ǰʌd ǰəd]	D
6a.	[coˈřəlˇ coˈřəlˇ]	S	6b.	[ži'ǰʌd ži'ǰəd]	D

7a. [co'řəlˇ co'řɑlˇ] D
8a. [co'řɑlˇ co'řəlˇ] D
9a. [co'řɑlˇ co'řɑlˇ] S
10a. [co'řəlˇ co'řɑlˇ] D

7b. [ži'ǰəd ži'ǰʌd] D
8b. [ži'ǰəd ži'ǰəd] S
9b. [ži'ǰəd ži'ǰʌd] D
10b. [ži'ǰʌd ži'ǰəd] D

1c. [xɨŋ xɨŋ] S
2c. [xɨŋ xʌŋ] D
3c. [xɨŋ xʌŋ] D
4c. [xʌŋ xʌŋ] S
5c. [xɨŋ xɨŋ] S
6c. [ɬlɑ'xɨŋ ɬlɑ'xɨŋ] S
7c. [ɬlɑ'xʌŋ ɬlɑ'xʌŋ] S
8c. [ɬlɑ'xɨŋ ɬlɑ'xʌŋ] D
9c. [ɬlɑ'xɨŋ ɬlɑ'xɨŋ] S
10c. [ɬlɑ'xɨŋ ɬlɑ'xʌŋ] D

1d. [c^{h}əʀ̌ c^{h}əʀ̌] S
2d. [c^{h}əʀ̌ c^{h}ɨʀ̌] D
3d. [c^{h}ɨʀ̌ c^{h}ɨʀ̌] S
4d. [c^{h}əʀ̌ c^{h}əʀ̌] S
5d. [ñu'c^{h}ɨʀ̌ ñu'c^{h}əʀ̌] D
6d. [ñu'c^{h}ɨʀ̌ ñu'c^{h}ɨʀ̌] S
7d. [ñu'c^{h}əʀ̌ ñu'c^{h}ɨʀ̌] D
8d. [ñu'c^{h}ɨʀ̌ ñu'c^{h}əʀ̌] D
9d. [ñu'c^{h}ɨʀ̌ ñu'c^{h}əʀ̌] D
10d. [ñu'c^{h}əʀ̌ ñu'c^{h}əʀ̌] S

1e. [dit^h dɨt^h] D
2e. [dɨt^h dɨt^h] S
3e. [dɨt^h dit^h] D
4e. [dit^h dit^h] S
5e. [gɛ'dit^h gɛ'dɨt^h] D
6e. [gɛ'dɨt^h gɛ'dɨt^h] S
7e. [gɛ'dit^h gɛ'dit^h] S
8e. [gɛ'dɨt^h gɛ'dit^h] D
9e. [gɛ'dit^h gɛ'dɨt^h] D
10e. [gɛ'dit^h gɛ'dɨt^h] D

1f. [pɩn pɨn] D
2f. [pɨn pɩn] D
3f. [pɨn pɩn] D
4f. [pɨn pɩn] D
5f. [l̃æ'pɨn l̃æ'pɨn] S
6f. [l̃æ'pɩn l̃æ'pɨn] D
7f. [l̃æ'pɩn l̃æ'pɨn] D
8f. [l̃æ'pɩn l̃æ'pɩn] S
9f. [l̃æ'pɨn l̃æ'pɨn] S
10f. [l̃æ'pɨn l̃æ'pɨn] S

Production of [ɑ ʌ ə ɨ]

All of these central vowels occur in some dialects of American English, but the last three usually in restricted environments, and with a great deal of dialect and idiosyncratic difference between speakers.

In addition to problems of dialect variation, and of fluctuation within dialects, we now face an additional problem in that two of the vowels which are being presented here, and the glides related to them, are often considered substandard in English. For example, [bəyd] bird, [wəyd] word, and [θəyd] third are considered 'Brooklynese' and the butt of many a joke all over the country, although this glide is used by millions of people in the New York City, Long Island, Westchester, and Northern New Jersey area, and is spreading. (Outsiders who try to mimic it in fun usually produce [ɔy] or [oy] instead, however.) Some Southern dialects have [əH] or [ə·] in but, cup, etc., and this makes it seem provincial to some people.

[ɨ] with or without glides occurs in the speech of almost all English-speaking people, but recognition is complicated by several factors. In some speakers it may not be phonemically separate from /ɩ/ or from /ʊ/ (depending on the speaker). That is, there is no contrast between [ɩ] and [ɨ], or between [ʊ] and [ɨ]. They may be in complementary distribution, for example, or there may be complete fluctuation between [ɨw] and [ʊw]. In other speakers they may be in contrast in some words, but the contrasts are very rare. They are almost in complementary distribution. The speaker is therefore not very aware of their contrastive function. Then, when the sound occurs, whether it is a full phoneme or not in a particular speaker, it more commonly occurs in unstressed syllables, which get less prominence, and are slurred over in English. This gives rise to the feeling that the sound represents sloppy speech. Elocution teachers try to teach people not to use it, although the elocution teachers are using it as they correct their pupils.

If you can get an objective sense of what actually occurs in your speech (and that of your classmates) it will be easier to isolate these sounds and reproduce them for other languages.

RE 20.3. Demonstration: Producing [ɑ ʌ ə ɨ]

a. One of the best ways to get a sense of the articulation of central vowels is to begin with [ɑ] and experiment with raising the center of the tongue. Be sure you start with [ɑ] and not [a] or [ɒ] or anything between. You can work

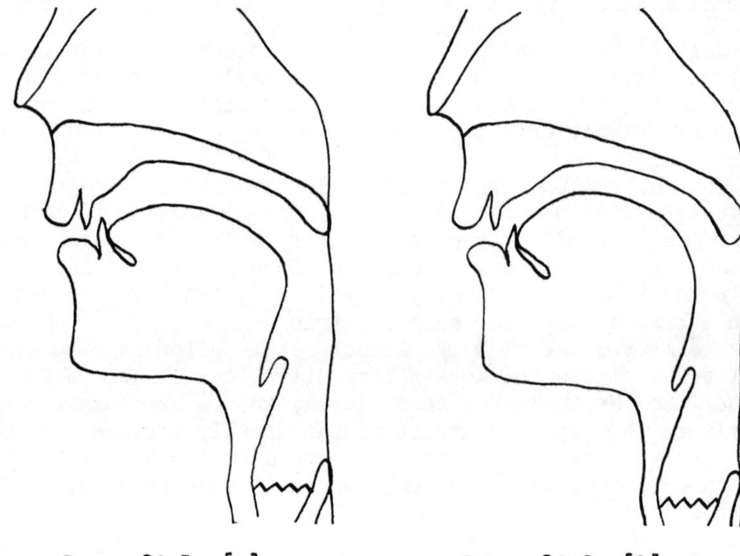

Sammy 20.1: [ɵ]   Sammy 20.2: [ɨ]

by slurring up and down, or by moving in short steps. Listen to the demonstration on the tape.

b. Mimic the tape on the following English sentences. These contrasts are natural to my speech. They may or may not be to yours. Get them by mimicry if you do not normally make them. Note how the stress patterns are nearly constant.

1. [ǰɩst] Give me the 'gist [of the conversation] ˌnow.

2. [ǰɛst] He's starting to 'jest ˌnow.

3. [ǰʌst] He'll be very 'just ˌnow.

4. [ǰɨst] I'm sure he 'left just now.

5. [ǰɩst] Give me the 'gist, ˌJudge.

6. [ǰɛst] Please let him 'jest, ˌJudge.

7. [ǰʌst] It's gotta be 'just, ˌJudge.

8. [ǰɨst] I wish you would just 'judge [and not do anything else].

c. Mimic the tape on the following English words. Get the contrasts by mimicry if you do not have them in your own speech. More of you will find that you do have them in your speech than think you do when you start.

1a.	['hɩťɩm]	hit him	vs.	1b.	['hɩťɨm]	hit them
2a.	['bɑyɩt]	buy it	vs.	2b.	['rɑyɨt]	riot
3a.	['lɑkɩt]	lock it	vs.	3b.	['lɑkɨt]	locket
4a.	['fɩytɩd]	fetid	vs.	4b.	['p^hɛtɨd]	petted
5a.	['rowzʌz]	Rosa's	vs.	5b.	['rowzɨz]	roses
6a.	['ne˅ymʌs]	name us	vs.	6b.	['fe˅ymɨs]	famous
7a.	['re˅ysʌs]	race us	vs.	7b.	['re˅ysɨz]	races

d. If you are able to locate [ɨ] and [ʌ], try to hit [ə] in between.

e. Many speakers of English have [ə] where I have [ʌ]. Mimic the following.

1a.	[k^hʌp^h]	1b.	[k^hə·p^h]	cup
2a.	[bʌt^h]	2b.	[bə·t^h]	but
3a.	[l˅ʌk^h]	3b.	[l˅ə·k^h]	luck
4a.	[fʌn]	4b.	[fə·n]	fun
5a.	[dʌn]	5b.	[də·n]	done

RE 20.4. Negative Practice

Mimic the substitution of different central vowels and others in the English words. Watch the transcription.

sister		roses		famous	
1a.	['sɨstr̩]	1b.	['rowzɨz]	1c.	['fe˅ymɨs]
2a.	['sɩstr̩]	2b.	['rowzɩz]	2c.	['fe˅ymɩs]
3a.	['sʌstr̩]	3b.	['rowzʌz]	3c.	['fe˅ymʌs]
4a.	['səstr̩]	4b.	['rowzəz]	4c.	['fe˅ymən]
5a.	['sɛstr̩]	5b.	['rowzɛz]	5c.	['fe˅ymɛs]

6a. ['sɑstr̩]	6b. ['rowzɑz]	6c. ['fe˅ymɑs]
7a. ['sɒstr̩]	7b. ['rowzɒz]	7c. ['fe˅ymɒs]
8a. ['sɩstr̩]	8b. ['rowzɩz]	8c. ['fe˅ymɩs]
9a. ['səstr̩]	9b. ['rowzəz]	9c. ['fe˅yməs]
10a. ['sɨstr̩]	10b. ['rowzɨz]	10c. ['fe˅ymɨs]

RE 20.5. Mimicry: [ɨ]

Mimic the tape and follow the transcription. Work with your buddy on this material. Use this exercise for transcription as well.

1a. [đɨ·]	1b. [đɨ·y]	1c. [đɨ·w]	1d. [đɨ·H]
2a. [mɨ·]	2b. [mɨ·y]	2c. [mɨ·w]	2d. [mɨ·H]
3a. [bɨ·]	3b. [bɨ·y]	3c. [bɨ·w]	3d. [bɨ·H]
4a. [žɨ·]	4b. [žɨ·y]	4c. [žɨ·w]	4d. [žɨ·H]
5a. [l^ɨ·]	5b. [l^ɨ·y]	5c. [l^ɨ·w]	5d. [l^ɨ·H]
6a. [ñɨ·k^h]	6b. [ñɨ·yk^h]	6c. [ñɨ·wk^h]	6d. [ñɨ·Hk^h]
7a. [xɨ·v]	7b. [xɨ·yv]	7c. [xɨ·wv]	7d. [xɨ·Hv]
8a. [gzɨ·m]	8b. [gzɨ·ym]	8c. [gzɨ·wm]	8d. [gzɨ·Hm]
9a. [ṱθɨ·š]	9b. [ṱθɨ·yš]	9c. [ṱθɨ·wš]	9d. [ṱθɨ·Hš]
10a. [tƚɨ·ŋŊ]	10b. [tƚɨ·yŋŊ]	10c. [tƚɨ·wŋŊ]	10d. [tƚɨ·HŋŊ]

RE 20.6. Mimicry: [ə]

Mimic the tape and follow the transcription. Work with your buddy. Then use the exercise for transcription.

1a. [đə·]	1b. [đə·y]	1c. [đə·w]	1d. [đə·H]
2a. [mə·]	2b. [mə·y]	2c. [mə·w]	2d. [mə·H]
3a. [bə·]	3b. [bə·y]	3c. [bə·w]	3d. [bə·H]
4a. [žə·]	4b. [žə·y]	4c. [žə·w]	4d. [žə·H]
5a. [l^ə·]	5b. [l^ə·y]	5c. [l^ə·w]	5d. [l^ə·H]

6a. [ñə•kʰ]	6b. [ñə•ykʰ]	6c. [ñə•wkʰ]	6d. [ñə•Hkʰ]
7a. [xə•v]	7b. [xə•yv]	7c. [xə•wv]	7d. [xə•Hv]
8a. [gzə•m]	8b. [gzə•ym]	8c. [gzə•wm]	8d. [gzə•Hm]
9a. [t̬θə•s]	9b. [t̬θə•ys]	9c. [t̬θə•ws]	9d. [t̬θə•Hs]
10a. [tɬə•ŋN̥]	10b. [tɬə•yŋN̥]	10c. [tɬə•wŋN̥]	10d. [tɬə•HŋN̥]

RE 20.7. Negative Practice: "Ten Little Indians"

Practice the vowel chart, including the new vowels, in the framework of the song demonstrated on the tape. Then continue with the other combinations listed below.

[ʔi] little, [ʔɩ] little, [ʔe] little Indians;

[ʔɛ] little, [ʔæ] little, [ʔa] little Indians,

[ʔɑ] little, [ʔɒ] little, [ʔɔ] little Indians,

[ʔo] little Indian boys.

[ʔu] little, [ʔʋ] little, [ʔo] little Indians,

[ʔɔ] little, [ʔɒ] little, [ʔɑ] little Indians,

[ʔʌ] little, [ʔə] little, [ʔɨ] little Indians,

[ʔɨ] little Indian boys.

a. [wi] little...

b. [yi] little...

c. [ri] little...

d. [pwi] little...

e. The same with other consonants, and other on-glides.

f. Off-glides.

RE 20.8. Differential: Tongue Height

Respond with HIGH, LOWER-HIGH, MID, LOWER-MID, LOW or LOWER-LOW. When you are able to do this well, use the exercise for transcription.

1. [Mmʌ] L		8. [R̃əftʰ] L-M		15. [cʰɒl˄] L-L			
2. [Mmɨ] L-H		9. [R̃ɨftʰ] L-H		16. [cʰɑl˄] L-L			
3. [Mmɑ] L-L		10. [R̃ʌftʰ] L		17. [cʰʌl˄] L			
4. [Mmɛ] L-M		11. [R̃ɑftʰ] L-L		18. [cʰal˄] L-L			
5. [Mmæ] L		12. [R̃ɨftʰ] L-H		19. [cʰəl˄] L-M			
6. [Mmɒ] L-L		13. [R̃ʌftʰ] L		20. [cʰæl˄] L			
7. [Mmɔ] L		14. [R̃əftʰ] L-M		21. [cʰɨl˄] L-H			

RE 20.9. Differential: FRONT or CENTRAL UNROUNDED, BACK ROUNDED or UNROUNDED

1. [myʌ] C U	6. [twɒz] B U	11. [frag] F U
2. [myɑ] C U	7. [twʌz] C U	12. [frɨg] C U
3. [myɨ] C U	8. [twɨz] C U	13. [frʌg] C U
4. [myɒ] B U	9. [twəz] C U	14. [frɑg] C U
5. [myə] C U	10. [twoz] B R	15. [frəg] C U

RE 20.10. Differential: Full Labels

Select one term from each column to make up your response. Keep the exercise covered while you do this.

HIGH	FRONT	ROUNDED
LOWER-HIGH	CENTRAL	UNROUNDED
MID	BACK	
LOWER-MID		
LOW		
LOWER-LOW		

1. [co] M B R	4. [cɨ] L-H C U	7. [cɒ] L-L B U
2. [cɒ] L-L B U	5. [cə] L-M C U	8. [ca] L-L F U
3. [cæ] L F U	6. [cʌ] L C U	9. [cɛ] L-M F U

10. [skʰeƀ] M F U
11. [skʰɔƀ] L B R
12. [skʰəƀ] L-M C U
13. [skʰɨƀ] L-H C U
14. [skʰaƀ] L-L f U
15. [skʰɑƀ] L-L C U
16. [skʰʌƀ] L C U
17. [skʰɨƀ] L-H C U
18. [skʰəƀ] L-M C U
19. [jʌt̤š] L C U
20. [jɛt̤š] L-M F U
21. [jət̤š] L-M C U
22. [jʋt̤š] L-H B R
23. [jɩt̤š] L-H F U
24. [jɨt̤š] L-H C U
25. [jət̤š] L-M C U
26. [jɑt̤š] L-L C U
27. [jʌt̤š] L C U

RE 20.11. Differential: Vowel Symbols

Give the name of the symbol by which the vowel is transcribed, or write the vowel. When you can respond with the correct symbol in every case, transcribe the utterance.

1. [bɑ] SCRIPT ɑ
2. [bʌ] CARET
3. [ba] PRINTED a
4. [bɨ] BARRED i
5. [bɩ] IOTA
6. [m̩bʋš] UPSILON
7. [m̩bəš] SHWA
8. [m̩bɔš] BACKWARDS c
9. [m̩bɒš] UPSIDE-DOWN ɑ
10. [m̩bɨš] BARRED i
11. [Mm̩bʌtš] CARET
12. [Mm̩bɑtš] SCRIPT ɑ
13. [Mm̩bətš] SHWA
14. [Mm̩bɔtš] BACKWARDS c
15. [Mm̩bætš] DIGRAPH
16. [Mm̩bɑtš] SCRIPT ɑ
17. [Mm̩bɨtš] BARRED i
18. [Mm̩batš] PRINTED a
19. [Mm̩bətš] SHWA
20. [Mm̩bʌtš] CARET

Vowel Clusters

Up to this time we have worked with single vowels, vowels separated by consonants, vowels with on-glides and off-glides, but never with clusters of vowels.

RE 20.12. Demonstration: Glides and Vowel Clusters

Listen, mimic the tape, and watch the transcription. Notice both the differences and similarities between the columns. Be careful not to get a glide between the vowels of column b.

1a. [nyʌ]	1b. [ni.ʌ]	1c. [niH]
2a. [kʰyʌ]	2b. [kʰi.ʌ]	2c. [kʰiH]
3a. [nwʌ]	3b. [nu.ʌ]	3c. [nuH]
4a. [kʰwʌ]	4b. [kʰu.ʌ]	4c. [kʰuH]
5a. [nrʌ]	5b. [nr̩.ʌ]	5c. [nr̩H]
6a. [kʰrʌ]	6b. [kʰr̩.ʌ]	6c. [kʰr̩H]
7a. [nyu]	7b. [ni.u]	7c. [niw]
8a. [kʰyu]	8b. [kʰi.u]	8c. [kʰiw]
9a. [nwi]	9b. [nu.i]	9c. [nuy]
10a. [kʰwi]	10b. [kʰu.i]	10c. [kʰuy]

Note the differences of timing and syllabicity between the middle column, and the other two. Remember that a glide is a non-syllabic movement, and note the relationship between the end points of the glides [y w H] and the vowels [i u ʌ] respectively. Note also the relationship between [r̩] (which is phonetically a vowel) and [r] (which is phonetically a glide). In making these comparisons we are not saying that every [y] glides to or from [i], every [w] to or from [u], etc. The glide refers to the direction of the movement, not to the end point (see Lesson 12, p. 174ff.).

RE 20.13. Demonstration: Vowel Clusters

In vowel clusters (such as in column b, above), each of the vowels has syllabicity, even though one may be more stressed than the other. Mimic the tape and follow the transcription, noting the syllabicity, stress, etc.

1a. [ˈɑˈi]	1b. [ɑˈi]	1c. [ˈɑ.i]	1d. [ɑy]
2a. [ˈɑˈe]	2b. [ɑˈe]	2c. [ˈɑ.e]	
3a. [ˈɑˈæ]	3b. [ɑˈæ]	3c. [ˈɑ.æ]	

4a. [ˈɑˈu]   4b. [ɑˈu]   4c. [ˈɑ.u]   4d. [ɑw]

5a. [ˈɑˈo]   5b. [ɑˈo]   5c. [ˈɑ.o]

6a. [ˈɑˈɔ]   6b. [ɑˈɔ]   6c. [ˈɑ.ɔ]

7a. [ˈɑˈɨ]   7b. [ɑˈɨ]   7c. [ˈɑ.ɨ]   7d. [ɑH]

8a. [ˈeˈɑ]   8b. [eˈɑ]   8c. [ˈe.ɑ]   8d. [eH]

9a. [ˈoˈɑ]   9b. [oˈɑ]   9c. [ˈo.ɑ]   9d. [oH]

10a. [ˈuˈe]   10b. [uˈe]   10c. [ˈu.e]   10d. [we]

Virtually any combination of two vowels becomes possible in a cluster, just as virtually any combination of vowel and glide is possible. Clusters of three vowels also occur.

RE 20.14. Demonstration: Clusters of Three Vowels

Listen, mimic, and watch the transcription. Avoid getting glides between the vowels. The [ʔ]'s in the first column are to help you get pure vowels. After you have practised it thoroughly, try your hand at transcription.

1a. [ʔoʔeʔʌ]   1b. [o.e.ʌ]   1c. [oˈe.ʌ]   1d. [o.eˈʌ]

2a. [ʔæʔiʔɔ]   2b. [æ.i.ɔ]   2c. [æˈi.ɔ]   2d. [æ.iˈɔ]

3a. [ʔɨʔeʔɑ]   3b. [ɨ.e.ɑ]   3c. [ɨˈe.ɑ]   3d. [ɨ.eˈɑ]

4a. [ʔɛʔʋʔæ]   4b. [ɛ.ʋ.æ]   4c. [ɛˈʋ.æ]   4d. [ɛ.ʋˈæ]

5a. [ʔɩʔʌʔu]   5b. [ɩ.ʌ.u]   5c. [ɩˈʌ.u]   5d. [ɩ.ʌˈu]

In all of these examples of vowel clusters we have given strong syllabicity to each of the vowels, and that is the way in which we will continue to treat them in this course. For the sake of the record, however, it should be pointed out that whereas vowel clusters in some languages constitute two or more separate syllables, in other languages such clusters may constitute only one syllable. Sometimes the distinctive syllable beat, which is characteristic of the air pressure reinitiating in the chest, is clearly audible with each vowel sound. Sometimes it is not clearly audible and it becomes very difficult to identify the shape of the phonetic syllables in terms of change of vowel quality, beat, loudness, duration, etc.

RE 20.15. Differential: GLIDE or VOWEL

Listen to the tape, and decide for each utterance whether that which follows the main stressed vowel (second syllable) is an off-glide or a second vowel with its own syllabicity.

1. [lo'kɑ.u] V
2. [lo'kɑw] G
3. [lo'kɑ.ʊ] V
4. [lo'kɑ.e] V
5. [lo'kɑy] G
6. [lo'kɑ.ɔ] V
7. [lo'kɑH] G
8. [sɛ'tɛ.ɨ] V
9. [sɛ'tɛH] G
10. [sɛ'tɛ.æ] V
11. [sɛ'tɛy] G
12. [sɛ'tɛ.i] V
13. [sɛ'tɛw] G
14. [sɛ'tɛ.ɨ] V
15. [ba'lɔ.ʌ] V
16. [ba'lɔ.ɩ] V
17. [ba'lɔw] G
18. [ba'lɔH] G
19. [ba'lɔ.e] V
20. [ba'lɔy] G
21. [ba'lɔ.i] V

RE 20.16. Differential: LONG or REARTICULATED

It is perfectly possible to have a sequence of two identical vowels, each with their own syllabicity. This may have the duration of a long vowel, but differs from a long vowel in having two syllable beats. Such a sequence is called a rearticulated vowel. The quality is the same throughout, but the presence of two syllable beats, or a change in stress within the vowel creates the rearticulation. Rearticulation is simply a special case of vowel clusters.

In the following exercise listen to the tape and decide whether the vowel is simply long, or whether it has two beats and so is rearticulated. Respond with LONG or REARTICULATED.

1. [sa'mu·] L
2. [sa'mu.u] R
3. [sa'mu.u] R
4. [sa'mu·] L
5. [sa'mu·] L
6. [tu'ko.o] R
7. [tu'ko·] L
8. [tu'ko·] L
9. [tu'ko·] L
10. [tu'ko.o] R
11. [pɑ'pa·] L
12. [pɑ'pʌ·] L
13. [pɑ'pɛ.ɛ] R
14. [pɑ'pɔ.ɔ] R
15. [pɑ'pɨ·] L

RE 20.17. Mimicry: Vowel Clusters

Use this exercise for transcription after you have learned to mimic it. The items will be built up for you on the tape.

1. [tu.o'tu.o.ɑ]
2. [le.o'lo.ɔ.ʌ]
3. [sɑ.ɑ'mʌ.ɑ.o]
4. [mɒ.u'lɔ.u.u]
5. [lʌ.ɔ'mɒ.ʌ.ɔ]
6. [sɑ.e'tɑ.ʌ.ɒ]
7. [yu.o.ɑ'tu.o]
8. [so.ɔ.ʌ'le.e]
9. [tʌ.ɑ.e'lɑ.i]
10. [lɔ.ɒ.æ'mɒ.ɨ]
11. [mɒ.ʌ.i'mi.ɔ]
12. [lɛ.u.ɒ'sɩ.æ]

<u>RE 20.18. Review: Long Vowels and Consonants</u>

Mimic the tape and follow the transcription. Practice for fluency.

1. ['bowɗu·]
2. ['tɨg·te]
3. ['kɛ·gʌy]
4. ['gowƥ·ə]
5. ['xid·aw]
6. ['xʌ·ɗɔ]
7. ['g·afɨ]
8. ['kɨwfɒ·y]
9. ['θ·ɑ·və]
10. ['θævə·y]

<u>Transcription</u>

Use RE 20.4, RE 20.6, and RE 20.8-RE 20.18.

<u>Reading</u>

Use RE 20.15-RE 20.18.

LESSON TWENTY-ONE

Double Stops and Nasals

	Labial	Alveolar	Alveo-palatal	Alveopalatal (retroflexed)	Velar
Stops					
Single					
Voiceless					
Unasp.	p	t	c	ṭ	k
Asp.	p^h	t^h	c^h	ṭ^h	k^h
Voiced	b	d	j	ḍ	g
Double					
Vl. Unasp.	^{k}p	(^{k}t)[1]			
Voiced	^{g}b	(^{g}d)			
Nasals					
Single					
Voiceless	M	N	Ñ		Ŋ
Voiced	m	n	ñ	ṇ	ŋ
Double, vd.	ŋm	(ŋn)			

Table 21.1: Double Stops and Nasals in Relation to Some Other Consonants

The new sounds of this lesson differ from previous stops and nasals in that they have two simultaneous points of articulation. There is a secondary back-velar closure along with the primary bilabial closure. As may be seen in Table 21.1, the primary articulation may also be tip-alveolar (or it may be tip-dental, tip-alveopalatal, or even tip-palatal), but such combinations are more rare, and will not be included in the course. If you meet them you will find that they work in analogous fashion to the sounds presented here.

The two articulations of the double stops and nasals are essentially simultaneous rather than sequential. In some

---

[1]Sounds represented by symbols in parentheses are perfectly possible, but will not be drilled in this course.

languages either the beginning or the end of the sound may not be simultaneous, but at least one or the other must be to produce a double stop or nasal. This is the reason for the symbolization of the sounds by showing the primary articulation [p b m] in regular position on the line, and the secondary articulation [^{k} ^{g} ^{ŋ}] in raised position. You will often find these same sounds symbolized <u>kp</u>, <u>gb</u>, <u>ŋm</u> in other sources.

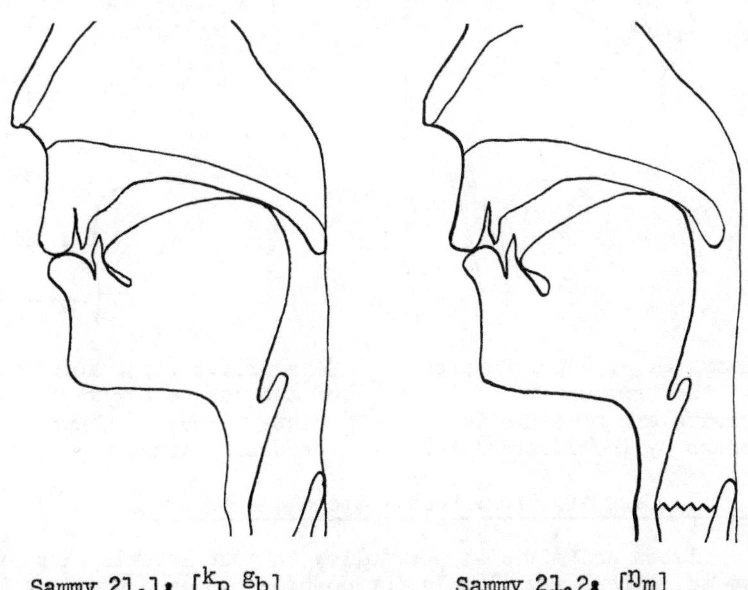

Sammy 21.1: [^{k}p ^{g}b] Sammy 21.2: [^{ŋ}m]

In many languages there is another ingredient to the articulation of [^{k}p ^{g}b] besides the double stop closure. This is a distinctive quality created by a tongue movement during the double stop and simultaneously with its release. The double stop creates a pocket of air in the mouth between the two points of articulation (see Sammy 21.1). The distinctive quality is produced by moving the tongue forward or backward to create air pressure or vacuum in the pocket of air. This distinctive quality is noticeable in double nasals as well, but not to the same degree.

In some languages the movement of the tongue forward, creating air pressure in the mouth just before the release of the consonant, results in a slight puffing of the cheeks. This is very noticeable in some dialects of Vietnamese, for example, when [^{k}p ^{ŋ}m] occur at the end of a phrase.[1]

---

[1] Double stops and nasals are not classified with clicks

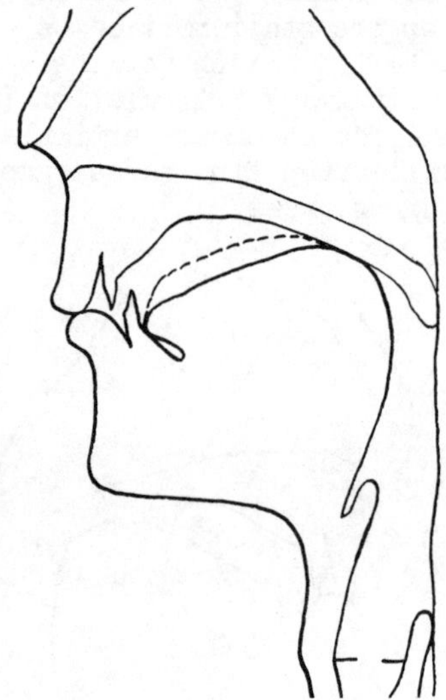

Sammy 21.3: [ᵏp]. Movement of the tongue forward to create air pressure is shown by the dotted line.

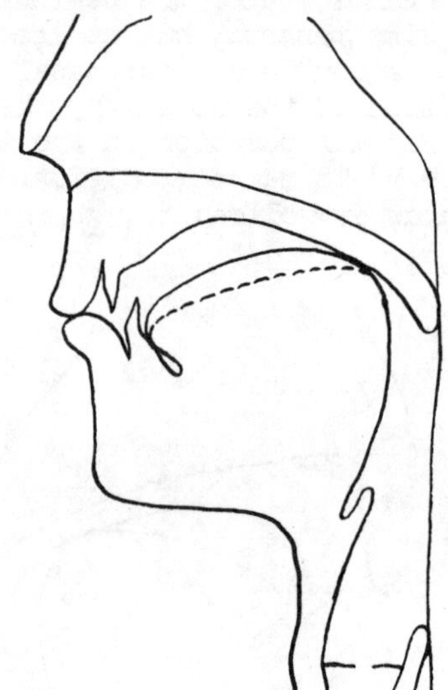

Sammy 21.4: [ᵏp]. Movement of the tongue backwards to create vacuum is shown by the dotted line.

RE 21.1. Demonstration: Double Stops and Nasals

Listen and mimic as you follow in your Manual. You will have to listen very closely for double stops and nasals. The recorder may not always produce them clearly, and the acoustic difference often seems slight to speakers of English under the best of conditions.

a. Some Americans make [ᵏp] when they are imitating a chicken which has laid an egg: [ˌᵏpʌ ˌᵏpʌ ˌᵏpʌ ˌᵏpʌ ᵏpɨˈkɑ·kɨ]. Don't fool yourself by saying the following and thinking it is the same thing: [ˌpʌk ˌpʌk ˌpʌk], etc.

b. If you can cackle by making [ᵏp], isolate it: [ᵏpʌ ᵏpɑ ᵏpe ᵏpo]. Change the stop: [ᵍbʌ ᵍbɑ ᵍbe ᵍbo].

c. Try the analogous nasal: [ᵑmʌ ᵑmɑ ᵑme ᵑmo].

(Lesson 31, p. 427) in spite of this feature (tongue movement creating an air stream) because the primary air stream is still lung air. The movement of the tongue creates a secondary air stream.

d. For another approach, try the following sequences fast, and see if they do not result in double articulation:

[ˈbʌgʌˈbʌgʌˈbʌgʌˈbʌgʌˈbʌgʌˈ^{g}bʌgˈ^{g}bʌgˈ^{g}bʌgˈ^{g}bʌg]

[ˈpʌkʌˈpʌkʌˈpʌkʌˈpʌkʌˈpʌkʌˈ^{k}pʌkˈ^{k}pʌkˈ^{k}pʌkˈ^{k}pʌk]

[ˈmʌŋʌˈmʌŋʌˈmʌŋʌˈmʌŋʌˈmʌŋʌˈ^{ŋ}mʌŋˈ^{ŋ}mʌŋˈ^{ŋ}mʌŋˈ^{ŋ}mʌŋ]

e. Another way to approach the double articulation is simply to make a [k] and a [p] at the same time, and to practice until you can release them simultaneously. Try it slowly and deliberately: [ɑ·^{k}pɑ·] [ɑ·^{g}bɑ·] [ɑ·^{ŋ}mɑ·].

f. Begin with some English sequences and follow a progression which may help you achieve the articulation. The tape will give each step three times. You may have to practice many times.

<u>make paste</u> (repeat several times)

[me˅ykˈpe˅yst] (without aspiration)

[me˅yk·ˈpe˅yst] (prolong [k] without releasing it)

[me˅·yˈ^{k}pe˅yst] (change the onset of stress and lengthen vowel)

[ˈ^{k}pe˅yst] (leave off the first syllable)

[ˈ^{k}pe ˈ^{k}pɑ ˈ^{k}pi ˈ^{k}pu]

g. Try the same kind of sequence to produce [^{g}b].

<u>big boy</u>

[bɩgˈboy]

[bɩg·ˈboy]

[bɩ·ˈ^{g}boy]

[ˈ^{g}boy]

[ˈ^{g}bo ˈ^{g}bɑ ˈ^{g}bi ˈ^{g}bu]

h. Try the same kind of sequence to produce [^{ŋ}m].

<u>bring mine</u>

[brɩŋˈmɑyn]

[brɩŋ•ˈmɑyn]

[brɩ•ˈᵑmɑyn]

[ˈᵑmɑyn]

[ˈᵑmɑ ˈᵑmo ˈᵑmi ˈᵑmu]

i. In order to get the distinctive quality of [ᵏp ᵍb] in some languages, you will need to move your tongue as shown in Sammy 21.3 and 21.4. Listen to the following and mimic.

Without Tongue Movement	With Tongue Movement
1a. [ɑ•ᵏpɑ•]	1b. [ɑ•ᵏpɑ•]
2a. [ᵏpo•]	2b. [ᵏpo•]
3a. [e•ᵍbe•]	3b. [e•ᵍbe•]
4a. [ᵍbe•]	4b. [ᵍbe•]

RE 21.2. Discrimination Drill: SAME or DIFFERENT

Respond orally to each pair with SAME or DIFFERENT. Don't peek. When you can do the exercise well, transcribe the items.

1a.	[ɑˈᵏpɑ ɑˈpɑ]	D	1b.	[aˈba aˈᵍba]	D
2a.	[eˈpe eˈᵏpe]	D	2b.	[ɩˈᵍbɩ ɩˈᵍbɩ]	S
3a.	[uˈᵏpu uˈᵏpu]	S	3b.	[oˈᵍbo oˈbo]	D
4a.	[æˈᵏpæ æˈpæ]	D	4b.	[ɛˈbɛ ɛˈbɛ]	S
5a.	[ᵏpɔ pɔ]	D	5b.	[bə ᵍbə]	D
6a.	[ᵏpʋ ᵏpʋ]	S	6b.	[ᵍbu bu]	D
7a.	[pɨ ᵏpɨ]	D	7b.	[bʌ ᵍbʌ]	D
8a.	[pʌ pʌ]	S	8b.	[ᵍbɨ ᵍbɨ]	S
9a.	[iᵏp iᵏp]	S	9b.	[ʋᵍb ʋb]	D
10a.	[ɛp ɛᵏp]	D	10b.	[ɔᵍb ɔᵍb]	S

1c.	[æ'ŋmæ æ'ŋmæ]	S	6c.	[mo ŋmo]	D
2c.	[e'ŋme e'me]	D	7c.	[ŋmɩ mɩ]	D
3c.	[ɑ'mɑ ɑ'mɑ]	S	8c.	[ŋma ŋma]	S
4c.	[ə'ŋmə ə'ŋmə]	S	9c.	[ɔŋm ɔm]	D
5c.	[ŋmɛ ŋmɛ]	S	10c.	[ʋm ʋŋm]	D

RE 21.3. Negative Practice: Double Stops and Nasals

Practice the following sentences with the indicated substitutions. Try to get fluency with these articulations.

1. ŋmake ŋmy ŋmonkey ŋmind ŋmother.

2. kpeter kpikper kpicked a kpeck of kpickled kpekppers.

3. The gbig gbad gboy gbent gbilly's gbike.

RE 21.4. Mimicry: Medial Double Stops and Nasals

1a. [ɑŋ'ŋmæ]	1b. [ɑg'gbæ]	1c. [ɑk'kpæ]
2a. [eŋ'ŋmɩ]	2b. [eg'gbɩ]	2c. [ek'kpɩ]
3a. [uŋ'ŋmɑ]	3b. [ug'gbɑ]	3c. [uk'kpɑ]
4a. [æŋ'ŋmə]	4b. [æg'gbə]	4c. [æk'kpə]
5a. [ɔŋ'ŋmɛ]	5b. [ɔg'gbɛ]	5c. [ɔk'kpɛ]
6a. [ʋ'ŋmo]	6b. [ʋ'gbo]	6c. [ʋ'kpo]
7a. [ɨ'ŋma]	7b. [ɨ'gba]	7c. [ɨ'kpa]
8a. [ʌ'ŋmɔ]	8b. [ʌ'gbɔ]	8c. [ʌ'kpɔ]
9a. [ɛ'ŋmʋ]	9b. [ɛ'gbʋ]	9c. [ɛ'kpʋ]
10a. [ə'ŋmi]	10b. [ə'gbi]	10c. [ə'kpi]

RE 21.5. Mimicry: Initial Double Stops and Nasals

1a. [ŋmɑ]	1b. [gbɑ]	1c. [kpɑ]
2a. [ŋme]	2b. [gbe]	2c. [kpe]

3a. [^{ŋ}mu] 3b. [^{g}bu] 3c. [^{k}pu]

4a. [^{ŋ}mæf] 4b. [^{g}bæf] 4c. [^{k}pæf]

5a. [^{ŋ}mɔt^{h}] 5b. [^{g}bɔt^{h}] 5c. [^{k}pɔt^{h}]

6a. [ˈ^{ŋ}mʋl^æ] 6b. [ˈ^{g}bʋl^æ] 6c. [ˈ^{k}pʋl^æ]

7a. [ˈ^{ŋ}mɨsɩ] 7b. [ˈ^{g}bɨsɩ] 7c. [ˈ^{k}pɨsɩ]

8a. [ˈ^{ŋ}mʌyɑ] 8b. [ˈ^{g}bʌyɑ] 8c. [ˈ^{k}pʌyɑ]

9a. [ˈ^{ŋ}mɛṭ^{h}o] 9b. [ˈ^{g}bɛṭ^{h}o] 9c. [ˈ^{k}pɛṭ^{h}o]

10a. [ˈ^{ŋ}məᵽi] 10b. [ˈ^{g}bəᵽi] 10c. [ˈ^{k}pəᵽi]

RE 21.6. Mimicry: Final Double Stops and Nasals

1a. [ʔɑ^{ŋ}m] 1b. [ʔɑ^{g}b] 1c. [ʔɑ^{k}p]

2a. [ʔe^{ŋ}m] 2b. [ʔe^{g}b] 2c. [ʔe^{k}p]

3a. [ʔu^{ŋ}m] 3b. [ʔu^{g}b] 3c. [ʔu^{k}p]

4a. [ʔæ^{ŋ}m] 4b. [ʔæ^{g}b] 4c. [ʔæ^{k}p]

5a. [ʔɔ^{ŋ}m] 5b. [ʔɔ^{g}b] 5c. [ʔɔ^{k}p]

6a. [l^æˈʔʋ^{ŋ}m] 6b. [l^æˈʔʋ^{g}b] 6c. [l^æˈʔʋ^{k}p]

7a. [zɩˈʔɨ^{ŋ}m] 7b. [zɩˈʔɨ^{g}b] 7c. [zɩˈʔɨ^{k}p]

8a. [yɑˈʔʌ^{ŋ}m] 8b. [yɑˈʔʌ^{g}b] 8c. [yɑˈʔʌ^{k}p]

9a. [ṭ^{h}oˈʔɛ^{ŋ}m] 9b. [ṭ^{h}oˈʔɛ^{g}b] 9c. [ṭ^{h}oˈʔɛ^{k}p]

10a. [ᵽiˈʔə^{ŋ}m] 10b. [ᵽiˈʔə^{g}b] 10c. [ᵽiˈʔə^{k}p]

RE 21.7. Differential: VOICED or VOICELESS

Respond orally with VOICED or VOICELESS as you listen to the double stop. Don't peek. Use this exercise for transcription when you can respond correctly to it.

1. [ɑ•ˈ^{k}pɑ] VL
2. [ɛ•ˈ^{g}bɛ] VD
3. [ʋ•ˈ^{k}pʋ] VL
4. [a•ˈ^{k}pa] VL
5. [ˈ^{k}pɩnu] VL
6. [ˈ^{g}bænu] VD
7. [ˈ^{g}bɔnu] VD
8. [ˈ^{g}bɨnu] VD
9. [ŋɩˈ^{g}bedæ] VD

10. [ŋɩ'^{k}podæ] VL
11. [ŋɩ'^{g}bidæ] VD
12. [ŋɩ'^{k}pʌdæ] VL

RE 21.8. Differential: DOUBLE or SINGLE

Respond DOUBLE if you hear a double stop or nasal [^{k}p ^{g}b ^{ŋ}m] and SINGLE if you hear an ordinary stop or nasal [p b m]. Don't peek.

1. [ɑ·'^{g}bɑ] D
2. [ɛ·'bɛ] S
3. [ʋ·'pʋ] S
4. [a·'^{k}pa] D
5. [ə·^{ŋ}mə] D
6. ['^{k}pɩve] D
7. ['mæve] S
8. ['^{ŋ}mɔve] D
9. ['bɨve] S
10. ['^{k}pʋve] D
11. [řɔ'belˆʌ] S
12. [řɔ'polˆʌ] S
13. [řɔ'bilˆʌ] S
14. [řo'^{k}pʌlˆʌ] D
15. [řɔ'^{ŋ}mɩlˆʌ] D

RE 21.9. Differential: SIMULTANEOUS or SEQUENTIAL

Respond SIMULTANEOUS if you hear a double stop or nasal [^{k}p ^{g}b ^{ŋ}m], or SEQUENTIAL if you hear a sequence of [k.p g.b ŋ.m]. Don't peek.

1. [ɑ·'^{g}bɑ] SI
2. [ɛ·g'bɛ] SE
3. [ʋ·k'pə] SE
4. [a·'^{k}pa] SI
5. [ə·ŋ'mə] SE
6. [t^{h}ik'pɩ] SE
7. [t^{h}i'^{ŋ}mæ] SI
8. [t^{h}iŋ'mɔ] SE
9. [t^{h}ig'bɨ] SE
10. [t^{h}i'^{k}pʋ] SI
11. [ẓag'beño] SE
12. [ẓa'^{k}poño] SI
13. [ẓa'^{g}biño] SI
14. [ẓak'pʌño] SE
15. [ẓaŋ'mɩño] SE

RE 21.10: Kaka.[1] Mimicry: [^{k}p p]

Follow the transcription as you mimic. On the tape you will hear the words read first down, and then across. Work for a fluent double stop articulation.

1. [^{k}pǫŋgi'la][2] 'blackboard'
2. ['^{k}pǫgɨ][2] 'box'
3. [^{k}pa'^{k}pa] 'toothbrush'
4. [^{k}pete] 'piece of manioc'

---

[1] Kaka is spoken in Cameroun. Recordings were obtained with the help of Dr. William D. Reyburn, Translations Consultant of the American Bible Society.

[2] The mark under the vowel indicates nasalization.

5. [ᵏpasate] 'true'
6. [pɔku] 'difficulty'
7. [potɔ•] 'break'
8. [pa'na] 'island'
9. ['pɛlte] 'half'
10. [papo˅] 'wing'

RE 21.11: Kaka. Mimicry: [ᵍb]

1. [ᵍboŋgo] 'valley'
2. [ᵍbisɔ˥] 'support'
3. [ᵍbakɔ^] 'branch'
4. [ᵍbe›kefe'kufu] 'owl'

RE 21.12: Maninka. Mimicry: [ᵍb]

1. [ᵍbɩ›ɾɩ›mɑ] 'shore'
2. [dʋ‹ ᵍbɛɾɛ›] 'other one'
3. [ᵍbɛ›dɛ›n] 'to be in need'
4. [ᵍbɩ› dɩ›] 'stick'
5. [tʋ‹l^ʋ‹ᵍbɩ›dɩ›ŋ] 'deaf'
6. [ᵍbʋ‹l^ʋ‹] 'leather'
7. [ᵍbʋ‹•ɾʋ‹] 'padlock'

RE 21.13: Vietnamese. Mimicry: Final [ᵑm ᵏp]

Whether you can hear the final double closure or not, mimic the tape, making the double articulation where it is indicated in the transcription.

1. [ˀʌwᵑm] 'grandfather'
2. [xʌwᵑm] 'no'
3. [dʌwᵑm] 'piastre'
4. [t̥ɑwᵑm] 'in'
5. [nɑwᵑm] 'to be hot'
6. [dɑwᵏp] 'read'
7. [dʋwᵑm] 'be exact'
8. [mʋwᵏp] 'ladle'
9. [cʋwᵏp] 'group of ten'

RE 21.14. Review: [j cʰ c]

Mimic the tape as you follow the transcription. Remember to keep your tongue tip down behind your lower teeth on these blade-alveopalatal stops. Remember that the articulation is analogous to [ñ l̃]. Remember to produce a slight [y] on-glide to the following vowel (or off-glide from the preceding vowel if the stop is in syllable-final position).

1a. [l̃ɑñɑjɑ]	1b. [l̃ɑñɑcʰɑ]	1c. [l̃ɑñɑcɑ]
2a. [l̃oñojo]	2b. [l̃oñocʰo]	2c. [l̃oñoco]
3a. [l̃eñeje]	3b. [l̃eñecʰe]	3c. [l̃eñece]
4a. [l̃ɔñɔjɔ]	4b. [l̃ɔñɔcʰɔ]	4c. [l̃ɔñɔcɔ]
5a. [l̃uñuj]	5b. [l̃uñucʰ]	5c. [l̃uñuc]
6a. [l̃ʌñʌj]	6b. [l̃ʌñʌcʰ]	6c. [l̃ʌñʌc]
7a. [l̃æñæj]	7b. [l̃æñæcʰ]	7c. [l̃æñæc]
8a. [l̃ɨñɨj]	8b. [l̃ɨñɨcʰ]	8c. [l̃ɨñɨc]
9a. [jɛñɛl̃]	9b. [cʰɛñɛl̃]	9c. [cɛñɛl̃]
10a. [jɒñɒl̃]	10b. [cʰɒñɒl̃]	10c. [cɒñɒl̃]

RE 21.15. Review Buildups

Mimic the tape and follow the transcription.

1. [ᵏpeˈbɑbɑ· ˈoᵍbuŋ.mi ˈᵑminoŋ]

2. [ˈɫlu.Mmɛŋ.kɨˈsɨlˀNno·ᵑmætʰiθi]

3. [cʌˈdasiẓi aˈjoŋʅřɛHcʰɛH]

4. [řapʰɨˈkʌřɑ ˈciŊŋolˀ ˈjɛnjɛŋ]

RE 21.16. Transcription

Use the special transcription form for RE 21.16 in the Workbook Supplement, pp. 57-58. Listen to the tape and fill in the blanks in the Supplement. If you find this easy, use a transcription form to transcribe the whole utterance. If you find it difficult, try transcribing any of RE 21.2, 21.4-21.9 instead. After each try, check your answers against the text below.

1. [c^{h}ʌ'r̰̃ɑks.l^ow]
2. ['ř̃æt•ιb.cʋŋ]
3. ['mɑr̋•ʌᵽiw]
4. ['sιt•æf.ši•l^]
5. [l̃æ'kæs•ɔm]
6. [^{k}pɛŋ'kʋb•ʋn]
7. ['l^ιf•kɛn.š•ɨ]
8. ['^{g}bɛb•anu•l^]
9. ['bɔt̤•e•x.zoy]
10. [yæ'šəl^ɛwm]
11. [zʌ'd̤ž̤ɔ^{g}bιñ]
12. [ñ̆u'pᵽabɛl^]
13. [t^{h}æw'^{ŋ}mɨyž.nɛ]
14. ['gɔθʋñ.Mmip^{h}]
15. [co'ɗel^.t̬θɑž]
16. [^{g}bɛŋ'^{k}puɫ•nɑ]
17. [ŧlu'jɔŋ.k^{h}ɨts]
18. [ts^{h}æv.jiw'l^ɛnt^{h}]
19. [zubɓə•'^{ŋ}mɛpᵽ]
20. [xʋp.t̤š̤^{h}oH'gɑw]

RE 21.17. Reading

Practice the following words to yourself, and read them aloud in the space provided before the tape recording. Have your buddy help you by listening to how closely you approximate the tape. If you need it, you can use RE 21.16 for the same purpose.

1. ['hɔp•ə]
2. ['hɔ•pə]
3. ['vit•^{h}uŋ]
4. [la•'t^{h}ɛ]
5. [n•o'pιz]
6. [^{k}pɔ'žʋ]
7. [tŧæ'^{ŋ}mιf]
8. [jɨ'l^ʌmp^{h}]
9. [ɗʌ'c^{h}ɛŋŊ]

LESSON TWENTY-TWO

Front Rounded Vowels; Glide Clusters

	Front U.	Front R.	Central U.	Central R.	Back U.	Back R.
High	i	ü				u
Lower-high	ɩ		ɨ			ʊ
Mid	e	ø				o
Lower-mid	ɛ		ə			
Low	æ	œ	ʌ			ɔ
Lower-low	a		ɑ		ɒ	

Table 22.1: Vowels to Date

The two dots over the ü are called umlaut /'ʊmlɑʊt/ or double dots. ü is therefore called "u umlaut," or "double-dotted u." ø is called "crossed o," and œ is called "o e" or "o digraph." When necessary, "a digraph" can be used to name [æ] to distinguish it from "o digraph." To write œ without lifting your pen, follow this sequence: ɔ, ɔ, œ

RE 22.1. Demonstration: Table 22.1

Listen repeatedly, and study the vowel chart as you do so. When you are familiar with the material read off the vowel chart with the tape. Get the new sounds as best you can by mimicry.

RE 22.2. Discrimination: SAME or DIFFERENT

Respond orally with SAME or DIFFERENT. Don't peek! Use this exercise for transcription when you can handle it orally.

1a.	[R̃ül^ R̃il^]	D	4a.	[R̃il^ R̃ül^]	D
2a.	[R̃ül^ R̃ül^]	S	5a.	[R̃ül^ R̃ül^]	S
3a.	[R̃il^ R̃il^]	S	6a.	[cɨ'R̃ül^ cɨ'R̃ül^]	S

7a. [cɨ'R̃ül^ cɨ'R̃il^] D

8a. [cɨ'R̃il^ cɨ'R̃ül^] D

9a. [cɨ'R̃ül^ cɨ'R̃ül^] S

10a. [cɨ'R̃ül^ cɨ'R̃il^] D

1b. [ceđ cøđ] D

2b. [cøđ cøđ] S

3b. [cøđ ceđ] D

4b. [ceđ cøđ] D

5b. [ceđ cøđ] D

6b. [xʌ'ceđ xʌ'cøđ] D

7b. [xʌ'ceđ xʌ'ceđ] S

8b. [xʌ'cøđ xʌ'cøđ] S

9b. [xʌ'cøđ xʌ'ceđ] D

10b. [xʌ'cøđ xʌ'cøđ] S

1c. [gœŋŊ gœŋŊ] S

2c. [gœŋŊ gæŋŊ] D

3c. [gœŋŊ gœŋŊ] S

4c. [gæŋŊ gœŋŊ] D

5c. [gœŋŊ gœŋŊ] S

6c. [dɨʋ'gæŋŊ dɨʋ'gœŋŊ] D

7c. [dɨʋ'gœŋŊ dɨʋ'gœŋŊ] S

8c. [dɨʋ'gœŋŊ dɨʋ'gæŋŊ] D

9c. [dɨʋ'gœŋŊ dɨʋ'gæŋŊ] D

10c. [dɨʋ'gæŋŊ dɨʋ'gæŋŊ] S

1d. [jør̃ jœr̃] D

2d. [jør̃ jür̃] D

3d. [jür̃ jür̃] S

4d. [jœr̃ jør̃] D

5d. [jør̃ jør̃] S

6d. [^{k}pe'jür̃ ^{k}pe'jør̃] D

7d. [^{k}pe'jœr̃ ^{k}pe'jœr̃] S

8d. [^{k}pe'jœr̃ ^{k}pe'jør̃] D

9d. [^{k}pe'jør̃ ^{k}pe'jür̃] D

10d. [^{k}pe'jør̃ ^{k}pe'jœr̃] D

1e. [ñɨp^{h} ñøp^{h}] D

2e. [ñøp^{h} ñəp^{h}] D

3e. [ñəp^{h} ñøp^{h}] D

4e. [ñøp^{h} ñøp^{h}] S

5e. [ñøp^{h} ñɨp^{h}] D

6e. [^{g}bi'ñəp^{h} ^{g}bi'ñøp^{h}] D

7e. [^{g}bi'ñøp^{h} ^{g}bi'ñəp^{h}] D

8e. [^{g}bi'ñøp^{h} ^{g}bi'ñøp^{h}] S

9e. [^{g}bi'ñəp^{h} ^{g}bi'ñøp^{h}] D

10e. [^{g}bi'ñəp^{h} ^{g}bi'ñəp^{h}] S

1f. [kœš kɨš] D

2f. [kəš kœš] D

3f. [kœš kœš] S

4f. [kœš kəš] D

5f.	[kɨš kɨš]	S	8f.	[ᵑmɑˈkœš ᵑmɑˈkœš]	S
6f.	[ᵑmɑˈkɨš ᵑmɑˈkœš]	D	9f.	[ᵑmɑˈkəš ᵑmɑˈkœš]	D
7f.	[ᵑmɑˈkœš ᵑmɑˈkəš]	D	10f.	[ᵑmɑˈkɨš ᵑmɑˈkœš]	D

Production of [ü ø œ]

We come now to the production of front rounded vowels, in which the tongue position is the same as that of the unrounded counterparts, and the lip position is the same as that of the back rounded counterparts. Knowledge of these positions may be of help to you in achieving the articulations, as may some of the suggestions in the following exercises, but as with all sounds, it is by mimicry that you achieve good production. It is very easy to fool yourself on the tongue and lip positions, and the slightest modification of the shapes of the cavities through which the air passes can bring strong acoustic differences, making sounds which seem utterly different from the ones intended. Work with a buddy on the production of all of these sounds.

For some of you the new sounds will not seem too strange as you had sounds of this kind in French or German, but do not rely on the habits you made there unless you are sure that they are good ones. Sometimes some bad substitutions go uncorrected in American students of these languages. There are, of course, differences in front rounded vowels from language to language, and the French ones are not identical with corresponding German ones.

RE 22.3. Demonstration: Producing [ü]

a. Say [i] but round your lips as you do so. The lip rounding should be tight, and the tongue really high front. Watch yourself in a mirror, experimenting with different degrees of lip rounding and tongue position until you can mimic the tape closely: [mü mü mü mü mü].

b. In trying to do this some people get the front of the tongue positioned well, but have a cup in the mid part of the tongue. This produces an [r]-like resonance. To eliminate it your tongue should have a natural, rounded contour from front to back. The tape demonstrates with and without the [r]-like resonance.

c. Practice saying He seems to see me with tightly rounded lips throughout.

d. Practice the following sequence many times. The

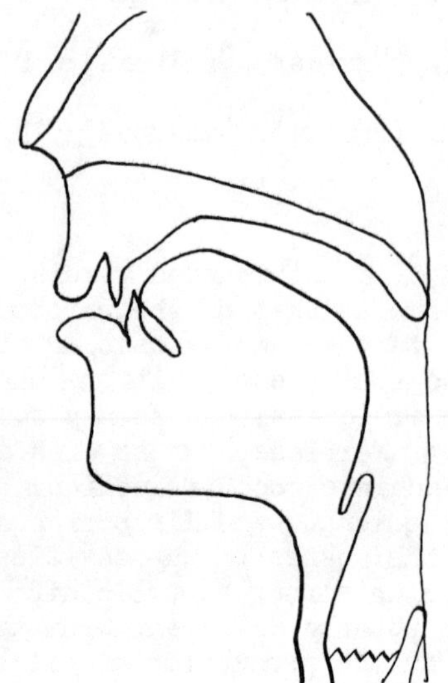

Sammy 22.1: [ü]   Degree of Lip Rounding for [ü]

phrases do not mean anything, but the first two are pronounced in English fashion. They help some people get the approximate lip and tongue combination, which can then be readjusted by trial and error. Eliminate the glide.

1. <u>fleece the geese</u> [ˈfli›ys đɨˈgi›ys]

2. <u>fluce the goose</u> [ˈflɨws đɨˈgɨws]

3. <u>fluce the guse</u> [ˈflüs đɨˈgüs]

e. Practice slurring from [i] to [ü] and back by beginning with [i] and rounding, then unrounding the lips, etc. Be careful not to move the tongue. Then practice slurring from [u] to [ü] and back by moving the tongue forwards and backwards.

RE 22.4. Demonstration: Producing [ø]

a. Say [e] and round your lips slightly less than you did for [ü]. Experiment as you did in front of the mirror for [ü]. Learn to produce [mø mø mø mø mø]. Watch out for an [r]-like resonance here also.

b. Practice saying <u>It's a gay May Day play</u> with rounded lips.

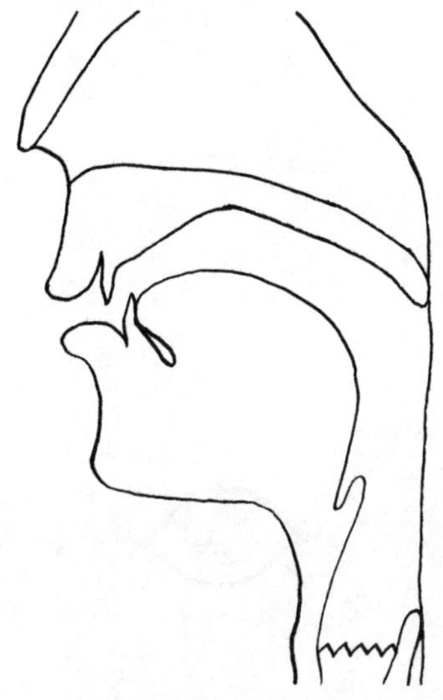

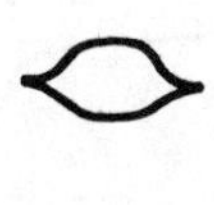

Sammy 22.2: [ø]   Degree of Lip Rounding for [ø]

c. Practice the following sequence many times.

1. make the cake ['meˇyk di'kʰeˇykʰ]

2. moke the coke ['mowk di'kʰowkʰ]

3. møke the cøke ['møk di'kʰøkʰ]

d. Practice slurring from [e] to [ø] and back by beginning with [e] and rounding, then unrounding the lips. Then slur from [o] to [ø] and back by moving the tongue forwards and backwards.

RE 22.5. Demonstration: Producing [œ]

a. Say [æ] and round your lips slightly. Experiment until you can say [mœ mœ mœ mœ mœ].

b. Practice saying Mad Mac mashed the can with slightly rounded lips.

c. Practice the following sequence many times.

1. back the stack ['bæk di'stækʰ]
2. balk the stalk ['bɔHk di'stɔHkʰ]
3. bœck the stœck ['bœk di'stœkʰ]

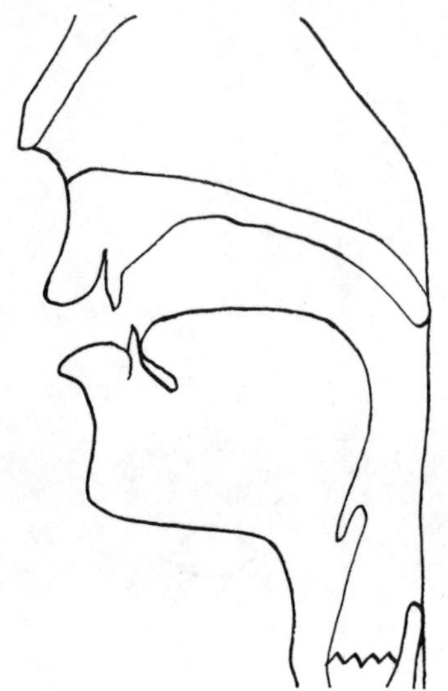

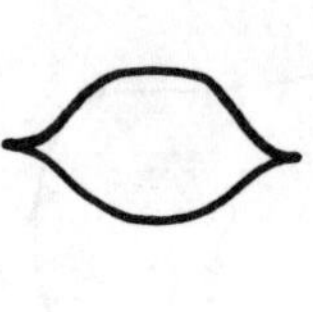

Sammy 22.3: [œ] Degree of Lip Rounding for [œ]

d. Practice slurring between [æ] and [œ] and back by changing lip rounding. Then slur between [ɔ] and [œ] by changing tongue position.

RE 22.6. Differential: ROUNDED or UNROUNDED

Respond orally to the tape. Don't peek. Use this exercise for transcription afterwards.

1.	[bü] R	5.	[m̩ˈbum] R	9.	[m̩ˈbemst] U
2.	[bi] U	6.	[m̩ˈbæm] U	10.	[m̩ˈbɨmst] U
3.	[bœ] R	7.	[m̩ˈbəm] U	11.	[m̩ˈbœmst] R
4.	[bø] R	8.	[m̩ˈbøm] R	12.	[m̩ˈbɛmst] U

RE 22.7. Differential: ROUNDED, UNROUNDED or MIXED

In this exercise you will hear three vowels in each utterance. Sometimes all of the vowels will be unrounded, sometimes all will be rounded, and sometimes they will be mixed. Respond accordingly. Don't peek. Use this exercise for transcription afterwards.

1. [ʔɩʔɨʔʌ] U 2. [ʔɔʔøʔü] R 3. [ʔuʔɔʔo] R

4. [ʔiʔαʔu] M
5. [ʔoʔæʔu] M
6. [ʔεʔɩʔα] U
7. [ʔɔʔæʔɨ] M
8. [ʔɔʔoʔø] R
9. [ʔaʔʌʔi] U
10. [ʔüʔoʔʊ] R
11. [ʔœʔüʔe] M
12. [ʔɩʔøʔʊ] M
13. [ʔəʔiʔε] U
14. [ʔœʔüʔu] R
15. [ʔüʔɔʔø] R

RE 22.8. Differential: GLIDED or NO

Front rounded vowels may be glided or they may be level, unglided vowels. In the following exercise respond GLIDED if you hear any kind of off-glide, and NO if you do not.

1. [fLüHt^h] G
2. [fLut^h] NO
3. [fLøt^h] NO
4. [fLœrt^h] G
5. [fLœt^h] NO
6. [fLüt^h] NO
7. [fLœyt^h] G
8. [fLøt^h] NO
9. [fLœHt^h] G
10. [fLüt^h] NO
11. [fLørt^h] G
12. [fLøwt^h] G

RE 22.9. Negative Practice: "The Walrus and the Carpenter"

Follow the same procedure as RE 16.12, p. 241, making the substitutions of [ü ø œ] as indicated in the three right-hand columns respectively. Practice this at many odd moments. The tape will start you off.

"The time has come, the Walrus said	1a. [süd]	1b. [sød]	1c. [sœd]
"To talk of many things	2a. [θüŋz]	2b. [θøŋz]	2c. [θœŋz]
Of shoes--and ships--and sealing wax--	3a. [wüks]	3b. [wøks]	3c. [wœks]
Of cabbages--and kings	4a. [k^{h}üŋz]	4b. [k^{h}øŋz]	4c. [k^{h}œŋz]
And why the sea is boiling hot—	5a. [hüt^h]	5b. [høt^h]	5c. [hœt^h]
And whether pigs have wings.	6a. [wüŋz]	6b. [wøŋz]	6c. [wœŋz]

\- - -

"A loaf of bread," the Walrus said	7a. [süd]	7b. [sød]	7c. [sœd]
"Is what we chiefly need:	8a. [nüyd]	8b. [nøyd]	8c. [nœyd]
Pepper and vinegar besides	9a. [süydz]	9b. [søydz]	9c. [sœydz]
Are very good indeed--	10a. [düyd]	10b. [døyd]	10c. [dœyd]
Now if you're ready, Oysters dear,	11a. [dür]	11b. [dør]	11c. [dœr]
We can begin to feed."	12a. [füyd]	12b. [føyd]	12c. [fœyd]

RE 22.10. Mimicry: [ü ø œ]

Mimic the tape and follow the transcription. When you can mimic well, try transcribing the exercise.

1a. [mü]	1b. [mø]	1c. [mœ]
2a. [θü]	2b. [θø]	2c. [θœ]
3a. [p^hü]	3b. [p^hø]	3c. [p^hœ]
4a. [ᵽü]	4b. [ᵽø]	4c. [ᵽœ]
5a. [^{k}pü]	5b. [^{k}pø]	5c. [^{k}pœ]
6a. [ksüf]	6b. [ksøf]	6c. [ksœf]
7a. [kxüp^h]	7b. [kxøp^h]	7c. [kxœp^h]
8a. [gǥül˄]	8b. [gǥøl˄]	8c. [gǥœl˄]
9a. [^{ŋ}müs]	9b. [^{ŋ}møs]	9c. [^{ŋ}mœs]
10a. [^{g}büŘ]	10b. [^{g}bøŘ]	10c. [^{g}bœŘ]

RE 22.11. Differential: Tongue Height

Respond with HIGH, LOWER-HIGH, MID, LOWER-MID, LOW, or LOWER-LOW. When you can do this well, use the exercise for transcription. Don't peek.

1. [cü] H 2. [cœ] L 3. [cø] M

4. [ce] M
5. [cü] H
6. [bægz] L
7. [bɨgz] L-H
8. [bøgz] M
9. [bœgz] L
10. [bügz] H
11. [Ññɛŋ] L-M
12. [ÑñΛŋ] L
13. [Ññøŋ] M
14. [Ññüŋ] H
15. [Ññüŋ] H

RE 22.12. Differential: FRONT, CENTRAL, or BACK

1. [ji] F
2. [jü] F
3. [jɨ] C
4. [ju] B
5. [pšøk^h] F
6. [pšək^h] C
7. [pšΛk^h] C
8. [pšœk^h] F
9. [^{k}peř] F
10. [^{k}poř] B
11. [^{k}pøř] F
12. [^{k}püř] F

RE 22.13. Differential: ROUNDED or UNROUNDED

1. [Ĩu] R
2. [Ĩø] R
3. [ĨΛ] U
4. [Ĩɛ] U
5. [Řřœx] R
6. [Řřæx] U
7. [Řřøx] R
8. [Řřex] U
9. [^{g}but^h] R
10. [^{g}büt^h] R
11. [^{g}bøt^h] R
12. [^{g}bΛt^h] U

RE 22.14. Differential: Full Labels

Select one term from each column to make up your response. Keep the exercise covered below.

HIGH	FRONT	ROUNDED
LOWER-HIGH	CENTRAL	UNROUNDED
MID	BACK	
LOWER-MID		
LOW		
LOWER-LOW		

1. [gge] M F U
2. [ggœ] L F R
3. [ggü] H F R
4. [ggu] H B R
5. [ggʋ] L-H B R
6. [ggü] H F R
7. [ggø] M F R
8. [gɛmt^h] L-M F U
9. [gœmt^h] L F R

10. [g̶əmt^{h}] L-M C U
11. [gemt^{h}] M F U
12. [gιmt^{h}] L-H F U
13. [gυmt^{h}] L-H B R
14. [gømt^{h}] M F R
15. [kwüŋ] H F R
16. [kwøŋ] M F R
17. [kwəŋ] L-M C U
18. [kwυŋ] L-H B R
19. [kwιŋ] L-H F U
20. [kwœŋ] L F R
21. [kwøŋ] M F R

RE 22.15. Differential: Vowel Symbols

Give the name of the symbol by which the vowel is transcribed, or write the vowel. When you can respond with the correct answer in every case, transcribe the utterance.

1. [pü] u UMLAUT
2. [pə] SHWA
3. [pø] CROSSED o
4. [pœ] o DIGRAPH
5. [pʌ] CARET
6. [m̩puts] u
7. [m̩pits] i
8. [m̩pɛts] EPSILON
9. [m̩pøts] CROSSED o
10. [m̩puts] u
11. [tm̩pœts] o DIGRAPH
12. [tm̩pəts] SHWA
13. [tm̩pɨts] BARRED i
14. [tm̩püts] u UMLAUT

RE 22.16. Negative Practice: "Ten Little Indians"

Practice the front rounded and front unrounded columns of the vowel chart as demonstrated on the tape.

a. [ʔi] little, [ʔü] little, [ʔι] little Indians;

[ʔe] little, [ʔø] little, [ʔɛ] little Indians;

[ʔæ] little, [ʔœ] little, [ʔa] little Indians;

[ʔi] little Indian boys.

b. Use the sequence [ü ø œ], [i e æ], [ι ɛ a], [ü] in the lines above.

Glide Clusters

Just as it is possible to have a sequence of vowels (p. 293 ff.) it is also possible to have a sequence of off-glides. This simply means that the non-syllabic tongue movement may go in more than one direction. This is often done partly simultaneously, and partly in rapid sequence.

Notice the difference in the /r/'s between English wreck and car, as spoken by people with retroflexed glides. Wreck begins with an [r] glide and simultaneous [w] glide. Car ends in an [r] glide without the [w] glide. Many speakers of English make a simple [r] glide in merry and a [Hr] glide cluster in Mary (/ˈmɛrɩy/ and /ˈmɛHrɩy/).

RE 22.17. Negative Practice: Off-glide Clusters

Mimic the following English words in the manner transcribed below and recorded on tape, whether you normally pronounce them this way or not. Notice the sequence of glides, and how these differ from sequences of vowel-glide-vowel.

1. fire	1a. [ˈfɑyr]	1b. [ˈfɑyr̩]
2. tower	2a. [ˈtʰɑwr]	2b. [ˈtʰɑwr̩]
3. care	3a. [ˈkʰe˅yr]	3b. [ˈkʰe˅yr̩]
4. fire	4a. [ˈfayH]	4b. [ˈfayə]
5. tower	5a. [ˈtʰawH]	5b. [ˈtʰawə]
6. buy you	6a. [ˈbɑyw]	6b. [ˈbɑyʊ˂w]
7. fooey	7a. [ˈfʊ˂wy]	7b. [ˈfʊ˂wi˃y]

RE 22.18. Mimicry: On-glide and Off-glide Clusters

Mimic and follow the transcription.

1a. [rwɑkʰ]	1b. [kʰɑwr]	1c. [ryɑkʰ]	1d. [kʰɑyr]
2a. [rwœpʰ]	2b. [pʰœwr]	2c. [ryœpʰ]	2d. [pʰœyr]
3a. [rwɩs]	3b. [sɩwr]	3c. [ryɩs]	3d. [sɩyr]
4a. [rwɔŋ]	4b. [ŋɔwr]	4c. [ryɔŋ]	4d. [ŋɔyr]
5a. [rwɨts]	5b. [stɨwr]	5c. [ryɨts]	5d. [stɨyr]

RE 22.19. Mimicry Review: Vowel Clusters

Mimic and follow the transcription.

1a. [te'miü] 1b. [sɑ't^hœo] 1c. [ku'pʌø]

2a. [te'mæü] 2b. [sɑ't^hœe] 2c. [ku'piø]

3a. [te'moü] 3b. [sɑ't^hœʋ] 3c. [ku'püø]

4a. [te'maü] 4b. [sɑ't^hœɔ] 4c. [ku'pɔø]

5a. [te'møü] 5b. [sɑ't^hœə] 5c. [ku'paø]

6a. [te'mɛü] 6b. [sɑ't^hœɑ] 6c. [ku'pʌø]

7a. [te'meü] 7b. [sɑ't^hœɩ] 7c. [ku'pʋø]

8a. [te'mʋü] 8b. [sɑ't^hœɨ] 8c. [ku'pæø]

RE 22.20. Mimicry Review: Long and Rearticulated Vowels

1a. [fu·t^h] 1b. [fuut^h]

2a. [fi·m] 2b. [fiim]

3a. [vü·m] 3b. [vüüm]

4a. [vwɛ·ŋ] 4b. [vwɛɛŋ]

5a. [sye·l^] 5b. [syeel^]

6a. [sø·l^] 6b. [søøl^]

7a. [l^æ·kf] 7b. [l^æækf]

8a. [l̃œ·kf] 8b. [l̃œœkf]

9a. [r̃ü·p] 9b. [r̃üüp]

10a. [ẓ̌a·x] 10b. [ẓ̌aax]

RE 22.21: German.[1] Mimicry [ü ø œ]

Listen and mimic as you follow along in your *Manual*. In addition to the front rounded vowels drilled here, German has

---

[1]This drill was prepared by Miss Rénate Wiesmann of Zurich, Switzerland. Her voice is recorded.

a fourth in lower-high front rounded position, but that is not included here.

1a. ['gü·tʰʌṛ̌][1] 'goods, estate'	1b. ['gø·tʰε›][1] 'Goethe'	1c. ['gœtʰʌṛ̌] 'gods'
2a. ['mü·lε›] 'mill'	2b. ['mø·nε›n] 'hum'	2c. ['mœnɕ][2] 'monk'
3a. ['fü·řε›ṛ̌] 'leader'	3b. ['fø·řε›] 'Scotch pine'	3c. ['fœřmʋɕ] 'formed'
4a. ['hü·nε›] 'Hun'	4b. ['hø·nε›n] 'jeer'	4c. ['hœl^ε›] 'hell'
5a. ['šü·řε›n] 'stir'	5b. ['šø·n] 'beautiful'	5c. ['šœl^tʰε›] 'I was scolding (subj.)'
6a. ['řü·šε›] 'ruche'	6b. ['řø·zlɑyn] 'little rose'	6c. ['řœslɑyn] 'little horse'
7a. ['gřü·sε›n] 'to greet'	7b. ['gřø·sε›ṛ̌] 'bigger'	7c. ['kʰœstʰl^ʋɕ] 'precious'
8a. ['ʔü·bʌṛ̌] 'over'	8b. [ʔø·l^] 'oil'	8c. ['ʔœstʰl^ʋɕ] 'eastern'
9a. ['bü·nε›] 'stage'	9b. ['bø·mε›] 'Bohemian'	9c. ['bœřzε›] 'exchange'
10a. ['mü·ε›] 'trouble'	10b. ['hø·ε›] 'height'	10c. ['hœkʰʌṛ̌] 'hump'

Transcription and Reading

Use RE 22.2, 22.6-22.15, 22.17-22.21, following the directions of earlier lessons.

---

[1] [ṛ̌] is a very light uvular flap. [ʌ ε›] sound slightly rounded.

[2] [ɕ] is an alveopalatal flat fricative.

LESSON TWENTY-THREE

Fronted and Backed Velar Consonants

	Fronted Velar (or Palatal)	Mid Velar	Backed Velar
Stops			
Voiceless			
Unaspirated	k̭	k	ḳ
Aspirated	k̭h	kh	ḳh
Voiced	g̭	g	g̣
Fricatives			
Voiceless	x̭	x	x̣
Voiced	ǥ̭	ǥ	ǥ̣
Affricates			
Voiceless			
Unaspirated	k̭x̭	kx	ḳx̣
Aspirated	k̭x̭h	kxh	ḳx̣h
Voiced	g̭ǥ̭	gǥ	g̣ǥ̣
Nasals			
Voiceless	Ŋ̭	Ŋ	Ŋ̣
Voiced	ŋ̭	ŋ	ŋ̣

Table 23.1: Fronted and Backed Velars

An examination of Table 23.1 will show that no new symbols are involved. Two diacritics are used in a way which may seem different from their previous use at first glance, but which may be thought of as essentially the same. [̭], for example, marked the "dental" series when used with the "alveolar" consonant symbols on p. 164. The dental series, however, is "fronted" in relation to the alveolar series, and it is in that meaning that the diacritic is used again here. [.], likewise, was used for "retroflexed" sounds on p. 164, but these retroflexed sounds are "backed" from the corresponding alveolars or alveopalatals, and it is backing which is intended when the diacritic is used with velar consonants. It was used for "uvular" trill on p. 246, but this trill is again "backed" from other trills.

To summarize: [̭] indicates fronting of tongue position. This gives dental position when it is an alveolar articulation which is fronted, and palatal position when it is a velar which is fronted. [.] indicates backing. The backing is simply a difference of position when used with the velars or the trills, but also involves retroflex quality when used with the alveolars or alveopalatals - not that backing cannot occur for them without retroflex quality, but we are using it to represent retroflex quality when it is associated with the alveolars and alveopalatals.

Notice also the difference between a back-velar consonant (i.e., one made with the back of the tongue against the velum, and a backed velar consonant (i.e., a velar consonant articulated in a backed position, farther from the front of the mouth).

You can easily gain a feeling for the difference between fronted (palatal) and mid velar articulations with the following English words. Say them slowly and deliberately, sensing the difference in point of articulation on the velar consonant. Prolong the velar consonant to help you feel it. As you hold the articulation of the consonant, put a pencil or pen in your mouth, and you will notice how much farther back it reaches with the second column than with the first. (See Sammies 23.1 and 23.2).

Fronted velar articulation		Backed velar articulation	
keel	[k̭^{h}i› yl˅]	call	[ḳ^{h}ɔHl˅]
skeet	[sk̭i› yt]	Scotch	[sḳɑc^{h}]
gain	[g̭e˅yn]	gone	[g̣ɔHn]
sing	[sɩŋ̭]	song	[sɔHŋ̣]

In English the degrees of fronting or backing of velar consonants are not significant, being automatically conditioned by the surrounding sounds, particularly vowels. There are languages, however, where there may be a two-way phonemic contrast, or a three-way one. That is, there may be a phonemic distinction between fronted and backed velar consonants (or mid and backed, or mid and fronted), or there may be a phonemic distinction between fronted, mid and backed.

From now on in this course, whenever you hear fronting or

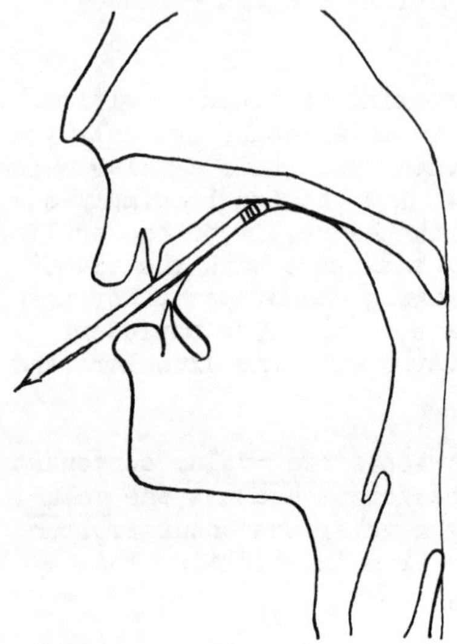

Sammy 23.1: Fronted velar (palatal) articulation, with a pencil in Sammy's mouth to show the relatively short distance it enters.

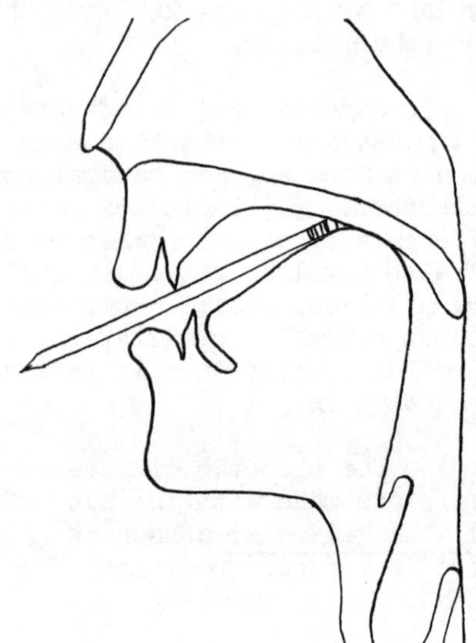

Sammy 23.2: Mid velar articulation, with a pencil in Sammy's mouth to show the longer distance it enters.

backing of velars, be sure to note it. In transcription, if you cannot distinguish fronting or backing, write the velar consonant but leave it without a diacritic mark.

RE 23.1. Demonstration: Fronted and Backed Velars

Follow the text as you mimic the tape.

a. If you can whistle with the back of your tongue, try "London Bridge is Falling Down." The last three syllables of the verse ("...fair lady.") give three points of articulation approximately like those on which we are working here. As I whistle the tune, however, the relationship between articulator and point of articulation on the final syllable is not exactly the same as that for the articulation of a backed velar consonant in languages where I have heard it. In the whistling the tongue bunches backward to reach the backed point of articulation. In languages where I have heard it, the tongue lies flat, and the part of it directly under the backed point of articulation rises to serve as articulator.

b. Use the two lists of English words above, getting the

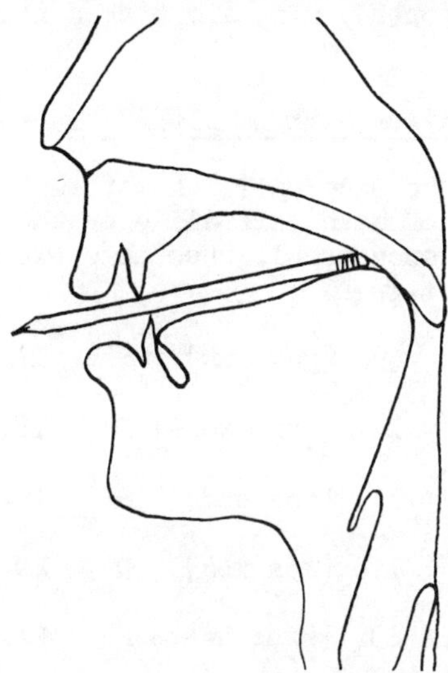

Sammy 23.3: Backed Velar Articulation. Note that the tongue is relatively flat and natural in the mouth, and that the articulator is the part of the tongue naturally under the point of articulation.

feel of the points of articulation for the velars, and then reversing them, using the mid velar articulation in the first column, and the fronted articulation in the second.

c. Use the fronted articulation of several consonants, such as [k̭ʰ g̭ x̭ ŋ̭] before and after each of the vowels on Table 18.1, p. 261.

d. Use the mid articulation before and after each of these vowels.

e. To help toward articulation in backed velar position, whisper an imitation of a donkey's hee haw repeatedly, and notice the articulation. Push the articulation of the second syllable back as far as you can, and this gives you [x̭i· x̣ɔ·].

f. If you can make a good [ɒ], articulate [ḳʰ g̣] with it. This should come very naturally.

g. Practice backed articulation with the vowels in Table 18.1, beginning with the lower-low back position and gradually moving to the front position, but keeping a backed point of articulation as nearly at the edge of the velum as you can.

h. Alternate fronted, mid, and backed articulations with the same vowels.

RE 23.2. Discrimination: SAME or DIFFERENT

Respond orally to each pair. An attempt is made to keep the vowel qualities of each pair alike on the tape, but this has not always been successful. Use this exercise for transcription also. Don't peek.

1.	[ɑk̭ʰɑ ɑḳʰɑ]	D	9.	[g̣ɑv g̣ɑv]	S	17.	[mɩx̣ mɩx̣]	S
2.	[ugu ugu]	S	10.	[ḳœθ k̭œθ]	D	18.	[nʊkxʰ nʊḳx̣ʰ]	D
3.	[ix̣i ixi]	D	11.	[g̭ud g̭ud]	S	19.	[ñəŋ̭ ñəŋ̭]	S
4.	[ɔgɔ ɔg̣ɔ]	D	12.	[xos x̣os]	D	20.	[l̃üx l̃üx]	S
5.	[eḳe eḳe]	S	13.	[ḳx̣ez k̭x̭ez]	D	21.	[lˆæk̭ʰ lˆæḳʰ]	D
6.	[o.k̭x̭o o.kxo]	D	14.	[ggeš ggeš]	S	22.	[lˇɛg̭g̭ lˇɛg̭g̭]	S
7.	[øŋ̭ø øŋ̭ø]	S	15.	[ŋ̭æž ŋ̭æž]	S	23.	[r̃ɨ̭g r̃ɨg]	D
8.	[ʌ.ggʌ ʌ.ggʌ]	S	16.	[k̭ʰɩp kʰɩp]	D	24.	[fag̣ fag̣]	S

RE 23.3. Negative Practice: Various Velar Consonants

Mimic the tape, and practice the production of each of the following English phrases with the substitutions indicated.

1. Come kitty!	1a. [kʰ]	1b. [k̭ʰ]	1c. [ḳʰ]
2. Can Kathy cough?	2a. [k]	2b. [k̭]	2c. [ḳ]
3. Cut capers	3a. [x]	3b. [x̭]	3c. [x̣]
4. Candy cane	4a. [kx]	4b. [k̭x̭]	4c. [ḳx̣]
5. Ghastly ghosts	5a. [g]	5b. [g̭]	5c. [g̣]
6. Gay gondolas	6a. [g]	6b. [g̭]	6c. [g̣]
7. Get gifts	7a. [gg]	7b. [g̭g̭]	7c. [g̣g̣]
8. Nasty noises	8a. [ŋ]	8b. [ŋ̭]	8c. [ŋ̣]
9. Nine nuts	9a. [ɴ]	9b. [ɴ̭]	9c. [ɴ̣]

RE 23.4. Differential: FRONTED or BACKED

Respond orally to the tape, and use the exercise for transcription. Don't peek.

1. [αḳʰα] B
2. [ok̭ʰo] F
3. [εk̭ʰε] F
4. [æḳʰæ] B
5. [ʋḳʰʋ] B
6. [k̭ʰɔ] F
7. [ḳʰe] B
8. [k̭ʰü] F
9. [ḳʰʌ] B
10. [k̭ʰo] F
11. [aḳʰ] B
12. [øḳʰ] B
13. [ɩḳʰ] B
14. [ɨk̭ʰ] F
15. [əḳʰ] B

RE 23.5. Differential: MID or BACKED

1. [ˈʋxʋ] M
2. [ˈæx̣æ] B
3. [ˈεx̣ε] B
4. [ˈoxo] M
5. [ˈαxα] M
6. [x̣ʌš] B
7. [x̣ež] B
8. [xør̃] M
9. [xɔR̃] M
10. [x̣œy] B
11. [ʔəx] M
12. [pɨx] M
13. [bɩx̣] B
14. [büx̣] B
15. [dax̣] B

RE 23.6. Differential: MID or FRONTED

1. [ˈɔg̭ɔ] F
2. [ˈɩgɩ] M
3. [ˈog̭o] F
4. [ˈαg̭α] F
5. [ˈœg̭œ] F
6. [gɨts] M
7. [güč] M
8. [g̭əč] F
9. [gadz] M
10. [gʋǰ] M
11. [Mmøg] M
12. [Ññeg̭] F
13. [Ññʌg̭] F
14. [ṇεg] M
15. [ṋæg̭] F

RE 23.7. Differential: DOT, CARET, or UNMARKED

In this exercise listen to the tape and respond orally or write your response as [.], [‸], or no mark. If this is too easy, transcribe the whole item. Don't peek.

1. [ˈiḳi] DOT
2. [ˈɔk̭ɔ] CARET
3. [ˈʌkʌ] UNM
4. [ˈækæ] UNM
5. [ˈoḳo] DOT
6. [g̣εŧ] DOT
7. [g̭ɨpf] CARET
8. [g̣ʋtθ] DOT
9. [geps] UNM

10. [g̭ubž] CARET
12. [ǰukx] UNM
14. [jaḳx̣] DOT
11. [čιkx] UNM
13. [cʰœḳx̣] DOT
15. [cɑk̭x̭] CARET

RE 23.8. Mimicry: Fronted, Mid, and Backed Velars

Mimic the tape as you follow in your Manual. Work consciously for the articulation you want in each case. Work with your buddy.

1a. [kʰu]
1b. [ḳʰu]
1c. [k̭ʰu]

2a. [ukʰu]
2b. [uḳʰu]
2c. [uk̭ʰu]

3a. [ki]
3b. [ḳi]
3c. [k̭i]

4a. [iki]
4b. [iḳi]
4c. [ik̭i]

5a. [gɔ]
5b. [g̣ɔ]
5c. [g̭ɔ]

6a. [ɔgɔ]
6b. [ɔg̣ɔ]
6c. [ɔg̭ɔ]

7a. [xæ]
7b. [x̣æ]
7c. [x̭æ]

8a. [æxæ]
8b. [æx̣æ]
8c. [æx̭æ]

9a. [gɨ]
9b. [g̣ɨ]
9c. [g̭ɨ]

10a. [ɨgɨ]
10b. [ɨg̣ɨ]
10c. [ɨg̭ɨ]

11a. [kxa]
11b. [ḳx̣a]
11c. [k̭x̭a]

12a. [a.kxa]
12b. [a.ḳx̣a]
12c. [a.k̭x̭a]

13a. [kxʰe]
13b. [ḳx̣ʰe]
13c. [k̭x̭ʰe]

14a. [e.kxʰe]
14b. [e.ḳx̣ʰe]
14c. [e.k̭x̭ʰe]

15a. [ggo]
15b. [g̣g̣o]
15c. [g̭g̭o]

16a. [o.ggo]
16b. [o.g̣g̣o]
16c. [o.g̭g̭o]

17a. [ŋʌ]
17b. [ŋ̣ʌ]
17c. [ŋ̭ʌ]

18a. [ʌŋʌ]
18b. [ʌŋ̣ʌ]
18c. [ʌŋ̭ʌ]

19a. [Ŋŋɑ]
19b. [Ŋ̣ŋ̣ɑ]
19c. [Ŋ̭ŋ̭ɑ]

20a. [ɑ.Ŋŋɑ]
20b. [ɑ.Ŋ̣ŋ̣ɑ]
20c. [ɑ.Ŋ̭ŋ̭ɑ]

RE 23.9. Mimicry: Mixed Sequences

Mimic the tape and follow in your Manual. Work with your buddy. When you have learned to produce these sequences, practice substituting other velar fricatives for these.

1. [k̭a'ḳa]	6. [k̭ʌ'ḳə]	11. [k̭ɔ'ḳɨ]
2. [k̭a'ḳɛ]	7. [k̭ə'ḳæ]	12. [k̭ɨ'ḳɑ]
3. [k̭ɛ'ḳu]	8. [k̭æ'ḳi]	13. [k̭ɑ'ḳü]
4. [k̭u'k̥ø]	9. [k̭i'ḳɒ]	14. [k̭ü'ḳo]
5. [k̭ø'ḳʌ]	10. [k̭ɒ'ḳɔ]	15. [k̭o'ḳœ]

RE 23.10. Review: Double Stops and Nasals

Mimic the tape and follow in your Manual.

1a. [ɑ·'kɑ·]	1b. [ɑ·'pɑ·]	1c. [ɑ·'^{k}pɑ·]
2a. [ɑ·'gɑ·]	2b. [ɑ·'bɑ·]	2c. [ɑ·'^{g}bɑ·]
3a. [ɑ·'ŋɑ·]	3b. [ɑ·'mɑ·]	3c. [ɑ·'^{ŋ}mɑ·]
4a. [k·e·]	4b. [p·e·]	4c. [^{k}p·e·]
5a. [g·e·]	5b. [b·e·]	5c. [^{g}b·e·]
6a. [ŋ·e·]	6b. [m·e·]	6c. [^{ŋ}m·e·]
7a. [o·k]	7b. [o·p]	7c. [o·^{k}p]
8a. [o·g]	8b. [o·b]	8c. [o·^{g}b]
9a. [o·ŋ]	9b. [o·m]	9c. [o·^{ŋ}m]

RE 23.11. Review: Alveopalatal Stops

Listen to the tape demonstration of alveopalatal stops in "Old MacDonald Had a Farm" and continue, practicing in the same manner, substituting the vowels of Table 22.1, p. 309.

RE 23.12: Finnish. Review Buildup: Long and Short Sounds; Vowel Clusters

Mimic the tape and follow along in your Manual. Be careful to mimic all features. Keep working on the exercise until you can recite the full sentence with perfect intonation, and solid control of the consonants and vowels and length. The sentence means "That little boy sat quietly, without moving, just now for a whole hour in the shadow of a bushy tree."

Note that when new words are introduced on the tape, they are first introduced alone, or in combination with words already introduced, before the full phrase is given. As the tape moves from single words to longer phrases, notice how some of the vowel clusters tend to become glides, and how the long consonants tend to become shorter.

1. ['poika]
2. ['poika'istui]
3. ['poika'istui 'vařyoe•a][1]
4. ['poika'istui 'li•k•umat•a'vařyoe•a]
5. ['poika'istui 'ayvan'li•k•umat•a 'vařyoe•a]
6. ['poika'istui 'ayvan'li•k•umat•a 'pu•n(ə)'vařyoe•a]
7. ['piεni'poika'istui 'ayvan'li•k•umat•a 'pu•n(ə)'vařyoe•a]
8. ['piεni'poika'istui 'æskεn 'ayvan'li•k•umat•a 'pu•n(ə) 'vařyoe•a]
9. ['piεni'poika'istui 'æskεn 'tun•in 'ayvan'li•k•umat•a 'pu•n(ə)'vařyoe•a]
10. ['piεni'poika'istui 'æskεn 'koko'tun•in 'ayvan'li•k•umat•a 'pu•n(ə)'vařyoea]
11. ['piεni'poika'istui 'æskεn 'koko'tun•in 'ayvan'li•k•umat•a 'tuoe•a 'pu•n(ə)'vařyoe•a]
12. ['peεni'poika'istui 'æskεn 'koko'tun•in 'ayvan'li•k•umat•a 'tuoe•a 'tu•hean'pu•n(ə)'vařyoe•a]

---

[1]The last consonant is not one which has been formally drilled. Mimic it as best you can.

13. ['tuo'piɛni'poika'istui 'æskɛn 'koko'tun•in 'ayvan'li•k•u-

mat•a 'tuoe•a 'tu•hean'pu•n(ə)'var̃yoe•a]

RE 23.13. Review Substitutions: General

Mimic the tape to drill these sequences, and follow along in your Manual. Work on them until you get them fluently. There is a buildup on the tape for the first item, but the following are given without buildup except for the pronunciation of the part being substituted.

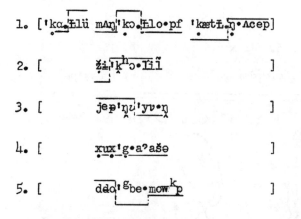

1. ['kɑ.ɫlü mʌŋ'kɔ.ɫlo•pf 'kætɫ.ŋ•ʌcep]

2. [žɨ'kʰɔ•ɫĩĩ]

3. [jep'ŋʊ'yʋ•ŋ]

4. [xux'g•aʔašə]

5. [ddɑ'ᵍbe•mowᵏp]

RE 23.14. Transcription

Use the special transcription form for RE 23.14 in the Workbook Supplement, pp. 59-60. Listen to the tape, and fill in the blanks in the Supplement. If you find this easy, use a transcription form to transcribe the whole utterance. If you find it difficult, try transcribing any of RE 23.2, 23.4-23.10 for preliminary practice.

1. [dʌm'deñɛkʰ]
2. [tʰə'nü•l^əy]
3. ['z•ɩMmʋʔɑy]
4. [neɑ.tšø•v'ɫl^i]
5. ['ᵍbɛgœ•gɔe]
6. [lᵛɨr̃ʋn•'ᵑmɛɔ]
7. [př̌ø•ñuyŊŋ•ʌʔ]
8. [ʌɔ'cʰʌ•yɔg]
9. [tsʰuɑ'džuHži]
10. [sya'm•uoyɛ•l^]
11. [ɫlɛkl^eu'ᵏpiH]
12. [l̃ɔʋkyeɔ'NnʌwᵑN m]
13. ['ʂɑ•tʂol^.č•æŋu]
14. [bɩθ'Ŋŋaütʰæ•H]

15. [ɵeuˈʔʌ•yžuo]
16. [ᵏpα•ˈkʰuH.ĩoα]
17. [Mmyøtoeyˈswʌycʰ]
18. [ˈθeotʰɔk̂iš]
19. [dʋyˈn•oepyɨ]
20. [ˈtʰüxɔÑñεʔε]

RE 23.15. Reading

Practice the following words to yourself, and read them aloud in the space provided before the recording. Have your buddy help you by listening to how closely you approximate the tape. If you need it you can use RE 23.14 for the same purpose.

1. [ƚlœˈšoH]
2. [ˈpʰüxɔ]
3. [ˈtʰɩĝεʔ]
4. [ˈθœᵏpu]
5. [ˈbʌwᵑmo]
6. [dœˈpa]
7. [cɩdɔ]
8. [ñœɨˈĩʌŋ]
9. [ᵍbαyˈpɨ]

... I SAID "HOW'S YOUR VOWEL MOVEMENT TODAY?"

LESSON TWENTY-FOUR

Nasalized and Oral Vowels

	Front U.	Front R.	Central U.	Central R.	Back U.	Back R.
High	į	ų̈				ų
Lower-high	ɩ̨		ɨ̨			ʊ̨
Mid	ę	ø̨				ǫ
Lower-mid	ɛ̨		ə̨			
Low	æ̨	œ̨	ʌ̨			ɔ̨
Lower-low	ą		ɑ̨		ɒ̨	

Table 24.1: Vowels to Date, Nasalized

The symbol for nasalization is called a "hook." Some people remember it as representing the open velic hanging down in the back of the mouth. Notice the use of the terminology nasal (consonant) for sounds like [m M n N ŋ Ŋ], etc., (Lesson 13, p. 192) and nasalized for the phenomenon introduced here. For a nasal consonant the mouth is closed off at the point of articulation but the velic is open and the air stream goes out the nose. For a nasalized sound the mouth is not closed off. The velic is open, and the airstream goes out both nose and mouth. The mouth remains the primary channel, and articulations in the mouth modify the quality of the sound in the same ways they do purely oral sounds. The nasal cavity provides the secondary channel, and the degree of opening at the velic determines the degree of nasalization. We can speak of "heavy" or "strong" nasalization, referring to sounds made with the velic wide open, or "weak, light" nasalization, referring to sounds made with the velic relatively (but not completely) closed.

This lesson has to do primarily with nasalized vowels, but it should be clear from the above discussion that any continuant (a sound which is not a stop) which we have had so far[1]

[1] This would be true of sounds in which the air stream originates in the lungs. For those where the airstream originates in the pharynx or the mouth (see Lessons 27, 29, and 31) the situation is more complicated.

can be nasalized if it is not already a nasal. The velic, for example, can be opened for [l s z x g r̃], etc. In the case of the voiceless sounds the difference you hear is slight, but with the voiced ones it is appreciable. Nasalized consonants will not be drilled in this lesson. We are only pointing out the possibility of finding them.

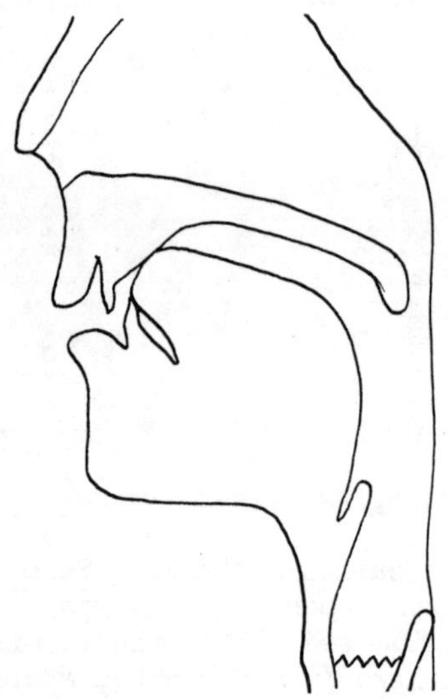

Sammy 24.1: [n]. Note the tongue articulation and open velic which produce a nasal consonant.

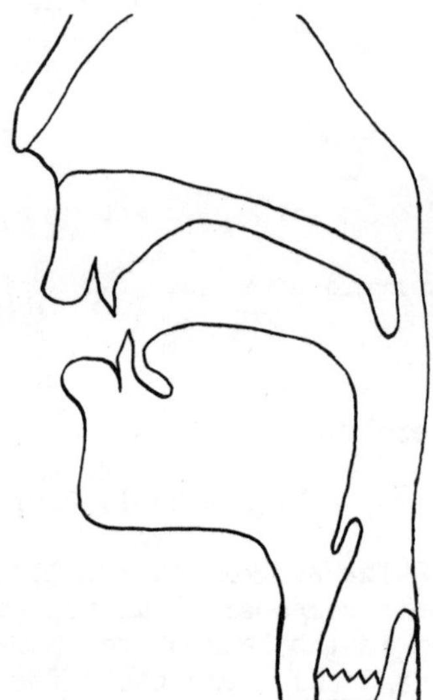

Sammy 24.2: [α̨] heavily nasalized, with velic wide open.

Speakers of American English do not seem to find making nasalized vowels particularly difficult, although some have trouble controlling the quality of those vowels, just as they do controlling the quality of other new sounds. For us, however, there is usually a great deal of difficulty in obtaining pure, oral (nonnasalized)[1] vowels in some contexts. Some of

---

[1]The use of the term oral for nonnasalized vowels is convenient, although it may be slightly misleading. All vowels are oral sounds. The oral cavity is the principal resonance chamber through which nasalized vowels as well as nonnasalized vowels pass. With this proviso kept in mind, there is no reason why the term oral cannot be used in the way it is used in this chapter.

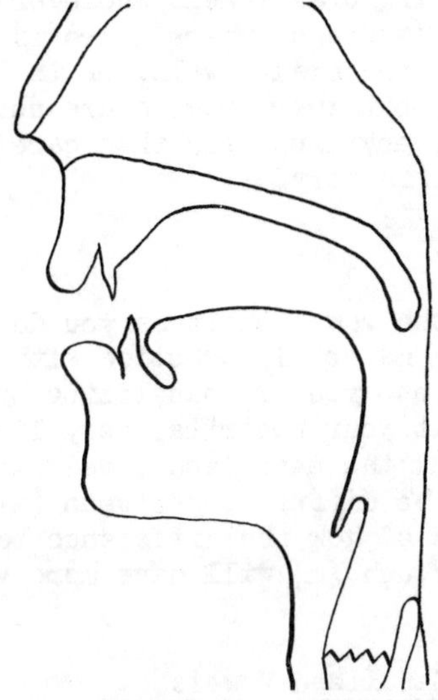

Sammy 24.3: [ą] lightly nasalized with velic slightly open.

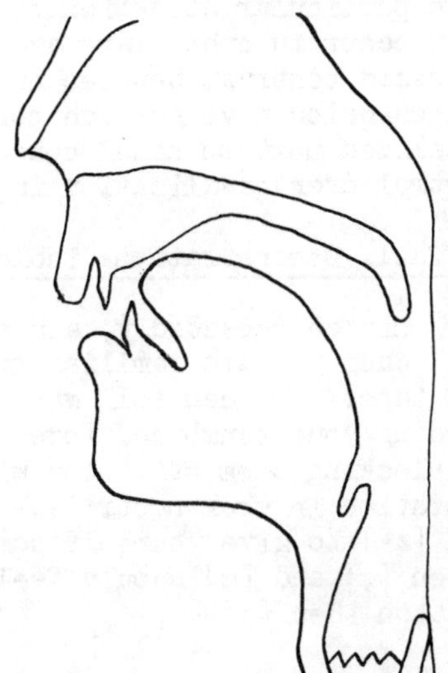

Sammy 24.4: [ą] nasalized because velic is open.

us are inclined to nasalize slightly a good deal of the time, and all of us have nasalized allophones of our vowels in the vicinity of our nasal consonants. This means that the timing on the opening and closing of the velic does not coincide with other articulations.

Notice the following diagrams:

With Slight Nasalization Without Nasalization

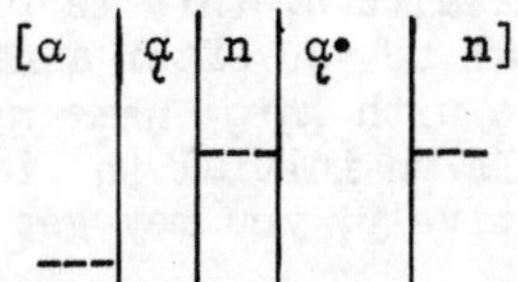

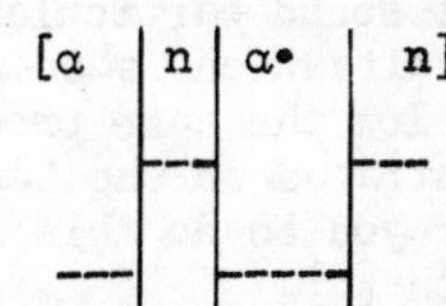

Oral closure

Velic closure

In the first diagram the [α] starts oral, but the velic quickly opens in anticipation of the nasal consonant, and remains open through the rest of the sequence, giving a slight nasalized quality to the latter part of the first vowel and all of the second. In the second case the velic opening coincides with the oral closure for the nasal consonant, leaving no trace of nasalization on the vowels.

Because of this habit in speaking English, we need to

give particular attention to producing oral vowels wherever they occur in other languages. In languages where there is a phonemic contrast between nasalized and oral vowels, or in languages which have no such contrast, but where vowels are not nasalized next to nasal consonants, anything less than careful control over nasalization is unsatisfactory.

RE 24.1. Demonstration: Table 24.1

Listen repeatedly, and study the vowel chart as you do so. When you are familiar with the material, practice with the tape. You can tell whether or not you are nasalizing by holding your thumb and forefinger at your nostrils, very lightly blocking them off. You will feel the nasalized vowels as vibration in your nostrils. Feel the difference between [m•] and [z•] to give yourself some idea of how the difference between [ą] and [ɑ] should feel, although [m] will have more vibration then [ą].

RE 24.2. Demonstration: Producing Nasalized Vowels

a. As you practice nasalized vowels be careful not to substitute a laryngealized "rasping" quality (Lesson 28) for nasalization. Some speakers of English, since they already nasalize vowels somewhat, add the laryngealization to force a contrast with what they already do. The tape demonstrates true simple nasalization and the addition of laryngealization. Avoid the latter.

b. To get a clear nasalized vowel, start with [ŋ•] and lower the tongue slowly to [ą], trying not to make any other changes in articulation. Chances are that you will naturally produce a nasalized vowel in this position. Feel it with your fingers at your nostrils. If you are doing so, and if it does not sound particularly nasalized, this is probably because nasalization is so natural to you after a nasal consonant. Follow the same procedure with [ŋ•ǫ• ŋ•æ̨• ŋ•ę•], etc., as demonstrated on the tape. If an initial [ŋ] is still too difficult for you to do this effectively, you may get the same effect with [n].

c. Isolate the nasalized vowels by beginning with the above procedure and then saying them after [ʔ]: [ŋ•ą• ʔą• ŋ•ǫ• ʔǫ•], etc. Then [ʔą• ʔǫ•], etc. Keep the same quality of nasalization throughout. Check it with your fingers at your nostrils. Be careful not to strain it with laryngealization.

d. Beginning in the same way, pronounce the nasalized vowels following [b d]: [ŋ•ą• b•ą• d•ą• ŋ•ǫ• b•ǫ• d•ǫ•], etc.

Be sure you keep the same degree of nasalization.

e. Using the same initial consonant to tune you up, produce the nasalized vowels between nonnasal consonants: [ŋ•ą̢• bą̢•b dą̢•d], etc. Check carefully with your fingers at your nostrils.

RE 24.3. Demonstration: Producing Oral Vowels

a. Get a clear nonnasalized vowel in a frame like [p...pʰ]. Follow the tape: [pɑ•pʰ pe•pʰ pu•pʰ], etc. Check yourself with your fingers at your nostrils. There should be not the slightest vibration.

b. Now do the same thing in a voiced frame. Make sure the vowel remains nonnasalized: [bɑ•b be•b bu•b], then [bɑ• be• bu•], etc.

c. Alternate [ɑ•b] and [ɑ•m], making sure the vowel in [ɑ•b] is an oral one, and that the one in [ɑ•m] is just like it. Follow the tape and keep your fingers at your nostrils: [ɑ•b ɑ•m u•b u•m æ•b æ•m], etc.

d. Alternate [bɑ•] and [mɑ•], making sure the vowel in [bɑ•] is nonnasalized, and that the one in [mɑ•] is just like it. Follow the tape, and keep your fingers at your nostrils: [bɑ• mɑ• bo• mo• be• me•], etc.

e. Follow the same procedure for the frames [b...b m...m].

RE 24.4. Demonstration: Table 24.1 and Oral Counterparts

Listen repeatedly, and study the vowel chart as you do so. The nasalized vowels of the chart will be contrasted with their oral counterparts. After you have listened sufficiently, practice with the tape.

RE 24.5. Discrimination: SAME or DIFFERENT

Respond orally with SAME or DIFFERENT. Don't peek! Use this exercise for transcription after you can handle it orally.

1. [bo• bǫ•]	D		5. [lə• lə•]	S
2. [mį mį]	S		6. [ʔəy ʔə̢y]	D
3. [ŋɛ̢ ŋɛ]	D		7. [ʔʊ̢•f ʔʊ̢•f]	S
4. [zu zų]	D		8. [ʔą̢ŋ ʔaŋ]	D

9. [ʔɔ̨p^h ʔɔ̨p^h] S

10. [ʔɛɪ̃ ʔɛɪ̃] S

11. [gøp^h gø̨p^h] D

12. [žʌ̨ŋ žʌ̨ŋ] S

13. [θew θew] S

14. [ñų̈·š ñü·š] D

15. [t^{h}ɔ̨ʔ t^{h}ɔ̨ʔ] S

16. [tŁɪ·k^h tŁɪ̨·k^h] D

17. [cɪ̨r̃ cɪr̃] D

18. [^{k}pɑyk ^{k}pɑyk] S

19. [ǰæ̨pf ǰæ̨pf] S

20. [ɪ̃ɨts ɪ̃ɨ̨ts] D

RE 24.6. Differential: NASALIZED or ORAL

Respond orally to the tape. Don't peek. Use this exercise for transcription afterwards.

1. [ʔa·] O
2. [ʔą·] N
3. [ʔę·] N
4. [ʔɔ̨·] N
5. [ʔø·] O
6. [ʔų·] N
7. [ʔe·] O
8. [mu·] O
9. [mɔ̨·] N
10. [mœ·] O
11. [mæ·] O
12. [mɨ·] O
13. [mœ̨·] N
14. [mʌ·] O
15. [bę·m] N
16. [bɒ·m] O
17. [bɪ·m] O
18. [bɛ̨·m] N
19. [bɑ̨·m] N
20. [bu·m] O
21. [bį·m] N

RE 24.7. Negative Practice: Nasalized and Oral Articulation

Practice reciting a nursery rhyme such as the following one in a fully nasalized style, then in oral style, making sure that there is no residual nasalization on any vowel, and finally alternating the lines, with one nasalized and the next oral. The tape demonstrates. Be careful of the vowels near nasal consonants when you are practicing nonnasalized articulation.

Mary, Mary quite contrary,

How does your garden grow?

With silver bells and cockle shells,

And pretty maids all in a row.

RE 24.8. Mimicry: Oral and Nasalized Vowels

Mimic the tape as you follow along in your Manual. Be careful to eliminate nasalization where it is not called for!

1a. [bo]   1b. [mo]   1c. [bǫ]   1d. [mǫ]

2a. [pɛ]   2b. [mɛ]   2c. [pɛ̨]   2d. [mɛ̨]

3a. [tʰʊ]   3b. [nʊ]   3c. [tʰʊ̨]   3d. [nʊ̨]

4a. [dɨ]   4b. [nɨ]   4c. [dɨ̨]   4d. [nɨ̨]

5a. [gʌ]   5b. [ŋʌ]   5c. [gʌ̨]   5d. [ŋʌ̨]

6a. [bæm]   6b. [mæm]   6c. [bæ̨b]   6d. [mæ̨b]

7a. [püm]   7b. [müm]   7c. [pų̈b]   7d. [mų̈b]

8a. [tim]   8b. [nim]   8c. [tįm]   8d. [nįm]

9a. [ḍẓ̌um]   9b. [ṇum]   9c. [ḍẓ̌ųm]   9d. [ṇųm]

10a. [køm]   10b. [ŋøm]   10c. [kø̨m]   10d. [ŋø̨m]

RE 24.9. Mimicry: Mixed Oral and Nasalized Sequences

Some languages have vowel clusters of which one vowel is oral and the other nasalized. Practice this exercise to help you learn to make these combinations.

1a. [ɑʔɑ̨]   1b. [ɑhɑ̨]   1c. [ɑɑ̨]   1d. [ɑ̨ɑ]

2a. [eʔę]   2b. [ehę]   2c. [eę]   2d. [ęe]

3a. [əʔə̨]   3b. [əhə̨]   3c. [əə̨]   3d. [ə̨ə]

4a. [œʔœ̨]   4b. [œhœ̨]   4c. [œœ̨]   4d. [œ̨œ]

5a. [ɪʔɪ̨]   5b. [ɪhɪ̨]   5c. [ɪɪ̨]   5d. [ɪ̨ɪ]

6a. [ɑʔę]   6b. [ɑhę]   6c. [ɑę]   6d. [ɑ̨e]

7a. [eʔə̨]   7b. [ehə̨]   7c. [eə̨]   7d. [ęə]

8a. [əʔœ̨]   8b. [əhœ̨]   8c. [əœ̨]   8d. [ə̨œ]

9a. [œʔɪ̨]   9b. [œhɪ̨]   9c. [œɪ̨]   9d. [œ̨ɪ]

10a. [ɪʔɑ̨]   10b. [ɪhɑ̨]   10c. [ɪɑ̨]   10d. [ɪ̨ɑ]

RE 24.10. Mimicry: Mixed Oral and Nasalized Sequences

1a. ['cǫ•saɛ]   1b. ['co•sąɛ]   1c. ['cǫ•saɛ̨]

2a. ['swį•saɛ]   2b. ['swi•sąɛ]   2c. ['swį·saɛ̨]

3a. ['ñų•saɛ]   3b. ['ñu•sąɛ]   3c. ['ñų•saɛ̨]

4a. ['ṭ^{h}ʌ̨•saɛ]   4b. ['ṭ^{h}ʌ•sąɛ]   4c. ['ṭ^{h}ʌ̨•saɛ̨]

5a. ['vø̨•saɛ]   5b. ['vø•sąɛ]   5c. ['vø̨•saɛ̨]

6a. ['Mmɔ̨•žɩo]   6b. ['Mmɔ•žɩ̨o]   6c. ['Mmɔ̨•zɩǫ]

7a. ['plų̈•žɩo]   7b. ['plü•zɩ̨o]   7c. ['plų•žɩǫ]

8a. ['k^{h}rə̨•žɩo]   8b. ['k^{h}rə•žɩ̨o]   8c. ['k^{h}rə̨•žɩǫ]

9a. ['tɬæ̨•žɩo]   9b. ['tɬœ•žɩ̨o]   9c. ['tɬœ̨•žɩǫ]

10a. ['kxį•žɩo]   10b. ['kxi•žɩ̨o]   10c. ['kxį•žɩǫ]

RE 24.11. Differential: Tongue Height

Respond with HIGH, LOWER-HIGH, MID, LOWER-MID, LOW, or LOWER-LOW. Don't peek. All of the vowels will be nasalized.

1. [jų̈] H   6. [đæ̨kx] L   11. [žɛ̨̣ŋN] L-M

2. [jœ̨] L   7. [đɨ̨kx] L-H   12. [žʌ̨̣ŋN] L

3. [jø̨] M   8. [đø̨kx] M   13. [žǫ̣ŋN] M

4. [ję] M   9. [đœ̨kx] L   14. [žə̨̣ŋN] L-M

5. [jų] H   10. [đįkx] H   15. [žɔ̨̣ŋN] L

RE 24.12. Differential: FRONT, CENTRAL, or BACK

1. [k̭į] F   5. [kø̨̣f] F   9. [^{g}bęŘ] F

2. [k̭ų̈] F   6. [kə̨̣f] C   10. [^{g}bǫŘ] B

3. [k̭ɨ̨] C   7. [kʌ̨̣f] C   11. [^{g}bɤ̨Ř] B

4. [k̭ų] B   8. [kœ̨̣f] F   12. [^{g}bąŘ] F

RE 24.13. Differential: ROUNDED or UNROUNDED

1. [ɬlų] R   2. [ɬlø̨] R   3. [ɬlʌ̨] U

4. [ɫlę̨]	U	7. [ᵑmǫn]	R	10. [cʰü̜lˆ]	R
5. [ᵑmœ̨n]	R	8. [ᵑmę̨n]	U	11. [cʰǫlˆ]	R
6. [ᵑmə̨n]	U	9. [cʰų̈lˆ]	R	12. [cʰɨ̨lˆ]	U

RE 24.14. Differential: Full Labels

Select one term from each column to make up your response. Keep the exercise covered below.

HIGH	FRONT	ROUNDED
LOWER-HIGH	CENTRAL	UNROUNDED
MID	BACK	
LOWER-MID		
LOW		
LOWER-LOW		

1. [k̂x̂ę]	M F U	10. [x̂ę̨nts]	M F U
2. [k̂x̂œ̨]	L F R	11. [x̂ɩ̨nts]	L-H F U
3. [k̂x̂ü̜]	H F R	12. [x̂ɨ̨nts]	L-H C U
4. [k̂x̂ų]	H B R	13. [x̂yæ̨ŋ]	L-L F U
5. [k̂x̂ʋ̨]	L-H B R	14. [x̂yę̨ŋ]	L-M F U
6. [k̂x̂ø̨]	M F R	15. [x̂yǫŋ]	L B R
7. [x̂ę̨nts]	L-M F U	16. [x̂yɑ̨ŋ]	L-L C U
8. [x̂œ̨nts]	L F R	17. [x̂yü̜ŋ]	H F R
9. [x̂ə̨nts]	L-M C U	18. [x̂yɩ̨ŋ]	L-H F U

RE 24.15. Differential: Vowel Symbols

As in the exercises above, all of the following vowels will be nasalized. Give the name of the symbol by which the vowel is transcribed, or write the vowel.

1. [dü̜]	u UMLAUT WITH HOOK	3. [dø̨]	CROSSED o WITH HOOK
2. [də̨]	SHWA WITH HOOK	4. [dœ̨]	o DIGRAPH WITH HOOK

5. [dʌ̨] CARET WITH HOOK

6. [ŋ̍kʰų̵ts] u̲ WITH HOOK

7. [ŋ̍kʰįts] i̲ WITH HOOK

8. [ŋ̍kʰɛ̨ts] EPSILON WITH HOOK

9. [ŋ̍kʰɔ̨ts] BACKWARDS c̲ WITH HOOK

10. [sn̩dɩ̨n] IOTA WITH HOOK

11. [sn̩dɨ̨n] BARRED i̲ WITH HOOK

12. [sn̩dąn] PRINTED a̲ WITH HOOK

RE 24.16: Kaka. Mimicry: Nasalized Vowels

1.	[dɑ̨]	'rigid'	5.	[ŋ̍'wɔ̨]	'fear'
2.	[kɑ̨]	'pride'	6.	[lɑŋ'sɑ̨]	'win'
3.	[kɔ̨]	'spear'	7.	[lų]	'to spear'
4.	[kwɑ̨]	'leave'	8.	[luku'sɑ̨]	'glory'

RE 24.17: Mano. Mimicry: Oral and Nasalized Vowels

1. [di˃] /dí/ 'spear'		8. [li·˃] /líí/ 'raffia'		15. [dį˅] /dí̃/ 'wait'	
2. [lɩ] /lé/ 'mouth'		9. [we·] /wéé/ 'word'			
3. [yɛ] /yɛ́/ 'to break'		10. [zɛ·] /zɛ́ɛ́/ 'dance rattles'		16. [mɛ̨·˅pɛ̨] /mɛ̃́ɛ̃pɛ̃́/ 'when?'	
4. [ka] /ká/ 'house'		11. [ka·] /káá/ 'to pour'		17. [ᵍbą] /gbã́/ 'dog'	
5. [tɔ˂] /kɔ́/ 'name'		12. [lɔ·˂] /lɔ́ɔ́/ 'week'		18. [tɔ̨w̨] /tɔ̃̀ũ̀/ 'kill'	

6. [go] /gó/ 13. [zo•] /zóó/

'to come from' 'doctor'

7. [lu] /lú/ 14. [wu•] /wúú/ 19. [dų] /dũ/

'daughter' 'breath' 'to squat'

RE 24.18: Mano. Mimicry: Vowel Glides and Nasalization

1. [ʔuey] /wéí/ 'urine' 4. [ʔuɛy] /wɛ̀i/ 'monkey'

2. [ʔueỵ] /wéĩ/ 'mortar' 5. [ʔuɛỵ] /wɛ̃̀ĩ̀/ 'to scatter'

3. [ʔuẹỵ] /wẽ̀ĩ́/ 'pestle'

As you mimic the following materials, notice the two different vowel glides, and the nasalization and lack of nasalization on each. Notice also that the nasalization extends over, or occurs solely on the non-syllabic glide [y]. The reasons for interpreting [ʔu] as /w/ and [y] as /i/ have to do partly with the possibility of the occurrence of nasalization, but of course we need much more data for that problem.

RE 24.19: Mano. Mimicry: Oral Vowels After [m n]

Mimic the clear oral vowels which come after these nasal consonants. Hold your fingers at your nostrils to make sure that your vowels are clear. One nasal vowel is included for contrast (No. 8).

1. [mɛ•] /méè/ 'large ship'

2. [nʌ•] /neè/ 'good friend of a woman'

3. [na•] /nàa/ 'someone else's father'

4. [na•ᵍbə] /nàagbe/ 'friend of a man'

5. [ᵍbono] /gbóné/ 'medicine test for lying'

6. [nɛ•] /nèe/ 'one's own mother'

7. [ɲô·] /nòo/ 'one's own mother'

8. [n̄ą̄·] /na̋̃ã/ 'to want'

Transcription and Reading

Use RE 24.5-24.6, 24.8-24.19.

... AND SO YOU THINK, PROFESSOR, THAT THIS CULTURE HAD MAINLY FRONT-ROUNDED VOWELS?

LESSON TWENTY-FIVE

Unreleased and Released Consonants; Clusters With [ʔ]

No new sounds are introduced in this lesson. We are rather concerned with some phonomena related to some sounds and combinations we have previously had.

Unreleased Sounds

You are already familiar with the difference between aspirated and unaspirated stops. Think now of an English voiceless bilabial stop at the end of a sentence, when you have nothing more to say and your mouth remains closed: He went by ship. In such a case the final /p/ is unaspirated, but it is more than that. It is unreleased. It is possible to say the same sentence, still with an unaspirated stop at the end, but with the lips closing only briefly for the stop. Such a stop is not unreleased, even though there is no audible release. An aspirated stop is, of course, released with aspiration.

There are many languages in which syllable-final unreleased stops are an important general feature of articulation. Whereas in English our handling of this is rather casual, with considerable latitude of free fluctuation in any speaker, there are languages where the use of the unreleased stop is the norm. This presents no difficulty to the English speaking person when he thinks about it, for he has no trouble making unreleased stops. Unless he forms a solid habit of doing so, however, he is likely to substitute the English pattern of variation and fluctuation.

When we need to specify an unreleased stop we may do so by a diacritic, as follows: [p⁻ t⁻ k⁻]. We will use this symbol in this lesson, and occasionally later when it seems appropriate, but in general from now on in this course you should consider voiceless unaspirated stops in syllable-final position as unreleased whether you have the symbol or not.

RE 25.1. Mimicry: Unreleased Stops

Mimic and follow the transcription. Practice what is written whether you hear the final stop distinction on the tape or not. Unreleased final stops are more difficult to distinguish than released ones.

1a. [t̬ʰɑ·p⁻] 1b. [t̬ʰɑ·t⁻] 1c. [t̬ʰɑ·k⁻]

2a. [zɩ•p¯] 2b. [zɩ•t¯] 2c. [zɩ•k¯]

3a. [ñɔ•p¯] 3b. [ñɔ•t¯] 3c. [ñɔ•k¯]

4a. [ᵏpɛ•p¯] 4b. [ᵏpɛ•t¯] 4c. [ᵏpɛ•k¯]

5a. [x̭u•p¯] 5b. [x̭u•t¯] 5c. [x̭u•k¯]

6a. [ṭʰi'tsa•p¯] 6b. [ṭʰi'tsa•t¯] 6c. [ṭʰi'tsa•k¯]

7a. [Ɫlo'ŋɨ•p¯] 7b. [Ɫlo'ŋɨ•t¯] 7c. [Ɫlo'ŋɨ•k¯]

8a. [Ṛ̃ɔ'Nnʋ•p¯] 8b. [Ṛ̃ɔ'Nnʋ•t¯] 8c. [Ṛ̃ɔ'Nnʋ•k¯]

9a. [bvə'ɪ̃ʌ•p¯] 9b. [bvə'ɪ̃ʌ•t¯] 9c. [bvə'ɪ̃ʌ•k¯]

10a. [ře'ḳʰæ•p¯] 10b. [ře'ḳʰæ•t¯] 10c. [ře'ḳʰæ•k¯]

Stops are not the only sounds which may be unreleased. In English nasals and laterals in final position are more consistently unreleased than are stops. In the latter there is fluctuation in the same words between unreleased stops and aspirated stops, whereas audible release of final nasals and laterals is more rare.

In a language like French, however, unreleased final nasals and laterals are much less common than are released ones.

Released "Final" Sounds

We have already discussed aspiration as one kind of release for stops. This is, of course, a voiceless release, and in strict phonetic terms we must say that the aspiration constitutes an additional phonetic segment after the stop, even though it patterns as part of the stop phoneme in English. In other words, if a stop is released with aspiration, the aspiration really constitutes an additional sound following the stop.

The same is true of voiced release after voiced stops in English. Occasionally we hear someone say a word like big with a voiced release of the /g/: ['bɩ•gə]. When the /g/ is released the voicing continues to give an unstressed vowel of central quality. At other times we may hear a voiceless release on the word big, as though it were very slightly aspirated: [bɩgʰ]. This aspiration is not as heavy as in a regular English voiceless aspirated stop.

RE 25.2. Demonstration: Releases on English Voiced Stops

Listen to the tape and watch the transcription as the points made above are illustrated for you.

	Unreleased	Voiced release	Voiceless release
1. big	1a. [bɩg⁻]	1b. [ˈbɩgə]	1c. [bɩgʰ]
2. bad	2a. [bæ·d⁻]	2b. [ˈbæ·də]	2c. [ˈbæ·dʰ]
3. cob	3a. [kʰɑ·b⁻]	3b. [ˈkʰɑ·bə]	3c. [kʰɑ·bʰ]

Strictly speaking, then, since audible release constitutes an additional sound segment, there is no such thing phonetically as a final sound with audible release. The audible release constitutes the final sound. Phonemically, of course, it is possible to speak of a final phoneme which is released, as in the pronunciations in the second and third columns above.

RE 25.3: French. Voiced Release

French has a phenomenon which some linguists interpret phonemically as voiced release of final consonants, as is illustrated in the transcription below. Other linguists analyze the final sound as a phonemic segment. Regardless of the analysis, it all comes out to the same pronunciation phonetically. Mimic the tape and follow the transcription.

1. [ˈfiyə̯][1]	/fiy/	fille	'daughter'
2. [ˈvilʼə̯]	/vil/	ville	'city'
3. [ˈšozə̯]	/šoz/	chose	'thing'
4. [ˈs̬ɛt̬ə̯]	/set/	cette	'this'
5. [ˈgɛpə̯]	/gep/	guêpe	'wasp'
6. [ˈlǫgə̯]	/lǫg/	langue	'language'
7. [ˈfr̃azə̯]	/fraz/	phrase	'sentence'
8. [ˈakt̬ə̯]	/akt/	acte	'act'
9. [ˈpor̃tə̯]	/port/	porte	'door'
10. [mǫˈt̬añə̯]	/mǫtañ/	montagne	'mountain'

---

[1] [̯] indicates a slight rounding of the vowel.

Close and Open Transition

Another way in which an unreleased stop may occur in English is in a word such as cupcake. We often form the articulation for the /k/ while the /p/ is still closed, so that when the lips are opened from the /p/, the result is a /k/ without any audible transition between the two. From a purely articulatory standpoint we have one long stop which begins bilabial and ends velar. Both the end of the /p/ and the beginning of the /k/ are inaudible. In this kind of a transition the /p/ is sometimes spoken of as unreleased, or as in close transition.

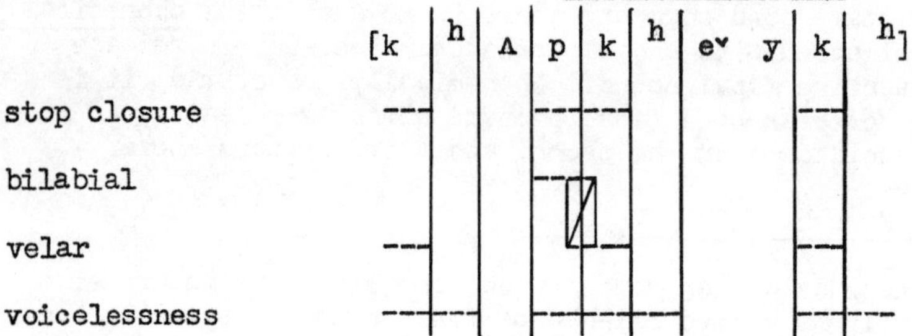

However, if someone were being very emphatic or overly precise, he might pronounce cupcake as [ˈk^hʌ$p^h$$k^h$e·y$k^h$], which has voiceless open transition (aspiration) between the consonants. We normally say bad boy as [ˈbæ·dˈboy] with close transition. However, in imitating an Italian talking English we might say [ˈbæ·dəˈboy] with voiced open transition. Each of these statements, of course, stands in relation to a presumed syllable-final phoneme. On purely phonetic grounds we can think of two consonants with aspiration between, or two consonants with a voiced central vowel between, respectively.

RE 25.4. Differential, CLOSE or OPEN

Respond according to whether the transition between the medial consonants is CLOSE or OPEN. Don't peek.

1. [ɑpˈtɑ·]	C	6. [k̭at^hˈkɔŋ]	O	11. [ḳɪnˈtʊf]	C
2. [epəˈtœ·]	O	7. [x̭ozəˈzɪm]	O	12. [x̣ɔŋəˈmɛz]	O
3. [ɔfˈsi·]	C	8. [g̭ætˈsül^]	C	13. [g̣el^ˈžɑb̶]	C
4. [ɛbˈdʌ·]	C	9. [ŋ̭ɑf^hˈfiw]	O	14. [ŋ̣ʌd̶ədež]	O
5. [ɨnəˈmɯ·]	O	10. [k̭^{h}ud̶ˈmɛy]	C	15. [ḳ^{h}æg̣əˈŋ̣ømM]	O

RE 25.5. Negative Practice: Open Transition

People learning English in Southeast Asia and many other areas tend to put an open transition in the middle of some English consonant clusters because these clusters do not occur in close transition in their own languages. The following English words are transcribed and recorded as such people might pronounce them. Mimic the tape and follow the transcription.

1. [səˈtɔp⁻]	*stop*	5. [səˈnek⁻]	snake
2. [səˈpil^]	*spill*	6. [səˈl^æp-]	*slap*
3. [səˈkin]	*skin*	7. [ˈmæsək-]	*mask*
4. [səˈmok⁻]	*smoke*	8. [ˈfæsət⁻]	*fast*

Clusters with [ʔ]

One kind of consonant cluster which needs special drill by English-speaking people is the cluster which includes [ʔ] as one of its members. Such clusters may consist of two consonants, or more rarely even three or four. [ʔ] may occur in virtually any position in the cluster, depending on the particular consonant sequence, and on the language.

RE 25.6. Demonstration: Clusters with [ʔ]

Many dialects of English do have clusters with [ʔ], although not so commonly in the initial and final positions which will be drilled in this lesson. Mimic the following English words as recorded on the tape and transcribed below. Make a clear, strongly articulated [ʔ].

1. *cotton*	[ˈkʰɑʔn̩]	4. *bottle*	[ˈbɑʔl̩]
2. (negative)	[ˈʔm̩ʔm̩]	5. *Scotland*	[ˈskɑʔlɨnd]
3. *button*	[ˈbʌʔn̩]	6. *flap 'em*	[ˈflæpʔm̩]

RE 25.7. Mimicry: Clusters of Nasals with [ʔ]

Perhaps the easiest clusters with [ʔ] to hear and produce are those where the [ʔ] is adjacent to nasals. In the following exercise the tape will read across from left to right, and then down the last column. Listen for the glottal stop and mimic with a clear, strong one.

1a. [ɑmˈʔmɑ] 1b. [ɑˈʔmɑ] 1c. [ʔmɑ]

2a. [en'ʔne] 2b. [e'ʔne] 2c. [ʔne]

3a. [ɔñ'ʔñɔ] 3b. [ɔ'ʔñɔ] 3c. [ʔñɔ]

4a. [ιŋ'ʔŋι] 4b. [ι'ʔŋι] 4c. [ʔŋι]

5a. [om'ʔmo] 5b. [om'ʔo] 5c. [omʔ]

6a. [ʌn'ʔnʌ] 6b. [ʌn'ʔʌ] 6c. [ʌṇʔ]

7a. [uñ'ʔñu] 7b. [uñ'ʔu] 7c. [uñʔ]

8a. [æŋ'ʔŋæ] 8b. [æŋ'ʔæ] 8c. [æŋʔ]

RE 25.8. Differential: GLOTTAL or NO

If you hear a glottal in sequence with a nasal, respond GLOTTAL. If you do not, respond NO. Each item will be given twice.

1. [ʔmɑ] GL 7. [onʔ] GL 13. ['ŋosɨ] NO

2. [me] NO 8. [æŋ] NO 14. ['ʔmɛfœ] GL

3. [ŋɔ] NO 9. [ʌŋʔ] GL 15. ['ñɔvι] NO

4. [ʔñɛ] GL 10. [añ] NO 16. ['sulañ] NO

5. [ni] NO 11. [ʊmʔ] GL 17. ['yøžʌŋʔ] GL

6. [ʔŋu] GL 12. [ønʔ] GL 18. ['θülιmʔ] GL

RE 25.9. Mimicry: Clusters of Laterals or Vowel Glides with [ʔ]

Mimic as you follow the transcription.

1a. [ol^'ʔl^o] 1b. [o'ʔl^o] 1c. [ʔl^o]

2a. [aw'ʔwa] 2b. [a'ʔwa] 2c. [ʔwa]

3a. [ɔy'ʔyɔ] 3b. [ɔ'ʔyɔ] 3c. [ʔyɔ]

4a. [ʌy'ʔyʌ] 4b. [ʌy'ʔʌ] 4c. [ʌyʔ]

5a. [ɨw'ʔwɨ] 5b. [ɨw'ʔɨ] 5c. [ɨwʔ]

6a. [øl^'ʔl^ø] 6b. [øl^'ʔø] 6c. [øl^ʔ]

RE 25.10. Differential: INITIAL or FINAL

Respond according to whether you hear the [ʔ] in INITIAL position or FINAL position. Each item will be given twice. Don't peek.

1. [mɨmʔ]	F	6. [ʔŋɛŋ]	I	11. [nɩnʔ]	F
2. [ʔnɨn]	I	7. [wæwʔ]	F	12. [ŋʋŋʔ]	F
3. [ʔyœy]	I	8. [ʔñɩñ]	I	13. [ʔmam]	I
4. [ñeñʔ]	F	9. [ʔl^ül^]	I	14. [ʔwɩw]	I
5. [l^əl^ʔ]	F	10. [yuyʔ]	F	15. [ʔnæn]	I

RE 25.11. Discrimination: SAME or DIFFERENT

Clusters in this exercise will be made up of voiced fricatives or voiced stops with [ʔ]. For each pair respond with SAME or DIFFERENT. The differences will be between single consonants and consonant clusters with [ʔ]. Don't peek.

1. [ʔzü zü]	D	11. [øl^ʔ øl^]	D
2. [ʔvœ ʔvœ]	S	12. [əy əyʔ]	D
3. [ʔbɨ bɨ]	D	13. [on on]	S
4. [ʔdɔ ʔdɔ]	S	14. [ʌwʔ ʌwʔ]	S
5. [gœ gœ]	S	15. [œnʔ œn]	D
6. [gi ʔgi]	D	16. [əŋ əŋʔ]	D
7. [žɑ ʔžɑ]	D	17. [umʔ umʔ]	S
8. [jɛ jɛ]	S	18. [ʋñ ʋñʔ]	D
9. [ʔḍe ḍe]	D	19. [ul^ʔ ul^ʔ]	S
10. [ʔẓ̌ʋ ʔẓ̌ʋ]	S	20. [ɩŋ ɩŋ]	S

RE 25.12. Mimicry: Clusters of Voiced Stops with [ʔ]

Mimic the tape as you follow the transcription. There will be a tendency for some of you to substitute similar-sounding (and similarly articulated) implosives (see Lesson 27) here. Keep your fingers lightly on your larynx. It should not pull sharply downward in the clusters here. Keep even pressure with your lungs. Be sure you get good voicing on the stops also.

1a. [ʌbˈʔbʌ]	1b. [ʌˈʔbʌ]	1c. [ʔbʌ]
2a. [ødˈʔdø]	2b. [øˈʔbø]	2c. [ʔdø]
3a. [ɛjˈʔjɛ]	3b. [ɛˈʔjɛ]	3c. [ʔjɛ]
4a. [ɨgˈʔgɨ]	4b. [ɨˈʔgɨ]	4c. [ʔgɨ]
5a. [ügˈʔgü]	5b. [ügˈʔü]	5c. [ügʔ]
6a. [ɑjˈʔjɑ]	6b. [ɑjˈʔɑ]	6c. [ɑjʔ]
7a. [œdˈʔdœ]	7b. [œdˈʔœ]	7c. [œdʔ]
8a. [abˈʔba]	8b. [abˈʔa]	8c. [abʔ]

RE 25.13. Mimicry: Clusters of Voiced Fricatives with [ʔ]

1a. [ɨđˈʔđɨ]	1b. [ɨˈʔđɨ]	1c. [ʔđɨ]
2a. [ævˈʔvæ]	2b. [æˈʔvæ]	2c. [ʔvæ]
3a. [øzˈʔzø]	3b. [øˈʔzø]	3c. [ʔzø]
4a. [ɩžˈʔžɩ]	4b. [ɩˈʔžɩ]	4c. [ʔžɩ]
5a. [əgˈʔgə]	5b. [əˈʔgə]	5c. [əgʔ]
6a. [œđˈʔđœ]	6b. [œˈʔđœ]	6c. [œđʔ]
7a. [ɨvˈʔvɨ]	7b. [ɨˈʔvɨ]	7c. [ɨvʔ]
8a. [ʋzˈʔzʋ]	8b. [ʋˈʔzʋ]	8c. [ʋzʔ]
9a. [əžˈʔžə]	9b. [əˈʔžə]	9c. [əžʔ]
10a. [egˈʔge]	10b. [eˈʔge]	10c. [egʔ]

RE 25.14. Differential: GLOTTAL or NO

Each item will be given twice. Don't peek.

1. [ʔzø] GL	4. [žɔ] NO	7. [œbʔ] GL
2. [ʔdʌ] GL	5. [ʔvɨ] GL	8. [iđʔ] GL
3. [gü] NO	6. [əgʔ] GL	9. [øž] NO

10. [oj]	NO	12. [ˈʔbɨsom]	GL	14. [ˈl^üšazʔ]	GL
11. [ˈdʌfun]	NO	13. [ˈzœxɩŋ]	NO	15. [ˈwɒθəvʔ]	GL

RE 25.15. Demonstration: Clusters of Voiceless Fricatives or Stops with [ʔ]

Since clusters of voiceless consonants with [ʔ] are harder to hear than those of voiced consonants, try the following exercise to warm up to them. Mimic the tape and follow the transcription.

a. Begin with the affricate [kf] and switch to [ʔf] following the tape and the transcription. The purpose of this exercise is to help you feel the release of a stop into a fricative on the [kf] and then switch to the desired [ʔf], maintaining the same "feel" of relationship.

[kfɑ kfɑ kfɑ kfɑ ʔfɑ ʔfɑ ʔfɑ ʔfɑ kfɑ ʔfɑ kfɑ ʔfɑ]

b. Use the same pattern for drilling the following pairs: [ksɑ ʔsɑ], [kšɑ ʔšɑ], [kxɑ ʔxɑ].

c. Get the feel of combinations with voiceless stops in the same way. Notice that there is an audible transition between the consonants even when no air escapes between them. The air released by the first stop rushes in to fill the cavity closed by the second stop. Use these pairs: [kpɑ ʔpɑ], [ktɑ ʔtɑ], [kcɑ ʔcɑ].

RE 25.16. Mimicry: Clusters of Voiceless Fricatives with [ʔ]

1a. [εθˈʔθε]	1b. [εˈʔθε]	1c. [ʔθε]
2a. [əfˈʔfə]	2b. [əˈʔfə]	2c. [ʔfə]
3a. [œsˈʔsœ]	3b. [œˈʔsœ]	3c. [ʔsœ]
4a. [ɒšˈʔšɒ]	4b. [ɒˈʔšɒ]	4c. [ʔšɒ]
5a. [ixˈʔxi]	5b. [iˈʔxi]	5c. [ʔxi]
6a. [øxˈʔxø]	6b. [øxˈʔø]	6c. [øxʔ]
7a. [ɨšˈʔšɨ]	7b. [ɨšˈʔɨ]	7c. [ɨšʔ]
8a. [ʌsˈʔsʌ]	8b. [ʌsˈʔʌ]	8c. [ʌsʔ]
9a. [æfˈʔfæ]	9b. [æfˈʔæ]	9c. [æfʔ]
10a. [ɩθˈʔθɩ]	10b. [ɩθˈʔɩ]	10c. [ɩθʔ]

RE 25.17. Mimicry: Clusters of Voiceless Stops with [ʔ]

1a. [ɑpˈʔpɑ]	1b. [ɑˈʔpɑ]	1c. [ʔpɑ]
2a. [øtˈʔtø]	2b. [øˈʔtø]	2c. [ʔtø]
3a. [ecˈʔce]	3b. [eˈʔce]	3c. [ʔce]
4a. [ɨkˈʔkɨ]	4b. [ɨˈʔkɨ]	4c. [ʔkɨ]

RE 25.18. Discrimination: SAME or DIFFERENT

Each pair will be given twice. Don't peek.

1. [ʔküͅ küͅ] D
2. [ʔfuͅ ʔfuͅ] S
3. [θɨͅ θɨͅ] S
4. [seͅ ʔseͅ] D
5. [ʔpʌͅ ʔpʌͅ] S
6. [šɔͅ šɔͅ] S
7. [xøͅ xøͅ] S
8. [tüͅ ʔtüͅ] D
9. [ceͅ ceͅ] S
10. [pœͅ ʔpœͅ] D
11. [ʔxœ ʔxœ] S
12. [ʔšü ʔšü] S
13. [kɨ ʔkɨ] D
14. [ʔθʌ θʌ] D
15. [ʔti ti] D
16. [ušʔ ušʔ] S
17. [œf œf] S
18. [ax axʔ] D
19. [ʋθʔ ʋθʔ] S
20. [ɛs ɛs] S

RE 25.19. Differential: GLOTTAL or NO

Each item will be given twice. Don't peek.

1. [ʔsø] GL
2. [pɔ] NO
3. [tɨ] NO
4. [ʔxʌ] GL
5. [fe] NO
6. [ʔku] GL
7. [œθʔ] GL
8. [ɩšʔ] GL
9. [üx] NO
10. [ɑfʔ] GL
11. [əsʔ] GL
12. [oš] NO
13. [ˈʔpiŋø] GL
14. [ˈkʋmü] NO
15. [ˈsaño] NO
16. [ˈʔtælˆɩ] GL
17. [ˈʔθɑnɨ] GL
18. [ˈʔfəwe] GL

RE 25.20: Quiotepec Chinantec.[1] Mimicry: Miscellaneous Nasal Clusters and Tones

Follow the transcription as you mimic the tape. You will hear the linguist giving the Spanish form before the Chinantec item.

1. [m·M]	'I ask for'	7. [m·ʔ]	'snake'
2. [m·M]	'sandal'	8. [ʔm·M]	'new'
3. [m·M]	'tick'	9. [ʔm·ʔ]	'underbrush'
4. [mM]	'thick (as a tree)	10. [MmM]	'blood'
5. [mʔ]	'pill'	11. [Mmʔ]	'tomato'
6. [ʔmʔ]	'cloth'	12. [Mm·M]	'water'

RE 25.21: Quiotepec Chinantec. Mimicry: Miscellaneous Nasal Clusters and Tones

Mimic and follow the transcription. Note the rearticulated [m] as well as the long ones. Note the meanings, also!

1a. [MmM]	'blood'	1b. [Mm·M]	'water'
2a. [Mm·M]	'my blood'	2b. [Mm·M]	'my water'
3a. [MmʔmM]	'your (sg.) blood'	3b. [Mm·mʔmM]	'your (sg.) water'
4a. [MmM]	'his blood'	4b. [MmmM]	'his water'

---

[1] Chinantec is spoken in the state of Oaxaca, Mexico. Data and recording were prepared and supplied by Dr. Frank Robbins of the Summer Institute of Linguistics. The recording is of the speech of Ramón García.

5a. [Mm•ʔ]	'our (incl.) blood'	5b. [Mm•ʔ]	'our (incl.) water'
6a. [Mm•'mʔmM]	'our (excl.) blood'	6b. [Mm•'mʔmM]	'our (excl.) water'
7a. [Mm•mʔ]	'your (pl.) blood'	7b. [Mm•mʔ]	'your (pl.) water'

RE 25.22: Quiotepec Chinantec. Mimicry: Miscellaneous Nasal Clusters and Tones

1a. [m•M]	'I ask for'	1b. ['ʔmʔm]	'I pinch'
2a. [m'ʔmM]	'you (sg.) ask for'	2b. ['ʔmʔm]	'you (sg.) pinch'
3a. [mM]	'he asks for'	3b. ['ʔm'm]	'he pinches'
4a. [m•ʔ]	'we (incl.) ask for'	4b. [ʔm•'mʔ]	'we (incl.) pinch'
5a. ['m•mʔmM]	'we (excl.) ask for'	5b. [ʔm•'mʔm]	'we (excl.) pinch'
6a. [m•'mʔmM]	'you (pl.) ask for'	6b. [ʔm•'mʔ]	'you (pl.) pinch'

Transcription and Reading

Use any of the following exercises for transcription: RE 25.1, 25.3-25.14, 25.16-25.19. For reading back try 25.1, 25.3, 25.4, 25.7, 25.12, 25.13.

LESSON TWENTY-FIVE R

Review

Consonants

The inventory of the symbols representing the consonant sounds so far is to be found in Table 25R.1 (p. 358). You are responsible for the production of all of these sounds except the ones in parentheses, which are included for reference only because they have not been drilled, but have been encountered in the actual language materials. You are not responsible for hearing the difference between dental and alveolar stops, nasals, and laterals. You should hear this difference in fricatives and affricates.

In addition to the consonant symbolization on the chart, review the affricates which are not included (p. 138), length (p. 269), syllabic consonants (p. 151), and the material on released and unreleased consonants, close and open transition, and consonant clusters, in Lesson 25 (p. 345).

TE 25R.1. Matching Consonant Symbols

After you have reviewed Table 25R.1, paying particular attention to the diacritic marks and the distinctions they represent, try TE 25R.1 in the Workbook Supplement (pp. 61-64). This exercise is to help you remember the symbols and their values.

Vowels

Tables 22.1 and 24.1 (pp. 309 and 333 respectively) chart the vowel qualities to date. Review the vowel symbols and the qualities they represent. Review also the on-glides [w y r] and the off-glides [w y r H] in Lesson 12 (p. 175), length in Lesson 18 (p. 269), and vowel clusters in Lesson 20 (p. 293).

TE 25R2. Matching Vowel Symbols

The increasing number of vowel symbols now needs attention to make sure that you remember what the individual symbols stand for, and their relation to each other in the chart. This exercise, which works on the same pattern as TE 25R.1 is designed to help you to establish these relationships. Repeat it as many times as necessary. The exercise will be found on pp. 65-68 of the Workbook Supplement.

	Double	Bilabial	Labio-Dental	Dental
STOPS				
Vl. unaspirated	^{k}p	p		ṱ
Vl. aspirated		p^{h}		ṱ^{h}
Voiced	^{g}b	b		ḓ
Vl. flap				
Vd. flap				
FRICATIVES				
Vl. flat		ᵽ	f	θ
Vd. flat		ƀ	v	đ
Vl. grooved				s̭
Vd. grooved				z̭
Vl. lateral				
Vd. lateral				
AFFRICATES[1]				
Vl. flat unaspirated		pᵽ	pf	ṱθ
Vl. flat aspirated		pᵽ^{h}	pf^{h}	ṱθ^{h}
Vd. flat		bƀ	bv	ṱđ
Vl. grooved unaspirated				ṱs̭
Vl. grooved aspirated				ṱs̭^{h}
Vd. grooved				ḓz̭
Vl. lateral unaspirated				
Vl. lateral aspirated				
Vd. lateral				

Alveolar	Alveopalatal	Retroflexed	Palatal	Mid Velar	Backed Velar	Uvular	Glottal
t	c	ṭ	k̭	k	ḳ		ʔ
t^h	c^h	$ṭ^h$	$k̭^h$	k^h	$ḳ^h$		
d	j	ḍ	g̭	g	g̣		
ť							
ď							
	(ɕ)		x̭	x	x̣		
			ǥ̭	ǥ	ǥ̣		
s	š	ṣ̌					
z	ž	ẓ̌					
ƀ							
ł							
			k̭x̭	kx	k̤x̤		
			$k̭x̭^h$	kx^h	$k̤x̤^h$		
			g̭ǥ̭	gǥ	g̤ǥ̤		
ts	č	t̤š̤					
ts^h	$č^h$	$t̤š̤^h$					
dz	ǰ	d̤ž̤					
tƀ							
$tƀ^h$							
dł							

	Double	Bilabial	Labio-Dental	Dental
NASALS				
Voiceless		M		Ṋ
Voiced	ŋm	m		ṋ
Voiced flap				
LATERALS[2]				
Voiceless				
Vd. high tongue				ḽˆ
Vd. low tongue				ḽˇ
Vd. flap				
TRILLS				
Voiceless				
Voiced				
FLAPS (cupped tongue)[3]				
Voiceless				
Voiced				

Table 25R.1:

[1] For affricates with different points of articulation on the stop and fricative, see p. 138.

[2] Lateral fricatives and affricates are shown under fricatives and affricates, respectively.

[3] Nasal flaps are shown under nasals, lateral flaps under laterals, and flat tongue flaps under stops.

Alveolar	Alveopalatal	Retroflexed	Palatal	Mid Velar	Backed Velar	Uvular	Glottal
N	Ñ	Ṇ	Ŋ^	Ŋ	Ŋ̣		
n	ñ	ṇ	ŋ^	ŋ	ŋ̣		
ň							
L							
l^	l̃						
lˇ							
ľ							
R̃						Ṛ̃	
r̃						ṛ̃	
Ř							
ř						(ṛ̌)	

Consonants to Date

Pitch and Syllables

Don't forget to review pitch in the early lessons if it gives you any difficulty, and the characteristics of syllables in Lesson 10 (p. 150).

Transcription

a. For any sounds which you have difficulty recognizing, use the differential drills in the lessons where they were introduced as transcription drills. Check your answers with the *Manual*.

b. Transcribe drills containing longer sequences. Redo some of the "fill in" transcription exercises in the *Workbook Supplement*.

In all of your transcription, study your mistakes in comparison with the correct form and see the reason for your errors if you can. Keep track of your errors on the Transcription Tally form in your *Workbook Supplement*.

Reading

Practice reading items from exercises in the *Manual*, and checking your production against the tape. Work with your buddy so that you can have some check on your production.

Sammies

Draw Sammies of [ṳ̹ ɨ̵ N̥ Ĩ] using Little Blank Sammies from the *Workbook Supplement*. Review the formation of any sounds of which you are not sure.

LESSON TWENTY-SIX

Back Unrounded Vowels; Modification of Vowel Quality

	Front		Central		Back	
	U.	R.	U.	R.	U.	R.
High	i	ü			ɯ	u
Lower-high	ɩ		ɨ			ʋ
Mid	e	ø			ɤ	o
Lower-mid	ɛ		ə			
Low	æ	œ	ʌ			ɔ
Lower-low	a		ɑ		ɒ	

Table 26.1: Vowels

With the present lesson we complete the inventory of basic vowel qualities which will be used as reference points for vowel production in this course. The symbols for the two new vowels are [ɯ] "inverted m" and [ɤ] "gamma." It may help to remember [ɯ] if you notice that [u], beside it, has the shape of an inverted n. ɯ is written by hand in analogous fashion to u. ɤ is not strictly speaking a Greek gamma, but looks enough like it so that we call it that for want of a better term.

RE 26.1. Demonstration: Table 26.1

Listen repeatedly, and study the vowel chart as you do so. When you are familiar with the material, read off the vowel chart with the tape. Get the new sounds as best you can by mimicry.

RE 26.2. Discrimination: SAME or DIFFERENT

Respond orally with SAME or DIFFERENT. Don't peek. Use this exercise for transcription if you can handle it well orally.

1a. [xɯm xum] D

2a. [xɯm xɯm] S

3a. [xum xɯm] D

4a. [xum xum] S

5a.	[xɯm xɯm]	D	8a.	[kl̩ˇ'xɯm kl̩ˇ'xɯm]	S
6a.	[kl̩ˇ'xɯm kl̩ˇ'xɯm]	D	9a.	[kl̩ˇ'xɯm kl̩ˇ'xɯm]	D
7a.	[kl̩ˇ'xɯm kl̩ˇ'xɯm]	S	10a.	[kl̩ˇ'xɯm kl̩ˇ'xɯm]	S
1b.	[žoꝑ žɤꝑ]	D	1c.	[sɨp sɯp]	D
2b.	[žɤꝑ žoꝑ]	D	2c.	[sɯp sɯp]	S
3b.	[žɤꝑ žoꝑ]	D	3c.	[sɨp sɨp]	S
4b.	[žoꝑ žoꝑ]	S	4c.	[sɯp sɨp]	D
5b.	[žɤꝑ žɤꝑ]	S	5c.	[sɨp sɯp]	D
6b.	[cɛ'žoꝑ cɛ'žɤꝑ]	D	6c.	[^{k}pɑ'sɯp ^{k}pɑ'sɨp]	D
7b.	[cɛ'žɤꝑ cɛ'žɤꝑ]	S	7c.	[^{k}pɑ'sɨp ^{k}pɑ'sɨp]	S
8b.	[cɛ'žoꝑ cɛ'žoꝑ]	S	8c.	[^{k}pɑ'sɯp ^{k}pɑ'sɯp]	S
9b.	[cɛ'žɤꝑ cɛ'žoꝑ]	D	9c.	[^{k}pɑ'sɨp ^{k}pɑ'sɯp]	D
10b.	[cɛ'žɤꝑ cɛ'žoꝑ]	D	10c.	[^{k}pɑ'sɯp ^{k}pɑ'sɯp]	S
1d.	[lˆəy lˆɤy]	D	1e.	[gɯw gɤw]	D
2d.	[lˆɤy lˆɤy]	S	2e.	[gɤw gɤw]	S
3d.	[lˆɤy lˆəy]	D	3e.	[gɯw gɤw]	D
4d.	[lˆəy lˆɤy]	D	4e.	[gɤw gɤw]	S
5d.	[lˆəy lˆəy]	S	5e.	[gɯw gɯw]	S
6d.	[ñe'lˆɤy ñe'lˆəy]	D	6e.	[ŋɔ'gɤw ŋɔ'gɯw]	D
7d.	[ñe'lˆɤy ñe'lˆɤy]	S	7e.	[ŋɔ'gɯw ŋɔ'gɤw]	D
8d.	[ñe'lˆəy ñe'lˆəy]	S	8e.	[ŋɔ'gɤw ŋɔ'gɯw]	D
9d.	[ñe'lˆɤy ñe'lˆəy]	D	9e.	[ŋɔ'gɤw ŋɔ'gɤw]	S
10d.	[ñe'lˆəy ñe'lˆɤy]	D	10e.	[ŋɔ'gɯw ŋɔ'gɯw]	S

RE 26.3. Demonstration: Producing [ɯ]

You will find it helpful to watch yourself in a mirror as you practice these steps. Work with your buddy.

a. Begin with a tight high back [u] and unround your lips to get [ɯ]. Experiment with modifying the position of the back of your tongue until you can mimic the tape closely: [dɯ· dɯ dɯ dɯ dɯ].

b. Start with [ɨ] and shift the highest part of the tongue up and back to get [ɯ].

c. Start with [g̊] and lower the tongue slightly so that it no longer produces a fricative. You should get close to [ɯ]. Practice [g̣ɯ· g̣ɯ g̣ɯ g̣ɯ g̣ɯ].

d. Most speakers of English do not have a high back sound in the words of the sentence we are going to use, but this is about the closest they come to it. Practice the sentence with unrounded lips and then modify your tongue position to match the tape. Avoid glides. A cool pool in the school.

e. Say what Miss Muffet said when the spider sat down beside her: [ʔɯ·]!

f. Practice the following sequence several times, experimenting with the last item to get a pronunciation which matches that of the tape.

1. fleece the geese ['fliʸys dɨ'giʸys]

2. fluce the goose ['flɨws dɨ'gɨws]

3. flɯce the gɯse. ['flɯs dɨ'gɯs]

g. Hold your tongue still and glide your lips into grin-pucker-grin, etc: [u·ɯ·u·ɯ·u·ɯ·u·ɯ·], [uɯuɯuɯuɯuɯ].

h. Hold your lips unrounded and glide your tongue back-front-back, etc. [i·ɯ·i·ɯ·i·ɯ·i·ɯ·], [iɯiɯiɯiɯiɯ].

RE 26.4. Demonstration: Producing [ɤ]

a. Begin with mid back [o] and unround your lips to get [ɤ]. Experiment with modifying the position of the back of your tongue until you can mimic the tape closely: [dɤ· dɤ dɤ dɤ dɤ].

b. Start with [ɘ] and shift the highest part of the tongue

up and back to get [ɤ].

c. Start with [g] and lower the tongue even more than for [ɯ], to get close to [ɤ]. Practice [g̣ɤ· g̣ɤ g̣ɤ g̣ɤ g̣ɤ] and [g̣ɯ· g̣ɤ· g̣ɯ· g̣ɤ· g̣ɯ· g̣ɤ·].

d. Start with [ɯ] and lower the tongue slightly to get [ɤ]. Practice [ɯɤɯɤɯɤɯɤ].

e. Practice the following sentence with unrounded lips and then modify your tongue position to match the tape. Avoid glides. <u>Will the show go on the road?</u>

f. Practice the following sequence several times. Experiment with the last item to get a pronunciation which matches that of the tape.

1. <u>make the cake</u> ['me˅yk ðɨ'k^he˅yk^h]
2. <u>moke the coke</u> ['mowk ðɨ'k^howk^h]
3. <u>mɤke the cɤke</u> ['mɤk ðɨ'k^hɤk^h]

g. Hold your tongue still and glide your lips into grin-pucker-grin, etc: [o·ɤ·o·ɤ·o·ɤ·o·ɤ·], [oɤoɤoɤoɤ].

h. Hold your lips unrounded and glide your tongue back-front-back, etc. [e·ɤ·e·ɤ·e·ɤ·e·ɤ·e·ɤ·], [eɤeɤeɤeɤeɤ].

<u>RE 26.5. Differential: ROUNDED or UNROUNDED</u>

Respond orally to the tape. Don't peek. Use this exercise for transcription afterwards.

1. [ĭu] R	5. [ĭɤd] U	9. [šĭɯdz] U
2. [ĭo] R	6. [ĭud] R	10. [šĭodz] R
3. [ĭɤ] U	7. [ĭod] R	11. [šĭɤdz] U
4. [ĭɯ] U	8. [ĭɯd] U	12. [šĭudz] R

<u>RE 26.6. Differential: ROUNDED, UNROUNDED or MIXED</u>

In this exercise you will hear three vowels in each utterance. Sometimes all of them will be unrounded, sometimes all will be rounded, and sometimes they will be mixed. Respond accordingly. Don't peek. Use this exercise for transcription afterwards.

1. [ʔuʔoʔɔ] R	5. [ʔɒʔoʔɯ] M	9. [ʔɔʔuʔɤ] M
2. [ʔɒʔɤʔɯ] U	6. [ʔɒʔɯʔɤ] U	10. [ʔɔʔoʔu] R
3. [ʔɤʔɒʔɯ] U	7. [ʔɤʔɯʔɤ] U	11. [ʔɒʔɯʔɤ] U
4. [ʔɯʔuʔɔ] M	8. [ʔoʔuʔɔ] R	12. [ʔoʔɔʔo] R

RE 26.7. Differential: GLIDED or NO

1. [ḳɯw] GL	5. [pʰɑˈx̣ɤz] NO	9. [šeˈŋ̣ɤf] NO
2. [ḳɤw] GL	6. [pʰɑˈx̣ɤHz] GL	10. [šeˈŋ̣ɯrf] GL
3. [ḳɯH] GL	7. [pʰɑˈx̣ɤyz] GL	11. [šeˈŋ̣ɯf] NO
4. [ḳɤm] NO	8. [pʰɑˈx̣ɤrz] GL	12. [šeˈŋ̣ɤts] NO

RE 26.8. Mimicry: [ɯ ɤ ɨ]

Mimic the tape and follow the transcription. When you can mimic well, try transcribing the exercise.

1a. [sɯ·]	1b. [sɤ·]	1c. [sɨ·]
2a. [sɯ·t]	2b. [sɤ·t]	2c. [sɨ·t]
3a. [swɯ·t]	3b. [swɤ·t]	3c. [swɨ·t]
4a. [snɯ·t]	4b. [snɤ·t]	4c. [snɨ·t]
5a. [skʰɯ·t]	5b. [skʰɤ·t]	5c. [skʰɨ·t]
6a. [kʰɯst]	6b. [kʰɤst]	6c. [kʰɨst]
7a. [yoˈkʰɯst]	7b. [yoˈkʰɤst]	7c. [yoˈkʰɨst]
8a. [zeˈpʰɯst]	8b. [zeˈpʰɤst]	8c. [zeˈpʰɨst]
9a. [zeˈpɯl^kʰ]	9b. [zeˈpɤl^kʰ]	9c. [zeˈpɨl^kʰ]
10a. [buˈpɯl^kʰ]	10b. [buˈpɤl^kʰ]	10c. [buˈpɨl^kʰ]

RE 26.9. Negative Practice: "This is the House that Jack Built"

Substitute the vowels as indicated in the lists below. The verse begins on p. 205 if you need to refer to it.

	a	b	c	d
House	[hɯs]	[hɤs]	[hɨs]	[həs]
Malt	[mɯl^t]	[mɤl^t]	[mɨl^t]	[məl^t]
Rat	[rɯt]	[rɤt]	[rɨt]	[rət]
Cat	[kʰɯt]	[kʰɤt]	[kʰɨt]	[kʰət]
Dog	[dɯg]	[dɤg]	[dɨg]	[dəg]
Cow	[kʰɯw]	[kʰɤw]	[kʰɨw]	[kʰəw]
Maiden	[mɯdn̩]	[mɤdn̩]	[mɨdn̩]	[mədn̩]
Man	[mɯn]	[mɤn]	[mɨn]	[mən]
Priest	[pʰrɯst]	[pʰrɤst]	[pʰrɨst]	[pʰrəst]
Cock	[kʰɯk]	[kʰɤk]	[kʰɨk]	[kʰək]
Farmer	[fɯmr̩]	[fɤmr̩]	[fɨmr̩]	[fəmr̩]

RE 26.10. Differential: Tongue Height

Respond with HIGH, LOWER-HIGH, MID, LOWER-MID, LOW, or LOWER-LOW. When you can do this well, use the exercise for transcription. Don't peek.

1. [l̃ɯ·] H
2. [l̃ə·] L-M
3. [l̃ɨ·] L-H
4. [l̃ʌ·] L
5. [l̃ɤ·] M
6. [ƀɤ·ŋ] M
7. [ƀœ·ŋ] L
8. [ƀø·ŋ] M
9. [ƀi·ŋ] H
10. [ƀɯ·ŋ] H
11. [řɨpf] L-H
12. [řøpf] M
13. [řɯpf] H
14. [řʌpf] L
15. [řɤpf] M

RE 26.11. Differential: FRONT, CENTRAL, or BACK

1. [Mmü·] F
2. [Mmə·] C
3. [Mmɤ·] B
4. [Mmɯ·] B
5. [kxɨ·θ] C
6. [kxœ·θ] F
7. [kxɒ·θ] B
8. [kxə·θ] C
9. [sɯ·tɬ] B
10. [sɤ·tɬ] B
11. [sü·tɬ] F
12. [sø·tɬ] F

RE 26.12. Differential: ROUNDED or UNROUNDED

1. [jɤ·] U
2. [jø·] R
3. [jü·] R
4. [jɨ·] U
5. [đə·ʔ] U
6. [đɯ·ʔ] U
7. [đœ·ʔ] R
8. [đü·ʔ] R
9. [g̤g̤ø·Ł] R
10. [g̤g̤ɨ·Ł] U
11. [g̤g̤ə·Ł] U
12. [g̤g̤ɒ·Ł] U

RE 26.13. Differential: Full Labels

Give the full label for each of the vowels you hear.

1. [^{k}pɤ·] M B U
2. [^{k}pʌ·] L C U
3. [^{k}pü·] H F R
4. [^{k}pɒ·] L-L B U
5. [^{k}pə·] L-M C U
6. [^{k}pø·] M F R
7. [^{k}pɯ·] H B U
8. [zwɒ·kl̩$^{\vee}$] L-L B U
9. [zwœ·kl̩$^{\vee}$] L F R
10. [zwɔ·kl̩$^{\vee}$] L B R
11. [zwɑ·kl$^{\vee}$] L-L C U
12. [zwɨ·kl$^{\vee}$] L-H C U
13. [zwi·kl$^{\vee}$] H F U
14. [zwɛ·kl$^{\vee}$] L-M F U
15. [s̭ɯ·č] H B U
16. [s̭ɒ·č] L-L B U
17. [s̭a·č] L-L F U
18. [s̭œ·č] L F R
19. [s̭ə·č] L-M C U
20. [s̭ü·č] H F R

RE 26.14. Differential: Vowel Symbols

Give the name of the symbol with which the vowel is transcribed, or write the vowel.

1. [t^{h}ɤ·] GAMMA
2. [t^{h}ü·] u UMLAUT
3. [t^{h}ʌ·] CARET
4. [t^{h}ɒ·] INVERTED ɑ
5. [t^{h}ɯ·] INVERTED m
6. [t^{h}ø·] CROSSED o
7. [ḓz̭œ·v] o DIGRAPH
8. [ḓz̭ɨ·v] BARRED i
9. [ḓz̭æ·v] a DIGRAPH
10. [ḓz̭ɑ·v] SCRIPT ɑ
11. [ḓz̭ɛ·v] EPSILON
12. [ḓz̭ɔ·v] BACKWARDS c

RE 26.15. Negative Practice: "Ten Little Indians"

Practice back rounded, back unrounded, and central unrounded columns of the vowel chart as demonstrated on the tape. Then continue with nasalized and oral vowels.

a. [ʔu] little, [ʔɯ] little, [ʔʊ] little Indians,

[ʔo] little, [ʔɤ] little, [ʔɔ] little Indians,

[ʔɒ] little, [ʔʌ] little, [ʔə] little Indians,

[ʔɨ] little Indian boys.

b. [ʔi] little, [ʔi$_\iota$] little, [ʔi] little Indians,

[ʔɩ] little, [ʔɩ$_\iota$] little, [ʔɩ] little Indians,

[ʔe] little, [ʔe$_\iota$] little, [ʔe] little Indians,

[ʔɛ] little Indian boys.

c. Continue around the whole vowel chart in this manner.

d. Reverse the sequence in b as follows:

[ʔi$_\iota$] little, [ʔi] little, [ʔi$_\iota$] little Indians,

[ʔɩ$_\iota$] little, [ʔɩ] little, [ʔɩ$_\iota$] little Indians,

[ʔe$_\iota$] little, [ʔe] little, [ʔe$_\iota$] little Indians,

[ʔɛ$_\iota$] little Indian boys.

e. Continue with the remainder of the chart.

Modification of Vowel Quality

We have been treating the vowels such as those represented on the vowel chart of Table 26.1 pretty much as though they were fixed norms which could be established with exactness. It must be pointed out now that any such treatment is at best a convenient fiction. Every difference in vowel sound is phonetically a different vowel, and it is virtually impossible to repeat the same vowel sound identically twice in a row so that an experienced phonetician cannot hear a difference. Furthermore, there is no absolute reason why the vowels which we have chosen for our norms should have been selected rather than others slightly differently placed in the mouth. There is nothing more basic about these than any of the thousands of other distinguishable vowel qualities.

However, for pedagogic convenience we have chosen the vowels represented in Table 26.1 as our approximate norms. We try to produce as close a consistency of articulation and hearing on them as we can, realizing that individual differences between speakers and within the production of any one speaker cannot be entirely eliminated. These areas are our reference points.

As we meet sounds in languages, however, they rarely hit our reference norms exactly. They may have allophones some of which are slightly higher, some slightly lower, some morefront and some more back than the general norms we have tried to establish. Phonetic flexibility involves the ability to adjust articulation to reproduce any such variations.

To represent such variations we will not add new symbols, but use arrow heads to show the relationship of the sounds to the norms. These diacritics may be used with any vowel symbol. For example, [e^] is slightly higher than [e], [ʋ˅] is slightly lower than [ʋ], [a˃] is slightly more back than [a], and [ɨ˂] is slightly more forward than [ɨ]. Note also that a combination like [o˂̂] indicates a vowel slightly higher and more forward than [o].

In addition to these indications of variation in tongue positions [ɩ̫] means slightly more rounded than [ɩ], and [u̯] slightly less rounded than [u], etc.

We will not ask you to use such symbols as these for transcribing in this course. They are suggested as an aid in actual language analysis and study. We will, however, practice making articulatory modifications from the vowel reference points with which we are working.

RE 26.16. Demonstration: Bracketing Vowels

In this exercise we will work on developing flexibility in vowels varying slightly from our norms by the "bracketing technique." To do this we pronounce two vowels, the first one being one which lies in the direction in which we want to modify our vowel, and the second the vowel we want to modify. We follow this with the modified position. Follow the transcription and mimic the tape.

1. [ʔɯ• ʔi• ʔi˃•] 3. [ʔø• ʔo• ʔo˂•] 5. [ʔɒ• ʔɑ• ʔɑ˃•]

2. [ʔə• ʔɛ• ʔɛ˃•] 4. [ʔœ• ʔɔ• ʔɔ˂•] 6. [ʔʌ• ʔæ• ʔæ˃•]

7. [ʔü• ʔø• ʔø^•]   9. [ʔɔ• ʔo• ʔo˅•]   11. [ʔi• ʔü• ʔi̭•]

8. [ʔɛ• ʔæ• ʔæ^•]   10. [ʔɛ• ʔe• ʔe˅•]   12. [ʔœ • ʔæ• ʔæ̨̭•]

RE 26.17. Review: Nasalized and Oral Vowels

Mimic the tape on these nasalized and oral vowels and follow along in the Manual. Be especially careful not to make extra tenseness or laryngealization substitute for a strong difference of nasalization, and be careful to have clear oral vowels when required. Hold your fingers at your nostrils to help you detect oral and nazalized vowels.

1a. [ti•]   1b. [tį•]   1c. [nį•]   1d. [ni•]

2a. [pü•]   2b. [pų̈́•]   2c. [mų̈•]   2d. [mü•]

3a. [cæ•]   3b. [cæ̨•]   3c. [ñæ̨•]   3d. [ñæ•]

4a. [k̭ɤ•]   4b. [k̭ɤ̨•]   4c. [ŋ̭ɤ̨•]   4d. [ŋ̭ɤ•]

5a. [ḳɯ•]   5b. [ḳɯ̨•]   5c. [ŋ̣ɯ̨•]   5d. [ŋ̣ɯ•]

6a. [ti•ŋ]   6b. [tį•k]   6c. [nį•k]   6d. [ni•ŋ]

7a. [pü•ŋ]   7b. [pų̈•k]   7c. [mų̈•k]   7d. [mü•ŋ]

8a. [cæ•ŋ]   8b. [cæ̨•k]   8c. [ñæ̨•k]   8d. [ñæ•ŋ]

9a. [k̭ɤ•ŋ]   9b. [k̭ɤ̨•k]   9c. [ŋ̭ɤ̨•k]   9d. [ŋ̭ɤ•ŋ]

10a. [ḳɯ•ŋ]   10b. [ḳɯ̨•k]   10c. [ŋ̣ɯ̨•k]   10d. [ŋ̣ɯ•ŋ]

RE 26.18. Review: Vowel Clusters and Glide Clusters

Mimic the tape and follow the transcription.

1. [l^ɔw'sewɯ]   8. [nɯH'swʌiṛ]

2. [l^ou'seɔɯ]   9. [nɯH'sɯʌiṛ]

3. [l^ɔw'seɤɯ]   10. [fwyew'ẋɯæy]

4. [l^ɤɯ'seɤɯ]   11. [fwiɛw'ẋɯæi]

5. [nuH'swʌyṛ]   12. [fwiɛɯ'ẋɯæy]

6. [nuʌ'swʌyṛ]   13. [ɗɤɑ'l˅ɤɔɯ]

7. [nɯH'swʌyṛ]   14. [ɗɤɒ'l˅ɤɔɯ]

RE 26.19: Vietnamese.[1] Transcription, Stress and Juncture

The following sentences from Vietnamese consist of thirty-nine different combinations of the same five words. Each of these variations has its own meaning. However, as you listen to the recording you will notice that juncture, stress, and intonation also change along with the word order.

For this exercise use pp. 69-74 of your Workbook Supplement, and do not refer to the text below until you have done the transcription. The Supplement does not have the juncture or stress transcribed for you. Listen to the tape recording as many times as you need to, and mark the primary stresses in the Supplement whenever you hear them.

Then listen for open juncture. This will not occur in every sentence. Indicate it by drawing a vertical line | where you hear it.

When you are satisfied with your transcription of stress and juncture check your transcription against the transcription below. Blanks for a second try are also given you so that you can try this exercise again another time. (Juncture is represented below by space in our usual fashion, see pp. 158-159.)

1. [ˈṣ̌a·wnɔˈɓa·wxʌŋmˈɗe>n] 'Why does he say that he won't come?'

2. [ṣ̌a·wˈɓa·wnɔxʌŋmˈɗe>n] 'Why do you say that he won't come?'

3. [ṣ̌a·wxʌŋmˈɓa·wnɔˈɗe>n] 'Why haven't you told him to come?'

4. [ṣ̌a·wxʌŋmˈɗe>n ˈɓa·wnɔ] 'Why didn't you come to tell him?'

5. [ˈṣ̌a·wnɔxʌŋmˈɓa·wɗe>n] 'Why didn't he tell you to come?'

6. [ˈṣ̌a·w ɗe>nˈɓa·wnɔxʌŋm] 'Well, did somebody come to tell him?'

7. [ˈṣ̌a·w ɓa·wnɔˈɗe>nxʌŋm] 'Well, have you told him to com come?'

---

[1]The examples are taken from Lê-văn-Ly, Le Parler Vietnamien, pp. 234-235. The recording is by Nguyễn-văn-Vạn.

8.	[nɔ'ɗe›n ʂ̌ɑ•wxʌŋm'ɓɑ•w]	'He came. Why haven't you told him?'
9.	[nɔ'ɗe›n xʌŋm'ɓɑ•wʂ̌ɑ•w]	'He is coming, but he is not saying anything.'
10.	[nɔɗe›n'ɓɑ•w xʌŋm'ʂ̌ɑ•w]	'He just said that it doesn't make any difference.'
11.	[nɔ'ɓɑ•w ʂ̌ɑ•wxʌŋm'ɗe›n]	'He said, "Why not come?"'
12.	[nɔɗe›n'ɓɑ•w ʂ̌ɑ•wxʌŋm]	'He came to say, "Why not?"'
13.	[nɔ'ɓɑ•w 'ɗe›nxʌŋm'ʂ̌ɑ•w]	'He said, "If you come, it doesn't matter."'
14.	[nɔ'ɓɑ•w xʌŋm'ɗe›nʂ̌ɑ•w]	'He said, "Aren't you coming?"'
15.	[nɔxʌŋm'ɓɑ•w ʂ̌ɑ•w'ɗe›n]	'He didn't say, so why come?'
16.	[nɔxʌŋmɓɑ•w'ɗe›nʂ̌ɑ•w]	'Didn't he say to come?'
17.	[nɔxʌŋmɗe›n'ɓɑ•wʂ̌ɑ•w]	'Didn't he come to tell you?'
18.	['ɓɑ•wnɔʂ̌ɑ•wxʌŋm'ɗe›n]	'Tell him why he didn't come.'
19.	['ɓɑ•wnɔ 'ɗe›nxʌŋm'ʂ̌ɑ•w]	'Tell him, "If he comes it doesn't matter."'
20.	['ɓɑ•w'ʂ̌ɑ•wnɔxʌŋm'ɗe›n]	'Tell why he didn't come.'
21.	[ɓɑ•wnɔ'ɗe›n ʂ̌ɑ•w'xʌŋm]	'Tell him to come. Why not?'
22.	['ɓɑ•wnɔxʌŋm'ɗe›nʂ̌ɑ•w]	'You say that he is not coming?'
23.	[ɓɑ•w'xʌŋm ʂ̌ɑ•wnɔ'ɗe›n]	'Somebody said, "No, why did he come?"'

24. ['ɓα·wṣ̌α·w nɔ'ɗe›nxʌŋm] 'What are you saying? Is he coming?'

25. [xʌŋm̩'ɓα·w š̥α·wnɔ'ɗe›n] 'Nobody told him why he had come.'

26. [xʌŋmɗe›n'ɓα·wnɔš̥α·w] 'Didn't you come to tell him?'

27. [xʌŋm'šα·w 'ɓα·wnɔ'ɗe›n] 'It doesn't make any difference. Tell him to come.'

28. [xʌŋm'ɓα·wnɔ'ɗe›nṣ̌α·w] 'Haven't you told him to come?'

29. [xʌŋm'ɗe›n ɓα·w'nɔ ṣ̌α·w] 'They aren't coming. What does one tell him?'

30. [xʌŋm'ɗe›n nɔ'ɓα·wṣ̌α·w] 'They aren't coming. What does he say?'

31. ['ɗe›n ɓα·wnɔxʌŋm'ṣ̌α·w] 'Go and tell him that it doesn't make any difference.'

32. ['ɗe›nxʌŋm 'ɓα·wnɔṣ̌α·w] 'Are they coming? What are we going to tell him?'

33. ['ɗe›nxʌŋm nɔ'ɓα·wṣ̌α·w] 'Are they coming? What does he say?'

34. ['ɗe›n ṣ̌α·wxʌŋm'ɓα·wnɔ] 'You are coming. Why didn't you tell him?'

35. ['ɗe›nɓα·wnɔ· ṣ̌α·w'xʌŋm] 'Go and say to him, "Why not?"'

36. ['ɗe›n ṣ̌α·wnɔxʌŋm'ɓα·w] 'You are coming. Why hasn't he said so?'

37. ['ɗe›n nɔɓα·wxʌŋm'ṣ̌α·w] 'Come! He says it doesn't make any difference.'

38. ['ɗe›n nɔxʌŋm'ɓα·wṣ̌α·w] 'They are coming, and he doesn't say anything'

39. ['ɗe›n ṣ̌α·w'ɓα·wnɔ'xʌŋm] 'You are coming. Why have you told him you are not?'

RE 26.20: Vietnamese. Differential: Intonation

Go through the tape recording of the previous exercise again, this time listening for the pitch on the last syllable of each sentence. Draw the pitch contour of this syllable on the blank sentences of the Workbook Supplement. Pay particular attention to cases where the same syllable comes out with different pitches. This is due to intonation (question vs. statement, etc.). Listen repeatedly until you feel that you have transcribed the pitch of the last syllable correctly in each case, and then check your transcription with the text above.

RE 26.21: Vietnamese. Mimicry

Now mimic the Vietnamese sentences of RE 26.19. Follow the transcription in the Manual as you do so. Pay particular attention to the stress, rhythm, juncture, and pitch. Mimic until you can do it fluently and easily. Work with your buddy.

Transcription and Reading

Use RE 26.2, 26.5-26.14, 26.17-26.18.

Suggested Reading

At this point in the course it would be helpful to read through some of the following materials, skipping any parts which you have already studied.

Eugene A. Nida, Learning a Foreign Language, pp. 86-140.

H. A. Gleason, An Introduction to Descriptive Linguistics, pp. 158-265 (1955 edition), or pp. 239-372 (1961 edition).

Charles F. Hockett, A Course in Modern Linguistics, pp. 62-119.

Charles F. Hockett, Manual of Phonology, pp. 23-42.

In this reading you may find an occasional difference in the symbolization of sounds. Note particularly the following equivalences in the vowels.

This Manual	Nida's LAFL (and others)	Other
u	ü	y
ø	ö	

This Manual	Nida's LAFL (and others)
œ	ɔ̈
ɯ	ï
ɤ	ë

WE HIRED HER TO TEACH DOUBLE STOPS!

LESSON TWENTY-SEVEN

Implosives; Fortis and Lenis Articulation

	Double	Bilabial	Dental/ Alveolar	Alveopalatal	Velar
STOPS					
Lung air					
Vl. unaspirated	^{k}p	p	t	c	k
Vl. aspirated		p^{h}	t^{h}	c^{h}	k^{h}
Voiced	^{g}b	b	d	j	g
Ingressive pharynx air					
Voiceless	^{k}ƥ	ƥ	ƭ	ƈ	ƙ
Voiced	^{g}ɓ	ɓ	ɗ	ʄ	ɠ
FRICATIVES[1]					
Lung air					
Voiceless		ᵽ	s	š	x
Voiced		ƀ	z	ž	ǥ
Ingressive pharynx air					
Voiceless		(ᵽ̔)	(s̔)	(š̔)	(x̔)
Voiced		(ƀ̔)	(z̔)	(ž̔)	(ǥ̔)

Table 27.1: Some Implosives

In this lesson we introduce an entirely new feature of articulation. This time, however, it does not relate to the relative positions of the organs in the mouth, but to a movement which produces an entirely different air stream from what we have had up to now.

---

[1]Only a sampling is given of the fricatives. Ingressive pharynx air fricatives will not be drilled in this course. Affricates may also be articulated with ingressive pharynx air.

In Sammy 27.1 the dotted arrow shows us the air stream on all sounds which we have practiced up to the present. This air stream originates in the lungs, through movement of the muscles in the chest and abdomen, and moves outward through the mouth, nose, or both. It may be stopped momentarily, impeded, or made to pass through air cavities of different shapes, but it is always an air stream which originates in the lungs and moves outward. It is egressive lung air. The majority of sounds in all languages are made with egressive lung air.[1]

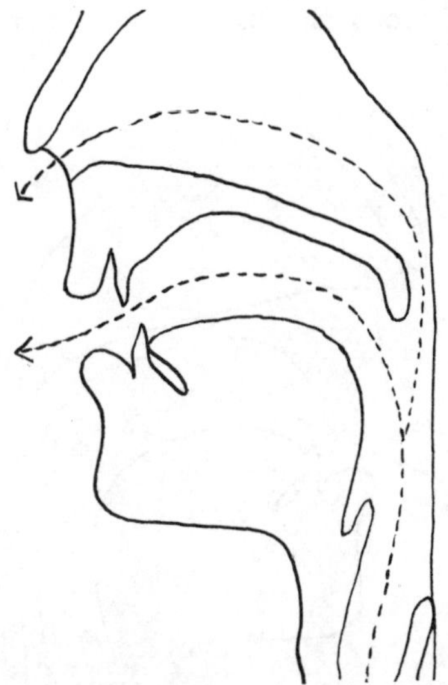

Sammy 27.1: Showing Egressive Lung Air

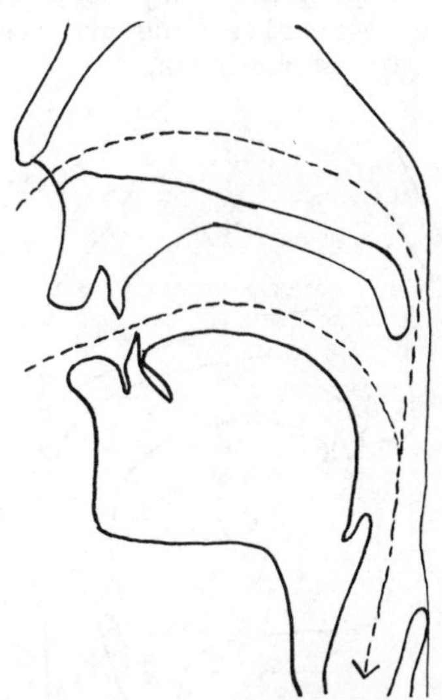

Sammy 27.2: Showing Ingressive Lung Air

But although egressive lung air sounds are by far the most common, Sammies 27.3 and 27.4 picture another source of air stream which occurs in languages scattered all over the world. It seems to be most common in Africa, with important occurrences in Asia, the Pacific, and in American Indian languages. To give two notable examples, it occurs frequently in such national Languages as Thai and Vietnamese, and can in no sence be considered marginal or uncommon.

---

[1]Ingressive lung air (talking while you breathe in) is perfectly possible, but very rare in languages. Hockett's Manual of Phonology mentions one language, Maidu, where two consonants regularly have ingressive lung air (p. 26). We do not drill it in this course.

The air stream for ingressive pharynx air sounds does not originate in the lungs, and it does not go out through the mouth and nose, but comes in. Ingressive pharynx air is produced by closing, or nearly closing, the vocal cords, and pulling the larynx downward while some articulation such as a stop is being made in the mouth, as in Sammy 27.3. This creates a partial vacuum in the air cavities (including the pharynx). When the articulation in the mouth is released, air comes in through the mouth to fill the partial vacuum, as shown in Sammy 27.4. The movement of an ingressive pharynx air sound is very rapid, and they occur in normal stream of speech surrounded by egressive lung air sounds without the slightest hesitation or awkwardness.

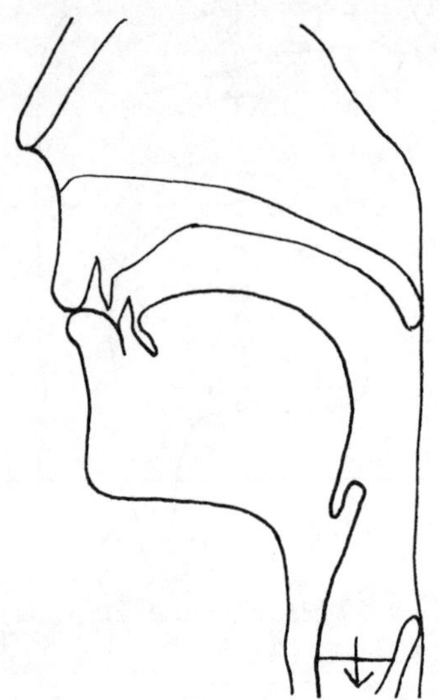

Sammy 27.3: Larynx Movement to Create Partial Vacuum for [ɓ]

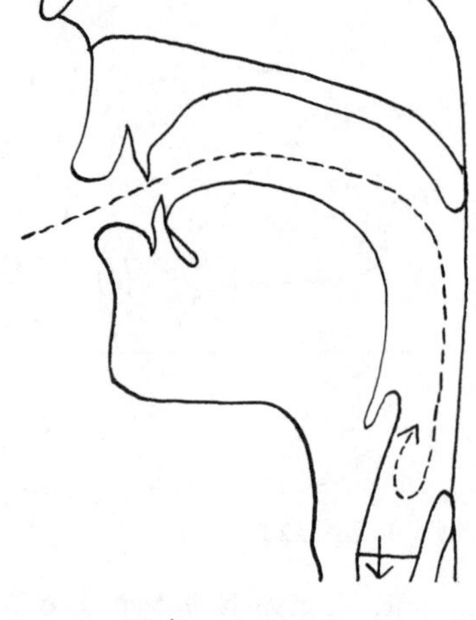

Sammy 27.4: Ingressive Air Stream After Labial Articulation is Released

If you will examine Table 27.1 you will see that we have listed a sampling of ingressive pharynx air stops and fricatives. The fricatives are more rare and will not be drilled in this course, although some of them will be used in the demonstrations to help you develop a feel for the proper larynx movement. The stops are often called implosives because of the ingressive air stream.

For symbols we use the usual ones for various articulations, modified by a hook which begins at the northwest corner of the symbol when there is such a corner, and at the northeast corner if there is a more convenient point of attachment there. From the standpoint of symbolization there is therefore only one new feature to learn (the hook), representing the one new feature of articulation.

One more point concerning implosives needs to be made. It has to do with voicing. Voicing, you remember, is an air movement through the vocal cords, such that a characteristic rumble is created (pp. 44-45). This involves the use of lung air. Voiced implosives, therefore, require two air streams. The primary air stream is ingressive pharynx air, created by the downward movement of the larynx. The secondary air stream is lung air allowed to leak up through the moving larynx into the pharynx. As the larynx moves down it is not quite closed, leaving enough aperture to create voicing. It moves downward, creating a partial vacuum in the pharynx. This vacuum is filled primarily by the air coming in through the mouth, but secondarily by air coming in from the lungs. Voiced and voiceless implosives are shown in Sammies 27.5 and 27.6 with their respective air streams.

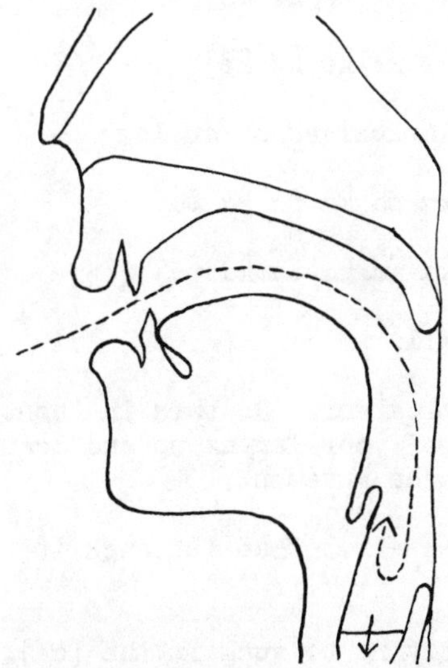

Sammy 27.5: [ƙ] Just Released. Note the single air stream.

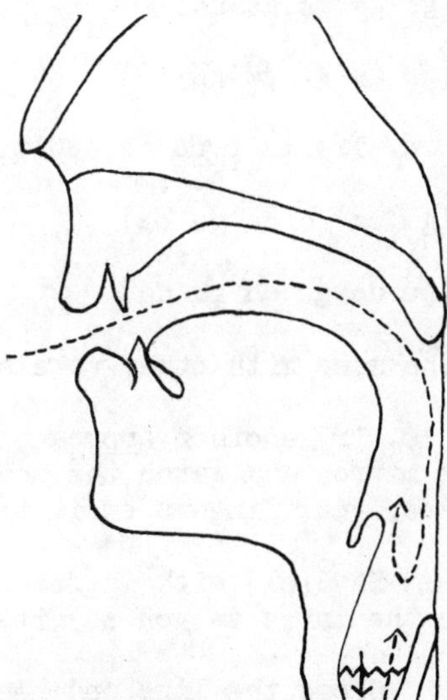

Sammy 27.6: [ɠ] Just Released. Note the two air streams going into the pharynx.

Production and Recognition of Implosives

In spite of the long explanation above, implosives are

not difficult to learn to make. Most people succeed on the first try, and others find that the combination "clicks" in a few days.

RE 27.1. Demonstration: Production of Implosives

Mimic the tape and follow in the *Manual*.

a. Some people make a [ɠ] when they imitate a frog croaking. Try it in mimicry of the tape: [ɠɤ ɠɤ ɠɤ ɠɤ ɠɤ].

b. Some people use [ƙ] to imitate water pouring from a bottle: [ƙ̹ ƙ̪ ƙ̂ ƙ ƙ̣].

c. If you can do either of the preceding articulations, put the implosive with a variety of vowels.

1. [ɠɑ ɠɑ ɠɑ ɠɑ ɠɑ]
2. [ɠu ɠu ɠu ɠu ɠu]
3. [ɠɛ ɠɛ ɠɛ ɠɛ ɠɛ]
4. [ɠø ɠø ɠø ɠø ɠø]
5. [ƙɑ ƙɑ ƙɑ ƙɑ ƙɑ]
6. [ƙu ƙu ƙu ƙu ƙu]
7. [ƙɛ ƙɛ ƙɛ ƙɛ ƙɛ]
8. [ƙø ƙø ƙø ƙø ƙø]

d. Try to produce additional implosives by analogy.

1. [ɠɑ ɓɑ ɠɑ ɓɑ ɠɑ ɓɑ]
2. [ɠɑ ɗɑ ɠɑ ɗɑ ɠɑ ɗɑ]
3. [ƙɑ ƥɑ ƙɑ ƥɑ ƙɑ ƥɑ]
4. [ƙɑ ƭɑ ƙɑ ƭɑ ƙɑ ƭɑ]

Do the same with other vowels as well.

e. Try another approach to implosives. Do this in front of a mirror and watch the movement of your larynx up and down, or keep your fingers on it to feel the movement.

Say [ɑ·] with ingressive lung air. That is, suck it into the lungs as you say it.

Close the lips and keep on trying to suck in the [ɑ·]. This may lead you to drawing down the larynx and producing [ƥ].

f. Many people actually produce implosives when they are trying to get strong voicing on a stop. Without releasing the bilabial articulation, try voicing and lowering the larynx at the same time. Do the same in alveolar and velar positions. Feel the movement of the larynx.

g. If you can make implosives, and if double stops are

not too difficult for you, you should have no trouble with [^{g}b ^{k}p]. Try these sequences.

1. [gɑ bɑ ^{g}bɑ ɠɑ ɓɑ ^{g}ɓɑ] 2. [kɑ pɑ ^{k}pɑ ƙɑ ƥɑ ^{k}ƥɑ]

h. In producing voiceless implosives you may find that you have a little difficulty with coordination between the release of the implosive and the onset of the vowel which follows. Because the implosive involves the closure of the vocal cords there is a danger of holding the [ʔ] too long, so that it is an additional segment between the implosive and the vowel. Listen to the tape as it demonstrates good transition and poor transition on the following sequences. Practice to produce the good transition.

Good Transition	Poor Transition
1a. [ƙɑ]	1b. [ƙʔɑ]
2a. [ƭɑ]	2b. [ƭʔɑ]
3a. [ƥɑ]	3b. [ƥʔɑ]

RE 27.2. Discrimination: SAME or DIFFERENT

1a.	[ɓɩ bɩ]	D	1b.	[ƭɛ tɛ]	D
2a.	[dɛ̢ ɗɛ̢]	D	2b.	[^{k}pu ^{k}pu]	S
3a.	[^{g}bu ^{g}bu]	S	3b.	[^{k}ƥɔ ^{k}pɔ]	D
4a.	[^{g}bɔ ^{g}ɓɔ]	D	4b.	[ƙɯ ƙɯ]	S
5a.	[ɠɯ ɠɯ]	S	5b.	[tɤ tɤ]	S
6a.	[ˈʔɣ̢ɗɤ ˈʔɣ̢ɗɤ]	S	6b.	[ˈʔøtü ˈʔøƭü]	D
7a.	[ˈʔøɗü ˈʔødü]	D	7b.	[ˈʔœƥɯ ˈʔœƥɯ]	S
8a.	[ˈʔœɓɯ ˈʔœɓɯ]	S	8b.	[ˈʔɒ^{k}ƥɤ ˈʔɒ^{k}pɤ]	D
9a.	[ˈʔɒ^{g}ɓɤ ˈʔɒ^{g}bɤ]	D	9b.	[ˈʔɯkɒ̢ ˈʔɯkɒ̢]	S
10a.	[ˈʔɯgɒ̢ ˈʔɯgɒ̢]	S	10b.	[ˈʔøkü ˈʔøƙü]	D
11a.	[ˈɠøzü ˈgøzü]	D	11b.	[ˈƥɨzɒ ˈpɨzɒ]	D
12a.	[ˈbɨzɒ ˈɓɨzɒ]	D	12b.	[ˈtʋzɤ ˈƭʋzɤ]	D
13a.	[ˈɗʋzɤ ˈdʋzɤ]	D	13b.	[ˈ^{k}ƥɛza ˈ^{k}pɛza]	D

RE 27.3. Differential: IMPLOSIVE or NO

1. [ɠɑ·]	I	5. [n̩ˈdo·]	NO	9. [yœnʌˈƙɔ]	I
2. [ƭɑ·]	I	6. [ŋ̩ˈgo·]	NO	10. [yœnʌˈtɔ]	NO
3. [cɑ·]	NO	7. [ŋ̩ˈᶢɓo·]	I	11. [yœnʌˈᵏpɔ]	NO
4. [ɓɑ·]	I	8. [m̩ˈƥo·]	I	12. [yœnʌˈɓɔ]	I

RE 27.4. Differential: LUNG or PHARYNX

In this exercise you will not be distinguishing anything different from what you were doing in the preceding exercise, but it gives you a chance to approach it from a different level of terminology.

1. [dü]	L	5. [sœˈᵏpɛ]	L	9. [wɨžiˈƥæ]	P
2. [ɓü]	P	6. [sœˈᶢɓɛ]	P	10. [wɨžiˈᶢɓæ]	P
3. [ƙü]	P	7. [sœˈjɛ]	L	11. [wɨžiˈbæ]	L
4. [pü]	L	8. [sœˈƭɛ]	P	12. [wɨžiˈɠæ]	P

RE 27.5. Differential: VOICED or VOICELESS

1. [ɠø]	VD	5. [ĩɩˈɓɨ]	VD	9. [sopʰʌˈƙu]	VL
2. [ƥø]	VL	6. [ĩɩˈᶢɓɨ]	VD	10. [sopʰʌˈɠu]	VD
3. [ɗø]	VD	7. [ĩɩˈƈɨ]	VL	11. [sopʰʌˈʄu]	VD
4. [ᵏƥø]	VL	8. [ĩɩˈɗɨ]	VD	12. [sopʰʌˈƭu]	VL

RE 27.6. Negative Practice: Implosives

Practice the following English sentences, or others like them, substituting the implosives indicated. Mimic the tape and follow the transcription.

1. ɓig ɓad ɓoy
2. ɠooey ɠreen ɠrapes
3. ɗoes ɗottie ɗream
4. ƥeck of ƥickled ƥeƥpers
5. ƙatheryn ƙissed her ƙousin
6. ƭake ƭommy ƭo the ƭrain

RE 27.7. Mimicry: Implosives

Mimic the tape, following the transcription as you do so.

1a. [ɓu]	1b. [uɓ]	1c. [ɓuɓ]	1d. [ɓuɓuɓ]
2a. [ɓe]	2b. [eɓ]	2c. [ɓeɓ]	2d. [ɓeɓeɓ]
3a. [ɗɔ]	3b. [ɔɗ]	3c. [ɗɔɗ]	3d. [ɗɔɗɔɗ]
4a. [ɗɪ]	4b. [ɪɗ]	4c. [ɗɪɗ]	4d. [ɗɪɗɪɗ]
5a. [ɠɨ]	5b. [ɨɠ]	5c. [ɠɨɠ]	5d. [ɠɨɠɨɠ]
6a. [ɠœ]	6b. [œɠ]	6c. [ɠœɠ]	6d. [ɠœɠœɠ]
7a. [ƥæ]	7b. [æƥ]	7c. [ƥæƥ]	7d. [ƥæƥæƥ]
8a. [ƥʋ]	8b. [ʋƥ]	8c. [ƥʋƥ]	8d. [ƥʋƥʋƥ]
9a. [ƭɛ]	9b. [ɛƭ]	9c. [ƭɛƭ]	9d. [ƭɛƭɛƭ]
10a. [ƭo]	10b. [oƭ]	10c. [ƭoƭ]	10d. [ƭoƭoƭ]
11a. [ƙi]	11b. [iƙ]	11c. [ƙiƙ]	11d. [ƙiƙiƙ]
12a. [ƙø]	12b. [øƙ]	12c. [ƙøƙ]	12d. [ƙøƙøƙ]

RE 27.8. Differential: GLOTTAL or IMPLOSIVE

When an implosive is articulated in strong, exaggerated fashion such as we have been demonstrating here for learning purposes, it does not sound much like clusters of [ʔ] plus voiced or voiceless stops practiced in Lesson 25 (pp. 349-354). In many languages, however, implosives are not so strongly articulated as this, and the acoustic difference between them and clusters with glottal stop becomes small. This is not difficult to understand because glottal closure is involved in either case. In this exercise decide whether you hear a cluster of [ʔ] plus stop or an implosive, and respond with GLOTTAL or IMPLOSIVE. Don't peek.

1. [ɠʌ]	I	6. [ʔtə]	G	11. [ɗü]	I
2. [ʔgʌ]	G	7. [ƭɛ]	I	12. [ƙa]	I
3. [ʔpɨ]	G	8. [ʔdu]	G	12. [ɗɪ]	I
4. [ƥe]	I	9. [ʔkø]	G	14. [ʔpœ]	G
5. [ɗɑ]	I	10. [ʔjœ]	G	15. [ʔtæ]	G

RE 27.9. Mimicry: Implosives and Clusters with [ʔ]

1a. [ɓɑ] 1b. [ɒˈɓɑ] 1c. [ʔbɑ] 1d. [ɒʔˈbɑ]

2a. [ɗø] 2b. [eˈɗø] 2c. [ʔdø] 2d. [eʔˈdø]

3a. [ʄə] 3b. [ɔˈʄə] 3c. [ʔjə] 3d. [ɔʔˈjə]

4a. [ɠɨ] 4b. [iˈɠɨ] 4c. [ʔgɨ] 4d. [iʔˈgɨ]

5a. [ƥʌ] 5b. [üˈƥʌ] 5c. [ʔpʌ] 5d. [üʔˈpʌ]

6a. [ƭɒ] 6b. [øˈƭɒ] 6c. [ʔtɒ] 6d. [øʔˈtɒ]

7a. [ƈe] 7b. [ɨˈƈe] 7c. [ʔce] 7d. [ɨʔˈce]

8a. [ƙʌ] 8b. [oˈƙʌ] 8c. [ʔkʌ] 8d. [oʔˈkʌ]

RE 27.10: Kaka. Mimicry: Implosives

1. [ɓo] '3rd plural'
2. [ɓɔ] 'rot'
3. [ɓe] 'hole'
4. [ʄè] 'eat'
5. [ʄɑ] 'village'
6. [ɗɔ] 'jump'
7. [ʄɔ̀] 'ton'
8. [ᵍbɑ] 'palm nut'

RE 27.11: Kaka. Mimicry: [ɓ]

1. [ɓoɓo] 'bedbug'
2. [ɓɔsoˇ] 'get wet'
3. [ɓokwɛ] 'joke'
4. [ɓɛmbɛ] 'manner'
5. [ɓulɓuseˇ] 'butterfly'
6. [ɓɑndoˇ] 'bind'
7. [ɓɑkiʄe] 'keep'
8. [ɓenoˇ] 'refuse'
9. [ɓembe] 'center'
10. [ɓɑɓo] 'compress'

11. [ɓendɔ] 'surroundings'
12. [ɓaŋgɛ›] 'plow'
13. [ɓe˅tite˅ři] 'domestic animals'
14. [ɓute˅] 'open'
15. [ɓuse˅] 'cover'
16. [ɓiřiki] 'perspiration'

RE 27.12: Kaka. Mimicry: [ɗ ʄ]

1. [ɗukwe] 'tear'
2. [ɗɑkwe] 'cord for hanging'
3. [ɗo˅kwe] 'become big'
4. [ɗite] 'fire'
5. [ʄɑ] 'village'
6. [ɗɔ̀] 'jump'
7. [ɗete] 'like that'

RE 27.13: Kaka. Mimicry: [ʄ ɗ]

1. [ʄɔŋgo˅] 'brain'
2. [ʄampi] 'war'
3. [ʄɑn] 'garbage'
4. [ʄe] 'eat'
5. [ɗiɓiʄe] 'protect'
6. [ɗiɓo] 'close'
7. [je˅mbo˅] 'sing'
8. [je˅mbiʄe˅] 'believe'
9. [ʄɔŋgwe˅ři] 'chamelion'
10. [ɗo˅kwe˅] 'become big'
11. [ɗɑkwe˅] 'cord for hanging'
12. [ʄɑ] 'village'

Fortis and Lenis Articulation

A little experimentation in your own speech tract will be enough to show you that speech articulations may be made with tense, tight muscle movements (which we will call fortis), or lax, light muscle movements (which we will call lenis). You can, for example, pronounce the English word pie in such a way as to barely touch the lips together for the initial stop. This light articulation gives you a lenis [p̹ʰ]. However, you can also say the same word beginning with a stop in which the lips are tightly and deliberately pressed together with tense muscle tone. In that case the word begins with fortis [p̎ʰ].

In English /b d g/ tend to be lenis, as opposed to /p t k/ which tend to be fortis. You will remember that in Lessons 5 and 7 (pp. 79ff. and 111ff.) when voiced stops were being introduced, it was pointed out that many speakers of English do not regularly voice /b d g/, but normally have voiceless unaspirated stops for these phonemes, at least in many positions. This statement remains true but we can now add as well that these English voiceless unaspirated stops are lenis, which helps to keep them separate from /p t k/.

The tenseness of articulation, therefore, is another variable in languages. Usually, relatively fortis or lenis quality is one factor along with many which go to make up the features by which one phoneme is distinguished from another. In some languages the contrast between fortis and lenis is the principal distinguishing feature of a set of phonemes. Korean, for example, has fortis consonants /p̎ t̎ c̎ k̎ s̎/ and lenis consonants /p̹ t̹ c̹ k̹ s̹/ as well as the aspirated set /p̹ʰ t̹ʰ c̹ʰ k̹ʰ/. The lenis set may be slightly aspirated (but not as much as the aspirated set) and has voiced allophones between voiced sounds.[1]

In this course we will not pay any further attention to the distinction between fortis and lenis other than what is included in this lesson.

RE 27.14. Differential: FORTIS or LENIS

This exercise will give you an opportunity to hear a distinction between fortis and lenis articulation of stops. As with many other features of articulation, it is not possible to eliminate every other variable like length. The fortis articulations may tend to be longer, but we will try to keep them constant.

1. [p̹ɑ] L	3. [c̹ɑ] L	5. [t̎ɑ] F
2. [p̎ɑ] F	4. [k̹ɑ] L	6. [t̹ɑ] L

---

[1]C. H. Park, An Intensive Course in Korean, Book I

7. [uku] F	11. [upu] L	15. [ʔɔc] F
8. [ucu] F	12. [upu] F	16. [ʔɔp] L
9. [ucu] L	13. [ʔɔt] L	17. [ʔɔt] F
10. [uku] L	14. [ʔɔk] F	18. [ʔɔk] F

RE 27.15: Red Bobo.[1] Transcription: Length and Tone

Use pp. 75-80 of your Workbook Supplement for this exercise. Without looking at the transcription below, listen to the tape as many times as necessary, and draw in the pitch contour wherever it is not indicated in the Workbook. Then go through the material again, inserting [• ' ˛] whenever you hear it. Use the "First Try" column on these repeated listenings until you are satisfied with your transcription. Use the "Second Try" column another day if you feel you need it.

The sentences are recorded in groups on the tape. Individual sentences are not repeated, but the groups are.

1. /oyiwa'yamuhe•le/ 'Doesn't he like the salt here?'

/oyiwa'bagahe•le/ 'Doesn't he like the gown here?'

/oyiwa'yo•muhe•le/ 'Doesn't he like the milk here?'

/oyiwa'ho•lehe•le/ 'Doesn't he like the sand here?'

2. /odiawa'yamuhe•le/ 'Did he leave our salt here?'

/odiawa'bagahe•le/ 'Did he leave our gown here?'

/odiawa'yo•muhe•le/ 'Did he leave our milk here?'

/odiawa'ho•lehe•le/ 'Did he leave our sand here?'

---

[1]Data are from the Ouarkoye dialect of Upper Volta. Analysis and recording was done by the Rev. James M. Ricciteli of the Christian and Missionary Alliance.

3. /o•nawa'yamuhę•le/ 'Will he give our salt here?'

/o•nawa'bagahę•le/ 'Will he give our gown here?'

/o•nawa'yo•muhę•le/ 'Will he give our milk here?'

/o•nawa'hǫ•lehę•le/ 'Will he give our sand here?'

4. /o•cawa'yamuhę•le/ 'Is he looking for our salt here?'

/o•cawa'bagahę•le/ 'Is he looking for our gown here?'

/o•cawa'yo•muhę•le/ 'Is he looking for our milk here?'

/o•cawa'hǫ•lehę•le/ 'Is he looking for our sand here?'

5. /^{g}ba•lala•/ 'They'll take the monkey.'

/^{g}ba•lala•/ 'They'll take an antelope.'

/^{g}balala•/ 'They took a monkey.'

/^{g}balala•/ 'They took an antelope.'

/^{g}ba•lala•/ 'They'll eat a monkey.'

/^{g}ba•lala•/ 'They'll eat an antelope.'

/^{g}balala•/ 'They ate a monkey.'

/^{g}balala•/ 'They ate an antelope.'

6. /ba·lala·/ 'A man took a monkey.'

/ba·lala·/ 'A man took an antelope.'

/ba·lala·/ 'A man ate a monkey.'

/ba·lala·/ 'A man ate an antelope.'

7. /ona·miahe/ 'The father isn't here.'

/ozamiahe/ 'The child isn't here.'

/oba·miahe/ 'The man isn't here.'

/ona·miahe/ 'The cow isn't here.'

/ona·miahe/ 'The scorpion isn't here.'

/ona·miahe/ 'The cow isn't here.'

/oha·miahe/ 'The snake isn't here.'

/oba·miahe/ 'The man isn't here.'

/oha·miahe/ 'The snake isn't here.' (not recorded)

/ona·miahe/ 'The scorpion isn't here.' (not recorded)

RE 27.16: Red Bobo. Mimicry

Replay RE 27.15 several times, mimicking carefully. Work particularly on the tone patterns. Follow the transcription.

Transcription and Reading

Use RE 27.2-27.5, 27.7-27.13.

LESSON TWENTY-EIGHT

Voiceless Vowels; Laryngealization

	Front		Central		Back	
	U.	R.	U.	R.	U.	R.
High	I	Ü				U
Lower-high			Ɨ			
Mid	E	Ø				O
Lower-mid						
Low	Æ	Œ				Ɔ
Lower-low			ɑ			

Table 28.1: Some Voiceless Vowels

All of the vowels practiced up to the present time have been voiced. Voiceless vowels also occur in many languages as diverse as French, Japanese, and Comanche. In most cases the voiceless vowels are allophones of phonemes which also have voiced members, but that does not lessen the necessity for recognizing them and being able to produce them.

Table 28.1 presents only a selection of voiceless vowels for drill purposes. Any vowel quality may be articulated without voicing. Voiceless vowels are indicated by capital letters on the analogy of voiceless nasals and laterals.

RE 28.1. Demonstration: Producing Voiceless Vowels

a. Start with English /h/ which is similar to, though not identical with, voiceless vowels. Mimic the tape and get the feel of English /h/ in different positions before different vowels. Prolong the /h/, and then isolate it. Read across.

1a. heat	1b. h•eat	1c. [I]
2a. hat	2b. h•at	2c. [Æ]
3a. hot	3b. h•ot	3c. [ɑ]
4a. hope	4b. h•ope	4c. [O]
5a. hoot	5b. h•oot	5c. [U]

The end product of this series is a voiceless vowel with an additional laryngeal quality (an additional constriction in the larynx) characteristic of English /h/. Note how the quality of the /h/ differs according to the quality of the following vowel.

b. Much the same effect can be obtained by whispering the five words above, or other English words. This time, however, the voicelessness continues throughout the vowel. Whispered vowels are voiceless, but again there is an additional constriction in the larynx which makes them easier to hear than as though the larynx were fully open for complete voicelessness.

c. Mimic the tape. This time you will deliberately turn off the voicing of vowels, but as you do so, try not to "whisper" them or give an /h/ quality to them. Maintain the oral articulation for the vowel and turn off the voicing, or turn it on as called for in the exercise. Be sure that your voiceless vowel is fully syllabic.

1a. [iI] 1b. [iIi] 1c. [Ii] 1d. [IiI]

2a. [eE] 2b. [eEe] 2c. [Ee] 2d. [EeE]

3a. [æÆ] 3b. [æÆæ] 3c. [Ææ] 3d. [ÆæÆ]

4a. [ɨƗ] 4b. [ɨƗɨ] 4c. [Ɨɨ] 4d. [ƗɨƗ]

5a. [ɑⱭ] 5b. [ɑⱭɑ] 5c. [Ɑɑ] 5d. [ⱭɑⱭ]

6a. [uU] 6b. [uUu] 6c. [Uu] 6d. [UuU]

7a. [oO] 7b. [oOo] 7c. [Oo] 7d. [OoO]

8a. [ɔƆ] 8b. [ɔƆɔ] 8c. [Ɔɔ] 8d. [ƆɔƆ]

9a. [üÜ] 9b. [üÜü] 9c. [Üü] 9d. [ÜüÜ]

10a. [øØ] 10b. [øØø] 10c. [Øø] 10d. [ØøØ]

11a. [œŒ] 11b. [œŒœ] 11c. [Œœ] 11d. [ŒœŒ]

d. Mimic the demonstration of Table 26.1 (p. 363), followed by Table 28.1.

RE 28.2. Differential: Full Labels

Give the description of the articulation of each of the voiceless vowels which you hear.

1. [pɑ] L-L C U	6. [nɔkØ] M F R	11. [tOnɨ] M B R
2. [pU] H B R	7. [nɔkI] H F U	12. [tEnɨ] M F U
3. [pÆ] L F U	8. [nɔkƆ] L B R	13. [tɑnɨ] L-L C U
4. [pƗ] L-H C U	9. [nɔkE] M F U	14. [tÆnɨ] L F U
5. [pŒ] L F R	10. [nɔkÜ] H F R	15. [tØnɨ] M F R

RE 28.3. Mimicry: Voiceless Vowels

Mimic the tape and follow the transcription.

1a. ['lɑpɑ]	1b. ['lɑpɑpɑ]	1c. ['lɑpɑpɑ]
2a. ['notO]	2b. ['notOto]	2c. ['notOtO]
3a. ['zecE]	3b. ['zecEce]	3c. ['zecEcE]
4a. ['rik̂I]	4b. ['rik̂Ik̂i]	4c. ['rik̂Ik̂I]
5a. ['sukU]	5b. ['sukUku]	5c. ['sukUkU]
6a. ['ɖøšØ]	6b. ['ɖøšØšø]	6c. ['ɖøšØšØ]
7a. ['fœxŒ]	7b. ['fœxŒxœ]	7c. ['fœxŒxŒ]
8a. ['wüθÜ]	8b. ['wüθÜθü]	8c. ['wüθÜθÜ]
9a. ['mɔɸƆ]	9b. ['mɔɸƆɸɔ]	9c. ['mɔɸƆɸƆ]
10a. ['ŋɨsƗ]	10b. ['ŋɨsƗsɨ]	10c. ['ŋɨsƗsƗ]
11a. ['ñæšÆ]	11b. ['ñæšÆšæ]	11c. ['ñæšÆšÆ]

RE 28.4: Comanche.[1] Mimicry: Voiceless Vowels

Mimic the tape and follow the transcription.

1. ['moʔO] 'hand' 2. ['pɑpI] 'hair'

---

[1] Data from Henry Osborn and William A. Smalley, "Formulae for Comanche Stem and Word Formation," Venda Riggs, "Alternate Phonemic Analyses of Comanche," William A. Smalley, "Phonemic Rhythm in Comanche," and Elliott D. Canonge, "Voiceless Vowels in Comanche." The recording is not by a native speaker.

3. [ˈtoˀI]	'pipe'	17. [ˈsɑhopA]	'broth'
4. [ˈpe•tI]	'daughter'	18. [ˈtosi•tO]	'hoof'
5. [ˈtsɑ•tI]	'good'	19. [ˈnɑƀo•pƗ]	'picture'
6. [ˈhi•pI]	'drink'	20. [ˈˀeᵽIᵽI]	'blue'
7. [ˈtɨ•pE]	'month'	21. [ˈtoˀInɨ•]	'pipes'
8. [ˈhu•pI]	'tree'	22. [ˈnɑkInɨ•]	'ears'
9. [ˈpu•kU]	'horse'	23. [ˈkupItɑˀ]	'a light'
10. [ˈpo•pƗ]	'drawing'	24. [ˈˀikƗsiˀ]	'it is right here'
11. [ˈko•ᵽE]	'face'	25. [ˈkWƗřiˀɑ]	'spill'
12. [ˈpiɑpƗ]	'big'	26. [ˈsikItɨˀuˀ]	'it is here'
13. [ˈtɨɑsE]	'again'	27. [ˈsokOřɨˀuˀ]	'it is over there'
14. [ˈmoɑkU]	'lots'	28. [ˈsukUřɨˀuˀ]	'it is out of sight'
15. [ˈtɨƀitsI]	'very'	29. [ˈnořiƀɑkikiˀuˀ]	'he came to pack'
16. [ˈhunuᵽI]	'creek'	30. [ˈnořiƀɑkIkiˀuˀ]	'he packed and came on'

Voiceless Glides

Many dialects of English have two voiceless glides, /W/ and /Y/. It might help you to review TE A.2 and A.3 (pp. 472 and 473). Note that the voiceless glides differ from the voiceless vowels in the same way that voiced glides differ from voiced vowels. They are non-syllabic, and constitute on-glides to syllabic vowels or off-glides from them.

RE 28.5. Mimicry: Voiceless Glides

Mimic and follow the transcription.

1a. [Wɑˀ]	1b. [ˀɑW]	1c. [Yɑˀ]	1d. [ˀɑY]
2a. [Wom]	2b. [moW]	2c. [Yom]	2d. [moY]
3a. [Weŋ]	3b. [ŋeW]	3c. [Yeŋ]	3d. [ŋeY]
4a. [Wʌlˆ]	4b. [lˆʌW]	4c. [Yʌlˆ]	4d. [lˆʌY]

5a. [Wœz] 5b. [zœW] 5c. [Yœz] 5d. [zœY]

6a. [Wɔg] 6b. [gɔW] 6c. [Yɔg] 6d. [gɔY]

7a. [Wæk] 7b. [kæW] 7c. [Yæk] 7d. [kæY]

8a. [Wɨf] 8b. [fɨW] 8c. [Yɨf] 8d. [fɨY]

9a. [kWɛñ] 9b. [ñɛWk^h] 9c. [kYɛñ] 9d. [ñɛYk^h]

10a. [sWađ] 10b. [đaWs] 10c. [sYađ] 10d. [đaYs]

RE 28.6. Differential: GLIDE or FRICATIVE

The articulation of [Y] is very similar to that of [x̭], and [W] to that of the initial part of [xw]. The difference lies only in the degree of stricture, the tongue being closer to the point of articulation in the fricative. In this exercise respond with GLIDE or FRICATIVE according to the voiceless glide or fricative you hear.

1. [Yʌt^h] GL
2. [x̭ʌt^h] FR
3. [xwʌt^h] FR
4. [Wʌt^h] GL
5. [ˈˀeWen] GL
6. [ˈˀexwen] FR
7. [ˈˀexwen] FR
8. [ˈˀexwen] FR
9. [ˈnoYoz] GL
10. [ˈnoYoz] GL
11. [ˈnox̭oz] FR
12. [ˈnox̭oz] FR

Voiceless Vowels, [h], and Aspiration

We have already pointed out that English /h/ is a voiceless vowel plus additional constriction in the larynx. Aspiration of stops is also technically non-syllabic voiceless vowel, usually of indeterminate central quality. Strictly speaking, then, aspiration is a voiceless on-glide corresponding roughly with the [H] off-glide in quality, but corresponding with [W] and [Y] in its voicelessness. This information does not affect our production or transcription of [^{h}], but simply fills out our picture somewhat.

RE 28.7. Mimicry: Contrasting Voiceless Vowels and Aspiration

You can distinguish regular aspiration from voiceless vowels following stops by the syllabic nature of the vowel, and the fact that different vowel qualities can be distinguished. Follow the transcription as you mimic the tape.

1a. [mak^{h}ˈsuˀ] 1b. [makOˈsuˀ] 1c. [makEˈsuˀ]

2a. [zet^{h}'yʌŋ]   2b. [zetÆ'yʌŋ]   2c. [zetU'yʌŋ]

3a. [^{k}pɨt^{h}'tʋv]   3b. [^{k}pɨtI'tʋv]   3c. [^{k}pɨtɑ'tʋv]

4a. [jøt^{h}'xœl^]   4b. [jøtU'xœl^]   4c. [jøtO'xœl^]

5a. [gɔt^{h}'miw]   5b. [gɔtɨ'miw]   5c. [gɔtɔ'miw]

RE 28.8. Mimicry: Postvocalic [h]

[h] does not occur in syllable-final position in English, so that is a position in which we need to practice it for some languages. In this case we will not be concerned with whether or not the sound is a pure voiceless vowel or has the additional constriction in the larynx characteristic of initial /h/ in English.

1a. [mɑh]   1b. ['mɑhso]   1c. ['mɑhsoh]

2a. [lɛh]   2b. ['lɛhk^{h}u]   2c. ['lɛhk^{h}uh]

3a. [wɔ•h]   3b. ['wɔ•hmü]   3c. ['wɔ•hmüh]

4a. [væh]   4b. ['væhɗʌ]   4c. ['væhɗʌh]

5a. [ŋɨh]   5b. ['ŋɨhñɩ]   5c. ['ŋɨhñɩh]

6a. [tü•h]   6b. ['tü•hna]   6c. ['tü•hnah]

7a. [ge•h]   7b. ['ge•hbə]   7c. ['ge•hbəh]

8a. [ʔœh]   8b. ['ʔœhr̃ʌ]   8c. ['ʔœhr̃ʌh]

RE 28.9. Mimicry: Preaspiration

Some languages have aspiration, or a short [h] which comes before stops rather than after. Mimic the tape and follow the transcription for [h] in this position. In the third column be careful not to substitute a voiceless nasal, lateral, etc., for [h].

1a. [hpo]   1b. [hpo'hpo]   1c. [hpom'hpom]

2a. [hpü]   2b. [hpü'hpü]   2c. [hpül^'hpül^]

3a. [hta]   3b. [hta'hta]   3c. [htan'htan]

4a. [hti]   4b. [hti'hti]   4c. [htil^'htil^]

5a. [hcə]   5b. [hcə'hcə]   5c. [hcəñ'hcəñ]

6a. [hcɔ]	6b. [hcɔˈhcɔ]	6c. [hcɔĩˈhcɔĩ]
7a. [hkœ]	7b. [hkoeˈhkœ]	7c. [hkœŋˈhkœŋ]
8a. [hkæ]	8b. [hkæˈhkæ]	8c. [hkæŋˈhkæŋ]

Laryngealized Vowels

Several of the features of articulation which we have worked with so far have originated in the larynx. These include glottal stop, the source of the air stream in implosives, voicing, and pitch. We mentioned also earlier in this chapter that English /h/ has a quality created in the larynx which makes it more than a simple voiceless vowel. All of these features might be called laryngeal features, as they result from movements or constrictions or configurations in the larynx, and some, in fact, are occasionally referred to as laryngeal in the linguistic literature. In this course, however, we are going to reserve the adjective <u>laryngeal</u> for a feature of articulation which we have not previously introduced, but which may occur to modify any vowel quality.[1]

RE 28.10. Demonstration: Laryngealized Vowels

Laryngealization does not occur as part of the English phonemic system, but does occur as an over-all voice quality under certain conditions and in the speech of some people.

a. Stretch as though ready for bed, and say in a sleepy, raspy voice: <u>I'm so sleepy!</u> [ˌʔɑ̉ỷm̉ sỏw̉ ˈslỉ›ỷpỉ›ỷ]. Mimic the tape.

b. Some children use this effect to imitate a machine gun or a stick being rubbed along a picket fence: [ɑ̉·]

c. Note the symbolization for laryngealization. It is a glottal stop written over the vowel. You can think of laryngealization as being a kind of glottal trill, and you see the significance of using the glottal symbol. Here is a selection of the vowels from the vowel chart. Listen to the tape demonstration and mimic it. (See Table 28.2)

RE 28.11. Differential: LARYNGEALIZED or NO

1. [mɩ̉] LA	2. [mœ̉] LA	3. [ma] NO

[1]Actually, it can probably occur with any voiced continuant as well, but we will practice it only on vowels.

	Front U.	Front R.	Central U.	Central R.	Back U.	Back R.
High	iˀ	üˀ			ɯˀ	uˀ
Lower-high			ɨˀ			
Mid	eˀ	øˀ			ɤˀ	oˀ
Lower-mid						
Low	æˀ	œˀ	ʌˀ			ɔˀ
Lower-low	aˀ		ɑˀ		ɒˀ	

Table 28.2. Some Laryngealized Vowels

4. [mɔˀ] LA — 7. [str̃ɛ] NO — 10. [pr̩̃lˆuv] NO

5. [str̃ɑ] NO — 8. [str̃ə] NO — 11. [pr̩̃lˆəv] NO

6. [str̃æˀ] LA — 9. [pr̩̃lˆʌˀv] LA — 12. [pr̩̃lˆüv] NO

RE 28.12. Mimicry: Laryngealization

1a. [bɑˀ·ʔ]	1b. [ˈbɑˀ·bɑˀ]	1c. [ˈbɑˀ·bɑ]
2a. [nɨˀ·ʔ]	2b. [ˈnɨˀ·nɨˀ]	2c. [ˈnɨˀ·nɨ]
3a. [lˆœˀ·ʔ]	3b. [ˈlˆœˀ·lˆœˀ]	3c. [ˈlˆœˀ·lˆœ]
4a. [ɓeˀ·ʔ]	4b. [ˈɓeˀ·ɓeˀ]	4c. [ˈɓeˀ·ɓe]
5a. [ᵍbøˀ·ʔ]	5b. [ᵍbøˀ·ᵍbøˀ]	5c. [ˈᵍbøˀ·ᵍbø]
6a. [zɛˀ·ʔ]	6b. [ˈzɛˀ·zɛˀ]	6c. [ˈzɛˀ·zɛ]
7a. [xʋˀ·ʔ]	7b. [ˈxʋˀ·xʋˀ]	7c. [ˈxʋˀ·xʋ]
8a. [fiˀ·ʔ]	8b. [ˈfiˀ·fiˀ]	8c. [ˈfiˀ·fi]

RE 28.13. Mimicry Review: Nasalization

1a. [sɑ·]	1b. [sɑ̨·]	1c. [sɑɑ̨]	1d. [sɑ̨ɑ]
2a. [đɩ·]	2b. [đɩ̨·]	2c. [đɩɩ̨]	2d. [đɩ̨ɩ]
3a. [gɔ·]	3b. [gɔ̨·]	3c. [gɔɔ̨]	3d. [gɔ̨ɔ]
4a. [fə·]	4b. [fə̨·]	4c. [fəə̨]	4d. [fə̨ə]

5a. [ṣ̌o•]   5b. [ṣ̌o̜•]   5c. [ṣ̌oo̜]   5d. [ṣ̌o̜o]

6a. [Wæ•]   6b. [Wæ̜•]   6c. [Wææ̜]   6d. [Wæ̜æ]

7a. [ma•]   7b. [ma̜•]   7c. [maa̜]   7d. [ma̜a]

8a. [nü•]   8b. [nü̜•]   8c. [nüü̜]   8d. [nü̜ü]

9a. [ñʌ•]   9b. [ñʌ̜•]   9c. [ñʌʌ̜]   9d. [ñʌ̜ʌ]

10a. [ŋʋ•]   10b. [ŋʋ̜•]   10c. [ŋʋʋ̜]   10d. [ŋʋ̜ʋ]

RE 28.14. Mimicry Review: Length

1a. [r̃ɨ]   1b. [r̃ɨ•]   1c. [gor̃ɨf]   1d. [gor̃ɨ•f]

2a. [R̃u]   2b. [R̃u•]   2c. [goR̃uf]   2d. [goR̃u•f]

3a. [ṛ̃e]   3b. [ṛ̃e•]   3c. [goṛ̃ef]   3d. [goṛ̃e•f]

4a. [ři]   4b. [ři•]   4c. [gořif]   4d. [gořɨ•f]

5a. [Ṛ̃œ]   5b. [Ṛ̃•œ]   5c. [ĩɛṚ̃oeš]   5d. [ĩɛṚ̃•oeš]

6a. [dø]   6b. [d•ǿ]   6c. [ĩɛdǿš]   6d. [ĩɛd•øš]

7a. [jɔ]   7b. [j•ɔ]   7c. [ĩɛjɔš]   7d. [ĩɛj•ɔš]

8a. [zɩ]   8b. [z•ɩ]   8c. [ĩɛzɩš]   8d. [ĩɛz•ɩš]

RE 28.15. Mimicry Review: Back Unrounded Vowels

1a. ['ɓɒlˇɒ•]   1b. ['ɓɤlˇɤ•]   1c. ['ɓɯlˇɯ•]

2a. ['ᵽɒ•lˇɒm]   2b. ['ᵽɤ•lˇɤm]   2c. ['ᵽɯ•lˇɯm]

3a. ['ṣ̌ɒŋɒh]   3b. ['š̥ɤŋɤh]   3c. ['šɯŋɯh]

4a. ['ẓ̌ɒ•nɒh]   4b. ['ẓ̌ɤ•nɤh]   4c. ['ẓ̌ɯ•nɯh]

5a. ['ɗɒmɒ•h]   5b. ['ɗɤmɤ•h]   5c. ['ɗɯmɯ•h]

6a. ['ɓɒhtɒ]   6b. ['ɓɤhtɤ]   6c. ['ɓɯhtɯ]

7a. ['ʄɒhtɒ•h]   7b. ['ʄɤhtɤ•h]   7c. ['ʄɯhtɯ•h]

8a. ['ɠɒ•tɒhp^h]   8b. ['ɠɤ•tɤhp^h]   8c. ['ɠɯ•tɯhp^h]

RE 28.16: Liberian English.[1] Mimicry: General Review

There is a wide variety of dialects of English spoken in Liberia. The characteristics of some brands of Liberian English are in some cases due to speech habits which come from the sound systems of African languages in the area. In this exercise we have listed English words, classified according to my pronunciation of the vowels, but read by a Liberian of the upper lower class. Mimic his pronunciation of these words.

You will notice several things about this brief sample of Liberian English. Many of the glides characteristic of American English do not occur. Vowel qualities are sometimes different. The degree of aspiration is considerably less than in American English, to the point where it is sometimes hard to hear whether or not there is any aspiration. Our transcription is doubtless quite inconsistent as a consequence of this difficulty. Another notable characteristic of this dialect is the extremely lenis articulation of some consonants. These have not been marked, but you should watch for them and mimic them. Note also that final nasals are replaced by nasalized vowels or glides. There is a slight tendency to laryngealize the vowels throughout.

a			b		
1.	[se^v•]	say	1.	[bɔ•y]	boy
2.	[me^v•]	may	2.	[t^{h}ɔ•y]	toy
3.	[fe^v•s]	face	3.	[k^{h}ɔ̨•y̨]	coin
4.	[le^v•s]	lace	4.	[c^{h}ə•ys]	choice
5.	[be^v•]	bay			
6.	[be^v•s]	base			
7.	[de^v•]	day			
8.	[pę^v•]	pain			
9.	[k^{h}e^v•s]	case			
10.	[ce^v•s]	chase			

[1] The recording was made in Monrovia, Liberia. The voice is that of Mr. Sammy Goe, then a houseboy in the service of Mr. and Mrs. Loren Nussbaum.

c

1. [p^{h}ɑ•y] pie
2. [t^{h}ɑ•y] tie
3. [tRɑ•y] try
4. [lɑ•y] lie
5. [nɑ•ys] nice
6. [ʔɑ•ys] ice
7. [lɑ•į] line
8. [mɑ•į] mine
9. [sɑ•į] sign
10. fɑ•į] fine

d

1. [sι̨•] sin
2. [ʔι•s] is
3. [hι•s] his
4. [pι̨]/[fι̨] pin
5. [mι•s] miss
6. [wik^{h}] wick
7. [rιp] rib
8. [rič] rich
9. [hι̨•] him
10. [p^{h}i•g^{h}] pig

e

1. [sį•] seen
2. [bį•] bean
3. [nį•] knee
4. [bį•] bee
5. [hi•] he
6. [mį•] me
7. [pi•s] peace
8. [pi•s] peas
9. [bi•č^{h}] beach
10. [fri•] free

f

1. [pʌp] pup
2. [dək^{h}] duck
3. [k^{h}ɔp^{h}] cup
4. [hə̧•yt^{h}] hut
5. [k^{h}ɔ< •t^{h}] cut
6. [tə̧•č] touch
7. [kɔ•m] come
8. [wɔ•n] one
9. [ñə•ŋg] young
10. [nə̨t^{h}] nuts

g

1. [ʔiɛ] ear
2. [fiɛ] fear
3. [biɛ] beer
4. [diɛ] dear
5. [niɛ] near

h (not recorded)

1. [p^{h}ʊt^h] put
2. [k^{h}u·d] could
3. [bʊk^h] book
4. [k^{h}ʊk^h] cook
5. [gu·d] good
6. [wu·d] wood

i (not recorded)

1. [p^{h}ɛ·t^h] pet
2. [nɛ$_\iota$·t^h] net
3. [tRɛk^h] treck
4. [mɛ·] men
5. [sɛ$_\iota$t^h] cent
6. [bɩɛ] bell
7. [sɩɛ] sell
8. [bɛ$_\iota$č^h] bench
9. [rɛ·d] red
10. [ǰɛs]/[ǰɛst] guest

j (not recorded)

1. [bæt^h] bat
2. [t^{h}æp^h] tap
3. [hæd] had
4. [ʔɛ·s]/[ʔæ·s] as
5. [ʔæ·nd] and
6. [k^{h}æ$_\iota$t^h] can't
7. [bæ$_\iota$ŋk^h] bang
8. [bæk^h] back
9. [næ$_\iota$p^h] nap
10. [tRæk^h]/[t^{h}æk^h] tack

k (not recorded)

1. [p^{h}uə] pole
2. [boə] bowl
3. [ʔoə]/[ʔo·d] old
4. [groəd]/[gro·] grow
5. [no·] know
6. [go·s] goes
7. [č^{h}ʊk^h] choke
8. [k^{h}ot^h] coat
9. [smok^h] smoke
10. [ro˂·d] road

RE 28.17. Transcription

Use your Workbook Supplement, pp. 81-82, for this exercise, and fill in the blanks. Don't peek until you have transcribed the "first try" to your satisfaction.

1. [ˈ^{g}bɔdža^{ʔ}yʌk^{h}]
2. [ɓæ•l^ˈk^{h}ɔl̆^i]
3. [ˈsɯsɨpfu]
4. [k^{h}ɑˈmi•ɗø]
5. [ˈñɤnŋomæ•š]
6. [^{ʔ}nɯHˈŋɒ̨wy̨•t^{h}]
7. [ˈɠɔsOɓetU]
8. [ˈfu̓•zɨ̓ŋWəy]
9. [ˈsOř̌ɛfpÆ]
10. [Upüˈřæ•ɗɨŋ]
11. [ŋ̩ˈẓ̌ʋhpɛɠɔ]
12. [bzǫtø̨ˈl̃ɑ̓•]
13. [θe^{ŋ}mɨˈžʋ^{ʔ}]
14. [nɑˈÑñɛtɔ]
15. [ˈhɔp•ɨtƀ̨p]
16. [n̩ˈɗɛšdɛ̓•n]
17. [hpekØˈtʌv]
18. [ˈ^{k}poyR̃n̩dy̨ht]
19. [bɤˈɠ̓akU]
20. [ḍoe^{ˈg}bo•sMą̧p^{h}]

Transcription and Reading

Use RE 28.2-28.9, 28.11-28.15.

LESSON TWENTY-NINE

Glottalized Consonants; More Consonant Clusters

	Double	Bilabial	Dental/ Alveolar	Alveopalatal	Velar
STOPS					
Lung air					
Vl. unaspirated	^{k}p	p	t	c	k
Vl. aspirated		p^h	t^h	c^h	k^h
Voiced	^{g}b	b	d	j	g
Ingressive pharynx air					
Voiceless	kƥ	ƥ	ƭ	ƈ	ƙ
Voiced	gɓ	ɓ	ɗ	ʄ	ɠ
Egressive pharynx air					
Voiceless		pˀ	tˀ	cˀ	kˀ
Voiced		(bˀ)	(dˀ)	(jˀ)	(gˀ)
FRICATIVES[1]					
Lung air					
Voiceless		ᵽ	s	š	x
Voiced		ƀ	z	ž	ǥ
Egressive pharynx air					
Voiceless		ᵽˀ	sˀ	šˀ	xˀ

Table 29.1: Some Glottalized Consonants

In Lesson 27 we worked with implosives, or ingressive pharynx air sounds. Now we turn to *egressive* pharynx air

---

[1]Only a sampling of fricatives is given in this chart. Others work in exactly the same way. See Lesson 33 for a more complete representation (p. 456). Affricates may also be glottalized, but are not shown.

sounds, which we will often call glottalized. These sounds are the exact reverse of the implosives. The larynx moves upward with the vocal cords closed during the articulation of the consonant, and this creates air pressure in the pharynx. When the consonant articulation is released, the air rushes out, thus creating an egressive air stream which originates in the pharynx. Sammies 29.1 and 29.2 picture this for you.

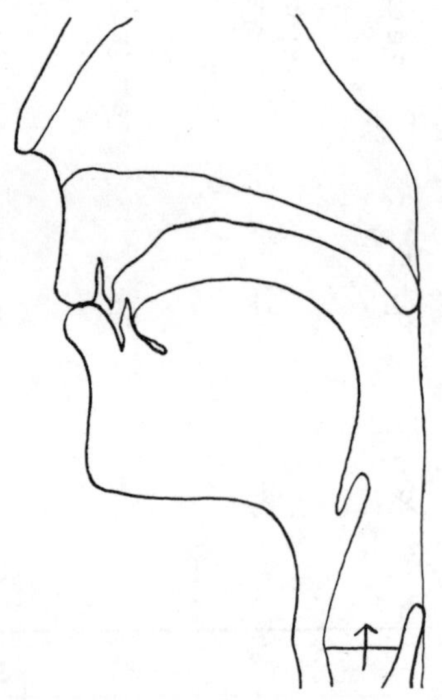

Sammy 29.1: Larynx Movement to Create Pressure for [pˀ]

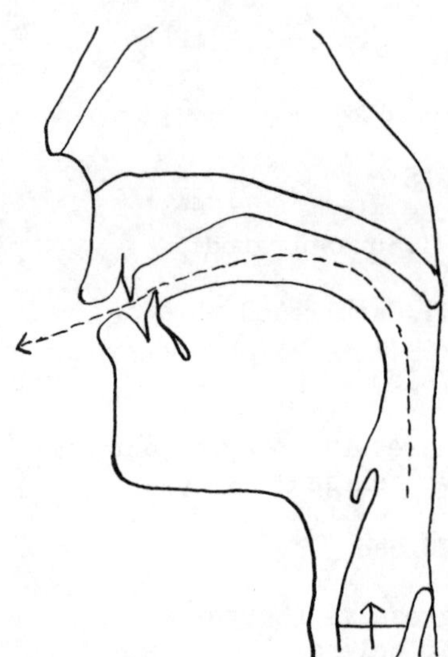

Sammy 29.2: Egressive Air Stream after Labial Articulation is Released

Egressive pharynx air sounds are called glottalized sounds because of the action of the vocal cords (glottis) in creating the pressure which makes possible the air stream. Actually the glottis is involved with implosives as much as it is here, but the term is convenient and we will use it. Our system of transcription for these sounds helps to reinforce the term, as we write glottalized consonants with a raised glottal stop [ˀ] after the usual consonant symbol.

As you study Table 29.1 you will notice that voiced egressive pharynx air sounds are included there for the record, but that they are not to be drilled in this course. They are relatively rare. In these sounds lung air builds up pressure behind the larynx and is leaked through into the pharynx simultaneously with the upward movement of the larynx in similar manner to that of voiced implosives.

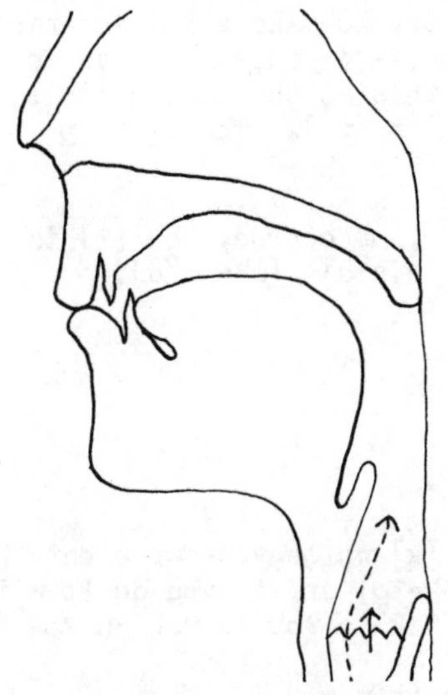

Sammy 29.3: [bˀ] Before Release. Note the air stream leaked into the pharynx.

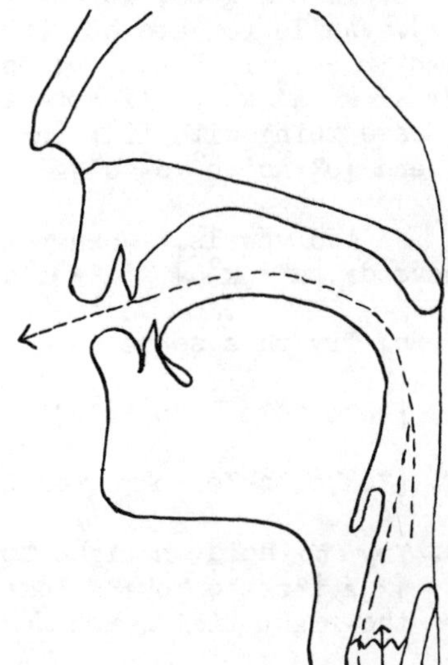

Sammy 29.4: [bˀ] At Time of Release

Glottalized consonants are not found quite so frequently as implosives, but they are a major part of the phonemic systems of many American Indian and African languages, including a language of such importance as Amharic, the national language of Ethiopia.

RE 29.1. Demonstration: Production of Glottalized Consonants

Like the implosives, glottalized consonants are not too difficult once you get the combination. People who have difficulty with them at first find that they work all of a sudden when the proper coordination of muscle movements is found. Here are some suggestions to help you. Mimic the tape.

a. Pretend you have a small piece of grass on the tip of your tongue. Pretend to spit it off by sticking your tongue tip out between your lips and drawing it back sharply, blowing the grass off. When some people do this they blow the grass off with a puff of air from the larynx, getting an interlabial glottalized stop. Change this now to [pˀ] by doing the same thing without sticking out your tongue tip. Say [pˀ pˀ pˀ pˀ]. Then add a vowel: [pˀɑ pˀɑ pˀɑ pˀɑ].

b. Make a good, strong [ʔ] after a vowel and hold it: [αʔ•]. While you are holding it, try to make a [k] several times in a row. Don't release the [ʔ•]! This may give you [αʔ• kˀ kˀ kˀ kˀ]. If you can do this as the tape does it, try the same thing with [t]: [αʔ• tˀ tˀ tˀ tˀ]. Then [αʔ• pˀ pˀ pˀ pˀ] and [αʔ• cˀ cˀ cˀ cˀ].

Add vowels. When you do so, of course, the [ʔ] is released: [αʔ• kˀα] [αʔ• tˀα] [αʔ• pˀα] [αʔ• cˀα].

c. Try this sequence:

1. [ʔoʔo ʔoʔo ʔoʔo ʔoʔo]

2. [ʔokʔo ʔokʔo ʔokʔo ʔokʔo]

3. Try to hold on tight to the [k] while you force out the [ʔ]: [ʔok•ʔo ʔok•ʔo ʔok•ʔo ʔok•ʔo] or, if you do it with the right timing and force: [ʔokˀʔo ʔokˀʔo ʔokˀʔo ʔokˀʔo].

4. Follow the same sequence with [t p c].

d. Get the feeling of the upward and downward movement of the larynx by singing from falsetto to base and back up again. Put your fingers on the larynx as you do it. Try to duplicate the movement without singing, simply by exercising the muscles in your throat.

Get the same effect by swallowing. Then try to move the larynx up and down rhythmically.

Get the feeling of the up and down movement by saying [hi• hɔ• hi• hɔ• hi• hɔ•]. Try to reproduce it by simply moving your muscles.

e. If you can "rock" the larynx, raising and lowering it in sequence, close your vocal cords in a [ʔ], and make a [k] repeatedly while you rock it. As the larynx goes up and down this gives you [kˀ ƙ kˀ ƙ kˀ ƙ]. Follow with [tˀ ƭ tˀ ƭ tˀ ƭ] and [pˀ ɓ pˀ ɓ pˀ ɓ].

f. "Rock" some fricatives like [f s š].

g. On any glottalized sound except [kˀ] be careful that the back of your tongue is not up against your velum. If it is, you are getting an egressive click instead, with mouth air rather than pharynx air. Listen to the tape as it gives you the correct sound and the much higher-pitched incorrect mouth air sound afterwards.

Correct	Incorrect
1a. [pˀ pˀ pˀ pˀ]	1b. [p→ p→ p→ p→]
2a. [tˀ tˀ tˀ tˀ]	2b. [t→ t→ t→ t→]
3a. [cˀ cˀ cˀ cˀ]	3b. [c→ c→ c→ c→]

h. In producing glottalized consonants you may find that you have a little difficulty with coordination between the release of the glottal and the onset of the vowel which follows. Glottalized consonants are very much like voiceless implosives in this respect (see p. 383). Because the glottalized consonant involves the closure of the vocal cords there is a danger of holding the [ʔ] too long. Listen to the tape as it demonstrates good transition from a glottalized consonant to a following vowel, and poor transition.

Good Transition	Poor Transition
1a. [kˀɑ]	1b. [kˀʔɑ]
2a. [tˀɑ]	2b. [tˀʔɑ]
3a. [pˀɑ]	3b. [pˀʔɑ]
4a. [cˀɑ]	4b. [cˀʔɑ]
5a. [sˀɑ]	5b. [sˀʔɑ]
6a. [fˀɑ]	6b. [fˀʔɑ]

RE 29.2. Discrimination: SAME or DIFFERENT

1.	[oˈpˀo oˈpˀo]	S	7.	[ʌˈpˀʌŋ ʌˈƥʌŋ]	D
2.	[eˈkˀe eˈƙe]	D	8.	[aˈƙaŋ aˈkˀaŋ]	D
3.	[æˈƈæ æˈcˀæ]	D	9.	[ˈkˀəwiŘ ˈƙəwiŘ]	D
4.	[ɨˈtˀɨ ɨˈtˀɨ]	S	10.	[ˈƈəwiŘ ˈcˀəwiŘ]	D
5.	[ɒˈfˀɒŋ ɒˈfˀɒŋ]	S	11.	[ˈsˀəwiŘ ˈsˀəwiŘ]	S
6.	[œˈƭœŋ œˈƭœŋ]	S	12.	[ˈpˀəwiŘ ˈƥəwiŘ]	D

RE 29.3. Differential: IMPLOSIVE or GLOTTALIZED

1. [ˈtˀømø] G 2. [ˈƙɨmɨ] I 3. [ˈtˀúmű] G

4. [ˈƥɛmɛ]	I	9. [ˀeˈpˀɔr̽ɔ]	G	14. [yonɔˈƙɨl^]	I
5. [ˈšˀimi]	G	10. [ˀeˈkˀʊr̽ʊ]	G	15. [yonɔˈtˀɑl^]	G
6. [ˈxˀumɯ]	G	11. [ˀeˈƙʌr̽ʌ]	I	16. [yonɔˈθˀæl^]	G
7. [ˀeˈƈɩr̽ɩ]	I	12. [ˀeˈƥær̽æ]	I	17. [yonɔˈpˀül^]	G
8. [ˀeˈƭər̽ə]	I	13. [yonɔˈcˀul^]	G	18. [yonɔˈƭɛl^]	I

RE 29.4. Negative Practice: Glottalized Consonants

Practice the following English sentences and others like them, substituting the glottalized consonants indicated. Mimic the tape and follow the transcription.

1. kˀween kˀatheryn kˀissed her kˀrotchety kˀousin.

2. tˀake tˀommy tˀo the tˀrain.

3. pˀeter pˀipˀer pˀicked a pˀeck of pˀickled pˀeppˀers.

4. fˀe fˀi fˀo fˀum

5. sˀisˀter sˀue sˀits sˀewing sˀocks.

RE 29.5. Mimicry: Glottalized Consonants

Follow the transcription as you mimic the tape.

1a. [pˀa]	1b. [pˀapˀa]	1c. [pˀapˀapˀ]
2a. [tˀi]	2b. [tˀitˀi]	2c. [tˀitˀitˀ]
3a. [cˀɨ]	3b. [cˀɨcˀɨ]	3c. [cˀɨcˀɨcˀ]
4a. [kˀø]	4b. [kˀøkˀø]	4c. [kˀøkˀøkˀ]
5a. [tsˀɩ]	5b. [tsˀɩ.tsˀɩ]	5c. [tsˀɩ.tsˀɩtsˀ]
6a. [ksˀə]	6b. [ksˀə.ksˀə]	6c. [ksˀə.ksˀəksˀ]
7a. [fˀœ]	7b. [fˀœfˀœ]	7c. [fˀœfˀœfˀ]
8a. [θˀɔ]	8b. [θˀɔθˀɔ]	8c. [θˀɔθˀɔθˀ]
9a. [sˀi]	9b. [sˀisˀi]	9c. [sˀisˀisˀ]
10a. [xˀu]	10b. [xˀuxˀu]	10c. [xˀuxˀuxˀ]

RE 29.6. Differential: Identification of Symbols

In this exercise respond by writing (or giving orally) the name of the symbol by which the consonant is written. Call the symbols for implosives HOOKED p, HOOKED g, etc. For the glottalized sounds call the symbols p RAISED GLOTTAL, g RAISED GLOTTAL, etc.

1.	[ʋ'ɓɛ]	HOOKED b	9.	[r̃ɨ'ƭoy]	HOOKED t
2.	[ʋ'ƙɛ]	HOOKED k	10.	[r̃ɨ'ɠoy]	HOOKED g
3.	[ʋ'tˀɛ]	t RAISED GL	11.	[r̃ɨ'cˀoy]	c RAISED GL
4.	[ʋ'fˀɛ]	f RAISED GL	12.	[r̃ɨ'ƥoy]	HOOKED p
5.	[ʋ'ɗɛ]	HOOKED d	13.	[r̃ɨ'kˀoy]	k RAISED GL
6.	[ʋ'pˀɛ]	p RAISED GL	14.	[r̃ɨ'^{g}ɓoy]	HOOKED ^{g}b
7.	[ʋ'xˀɛ]	x RAISED GL	15.	[r̃ɨ'čˀoy]	č RAISED GL
8.	[ʋ'tsˀɛ]	ts RAISED GL	16.	[r̃i'ʄoy]	HOOKED j

RE 29.7. Negative Practice: "Ten Little Indians"

The tape will demonstrate. Practice in odd moments to develop freedom and fluency in the production of implosives and glottalized consonants.

a. [pˀɔ] little, [ƥɔ] little, [ɓɔ] little Indians,

[tˀɔ] little, [ƭɔ] little, [ɗɔ] little Indians,

[kˀɔ] little, [ƙɔ] little, [ɠɔ] little Indians,

[ʄɔ] little Indian boys.

b. Follow the same sequence, using other vowels.

RE 29.8. Zulu.[1] Mimicry: Bilabial Stops

The tape reads down each column and then across the first three lines. Mimic and follow the transcription. Each item is read once, but you can replay the tape for more practice.

---

[1]Zulu materials in this book are taken from recordings of the Special Phonetics of the Wycliffe Language Course (England), and used by permission.

	a		b	
1.	[ˈɓα•ɓa]	'bitter'	[ˈpα•pa]	'flutter violently'
2.	[ˈɓu•l^a]	'to peel off'	[ˈpu•l^a]	'to divine'
3.	[ˈɓoᵛ•l^a]	'to rot'	[ˈpoᵛ•l^a]	'to bore'
4.	[isiˈɓi•ɓα]	'anti-snake preparation'	[ukuˈpi•pa]	'to flap'
5.	[ˈɓε^•ɓa]	'carry on back'	[ˈpεᵛ•ma]	'to smoke'
6.	[umˈɓε^•l^ε^]	'teat of an udder'	[umˈpε^•l^ε^]	'a surname'
7.	[umˈɓoᵛ•ni]	'on-looker'	[imˈpoŋkoˈoᵛl^o]	'donkey'

	c		d	
1.	[ˈpʰα•pʰa]	'fly gently'	[imˈpʾα•ma]	'slap'
2.	[ˈpʰu•ma]	'get out'	[imˈpʾu•nzi]	'kind of deer'
3.	[ˈpʰoᵛ•l^a]	'to cool'	[impʾumaˈl^α•ŋka]	'east'
4.	[ˈpʰinta]	'repeat'	[imˈpʾi•ni]	'at war'
5.	[ˈpʰε•k a]	'to cook'	[imˈpʾε^•l^a]	'really'
6.	[pʰuˈmu•za]	'relieve him'	[umpʾuˈmu•za]	'place name'
7.	[isiˈpʰu•ku]	'skin-blanket'	[pʾɔ•mpʾa]	'to blab'

RE 29.9. Mimicry: Miscellaneous

1. [ˈtεsʾi̯] 2. [ˈkokʾa] 3. [kʾαkʾ]

4. [ˈtˀɩkʰʅ] 7. [tˀʋˈzi·] 10. [pˀoˈtæ]

5. [ˈpˀɔšteˀ] 8. [ˈtˀeˀne] 11. [tɑˈˀɑkˀe]

6. [nʌˈfˀi] 9. [sˀɑkʰ] 12. [ta·ˈˀatˀɛ]

More Consonant Clusters

Up to the present we have emphasized consonant clusters consisting of stop plus fricative (affricates), clusters involving [ˀ], clusters with voiceless and voiced nasals or voiceless and voiced laterals, etc. In addition, there have been many different clusters included in more random fashion in the drills from time to time, so that you have had considerable exposure to certain kinds of consonant clusters before. In this following section we are going to drill some of these same kinds of combinations and then go on to a sampling of some longer consonant clusters.

RE 29.10: Kuy. Mimicry: [ˀŋ̩k ˀŋ̩kl]

1. [ˀŋ̩ˈka·ˀ] 'coarse, rough'
2. [ˀŋ̩ˈkɤŋ̩] 'tomatoes'
3. [ˀŋ̩ˈkat] 'to press'
4. [ˀŋ̩ˈkɛh] 'short'
5. [ˀŋ̩ˈkɑw] 'husked rice'
6. [ˀŋ̩ˈkl^ ɑ·ŋ] 'carry on pole between people'
7. [ˀŋ̩ˈkl^ɒ·ŋ] 'large red ants'
8. [ˀŋ̩ˈkl^ɛ·l^] 'gnaw'

RE 29.11: Kuy. Mimicry: [ˀŋ̩ˀ]

1. [ˀŋ̩ˈˀañ] 'to be angry'
2. [ˀŋ̩ˈˀɑ·p] 'to yawn'
3. [ˀŋ̩ˈˀɩ·ˀ] 'to lean against'
4. [ˀŋ̩ˈˀi·t] 'narrow'
5. [ˀŋ̩ˈˀɑ·l^] 'large black ants'

RE 29.12: Kuy. Mimicry: [ˀŋ̩h]

1. [ˀŋ̩ˈhat] 'to be quiet'
2. [ˀŋ̩ˈhɑ·l^] 'to be light'
3. [ˀŋ̩ˈhɑ·m] 'blood'
4. [ˀŋ̩ˈhɑ·y] 'far'
5. [ˀŋ̩ˈhɒ·ˀ] 'to cough'
6. [ˀŋ̩ˈhu·ˀ] 'to snore'
7. [ˀŋ̩ˈhɑ·ŋ] 'bones'

RE 29.13: Kuy. Mimicry: Miscellaneous Clusters

1. [Ll̬ɒ·] 'to make (for curries)'
2. [Ll̬ɑ·] 'leaves'

3. [Ll̆ᵛα·p] 'wings'

4. [ˀm̩'Mmɩ·] 'to steam sticky rice'

5. [ˀm̩'Mmʋ·c] 'ants'

6. [ˀm̩'Mmoᵛ·l^] 'chicken lice'

7. [ˀm̩'Mml^añ] 'fish net'

8. [ˀn̩'Nnɛ·n] 'to aim'

9. [ˀn̩'Nnaˀ] 'mattress'

10. [ˀn̩'Nnα·m] 'scar'

11. [ˀn̩'Nnα·p] 'first growth of rice'

12. [ˀn̩'Nnoh] 'nest'

13. [ˀñ̩'Ññɤ·] 'to wake up, become conscious'

14. [ˀñ̩'Ññɯ·t] 'to inhale, sniff'

RE 29.14: Kuy. Mimicry: [ɓ mb]

1. [ɓʋ·ˀ] 'to launder'

2. [ɓɯ·n] 'can'

3. [ɓʋm] 'suck'

4. [ɓu·l^] 'be drunk'

5. [ɓɤ·ˀ] 'to open'

6. [ɓʌ˃t] 'to light fire'

7. [ɓɯˀ] 'prick, wound'

8. [m̩'biɩˀ] 'trouble'

9. [m̩'bɯˀ] 'to bleach'

10. [m̩'bʋʌˀ] 'bark of tree'

RE 29.15. Mimicry: Longer Clusters

1a. ['αm.spflᵛα]	1b. ['αm.spfl̩ᵛ]	1c. [m̩'spflᵛα]
2a. ['oŋ.zdvlᵛo]	2b. ['oŋ.zdvl̩ᵛ]	2c. [ŋ̩'zdvlᵛo]
3a. [ɛp.tɫ̩'xR̃ɛ]	3b. [ɛp.tɫ̩'xR̩̃]	3c. [ptɫ̩'xR̃ɛ]
4a. [ɔg.dž'br̃ɔ]	4b. [ɔg.dž̩'br̩̃]	4c. [gdž̩'br̃ɔ]
5a. ['æx.tx̩.pfæ]	5b. ['æx.tx̩pf̩]	5c. ['x̩.tx̩.pfæ]
6a. ['ʌg.dm̩.dzʌ]	6b. ['ʌg.dm̩dz̩]	6c. ['g̩.dm̩dzʌ]
7a. [ʋvz.lr̩̃'ŋʋ]	7b. [ʋvz.lr̩̃ŋ]	7c. [vz̩.lr̩̃'ŋʋ]
8a. [ɩfxɫ'Ññɩ]	8b. [ɩfxɫ'Ññ̩]	8c. [fx̩ɫ'Ññɩ]

RE 29.16. Mimicry Review: Fronted and Backed Velar Consonants

1a. ['k̇ʰune]	1b. ['kʰune]	1c. ['k̂ʰune]
2a. ['k̇αzɩ]	2b. ['kαzɩ]	2c. ['k̂αzɩ]
3a. ['ġʋdɔ]	3b. ['gʋdɔ]	3c. ['ĝʋdɔ]

4a. [ˈŋ̣ɛt^{h}ɨ] 4b. [ˈŋɛt^{h}ɨ] 4c. [ˈŋ̭ɛt^{h}ɨ]

5a. [ṛ̃oˈḳ^{h}une] 5b. [ṛ̃ɔˈk^{h}une] 5c. [ṛ̃uˈk̭^{h}une]

6a. [ṛ̃oˈḳɑzɩ] 6b. [ṛ̃ɔˈkɑzɩ] 6c. [ṛ̃uˈk̭ɑzɩ]

7a. [ṛ̃oˈg̣ʋdɔ] 7b. [r̥̃ɔˈgʋdɔ] 7c. [ṛ̃uˈg̭ʋdɔ]

8a. [ṛ̃oˈŋ̣ɛt^{h}ɨ] 8b. [ṛ̃ɔˈŋɛt^{h}ɨ] 8c. [ṛ̃uˈŋ̭ɛt^{h}ɨ]

RE 29.17. Mimicry Review: Released and Unreleased Consonants

1a. [ˈžep^{h}mep^{h}me] 1b. [ˈžep.mep.me]

2a. [ˈkɔpəmɔpəmɔ] 2b. [ˈkɔp.mɔp.mɔ]

3a. [meˈžep^{h}mep^h] 3b. [meˈžep.mep]

4a. [mɔˈkɔpəmɔpə] 4b. [mɔˈkɔp.mɔp]

5a. [ŋoˈƀæp^{h}tæk^h] 5b. [ŋoˈƀæp.tæk]

6a. [hʋˈl̃ipətikə] 6b. [hʋˈl̃ip.tik]

7a. [yøsədøŋəˈdø] 7b. [yøs.døŋˈdø]

8a. [k^{h}ǫvęnǫtęˈñǫ] 8b. [k^{h}ǫv.nǫt.ñǫ]

9a. [dœˈyœsədœŋə] 9b. [dœˈyœs.dœŋ]

10a. [ñǫˈk^{h}ǫvęnǫtę] 10b. [ñǫˈk^{h}ǫv.nǫt]

RE 29.18. Mimicry Review: Implosives

1a. [ˈɓømu] 1b. [ˈɓømuɓa] 1c. [ɓʋˈɓømuɓa]

2a. [ˈɗʌnü] 2b. [ˈɗʌnüɗɨ] 2c. [ɗøˈɗʌnüɗɨ]

3a. [ˈʄañi] 3b. [ˈʄañiʄɛ] 3c. [ʄɔˈʄañiʄɛ]

4a. [ˈɠoeŋɨ] 4b. [ˈɠœŋɨɠo] 4c. [ɠɩˈɠoeŋɨɠo]

5a. [ˈƥümø] 5b. [ˈƥümøƥe] 5c. [ƥʌˈƥümøƥe]

6a. [ˈƭʋnæ] 6b. [ˈƭʋnæƭɔ] 6c. [ƭœˈƭʋnæƭɔ]

7a. [ˈƈoña] 7b. [ˈƈoñaƈæ] 7c. [ƈɨˈƈoñaƈæ]

8a. [ˈƙɑŋü] 8b. [ˈƙɑŋüƙu] 8c. [ƙɨˈƙɑŋüƙu]

RE 29.19. Substitution

1. [tˀaɬˈkˀəkˀ ˈMmovupˀin yɛžpˀˈtoŋi]

2. [ˈr̃eɓwɔ]

3. [ˈyudɬɛŋ]

4. [ˈsæ̰̃lʌ̰]

5. [ˈcøšcø]

Transcription and Reading

Use RE 29.2-29.3, 29.5-29.6, 29.8-29.18.

THEY SAY SHE'S GREAT ON THE BILABIAL FLAP!

LESSON THIRTY

Retroflexed Vowels; Breathy Vowels; Voiced Aspirated Stops

	Front		Central		Back	
	U.	R.	U.	R.	U.	R.
High	ị					ụ
Lower-high	ɩ̣		ɨ̣			ʊ̣
Mid	ẹ					ọ
Lower-mid	ɛ̣		ə̣			
Low	æ̣		ʌ̣			ɔ̣
Lower-low	ạ		ɑ̣			

Table 30.1: Retroflexed Vowels

We introduced the [r] glide on pp. 179-181, and syllabic [r̩] was included in the drills on syllabic consonants (p. 152ff.). The retroflexed vowels with which we are now working involve exactly the same retroflexed articulation pictured in Sammy 12.9, p. 180. In this lesson we simply expand what we have done before to produce retroflexed quality on a much wider variety of vowels. As a matter of fact, [r] glide is to [ɨ] as [y] is to [i] or [w] to [u]. In each case the glide is a movement to the approximate position of the vowel. [r̩] was introduced earlier because in English it is so important and involves consonant function, as does [m̩ n̩ l̩], etc. Strictly speaking, however, [r̩] is the same as [ɨ̣] or [ə̣].

Our symbolization simply adds a dot diacritic under any vowel which is said with tongue curled up. The symbolization, therefore, is like that of retroflexed consonants. You identify the nearest vowel quality and write that with the dot under it. We think of retroflexed quality as a modification superimposed on the basic vowel articulations, as was nasalization in Lesson 24.

RE 30.1. Demonstration: Table 30.1

Listen repeatedly, and study the vowel chart as you do so. Learn to read off the vowel chart with the tape. Get the new sounds as best you can by mimicry.

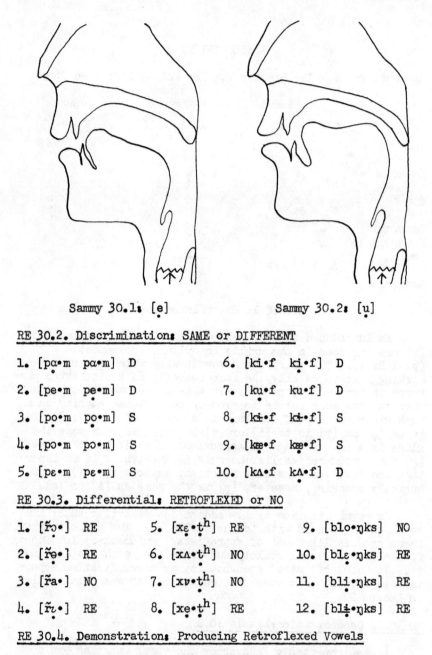

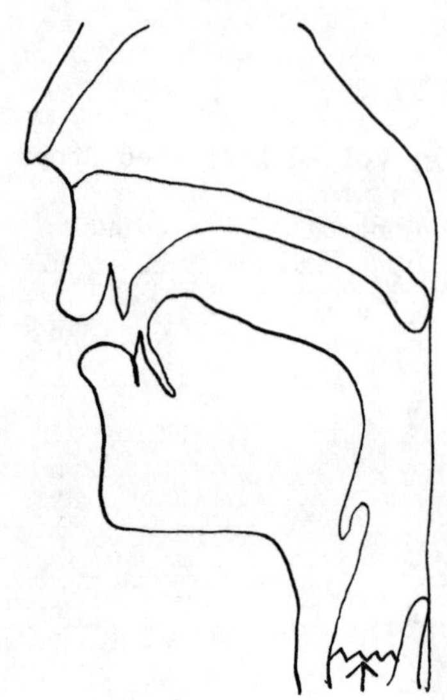

Sammy 30.1: [ẹ] Sammy 30.2: [ụ]

RE 30.2. Discrimination: SAME or DIFFERENT

1.	[pα̥·m pα·m]	D	6.	[ki·f kị·f]	D
2.	[pe·m pẹ·m]	D	7.	[kụ·f ku·f]	D
3.	[pọ·m pọ·m]	S	8.	[kɨ·f kɨ·f]	S
4.	[pɔ·m pɔ·m]	S	9.	[kæ̣·f kæ̣·f]	S
5.	[pɛ·m pɛ·m]	S	10.	[kʌ·f kʌ̣·f]	D

RE 30.3. Differential: RETROFLEXED or NO

1.	[r̃ɔ̣·]	RE	5.	[xɛ̣·ṭ^h]	RE	9.	[blo·ŋks]	NO
2.	[r̃ə̣·]	RE	6.	[xʌ·ṭ^h]	NO	10.	[blɛ̣·ŋks]	RE
3.	[r̃a·]	NO	7.	[xɒ·ṭ^h]	NO	11.	[blị·ŋks]	RE
4.	[r̃ɩ̣·]	RE	8.	[xẹ·ṭ^h]	RE	12.	[blɨ̣·ŋks]	RE

RE 30.4. Demonstration: Producing Retroflexed Vowels

Retroflexed vowels are not difficult to produce. You have probably produced them perfectly well by mimicry already. In case you are having difficulty, or are unsure of yourself, the following suggestions may help.

a. Start with a retroflexed [ṭ] and get the feeling of the tongue contour of a retroflexed sound. Then say [ṭα̣ ṭæ̣ ṭẹ ṭị ṭụ ṭọ] followed by [α̣ æ̣ ẹ ị ụ ọ].

b. Deliberately point your tongue tip upward, and experiment saying a sound as close to [α] as you can with the tongue in this position. Follow with other vowels, trying to get as close to [ʌ i ɔ o ɒ ɩ e ɛ] as you can. These will be retroflexed vowels of these different qualities.

c. Practice reading and talking with your tongue kept in retroflexed position. The tape demonstrates the reading of this paragraph in retroflexed negative practice. Practice talking to your buddy with your tongue tip curled up.

RE 30.5. Mimicry: Retroflexed Vowels

Follow the transcription as you mimic the tape.

1a. [ṭẹṭẹ] 1b. [kẹkẹ] 1c. [pẹpẹ]

2a. [ṇʌ̣ṇʌ̣] 2b. [ŋʌ̣ŋʌ̣] 2c. [mʌ̣mʌ̣]

3a. [ẓ̌α̣ẓ̌α̣] 3b. [gα̣gα̣] 3c. [bα̣bα̣]

4a. [ḍæ̣ḍæ̣] 4b. [gæ̣gæ̣] 4c. [bæ̣bæ̣]

5a. [ṭʰɩ̣ṭʰɩ̣] 5b. [kʰɩ̣kʰɩ̣] 5c. [pʰɩ̣pʰɩ̣]

RE 30.6. Differential: Vowel Symbols

Respond with the name of the symbol or write the symbol which corresponds to the quality of each of the following retroflexed vowels. Don't peek.

1. [yọkʰ] o
2. [yα̣kʰ] SCRIPT α
3. [yɨ̣kʰ] BARRED i
4. [yɔ̣kʰ] BACKWARDS c
5. [yạkʰ] PRINTED a
6. [yɛ̣kʰ] EPSILON
7. [Wịf] i
8. [Wẹf] e
9. [Wʌ̣f] CARET
10. [Wọf] o
11. [Wæ̣f] a DIGRAPH
12. [Wɩ̣f] IOTA

RE 30.7. Negative Practice: "This is the House that Jack Built"

Refer to the text of RE 14.4, p. 205, if you need to. Retroflex the vowels of each of the words which are constantly repeated through this verse. The tape demonstrates how the drill works but does not give the full exercise. The words in which the retroflexed vowels are to be substituted are: house, malt, rat, cat, dog, cow, maiden, man, priest, cock, farmer.

Breathy Vowels

Another modification of vowels we call breathiness. This time the difference in sound is caused in the larynx by a different positioning of the vocal cords from that either of voicing or of voicelessness. It sounds like a little bit of both, as will be demonstrated on the tape.

Some languages have two vowel systems, one breathy and the other non-breathy, just as others have two systems, one nasalized and the other non-nasalized. Some other languages have breathy vowels associated with particular tones or particular consonants.

We symbolize breathiness by a plus mark under the vowel [̟].

	Front		Central		Back	
	U.	R.	U.	R.	U.	R.
High	i̟	ü̟			ɯ̟	u̟
Lower-high	ɩ̟		ɨ̟			ʊ̟
Mid	e̟	ø̟			ɤ̟	o̟
Lower-mid	ɛ̟		ə̟			
Low	æ̟	œ̟	ʌ̟			ɔ̟
Lower-low	a̟		ɑ̟		ɒ̟	

Table 30.2: Some Breathy Vowels

RE 30.8. Demonstration: Table 30.2

Listen repeatedly, and study the vowel chart as you do so. Read off the vowel chart with the tape. Learn the breathy quality by mimicry.

RE 30.9. Discrimination: SAME or DIFFERENT

1. [kʰɑ̟•m kʰɑ•m] D
2. [kʰe•m kʰe̟•m] D
3. [kʰo̟•m kʰo̟•m] S
4. [kʰɔ•m kʰɔ•m] S
5. [kʰɛ•m kʰɛ•m] S
6. [si•w si̟•w] D
7. [sʊ̟•w sʊ•w] D
8. [si•w si•w] S
9. [sæ̟•w sæ̟•w] S
10. [sʌ•w sʌ̟•w] D

RE 30.10. Differential: BREATHY or NO

1. [vɔ̟•] BR
2. [və̟•] BR
3. [va•] NO
4. [vɪ̟•] BR
5. [xɛ̟•tʰ] BR
6. [xʌ•tʰ] NO
7. [xʊ•tʰ] NO
8. [xe̟•tʰ] BR
9. [blo•ŋks] NO
10. [blɛ̟•ŋks] BR
11. [bli̟•ŋks] BR
12. [blɨ̟•ŋks] BR

RE 30.11. Differential: RETROFLEXED or BREATHY

1. [ᵽa̟•nN] BR
2. [ᵽạ•nN] RE
3. [ᵽʊ̟•nN] BR
4. [ᵽɨ̣•nN] RE
5. [gu̟•cʰ] BR
6. [gɑ̣•cʰ] RE
7. [gɛ̟•cʰ] BR
8. [go̟•cʰ] BR
9. [vye̟•pˀ] BR
10. [vyʌ̣•pˀ] RE
11. [vyʊ̣•pˀ] RE
12. [vyæ̟•pˀ] BR

RE 30.12. Demonstration: Producing Breathy Vowels

Breathy vowels are not difficult to produce. Here are some suggestions.

a. Breathy vowels are often associated with "spookiness" in English, as in this simulated call of the owl: [u̟• u̟• u̟•].

b. They are also associated with sultry glamor. Listen to the following anecdote read with breathy voice quality. Practice reading and talking yourself with breathy quality.

"A linguist who had experience with breathy vowels through his knowledge of the Meo language was asked to demonstrate them. He replied, 'Marilyn Monroe.' 'Is that Meo?' he was asked. 'No,' he replied, 'she's female.'"

RE 30.13. Mimicry: Breathy Vowels

1a. [sɑ̟·]	1b. [sɑ·sɑ̟·]	1c. [sɑ̟·sɑ·sɑ̟·]
2a. [nu̟·]	2b. [nu·nu̟·]	2c. [nu̟·nu·nu̟·]
3a. [l^æ̟·]	3b. [l^æ·l^æ̟·]	3c. [l^æ̟·l^æ·l^æ̟·]
4a. [tsɔ̟·]	4b. [tsɔ·tsɔ̟·]	4c. [tsɔ̟·tsɔ·tsɔ̟·]
5a. [ti̟·]	5b. [ti·ti̟·]	5c. [ti̟·ti·ti̟·]
6a. [kˀɨ̟·]	6b. [kˀɨ·kˀɨ̟·]	6c. [kˀɨ̟·kˀɨ·kˀɨ̟·]

RE 30.14. Mimicry: Various Vowel Modifications

1a. [ƀəˀx]	1b. [ƀəͅx]	1c. [ƀə̟x]	1d. [ƀə̣x]
2a. [pᵽɩˀx]	2b. [pᵽɩͅx]	2c. [pᵽɩ̟x]	2d. [pᵽɩ̣x]
3a. [Mmaˀx]	3b. [Mmaͅx]	3c. [Mma̟x]	3d. [Mmạx]
4a. [bvɔˀx]	4b. [bvɔͅx]	4c. [bvɔ̟x]	4d. [bvɔ̣x]
5a. [pʰiˀx]	5b. [pʰiͅx]	5c. [pʰi̟x]	5d. [pʰị x]
6a. [kʰɛˀv]	6b. [kʰɛͅv]	6c. [kʰɛ̟v]	6d. [kʰɛ̣v]
7a. [gʌˀv]	7b. [gʌͅv]	7c. [gʌ̟v]	7d. [gʌ̣v]
8a. [ŋoˀv]	8b. [ŋoͅv]	8c. [ŋo̟v]	8d. [ŋọv]
9a. [Ŋŋɑˀv]	9b. [Ŋŋɑͅv]	9c. [Ŋŋɑ̟v]	9d. [Ŋŋɑ̣v]
10a. [kxuˀv]	10b. [kxuͅv]	10c. [kxu̟v]	10c. [kxụv]

Voiced Aspirated Stops

	Bilabial	Alveolar/ dental	Alveo- palatal	Retro- flexed	Velar
Vl. unasp.	p	t	c	ṭ	k
Vl. asp.	pʰ	tʰ	cʰ	ṭʰ	kʰ
Vd. unasp.	b	d	j	ḍ	g
Vd. asp.	b̟ʰ	d̟ʰ	j̟ʰ	ḍ̟ʰ	g̟ʰ

Table 30.3: Some Voiced Aspirated Stops

In Lesson 28 we discussed the relationship between voiceless vowels and aspiration of voiceless stops. Voiced stops occur with aspiration also, but the aspiration is breathy. In other words, the aspiration of a voiceless stop is to a voiceless vowel as the aspiration of a voiced stop is to a breathy vowel. Aspiration of voiced stops is extremely important in India, Pakistan and Ceylon.

RE 30.15. Demonstration: Production of Voiced Aspirated Stops

The principal problem in the production of voiced aspirated stops is keeping a very close transition between the stop and the aspiration so that the breathy aspiration does not become syllabic. Try these suggestions:

a. Start with a sequence like Tab Hunter and make the following adaptations in mimicry of the tape.

1. Tab Hunter

2. [tʰæ·b'hʌntr̩]

3. [tʰæ·'b̟ʰʌntr̩]

b. Try the same procedure with bad harvest, and big hangar.

c. Mimic the tape on the following sequence. Be sure the vowel coming after the aspiration is not breathy.

1. [ɑbɑhɑ]

2. [ɑbɑ̟]

3. [ɑb̟ʰɑ]

RE 30.16. Negative Practice: Voiced Aspirated Stops

Mimic the tape and follow the transcription as you substitute voiced aspirated stops in these English sequences.

1a. baby	1b. b̟ʰaby	1c. b̟ʰab̟ʰy
2a. dodo	2b. d̟ʰodo	2c. d̟ʰod̟ʰo
3a. gagging	3b. g̟ʰagging	3c. g̟ʰagg̟ʰing

4. b̟ʰig b̟ʰad b̟ʰoy

5. g̟ʰooey g̟ʰooey g̟ʰumdrops

6. d̟ʰon't d̟ʰunk d̟ʰonuts

RE 30.17. Differential: VOICED or VOICELESS

The distinction between voiced and voiceless aspirated stops is not difficult to hear. Respond with VOICED or VOICELESS. Don't peek!

1. [pʰɔ] VL	5. [tʰay] VL	9. [ŋə'tʰɔs] VL
2. [b̟ʰɒ] VD	6. [d̟ʰɩy] VD	10. [ŋə'j̟ʰæs] VD
3. [cʰe] VL	7. [ḍ̟ʰɨy] VD	11. [ŋə'kʰɑs] VL
4. [g̟ʰæ] VD	8. [b̟ʰʌy] VD	12. [ŋə'g̟ʰus] VD

RE 30.18. Differential: ASPIRATED or IMPLOSIVE

1. [ḍ̟ʰo] A	5. [ʔi'd̟ʰɨ] A	9. [r̃ʌ'd̟ʰaŘ] A
2. [ɠə] I	6. [ʔi'ɗi] I	10. [r̃ʌ'ɓøŘ] I
3. [b̟ʰɛ] A	7. [ʔi'g̟ʰɒ] A	11. [r̃ʌ'ɗ̣ɩŘ] I
4. [j̟ʰœ] A	8. [ʔi'ʄe] I	12. [r̃ʌ'ɠuŘ] I

RE 30.19. Mimicry: Voiced Aspirated Stops

1a. [ɑ·'b̟ʰɑ]	1b. [ɑ·'b̟ʰɑb̟ʰɑ]	1c. ['b̟ʰɑb̟ʰɑb̟ʰɑ]
2a. [ɔ·'d̟ʰɔ]	2b. [ɔ·'d̟ʰɔd̟ʰɔ]	2c. ['d̟ʰɔd̟ʰɔd̟ʰɔ]
3a. [e·'j̟ʰe]	3b. [e·'j̟ʰej̟ʰe]	3c. ['j̟ʰej̟ʰej̟ʰe]
4a. [æ·'ḍ̟ʰæ]	4b. [æ·'ḍ̟ʰæḍ̟ʰæ]	4c. ['ḍ̟ʰæḍ̟ʰæḍ̟ʰæ]
5a. [œ·'g̟ʰœ]	5b. [œ·'g̟ʰœg̟ʰœ]	5c. ['g̟ʰœg̟ʰœg̟ʰœ]
6a. ['b̟ʰɛřu]	6b. [b̟ʰɛ'b̟ʰɛřu]	6c. ['b̟ʰɛřub̟ʰɛ]
7a. ['d̟ʰɩřu]	7b. [d̟ʰɩ'd̟ʰɩřu]	7c. ['d̟ʰɩřud̟ʰɩ]
8a. ['j̟ʰɔřu]	8b. [j̟ʰɔ'j̟ʰɔřu]	8c. ['j̟ʰɔřuj̟ʰɔ]
9a. ['ḍ̟ʰořu]	9b. [ḍ̟ʰo'ḍ̟ʰořu]	9c. ['ḍ̟ʰořuḍ̟ʰo]
10a. ['g̟ʰiřu]	10b. [g̟ʰi'g̟ʰiřu]	10c. ['g̟ʰiřug̟ʰi]

RE 30.20: Kuy. Mimicry: [u̟•]

1.	[cu̟•n]	'to send'	6.	[mu̟•l^]	'to roll'
2.	[cu̟•y]	'to help'	7.	[mu̟•t]	'to enter'
3.	[kʌ'n̆u̟•]	'to push'	8.	[n̩tr̽u̟•ñ]	'termites'
4.	[kʌ'tu̟•ŋ]	'to transplant rice'	9.	[plu̟•ʔ]	'to fall (for trees)'
5.	[klu̟•p]	'to cover a plant with a basket'	10.	[tu̟•h]	'yonder'

RE 30.21: Kuy. Mimicry: [u u̟ u• u̟•]

The Kuy language has a whole series of breathy vowels (both long and short) which contrasts with non-breathy vowels (both long and short). In this and the succeeding exercises two of the Kuy breathy vowels are drilled, together with some contrast with non-breathy vowels. In order to accentuate the difference, Kuy non-breathy vowels are generally more tense than English vowels, with a greater constriction of the muscles at the opening of the throat (faucal pillars). This kind of vowel modification (faucalization) is not being drilled in this course, but imitate it as best you can.

1.	[ɗuʔ]	'often'	3.	[l^u̟ʔ]	'to mix together'
2.	[kʌyu•ʔ]	'sorghum'	4.	[plu̟•ʔ]	'to fall (for trees)'

RE 30.22: Kuy. Mimicry: [o̟•]

1.	[l^o̟•t]	'to jump'	7.	[ko̟•ʔ]	'forest'
2.	[mo̟•ŋ]	'crazy'	8.	[ko̟•n]	'trunk of tree'
3.	[n̩'no̟•l^]	'to be puffed up'	9.	[kʌ'po̟•k]	'firecracker'
4.	[n̩'tr̽o̟•y]	'to loosen soil'	10.	[l^o̟•h]	'to escape'
5.	[n̆o̟•m]	'laymen'	11.	[ŋ̩'ko̟•p]	'a kind of frog'
6.	[ko̟•]	'cow'			

RE 30.23: Kuy. Mimicry: [oˇ o̟ˇ o• o̟•]

1.	[kloˇŋ]	'sock woven of leaves'	2.	[kʌ'yo•l^]	'red "bud" of banana'

3. [m̩'pọ̟ˇŋ] 'brace' 4. [mọ̟•ŋ] 'crazy'

<u>Transcription and Reading</u>

Use RE 30.2-30.3, 30.5-30.6, 30.9-30.11, 30.13-30.14, 30.17-30.23.

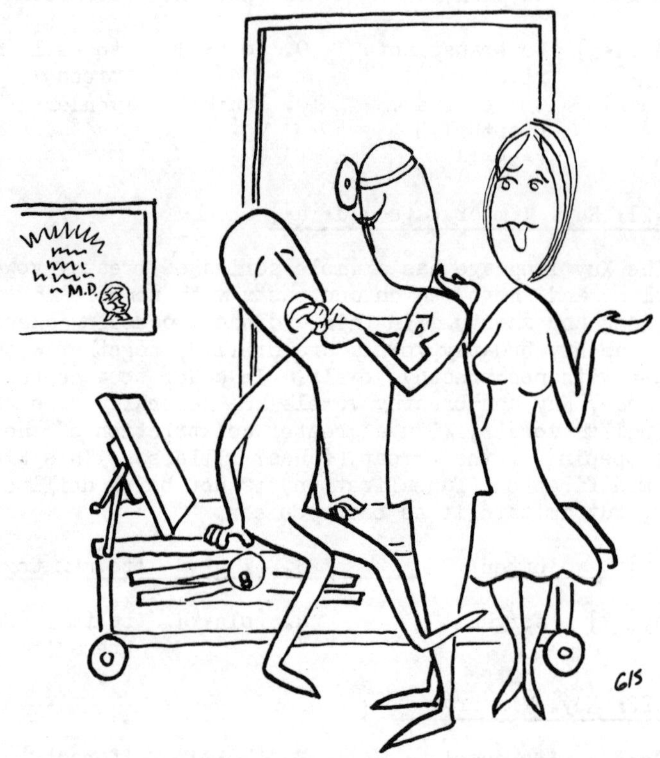

WELL, DOCTOR, HE WAS TRYING TO PRONOUNCE A RETROFLEXED SYLLABIC "s̩" AND GOT A KNOT IN HIS TONGUE!

LESSON THIRTY-ONE

Clicks

	Bilabial	Dental	Alveolar	Alveopalatal	Retroflexed
Central[1]					
Vl. unaspirated	p←	ṱ←	t←	c←	ṭ←
Vl. aspirated	pʰ←	ṱʰ←	tʰ←	cʰ←	ṭʰ←
Voiced	b←	ḓ←	d←	j←	ḍ←
Nasalized	m←	ṋ←	n←	ñ←	ṇ←
Lateral					
Vl. unaspirated			tŁ←		
Vl. aspirated			tŁʰ←		
Voiced			dŁ←		
Nasalized			nŁ←		

Table 31.1. Some Clicks

Not only do we have the vast majority of speech sounds made with air coming out of the lungs, and the smaller but important number of pharynx air sounds, where the air stream is drawn in or pushed out by the lowering or raising action of the larynx (Lessons 27 and 29), but we also have speech sounds in which the air stream is initiated in the mouth. These are called clicks.

---

[1]Central clicks (as opposed to lateral ones) have a release which is over the center and tip of the tongue. When these are affricated (as most central clicks except retroflexed ones are) the fricative quality is at the nearest point of articulation to that of the stop feature of the click. (Even nasalized clicks have a stop feature.) In lateral clicks, however, the fricative quality is [Ł] no matter what the point of articulation of the stop feature of the click.

As non-speech sounds some clicks occur everywhere, but as full-fledged consonants they are restricted to South Africa. The clicks are not at all difficult to do in isolation as we have used them for a wide variety of non-linguistic purposes all of our lives. These activities include kissing (voiceless bilabial click),[1] expressing mild reproval : "tsk tsk" (voiceless dental click), "giddeap" (voiceless lateral affricated click), etc.

If you examine Sammy 31.1 you will see that there are two closures in the mouth, just as for a double stop. However, in a click, which is an ingressive mouth air sound,[2] the back of the tongue moves backward, creating a partial vacuum in the mouth, and the sound is created by the air going into the mouth after the release (Sammy 31.2). Double stops differ in that they involve lung air. Double stops sometimes have a click articulation associated with them as was shown in Sammy 21.4, p. 300, but this mouth air articulation is secondary. The primary airstream comes from the lungs. Voiced and nasalized clicks introduced below involve lung air for the voicing and nasalization, but this is simultaneous with the click and does not alter its mouth air articulation.

Our symbolization does not show it, but all clicks except retroflexed ones tend to have a voiceless affricated release which you will hear on the tape. If you test this out with a kiss (a bilabial one) you will see that the bilabial articulation is opened slightly while the tongue is still pulling backward to give what we could transcribe more precisely as [pp←].

RE 31.1. Demonstration: Producing Voiceless Clicks

The simple voiceless clicks should not give you any trouble once you have heard them demonstrated.

a. [p←] is nothing more than a kiss. Mimic the tape in the following sequence:

1. [p← p← p← p← p←]

2. [αp← αp← αp← αp← αp←]

3. [p←α p←α p←α p←α p←α]

---

[1] You'll get a bigger kick
From a quadrilabial click
With a bilabial chick.

[2] Egressive mouth air is also possible, but will not be included here.

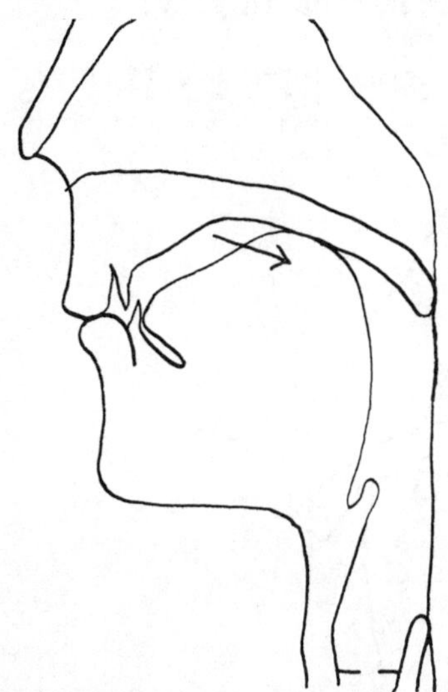

Sammy 31.1: Voiceless Bilabial Click [p←] Before Release

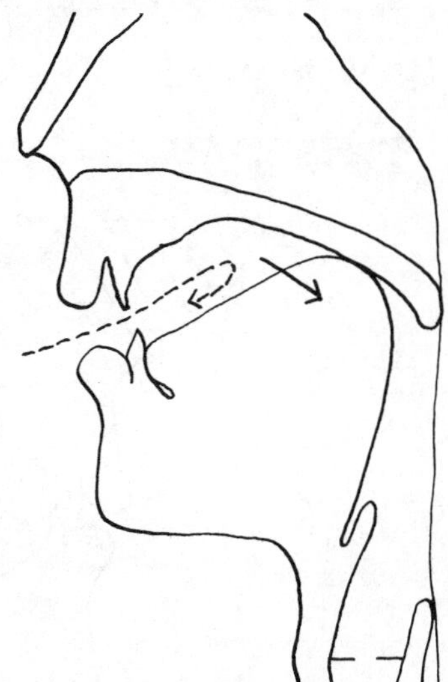

Sammy 31.2: [p←] After Release of Bilabial Closure

b. [ṱ←] or [t←] is simply the sign of mild reproach used by speakers of English and represented by "tsk, tsk" in the comic strips. The difference between [ṱ← t←], of course, is in the point of articulation, whether it is dental or alveolar.

1a. [ṱ← ṱ← ṱ← ṱ← ṱ←] 1b. [t← t← t← t← t←]

2a. [ɑṱ← ɑṱ← ɑṱ← ɑṱ← ɑṱ←] 2b. [ɑt← ɑt← ɑt← ɑt← ɑt←]

3a. [ṱ←ɑ ṱ←ɑ ṱ←ɑ ṱ←ɑ ṱ←ɑ] 3b. [t←ɑ t←ɑ t←ɑ t←ɑ t←ɑ]

c. [tł] is the "giddeap" click of the American farmer to his horse.

1. [tł← tł← tł← tł← tł←]

2. [ɑtł← ɑtł← ɑtł← ɑtł← ɑtł←]

3. [tł←ɑ tł←ɑ tł←ɑ tł←ɑ tł←ɑ]

d. [c←] can be easily made on the analogy of [t←]. Just keep the tongue tip down behind the lower teeth.

1. [c← c← c← c← c←]

2. [ɑc← ɑc← ɑc← ɑc← ɑc←]

3. [c←ɑ c←ɑ c←ɑ c←ɑ c←ɑ]

e. [ṭ←] is a familiar sound often made in play.

1. [ṭ← ṭ← ṭ← ṭ← ṭ←]
2. [ɑṭ← ɑṭ← ɑṭ← ɑṭ← ɑṭ←]
3. [ṭ←ɑ ṭ←ɑ ṭ←ɑ ṭ←ɑ ṭ←ɑ]

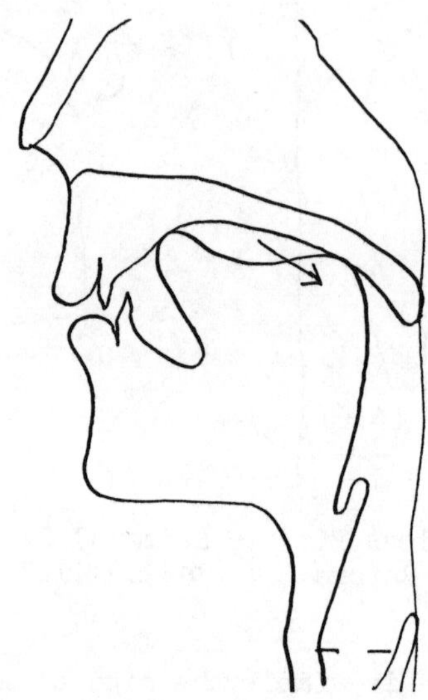

Sammy 31.3: [ṭ←]

f. With a little practice, aspiration can be added to any of these.

1. [p^{h}←ɑ p^{h}←ɑ p^{h}←ɑ p^{h}←ɑ p^{h}←ɑ]
2. [ṱ^{h}←ɑ ṱ^{h}←ɑ ṱ^{h}←ɑ ṱ^{h}←ɑ ṱ^{h}←ɑ]
3. [t^{h}←ɑ t^{h}←ɑ t^{h}←ɑ t^{h}←ɑ t^{h}←ɑ]
4. [c^{h}←ɑ c^{h}←ɑ c^{h}←ɑ c^{h}←ɑ c^{h}←ɑ]
5. [ṭ^{h}←ɑ ṭ^{h}←ɑ ṭ^{h}←ɑ ṭ^{h}←ɑ ṭ^{h}←ɑ]
6. [tɬ^{h}←ɑ tɬ^{h}←ɑ tɬ^{h}←ɑ tɬ^{h}←ɑ tɬ^{h}←ɑ]

<u>RE 31.2. Differential: CENTRAL or LATERAL Release</u>

If the release of the click is lateral respond with LATERAL. Otherwise respond with CENTRAL.

1. [α'tƚ←α] L
2. [e'ṭ←o] C
3. [o'c^h←ε] C
4. [ε'p^h←ʋ] C
5. [pʋ'ṱ←ɔ] C
6. [tɔ'tƚ^h←ɨ] L
7. [cɨ't^h←æ] C
8. [kæ'p←u] C
9. [mu'ṱ^{h}←ʌy] C
10. [nʌ'tƚ←ɩy] L
11. [ñɩ'tƚ^h←əy] L
12. [ŋə'c←αy] C

RE 31.3. Differential: GLOTTALIZED or CLICK

The sound of a glottalized consonant is readily distinguishable from a click if the two are pronounced in exaggerated or deliberate fashion. If they are produced in a more lenis way, however, they sound somewhat more alike, although there still is an appreciable difference. Don't peek.

1. [α't$^?$α] G
2. [e'ṭ←o] C
3. [o'c$^?$ε] G
4. [ε'p←ʋ] C
5. [i'p$^?$ɨ] G
6. [ᵽʋ'k$^?$ɔ] G
7. [fɔ't$^?$ɨ] G
8. [θɨ't←æ] C
9. [sæ'p←u] C
10. [si'ṱ←i] C
11. [mu'tƚ←ʌy] C
12. [nʌ'k$^?$ɩy] G
13. [ñɩ'p$^?$əy] G
14. [ŋə'c←αy] C
15. [l̃α't←ɔy] C

RE 31.4. Differential: IMPLOSIVE or CLICK

When you make a voiceless implosive, with the exception of [ƙ], there is a temptation to substitute a mouth air sound - a click without affrication, or at least with less than what we usually practice. Implosives and clicks are both ingressive, the one with pharynx air and the other with mouth air. The implosives are lower-pitched than the clicks. Respond with IMPLOSIVE or CLICK. Don't peek.

1. [α'ƭα] I
2. [e'ṭ←o] C
3. [o'ƈε] I
4. [i'ƥɨ] I
5. [ε'p←ʋ] C
6. [šɨ'ṱ←i] C
7. [sæ'p←u] C
8. [fɔ'ƭɨ] I
9. [θɨ't←æ] C
10. [ᵽʋ'ƙɔ] I
11. [mu'tƚ←ʌw] C
12. [ŋa'c←αw] C
13. [nʌ'ƥɩw] I
14. [ñɩ'ƈəw] I
15. [l̃α't←ɔw] C

RE 31.5. Differential: ASPIRATED or UNASPIRATED

1. [ε'p^h←ʋ] A
2. [i'p←ɨ] U
3. [o'c←ε] U

4. [e'ṭʰ←o] A	7. [fɔ'ṱʰ←ɨ] A	10. [ñɩ'tʰ←əH] U
5. [ᵽʋ'ṭ←ɔ] U	8. [šɨ'ṱ←i] U	11. [ñʌ'tᴌʰ←ɩH] A
6. [θɨ't←æ] U	9. [l̃ɑ'cʰ←ɔH] A	12. [ŋə'tᴌ←ɑH] U

RE 31.6. Differential: Point of Articulation

Respond to the clicks you hear with LABIAL, DENTAL, ALVEOLAR, ALVEOPALATAL, or PALATAL (for retroflexed clicks). Don't peek.

1. [ɑ'ṭ←ɑ] PA	6. [ᵽʋ'cʰ←ɔ] AP	11. [mu'tᴌʰ←ʌr] AL
2. [e'p←o] LA	7. [fɔ'tʰ←ɨ] AL	12. [nʌ'c←ɩr] AP
3. [o'ṱ←ɛ] DE	8. [θɨ'ṭʰ←u] PA	13. [nɩ'p←ər] LA
4. [ɛ'tᴌ←ʋ] AL	9. [sæ'pʰ←u] LA	14. [ŋə'tʰ←ɑr] AL
5. [i't←ɨ] AL	10. [šɨ'ṱʰ←i] DE	15. [lɑ'ṭ←ɔr] PA

RE 31.7. Mimicry: Voiceless Clicks

1a. [p←ɑ]	1b. [pʰ←ɑ]	1c. [p←xɑ]	1d. [p←kɑ]
2a. [ɑp←]	2b. [ɑhp←]	2c. [ɑxp←]	2d. [ɑkp←]
3a. [ṱ←ø]	3b. [ṱʰ←ø]	3c. [ṱ←xø]	3d. [ṱ←kø]
4a. [øṱ←]	4b. [øhṱ←]	4c. [øxṱ←]	4d. [økṱ←]
5a. [t←a]	5b. [tʰ←a]	5c. [t←xa]	5d. [t←ka]
6a. [at←]	6b. [aht←]	6c. [axt←]	6d. [akt←]
7a. [c←æ]	7b. [cʰ←æ]	7c. [c←xæ]	7d. [c←kæ]
8a. [æc←]	8b. [æhc←]	8c. [æxc←]	8d. [ækc←]
9a. [ṭ←i]	9b. [ṭʰ←i]	9c. [ṭ←xi]	9d. [ṭ←ki]
10a. [iṭ←]	10b. [ihṭ←]	10c. [ixṭ←]	10d. [ikṭ←]
11a. [tᴌ←u]	11b. [tᴌʰ←u]	11c. [tᴌ←xu]	11d. [tᴌ←ku]
12a. [utᴌ←]	12b. [uhtᴌ←]	12c. [uxtᴌ←]	12d. [uktᴌ←]

Nasalized Clicks

If you will experiment a little bit and "pucker up" for a bilabial click without releasing it, you can say a simultaneous [m] with it. Sammy 31.4 shows you why. The click mechanism is completely in the mouth, and does not obstruct the passage from the lungs out through the velic opening and nose which makes possible a nasal consonant. A nasalized click is one in which there is a nasal articulation preceding and simultaneous with a click, as in Sammy 31.5, or in the following segmental diagram.

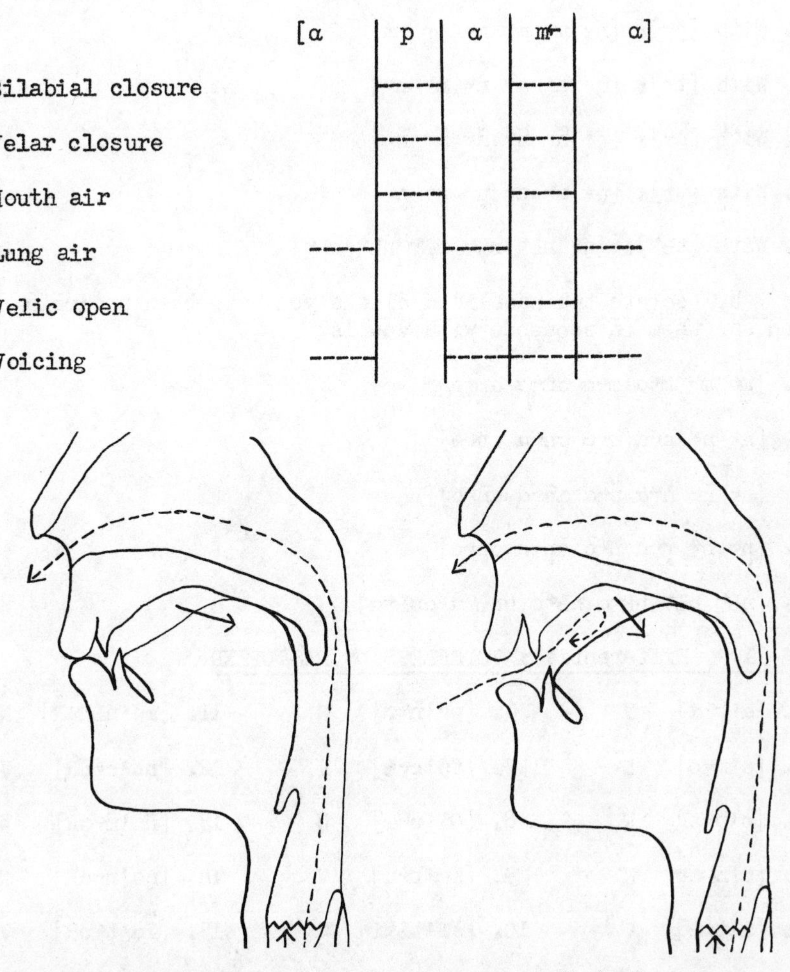

Sammy 31.4: Voiced Nasalized Bilabial Click [m←] Before Release

Sammy 31.5: [m←] After Release of Bilabial Closure

Don't let the symbolization fool you. [m←] is a [p←] with a simultaneous nasal quality. Or, you can think of it as [ŋ] and [p←] at the same time ([ŋ] because the back of the tongue is articulated against the velum to move backwards and produce the ingressive mouth air stream). In the same manner, [n←] is [t←] with a simultaneous [ŋ], etc.

RE 31.8. Demonstration: Nasalized Clicks

a. Make a long [ŋ••] and without releasing it say several clicks in a row simultaneously with it.

1. With [p←]: [ŋ• m← m← m← m← m←]

2. With [t←]: [ŋ• n← n← n← n← n←]

3. With [c←]: [ŋ• ñ← ñ← ñ← ñ← ñ←]

4. With [ṭ←]: [ŋ• ṇ← ṇ← ṇ← ṇ← ṇ←]

5. With [tƀ←]: [ŋ• nƀ← nƀ← nƀ← nƀ← nƀ←]

b. Isolate the nasalized clicks you have been producing and say them in sequence with vowels.

1. [m← m← m←α m←α αm←α αm←α]

2. [n← n← n←α n←α αn←α αn←α]

3. [ñ← ñ← ñ←α ñ←α αñ←α αñ←α]

4. [ṇ← ṇ← ṇ←α ṇ←α αṇ←α αṇ←α]

5. [nƀ← nƀ← nƀ←α nƀ←α αnƀ←α αnƀ←α]

RE 31.9. Differential: VOICELESS or NASALIZED

1. [α'ṭ←α]	V	6. [ᵽʋ'ñ←ɔ]	N	11. [mɯ'nƀ←ʌR̃]	N
2. [e'm←o]	N	7. [fɔ'c←ɨ]	V	12. [nʌ'c←ɩR̃]	V
3. [o'n̬←ɛ]	N	8. [θɨ'n̦←æ]	N	13. [ñɩ'm←əR̃]	N
4. [ɛ'nƀ←ʋ]	N	9. [sæ'p←u]	V	14. [ŋə'n←αR̃]	N
5. [i't←ɨ]	V	10. [š̌ɨ'tƀ←i]	V	15. [l̃α'ṭ←ɔR̃]	V

RE 31.10. Mimicry: Nasalized Clicks

1a. [ɩŋ'm←ɛ] 1b. [ɩ'm←ɛ] 1c. [m←ɛ]

2a. [εŋ'n̺←ə] 2b. [ε'n̺←ə] 2c. [n←ə]

3a. [əŋ'n←ü] 3b. [ə'n←ü] 3c. [n←ü]

4a. [üŋ'ñ←ɔ] 4b. [u'ñ←ɔ] 4c. [ñ←ɔ]

5a. [ɔŋ'ṇ←e] 5b. [ɔ'ṇ←e] 5c. [ṇ←e]

6a. [eŋ'nƀ←ʌ] 6b. [e'nƀ←ʌ] 6c. [nƀ←ʌ]

RE 31.11. Mimicry. Voiceless and Nasalized Clicks

1a. [r̃ø'p←oz] 1b. [r̃ø'm←oz] 1c. [r̃øp←om←]

2a. [r̃œ't̺←ʋz] 2b. [r̃œ'n̺←ʋz] 2c. [r̃œt̺←ʋn←]

3a. [r̃a't←iz] 3b. [r̃a'n←iz] 3c. [r̃a't←in←]

4a. [r̃u'c←ʌz] 4b. [r̃u'ñ←ʌz] 4c. [r̃u'c←ʌñ←]

5a. [r̃ɩ'ṭ←ɔz] 5b. [r̃ɩ'ṇ←ɔz] 5c. [r̃ɩ'ṭ←ɔṇ←]

6a. [r̃ə'tƀ←ez] 6b. [r̃ə'nƀ←ez] 6c. [r̃ə'tƀ←enƀ←]

Voiced Clicks

Voiced clicks are produced in a way analogous to nasalized ones, except that the velic is closed (Sammies 31.6 and 31.7). Lung air causes voicing by moving into the pharynx preceding and simultaneous with the click. A segmental diagram would differ from the one shown on p. 433 only by removal of the open velic.

The symbolization follows the same logic as that of nasalized clicks. [b←] is a [p←] with simultaneous voicing. Or, you can think of it as [g] and [p←] at the same time, because the back of the tongue is up simultaneously with the voicing.

RE 31.12 Demonstration: Voiced Clicks

a. Start with the sequence [gɑ gɑ gɑ gɑ] and then continue, making simultaneous clicks with it.

1. With [p←]: [gɑ gɑ gɑ gɑ b←ɑ b←ɑ b←ɑ b←ɑ]

2. With [t←]: [gɑ gɑ gɑ gɑ d←ɑ d←ɑ d←ɑ d←ɑ]

3. With [c←]: [gɑ gɑ gɑ gɑ j←ɑ j←ɑ j←ɑ j←ɑ]

4. With [ṭ←]: [gɑ gɑ gɑ gɑ ḍ←ɑ ḍ←ɑ ḍ←ɑ ḍ←ɑ]

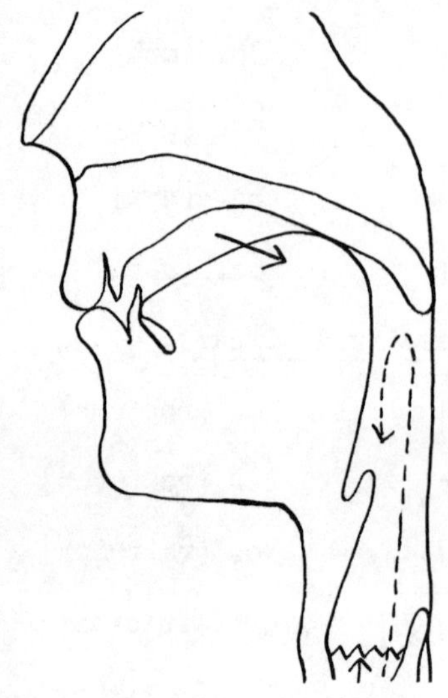

Sammy 31.6: [b←] Before Release

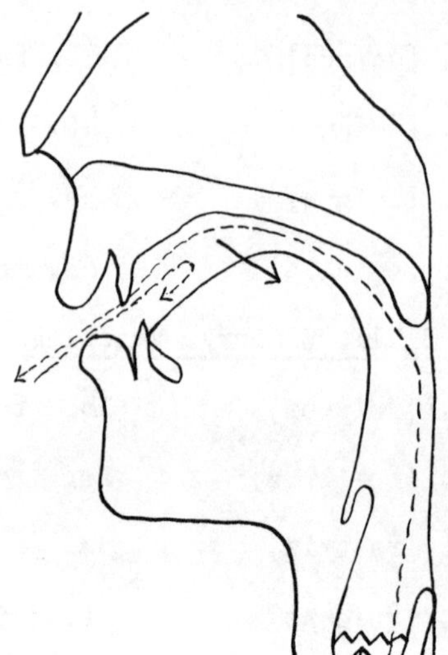

Sammy 31.7: [b←] After Release

5. With [tƚ←]: [gα gα gα gα dƚ←α dƚ←α dƚ←α dƚ←α]

b. Make a long vowel, and then articulate a [g] and the proper click simultaneously.

1. With [p←]: [α·'b←α α·'b←α]

2. With [t←]: [α·'d←α α·'d←α]

3. With [c←]: [α·'j←α α·'j←α]

4. With [ṭ←]: [α·'ḍ←α α·'ḍ←α]

5. With [tƚ←]: [α·'dƚ←α α·'dƚ←α]

RE 31.13. Differential: VOICED or VOICELESS

1.	[ɛ'ḍ←ɔ]	VD	5.	[xα't̂←œ]	VL	9.	[gɨ'ṭ←amM]	VL
2.	[ɔ'c←æ]	VL	6.	[xœ'b←ʋ]	VD	10.	[ga'd←ümM]	VD
3.	[æ'j←u]	VD	7.	[xʋ'dƚ←o]	VD	11.	[gü'tƚ←imM]	VL
4.	[u'p←α]	VL	8:	[xo'd←ɨ]	VD	12.	[gi'ḍ←umM]	VD

RE 31.14. Differential: VOICED or NASALIZED

1. [u'b←α]	V	6. [xo'n←ɨ]	N	11. [gɨ'ḍ←amM]	V
2. [æ'ñ←u]	N	7. [xα'ḓ←œ]	V	12. [gu'dŁ←imM]	V
3. [ɔ'j←æ]	V	8. [xoe'b←ü]	V	13. [ga'ṋ←ümM]	N
4. [e'dŁ←ε]	V	9. [xʋ'nƀ←ε]	N	14. [gi'ṇ←ʋmM]	N
5. [ε'ṇ←ɔ]	N	10. [xœ'm←ʋ]	N	15. [gʋ'd←œmM]	V

RE 31.15. Differential: CLICK or IMPLOSIVE

1. [ε'ḍ←ɔ]	C	5. [xα'ɗ̭œ]	I	9. [gɨ'ɗ̣amM]	I
2. [ɔ'ʄæ]	I	6. [xœ'b←ʋ]	C	10. [ga'ḓ←ümM]	C
3. [æ'j←u]	C	7. [xʋ'dƀ←o]	C	11. [gu'dŁ←imM]	I
4. [u'ɓα]	I	8. [xo'ɗɨ]	I	12. [gi'd̥←ʋmM]	C

RE 31.16. Mimicry: Voiced Clicks

1a. [ɩg'b←ε]	1b. [ɩ'b←ε]	1c. [b←ε]
2a. [εg'ḓ←ɵ]	2b. [ε'ḓ←ɵ]	2c. [ḓ←ɵ]
3a. [ɵg'd←ü]	3b. [ɵ'd←ü]	3c. [d←ü]
4a. [ug'j←ɔ]	4b. [u'j←ɔ]	4c. [j←ɔ]
5a. [ɔg'ḍ←e]	5b. [ɔ'ḍ←e]	5c. [ḍ←e]
6a. [eg'dŁ←ʌ]	6b. [e'dƀ←ʌ]	6c. [dƀ←ʌ]

RE 31.17. Mimicry: Voiced and Nasalized Clicks

1a. [ñø'm←oc^h]	1b. [ñø'b←oc^h]	1c. [ñø'm←ob←]
2a. [ñœ'ṋ←ʋc^h]	2b. [ñœ'ḓ←ʋc^h]	2c. [ñœ'ṋ←ʋd←]
3a. [ña'n←ic^h]	3b. [ña'd←ic^h]	3c. [ña'n←id←]
4a. [ñu'ñ←ʌc^h]	4b. [ñu'j←ʌc^h]	4c. [ñu'ñ←ʌj←]
5a. [ñɩ'ṇ←ɔc^h]	5b. [ñɩ'ḍ←ɔc^h]	5c. [ñɩ'ṇ←ɔḍ←]
6a. [ñə'nƀ←ec^h]	6b. [ñə'dƀ←ec^h]	6c. [ñə'nƀ←edƀ←]

RE 31.18. Negative Practice: Clicks

Make the indicated substitutions in the following English sentences.

1. p←eter p←ip←er p←icked a p←eck of p←ickled p←epp←ers

2. b←ig b←ad b←oy

3. m←other m←ake m←e m←uch m←ore m←ush

4. t←ake t←ommy t←o the t←rain

5. d←oes d←otty d←ream

6. n←ed n←ever kn←ew n←ancy's n←ew n←umber

7. t̥←ake ṭ←ommy ṭ←o the ṭ←rain

8. ḍ←oes ḍ←otty ḍ←ream

9. ṇ←ed ṇ←ever ṇ←ew ṇ←ancy's ṇ←ew ṇ←umber

RE 31.19: Zulu. Mimicry: Click Song

Listen to this song repeatedly and learn to sing it. When you can do it well with [ṭ←], substitute other clicks.

['ṭ←uɑ 'ṭ←ɑwɑ 'ṭ←uɑ 'ṭ←ɑ] (Repeat)

['ṭ←uɑ 'ṭ←ɑwɑ 'ṭ←i pil^i ṭ←i'ṭ←o˅] (Repeat)

[ṭ←i'ṭ←o˅l^iɑm ṭ←i'ṭ←o˅l^iɑm ṭ←i'ṭ←o˅l^iɑm ṭ←i'ṭ←o˅] (Repeat)

RE 31.20: Zulu. Mimicry: Clicks

Mimic the tape as it reads down each column. Each item is given only once, so you may want to repeat each column several times.

	Set 1		Set 2	
1.	['t←i•ma]	'extinguish'	['ṭ←i•na]	'too clean'
2.	[i't←i•t←i]	'ear ring'	[i"ṭ←ɑ•ṭ←ɑ]	'polecat'
3.	[isit←ɑ'tʰu•l^o]	'shoe'	[um'ṭ←ɑ•l^a]	'neck'

	Set 1		Set 2	
4.	['t←oˇ·l^a]	'setting the hair'	[i't←oˇ·t←o]	'to bully'
5.	[ɑmɑ't←u·l^o]	'they are hymns'	[ugu't←oˇ·nta]	'to understand'

	Set 3		Set 4	
1.	[ugu'tƚ←i·na]	'urge to hurry'	['tʰ←i·nsʔa]	'sprinkle'
2.	[tƚ←ɑ'tƚ←ɛ·la]	'relate'	['tʰ←ɑ·tʰ←ɑ]	'clean'
3.	[u'tƚ←ɑ·mu]	'frog'	['tʰ←oˇ·ma]	'to stick up'
4.	[i'tƚ←oˇ·tƚ←o]	'toad'	[u'tʰ←u·ku]	'trouble'
5.	[u'tʰi·tƚ←o]	'God'		

	Set 5		Set 6	
1.	[tʰ←ɑ·tʰ←a]	'to tear apart'	[tLʰ←tLʰ←i·ma]	'be excited'
2.	[itʰ←u'tL←ɑ·nɛ]	'it is a hut'	[i'tƚʰ←i·ba]	'cookhouse'
3.	[ugu'tʰ←u·ma]	'to burst'	[ugu'tƚʰ←u·ma]	'to join'
4.	[ugu'tʰ←u·tʰ←a]	'to shiver'	['tƚʰ←u·tƚʰ←a]	'boil something thick'
5.			[tƚʰ←u'tLʰ←u·ma]	'to be restless'

	Set 7		Set 8	
1.	[in←wɑ·ti]	'it is a book'	[i'n←i·na]	'the hunt'

2.	[ka'n←α•nε^]	'little'	[umvεli"n←α•ŋk?i]	'God'
3.	[i"n←wi•n←wi]	'honeybird'	['n←ε•na]	'lazy'
4.	[i"n←wα•n←wa]	'paste'	[i'si•n←ε]	'small of back'
5.			[n←oᵛŋk?a]	'pile up'
6.			[i'n←oᵛ•l^a]	'wagon'

	Set 9		Set 10	
1.	[i"nƀ←i•wa]	'abandoned site'	[d←i•na]	'to end'
2.	[nƀ←a]	'if'	[d←α•ɓa]	'to incise'
3.	['nƀ←α•pʰa]	(exclamation)	[d←wα•l^a]	'to fill'
4.	[nƀ←ul^u'pe•ni]	'place'	[d←oᵛ•na]	'to tease'

	Set 11		Set 12	
1.	[d←in's i•l^a]	'slam down'	['dƀ←i•l^a]	'sink into'
2.	['d←i•za]	'ankle decoration'	['dƀ←α•za]	'to ooze out'
3.	['d←i•ba]	'cover'	['dƀ←oᵛ•ba]	'smash'
4.	['d←u•ma]	'to groan'	[dƀ←u'mε^•ga]	'plunge into ground'
5.			['dƀ←u•ma]	'to jump'

LESSON THIRTY-TWO

Pharyngealized Sounds

	Front U.	Front R.	Central U.	Central R.	Back U.	Back R.
High	ḭ					ṵ
Lower-high	ɪ̰		ɨ̰			ʊ̰
Mid	ḛ					o̰
Lower-mid	ɛ̰		ə̰			
Low	æ̰		ʌ̰			ɔ̰
Lower-low	a̰		ɑ̰			

Table 32.1: Pharyngealized Vowels

Pharyngealization is a modification of articulation such that the pharyngeal cavity is constricted, usually by drawing the root of the tongue back into it as in Sammies 32.1 and 32.2. Any vowel or consonant may be pharyngealized, but the pharyngealization is not heard as easily on consonants as on vowels. In those languages where pharyngealized consonants occur some of the pharyngealized consonants are detected primarily by the fact that the surrounding vowels are colored by the pharyngealization as well. On some consonants pharyngealization is more easily heard than others, and we will emphasize them.

Pharyngealized consonants are symbolized in the same way as pharyngealized vowels, by a wavy line under the usual symbol for the basic articulation. This gives us [f̰ s̰ l̰ n̰], etc. Sammies 32.3 and 32.4 give the articulations for two pharyngealized consonants.

Pharyngealization is extremely important in Arabic and some related languages of the Middle East and North and East Africa. It is to be found in some other languages as well.

RE 32.1. Demonstration: Producing Pharyngealized Vowels

a. Start with the vowel [ɑ] and pull the root of the tongue downwards (opening up a larger cavity in the back of the mouth) and backwards (pushing into the pharyngeal cavity

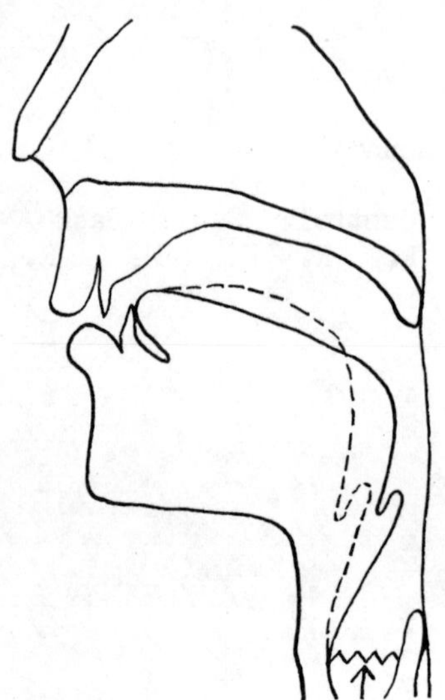

Sammy 32.1: [ɛ̰]. The pharyngealized vowel is shown by the solid line. A non-pharyngealized [ɛ] is shown by the broken line.

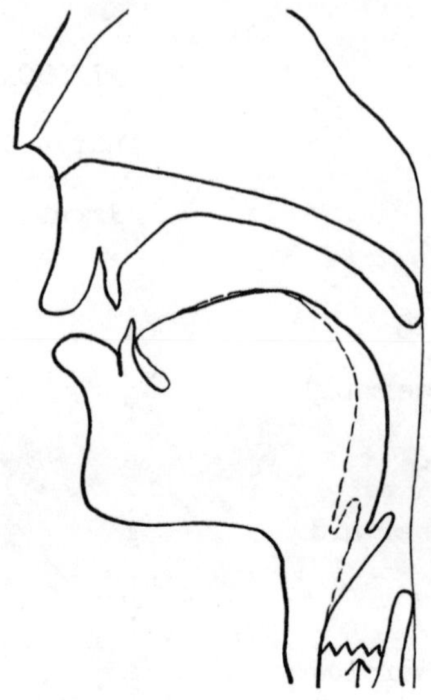

Sammy 32.2: [o̰]. The solid line shows the pharyngealized vowel and the broken one the corresponding non-pharyngealized vowel.

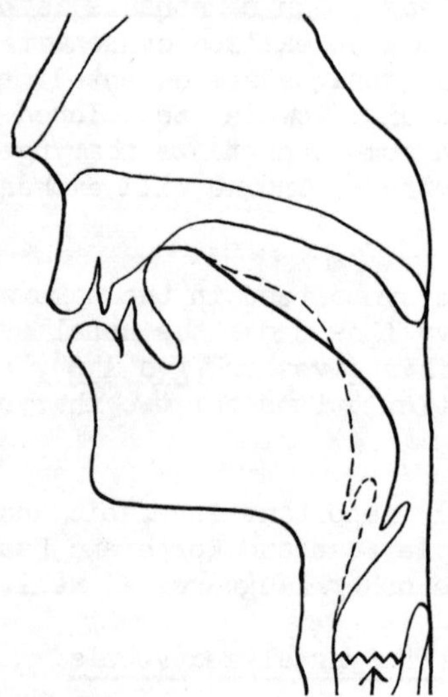

Sammy 32.3: [l̰]

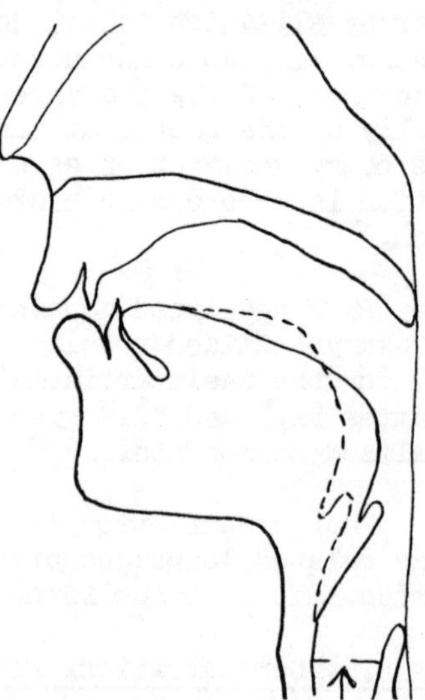

Sammy 32.4: [f̰]

and making it smaller). This gives you [ɑ· ɑ̰·]. Move the root of the tongue backwards and forwards to get [ɑ·ɑ̰·ɑ·ɑ̰·ɑ·ɑ̰·ɑ·].

b. If you have difficulty doing this, press the back of your tongue down and back with the handle of a spoon or with a pencil and say [ɑ̰·] as you do in the doctor's office. By moving the spoon or pencil, help yourself get the feel of [ɑ· ɑ̰· ɑ· ɑ̰· ɑ· ɑ̰·].

c. With your thumb and forefinger on your throat just under the chin and above the larynx, push inward and downward on your throat gently as you say [ɑ·]. Then push in and out to get [ɑ·ɑ̰·ɑ·ɑ̰·ɑ·].

d. Stand in front of a mirror and watch the back of your tongue as you practice going from [ɑ·] to [ɑ̰·].

e. Practice talking English with the root of your tongue way down and back. Read this paragraph in this style in the same manner the tape does.

f. Follow these same procedures on other vowels to give you sequences like these:

1. [ɔ· ɔ̰· ɔ· ɔ̰· ɔ· ɔ̰·]	3. [o· o̰· o· o̰· o· o̰·]
2. [æ· æ̰· æ· æ̰· æ· æ̰·]	4. [e· ḛ· e· ḛ· e· ḛ·]

g. Listen repeatedly to the tape demonstration of the vowels in Table 32.1. Learn to read off the vowel chart with the tape.

RE 32.2. Differential: LARYNGEALIZED or PHARYNGEALIZED

You may have noticed in the demonstrations above that the pharyngealized vowels had something of the same rasping quality as the laryngealized vowels of Lesson 28. This may have been due in part to actual laryngealization along with the pharyngealization, but not entirely. The constriction in the pharynx caused by the pulling back of the root of the tongue can create a rasping quality reminiscent of laryngealization.

Regardless of the similarity, however, laryngealized and pharyngealized vowels can be distinguished because of the other differences of quality. The more open mouth cavity and the more constricted pharyngeal cavity in pharyngealization produces a sound quite different from the laryngealized vowel. Listen to the tape and decide whether the vowel is LARYNGEALIZED or PHARYNGEALIZED. Don't peek!

1. [ɑ̰·] P	6. [zỏ·] L	11. [nu'vủ·] L
2. [ɑ̉·] L	7. [zỉ·] L	12. [nu'vḛ·] P
3. [ẻ·] L	8. [zɛ̰·] P	13. [nu'vɩ̉·] L
4. [æ̰·] P	9. [zʌ̰·] P	14. [nu'vʌ̉·] L
5. [ɔ̰·] P	10. [zo̰·] P	15. [nu'vɑ̰·] P

RE 32.3. Mimicry: Pharyngealized Vowels

1a. [ɑ̰·]	1b. [lˇɑ̰·]	1c. [yo'tʰɑ̰·]
2a. [æ̰·]	2b. [lˇæ̰·]	2c. [yo'tʰæ̰·]
3a. [ɔ̰·]	3b. [lˇɔ̰·]	3c. [yo'tʰɔ̰·]
4a. [ʌ̰·]	4b. [lˇʌ̰·]	4c. [yo'tʰʌ̰·]
5a. [o̰·]	5b. [lˇo̰·]	5c. [yo'tʰo̰·]
6a. [ɛ̰·]	6b. [lˇɛ̰·]	6c. [yo'tʰɛ̰·]
7a. [ḛ·]	7b. [lˇḛ·]	7c. [yo'tʰḛ·]
8a. [ɨ̰·]	8b. [lˇɨ̰·]	8c. [yo'tʰɨ̰·]

Pharyngealized Glides

The Arabic languages have two sounds which are actually pharyngealized vowel glides, although they are used as consonants in the phonemic system. This should not be surprising, since English glides such as [y w r] are used as consonants also. In Arabic these pharyngealized glides are called ayin and ha, and are voiced and voiceless respectively. They are distinguished from pharyngealized vowels by the fact that they are non-syllabic, that they do not carry the syllable beat. They move into, or out of, roughly an [ɑ̰] position.

The symbols which we will use for these two glides are [9̰] for the voiced one and [h̰] for the voiceless. In the latter case a "pharyngealized h" makes a good description of the sound, so the symbol is appropriate. The symbol 9, however, is arbitrary. It does have the advantage that the English word nine sounds something like the Arabic word ayin for anyone who happens to remember it.

RE 32.4. Demonstration: Pharyngealized Glides

a. [ʕ̰] is a movement into or out of [ɑ̰] position. Mimic the demonstration in various positions:

1. [ɑʕ̰ɑ ɑʕ̰ɑ ʕ̰ɑ ʕ̰ɑ ɑʕ̰ ɑʕ̰]   3. [eʕ̰e eʕ̰e ʕ̰e ʕ̰e eʕ̰ eʕ̰]

2. [ɔʕ̰ɔ ɔʕ̰ɔ ʕ̰ɔ ʕ̰ɔ ɔʕ̰ ɔʕ̰]   4. [uʕ̰u uʕ̰u ʕ̰u ʕ̰u uʕ̰ uʕ̰]

b. To produce [h̰] say [h] and pull the root of the tongue back and down. The stricture in the pharynx does not need to be quite so great as for [ʕ̰]. Use the same devices as in RE 32.1 to help you get the pharyngeal constriction. Or, say [ʕ̰] without voicing. Practice these sequences:

1. [ɑh̰ɑ ɑh̰ɑ h̰ɑ h̰ɑ ɑh̰ ɑh̰]   3. [eh̰e eh̰e h̰e h̰e eh̰ eh̰]

2. [ɔh̰ɔ ɔh̰ɔ h̰ɔ h̰ɔ ɔh̰ ɔh̰]   4. [uh̰u uh̰u h̰u h̰u uh̰ uh̰]

RE 32.5. Differential: GLOTTAL or PHARYNGEALIZED

[ʕ̰], when pronounced rapidly, may be confused with [ʔ]. Respond with GLOTTAL or PHARYNGEALIZED.

1. ['zɑʔɑ] G	5. ['fiʕ̰ɑl^u] P	9. ['ʔunoveŋ] G
2. ['zɑʕ̰ɑ] P	6. ['fḭʕɑl^u] P	10. ['ʕ̰unoveŋ] P
3. ['zɑʕ̰ɑ] P	7. ['fiʔɑl^u] G	11. ['ʕṵnoveŋ] P
4. ['zɑʔɑ] G	8. ['fiʕɑ̰l^u] P	12. ['ʔunoveŋ] G

RE 32.6. Differential: [h] or PHARYNGEALIZED

1. ['zɑhɑ] h	5. ['fih̰ɑl^u] P	9. ['hunoveŋ] h
2. ['zɑh̰ɑ] P	6. ['fih̰ɑl^u] P	10. ['h̰unoveŋ] P
3. ['zɑhɑ] h	7. ['fihɑl^u] h	11. ['hṵnoveŋ] P
4. ['zɑh̰ɑ] P	8. ['fih̰ɑl^u] P	12. ['hunoveŋ] h

RE 32.7. Mimicry: [ʕ̰]

1a. [sɨ'ʕ̰ɒŋæ]	1b. [ʕ̰ɒ'ŋæsɨ]	1c. ['ŋæsɨʕ̰]
2a. [sʌ'ʕ̰oŋɩ]	2b. [ʕ̰o'ŋɩsʌ]	2c. ['ŋɩsʌʕ̰]
3a. [sɔ'ʕ̰øŋə]	3b. [ʕ̰ø'ŋəsɔ]	3c. ['ŋəsɔʕ̰]

4a. [se'9̰aŋi]   4b. [9̰a'ŋise]   4c. ['ŋise9̰]

5a. [su'9̰œŋu]   5b. [9̰œ'ŋusu]   5c. ['ŋusu9̰]

6a. [sɨ'9̰əŋɑ]   6b. [9̰ə'ŋɑsɨ]   6c. ['ŋɑsɨ9̰]

7a. [sɩ'9̰oŋɔ]   7b. [9̰o'ŋɔsɩ]   7c. ['ŋɔsɩ9̰]

8a. [sɛ'9̰æŋʋ]   8b. [9̰æ'ŋʋsɛ]   8c. ['ŋʋsɛ9̰]

RE 32.8. Mimicry: [h̰]

1a. [šɨ'h̰ʋṇæ]   1b. [h̰ʋ'ṇæšɨ]   1c. ['ṇæšɨh̰]

2a. [šʌ'h̰oṇɩ]   2b. [h̰o'ṇɩšʌ]   2c. ['ṇɩšʌh̰]

3a. [šɔ'h̰øṇə]   3b. [h̰ø'ṇəšɔ]   3c. ['ṇəšɔh̰]

4a. [še'h̰œṇu]   4b. [h̰œ'ṇuše]   4c. ['ṇušeh̰]

5a. [šü'h̰aṇi]   5b. [h̰a'ṇišü]   5c. ['ṇišüh̰]

6a. [šɨ'h̰əṇɑ]   6b. [h̰ə'ṇɑšɨ]   6c. ['ṇɑšɨh̰]

7a. [šɩ'h̰oṇɔ]   7b. [h̰o'ṇɔšɩ]   7c. ['ṇɔšɩh̰]

8a. [šɛ'h̰æṇʋ]   8b. [h̰æ'ṇʋšɛ]   8c. ['ṇʋšɛh̰]

RE 32.9. Mimicry: [9̰][1]

1a. ['tɑ9̰ɑ]   1b. [9̰u·d]   1c. [be'l^ɑ9̰]

2a. ['zɑ9̰ɑl^]   2b. [9̰ɑ·l^]   2c. [bʌ'l^ɩ9̰]

3a. [mʌl^'9̰ɑb]   3b. [9̰i·ř]   3c. [dʌ'fɑ9̰]

4a. ['zum9̰ɑ]   4b. ['9̰ɩlbi]   4c. [xʌ'l^ɑ9̰]

5a. [mɑ9̰'mu·l^]   5b. ['9̰i·řʌ]   5c. [bɩ'šɩ9̰]

6a. [tɑ9̰'kæ·n]   6b. ['9̰ɑ·l^i]   6c. [l^ʌ'mɑ9]

Pharyngealized Consonants

Pharyngealized consonants are made by lowering the back of the tongue and constricting the pharyngeal cavity, just as

---

[1]Examples from Robert E. Maston, Lebanese Spoken Arabic. Recording is simulated from the transcription.

	Bilabial	Dental	Alveolar	Velar	Glide
Vl. stops	p̰		t̰	k̰	
Vd. stops	b̰		d̰	g̰	
Vl. fricatives		f̰	s̰	x̰	
Vd. fricatives		ṽ	z̰	g̰	
Nasals	m̰		n̰		
Lateral			l̰		
Flap			ř̰		
Voiceless					ḛ
Voiced					ʕ̰

Table 32.2: Some Pharyngealized Consonants and Glides. Theoretically nearly any consonant can be pharyngealized, but these are presented as a sample.

are pharyngealized vowels. The regular consonant articulation is otherwise maintained as nearly as possible (Sammies 32.3 and 32.4). In the case of a continuant like a fricative or nasal, it is sometimes possible to hear the actual pharyngeal quality during the articulation of the consonant, but in any case pharyngealized consonants are more readily recognizable by the resulting pharyngealization on an adjacent vowel. The pharyngealization of the vowel may be non-phonemic, but it may provide the necessary clue to the pharyngealized consonant.[1]

RE 32.10. Producing Pharyngealized Consonants

a. Follow this sequence in mimicry of the tape:

1. [α·ʕ̰·α·ʕ̰·α·ʕ̰·α·] 3. [z·z̰·z·z̰·z·z̰·z·]

2. [m·m̰·m·m̰·m·m̰·m·] 4. [l·l̰·l·l̰·l·l̰·l·]

[1]This is not an unusual phenomenon. In fact, the acoustic clues of most sounds overlap. Since voiceless stops, for example, are completely noiseless, we cannot distinguish them on the sounds of the stops themselves, but on the basis of the different quality they give adjacent sounds.

5. [v·v̰·v·v̰·v·v̰·v·]

b. Place the pharyngealized consonants between pharyngealized vowels:

1. [ɑ̰m̰ɑ̰ ḛm̰ḛ ṵm̰ṵ æ̰m̰æ̰ ɨ̰m̰ɨ̰ ɔ̰m̰ɔ̰]

2. [ɑ̰z̰ɑ̰ ḛz̰ḛ ṵz̰ṵ æ̰z̰æ̰ ɨ̰z̰ɨ̰ ɔ̰z̰ɔ̰]

3. [ɑ̰l̰ɑ̰ ḛl̰ḛ ṵl̰ṵ æ̰l̰æ̰ ɨ̰l̰ɨ̰ ɔ̰l̰ɔ̰]

4. [ɑ̰v̰ɑ̰ ḛv̰ḛ ṵv̰ṵ æ̰v̰æ̰ ɨ̰v̰ɨ̰ ɔ̰v̰ɔ̰]

c. Continue to practice talking with the back of your tongue down and the base pulled back into the pharyngeal cavity.

RE 32.11. Mimicry: Non-pharyngealized and Pharyngealized Sequences

1a. [ɑzɑ ɑ̰z̰ɑ̰ ɑzɑ ɑ̰z̰ɑ̰] 1b. [ɑ̰z̰ z̰ɑ̰ ɑz zɑ]

2a. [ɑmɑ ɑ̰m̰ɑ̰ ɑmɑ ɑ̰m̰ɑ̰] 2b. [ɑ̰m̰ m̰ɑ̰ ɑm mɑ]

3a. [æbæ æ̰b̰æ̰ æbæ æ̰b̰æ̰] 3b. [æ̰b̰ b̰æ̰ æb bæ]

4a. [ælæ æ̰l̰æ̰ ælæ æ̰l̰æ̰] 4b. [æ̰l̰ l̰æ̰ æl læ]

5a. [ořo o̰ř̰o̰ ořo o̰ř̰o̰] 5b. [o̰ř̰ ř̰o̰ oř rǒ]

6a. [oko o̰ḵo̰ oko o̰ḵo̰] 6b. [o̰ḵ ḵo̰ ok ko]

7a. [ete ḛṯḛ ete ḛṯḛ] 7b. [ḛṯ ṯḛ et te]

8a. [eve ḛv̰ḛ eve ḛv̰ḛ] 8b. [ḛv̰ v̰ḛ ev ve]

RE 32.12. Negative Practice: "Old MacDonald Had a Farm"

Get a thorough review of some of the vowel qualities and the modifications of vowel quality by singing "Old MacDonald" with the following progressions. The tape demonstrates some of them.

a. Back unrounded: "With a [ʔɯ ʔɯ] here..." Continue with [ɤ ɒ].

b. Front rounded: [ü ø œ]

c. Central unrounded: [ʌ ə ɨ]

d. Nasalized: [ą æ̨ ɛ̨ ę ɩ̨ į ɔ̨ ǫ ʋ̨ ų ɑ̨ ʌ̨ ə̨ ɨ̨ œ̨ ø̨ ų̈ ɒ̨ ɤ̨ ɯ̨]

e. Voiceless: [I E Æ A Ɔ O U]

f. Laryngealized: [æ̉ ẻ ỉ ɑ̉ ʌ̉ ɔ̉ ỏ ủ]

g. Pharyngealized: [æ̰ ḛ ḭ ɑ̰ ʌ̰ ɔ̰ o̰ ṵ]

h. Breathy: [æ̟ e̟ i̟ ɑ̟ ʌ̟ ɔ̟ o̟ u̟]

i. With off-glides [y w r H ʕ̰ Y W h ẖ]

j. With on-glides [y w r ʕ̰ Y W h ẖ]

k. Clusters [eɑ ɛɨ æɔ ɔʌ iæ]

l. Long: [a· æ· ɛ· e· ɩ· i· ɔ· o· ʋ· u· ɑ· ʌ· ə· ɨ· œ· ø· ü· ɒ· ɤ· ɯ·]

RE 32.13: Gola. Review: Pitch, Consonants, Vowels, Nasalization

The text of this exercise will be found as RE 8.18 (pp. 131-135). There was not time to include it in the tape for that lesson, so it is being included here on the tape for this lesson as a review, without repeating the text from Lesson 8. Mimic consonants, vowels, and tone very carefully.

RE 32.14: Mano. Review: Pitch, Consonants, Vowels, Nasalization

Mimic the following exercise closely. As you go over it several times, study the difference in tone on [yi] (the last syllable) in Nos. 1, 4, and 5. This shows the effect of intonation on the inherent tone of the syllable. In phrase final position the mid tone falls for statements, negative imperatives, and questions containing question words. It is level for affirmative commands, and rising (or slightly higher level) for questions without question words.

1.	[agɛ̨yi]	a gɛ̃̀ yi	'He saw it there.'
2.	[ɓa·gɛ̨yi]	ɓáá gɛ̃̀ yi!	'Don't look at it there!'
3.	[mɛ̨·pɛ̨lɛ̨ agɛ̨yi]	mɛ́ɛ̃ pɛ̃́ lɛ́ a gɛ̃̀ yi?	'When did he see it there?'
4.	[agɛ̨yi]	à gɛ̃̀ yi!	'Look at it there.'

5. [agɛyi] a gɛ̀ yi? 'Did he see it there?'

6. [agɛyi] a gɛ̀ yi 'He saw it there.'

7. [agɛyi] à gɛ̀ yi! 'Look at it there.'

8. [agɛyi] a gɛ̀ yiʔ 'Did he see it there?'

RE 32.15: Mano. Review: Longer Sequences

In this exercise mimic closely, watching for the differences of tone in the initial syllables, and reproducing accurately the vowel qualities and nasalization.

1. [ˌyɩřiˌwaˈyi] yílí wá yi
   'Trees are not there.'
2. [ˌzʊřuˌwaˈyi] zulu wá yi
   'Driver ants are not there.'
3. [ˈwi·waˈyi] wìì wá yi
   'Animals are not there.'
4. [ˌkoˈka ˌgɛyaˈřa] ko ka gɛ̀ yalá
   'We saw a house yesterday.'
5. [ˌkoˈgɔ· ˌgɛyaˈřa] ko gɔɔ gɛ̀ yalá
   'We saw a canoe yesterday.'
6. [ˌkoˈdi· ˌgɛyaˈřa] ko dìì gɛ̀ yalá
   'We saw a cow yesterday.'
7. [ˈsi·ˌeˈyɩHlɛˌᵍbe›ˌke›ˈnɩ] síí e yía lɛ gbèkènĩ
   'That hawk is far away.'
8. [ˈziʔ ˌeˈyɩHlɛˌᵍbe›ˌke›ˈnɩ] zi e yía lɛ gbèkènĩ
   'That road is far away.'
9. [ˌmɛnɛ eˈyɩHlɛˌᵍbe›ˌke›ˈnɩ] m̀ɛnɛ̀ e yía lɛ gbèkènĩ
   'That tsetse fly is far away.'

RE 32.16. Transcription

Use the special transcription form for RE 32.16 in the

Workbook Supplement, pp. 101-102. Listen to the tape, and fill in the blanks in the Supplement.

1. [pʰønʋˈzã̰ˀ·ʔɨ̰]
2. [yʌ·ˈlˆ ɔ̟kʰɛdu]
3. [ˈmiřœpɔ·ja]
4. [yʌ̰dü·cʰṻˈgɨ]
5. [sɩˈwǿñob̰ḭ]
6. [tɔ·ˈtʰɨ̰p̰ǿlˆ Æ·]
7. [šAˈbʋẓ̌ʋkʰə·]
8. [wḛ̃ˀŋəhʌˈye]
9. [roxAˈwu·mI]
10. [ˈhɛ·fʌy̰ɑ̰pʰu]
11. [pʰeˈm←iŋʋkʔ]
12. [ᵏposiˈɗɑgɑ]
13. [ḳiˈsʔɛʔnɔl̃i]
14. [batʰɛv·aˈƙe]
15. [pʔɩḍʌˈwɔfʔ]
16. [nəb·ʔ̰æˈɠæy]
17. [h̰ɩˈlˆ o̰habʰ̟ɨ]
18. [ˈɓʌj̟ʰen·otʔ]
19. [z̰ɑ̰ʔ̰iˈžɩŋƭu]
20. [ˈtɓ←ɔtʰʌz·æcʔ]

Reading

Use RE 23.2-32.3, 32.5-32.9, 32.14-32.16.

PS: Phonetician's Theme Song

As the last recorded item in this, the last regular lesson of this Manual, we present a song composed by Ray Williamson, and performed by Joe Karcher, Nancy Karcher, and Hank Schaftsmaa at the Missionary Training Conference, Meadville, Pa., July, 1958.

I was a simple soul with just one language grid;
I spoke the English tongue - 'twas all I ever did,
But at phonetics school my tongue began to skid.
Now I say, [u· i· u ɑ ɑ

tʰɩ·ŋ tʰæ·ŋ wɑlɑ wɑlɑ bɩŋ bæŋ

u· i· u ɑ ɑ

tʰɩŋ tʰæŋ wɑlɑ wɑlɑ bɩŋ bæŋ]

You've been makin' sounds at us
Just like you were a chicken.

For glottal stops we never had to beg.
Now you do very well at this,
    But there's one thing we wonder -
We'd really like to see you lay an egg.

The only witch doctors are not in Timbuctoo.
For there are several here who sit right there with you.
And they will teach you how to gargle, trill, and coo,
And you'll say, [u· i· u ɑ ɑ

tʰɪ·ŋ tʰæ·ŋ wɑlɑ wɑlɑ bɪŋ bæŋ

u· i· u ɑ ɑ

tʰɪŋ tʰæŋ wɑlɑ wɑlɑ bɪŋ bæŋ]

(Repeat the chorus nasalized and then whispered.)

HEAVENS NO, OLD CHAP! NOT VOO-DOO!
IT'S AN ARTICULATORY PHONETICS DRILL!

LESSON THIRTY-THREE

Review and Summary

Previous review lessons have not involved recorded materials, but in this lesson we give a tape summary of much of the course, as well as the usual content of review lessons. Students who have completed the course would not want to have a complete set of thirty-two tapes but may find that by owning the one tape for this lesson they have something to refer to and to review by in the future.[1]

Consonants

In Table 33.1 you have all of the types of consonants of the course symbolized, plus an additional number in parentheses which have not been drilled, although in some cases they may be as common as some which were drilled. We cannot emphasize strongly enough that you must not assume that this table is complete in any sense of the word. The best we can say is that is is representative of most of the general types of consonantal speech sounds (as defined in terms of articulation) to be found in natural languages of the world.

Almost all of these consonant types can be modified in a variety of ways, of which some are included below and some are not. It would have been possible to devise a chart with more points of articulation, and more varieties of manner. It would have been possible to fill in some of the blanks on the chart we now have. Theoretically the number of possible consonant sounds is ever so much larger than this. Our chart simply gives us some of the major types around which most of the others can be grouped as modifications.

RE 33.1. Mimicry: Table 33.1

In this exercise we demonstrate all of the consonants of Table 33.1 except for those in parentheses. The tape reads across each line, using the frame [...α ...α ...α α...α α...α α...α α... α... α...] for each consonant. On the first few sounds you are given the labels as well to help you orient yourself until you get in the rhythm of the thing. The vowel is occasionally changed for variety. Follow along in Table 33.1 as you mimic the tape.

---

[1]A notice of where tapes are obtainable is included elsewhere in this book.

	Double	Bilabial	Labio-Dental	Dental
EGRESSIVE LUNG AIR				
STOPS				
Vl. unaspirated	^{k}p	p	(p̭)	ṱ
Vl. aspirated		p^h	(p̭^{h})	ṱ^h
Vd. unaspirated	^{g}b	b	(b̭)	ḓ
Vd. aspirated		b̟^{h}	(b̭̟^{h})	ḓ̟^{h}
Vl. flap				(ṱ̆)
Vd. flap				(ḓ̆)
FRICATIVES				
Vl. flat		ᵽ	f	θ
Vd. flat		ƀ	v	đ
Vl. grooved				s̭
Vd. grooved				z̭
Vl. lateral				(ɬ̭)
Vd. lateral				(ɫ̭)
AFFRICATES[2]				
Vl. flat unaspirated		pᵽ	pf	ṱθ
Vl. flat aspirated		pᵽ^h	pf^h	ṱθ^h
Vd. flat		bƀ	bv	ḓđ
Vl. grooved unaspirated				ṱs̭
Vl. grooved aspirated				ṱs̭^{h}
Vd. grooved				ḓz̭
Vl. lateral unaspirated				(ṱɬ̭)
Vl. lateral aspirated				(ṱɬ̭^{h})

Alveolar	Alveopalatal	Retroflexed	Palatal	Mid Velar	Backed Velar	Uvular	Glottal
t	c	ṭ	k̭	k	ḳ		ʔ
t^h	c^h	ṭ^h	k̭^{h}	k^h	ḳ^h		
d	j	ḍ	g̭	g	g̣		
d̟^{h}	j̟^{h}	ḍ̟^{h}	g̭̟^{h}	g̟^{h}	g̣̟^{h}		
ť		(ṭ̌)	(ḍ̌)				
ď							
(θ)	(ȼ)		x̭	x	x̣		h
(đ)	(ɉ)		ǥ̭	ǥ	ǥ̣		
s	š	ṣ̌	(x̭	x	x̣)[1]		
z	ž	ẓ̌	(ǥ̭	ǥ	ǥ̣)[1]		
ƚ	(ƚ̌)	(ƚ̣)	(ƚj̭)	(ƚj)			
ł	(ł̌)	(ł̣)	(łj̭)	(łj)			
			k̭x̭	kx	ḳx̣		
			k̭x̭^{h}	kx^h	ḳx̣^{h}		
			g̭ǥ̭	gǥ	g̣ǥ̣		
ts	č	ṭṣ̌					
ts^h	č^h	ṭṣ̌^{h}					
dz	ǰ	ḍẓ̌					
tƚ	(cƚ̌)	(ṭƚ̣)	(k̭ƚj̭)	(kƚj)			
tƚ^h	(cƚ̌^{h})	(ṭƚ̣^{h})	(k̭ƚj̭^{h})	(kƚj^h)			

	Double	Bilabial	Labio-Dental	Dental
Vd. lateral				(ḓɫ̭)
NASALS				
Voiceless		M	(Ɱ)	Ṋ
Voiced	ŋm	m	(ɱ)	ṋ
Vd. flap				(ṋ̌)
LATERALS[3]				
Voiceless				(Ḽ)
Vd. high tongue				ḽˆ
Vd. low tongue				ḽˇ
Vd. flap				(ḽ̌)
TRILLS				
Voiceless		(p̃)		(R̭̃)
Voiced		(b̃)		(r̭̃)
FLAPS (cupped tongue)[4]				
Voiceless				(Ř̭)
Voiced				(Ř̭)
<u>EGRESSIVE PHARYNX AIR (GLOTTALIZED)</u>				
STOPS				
Vl. unaspirated		pˀ		ṱˀ
Vd. unaspirated		(bˀ)		(ḓˀ)
FRICATIVES				
Voiceless		ɸˀ	fˀ	θˀ
<u>INGRESSIVE PHARYNX AIR (IMPLOSIVE)</u>				
STOPS				
Vl. unaspirated	kƥ	ƥ		ƭ̭
Vd. unaspirated	gɓ	ɓ		ɗ̭

Alveolar	Alveopalatal	Retroflexed	Palatal	Mid Velar	Backed Velar	Uvular	Glottal
dɫ	(j̃ɫ)	(d̤ɫ)	(gɫ̡)	(gɫ̡)			
N	Ñ	Ṇ	Ŋ̭	Ŋ	Ŋ̣		
n	ñ	ṇ	ŋ̭	ŋ	ŋ̣		
ň		(ṇ̌)					
L	(L̃)	(Ḷ)	(Ḽ̡)	(L̡)			
l^	l̃		(ḽ̡)	(l̡)			
lˇ		(ḷ)					
ľ		(ḷ̌)					
R̃						Ṛ̃	
r̃						ṛ̃	
Ř							
ř						(ṛ̌)	
tʔ	cʔ	ṭʔ	k̭ʔ	kʔ	ḳʔ		
(dʔ)	(jʔ)	(ḍʔ)	(g̭ʔ)	(gʔ)	(g̣ʔ)		
sʔ	šʔ	ṣ̌ʔ	x̭ʔ	xʔ	x̣ʔ		
ƭ	ƈ	ƭ̣	ƙ̭	ƙ	ƙ̣		
ɗ	ʄ	ɗ̣	ɠ̭	ɠ	ɠ̣		

	Double	Bilabial	Labio-Dental	Dental
FRICATIVES				
Voiceless		(ɸ)	(f)	(θ)
Voiced		(β)	(v)	(ð)
INGRESSIVE MOUTH AIR (CLICK)				
CENTRAL				
Vl. unaspirated		p←		ṱ←
Vl. aspirated		p^h←		ṱ^h←
Voiced		b←		ḓ←
Nasalized		m←		ṋ←
LATERAL				
Vl. unaspirated				
Vl. aspirated				
Voiced				
Nasalized				

Table 33.1: Consonants Studied

---

[1]We have not distinguished between flat and grooved fricatives in velar position, although both are possible. We have used either, indiscriminately.

[2]For affricates with different points of articulation on the stop and fricative, see p. 138.

[3]Lateral fricatives and affricates are shown under fricatives and affricates, respectively.

[4]Nasal flaps are shown under nasals, lateral flaps under laterals, and flat tongue flaps under stops.

Alveolar	Alveopalatal	Retroflexed	Palatal	Mid Velar	Backed Velar	Uvular	Glottal
(ś)	(š)	(ṣ̌)	(x̂)	(x)	(x̣)		
(ź)	(ž)	(ẓ̌)	(ĝ)	(g)	(g̣)		
t←	c←	ṭ←					
tʰ←	ch←	ṭʰ←					
d←	j←	ḍ←					
n←	ñ←	ṇ←					
tƀ←							
tƀʰ←							
dƀ←							
nƀ←							

in This Course, And Some Others

RE 33.2. Mimicry: Additional Modifications to Consonants

Each of the consonants in Table 33.1 can be modified in many ways, some of which are reviewed in this exercise. Each modification is demonstrated with a small number of consonants. When possible, the same frame will be used as in the preceding drill. Mimic the tape and follow along in the *Manual*. The pages where these modifications are discussed are indicated in parentheses. The modifications will often carry over the vowels as well.

a. Long (p. 269): [m· l· k· j· v·]

b. Syllabic (p. 152): [n̩p l̩p z̩p x̩p r̩p] and [pn̩ pl̩ pz̩ px̩ pr̩].

c. Pharyngealized (p. 446): [ŋ̰ l̰ p̰ d̰ ƀ̰]

d. Unreleased (p. 345): [b- ñ- k- t-]

e. With voiced release (p. 345): [bə ñə kə tə]

f. With voiced open transition (p. 348): [bən təl sək ñəd]

g. With voiceless open transition (p. 348): [t^hn p^hd c^hz]

h. With close transition (p. 348): [bn sk pd tl]

i. Fortis (p. 387): [p̯ s̤ p̤ʔ t̤←]

j. Lenis (p. 387): [p̨ ş p̨ʔ ţ←]

k. Nasalized (p. 333): [l̨ z̨ v̨ g̨]

The following modifications have not been specifically discussed in connection with consonants in this Manual, but they are also possible. These are not recorded.

l. Laryngealized: [m̉ n̉ l̉ z̉ b̉]

m. Breathy: [m̟ n̟ l̟ z̟ v̟]

n. Rounded: [t̮ m̮ f̮ t̮s̮]

o. Unrounded: [š̭ r̭̃ s̭ z̭]

p. Fronted: [n‹ l‹ ṭ‹ x‹]

q. Backed: [n› l› ṭ› x›]

r. Faucalized (muscles at the opening to the throat drawn together to constrict the opening).

Vowels

In Table 26.1 (p. 363) you have all of the basic vowel symbols of this course. They represent a variety of vowel pronunciations even more difficult to specify unambiguously than the consonants. The same cautions which were made concerning absolutizing the table of consonants apply here even more strongly.

RE 33.3. Mimicry: Table 26.1

The vowel sounds represented in the table are given you in a "buildup" frame: [t... t...t... t...t...t...]. Mimic the tape and follow the chart on p. 363.

RE 33.4. Mimicry: Modification of Vowels

The first six modifications will be given on the tape in the form of a "bracketing drill" (see p. 371). It is the third vowel in each series which is the one indicated in the modified transcription below.

a. Raised (p. 371): [æ^ ɔ^ o^ ɨ^]

b. Lowered (p. 371): [ɩˇ uˇ ü̈ˇ æˇ]

c. Fronted (p. 371): [ʌ< o< ɨ< ɑ<]

d. Backed (p. 371): [i> ɛ> ü> ə>]

e. Rounded (p. 371): [ɨ̫ e̫ ə̫ a̫]

f. Unrounded (p. 371): [ṷ̈ ṷ ɔ̭ ʋ̭]

The following are placed in the same kind of frame as for RE 33.3.

g. Long (p. 269): [e· ɤ· ɒ· ɯ·]

h. Voiceless (p. 392): [Æ O U A]

i. Nasalized (p. 333): [œ̨ æ̨ ɑ̨ ɩ̨]

j. Retroflexed (p. 417): [ạ ʌ̣ ọ ɔ̣]

k. Breathy (p. 420): [ø̟ ɣ̟ ɤ̟ ɛ̟]

l. Laryngealized (p. 398): [ủ ỉ ə̉ ɑ̉]

m. Pharyngealized (p. 441): [o̰ ɩ̰ a̰ ʌ̰]

Glides

	High Front	High Back	Retro-flex	Central-izing	Laryn-geal	Pharyn-geal
Voiced	w	y	r	H		9̰
Voiceless	W	Y			h	h̰

Table 33.2: Glides Studied in This Course

RE 33.5. Mimicry: Table 33.2

For this drill the glides are placed in the same frame as

that used for RE 33.1. [H] is not given in initial position. Mimic the tape as you follow along on the chart.

Pitch

For a review of pitch we include one exercise from Thai, where the pitches are often glides, and one from Hausa, where the pitches are generally level.

RE 33.6: Thai. Mimicry: Pitch

a		b	
1. [ma·]	'come'	11. [ma·]	'to pickle'
2. [mʌn]	'greasy'	12. [mʌn]	'industrious'
3. [fʌŋ]	'to listen'	13. [dʌŋ]	'similar to'
4. [nay]	'in'	14. [mʌy]	'new'
5. [liŋ]	'monkey'	15. [r̃iŋ]	'species of rat'
6. [na·m]	'name'	16. [ʔa·n]	'read'
7. [mɛ·w]	'cat'	17. [cɛ·w]	'a condiment'
8. [pʰɛ·ŋ]	'expensive'	18. [kʰɛ·ŋ]	'to race'

c		d	
21. [na·]	'face'	31. [ma·]	'horse'
22. [mʌŋ]	'engaged'	32. [nʌn]	'that'
23. [nʌŋ]	'sit'	33. [r̃ʌŋ]	'haul, pull'
24. [hay]	'to let'	34. [ma·y]	'tree'

25. [pɩŋ] 'to roast' 35. [tʰɩŋ] 'throw away'

26. [ha·m] 'to forbid' 36. [na·m] 'water'

27. [kɛ·w] 'glass' 37. [l^ɛ·w] 'already'

28. [hɛ·ŋ] 'dry' 38. [l^ɛ·ŋ] 'dry (weather)'

e

41. [ma·] 'dog' 45. [pʰɩŋ] 'to warm by fire'

42. [mʌn] 'sterile' 46. [nɑ·m] 'thorns'

43. [nʌŋ] 'hide, skin' 47. [tʰɛ·w] 'row, line'

44. [hɑy] 'pickling jug' 48. [pʰɛ·ŋ] 'bamboo partition'

RE 33.7: Hausa. Mimicry: Pitch

1. [ajal^i] 'allotted time' 8. [itačʰe] 'wood'

2. [idanu] 'eyes' 9. [dʌŋgana] 'resignation'

3. [alama] 'sign' 10. [tasoši] 'dishes'

4. [fʌrtʰañɑ] 'hoe' 11. [al^·unɑ] 'slates'

5. [amfani] 'usefulness' 12. [ɑl^u·řa] 'needle'

6. [wʌhal^a] 'trouble' 13. [asal^i] 'origin'

7. [tal^aka] 'poor person' 14. [ɑwgwɑwgwɑ] 'duck'

15. [al^heri] 'goodness'
16. [sa•bul^u] 'soap'
17. [asi•ri•] 'secret'
18. [mut^ha•ne] 'people'
19. [iiyok^ha] 'limit'
20. [buk^ha•t^ha] 'need'
21. [ajiye] 'put (it) down!'
22. [ja•hil^i] 'ignorant'
23. [saurayi] 'young man'
24. [dal^il^i] 'reason'
25. [gaysuwa•] 'greetings'
26. [ga•fara] 'forgiveness'
27. [al^kal^i] 'judge'
28. [jawabi] 'reply'
29. [duwats^?u] 'stones'
30. [l^ttafi] 'book'

RE 33.8. Negative Practice: Miscellaneous

Practice talking with the various articulation styles listed below and demonstrated on the tape. The tape uses the following three sentences for this negative practice.

1. We spared the rod for all these years, and look what we wound up with -- the beat generation.

2. All men are not homeless, but some are home less than others.

3. A woman may be taken for granted, but she never goes without saying.

a. Nasalized
b. Fronted
c. Retroflexed
d. Pharyngealized
e. Laryngealized
f. Breathy
g. Rounded lips
h. Spread lips
i. Even syllable timing
j. Even pitch

k. Rising pitch

l. Falling pitch

m. Rising and falling pitch

TE 33.1. Matching Symbols

This exercise is to be found in the Workbook Supplement, pp. 103-106. It is to help you remember the symbols and their values.

Transcription Review

a. For any sounds which you have difficulty recognizing, use the differential drills in the lessons where they were introduced as transcription drills. Check your answers with the Manual.

b. Transcribe drills containing longer sequences. Redo some of the "fill in" transcription exercises in the Workbook Supplement.

In all of your transcription, study your mistakes in comparison with the correct form and see the reason for your errors if you can. Keep track of any mistakes on the Transcription Tally form in your Workbook Supplement.

Reading Review

Practice reading items from exercises in the Manual, and check your production against the tape. Work with your buddy so that you will have someone to check your production.

Sammies

Be sure you can draw the Sammies for all articulations represented in this review lesson. Pay special attention to clicks, implosives, and glottalized consonants.

I LEARNED "MOLL"ESE SO WELL IN LINGUISTICS STUDIES THAT I WANT TO TRANSFER TO "MOLLAND"!

Appendix

LESSON A

English Consonant Phonemes[1]

Here are three objectives for this lesson:

1. To begin to make you conscious of the consonant phonemes (sound distinctions) of English as over against the spelling of English, which is often very misleading.

2. To help you get used to some consonant symbols which you will need throughout the course, as quickly and as painlessly as possible. This will be done by using them for the transcription of English.

3. To help you begin to get the habit of transcribing what you hear in a consistent way, using one symbol for each different sound you distinguish. In other words, to transcribe both cable and Kate with the same initial symbol.

Chart of English Consonant Phonemes

In Table A.1 there is a chart of all of the consonant phonemes in the author's English speech. These phonemes are symbolized by letters of the English alphabet, plus modified letters since there is need for more than the regular alphabet provides us. The symbols will be used to transcribe similar sounds in other languages as well.

The phoneme symbols are enclosed in slant lines / / (which are also spoken of sometimes as diagonals). The majority of the phoneme symbols have English spelling values, except where they are complicated by English spelling inconsistencies. For example /k/ is no problem to read because of associations in English spelling with key, kind, kill, etc., but in phonemic transcription the student has to be careful also to use it in ache, cat, etc. The remainder of the symbols will have to be learned outright. Exercises in this lesson will give you an opportunity to make the necessary sound-symbol associations.

Names of the Symbols

In spelling transcriptions aloud, or in talking of the

---

[1]This lesson should be prepared before Lesson 3.

Table A.1: English Consonant Phonemes

Bilabial	Labio-dental	Tip-dental	Alveolar	Alveo-palatal	Back-velar
/p/ pea ape			/t/ tea ate		/k/ key ache
/b/ buy ebb			/d/ die Ed		/g/ guy egg
/m/ mit Tim			/n/ knit tin		/ŋ/[1] sing
				/č/ chick pitch	
				/ǰ/ Jill fudge	
	/f/ fie if	/θ/ thigh pith	/s/ sigh Tess	/š/ shy Assher	
	/v/ vie live	/đ/ thy withe	/z/ Z wise	/ž/[1] Zsa Zsa azure	
			/l/ lit till		
/w/ wit throw				/y/ you May	
/W/[1] when				/Y/[1] huge	
	/r/ writ tear		/h/[1] hit		

[1] /ŋ/ and /ž/ do not occur at the beginning of normal English words. /ŋ/ does not occur at the beginning of any English syllable. /h/, /W/, and /Y/ do not occur at the end of any English syllable.

[2] The dividing lines on the chart separate groups of consonants whose manner of articulation (formation in the mouth) are quite different.

symbols, it is convenient to have names for them. Wherever possible, the names are those which the symbols are given in regular English spelling, as kay for the symbol /k/, and em for /m/. Where the symbol does not occur in traditional English spelling, however, new names have to be learned through use. Table A.2 lists the names of such symbols as occur in this lesson.

Symbol	Name[1]	Phonemic transcription of name[2]	Notes
/ŋ/	eng	/ɛŋ/	analogy of m and n /ɛm/ and /ɛn/
	velar n	/ˈvɩylr̩ ˌɛn/	
/č/	c wedge	/ˈsɩy ˌwɛǰ/	wedge is the term for the diacritic ˇ wherever it is found
/ǰ/	j wedge	/ˈjɛy ˌwɛǰ/	
/š/	s wedge	/ˈɛs ˌwɛǰ/	
	esh	/ɛš/	analogy of f /ɛf/ and s /ɛs/
/ž/	z wedge	/ˈzɩy ˌwɛǰ/	
/θ/	theta	/ˈθɛytʌ/	name of the corresponding letter of the Greek alphabet
/đ/	barred d	/ˌbɑHrdˈdɩy/	i.e., d with a bar

Table A.2: Names of Some Consonant Symbols

Transcription Exercises

We now give you some written exercises to help you get facility in the transcription of English consonant phonemes. These transcription exercises are not recorded on tape. It is the purpose of this lesson to help you learn to transcribe your own speech, not someone else's. In this lesson the transcription exercises (TE) will be limited to transcribing the initial consonant (if there is only one) or consonants (if there are more than one) in English words, as you pronounce them (not as they are written). That is, you will transcribe all of the consonants in a word until you come to the first vowel. You will not transcribe the vowel, or any of the remaining

---

[1] Alternative names are given in some cases.

[2] Ignore this column for now if it is confusing to you.

consonants in the word. Remember that we are not concerned with the written consonants or vowels, but with spoken ones. This should become clear as you try the exercises.

In any phonemic (or phonetic) transcription please observe the following conventions:

1. Print with separate symbols rather than joining them together. You will accumulate a variety of symbols in time, and some of them will be confusing if you do not develop the habit of printing each one separate from the ones preceding and following it.

2. Do not use capital letters unless the capitals are themselves the symbols for the sound you want. For example, in Table A.1 you find /Y/ and /W/ as distinguished from /y/ and /w/ (representing a distinction in my speech and in that of many other speakers of English). You will later learn values for other capitals for use in other languages. If the symbol given you is a lower-case letter, then do not make it a capital, not even for a proper name or the beginning of a sentence. Remember that you are transcribing speech, and your speech does not "capitalize" names or anything else.

3. Be careful of the wedge (ˇ) on /č ǰ š ž/. Do not get it upside down. Think of it as a pair of horns. We will have use for the upside down variety later.

4. In some cases there may be a slight problem because of differences between your English and mine. Dialect differences inevitably occur in any group of English-speaking people. This means that transcriptions of my speech will differ from yours, sometimes only at a few points, and sometimes at many points, depending on the speech differences between us. These differences are not as great in the consonants as they would be in the vowels. There tend also to be more of them in combinations of consonants (consonant clusters) than there are in single initial consonants in English. These differences will come out when you compare your transcription of your own speech with your classmates' and with that of this book or of your instructor. Remember that differences do not mean that your speech is any more or less "correct". They are simply objective, observable differences such as occur in all languages, and which are inevitably part of the problem in any language learning.

5. Be sure to use a normal pronunciation as a basis of your transcription. Say the word or phrase which you are transcribing to yourself several times, and write what you hear. Do not strive for some artificial "correct" or over-precise pronunciation, but write what you normally say. Do not say the

word too slowly. This may distort your pronunciation. Say it naturally and easily. _Do not look up any words in a dictionary._ If you never use a given word which is listed for your transcription, leave it blank. If you do use the word, transcribe the pronunciation you use.

The transcription exercises which follow have two parts. The first consists of the directions and examples, which are incorporated in the text of the chapter. The second consists of the exercises proper with blanks to be filled out by the student. These will be found in the _Workbook Supplement_.

Transcription Exercise A.1: Initial /š θ đ č ǰ/

Study the following five lists of examples, with transcription of the initial consonant as it occurs in my speech. Read down the lists carefully to see whether or not the initial sounds are all alike in each list in your pronunciation. It is possible that at a few points your pronunciation may differ from mine. If you think you find a word which does not "fit" as you pronounce it, mark it in some way. What symbol would you use to transcribe it?

/š/		/θ/		/đ/	
1a. she	/š/	1b. thin	/θ/	1c. then	/đ/
2a. shape	/š/	2b. think	/θ/	2c. this	/đ/
3a. Schaeffer	/š/	3b. thigh	/θ/	3c. thy	/đ/
4a. ship	/š/	4b. thousand	/θ/	4c. thou	/đ/
5a. shot	/š/	5b. thistle	/θ/	5c. there	/đ/

/č/		/ǰ/	
1d. chain	/č/	1e. Jane	/ǰ/
2d. cheap	/č/	2e. jeep	/ǰ/
3d. chest	/č/	3e. jest	/ǰ/
4d. chosen	/č/	4e. Joseph	/ǰ/
5d. chin	/č/	5e. gin	/ǰ/

Now transcribe the initial consonant of each of the words of TE A.1 (_Workbook Supplement_, p. 5) in the same way that they are transcribed between the diagonals above. All of the initial consonants of these words in my speech are transcribed with one of the above five symbols. However, you may find that in your speech one or more of the words needs some other symbol. In that case see if you can find what you need in Table A.1.

Transcription Exercise A.2: Initial /h W w/

At this point we have some marked dialect differences in English. Some speakers have no distinction between /W w/ such and I have. In that case they have only /h w/ instead of the three phonemes illustrated here. Other speakers have all three, but differ from me in the words which begin with /w/ and those which begin with /W/. Other speakers may differ occasionally between words beginning with /h/ and those beginning with /W/. This is not a question of right and wrong, but a question of usage.

Study the following columns, which are listed as the words occur in my speech. That is, in my speech all of the words in Column a begin with /h/, those in Column b with /W/, and those in Column c with /w/. Notice that the words rhyme across. Except for the differing initial phonemes, the words in a line across are exactly alike in my speech.

Read down each list several times to see whether or not all the words in a given column begin with the same sound in your speech. Mark any which do not, and indicate the symbol for your pronunciation in the space provided (when it differs from mine).

Then read across each line. Do you make a difference in the initial sounds across? Do you have a three-way difference or a two-way difference? Wherever your speech differs from mine, transcribe the difference in the initial consonant phoneme. Do not bother to make a transcription if your speech is the same as that indicated by the columns. Some of you may notice a fluctuation in your speech. On which of these words does it occur?

/h/	/W/	/w/
1a. hitch / /	1b. which / /	1c. witch / /
2a. heather / /	2b. whether / /	2c. weather / /
3a. hither / /	3b. whither / /	3c. wither / /
4a. hen / /	4b. when / /	4c. wen / /

/h/	/W/	/w/
5a. heel / /	5b. wheel / /	5c. weal / /
6a. hack / /	6b. whack / /	6c. WAC / /
7a. hey! / /	7b. whey / /	7c. way / /
8a. hail / /	8b. whale / /	8c. wail / /

After you have followed the directions above, determining whether or not your transcription should be the same as mine and filling in the differences, then go on to transcribe the initial consonants in TE A.2 (Workbook Supplement, p. 5) as you pronounce them. They are in random order.

Transcription Exercise A.3: Initial /y Y/

Pronounce you and hue. Are the initial consonants different in your speech? If so, you would transcribe them with /y/ and /Y/ respectively. If not, you have /y/.

Transcribe the initial consonant of each of the words of TE A.3 as you say it. Do not let the initial written vowels confuse you. Write what you say. (Workbook Supplement, p. 5)

Transcription Exercise A.4: Some Initial Consonant Clusters

Transcribe the initial consonant clusters of the words of TE A.4. In other words, transcribe all of the consonants up to the first vowel phoneme (the first pronounced vowel). Some examples are given here, from my speech. Go back to Table A.1 for any symbols you need. (Workbook Supplement, p. 6)

please	/pl/	tray	/tr/	Sphinx	/sf/
clean	/kl/	scratch	/skr/	smash	/sm/
split	/spl/	three	/θr/	shrewd	/šr/

Transcription Exercise A.5: Some Initial Clusters with /w y/

Compare the words in Column a with those in Column b, and those in Column c with those in Column d. In my speech they differ only by the presence or absence of /y/ (in the first pair) or of /w/ (in the second pair). Note the importance of the /y/ to distinguish between booty and beauty, for example. The /y/ or the /w/, as the case may be, forms a part of the initial consonant cluster. Mark any cases where your pronunciation differs from mine. You can determine this by reading down the column to see whether there are any words which you pronounce with or without the /w/ or /y/ in a contrary way to what I have indicated for my pronunciation.

With /y/		Without /y/	
1a. beauty	/by/	1b. booty	/b/
2a. pure	/py/	2b. poor	/p/
3a. few	/fy/	3b. foo	/f/
4a. fjord	/fy/	4b. Ford	/f/
5a. mute	/my/	5b. moot	/m/

With /w/		Without /w/	
1c. twinge	/tw/	1d. tinge	/t/
2c. quick	/kw/	2d. kick	/k/
3c. thwack	/θw/	3d. Thackeray	/θ/
4c. sway	/sw/	4d. say	/s/
5c. square	/skw/	5d. scare	/sk/

After you have studied the words above to determine whether or not your speech differs from mine on any of them, transcribe the initial clusters (including the /w/ or /y/, if any) of the words in TE A.5. Expect some dialect difference between your speech and that of your classmates. (Supplement, p. 6)

Suggested Readings

The following readings are selected because they discuss English consonant phonemes from one standpoint or another. They inevitably introduce also material which we have not yet covered. This should provide excellent background for your further study.

Charles F. Hockett, A Course in Modern Linguistics, pp. 15-32.

H. A. Gleason, An Introduction to Descriptive Linguistics, pp. 14-26.

One further caution may be helpful to you as you do reading about English consonant phonemes in other books, either the ones suggested here or ones which you may run across. Most of the consonant symbols in any modern work in linguistics written in the United States will differ very little from the symbols used in this lesson. You will find a few such differences, however. In Table A.3 we tabulate the differences which you are most likely to meet in your reading. Blanks in the chart indicate that the symbol used is the same as ours. The last column shows you other representations by a variety of authors whose works you may find. Although this table may not give the equivalence for the author you are reading, you should easily figure out the values of his English phoneme symbols from the range of possibilities presented here.

Ours	Nida	Pike	Hockett, Bloomfield	Gleason, ELI	Trager and Smith	Others
đ						
č					c	tš, t
ǰ					j	dž, d
š						
ž						
y			j			
W	hw,W	w̲	hw	hw	hw	ʍ
Y	hy,Y	y̲	hj	hy	hy	ç

Table A.3: Equivalent English Consonant Phoneme Symbols[1]

---

[1]In addition to the suggested readings listed above, the following works are specifically covered in this table. The last column represents a wide variety of works which we will not list.

Eugene A. Nida, *Morphology* (first column) and *Learning a Foreign Language* (second column).

Kenneth L. Pike, *Phonemics*

Leonard Bloomfield, *Language*

English Language Institute (ELI), *English Pronunciation*

George L. Trager and Henry Lee Smith, Jr., *An Outline of English Structure*

LESSON B

English Vowel Phonemes[1]

In Lesson A we gave you a chart of English consonant phonemes with illustrations of English words containing them, and you were able on the basis of this information to learn to transcribe the consonants of your speech with relatively little difficulty. Since then you have learned that these phonemes were phonetically far more complex than you dreamed at the time, many of them consisting of several different allophones (different kinds of sounds comprising /l/, different kinds of sounds comprising /t/, etc.), but this does not affect the validity of the phonemic contrasts which you symbolized in Lesson A. Phonemes are often made up of more than one sound.

When we come now to English vowel phonemes, however, our approach cannot be as simple and direct because the analysis of English vowel phonemes is quite complicated. The complications arise both from the fact that the vowel system of any one speaker of English is complex, and from the fact that speakers of English vary tremendously from region to region and from social dialect to social dialect in their vowel systems. We cannot, therefore, present a ready-made system with ready-made examples and expect it to fit your speech. Rather, you will have to figure out your own vowel system.

There are really three goals in this lesson:

1. Working on your vowel system and comparing it with that of your classmates will help you gain in phonetic perceptiveness, and thus contribute directly to the purpose of this textbook and course.

2. An understanding of your phonemic system is a help toward understanding the learning problems which you face in <u>another language</u>.

[1]This lesson may begin as early as Lesson 11, with TE B.1-3, but the remainder is intended to come after Lesson 20, when the phonetic vowel distinctions needed have been covered. Unlike the other lessons in this book, it is not intended for a single classroom period, but should be stretched out over several periods interspersed with the remaining phonetics lessons. Also unlike the phonetics lessons, the exercises of this lesson are designed to be worked out before being discussed in class, with the exception of TE B.1. For further suggestions to the instructor see the <u>Teacher's Guide</u>.

3. Working toward a preliminary analysis of one kind of complicated phonemic problem (your vowel system) will give you a greater understanding of the phonemic structure of language in general, and thus contribute to your sophistication in approaching language learning.

Reading

Several valuable and relatively readable discussions of English vowel phonemes are available, and you should read them in connection with this chapter. Perhaps if you keep returning to them as you go through this chapter, step by step, it will help you understand what you are doing, and help you perform the steps. There is no point in repeating this excellent material here.

H. A. Gleason, Introduction to Descriptive Linguistics (either edition), pp. 27-39.

Charles F. Hockett, A Course in Modern Linguistics, pp. 15-32.

Archibald A. Hill, Introduction to Linguistic Structures, pp. 62-67.

As you do this reading, bear in mind that the phonemic symbols used /i e æ ɨ ə a u o ɔ/ do not necessarily have exactly the same phonetic qualities which we have assigned them in this course. Phonetic qualities in English vary from one dialect to another, and more important yet, different qualities may be united in the same phoneme. I have [i˃] and [ɩ] as two of my English vowel sounds. However, both of these belong to the same phoneme, the difference between them being conditioned by the sound environment. ([i˃] occurs before [y], [ɩ] does not, etc.) I therefore write them phonemically the same way. In this book I have written the phoneme as /ɩ/ as in /bɩt/ bit and /bɩyt/ beat. The books which you read will write this same phoneme /i/, giving them /bit/ bit and /biyt/ beat. The choice of symbol is arbitrary, except that I wanted to make the phonemics coincide more closely with the phonetic symbolization, and the other authors you will be reading wanted to use the more commonly used letter i. So far as the phonemic principles are concerned, they are exactly equivalent.

It might be well to make an explanation of some other systems of analyzing or transcribing English which you may find commonly. Some, like that of Leonard Bloomfield's Language, date from an earlier stage in linguistics. One very important one, that of Kenneth L. Pike's Phonemics stems from a slightly different approach to phonemics, and ignores some of the contrasts of lower functional load which we include. The English teaching materials of the English Language Institute follow Pike, and Pike's system does have some advantages for teaching English, as the contrasts omitted vary tremendously among speakers of English and do not carry a high functional load.

TE B.1. Sorting Words by Vowel Nuclei

The first step toward an analysis of the vowel phonemes of your speech is to make a preliminary sorting according to the pronunciation of the stressed vowel nuclei in your English words. By "vowel nuclei" we refer for the time being to what is traditionally considered to be the spoken vowel of the syllable (not the written symbol). For example, here are some vowel nuclei in my speech.

Spelling	Nucleus
bid	pronunciation symbolized by i
bead	pronunciation symbolized by ea
yes	pronunciation symbolized by e
queen	pronunciation symbolized by ee[1]

To do this exercise use the list of words which follows these instructions, sorting them into groups on scrap paper by use of the following procedure.

a. Read any two words aloud together, one after the other. If the vowel nuclei have the same sound (the spelling is totally irrelevant) list the two words together in the same list. If the vowel nucleus of one word is different from that of the other use them to start two separate lists. Your only consideration is that of the sameness or difference in the sound of the vowel nuclei.

b. Try the third word in comparison with the two previous words. If the two previous words went into the same list read the new word aloud with those two words. Preferably place it between them as you read, pronouncing the words in the order of first word, new word, second word. Putting it in the middle

---

[1]Note that the pronunciation symbolized by u was covered under the /w/ consonant of Appendix A. Note also that in my speech the vowel nucleus of bead and that of queen are the same, although they are spelled differently.

makes comparison easier than in initial or final position where the intonation is likely to affect it. If the vowel nucleus sounds the same as the nucleus of the two words, list it with them. If it sounds different, put it in a different list.

Or, if the original two words went into different lists try the new word with each of the original two separately. If it is the same as either one list it with that one. If it is different from both of them use it to start a new list.

c. Continue with each succeeding word. Include it with any previous list if the vowel nucleus sounds the same as the nuclei already in the list. Start a new list if it is not the same as the nucleus in any list. When there is a list of two or more items with which you are comparing it say the new word in the middle of the list. Say the whole list aloud.

d. As you work along you will occasionally realize that a word which you had previously classified in a given list really does not belong there with the others because it sounds different, a difference which you had not detected before. In that case take it out and reclassify it where it belongs.

Your lists will not necessarily be the same as those prepared by anyone else because there are wide dialect differences in English vowel nuclei. We are not concerned with any notion you may have about English "correctness." List the words as you normally say them. If you find that you fluctuate in any word, pronouncing it sometimes one way and sometimes another, put it in both lists.

Here are the words to use.

boy	Ben	hate	hop	lard	loud
bow	mine	heft	bite	foot	sound
boa	bound	hat	buy	boot	nut
bean	boon	hot	height	low	ton
bin	bond	hut	bad	year	us
bone	spa	hoot	bat	yea	hit
ban	spill	hoof	bid	cow	in
bun	heat	roof	bead	bout	ink
bane	hit	hope	led	now	sift

stop	too	pun	prow	bond	many
cod	kit	buck	bed	shreek	penny
balm	cat	nook	bait	shrink	end
ten	pin	neck	fuss	shrank	and
tin	pen	Hoyt	fuzz	shrunk	greasy
two	pan	pry	thank	any	soft

TE B.2. Checking for Additional Nuclei and Examples

During and after class discussion of the results of the previous exercise, you will need to take another look and see if you can find other nuclei which you have missed.

a. As a result of class discussion you may have recognized that you combined two phonetically different nuclei into the same list. Revise your work to separate them.

b. In the class discussion new words may have come up which give you new nuclei, or examples for lists where you do not have enough examples. Incorporate this material. Make sure you incorporate it only as you pronounce it. You may not list it with the same words another person does, because his pronunciation may be different from yours.

c. Check the following words against your lists. Where necessary because you find new nuclei, start new lists. Fill out lists for which you do not have enough examples. Some of these words contain more than one syllable. You are concerned with the stressed syllable only.

alcohol	pot	about	starry
lawn	cash	cot	mourning
garage	louse	our	oral
thank	tomorrow	gregarious	caught
loin	horrible	Jewry	board
out	Shaw	ferry	pill
look	warrant	Erie	wiggle
whole	light	coarse	balm

waffle	ice	flour	Oz
end	try	Mary	portion
fine	bomb	Gary	dear
off	tugs	sorry	balk
joint	bond	door	vary
bird	bask	fairy	Pa
tune	his	coal	father
flute	stop	welter	poor
sister	pony	miracle	merry
proud	boat	bah	bard

TE B.3. Looking for More Nuclei and Examples

In this exercise you should add at least fifty new words to the lists you are collecting, or to new lists you may have to start because new nuclei come to light. The words may be of more than one syllable, but you are concerned only with the stressed syllable.

Continue to expand your lists on paper, finding as many different groups as you can - that is, as many different stressed vowel nuclei as you can. You may notice certain problems, and perhaps these suggestions will help you:

a. For some vowel nuclei you will immediately think of many words. Ten words or so are enough for any one list, but be sure to make the words as varied as possible. A list like hit, sit, fit, bit, wit is not as useful for later stages of this work as hit, in, ink, sift, interest.

b. For other vowel nuclei you may be able to think of only one example. Try to find more, but if you cannot, keep the one as a separate list. Do not discard it or combine it with another list simply because it is small.

c. You will likely find your pronunciation of many words to be different in different contexts, or when spoken at different speeds. As you say your words, try to keep a uniform natural pronunciation, not an overly "precise" one. But when you find fluctuation in pronunciation anyhow, or different pronunciations in different contexts, put the word in each of the appropriate columns. For example, I say Can I [ˈkʰænɑy], but I can [ˌɑyˈkʰæHn]. Thus the word illustrates [æ] and [æH], but I must keep track of the difference of context. Make a notation beside each pronunciation of the different context in which you found it.

d. You may find a difference in length. In my speech, for example, I have hot, stop, cot with [ɑ] and bar, balm, spa with [ɑ·˃]. These should be kept in separate lists although you are not yet concerned with the phonetic transcription of your lists.

e. To save time and give you ideas you may use a dictionary or any other source to remind you of words, but list them as you pronounce them, not as the dictionary says they should be pronounced. Use only words which are natural to you. If the list is alphabetical, skip through it in order not to have your words all begin with the same few letters of the alphabet.

TE B.4. Preliminary Charting of Vowel Nuclei

Up to now you have been collecting data and sorting it into groups of words which have the same vowel nuclei. The next step is to make up a set of vowel charts for what you have been finding. You will need one chart for unglided nuclei, one for nuclei with [y], one for nuclei with [w], and one for nuclei with [H]. If you have found some nuclei with long vowels and others with short, these should be charted separately.

As the first step in making these charts, make a phonetic notation of the nucleus for each list. In my speech, for example, I would write [ɩ] beside a list consisting of sit, in, ink, spit, sprinkle, etc. Similarly, the appropriate notation would be made beside each other list.

At this point the phonetic nature of what we have labeled "vowel nuclei" becomes a little more apparent. We refer to pure vowels which are not followed by glides, and to vowels plus [w y H]. For example, here are some illustrations of vowel nuclei in various words in my speech.

Word		Vowel Nucleus
bid	[bɩd]	[ɩ]
bead	[bi˃yd]	[i˃y]
led	[lɛd]	[ɛ]
laid	[le˅yd]	[e˅y]

foot	[fʊ˂t]	[ʊ˂]
boot	[bɨwt]	[ɨw]
low	[low]	[ow]
period	[ˈpʰɩri˅Hd]	[ɩ] [i˅H]
yeah	[yɛH]	[ɛH]

Note that the [r] off-glide does not enter into English phonemic vowel nuclei in the same way that do [w y H]. We simply tell you this to make the exercises easier. Handle English /r/ even after vowels as a full consonant, as you did in Lesson A, although you are handling other post-vocalic glides as parts of vowel nuclei.

After you decide upon the phonetic notation for the nucleus of each list, then these nuclei should be entered in the blank vowel charts in the *Workbook Supplement*, p. 83-84. It would be wise to use pencil, as you may make changes. Thus, for my list in the previous paragraph, I would enter [ɩ] in the lower-high front unrounded position of Blank Vowel Chart 1. [ow] would be entered in the mid back rounded position of Chart 3, writing in both vowel and glide. [i˃y] I would enter in the high front unrounded position of Chart 4. The diacritic [˃] shows the fact that it is slightly backed from this position.

The phonetic transcription of the nucleus of every one of your lists should be entered somewhere on one of these charts. Do not expect all of the charts to be filled out. No dialect of English has that great a variety of vowel nuclei. However, where there are gaps keep on the lookout for words you have overlooked which might have nuclei to fill them.

TE B.5. Looking for Minimal Pairs Within Chart 1

At this point you begin to make a phonemic analysis of your vowel system based on the data which you have been collecting and sorting. The first step is to find minimal pairs between as many of the phonetic entries in the five charts of the previous exercise as you can. For the purposes of our work now, a minimal pair is any pair of words in your speech which differ in their vowel, and only in their vowel. The remainder of the word is the same. The words must have different meanings. For example, in my speech *tin* and *ten* are a minimal pair. The vowels [ɩ] and [ɛ] constitute the only difference between these words for me. The words are otherwise the same. For some speakers of English, however, these two words are not minimal pairs, because they are pronounced the same way. There is no difference between them for these speakers.

Kit and *cat* are minimal pairs in my speech. The distinction is in [ɩ] and [æ]. Do not let the fact that the consonant phonemes are spelled differently fool you. From a pronunciation standpoint the only difference is in the nucleus.

Two and *too* are not minimal pairs in my speech. They are pronounced the same way. Neither are *rim* and *ran*, for there is a consonant difference as well as a vowel difference. *Ram* and *ran* are, of course, minimal pairs, but are of no use to us here, because we want minimal pairs which differ by vowel nucleus.

First of all, you want to look for minimal pairs within Chart 1 of TE B.3. For example, Blank Vowel Chart 1 (p. 83) may look like this (which is one possibility, but not the only one among English dialects):

ɩ		ʊ‹
ɛ		
æ	ʌ	ɔ
	ɑ	

If this is what your chart looks like, you will now look for minimal pairs between [ɩ ɛ], [ɩ æ], [ɩ ʌ], [ɩ ɑ], [ɩ ʊ‹], [ɩ ɔ], [ɛ æ], [ɛ ʌ], etc. It helps a great deal if you can find a minimal series like *pin*, *pen*, *pan*, *pun*, taking care of [ɩ ɛ], [ɩ æ], [ɩ ʌ], [ɛ æ], [ɛ ʌ], and [æ ʌ] all at once. When you cannot find a series like this you have to work by individual pairs like *book*, *buck* [ʊ‹ ʌ], *nook*, *neck* [ʊ‹ ɛ], etc. around the chart.

This step is a very important step, for when you find minimal pairs, they prove that the sounds which make the difference between the words do not belong to the same phoneme but to different phonemes. If you can find minimal pairs separating all of your sounds in Chart 1, these sounds are all different phonemes. You do not yet know the full story about these phonemes, but you have established these particular phonetic qualities as belonging to separate phonemes in your dialect of English.

Page 85 in the *Workbook Supplement* will help you in recording your *minimal pairs for Chart 1*. Enter each pair of phonetic nuclei on the left between the slant lines. Slant lines are used because if you have a minimal pair for the two sounds, you have proved a phonemic difference. Then write in the English words which are a minimal pair separating these vowels in your speech. You do not have to restrict yourself to words already in your preliminary lists. Any words in your natural speech may be used as minimal pairs.

TE B.6. Looking for Minimal Pairs Within Charts 2-5

Continue the procedure of the preceding exercise within each of the remaining charts. Blanks for the recording of minimal pairs for each chart are to be found on pp. 87-88 of the Workbook Supplement. On Chart 4, for example, in my dialect heat, hate, height, Hoyt would provide pairs for phonetic nuclei [i˃y e˅y], [i˃y ʌy], [i˃y ɔy], [e˅y ʌy], [e˅y ɔy], [ʌy ɔy].

Be sure to keep track of pairs of sounds for which you cannot find any minimal pairs.

TE B.7. Looking for Minimal Pairs Between Charts 3-5

In turning to look for minimal pairs between charts we keep the same principle in mind, that we want to find words which have only one difference between them. For example, in my speech boy [boy] and bow [bow] are a minimal pair. The nucleus of boy is in Chart 4 (Workbook Supplement, p. 84) and that of bow is in Chart 3 ([oy] and [ow] respectively). The minimal difference lies in the glide part of the nucleus, the difference between [w] and [y]. For my speech, then, the [w] off-glide and the [y] off-glide belong to separate phonemes.

If I go on to compare Chart 5, I find that I have the word boa [boH] in minimal contrast with boy and bow, giving me a third phoneme /H/.[1]

---

[1]By way of interest we might mention that the phonemes /y w/ in English pattern as consonants in English when they are on-glides (see Lesson A) and as parts of English vowel nuclei when they are off-glides. The same phonemes, then, sometimes have a consonant function and sometimes a function as part of the vowel nucleus phonemically although they are both vowel glides phonetically. The reasons for such an analysis go beyond the scope of this book. /H/ presents some subject of controversy among linguists. Some combine it with the phoneme /h/ on the basis of complementary distribution, while others do not, feeling that there is not enough phonetic similarity. /r/ patterns as a consonant whether it is an on-glide or an off-glide, which is why we did not bring it into our discussion of nuclei.

Study your Charts 3-5 and look for minimal pairs between them, in the manner just illustrated. Record this information on p. 89 of the <u>Workbook Supplement</u>.

<u>TE B.8. Looking for Minimal Pairs Between All the Charts</u>

Continue the process which you began in the previous exercise by adding the charts which do not have off-glides as part of the nucleus. Make your comparisons for minimal pairs between Charts 1 and 2, and then between these charts and Charts 3-5, comparing Chart 1 with Chart 3, Chart 1 with Chart 4, etc. Remember that for there to be a minimal pair there must be only one difference in sound. For example, <u>nut</u> and <u>night</u> are a minimal pair in my speech, [nʌt] and [nʌyt] respectively. They are the same except for the presence and absence of [y]. However, for me <u>bit</u> [bɩt] and <u>beat</u> [bi˃yt] are not a minimal pair. They differ in vowel quality as well as in glide.

Record your minimal pairs in the <u>Workbook Supplement</u>, p. 89, as you did before.

Theoretically you should search for a pair to represent every possible pair of nuclei between all of the charts, but this becomes a pretty large task. Instead look for pairs where the vowels are the same or very similar, and compare these.

<u>TE B.9. Looking for Complementary Distribution</u>

In our search for minimal pairs we have been finding evidence for separating sounds into different phonemes, or separating nuclei. <u>Bit</u> and <u>bet</u> in my dialect separate [ɩ ɛ] into separate phonemes. The minimal pairs prove that they contrast phonemically. <u>Bit</u> and <u>beat</u> separate the two nuclei [ɩ i˃y], but the second nucleus is not a single sound, but a vowel plus a glide. Is there any relationship between the vowels of the two? Certainly they are very close phonetically, but what is their phonemic relationship? Are [ɩ] and [i˃] different phonemes in my dialect? And what about [iˇ] as in [iˇH]? (See my "front unrounded" column reproduced in the preceding exercise.)

When I look at my charts, however, or the parts of them reproduced above, I notice immediately that I never get [i˃] except with a following [y], never get [iˇ] except with a following [H], and never get [ɩ] with either glide. These three vowels are very similar. Their slight differences are associated with the presence or absence of particular glides. I notice that there is a similar relationship between [ɛ eˇy] except that it is simpler in that there is not a third variety before [H]. These shades of difference in vowel are in complementary distribution[1] according to the presence or absence of the glide.

These similar vowels in complementary distribution belong to the same phoneme. In the examples above [ɩ i˃ iᵛ] all belong to one phoneme /ɩ/ (or /i/ if you prefer), and they take these different phonetic forms when found in these different complementary environments.

It is not evident from my charts, but in my dialect [ɛ ɛ•] are also in complementary distribution. I cannot find any minimal pairs to separate them, so I look at the words in which they occur. I find that the long vowel occurs before voiced consonants, and the short vowel occurs in other environments. This shows up in pairs like bet, bed; fuss, fuzz; etc. The vowel in the first word is short and that in the second is long. This would not mean anything if I found minimal pairs to separate them, but it is impossible to find minimal pairs to separate sounds which are in complementary distribution. The fact that they are in complementary distribution means that they have no sound environment which is identical, and in minimal pairs the sound environment must be identical.

In the Workbook Supplement (p. 91) there is a form to help you work out the complementation of similar sounds. Take up first the charts, and the complementation which they show, and then turn to other similar vowels for which you have not been able to find minimal pairs.

In working out the complementary distribution deal with the sounds which would go together to make up one phoneme, and work out the rules for them. Then turn to those which would make up another phoneme, etc.

Enter the sounds in complementary distribution in the appropriate place, and for each one give the environment (the distribution) which is peculiar to it.

It is quite likely that you will need occasional help from an experienced person when you are working with complementary distribution. If you do not get enough help in class, ask for it from your instructor on the side.

---

[1]Sounds are distributed through words. The sounds [ɩ i˃ iᵛ] complement each other in their distribution in relation to glides. They together have a distribution with and without glides, but no one of them has the same distribution as any other.

TE B.10. Analyzing Free Fluctuation

When you were collecting your lists you found some words in which your pronunciation fluctuated, and you listed the words in more than one list. Now you want to study the phonemic significance of that fluctuation.

Pick out the words which fluctuated, and on the basis of what you have so far discovered about your phonemes, try to determine for each word whether your fluctuation was between two phonemes or not. Was the fluctuation between two sounds proved to be separate phonemes because you have minimal pairs for them? Or was the fluctuation between sounds which are not in contrast, for which you cannot find minimal pairs?

If the sounds are separate phonemes, you recognize that on some words you fluctuate between these phonemes (though not on all words). You can record this information concerning these words on p. 93 of the Workbook Supplement.

If the sounds are not separate phonemes, your fluctuation is within the allophones (sounds which comprise a phoneme). There is place for you to record this on p. 94 of the Workbook Supplement.

Sometimes the fluctuation will be between an unglided vowel and a glided one, particularly one glided with [H]. For the purposes of this exercise, handle the presence and absence of [H] as phonemic. That is, consider the fluctuation between [æ æH], if you have it, to be a phonemic one.

TE B.11. Making a Tentative Phonemic Vowel Chart

Charts 1-5 which you made before in the Workbook Supplement were phonetic charts. You have now been working with them to see which of these sounds are separate phonemes, and which belong to the same phoneme as allophones either because of complementary distribution or because of free fluctuation. For this purpose you do not include the glides in the chart, but the vowels alone. You choose one symbol for each phoneme, no matter how many allophones it has. This you can do in the Workbook Supplement, p. 95.

Under the chart, list the allophones which go with each phoneme. All of the vowel qualities in your previous charts should be included among these allophones.

You may find a problem in that you still have vowel sounds for which you do not have minimal pairs, and for which you cannot find complementary distribution or free fluctuation. For the purposes of this exercise consider them separate phonemes.[1]

TE B.12. Phonemic Transcription

Your analysis of your English phonemes is not technically complete, but this is as far as we are going to take it. With this much knowledge of your vowel phonemes, plus what you know about your consonant phonemes, you should be able to make an approximate phonemic transcription of your consonants and vowels. Try this out with the words in the *Workbook Supplement*, p. 96. Write the full word *phonemically*. Remember that *this* means you will not write aspiration because aspirated and unaspirated stops belong to the same phoneme. If in doubt, review Lesson A.

TE B.13. Phonemic Transcription

Transcribe phonemically the sentences on pp. 99, 100 of the *Workbook Supplement* in the space provided.

---

[1]There are other phonemic techniques to help in the analysis of such residual problems, but they are beyond the scope of this course, which is one in phonetics, and where the present phonemics exercise is introduced because of the strong phonetic reinforcement which it provides.

LESSON C

Descriptive Summary of Speech Articulation

In the preceding chapters our approach to understanding articulatory phonetics has been guided by pedagogical considerations rather than descriptive ones. We introduced new information piecemeal, and in the order which we had found by experience was the easiest to teach to North American students. Considerations of what students are able to hear and produce in the most efficient order were paramount. With the myriad detail and variety in speech sounds, however, some students may not have seen the over-all picture. For that reason we append this brief chapter to give a systematic though brief summary of human speech articulation. There will be little new information here. Nor will there be as much detail as can be found in some of the lessons which constitute the main part of this book, and to which cross-reference will be made. This will be strictly a descriptive overview, a reorganization of the facts of articulation into a more "logical" pattern of presentation.

The Air Stream

A movement of air out of, or into the human head is a fundamental requisite of normal human speech sounds. The movement of this air stream sets up vibrations which are those sounds. The air stream is modified (its sound frequencies are modified) by variations in the shape of the parts of the head and throat through which it travels. In the most general terms this is a full description of what articulatory phonetics is all about. The rest is a matter of filling in the detail (and learning the skills) of specific features of articulation.

The most important organs for originating airstreams used in speech are the lungs. All languages use lung air (pp. 378-379) for a substantial number of speech sounds. None of the other airstream mechanisms to be described below are as universal. The most important direction of movement for the lung air stream is egressive (going out of the body), moving from the lungs through the throat and then the mouth or nose or both. Ingressive lung air, with the lungs pulling the air in rather than pushing it out, is fully possible but very rare as a part of normal speech. Children at play, or anyone else who wants to try it, can say short sentences in English with continuous ingressive lung air. They simply draw in the air as they talk rather than expelling it.

The egressive lung air stream of normal speech does not

come out with the same even flow which is characteristic of quiet breathing. Rather it comes out in pulses of varying lengths. This pulsation is caused by movement of the muscle system in the chest and abdomen. These pulses of air are integrated with articulations in the throat and mouth to produce syllables (pp. 150-154), differences of degree of stress (pp. 154-158) and loudness, breath groups, and other modifications in the stream of speech. These modifications stemming from the chest pulsations usually cover a sequence of sounds rather than isolated individual sounds.

A second initiator of speech air streams is the pharynx, or the cavity in the throat above the larynx and below the faucal pillars (muscles at the entrance to the throat from the mouth), uvula, etc. By closing (or nearly closing) the vocal cords and pushing the larynx upward air is expelled from the pharyngeal cavity, making an egressive air stream (pp. 405-411). By pulling the larynx downward an ingressive pharynx air stream (pp. 378-387) is produced. Pharynx air streams are never the only basis of speech sounds in any language, nor are they to be found in every language, but they are very commonly found in African, Asian, and American Indian languages, and are occasionally heard as alternate forms in English.

A third place where speech air streams begin is in the mouth. The mouth air stream (pp. 427-440) is created by forming a cup with the tongue against the roof of the mouth in various positions. By releasing one point of the cup and by pushing the air out with the tongue an egressive mouth air stream can be formed. More commonly, however, the tongue lowers to create a partial vacuum in the cup just as the one point is released, and an ingressive air stream results. "Clicks" which mouth-air sounds are called, form a functioning part of speech only in Africa (especially southern Africa), but are widely used elsewhere in play, verbal gesture, exclamation, and communication with animals.

The various air streams occur in combination in some speech sounds. Pharynx and lung air are both involved in voiced pharynx air sounds (p. 381), for voicing requires lung air. Mouth and lung air are used together in voiced and nasalized clicks (pp. 433-437) and in some varieties of double stops (pp. 299-300). Other combinations are theoretically possible but probably do not enter into the speech sounds of actual languages.

Effect of the Larynx on Lung Air

Various positions of the vocal cords in the larynx modify an air stream originating in the lungs in different ways. They naturally do not have this same effect on other airstreams because these do not pass through the larynx.

One extremely important pair of modifications created in the larynx is the contrast between voicing and voicelessness (pp. 43-48 and many others). Voicing is created by a narrowed passage between the vocal cords such that the air stream passing through develops a buzz as it causes these membranes to vibrate. With a wider, more relaxed position the vocal cords do not impede the air stream as much, nor do they set up the vibration of voicing.

A second extremely important modification created by the larynx is that of pitch (pp. 26-42, and others). All voiced speech has the possibility of a variation in pitch frequency, and all languages use this possibility, though in varying ways. Tone systems and intonation systems are in large part based on this kind of modification, although pitch is probably never the only ingredient in them.

The vocal cords may close momentarily to stop the air stream and produce a glottal stop (pp. 102-108). In another configuration they modify the air stream to provide the basis for the various forms of [h] (pp. 392, 396-398).

Two other modifications, laryngealization (pp. 398-399) and breathiness (pp. 420-426), do not have the same universality as the preceding, but they are nevertheless extremely important modifications of the air stream caused by changes of configuration within the larynx. Falsetto and whisper are also modifications made there.

The Cavities and their Modifications

The three principal cavities (pp. 1-2) through which air streams may pass are the pharyngeal cavity, the oral cavity, and the nasal cavity. All lung air must pass through the pharyngeal cavity, but then may pass through the oral cavity (without the nasal) to produce oral sounds, through the nasal cavity (without the oral) to produce nasal sounds, or through both (the oral being predominant, but the nasal cavity also open) to produce nasalized sounds.

When the oral cavity is closed off the closure may be at different points in the mouth, as described in the next section. If the closure is velar (to produce [ŋ]) the oral cavity figures very little in the formation of the nasal sound, but if the closure is farther front in the mouth (to produce [n] or [m], for example) there is an oral cavity behind the tongue which provides a resonance chamber off of the direct line of the air stream going out the nose (pp. 10-17).

If the oral cavity is open the nasal cavity may or may not be closed off. There is only one position at which this closure can take place. It is articulated only by the velic. However, various degrees of closure are possible ranging from a wide-open access to the nasal cavity to a very slight aperture. The degree of opening affects the degree of nasalization (pp. 333-340).

Modifications in the pharyngeal cavity consist of various degrees of enlargement and constriction of the cavity by movement of the tongue root forward or back. Extreme constriction produces pharyngealization (pp. 441-449). Extreme openness produces a deep, hollow sound. At the mouth of the pharyngeal cavity lie the faucal pillars. These may be narrowed to produce a tense, strained, or "bright" modification of speech.

Modifications in the oral cavity (the articulations of speech) will be discussed in the next section.

Other air streams than the lung air stream use fewer cavities because any air stream uses only cavities between its origin and its point of egress or ingress. Mouth air uses only the oral cavity (p. 429). Pharynx air theoretically can use both oral and nasal cavities but in actual practice is almost always restricted to oral (pp. 380-381). The simultaneous nasalization or voicing which occurs with clicks (mouth air sounds) is produced by lung air, and not by mouth air (pp. 433-436).

Articulators and Points of Articulation (pp. 3-11)

The mouth contains the greatest potential for variety in the modification of the air stream primarily because of the great flexibility and agility of the tongue. The root of the tongue may move back to or near the pharyngeal wall, as was mentioned under modifications in the pharyngeal cavity (p. 442). The back of the tongue may articulate at or near the uvula, the lower rim of the velum, or any upper surface of the mouth as far forward as the palate (pp. 322-329). It normally articulates as far forward as the front edge of the velum.

The tongue mid is capable of articulating from the uvula to the upper lip, but for languages it is found typically articulating in the area of the palate which lies above it (p. 324).

For people with a bit of agility the tongue blade and tip likewise are capable of articulating from the uvula to the upper lip. In actual languages the blade normally articulates against the palate, alveopalatal region (pp. 193-194, 275-281), or the alveolar ridge (pp. 20-22). The tip articulates anywhere from the palate to the teeth (pp. 164-171). Tip-palatal and some tip-alveopalatal articulations are retroflexed.

The lower lip is capable of articulating from the alveopalatal region to the upper lip. It is actually found articulating against the upper teeth and upper lip (pp. 48-52).

Various degrees of distance from articulator to point of articulation are possible, giving the manners of articulation which will be discussed in the next section. Different configurations of the tongue as articulator are also possible, as will be seen under the section on manners of articulation and under the one on vowels.

Manners of Articulation

Various relative positions of articulator and point of articulation, various uses of the cavities, and various configurations of the tongue produce modifications of the air stream which are called manners of articulation. Fig. C.1 portrays the classification of these manners of articulation which we will follow in the discussion. Many of these manners of articulation may be produced with any or most of the combinations of articulator and point of articulation listed above.

Non-continuant sounds are ones in which the air stream is interrupted by the articulation, or in which the "sound" itself consists of such an interruption. Stops are the most widespread form of non-continuant (pp. 12-13, 79-83, 108-116). A stop consists of a closure between articulator and point of articulation such that the airstream is fully cut off. It requires a simultaneous closure of the velic so that air does not escape through the nose. A stop may be voiced, which requires that an air stream move through the larynx to create a vibration there, but it may not pass through the point of articulation in the mouth during the brief duration of the stop.

Stops occur single or double (pp. 298-305). That is, in addition to the velic closure there may be a single stop articulation or two. If there are two, one of these is a back-velar articulation. The other is commonly bilabial, but may be articulated with the tongue tip against the teeth, alveolar ridge, or alveopalatal region.

Flaps are very brief stops[1] in which the articulator flips

---

[1]Nasal and lateral flaps are continuants (p. 246).

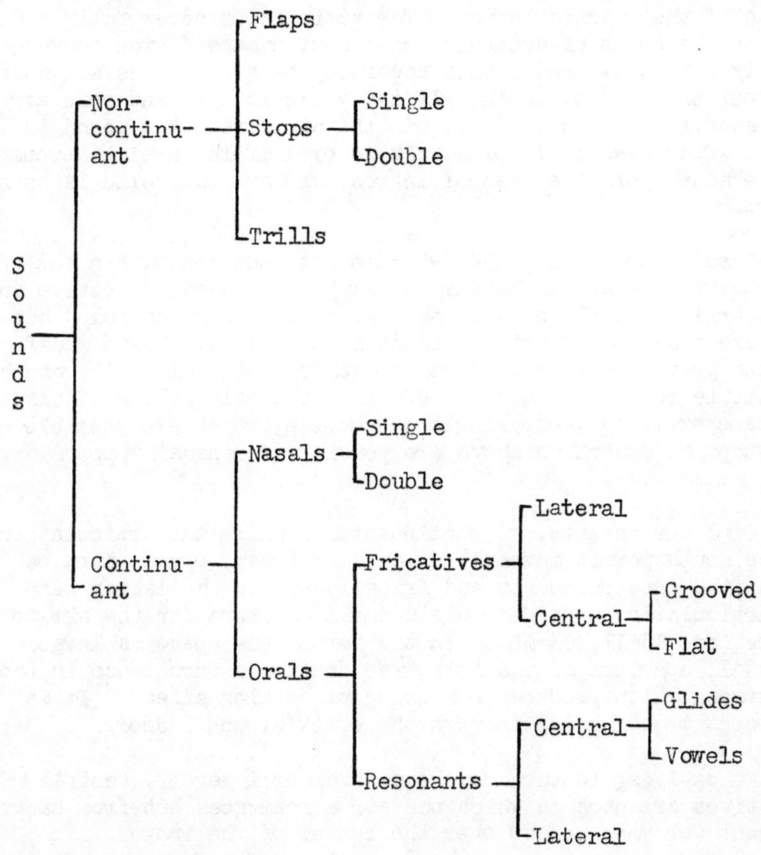

Fig. C.1: Manners of Articulation[1]

against the point of articulation (pp. 246-250). Trills consist of a very rapid series of flaps (pp. 250-255). It would be possible to classify a trill as a continuant ecause the sound continues through a series of several such rapidly articulated flaps. If so classified, however, it would be a continuant which stops repeatedly! Both flaps and trills are typically articulated with the tongue tip in the alveolar or alveopalatal region, or with the uvula against the back of the tongue.

Continuants are sounds which are not interrupted during the

[1]Schematic classification modified from Kenneth L. Pike, Phonetics, p. 142 and classroom presentations at the Summer Institute of Linguistics.

course of their articulation. The articulator never fully touches the point of articulation. Continuants divide conveniently into orals and nasals according to whether the air stream goes out the nose or mouth. If the velic is open and some articulator in the mouth closes off the air stream the sound is nasal. Otherwise it is oral. It is oral if the articulations in the mouth permit egress or ingress whether the velic is open or not.

Nasals (pp. 16-17, 192-199) are not modified within the nasal cavity in actual languages (although a nasal fricative and nasal trill articulated with the velic are fully possible) but they are modified by articulations in the mouth. These modifications provide different sizes and shapes of oral cavity which constitute resonance chambers off from the main column of air. The same articulations, single and double, which are possible for stops as described above are possible for nasals (pp. 298-306).

Oral continuants, or continuants in which the articulations in the mouth permit movement of the airstream, may in turn be classified into resonants and fricatives. In the latter case the articulation provides only a small aperture for the air to escape (pp. 13-17, 43-60). In the former the space is larger. The small aperture of the fricative creates a turbulance in the air stream which produces a hissing or buzzing effect. It is analogous to air going through the crack around a door.

Fricatives, in turn may be central or lateral. Central fricatives are ones in which the air stream goes out from back to front (or vice versa) over the center of the tongue. In lateral fricatives the center of the tongue touches the point of articulation and air movement through this articulation is impossible. However, one or both sides of the tongue leave an opening permitting the air stream to move (pp. 217, 221-225).

Central fricatives may be flat or grooved (pp. 167-168). Flat fricatives have a flat or convex configuration of the top surface of the tongue when seen from the front. Grooved fricatives have a concave configuration.

Resonant orals, or oral sounds with a large aperture between articulator and point of articulation may likewise be central or lateral. That is, the airstream may go out over the center of the tongue or over the side, as described for fricatives. Laterals vary according to the configuration of the tongue behind the point of articulation, or according to the point itself (pp. 217-229).

Each of the manners of articulation mentioned above is

classified as a consonant articulation. Central resonant orals are vowel and vowel glide articulations. Because of their complexity they will be handled separately in the following section.

Vowels and Vowel Glides

Central resonant oral continuants are vowels and vowel glides. The distinguishing feature of glides lies in their audible movement (pp. 175-187). Most typically this change in position is a movement toward or away from the upper front of the mouth, the upper back of the mouth (with a simultaneous lip rounding), the center of the mouth, or retroflexed tongue position. Glides may be on-glides in which case the movement is away from the general area indicated into the position of the vowel which follows. Or they may be off-glides, in which they move from the position of the vowel in the direction of the glide.

Vowels are less easily classified and described than consonants because of their complexity. Differences of vowel sound are created by subtle differences of configuration on the surface of the tongue without any points of articulation against which reference may be made. All sounds are formed by the shape of the cavities through which the air stream passes, but with vowels there is nothing as readily definable as the articulators and points of articulation of the consonants (pp. 174-175, 201-202).

Vowels are classified according to the degree of lip rounding (rounded or unrounded), the general part of the tongue which is highest in the formation of the vowel (front, central, back), and the relative height of that part of the tongue (high, lower-high, mid, lower-mid, low, lower-low). Further modifications include the degree of bunching, cupping, curling (retroflex, pp. 417-420), etc. of the tongue. Vowels are most commonly voiced. In many languages they sometimes occur voiceless, however (pp. 392-396). All vowel articulations may be combined with such features as nasalization (pp. 333-340), breathiness (pp. 420-426), laryngealization (pp. 398-399).

Other Features

There are many other ways in which the air stream can be modified, a few of which will be mentioned now. Rounded or spread lips, with various degrees between may be characteristic of consonants as well as of vowels and glides.

Sounds may be articulated with varying degrees of length (pp. 269-274). They can be held for extremely brief periods, or longer ones. Articulation can be smooth and unbroken, or there

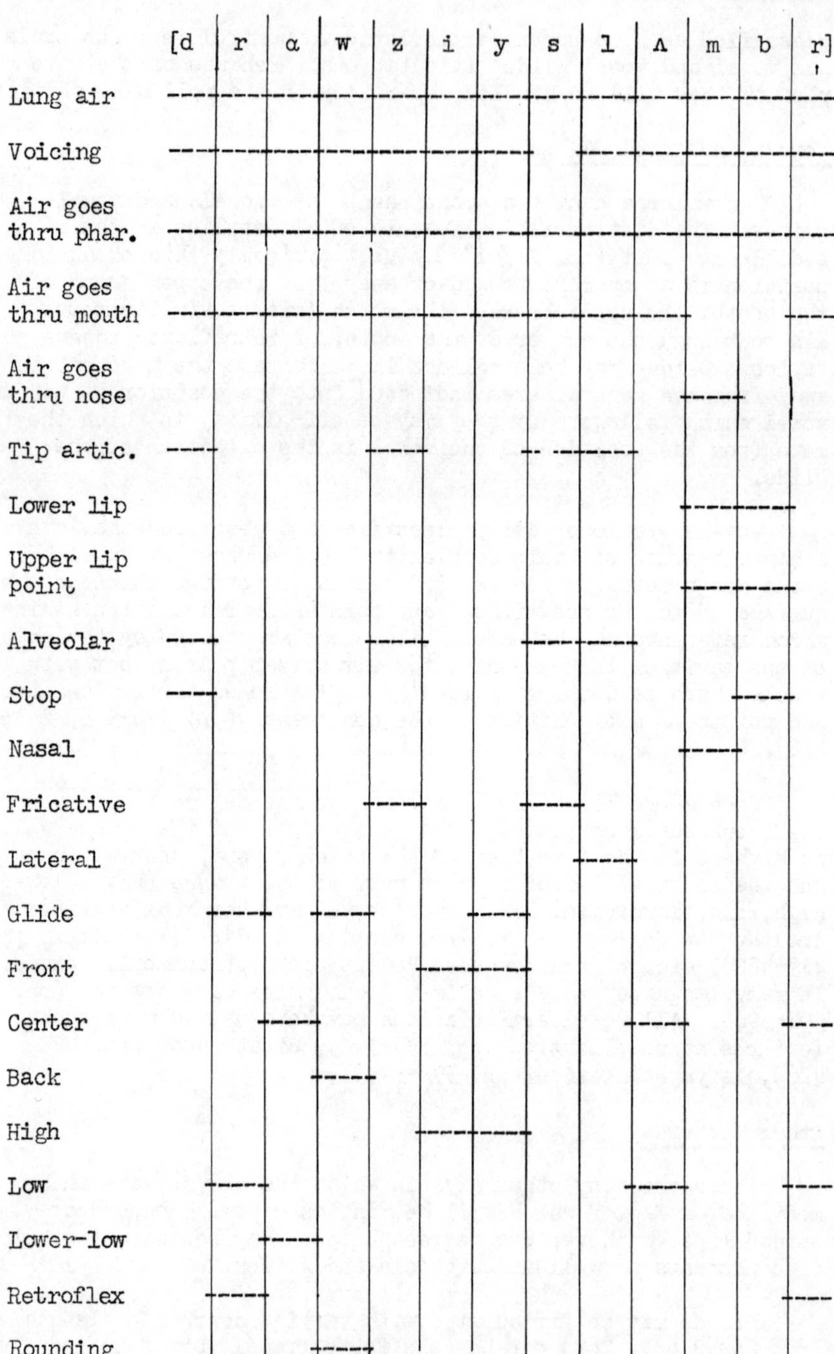

Fig. C.2: Segmentation Diagram

may be a juncture (pp. 158-159), a slight hesitation or pause between sounds. Sounds may be forcibly articulated (fortis) because of extra lung pressure and/or extra tenseness of the articulator, or the articulation may be lenis (pp. 387-389).

Sounds are often grouped together into syllables by chest pulses and other factors of articulation. Each syllable has one sound which is syllabic, and the others are non-syllabic.[1] The syllabic is most typically a vowel, but may often be a consonant (pp. 150-153). Nasal and lateral consonants (except lateral fricatives) most readily lend themselves to syllabic articulation.

Some syllables are stressed more heavily than others, the stress being created by a more forceful pump of the airstream associated with additional length, change in pitch and vowel quality (pp. 154-158).

Combining the Features of Articulation: Segmentation

The miracle of speech articulation is that the enormous complexity which we have been describing is coordinated and intertwined into a code system with enormous rapidity, and that people who know the code (the language) can decipher the meaning of the stream of sounds which come at such a great rate. Some of the interplay of the various elements of articulation can be seen in the vastly oversimplified schematic diagram in Fig. C.2. Articulations do not start and stop with the abrupt precision pictured here, and there are many more factors than are listed, but the diagram serves to show some of the complexity involved in the simple expression drowsy slumber. Note that although the various aspects of speech production are intertwined, and turned off and on at various rates and positions, each sound shows various features in different combinations, and it is this which gives us the distinction between sounds as well as the impression of segmentation, the impression that one discreet sound succeeds another.

Suggested Reading

Kenneth L. Pike, *Phonetics*, pp. 83-156.

H. A. Gleason, *An Introduction to Descriptive Linguistics*, pp. 239-256.

Charles F. Hockett, *A Course in Modern Linguistics*, pp. 62-83.

Charles F. Hockett, *A Manual of Phonology*, pp. 23-42.

BIBLIOGRAPHY

Bloch, Bernard, and George L. Trager, Outline of Linguistic Analysis. L. S. A. Waverly Press, Inc., Baltimore, Md., 1942.

Bloomfield, Leonard, Language. Henry Holt and Co., New York, 1933.

Canonge, Elliott D., "Voiceless Vowels in Comanche," International Journal of American Linguistics, Vol. 23, No. 2 (April, 1957), pp. 63-67.

English Pronunciation. English Language Institute, University of Michigan, Ann Arbor, Mich.

Francis, W. Nelson, The Structure of American English. The Ronald Press Co., New York, 1958.

Gleason, H. A., An Introduction to Descriptive Linguistics. Henry Holt and Co., New York, 1955, revised 1961.

Heffner, R. M. S., General Phonetics. University of Wisconsin Press, Madison, Wisc., 1952.

Hill, Archibald A., Introduction to Linguistic Structures. Harcourt, Brace and Co., New York, 1958.

Hockett, Charles F., A Course in Modern Linguistics. Macmillan, New York, 1958.

Hockett, Charles F., Manual of Phonology. Waverly Press, Baltimore, Md., 1955 (Memoir 11 of the International Journal of American Linguistics).

Kaiser, L. (ed.), Manual of Phonetics. North Holland Publishing Co., Amsterdam, 1957.

Lê-van-Ly, Le Parler Vietnamien. Huong Anh Press, Paris, 1948.

Maston, Robert E., Lebanese Spoken Arabic (reproduced by ditto process). Beirut, 1955.

Nida, Eugene A., Learning a Foreign Language. Friendship Press, New York, 1957.

Osborn, Henry, and William A. Smalley, "Formulae for Comanche Stem and Word Formation," *International Journal of American Linguistics*, Vol. 15, No. 2 (April, 1959), pp. 93-99.

Park, C. H., *An Intensive Course in Korean, Book I.* Yonsei University Press, Seoul, Korea, 1961.

Pike, Kenneth L., *The Intonation of American English.* University of Michigan Publications, Linguistics, Vol. I. University of Michigan Press, Ann Arbor, Mich., 1947.

Pike, Kenneth L., *Tone Languages.* University of Michigan Press, Ann Arbor, Mich., 1948.

Pike, Kenneth L., *Phonemics; A Technique for Reducing Languages to Writing.* University of Michigan Publications, Linguistics, Vol. III. University of Michigan Press, Ann Arbor, Mich. 1947.

Pike, Kenneth L., *Phonetics.* University of Michigan Press, Ann Arbor, Michigan, 1943.

Riggs, Venda, "Alternate Phonemic Analyses of Comanche," *International Journal of American Linguistics*, Vol. 15, No. 4 (October, 1949), pp. 229-231.

Smalley, William A., *Outline of Khmu' Structure.* American Oriental Society, New Haven, Conn., 1961.

Smalley, William A., "Phonemic Rhythm in Comanche," *International Journal of American Linguistics*, Vol. 19, No. 4, October, 1953. pp. 297-301.

Smalley, William A., and Nguyễn-Văn-Vạn, *Vietnamese for Missionaries; A Course in the Spoken and Written Language of Central Vietnam.* Trial Edition. Imprimerie Evangelique, Dalat, Vietnam, 1954.

Trager, George, and Henry Lee Smith, *An Outline of English Structure.* American Council of Learned Societies, Washington, D. C., 1956.

Westerman, D., and Ida C. Ward, *Practical Phonetics for Students of African Languages.* Oxford University Press, London, 1933.

Wise, Claude Merton, *Applied Phonetics.* Prentice-Hall, Inc., Englewood Cliffs, N.J., 1957

INDEX

Phonetic symbols not a part of the usual English alphabet are combined with it in the index below. The order in which they appear follows. Other symbols, not shown in this listing are included in the index as subheadings under the basic symbol they most resemble, with [ǫ] under [o], [b̰] under [b], etc.

a ɑ ɒ æ b ƀ c č d đ e ə ɛ f g ᵍb ǥ h i ɨ ɩ j ǰ k ᵏp l ƚ m ɯ n ñ
ŋ ᵑm o ø ɔ œ p ᵽ q r r̃ ř s š t u ü ʋ v ʌ w x y z ž ˀ 9̰ θ ɾ.

[a] lower-low front unrounded oral vowel 261ff. [a·] long 269ff. [ą] nasalized 333ff. [a̓] laryngealized 398f. [ạ] retroflexed 417ff. [a̟] breathy 420ff. [a̰] pharyngealized 441ff. [a^] raised 370ff. [aᵛ] lowered 370ff. [a‹] fronted 370ff. [a›] backed 370ff. [a̹] with very slight rounding 370ff. [A] voiceless 392ff.
Affricates 136ff, 148, 229f, 277, 454ff; aspirated and unaspirated 139ff; dental 166f; flat and grooved 167; lateral 259n; laterally released 228f; retroflexed 168; velar 143; voiced 139f.
Air stream: Sammy 78, 379ff, 406f, 429f, 433, 436; 77ff, 378ff, 405ff, 427ff, 490ff.
Alveolar 3ff, 20, 85ff, 148, 166f, 170, 278.
Alveopalatal 3ff, 20ff, 75f, 85ff, 148, 164, 170, 193ff, 196, 218, 225f, 275ff.
Amoy 30ff, 61f.
Articulation 3ff, 490ff; manners of 11ff, 490ff; points of 3ff, 493ff.
Articulators 9ff, 493ff.
Aspiration 108ff, 113ff, 229, 277, 396f.

[ɑ] lower-low central unrounded oral vowel: Sammy 175; 174f, 187ff, 263ff, 335. [ɑ·] long 269ff. [ɑ̨] nasalized: Sammy 334f; 333ff. [ɑ̓] laryngealized 398f. [ɑ̣] retroflexed 417ff. [ɑ̟] breathy 420ff. [ɑ̰] pharyngealized 441ff. [ɑ^] raised 370ff. [ɑᵛ] lowered 370ff. [ɑ‹] fronted 370ff. [ɑ›] backed 370ff. [ɑ̹] with slight rounding 370ff. [Ɑ] voiceless 392ff.

[ɒ] lower-low back unrounded oral vowel: Sammy 264; 261ff. [ɒ·] long 269ff. [ɒ̨] nasalized 333ff. [ɒ̓] laryngealized 398f. [ɒ̣] retroflexed 417ff. [ɒ̟] breathy 420ff. [ɒ̰] pharyngealized 441ff. [ɒ^] raised 370ff. [ɒᵛ] lowered 370ff. [ɒ‹] fronted 370ff. [ɒ›] backed 370ff. [ɒ̹] with slight rounding 370ff. [Ɒ] voiceless 392ff.

[æ] low front unrounded oral vowel: Sammy 235; 232, 234ff, 263ff. [æ·] long 269ff. [æ̨] nasalized 333ff. [æ̓] laryngealized 398f. [æ̣] retroflexed 417ff. [æ̟] breathy 420ff. [æ̰] pharyngealized 441ff. [æ^] raised 370ff. [æᵛ] lowered 370ff. [æ‹] fronted 370ff. [æ›] backed 370ff. [æ̹] slightly rounded 370ff. [Æ] voiceless 392ff.

consonant release 347.

[ε] lower-mid front unrounded oral vowel: Sammy 175; 174, 187f, 190, 201. [ε·] long 269ff. [ε̨] nasalized 333ff. [ε̉] laryngealized 398f. [ε̥] 417ff. [ε̤] breathy 420ff. [ε̴] pharyngealized: Sammy 442; 441ff. [ε^ εᵛ ε‹ ε› ε̹] raised, lowered, fronted, backed, and with slight rounding 370ff.

[f] voiceless flat labiodental fricative with egressive lung air: Sammy 14, 49; 43ff, 48, 87, 148, 454. [f·] long 269ff. [f̹] rounded 460. [f̴] pharyngealized: Sammy 442; 446ff. [f˝] with egressive pharynx air 456.
Faucalization, Faucal pillars 425, 493.
Fall, Falling. see Pitch, Glides.
Finnish 272ff, 329ff.
Flaps 246ff, 249, 253f, 256, 281, 456, 494f.
Foe 282.
Fortis 388.
Free fluctuation 488ff.
French 27, 221, 219, 346f.
Fricatives: Sammy 49; 13ff, 43ff, 48ff, 52ff, 55ff, 75f, 80f, 87f, 116f, 143, 148, 166, 172, 454ff; flat 167, 454, 496; grooved 167, 454f, 496; lateral 217, 221ff, 496.
Front. see Mouth, Vowels.
Fronted velar articulation: Sammy 324.

[g] voiced velar stop with egressive lung air: Sammy 78; 79ff, 148, 455. [g̑] fronted 322ff, 455. [g̣] backed 322, 455. [gʱ] with voiced aspiration 422, 455. [g·] long 269ff. [g̴] pharyngealized 446ff. [g̃ə] with voiced release 346f. [ɠ] with ingressive pharynx air: Sammy 381; 378, 457.
"Gamma" 363. see [ɤ].
German 320f.
Glides. see Pitch, Vowels.
Glottal stop. see Stops, [ʔ].
Glottalized consonants 456ff.
Glottis. see Vocal cords.
Gola 131ff, 449.

[ᵍb] voiced double stop with egressive lung air: Sammy 299; 298ff, 306, 454. [ᵍɓ] with ingressive pharynx air 378, 456.

[ɡ̶] voiced flat velar fricative with egressive lung air: Sammy 53; 48, 52ff, 56, 148, 200, 455. [ɡ̶ ɡ̶] fronted, backed, 322ff, 455. [ɡ̶·] long 269ff. [ɡ̶] nasalized 333f. [ɡ̶] pharyngealized 446ff. [gɡ̶] affricate 138ff, 148, 455.

[h] voiceless glottal fricative 182f, 396f, 445, 492.
[H] voiced centralizing glide: Sammy 181; 181f.
[ḥ] voiceless pharyngeal glide 444ff.
[ʰ] aspiration 108ff, 140, 182f, 229, 277, 396f, 422ff.
[ʱ] voiced aspiration (breathy) 422ff, 454f.
"Hat with the Bird" 93f, 118ff, 271.
Hausa 33ff, 161f, 463f.
"House that Jack Built" 205, 238f.
"Hook," "Hooked" 333, 411.
Huli 143
High. see Pitch, Tongue.
"High tongue l̲" 218. see [l^].

[i] high front unrounded oral vowel: Sammy 235; 232ff. [i·] long 269ff. [į] nasalized 333ff. [ỉ] laryngealized 398f.